Northern Ireland Social Work Law

To Úna, Cormac, Liadh and Saorla

Northern Ireland Social Work Law

by

Ciaran White BL

Senior Lecturer in Law at the University of Ulster, Jordanstown

with contributions from

Maura McCallion LLB (Hons) LLM, Solicitor (Chapter 10)
and
Michael Potter LLB LLM BL (Chapter 11)

LexisNexis™

Members of the LexisNexis Group worldwide

Ireland	LexisNexis, 24–26 Upper Ormond Quay, DUBLIN 7
Argentina	LexisNexis Argentina, BUENOS AIRES
Australia	LexisNexis Butterworths, CHATSWOOD, New South Wales
Austria	LexisNexis Verlag ARD Orac GmbH & Co KG, VIENNA
Canada	LexisNexis Butterworths, MARKHAM, Ontario
Chile	LexisNexis Chile Ltda, SANTIAGO DE CHILE
Czech Republic	Nakladatelství Orac sro, PRAGUE
France	Editions du Juris-Classeur SA, PARIS
Germany	LexisNexis Deutschland GmbH, FRANKFURT and MUNSTER
Hong Kong	LexisNexis Butterworths, HONG KONG
Hungary	HVG-Orac, BUDAPEST
India	LexisNexis Butterworths, NEW DELHI
Italy	Giuffrè Editore, MILAN
Malaysia	Malayan Law Journal Sdn Bhd, KUALA LUMPUR
New Zealand	LexisNexis Butterworths, WELLINGTON
Poland	Wydawnictwo Prawnicze LexisNexis, WARSAW
Singapore	LexisNexis Butterworths, SINGAPORE
South Africa	LexisNexis Butterworths, DURBAN
Switzerland	Stämpfli Verlag AG, BERNE
United Kingdom	LexisNexis UK, LONDON and EDINBURGH
USA	LexisNexis, DAYTON, Ohio

© Chapters 1–9 Ciaran White
© Chapters 10 and 11 Butterworth Ireland Ltd, 2004

Published by LexisNexis

A CIP Catalogue record for this book is available from the British Library.

ISBN 1 854 75218 9

Printed and bound in Great Britain by Antony Rowe, Chippenham, Wiltshire

Typeset by Kerrypress Ltd, Luton http://www.kerrypress.co.uk

Visit LexisNexis at www.lexisnexis.ie

Preface

This is a textbook primarily for social work students and a reference work for social work practitioners and their legal advisers. It unravels the law relating to the specialist functions performed by social workers, allowing rapid comprehension of the relevant law and, where appropriate, practice. Written in an accessible style, it makes extensive use of Northern Ireland case law and other materials with a uniquely Northern Ireland flavour. *Northern Ireland Social Work Law* details the legal information relating to social work practice, including child protection, adoption and fostering, community care, mental health and the criminal justice system. It also provides a context for that legal knowledge by outlining the operation of the legal system, the accountability of social workers, the role of social workers in court and the requirements of equality law.

The transfer of legislative competence to the Northern Ireland Assembly, the establishment of a range of new agencies (such as the Human Rights Commission, the Equality Commission and the Children's Commissioner) as well as the integrated nature of health and social services provision in the region, mean that social work law in Northern Ireland has its own distinctive features. This distinctiveness is enhanced by a separate statute book whose content will increasingly reflect the devolution of legislative power and embody innovative legislative solutions to contemporary problems.

The rapid and substantial change in the legal rules that impact upon social work practice in Northern Ireland in the years since a similar textbook was produced has meant that it is necessary to produce a new, discrete textbook to service that profession and to aid those legal practitioners that advise social workers. There has also been sufficient institutional change in the jurisdiction to require an holistic treatment of the law of social work practice in Northern Ireland. These institutional changes have included those outlined above but have also seen the establishment of the Northern Ireland Social Care Council, the new body responsible for the training and professional regulation of social workers. Changes are also afoot in the field of criminal justice, arising from the Criminal Justice Review Commission's recommendations. In short, after many years of piecemeal development during the years of direct rule, much of it simply aping developments in England and Wales, Northern Ireland is undergoing significant political and legal reform and these reforms have considerable impact on social work law.

The breadth and depth of knowledge expected of social workers is quite considerable and the pace of change in the law means that there is an almost constant evolution in social work law. Allied to this, there is a developing awareness among the general public, including social services' clientele, of the power of the law to achieve outcomes that are satisfactory to them. This development can be traced to the growing litigiousness of society generally but also to the manner in which litigation in Northern Ireland in particular has become another way in which political disputes, about human rights and other matters, have been reshaped.

There is a growing recognition of the distinctive nature of social work law as a discrete legal subject and the implications of that for training social work students and practitioners. This is a topic discussed in chapter one. The scale of the task facing social workers studying law is indicated by the fact that social work law involves digesting significant amounts of legal texts, understanding the interaction of a range of different legal actors and the implementation of very different legal rules and sanctions. These include matters as diverse as judicial review of decisions of Health and Social Services authorities and the liability of social workers in negligence. And layered across all social work law, as with all other areas of public law generally, is the Human Rights Act 1998.

The replacing of the Diploma in Social Work with a three-year, full-time degree course and the establishment of Social Care Councils across the UK makes this an opportune time to re-evaluate the teaching of social work law and to reconsider the role of law in the social care services sector. This book attempts to provide as much depth as is possible in a general text, recognising the fact that social workers involved in different elements of the social care sector, and at different levels of managerial responsibility, will require different levels of information. Where relevant, the reader is referred to other sources of information to allow them to deepen their knowledge. Although the text is written specifically for social workers, much of it will also be of benefit to other social care workers, like, for example, community care workers.

Ciaran White
University of Ulster

Contents

Table of Statutes

References in the right-hand column are to paragraph number. Paragraph references printed in **bold** type indicate where the Act is set out in part or in full.

Northern Ireland

Table of Statutory Instruments

References in the right-hand column are to paragraph number. Paragraph references printed in **bold** type indicate where the Act is set out in part or in full.

PARA

England

Northern Ireland

Second Legislation Directives

Table of Conventions

References in the right-hand column are to paragraph number. Paragraph references printed in **bold** type indicate where the Act is set out in part or in full.

Table of Cases

PARA

Chapter 1

Introduction to the Legal System

Introduction

1.1 This chapter provides a wide-ranging introduction to the legal system of Northern Ireland for those unfamiliar with it. Its aim is to make social workers aware of the sources of law and the manner in which the legal system operates as it affects the social work (and social care) professions, thereby underpinning the substantive knowledge that follows in later chapters. Thus, it will explain the sources of law, and the structure of the court system, the influence of human rights on the Northern Irish legal system, as well as examining the role of a number of different participants in the legal system. In doing so it explains how law is made, or developed, and offers some perspectives on how it is applied.

1.2 Law is not a social workers' domain and a social worker cannot be expected to have as detailed an understanding of the development and application of law as solicitors and barristers, but he or she is expected to have a certain degree of legal understanding, and to be comfortable with using, and applying, legal materials to allow them to fulfil their functions. Indeed, on occasion, social workers will be expected to contribute to discussions about legal reform of matters with particular relevance for their profession. In particular, social workers are expected to understand '(i) that the law gives [them] their mandate to practise; (ii) that legally accountable powers, when appropriately used, can promote and encourage good social work practice; (iii) that the exercise of legal powers may be oppressive or discriminatory if not used in ways that avoid discrimination and respect client's rights; (iv) and the tension between legal and ethical rights.'[1]

---

[1] Law for Social Workers in Northern Ireland, Improving Social Work Education and Training, 22 CCETSW, Belfast 1997, p 10.

Conceptualising 'social work law'

1.3 It is useful at the outset to consider the interaction of the social worker with the legal system in a little detail. Law impacts upon social work practice in a number of different ways. Most obviously, much social work practice, like child protection for example, is often underpinned by statute, providing social workers with their powers and duties, but also setting limits on the range of lawful options open to them. Where social workers have a direct involvement with such legislation then that legal knowledge can be considered core to the social work profession. However, social workers can also have a less direct interest in the law. Other aspects of social work practice, like the formulation or development of social care policy, might not, at first glance, appear to attract legal regulation, but such activity might well be the subject of judicial review proceedings.[1] Aggrieved clients, or perhaps other social workers, may wish to challenge elements of practice by alleging discrimination, thereby requiring social workers to have knowledge of equality law.[2] In other situations legal knowledge is necessary to help inform the social worker's understanding of, and ability to fulfil, his or her role, even though the social worker may have no direct role to play in the legal issue in question. This range of matters includes domestic violence and other family related legal matters,[3] and the criminal justice system.[4]

[1]   See chapter 2, paras 2.105 ff.
[2]   See chapter 4.
[3]   See chapter 9.
[4]   See chapter 5.

1.4   Preston-Shoot, Roberts and Vernon, in 'Social Work: from interaction to integration',[1] have argued that a new academic discipline, 'social work law', has emerged. Such a discipline is:

> 'much more complex than just what law (including its status) the social worker knows; it is how that knowledge is used. The methodology of social work law is, therefore, not just concerned with mapping and describing the boundaries of its jurisprudential terrain in terms of substantive rules, but it is also concerned to analyse how these rules are experienced, conceptualized and "functional-ized" by practising social workers, and how they are interpreted by the courts. It is the dynamic of the relationship between these substantive legal rules, the administrative context of social work practice, and the superstructure of social work values and knowledge which gives social work law its particular identity.'[2]

[1]   (1998) 20 JSWL 65–80.
[2]   (1998) 20 JSWL 15 at 76.

1.5   Social work law, they contend, has three distinct strands: first, the legal powers and duties that mandate social work practice; secondly, social work ethics and values incorporated into certain statutory provisions and thirdly, aspects of administrative law that render social workers, and more particularly their public sector employers, accountable. Examples of the first category would include the Children Order[1] and mental health[2] and community care legislation.[3] The second category includes a myriad of singular provisions that support or reinforce values such as self-determination, the maintenance of social order, and the cultural needs of clients, for example. Examples of such provisions, they argue, are the Children Act 1989, ss 1(3) and 22(5), which advance 'equal opportunities' and also relate to the 'cultural needs' of clients.[4] Similarly, they argue, the Carers (Recognition of Services) Act 1995 –

which provides for the assessment of carers' needs[5] – promotes the concept of 'partnership', presumably because it aids the development of a partnership approach to the care of vulnerable and elderly persons by social work and volunteer carers. Very often there is little or no coherence to the manner in which these provisions are enacted and the authors do admit that there is 'variable endorsement of social work's knowledge base'.[6] The third strand of this new academic discipline, the authors suggest, includes judicial review, and the less legalistic forms of redress offered by the various statutory Ombudsmen,[7] all of which arise from the public sector setting in which social work is practised and which serve to make social workers accountable for their actions.

[1] See chapter 6.
[2] See chapter 11.
[3] See chapter 10.
[4] The equivalent of these provisions in Northern Ireland law are art 1(3) (ie the 'welfare checklist'), and art 26(3) of the Children (Northern Ireland) Order 1995 (ie duty on authority looking after child to have regard to his or her wishes, religious, cultural or racial background).
[5] The equivalent legislation in Northern Ireland is the Carers and Direct Payments Act (Northern Ireland) 2002, see chapter 10, para 10.8.
[6] (1998) 20 JSWL 65 at 72.
[7] See chapter 2, para 2.45.

1.6 They expand on this thesis in a later article, 'Working Together in Social Work Law',[1] in which the differing working relationships between lawyers and social workers are elaborated. The relationships between lawyers and social workers differ from context to context because the nature of the work in which they are jointly engaged can vary. Thus the authors imagine social work law as a continuum, at one end of which, the language, methodology and values of the law predominate. An example of this interaction would be a plea in mitigation in the criminal courts after the presentation of a pre-sentence report.[2] They suggest that the 'the middle ground of the continuum is represented by an application for a Care Order by a local authority lawyer. At the opposite end of the continuum, the language, methodology and values of social work prevail, and lawyers are rarely involved. Community care assessments and care management are examples of this.'[3]

[1] (1998) JSWL 137–150.
[2] For an explanation of pre-sentence report, see chapter 5, para 3.78.
[3] (1998) JSWL 139.

1.7 This new discipline is not to be confused with social welfare law, which, in their view, includes anti-discrimination law, housing law and 'legislation with which social workers must be familiar if they are to respond appropriately to people's needs'.[1] As one might expect, they consider that descriptions such as 'law for social workers' or 'social workers and the law' should be dispensed with. Without necessarily adopting their views in full, these views do offer an interesting perspective that informs, to a degree, the approach taken in this book. Thus, this book does not attempt to provide a guide to housing or social security law, two aspects of legal regulation with which social workers have traditionally been required to be familiar.[2] The highly specialised nature of these fields of law, and the pace of change in each, means that social workers can only ever hope to provide the most general of advice and in most cases will simply direct clients to the specialised agencies involved in these areas.[3] This book concentrates on those matters that social workers directly administer or which are directly related to those areas of activity, requiring social workers to have some basic knowledge of them. However, the observant reader will have noted, that this book includes equality law within its contents and thus steps over into the territory referred to by Preston-Shoot et al as 'social welfare law'. The importance of equality law in Northern Ireland and the centrality of anti-discriminatory values in social work education and practice justify the inclusion of equality law in a text such as this.

[1] (1998) 20 JWSL 65 at 70.
[2] The Northern Ireland Framework Specification for the Degree in Social Work, March 2003, DHSSPS, does, it must be said, require social work students to 'have knowledge and understanding of legislation and social policy relating to', *inter alia*, 'education, housing and welfare rights' (para 3.2).
[3] Public housing in Northern Ireland is administered by the Northern Ireland Housing Executive, and the Housing Rights Service is the most pertinent NGO in that field. Social security benefits are administered by the Social Security Agency and rights of appeal to Appeal Tribunals exist, with advocacy services in those Tribunals being provided by the Northern Ireland Association of Citizen Advice Bureaux.

1.8 A number of factors will affect the development of any such discipline, I suggest. First, social workers are not autonomous agents but are employed by statutory and non-statutory agencies to advance their programmes of work or fulfil statutory duties. The relationship of lawyer/social worker, or the interaction between them is, therefore, often not a direct one, and is in fact usually mediated through the employer. This may mean that the employer is the agency with whom the lawyer must, at a technical level at any rate, engage, or it may mean that the autonomy of the employed social worker is circumscribed by the policies, guidelines or instructions issued by the employer.

More particularly, it might be argued, social workers are a peculiar consequence of the development of the post-World War Two welfare state and the roles that they fill will contract or expand, according to the adjustments made by successive governments in welfare state provision. As a result, the nature and location of their engagement with law, and lawyers, may not be of their choosing.

Secondly, while there is widespread general knowledge of the role that social workers play, the social worker's legal status is merely a developing one. Apart from reference to Approved Social Workers in the Mental Health (Northern Ireland) Order 1986,[1] and references in criminal justice legislation to social workers acting as appropriate adults,[2] no other statutory references were made to the role prior to the Health and Personal Social Services Act (Northern Ireland) 2001, which established the Northern Ireland Social Care Council to oversee the social work profession.[3] In all other respects the social worker has generally been invisible in legislation. For example, the courts' power under the Children (Northern Ireland) Order 1995 to require the compilation of court welfare reports makes reference not to 'social workers', but to 'suitably qualified persons'.[4] This, of course, broadens the court's options in choosing the most appropriate person to compile the report, but highlights the insubstantial legislative existence of the social worker.

[1] See chapter 11, para 11.16.
[2] See chapter 6, para 5.46.
[3] See chapter 2, para 2.9.
[4] Children (Northern Ireland) Order 1995, art 3.

1.9 Although social workers are often working within statutory boundaries, they are nevertheless usually implementing those duties on behalf of other bodies. Their relationship to the law and legal institutions therefore is often tangential and indirect, and the law organises itself with only passing reference to the role played by the social worker, rather than using the social worker as a reference point, as one might expect it to, if a discipline entitled 'social work law' existed as a coherent one.

1.10 Nevertheless, the role played by social workers is undoubtedly a recognisable one, to both the public and legal practitioners, and their child and family work might well be said to be the irreducible core of the profession. Furthermore, the nature of the tasks they perform means that certain legal knowledge is fundamental to the social worker's role. And, in the future, the development of the Northern Ireland Social Care Council, and its counterparts in the remainder of the UK, may result in the establishment of a discipline matching the description offered by Preston-Shoot et al. In the meantime, this textbook offers an approach to law and the study and operation of legal rules having a relevance for social work practice, that recognises the different types of interaction occurring along the continuum described by the authors in their second, follow-up article. It is important for social workers not only to be aware of the substantive rules underpinning their practice, but the interconnection between matters as apparently diverse as judicial review, human rights law and their routine tasks, for example. This appreciation of these legal elements must then occur in the context of the administrative structures that have responsibility for implementing or adhering to these legal rules. It is law that validates social work practice and simultaneously makes social workers accountable for their actions. As a consequence, social workers must have a rounded understanding of the impact of law on their profession.

Classifying law

1.11 Northern Ireland is one of three jurisdictions in the UK, Scotland and England and Wales being the other two. Northern Ireland is a common law jurisdiction, and has a legal system similar to that of England and Wales. (The Republic of Ireland is also a common law jurisdiction and there are broad similarities between the two legal systems in Ireland). This means that judge-made law or precedent[1] plays a significant part in the legal system and is one of the two main sources of law. The Scottish legal system, by contrast, is a civil law system, and as a consequence places much less emphasis on case law as a source of its legal rules.

[1] See para 1.48.

1.12 The fact that Northern Ireland is a separate jurisdiction within the UK means that social workers should be alert to the fact that there may be substantive legal differences not only between the law in Northern Ireland and England and Wales, but also between the law in Northern Ireland and Scotland. Indeed, the advent of devolution has made it more likely that there will be substantive differences between the constituent jurisdictions of the UK. The legislative basis for social work practice in Northern Ireland certainly differs from that applying elsewhere in the UK. In addition, the separate status of the three jurisdictions means that the enforcement in Northern Ireland of court orders issued in one of the other two jurisdictions, particularly in the field of family law, can be cumbersome. For example, the Children Order Advisory Committee, in its Second Report, highlighted one such anomaly. No legislative provision exists allowing for the Transfer of Care Orders from Northern Ireland to England and Wales, though there are regulations allowing for Transfer of Care Orders in the other direction.[1]

[1]   Children Order Advisory Committee Second Report, 2001, para 16.

Criminal law and civil law

1.13   Generally the easiest way of classifying law is to divide it into its criminal and civil branches. Most people are familiar with the criminal law and its salient characteristic is that it punishes certain behaviour or activity. Civil law, on the other hand, refers to non-criminal legal matters, usually between private legal persons, or between private legal persons and the state, in which the parties are seeking to uphold their legal rights or entitlements.

Parties to legal actions

1.14   The terminology used in respect of the civil law and the criminal law is also different. In a civil case the person or entity bringing the case is known as the 'plaintiff', or the 'applicant', while the other party is known as the 'defendant' or 'respondent'. To speak of one party suing the other indicates that the matter in dispute is a civil law one, because the proper term to describe a criminal action is 'prosecution' and hence the verb 'prosecuting' is generally reserved for criminal cases. Prosecutions are brought in the name of the Crown and the person being tried is known as the defendant. The criminal justice system is examined in chapter 5. The material in all other chapters can be classified as civil law.

Public law and private law

1.15   It is useful to imagine a further sub-division, within civil law, between public and private law, the former relating to the relationships between the State and individuals, and the latter referring to the law of private individuals only. Judicial review, which is examined in chapter 2,[1] is an example of public law, while the Residence and Contact Orders, explained in chapter 9,[2] are examples of private law proceedings.

[1] See para 2.105.
[2] See para 9.99.

Domestic and international law

1.16 Law may also be classified by reference to whether it applies domestically or internationally. Domestic law applies, for our purposes, within the UK, while international law applies between nation states. This distinction is normally irrelevant to social work practice, but in the last few years, aspects of international human rights law have begun to influence domestic law in a manner which did not happen previous to this. The sum of these developments, which are discussed later,[1] is that the language of human rights has greater relevance to social workers and their client groups than was the case in the past. An explanation of how international human rights law may impact upon social work practice is given later, but for the present it is sufficient to understand that law may be classified according to whether it is domestic or international law.

[1] See paras 1.66 ff.

Types and sources of law

1.17 There are two main sources of law: legislation and common law. Social workers are likely in practice to be more concerned with the former than the latter as great swathes of their practice is regulated by legislation. The two sources are examined in turn.

Legislation

1.18 Legislation is made by, or with the authority of, the competent legislature or parliamentary body, of which there have been many in Northern Ireland's history. Legislation can be primary or secondary. Primary legislation is the more important of the two in that it contains the important legal principles, with the details of implementation being left to the secondary legislation.

Primary and secondary legislation

1.19 Primary legislation is enacted in the form of Acts and Orders in Council (explained below), while secondary legislation comes in the form of statutory regulations or statutory rules and is usually recognisable by the inclusion of the words 'rules' or 'regulations' in the title. The crucial difference between the two is that secondary legislation can only be enacted under the authority of, and in compliance with, the primary legislation. If it is not within the competence granted by the primary legislation, it is invalid. Because secondary legislation usually deals with less important matters, or more detailed issues, than those with which the primary legislation deals, the legislature often delegates the authority to make secondary legislation to another body or person, and consequently this legislation is sometimes referred to as 'delegated legislation'. The Department of Health and Social Services and Public Safety (DHSSPS) often has the power to make regulations delegated to it, and there are numerous examples throughout this book.

1.20 An example may help to clarify the difference between the two types of legislation. The primary legislation that has most significance for children and childcare is the Children (Northern Ireland) Order 1995.[1] Secondary legislation enacted under that Order includes the Children (Allocation of Proceedings) Order (Northern Ireland) 1996, the power for which is found in the Children (Northern Ireland) Order 1995, art 164(5) and Sch 7. The provisions of the Children (Northern Ireland) Order 1995 allow cases to be re-allocated to other courts under various circumstances, but leaves it to the Lord Chancellor to set out the detail, in secondary legislation, of how and when that may be done. This then is the function of the Allocation of Proceedings Order 1996.

[1] See chapter 6.

1.21 Similarly, the 'Definition of Independent Visitors (Children) Regulations (Northern Ireland) 1996' are also an example of secondary legislation made under the 1995 Children Order, in this case article 31(7). Article 31(7) is designed to ensure that children being looked after by Boards or Trusts, who are not being visited regularly by their parents or relatives, are visited by an independent person. As the title of the regulations suggests, they set out in detail how one should define an independent visitor for this purpose.

1.22 The legislative competence in respect of many areas of social work practice now resides with the 108-member Northern Ireland Assembly, as a result of the Northern Ireland Act 1998, which is the Act implementing the Belfast/Good Friday Agreement into law. Legislation enacted by the Assembly is referred to as an Act. Prior to 2000, and dating back to the introduction of Direct Rule in 1972, most legislation made for Northern Ireland was in the form of Orders in Council enacted under the authority of the Northern Ireland Act 1974. From 1921 to 1972, legislation for Northern Ireland was enacted largely by the Stormont Parliament, though Westminster did retain residual legislative powers, particularly in relation to defence, taxation and other 'excepted' or 'reserved' matters. Thus, for example, the first pieces of Fair Employment legislation were enacted as Westminster Acts of Parliament in 1976 and 1989 respectively.[1]

[1] Fair Employment (Northern Ireland) Acts 1976–1989.

Orders in Council

1.23 Orders in Council are a less common type of legislation that have the merit, from the government's point of view, of requiring less parliamentary time than full-blown Acts of Parliament. They derive their titles from the fact that, technically, they are Orders made by the Queen on the advice of the Privy Council,[1] although in practice they are enacted by Parliament. Curiously, and perhaps confusingly, Orders in Council are in fact a form of secondary legislation because they are enacted under the authority of an Act of the Westminster Parliament, in this case the Northern Ireland Act 1974. However, during the period of Direct Rule this was the chief method of enacting legislation for Northern Ireland, particularly legislation which was identical, or similar, to legislation that had already been enacted in England and Wales, and thus Orders in Council often contain provisions more usually found in primary legislation in England and Wales. For example, the Children (Northern Ireland) Order 1995 is the near equivalent of the Children Act 1989 for England and Wales.

[1] The Privy Council is a body which historically advised the Monarch and therefore had an influential role in government and administration. Its role is greatly reduced in the modern era.

Enacting Orders in Council

1.24 We have already encountered an example of an Order in Council above, namely the Children (Northern Ireland) Order 1995. The procedure for the enactment of Orders in Council involves the full draft Order in Council being laid before the Westminster Parliament, and there are two forms of adopting such a draft: the affirmative procedure and the negative procedure. With the former the draft is passed by an affirmative resolution of the House of Commons and the House of Lords. The latter procedure means that the draft laid before Parliament is considered accepted by the Commons and the Lords, without a vote, unless a resolution of either House is adopted rejecting the draft within 40 days of it being laid before Parliament.[1] It is not possible to amend a draft Order in Council duly laid before Parliament. It must simply be voted on in its entirety. This means that the period of consultation on the proposal for a draft Order that precedes the parliamentary process is crucial in terms of influencing the content of the final Order in Council.[2] As the Assembly is a relatively new legislature, much of the present Northern Ireland statute book is made up of Orders in Council enacted during the Direct Rule era, and consequently you will encounter examples of them throughout this book. Over time, assuming the Northern Ireland Assembly remains operative, these Orders in Council are likely to be replaced by Acts of that Assembly as it proceeds to amend and update the statute book.

[1] Northern Ireland Act 1974, Sch 1, para 1(5).
[2] Consultation exercises usually take place, but there is no statutory requirement to carry one out.

Transferred, excepted and reserved matters

1.25 As a result of the 1998 Act, the Assembly has competence to enact legislation dealing with what are referred to as 'transferred' matters. Transferred matters are not enumerated in the Act, but instead are described as matters which are not 'excepted' or 'reserved' matters.[1] 'Excepted' or 'reserved' matters remain within the competence of the Westminster Parliament. 'Excepted' matters are outlined in the Northern Ireland Act 1998, Sch 2, and deal with such matters as the Crown, international law and relations, taxation, nationality, immigration and national security. Reserved matters, explained in Schedule 3, include a wide variety of subjects including the criminal law, the police, human genetics, embryology and fertilisation and surrogacy. The Assembly may, however, with the consent of the Secretary of State, enact legislation dealing with excepted matters where they are ancillary to reserved or transferred matters or where they relate directly to reserved matters.[2]

[1]   Northern Ireland Act 1998, s 4(1).
[2]   Northern Ireland Act 1998, s 8(b).

Extending the Assembly's competence

1.26   The Secretary of State has the power to extend, or contract, the legislative competence of the Assembly by designating a reserved matter as a transferred one, and vice versa.[1] It is generally considered, for example, that the Assembly will eventually be given the legislative competence to deal with criminal law and law enforcement matters. In the meantime, however, criminal law legislation and legislation dealing with the police will continue to be enacted in Westminster, either as Orders in Council or as Acts of that Parliament.[2] However, 'excepted' matters will never be transferred, and the Westminster Parliament will always retain competence in respect of them. Issues such as immigration and nationality then, will always remain within the control of the Westminster Parliament. Excepted matters are likely to be dealt with by way of Acts of the Westminster Parliament, but it will also be possible to legislate for them by way of an Order in Council that applies solely to Northern Ireland. The Assembly may modify any provision made by an Act of the Westminster Parliament in so far as it is part of the law of Northern Ireland[3] thus ensuring that amendment of any Westminster legislation that applies to Northern Ireland does not require further legislation at Westminster. Westminster retains the competence to enact legislation for Northern Ireland in respect of 'transferred matters' but in practice is unlikely to avail itself of that power.[4]

[1]   Northern Ireland Act 1998, s 4(2).
[2]   See, for example, the Police (Northern Ireland) Act 2000.
[3]   Northern Ireland Act 1998, s 5(6).
[4]   Northern Ireland Act 1998, s 5(6).

1.27   Transferred matters, therefore, include many of the matters that social workers will encounter in practice and that are dealt with in this book, including adoption, family and child law including child protection, the accountability of social workers, mental health law, many aspects of community care law and anti-discrimination and equality law. Legislation enacted by the Assembly in respect of matters not within its competence would be invalid.[1]

[1]   Northern Ireland Act 1998, s 6.

Suspension of the Assembly

1.28 In the event of the suspension of the Assembly, under the Northern Ireland Act 2000, s 1, (as occurred in October 2002) Northern Ireland legislation can be enacted by the Order in Council procedure. The legal device for suspending the Assembly is an order by the Secretary of State for Northern Ireland made under the Northern Ireland Act 2000, s 1. Similarly, the Secretary of State can also restore the Assembly, by order, under s 2 of that Act. Orders in Council made while the Assembly has been suspended must, however, be made using the affirmative resolution procedure unless the urgency of the situation requires otherwise.[1] A number of Orders in Council were made during the period of suspension beginning in October 2002, largely to do with matters which had originally been the subject of Bills before the Assembly prior to its suspension.[2]

[1] Northern Ireland Act 1998, Sch 1, para 2.
[2] A prominent example featured in this chapter, is the Commissioner for Children and Young Persons (Northern Ireland) Order 2003. See para 1.96. At the time of writing, the Assembly continued to be suspended.

Enacting Acts of the Assembly

1.29 All legislative proposals begin their life in the Assembly as Bills, although some form of consultation process will usually have preceded that stage. A Bill will also usually be accompanied by an Explanatory and Financial Memorandum, which sets out the effect of the Bill, clause by clause, in an accessible form, as well as outlining the financial impact of the Bill, if enacted, on the administration. Each Bill must be accompanied by a statement from the relevant Minister to the effect that in his or her view the legislative proposal is within the competence of the Assembly.[1]

[1] Northern Ireland Act 1998, s 9.

1.30 There is no obligation on the Assembly to engage in consultation before a legislative proposal is presented as a Bill to the Assembly. The one exception is where the Bill might have an adverse impact on one of the protected categories of persons under the Northern Ireland Act 1998, s 75, commonly referred to as the 'statutory duty'.[1] However, it is sufficient at this stage to note that the Explanatory and Financial Memorandum will usually carry a statement as to whether the Bill will have an adverse impact on one of the categories of persons mentioned in s 75. If the Bill does have such an impact, some consideration must be given to reducing that impact, if possible, and whether the adverse impact can be justified on some basis. The Health and Personal Social Services Act (Northern Ireland) 2001, which amongst other things, established the Northern Ireland Social Care Council,[2] will be used as an example to illustrate the Assembly's legislative procedures.

[1] This 'statutory duty' is explored in greater detail in chapter 4, paras 4.75 ff.
[2] See chapter 2, para 2.9.

1.31 There are seven steps in the enactment of a Bill. The 'first stage' involves the introduction of the Bill on the floor of the Assembly by a Minister of the Executive, a Member of the Legislative Assembly or by a Statutory Committee. (The then Minister for Health and Personal Social Services and Public Safety, Bairbre de Brún, introduced the Health and Personal Social Services Bill). This is usually a short, formal stage, with no substantive discussion of the Bill.

1.32   The 'second stage' is a general debate on the Bill's provisions after which the Members of the Assembly vote to determine whether it may proceed to the 'Committee stage'. In the second stage of the Health and Personal Social Services Act (Northern Ireland) 2001, the Minister introduced the Bill explaining its function and genesis, and how it might operate, and there then followed a wide-ranging discussion on the matters dealt with by the Bill. The Minister then addressed questions and issues raised in that debate before the debate was closed.

1.33   In the third stage, a Committee of Members considers the Bill in detail. The committee to which the Bill will be sent for consideration will depend on the substance of the Bill. There are various statutory committees, provided for in the Northern Ireland Act 1998, s 29, whose function it is to 'advise and assist' the relevant Minister and Government department, in effect to 'shadow' the department and its minister. Ten Departmental Committees shadow the various departments and Ministers, and would usually be expected to undertake the Committee stage for any legislation affecting the department's activity. There are also a number of Standing Committees, of which the Committee of the Centre is the most important because it shadows the Office of First Minister and Deputy First Minister, with responsibility for non-departmental matters. Lastly, on occasion Ad Hoc Committees are established to deal with particular issues or legislative proposals.[1] The Committee stage of the 2001 Act was taken by the Health, Social Services and Public Safety Committee, which considered the proposed legislation, at a number of hearings, over a six-week period.

[1]   A prominent example touching on some of the subject matter in this book was the Ad Hoc Committee on the Justice (Northern Ireland) Bill 2002.

1.34   Social workers might find themselves involved in the legislative process at this point because the relevant committee may gather written and/or oral evidence from individuals and organisations with an interest in the subject matter of the Bill in question. Depending on the nature of their practice and the content of the Bill, social workers might be required by employers, for example, to make submissions to the Committee considering a particular piece of proposed legislation. This Committee then reports back to the Assembly on the Bill, and this report then forms the basis of the next stage, referred to as the 'Consideration Stage'. The Committee Stage of the 2001 Act involved the Health and Social Services and Public Safety Committee taking evidence from the social work training body, CCETSW, and Social Services Inspectorate staff, for example.

1.35   In the Consideration stage, the Assembly votes on the detail of the Bill and amendments may be tabled and voted on. A 'Further Consideration' stage, the penultimate stage in the Assembly, then follows the Consideration stage. It also allows members to make further amendments to the Bill and the detailed provisions of the

Bill are once again voted upon. Aside from the Committee Stage, the Consideration Stages are usually the longest and most detailed parts of the enactment process. The 'Final Stage' involves the members passing or rejecting the Bill in the form in which it has emerged from the 'Further Consideration' stage. As one would expect, there are no further opportunities to amend the Bill at this stage. The last stage in the process involves the granting of Royal Assent. It is this final stage that gives the Bill its legal force and although it is theoretically possible for the Monarch to refuse her assent such a course of action hasn't been taken for centuries.

Civic Forum

1.36   A brief mention should be made of the Civic Forum, the consultative body provided for in para 34 of Strand One of the Belfast/Good Friday Agreement and given its statutory basis in the Northern Ireland Act 1998, s 56. The Forum is composed of 60 members, with members being appointed rather than elected, and was established by the First and Deputy First Ministers. It represents a wide range of 'constituencies' including, amongst others, the business, the trade union, and the voluntary and community sectors, community relations, victims and education, with members being appointed rather than elected. At first glance, the Forum might be considered an upper house in the Northern Ireland parliamentary system, in the manner of the House of Lords and Seanad Éireann in the British and Irish systems respectively. However, the one significant difference between the Civic Forum and these other two bodies is that the Forum has no direct role in the legislative process, being merely confined to offering advice to the Assembly on 'social, economic and cultural matters'.[1] However, social workers may also find themselves asked to engage with the Forum on particular matters of interest to the social work profession, as the Forum has in the past addressed issues such as social inclusion, for example,[2] and the role of the Children's Commissioner.

[1]   Northern Ireland Act 1998, s 56.
[2]   See the Civic Forum's, 'A Regional Strategy for Social Inclusion', May 2002.

Finding, reading and citing legislation

1.37   Perceptions of a social worker's professional competence are greatly enhanced by his or her ability to understand and cite legislation correctly. It will also make it easier for others to understand a point being made by a social worker, which requires reference to statute, if the legislation is properly cited.

It should be clear from the explanation above of the various sources of legislation in Northern Ireland that establishing what legislation governs a particular topic might not always be straightforward. It could involve examining the legislative enactments of a number of different legislative bodies, namely the Assembly, the Westminster Parliament, or the Stormont Parliament.

Finding legislation

1.38 Primary legislation for Northern Ireland, enacted by any of the three parliaments mentioned above, is collected in a series entitled 'Northern Ireland Statutes', with volumes produced on an annual basis. All secondary legislation is also published annually in bound volumes and there is also an Index to the Statutory Rules and Orders for Northern Ireland, ie an index to secondary legislation.

1.39 Aside from finding legislation in hard copy format in University libraries and the like, legislation is now also available on the Internet, thereby reducing the difficulty in obtaining such material. The Stationery Office site (www.hmso.gov.uk) provides links to the legislation, both primary and secondary, of the Westminster Parliament and of the Assembly, as well as the UK's other devolved legislatures, enacted in recent years. In particular it allows access to all Orders in Council for Northern Ireland between 1981 and present, and statutory rules from 1991. Quite helpfully, it also provides links to Acts of the Westminster Parliament, and secondary legislation enacted by Westminster that apply exclusively, or primarily, to Northern Ireland.[1] Access to some UK and Northern Ireland legislation is also available on other sites, such as the British and Irish Legal Information Institute (www.bailii.org) and the Irish Legal Information Institute (www.irlii.org) sites. (These last two sites also provide access to selected judgments of the Northern Ireland courts, as does the Northern Ireland Court Service website www.courtserviceni.gov.uk.) Commercial websites, such as Butterworths (www.lexis-nexis.com/professional) also provide access to Westminster legislation, (as well as to Northern Irish and English cases).

[1]   It also, of course, allows access to legislation that applies to all of the UK, and thus to Northern Ireland as well.

Territorial extent

1.40 When establishing the applicable legislation governing a particular topic, it is often necessary to ascertain the extent to which legislation enacted at Westminster applies to Northern Ireland, whether it is still in force, and whether it has been amended or even repealed. It is important to establish the extent of the applicability of a Westminster Act because some of them only apply in part to Northern Ireland. For example, only certain sections of the Criminal Justice and Court Services Act 2000 apply to Northern Ireland. (Whether an Act of the Westminster Parliament applies to Northern Ireland can usually be ascertained by examining the section in the Act entitled 'Extent').

1.41 A useful tool in establishing what statutes govern a particular topic in Northern Ireland is the 'Index to the Statutes', although the most recent edition dates to 1996. This Index sets out the legislation, on various matters, organised on a topic-by-topic basis. There is also a Chronological Table of Northern Ireland Statutes and a series known as 'Statutes Revised', which reproduces amended statutes, thereby removing some of the difficulties in establishing the applicable legislation on a topic. The HMSO website also provides access to the Updated Statutes of Northern Ireland 1921 to 2002.

Citing legislation

1.42   Each individual provision in an Act is a section, and sections are divided into subsections. Where subsections are divided the component elements are referred to as paragraphs, and if these paragraphs are sub-divided, as they sometimes are in complicated legislation to do with social work practice, the sub-divisions are known as sub-paragraphs. This typology applies to Westminster legislation as it does to Acts of the Northern Ireland Assembly, and indeed to the Acts of the defunct Stormont Parliament.

1.43   The nomenclature used to cite Orders in Council is slightly different, however, and these differences can often cause confusion. The provisions of Orders are called articles, with sub-divisions referred to as paragraphs and sub-paragraphs. It may seem obvious, but always give the full, correct title and year when citing legislation, especially in reports.

1.44   The placing of the words 'Northern Ireland' in the title of the legislative instrument in question will indicate which legislature is responsible for enacting it and where one might look to find it. Thus, legislation enacted by Westminster will have the words 'Northern Ireland' before the word 'Act' or 'Order', while legislation enacted by the Assembly, or the Stormont Parliament prior to 1972, will have the words 'Northern Ireland' after the word Act in the title. For example, it should now be clear that the Chronically Sick and Disabled Persons (Northern Ireland) Act 1978 was enacted at Westminster, while the Family Law Act (Northern Ireland) 2001 was enacted by the Northern Ireland Assembly.

Understanding the subject matter of legislation

1.45   A swift way of determining the subject matter of an Order in Council is to read the 'explanatory note' at the end of the Order which, although not part of the Order in any proper sense, provides a short summary of its effect. When dealing with an Act of the Assembly, or of the Westminster Parliament, the easiest way to ascertain the general effect of the Act is to read the long title of the legislation, located just below the short, or commonly used, title of the legislation. This is because Acts do not have an 'explanatory note' at the end.

1.46   Remember that it may be necessary to obtain relevant secondary legislation to establish particular detail relevant to the implementation of the statute. Ascertaining the precise meaning of terms used in legislation is often necessary and to this end particular terms used in an Act or Order in Council may be specially defined. These definitions are usually contained in the definition or interpretation sections and, in the case of an Act, are usually found towards the end, while those in Orders in Council are usually found near the beginning.

Commencement of legislation

1.47   Another point worth noting is that most modern legislation does not come into force at the end of the enactment process. Instead, the usual practice is to make provision in the primary legislation for it to be brought into force by way of secondary legislation, usually called a 'commencement order'. Sometimes a number of commencement orders will be made for an Act or Order because its provisions are being introduced on a gradual basis. This is usually to allow for preparations to be made for the future implementation of the legislation. This means that although an Act or Order may be on the statute book, it nonetheless has no legal force until its provisions have been commenced. For example, the Health and Personal Social Services (2001 Act) (Commencement No 2) Order (Northern Ireland) 2001 brought certain sections of the Health and Personal Social Services (Northern Ireland) Act 2001 into force in September of that year even though the legislation had been enacted since March. The sections in question were those relating to the Northern Ireland Social Care Council's duties, and its powers to make regulations, as well as that provision bringing its predecessor body, CCETSW, to an end.

Common law and the court structure

1.48   The other main source of law is judge-made law, or common law as lawyers more usually call it, and it arises from decisions of the courts where a significant point of law is involved. Such decisions are often referred to as precedent. It is this feature of the common law system that gives it its unique dimension. Students should appreciate that the role of the judge is not simply about interpreting and implementing the will of Parliament as expressed in legislation, but also about divining the applicable rules where there is no legislation dealing with a particular legal dispute. This may involve the judge assessing the value of precedents established in earlier cases or indeed in formulating a new precedent where there are little or no common law authorities on the legal point. (An example of this latter situation can be seen in the *Gillick* case discussed below).[1]

[1]   See para 1.52.

Northern Ireland court structure

1.49   To understand the significance of common law it is necessary to appreciate the hierarchical structure of the courts. A diagram of the court structure, including both civil and criminal courts, on the next page helps to simplify matters. At the lowest level of the court hierarchy is the magistrates' court, which hears both civil and criminal matters. At the next level are the county courts, hearing civil matters and criminal appeals from the magistrates' courts. The High Court (known as the Crown Court when it exercises its criminal jurisdiction) is superior to the county courts, while the highest court sitting in Northern Ireland is the Northern Ireland Court of Appeal. The High Court has three divisions, the Family Division, the Queen's Bench Division and the Chancery Division.

1.50   The third division does not concern us here and we will examine the role of the second named division in chapter 2, when the impact of judicial review on social work activity is explained.[1] The Family Division is of most relevance to social work practice and is relevant to the material explored in chapters 6, 7 and 8, which deal with child protection, adoption and fostering and relationship breakdown respectively. Appeals from the Northern Ireland Court of Appeal may be made to the House of Lords in London, which sits at the apex of the judicial system in the UK.

	The Court Structure in Northern Ireland[2]	
	House of Lords *Final court of appeal in* *UK, hearing appeals on* *points of law in cases of* *major importance*	
	The Court of Appeal *Hears appeals on points of* *law in civil and criminal* *cases*	
High Court		*Crown Court*
Hears appeals from county court, *judicial review applications, wardship* *and other complex cases*		*Hears indictable criminal cases*
Has three divisions		
	Queens *Bench* *Division*	
	Family *Division*	
	Chancery *Division*	
	County Courts *(including Care Centres)* *Hears civil actions and* *appeals from magistrates'* *courts* *(7 divisions)*	

	Magistrates' Courts *(including Family Proceedings Courts and Youth Court)* *Hears civil and summary criminal matters and preliminary matters in indictable criminal trials (21 Petty Sessions Districts)*	

[1]   See para 2.105.
[2]   This diagram is partly based on that used by the Northern Ireland Court Service in 'Judicial Statistics 2002', July 2003, p 3.

1.51   The doctrine of precedent requires courts lower down the hierarchy to apply principles of law determined by higher courts on a previous occasion, in cases raising similar issues. In this way, lawyers speak of a court being bound by precedent. Each level of court then binds those courts below it, and the House of Lords is generally bound by its own decisions though it may depart from them in certain instances. It is important to remember that the binding element is not the result of the case, but the reasoning involved in reaching that decision. Lawyers refer to this element of a judgment as the *ratio decidendi*. Establishing the ratio of a case is not a straightforward task as judges rarely indicate its presence in the text of their speeches. The ratio is often constructed then, by considering the judgments handed down by the court and deducing the reason, or reasons, for its decision from the judges' speeches. It is useful to choose a particular case to illustrate these points.

Establishing the precedent

1.52   The case of *Gillick v West Norfolk and Wisbech Area Health Authority*[1] is perhaps one of the most significant decisions affecting social work practice that the House of Lords has made in decades, and is a useful example to use to understand how a precedent is established. The mother of teenage daughters challenged the right of the local health authority to authorise its doctors to provide contraceptives to girls below 16 years of age, the age of consent then applying in England and Wales. The House of Lords was divided as to the lawfulness of this authorisation, with three Law Lords (Lords Fraser, Scarman and Bridge) considering it to be lawful and two (Lords Brandon and Templeman) declaring it to be unlawful. Each of the judges who considered the direction to be lawful handed down a speech outlining his reasons. Constructing the ratio in the *Gillick* case, then, is a matter of considering all three speeches of the majority and devising a common reason, or reasons, for their decision. Lord Bridge largely agreed with Lords Fraser and Scarman. Both these Law Lords were agreed that there was no statutory prohibition on a doctor prescribing contraceptives to girls under 16 and also that parental rights gave way to children's rights accordingly as the child matured. Lord Fraser appeared to set a number of conditions on the circumstances in which doctors could prescribe contraceptives to under 16 year old girls when he advise that the doctor should be satisfied of the following matters:

'(1) that the girl (although under 16 years of age) will understand his advice; (2) that he cannot persuade her to inform her parents or to allow him to inform the parents that she is seeking contraceptive advice; (3) that she is very likely to begin or to continue having sexual intercourse with or without contraceptive treatment; (4) that unless she receives contraceptive advice or treatment her physical or mental health or both are likely to suffer; (5) that her best interests require him to give her contraceptive advice, treatment or both without the parental consent.

That result ought not to be regarded as a licence for doctors to disregard the wishes of parents on this matter whenever they find it convenient to do so. Any doctor who behaves in such a way would be failing to discharge his professional responsibilities, and I would expect him to be disciplined by his own professional body accordingly.'

[1] [1986] AC 112, [1985] 3 All ER 402.

1.53 Lord Scarman imposed similar, though not identical, limitations or conditions on a doctor in such a situation:

'He would know that it was his duty to seek to persuade the girl to let him bring into consultation her parents (or one of them). If she refused, he (or the counsellor to whom the girl had gone) must ask himself whether the case was one of those exceptional cases in which the guidance permitted a doctor to prescribe contraception without the knowledge or consent of a parent (provided always that in the exercise of his clinical judgment he thought this course to be in the true interest of his patient). In my judgment the guidance clearly implies that in exceptional cases the parental right to make decisions as to the care of their children, which derives from their right of custody, can lawfully be overridden, and that in such cases the doctor may without parental consultation or consent prescribe contraceptive treatment in the exercise of his clinical judgment. And the guidance reminds the doctor that in such cases he owes the duty of confidentiality to his patient, by which is meant that the doctor would be in breach of his duty to her if he did communicate with her parents.'

1.54 Lord Scarman, in particular, made specific and repeated reference to the child reaching a 'sufficient understanding and intelligence' to be capable of making up its own mind,[1] suggesting a slightly higher threshold than mere understanding, as indicated in Lord Fraser's speech. And this reference to the child's 'sufficient intelligence and understanding' forms part of the accepted ratio of the case, and more importantly, of the legal language relating to children's competence. The generally accepted view is that *Gillick* is authority for the proposition that a child may be competent to consent to medical treatment, irrespective of the parents' views, if the medical practitioner considers the child to be sufficiently intelligent and mature enough to understand the significance of the treatment to which he or she consents. This is the notion now commonly referred to as '*Gillick* competency' and is likely to surface at some point in a social worker's practice. But the point that needs to be understood for present purposes is that one can see that this principle is derived from a synthesis of the various judgments.

¹   [1985] 3 All ER 402 at 423.

Applying the precedent

1.55   There are a number of features of this ratio that are worth considering and that help one to understand the importance of precedent. The most obvious is that the principle of '*Gillick* competency' is not confined to receiving contraceptive or reproductive advice, but can apply to all medical treatment. Lawyers sometimes refer to this as the 'elasticity of the ratio'. In other words, the significance of precedents in general is that they may apply to a broader range of factual circumstances than those that gave rise to the case in the first place. The principles underlying such decisions can be generalised to a certain degree and applied to analogous situations, and are not confined to identical scenarios to that which gave rise to the case in the first place.

1.56   Furthermore, the doctrine of precedent stipulates that the lower court is only bound to follow the higher court if the principle of law determined by the higher court is applicable in the case before it. If the lower court can distinguish the case it is hearing from that in which the higher court made its decision, then it is not required to apply the principle developed by the higher court. 'Distinguishing' one case from another is done by identifying legal and/or factual differences between the two cases, thereby demonstrating that the principle in the first cannot apply to the second.¹ An example will illustrate this point. In *Re R (a minor) (wardship: consent to treatment)*,² the Court of Appeal was faced with the situation where a girl in a adolescent psychiatric unit, where the proposed programme of treatment included the compulsory administration of certain anti-psychotic drugs, refused to consent to taking those drugs. When she had periods of lucidity she was considered to be '*Gillick* competent'. The court distinguished *Gillick* and held that it only applied to situations where the child wished to consent to medical treatment, and not to situations where the child, as a ward of court, wished to refuse his or her consent. Indeed, where the child refused to consent, others, like parents with the power to consent, could do so. As a result, the court in that case could make an order allowing the administration of the drugs.

¹   Another example of distinguishing cases can be seen in the cases of *Barry* and *Tandy* discussed in chapter 10, para 10.28.
²   [1992] Fam 11, [1991] 4 All ER 177, [1992] 1 FLR 190, [1992] 2 FCR 229.

1.57   However, notwithstanding the importance of the doctrine of precedent, social workers should be aware that most cases are decided on their own facts, and disputes about points of law are rare. More often than not the nature of the evidence made available to the court is the decisive factor in its decision. This evidence will come to the court by way of oral testimony and/or documentary evidence. Thus, the contemporaneous recording of evidence, whether this involves the maintenance of case or file notes, for example, or the production of accurate minutes of meetings and consultations with clients, is crucial in the social worker's interaction with the legal system. These matters are the subject of chapter 3.

Courts exercising special or particular jurisdiction

1.58   Occasionally courts are given a special jurisdiction by statute and as a result have a particular designation, or title, when exercising its powers under that legislation. In practice they will be known by these titles and it is useful to be aware of them. Social workers should be particularly aware that the court structure for hearing cases under the Children (Northern Ireland) Order 1995 has been specially designed for that purpose. Thus the Family Proceedings Court (FPC), for example, is the magistrates' court exercising its jurisdiction under the Children (Northern Ireland) Order 1995 to hear 'family proceedings'.[1] The FPC, however, differs from the magistrates' court in that, like the Youth Court, lay panellists sit with the magistrate.[2] The county courts involved in hearing family proceedings are referred to as 'Care Centres'.[3]

[1]   Defined in art 8(3) of that Order and including adoption, matrimonial and Children Order cases, amongst others. See chapter 6, para 6.28.
[2]   This arises from the Children (Northern Ireland) Order 1995, art 164(4).
[3]   The operation of the family court structure is explained in more detail in chapter 6, see para 6.45.

1.59   Social workers may also encounter references to the 'Domestic Proceedings Court', which is the magistrates' court hearing cases about financial support for family members under the Domestic Proceedings (Northern Ireland) Order 1980[1] and about domestic violence under the Family Homes and Domestic Violence (Northern Ireland) Order 1998.[2] The 'Divorce Court' is a common term used to describe the county court or the High Court exercising its jurisdiction under the Matrimonial Causes (Northern Ireland) Order 1978 to hear, and grant, divorce petitions.[3] Finally, the Youth Court is the new name for the juvenile court, and deals with juveniles under the age of 17, who are suspected of committing criminal offences. The Youth Court is presided over by a three-member panel, one of whom is a qualified lawyer and the other two of whom are lay panellists. Specialist tribunals also play important roles in the legal system. For example, the Mental Health Review Tribunal ascertains whether persons detained under mental health legislation should continue to be detained[4] while the Industrial Tribunal and the Fair Employment Tribunal deal with employment law matters, including discrimination complaints.[5]

[1]   See chapter 9, para 9.79.
[2]   Family Homes and Domestic Violence (Allocation of Proceedings) Order (Northern Ireland) 1999, art 4. See chapter 9, para 9.18.
[3]   See chapter 9, para 9.50.
[4]   See chapter 11, para 11.88.

⁵ See chapter 4, para 4.45.

Participants in the legal system

1.60 This also seems the appropriate place to offer a brief explanation of the role those involved in the administration of the legal system. The legal profession in Northern Ireland is composed of two branches, solicitors and barristers. The former usually provide advice and assistance to clients up to the commencement of court proceedings. The latter, on the other hand, are generally responsible for the preparation of court applications and the presentation of cases in court. Generally, barristers may only be briefed by solicitors, so in order to access a barrister a member of the public must first engage a solicitor. Barristers are sole practitioners who are self-employed. They are based in the Bar Library in the Royal Courts of Justice, Chichester Street, Belfast. Solicitors can, and do, operate from offices located anywhere in Northern Ireland, either as sole practitioners, or as part of a firm.

1.61 The judiciary in Northern Ireland is appointed by the Lord Chancellor and is administered by the Northern Ireland Court Service.[1] The most senior judge in the jurisdiction is the Lord Chief Justice of Northern Ireland, and there are three Lord Justices who sit in the Court of Appeal. There are seven High Court judges, one of whom is appointed to the Family Division, while five of them are appointed to the Queen's Bench Division. The county court judges, magistrates and district judges make up the remainder of the judiciary. (The last mentioned administer the Small Claims Courts, but also, more crucially from the social workers' point of view, hear applications about child-care and financial matters arising from county court divorces).

[1] At present the appointments process is overseen by a Commissioner for Judicial Appointments for Northern Ireland, and there are plans to establish a Judicial Appointments Commission for Northern Ireland, which would make, rather than supervise, appointments.

1.62 A noticeable development in the Northern Irish legal system in the last number of years has been the vibrancy of Non-Governmental Organisations (NGOs). Notable NGOs, whose work is legal in nature and touches upon social work practice include the Law Centre (Northern Ireland) and the Children's Law Centre. The work of the former embraces, amongst other areas, the delivery of community care services, whilst the latter, as it title suggests, is concerned with the law relating to children in Northern Ireland, in particular whether children's rights are being vindicated in law and in practice. 'Children (Northern Ireland)'[1] is another such NGO and is an umbrella organisation for organisations working with, or on behalf of, children in Northern Ireland. Its main focus is on making interventions about policy matters relating to children's rights. Social workers in practice may find it useful to direct clients to these NGOs or perhaps to direct appropriate issues that come to their attention to them.

[1] Formerly known as 'ChildCare (Northern Ireland)'.

High Court Masters

1.63 Some other notable office holders that social workers may encounter include High Court Masters, and the Official Solicitor. High Court Masters, of whom there are eight, fulfil important administrative and quasi-judicial functions in the legal system, because they deal with procedural matters and minor legal issues arising out of court actions. There are two High Court Masters whose activity may have a particular impact on social work practice, namely the Master (Care and Protection) and the Master (Probate and Matrimonial), and therefore are worthy of mention here.

1.64 The former exercises functions in respect of wardship, adoption, guardianship, abduction of minors, mental health patients, and Children Order proceedings that are not part of a pending matrimonial action.[1] The latter is concerned with all other Family Division business[2] which includes all matrimonial actions, and will deal, for example, with child residence and contact issues on divorce.

---

[1] Rules of the Supreme Court (Northern Ireland) 1980, Order 1, r 17. For more on the Office of Care and Protection, see chapter 11, para 11.79.
[2] Rules of the Supreme Court (Northern Ireland) 1980, Order 1, r 16.

Official Solicitor

1.65 The Official Solicitor is a court officer,[1] who may on occasion represent children in particular legal actions, particularly those cases with a wider legal importance or, more usually, where there is no other suitable person or agency to represent the child. In the past, the Official Solicitor principally dealt with wardship, adoption and, on occasion, childcare proceedings where he or she would act as a guardian ad litem. The development of guardians ad litem[2] for use in public law childcare proceedings, in particular, has significantly reduced this latter role. Further, as wardship has become less frequent under the regime set out in the Children (Northern Ireland) Order 1995,[3] the Official Solicitor's role has changed to some degree. However, it still plays an important role in the Official Solicitor's work, with 43 of the office's 486 cases relating to minors in 2002 being composed of wardship cases, and 139 of them composed of Children Order cases.[4] Social workers might also encounter the Official Solicitor in cases relating to adoption or guardianship or in some matrimonial cases.[5]

---

[1] Established under the Judicature (Northern Ireland) Act 1978, s 75.
[2] See chapter 6, para 6.63.
[3] Article 173.
[4] Northern Ireland Court Service, Judicial Statistics 2002, Table B41, combining cases 'received' and 'current cases' for that year. These two areas comprise the two largest areas of work for the Official Solicitor.
[5] The circumstances in which the Official Solicitor will act in family proceedings are summarised in the Children Order Advisory Committee's 'Best Practice Guidance' note: July 2003, Section 11.

The human rights dimension to the Northern Ireland legal system

1.66   Recent years have seen human rights related developments that have particular significance for social work practice and for social work clients. These developments have ensured that various elements of the public sector must respect certain rights of individuals. The developments discussed here are: (i) the implementation of the Human Rights Act 1998 (hereafter 'HRA'); (ii) the establishment of the Northern Ireland Human Rights Commission; and (iii) the appointment of a Children's Commissioner for Northern Ireland. One final matter worth mentioning in respect of human rights legal developments is that the equality dimension to Northern Ireland's legal system has increased significantly. This has resulted in the mainstreaming of principles of equality of opportunity in policymaking, and service delivery. However, this aspect of Northern Ireland's legal system is dealt with in more detail in chapter 4.[1]

[1]   See para 4.75.

1.67   Taken together these developments might be said to represent a mainstreaming of human rights principles in public policymaking and implementation. In practical terms they offer an opportunity to social workers, and their employing organisations, to ensure that their clients' rights and interests are protected and thus they amount to a significant addition to the manner in which the legal system operates. In summary, the significance of these human rights developments is that they alter the nature of the discourse between social workers, public agencies and their clients. The external standards provided by international human rights law will now form part of the accountability mechanisms for agencies and bodies engaged in areas relevant to social work practice. Where the practice, or the law governing it, amounts to a violation of individual human rights, then appropriate alterations will have to be made to ensure the compatibility of that law and/or practice with human rights law.

Understanding international human rights law

1.68   Before explaining the impact of these three developments, it is necessary to provide some explanation of international human rights law. International human rights law derives from treaties agreed by States, and by ratifying the treaties the States undertake to implement the terms of the treaties in their domestic jurisdictions. These treaties usually apply at a global or a regional level, that is they are either open to all countries for their signature, or only to those countries within a particular region such as Europe, for example. An example of a global treaty is the United Nations Convention on the Rights of the Child (UNCRC) while the European Convention of Human Rights (ECHR) is an example of a regional treaty. Broadly speaking, there are two main ways of enforcing human rights treaties, and it is through these that social workers may become aware of this dimension of the legal system. The first is by application to a specially created court or tribunal, whose purpose is to interpret the treaty, and the second is by way of report to a committee specifically tasked with monitoring the States' implementation of the obligations in the treaty.

1.69 The ECHR is enforced by the first of these two methods. Applications can be made, against the UK, to the European Court of Human Rights sitting in Strasbourg. (This is not an appeal from the decision of the domestic court but a separate and distinct case, even though the issue will probably also have been dealt with by the UK courts).

1.70 The UNCRC, on the other hand, is enforced in the second manner described above, ie by way of a report to a committee. The UK is required to make periodic reports to the UNCRC explaining the manner in which it is observing its obligations under that Convention. The UK is then quizzed on that report at hearings in Geneva, after which the Committee produces written comments and observations. The expectation is that the country's next report to the Committee will address those comments and observations. The UK's second, and most recent, report was considered at a hearing in September 2002.[1] The UNCRC published its observations on this report in October 2002.[2] The Committee's observations were broad-ranging, featuring criticisms of the UK's failure to incorporate the terms of the UNCRC into domestic law[3] and the lack of a 'rights-based approach to policy development' in respect of children's policy matters, for example.[4] It made specific reference to Northern Ireland in its recommendations that 'plastic bullets' no longer be used for riot control[5] and that anti-terrorist legislation be reviewed to take account of its affect on juveniles.[6]

[1]   The Committee has asked the UK to combine its third and fourth reports and present the next report 18 months before 15 July 2007: Concluding observations of the Committee on the Rights of the Child: United Kingdom of Great Britain and Northern Ireland CRC/C/15/Add 188, para 66.
[2]   Concluding observations of the Committee on the Rights of the Child: United Kingdom of Great Britain and Northern Ireland CRC/C/15/Add 188, 9 October 2002.
[3]   Concluding observations of the Committee on the Rights of the Child: United Kingdom of Great Britain and Northern Ireland CRC/C/15/Add 188, 9 October 2002, para 9.
[4]   Concluding observations of the Committee on the Rights of the Child: United Kingdom of Great Britain and Northern Ireland CRC/C/15/Add 188, 9 October 2002, para 15.
[5]   Concluding observations of the Committee on the Rights of the Child: United Kingdom of Great Britain and Northern Ireland CRC/C/15/Add 188, 9 October 2002, para 28.
[6]   Concluding observations of the Committee on the Rights of the Child: United Kingdom of Great Britain and Northern Ireland CRC/C/15/Add 188, 9 October 2002, para 54(c).

1.71 It is worth noting that the Children's Law Centre and Save the Children Fund produced a report, called 'Getting it Right?', to parallel the UK's second report, highlighting what it considered to be the areas of concern in the implementation of the UNCRC in Northern Ireland.[1] Social workers might find themselves involved in this UN reporting process as a result of contributions to reports like 'Getting it Right?' or to similar attempts to present a non-governmental perspective on the UK's compliance with the UNCRC in Northern Ireland.

[1]   Children's Law Centre and Save the Children, Belfast, 1999.

1.72 The two enforcement methods are very different in a number of respects. Applications to a court are about specific instances of human rights abuse and usually focus on a discrete number of rights. The focus of the court is on the circumstances of the applicant only. Whilst that allows the applicant to obtain a remedy it may not provide an opportunity to address more systemic human rights violations or to deal with a multiplicity of problems in the implementation of a particular treaty. Where a committee is considering a State's report, however, because the report deals with all actions of the State in respect of the obligations over the previous number of years since the last report, the committee is necessarily taking quite a broad view of various issues and matters. A committee will not usually focus on a particular case, for example, and so it is not useful to the individual seeking to have a determination made about his or her case. In both cases, however, the obligation to respond is on the State. Whichever method of enforcement is used, the obligation on States is to take remedial action to ensure compatibility between domestic law and international law. In this way there is a 'trickle-down' effect from the international to the domestic legal spheres, with the resultant improvement in human rights protection within a State's territory.

Types of international human rights treaties

1.73   There are a wide variety of international human rights law treaties, establishing rights for a broad category of persons. Examples of treaties other than those mentioned include the United Nations Covenant on Civil and Political Rights (CCPR), and the Covenant on Economic, Social and Cultural Rights (CESCR), as well as the Convention for the Elimination of Discrimination against Women (CEDAW), and the Convention for the Elimination of All Forms of Racial Discrimination (CERD).[1] All of these treaties have been ratified by the UK and were utilised by the Northern Ireland Human Rights Commission in drawing up the draft Bill of Rights for Northern Ireland (see later).[2] However, the two examples mentioned earlier, the UNCRC and the ECHR, are likely to have the greatest relevance for social work practice for reasons which will become clearer as we explore the human rights developments that have directly affected Northern Ireland.

[1]   The NI Human Rights Commission has produced a guide to this last named Convention.
[2]   See para 1.109.

Human Rights Act 1998

1.74   The Human Rights Act 1998, which came into force in November 2000, incorporates the European Convention of Human Rights into domestic law. This means that the rights protected by that Convention – referred to in the HRA[1] and throughout this book as 'Convention rights' – are now protected in the domestic courts of the UK, removing the necessity of applying to the European Court of Human Rights to have one's Convention rights protected.

[1]   HRA, s 1.

1.75 Social workers employed by public sector organisations should therefore be aware of the HRA, as they may encounter rights-based arguments at some point in their employment, particularly if engaged in child and family work. The effect of the HRA is that, in delivering services, and in formulating or amending policies, or in performing any other functions, boards and trusts (or others carrying out 'public functions') must not interfere improperly with individuals' Convention rights. Where this does happen, the courts will declare the action to be unlawful.

1.76 The specific obligation on public authorities or 'any person certain of whose functions are functions of a public nature', is that they must act in a manner that is compatible with 'Convention rights'.[1] The expression 'public authorities' clearly includes the DHSSPS, the health boards, the Health and Social Services Trusts and any special agencies.[2] Furthermore, the reference to 'any person certain of whose functions are functions of a public nature' could include private sector organisations to whom boards and trusts have contracted-out certain activity that the courts recognise as being public in nature. The significance of this for social workers and their employing organisations is discussed below,[3] but first it is necessary to offer a general guide to the Convention rights protected by the HRA.

---

[1] HRA, s 6.
[2] For descriptions of these entities, see para 1.110.
[3] See para 1.87.

Understanding Convention rights

1.77 A full exposition of all the Convention rights and their potential impact on social work practice is beyond the scope of this book, but social workers should be aware that they will have implications for aspects of their work.[1] Certain rights are, however, discussed in more detail in the appropriate chapters, and therefore, article 8, the right to privacy and family life, the right that practising social workers are mostly likely to encounter, is explored in chapter 6 in particular, but also in chapters 7 and 9. Consideration is also given, where appropriate, to other Convention rights, or aspects of them – like article 3 (freedom from torture, inhuman and degrading treatment),[2] article 5 (right to liberty),[3] article 6 (right to a fair trial)[4] and article 14 (the right not to be subject to discrimination).[5] In the meantime a general explanation is offered here of some more salient rights for social work practice.

---

[1] For comprehensive treatment of ECHR jurisprudence see Harris, O'Boyle and Warbrick, 'Law of the European Convention on Human Rights' (2nd edn) Butterworths.
[2] See chapter 6, para 6.21.
[3] See chapter 11, para 11.10.
[4] See chapter 6, para 6.23.
[5] See chapter 9, para 9.11.

1.78 These Convention rights include, amongst others, the right to life, the right not to be subject to torture or inhuman or degrading treatment or punishment, the right to privacy and family life and the rights to freedom of expression, assembly, and thought as well as the right to education. One might think that some of these rights would have little application to social work practice, but the application of them has been novel and a few case examples will demonstrate the extent to which these rights might indeed have significance for social work practice.

ARTICLE 3: TORTURE, INHUMAN AND DEGRADING TREATMENT

1.79   The right not to be subject to torture, inhuman or degrading treatment or punishment (article 3 of the Convention) has featured in a number of corporal punishment cases against the UK. The most recent of these, *A v United Kingdom*,[1] concerned a stepfather who had been acquitted of assaulting his stepchild when he had punished him by beating him with a cane. The European Court of Human Rights found that the UK had failed to protect the child's right not to be subject to degrading punishment because the law, which allowed a child to be 'reasonably chastised' by its parents or guardian, was too vague and didn't therefore provide enough protection for children from degrading punishment. As a result, the law in this area must be amended and at present a consultation process has been completed to determine the nature of the amendments that are required in Northern Ireland law.[2]

[1]   (1998) 27 EHRR 611.
[2]   See the consultation document issued by the Office of Law Reform, 'Physical punishment in the home – thinking about the issues, looking at the evidence', September 2000.

1.80   In another case, *ZP and TM v United Kingdom*,[1] the European Court considered that the failure by social services authorities to apply to the courts to have children taken into care where they were clearly suffering horrendous abuse and neglect was a breach of their article 3 rights.[2] Even though the abuse and neglect was being caused by private persons, and not the State, the State had a duty – a positive obligation – to protect the children's rights vis-à-vis third parties by intervening to bring the harm to an end. Positive obligations of this nature – requiring the State to actually do something, in contrast to negative obligations that prohibit the State from interfering – have been declared to exist in a number of Convention rights articles, most notably, from a social worker's perspective, in article 8, the right to privacy and family life.

[1]   [2001] 2 FCR 246, [2001] 2 FLR 612, 10 BHRC 38G, E Ct HR.
[2]   This case is discussed further in chapter 2 in the context of social workers' liability in negligence.

ARTICLE 5: RIGHT TO LIBERTY

1.81   Article 5 provides a guarantee that no one shall be deprived of their liberty except in a number of prescribed circumstances, and if a person's detention does not fall within one of these prescribed circumstances it will be a violation of his or her right to liberty, no matter what other reason is advanced for their detention. It also provides detained persons with certain rights to challenge the lawfulness of their detention. The two circumstances that have most relevance for social work practice are:[1]

- the detention of a minor by lawful order for the purpose of educational supervision or his lawful detention for the purpose of bringing him before the competent legal authority;
- the lawful detention of persons for the prevention of the spreading of infectious diseases, of persons of unsound mind, alcoholics or drug addicts or vagrants.

[1] Convention right, arts 5(1)(d) and 5(1)(e) respectively.

1.82 The first of these circumstances justifies the detention of minors in secure accommodation, while the second allows detention of persons with mental health problems or substance abuse problems.[1] In respect of the first of these matters, note that the detention of the minor must be for his or her 'educational supervision' and detention purely as a form of punishment or control, would be incompatible with the Convention.[2]

[1] Detention of persons with mental health problems features in chapter 11, paras 11.28 ff.
[2] For more on this element of Convention right, art 5, see chapter 6, para 6.109.

ARTICLES 6 AND 8: FAIR TRIAL AND FAMILY LIFE

1.83 Two further Convention rights that will be referred to here are articles 6 and 8. Article 6 provides that:

'In the determination of his civil rights and obligations or of any criminal charge against him, everyone is entitled to a fair and public hearing within a reasonable time by an independent and impartial tribunal established by law.'

1.84 Article 8 (commonly referred to as the right to privacy and family life)[1] is highly relevant to core areas of social work practice, like adoption and child and family work. The right will be more closely examined in chapters 6–8.[2] The intention here is to give a flavour of the operation of both these rights by focusing on *P, C and S v United Kingdom*,[3] a case involving a breach of both these rights.

[1] For text of art 8, see chapter 6, para 6.12.
[2] See in particular chapter 6, paras 6.11 ff.
[3] (2002) 35 EHRR 1075, E Ct HR.

1.85 S was the child of P and C, and had been the subject of an Emergency Protection Order, a Care Order[1] and, ultimately, a Freeing Order[2] allowing her to be adopted. The reason for the removal of the child from its parents and its placement for adoption lay chiefly in the fact that P was believed to be suffering from Munchausen's Syndrome by Proxy, which had caused her to abuse another child born to her some years previously. P was forced to conduct her own defence to the Care Order and Freeing Order proceedings because her legal representatives had withdrawn owing to the unreasonableness of her instructions. The judge considered that the case could proceed with P presenting her own case. In light of the complexity of the case, this lack of legal representation resulted in the European Court of Human Rights concluding that she had not had a fair trial, as required by article 6. It also concluded that the relatively short period of time between the Care Order and Freeing Order applications – a mere week – further infringed the article 6 rights of P and C.

3   See chapter 6, para 6.119.
4   See chapter 8, para 8.45.

1.86   Furthermore, it considered that the issuing of an Emergency Protection Order in the circumstances of the case, authorising the removal of the child from its mother within 12 hours of its birth as she recuperated in the hospital, was a Draconian response that was not 'necessary in a democratic society', and thus it breached the parents' right to family life, under article 8.

Bodies subject to the Human Rights Act 1998

1.87   As outlined above, all public bodies are subject to the HRA, but so too are those private bodies carrying out public functions. In a number of cases the courts have had to address the issue of when a private body must act in compliance with the HRA.

1.88   The Court of Appeal in England considered that the Leonard Cheshire Foundation (LCF), in fulfilling a contract made between it and a local authority to provide accommodation services for the authority, thereby allowing the authority to fulfil its statutory duty,[1] was not performing public functions under the HRA.[2] The fact that LCF was receiving public funding was not enough to determine whether the functions were public or private. The Foundation was not performing statutory powers, nor did the fact that the authority was acting under statute confer powers on the Foundation. LCF was not, the court concluded, 'standing in the shoes of the local authorities'.[3]

1   Under the National Assistance Act 1948, s 21.
2   *R (Heather) v Leonard Cheshire Foundation* [2002] 2 All ER 936, [2002] EWCA Civ 366.
3   *R (Heather) v Leonard Cheshire Foundation* [2002] 2 All ER 936, [2002] EWCA Civ 366 at [35].

1.89   Further consideration was given to this issue in *Poplar Housing and Regeneration Community Association Ltd v Donoghue*.[1] There, a tenant of the housing association was resisting eviction on the basis that eviction interfered with her right to family life, under article 8.[2] The main issue for the Court of Appeal was whether the housing association was performing public functions. The association was not a public body merely because it performed activities on behalf of a public body, in this case a local housing authority. But the court did consider that on this occasion the association's activities were so closely assimilated to those of the local housing authority to justify the conclusion that it was a 'functional public authority'.[3] The housing association was set up by the local authority to take the transfer of some of its housing stock and some of the local authority members were also members of the housing association. Thus the HRA applied to the housing association.

1   [2001] EWCA Civ 595, [2002] QB 48, [2001] 4 All ER 604.

1.90 Similarly, in another case the issue was whether a Church of England Parochial Church Council was to be considered a public authority because it was created and empowered by law, exercised functions which could be enforced in the courts, and had powers that private individuals did not have.[1] However, the House of Lords considered that such a body could not be considered a 'core' public authority as it had a religious mission and was not exercising governmental power. In *R (A) v Partnerships in Care Ltd*[2] a private psychiatric hospital was a public body for the purposes of the HRA, because it was operating to certain statutory requirements effectively delegated to it in its contractual arrangements with the relevant health authorities.

1 *Aston Cantlow and Wilmcote with Billesley Parochial Church Council v Wallbank* [2001] EWCA Civ 713, [2001] 3 All ER 393; revsd [2003] UKHL 37, [2003] 3 All ER 1213.
2 [2002] EWHC 529 (Admin), [2002] 1 WLR 2610.

1.91 These cases mean that where a social worker's employing organisation is effectively 'standing in the shoes' of the board or trust, in that it is, for all practical purposes, exercising the statutory functions – as opposed to helping the Board or Trust to facilitate its statutory brief – it too is a public body which must act in accordance with the HRA, even though it may, for other purposes, be a private organisation.

Incompatibility with Convention rights

1.92 There are two main ways in which incompatibility with Convention rights can be argued. First, the applicant may argue that the legislation that a public body relies upon to authorise its actions is in breach of the applicant's Convention rights. Secondly, the applicant may assert that the public body had not acted in a manner that is compatible with those Convention rights, either because it has not considered the applicant's rights, or because it has misapplied the principles that govern them.

1.93 Faced with an allegation that a legislative provision infringes an individual's Convention rights the courts must interpret the provision and it 'must be read and given effect in a way which is compatible with the Convention rights' so far as it is possible to do so.[1] If this is not possible and the court concludes that the legislation improperly infringes an individual's rights, then the High Court can be asked to issue a 'declaration of incompatibility', thereby indicating that the legislation is incompatible with the HRA.[2] This will usually result in the legislation being amended to ensure it no longer infringes Convention rights, although there is no obligation on Parliament to do so. Until appropriate amendments are made, however, primary legislation of the Westminster Parliament can continue to be operated or enforced and its validity is not affected.[3] However, secondary legislation, which, confusingly, in this context includes Northern Ireland Orders in Council and Acts of the Assembly, will be invalid and inoperable once the declaration of incompatibility is made, provided that the fault lies purely with the secondary legislation and that the primary legislation does not prevent the incompatibility being removed.[4]

1   HRA, s 3.
2   HRA, s 4.
3   HRA, s 3(2).
4   HRA, s 4.

1.94   Where the allegation made is that the public body did not act in a manner that is compatible with Convention rights, the court must examine the actions of that body, and measure them against the principles outlined in the Convention right and those deriving from the jurisprudence of the European Court of Human Rights in Strasbourg. This assessment of whether the public body did in fact have regard for the applicant's Convention rights has led to the courts requiring documentary evidence of HRA assessments in some cases, and not allowing the public body to simply assert that it has considered the applicant's Convention rights.[1] This has a practical dimension for social workers employed by public bodies because it means that, ideally, they should be documenting their assessments of the compatibility of their actions with Convention rights, so that they may be produced at a later date, if necessary.

1   See *R(A) v National Probation Service* [2003] EWHC 2910 (admin), [2003] All ER (D) 241 (Nov), where the court noted the failure of the Probation Services' risk assessment to explicitly balance A's art 8 rights before deciding to release details of his conviction. The decision to make that disclosure was unlawful.

Pleading Convention rights

1.95   Arguments that an individual's rights have been violated by a public body or a body carrying out a public function can be made in any court proceedings at any court level, even the magistrates' courts, for example. Furthermore, because the courts are deemed to be 'public authorities'[1] they must ensure that there has been no violation of an individual's rights, even if that person's legal advisers make no such claim. The effect of this is that Convention rights may arise in almost any court proceeding, whether civil or criminal. For example, a father might argue that his right to family life had been infringed in the making of an order refusing him contact with his children. Or a defendant in a criminal trial might argue that the public order offence with which he or she was charged might amount to a breach of his right to freedom of expression or assembly. Or in a judicial review, a community care user might argue that the refusal of a trust to provide her with further assistance, by way of social services or otherwise, was a breach of the positive obligation on the State to protect her article 8 rights to family life.

1   HRA, s 6(3)(b).

Children's Commissioner

1.96   The Commissioner for Children and Young People for Northern Ireland, to give it its full title, was established under the Commissioner for Children and Young

People (Northern Ireland) Order 2003, and appointed by the First and Deputy First Ministers, with the principal aim of safeguarding and promoting the rights and best interests of children.[1] Note that no definition of these 'rights' is provided, and therefore it should be open to the Commissioner to argue for an inclusive approach, making use of the full range of treaties mentioned earlier.[2] The Commissioner is, as one would expect, to have regard to the UNCRC when exercising his or her functions.[3] As with the office of the Ombudsman,[4] the effectiveness of the Commissioner may depend upon the incumbent's view of his or her role. It is to be hoped that the Commissioner will seize the opportunity to assess children's services and facilities from a children's rights perspective, assessing what additional role the Commissioner's office can play in the panoply of accountability mechanisms available in Northern Ireland,[5] and not be put off unduly by the existence of other legal or statutory remedies for the assessment of these matters.

[1]   Commissioner for Children and Young People (Northern Ireland) Order 2003, art 6.
[2]   See para 1.73.
[3]   Commissioner for Children and Young People (Northern Ireland) Order 2003, art 6(3)(b).
[4]   See chapter 2, para 2.45.
[5]   See chapter 2 generally.

1.97   In particular, the Commissioner is required to promote: (1) an understanding of the rights and interests of children and young people, (2) an awareness of the importance of those rights; and (3) an awareness of matters relating to the best interests of children and young persons.[1] The Commissioner is also required to review the 'adequacy and effectiveness of law and practice' relating to children's rights and to service delivery for children.[2] (The Northern Ireland Human Rights Commission has a similar duty in respect of the human rights of the general populace (see below)).[3]

[1]   Commissioner for Children and Young People (Northern Ireland) Order 2003, art 7.
[2]   Commissioner for Children and Young People (Northern Ireland) Order 2003, art 7(2).
[3]   See para 1.106.

Commissioner's powers

1.98   To achieve these functions, the Commissioner has a diverse range of powers facilitating the commissioning of research, the issuing of best practice guidance, conducting investigations, publishing relevant information or material relating to children's rights and making representations to any body of persons concerning children's rights.[1] More importantly, the Commissioner has a number of powers of investigation or review. There are four types of such investigation or review that the Commissioner may conduct. First, a general review of specified activities performed by boards and trusts; secondly, a review of those activities prompted by a particular child's case; thirdly, an investigation of a child's complaint that its rights have been affected, and fourthly, a 'formal investigation'.

[1]   Commissioner for Children and Young People (Northern Ireland) Order 2003, art 8.

GENERAL REVIEW OF SPECIFIC ARRANGEMENTS

1.99   The Commissioner has the power to review arrangements made by boards, trusts, schools, children's homes, and various other establishments, for handling complaints from children about a range of matters. These matters include systems for protecting 'whistle-blowers', or for providing advocates for children, or for inspecting the facilities where children are detained, looked after, or where they are educated or receive health or welfare services.[1] The Commissioner may review the operation of these arrangements to ascertain whether, and to what extent, these arrangements are effective in safeguarding and promoting the rights and best interests of children and young persons.[2] These reviews can also be conducted of the relevant arrangements kept in place by bodies such as the Probation Board for Northern Ireland, the Chief Inspector of Criminal Justice, the Policing Board and the Youth Justice Agency.[3]

[1]   Commissioner for Children and Young People (Northern Ireland) Order 2003, art 9.
[2]   Commissioner for Children and Young People (Northern Ireland) Order 2003, art 9(2).
[3]   In carrying out such a review the Commissioner can adhere to the procedure set out in Sch 2 to the Order if he or she wishes: art 9(6). Note, however, that no formal investigation can be carried out of these arrangements maintained by those bodies listed here: art 16(1)(a).

REVIEW OF SPECIFIED ACTIVITIES INITIATED BY SPECIFIC CASE

1.100   More significantly, the Commissioner may investigate the circumstances of a particular child in respect of the matters outlined in the paragraph above (as opposed to simply reviewing them generally), though the power to do so is circumscribed by the fact that the Commissioner must have reasonable grounds for believing that the arrangements in question were ineffective, or didn't operate properly.[1]

[1]   Commissioner for Children and Young People (Northern Ireland) Order 2003, art 10.

CHILD INITIATED COMPLAINT

1.101   The Commissioner can also entertain, and investigate, individual complaints from children that the action of a 'relevant authority'[1] has infringed his or her human rights, or adversely affected the child's interests, if the Commissioner considers that the complaint raises a question of principle and does not fall within the remit of existing statutory complaints systems.[2] These investigations are to be distinguished from 'formal investigations', which are discussed later. Child-complainant investigations cannot be conducted where the child has another remedy, whether court-based or otherwise, nor can they be conducted into the conduct of court proceedings or where a local or public inquiry has already dealt with the substance of the complaint, nor where, in the opinion of he Commissioner, there has been unreasonable delay.[3] The Commissioner can provide assistance, financial or otherwise, to individual complainants to bring their complaints before other bodies, although only where there is no other agency or body likely to provide such assistance.[4]

[1]   Commissioner for Children and Young People (Northern Ireland) Order 2003, which includes bodies

subject to the Ombudsman's jurisdiction, boards and trusts and bodies such as the Youth Justice
Agency and the Probation Board amongst others: art 4.
2   Commissioner for Children and Young People (Northern Ireland) Order 2003, art 12.
3   Commissioner for Children and Young People (Northern Ireland) Order 2003, art 13.
4   Commissioner for Children and Young People (Northern Ireland) Order 2003, art 11.

FORMAL INVESTIGATIONS

1.102   Formal investigation powers are another significant weapon in the Commissioner's armoury. These are investigations into matters that might be dealt with in
any of the three previous forms of investigation examined above, namely general
review of specific activities, reviews initiated by specific cases, or investigations
initiated by a child-complainant.[1] How then do formal investigations differ from
those already examined? First, the Commissioner's formal investigation powers are
more formidable, with the Commissioner being allowed to require the production of
evidence in terms similar to the High Court, and being allowed to enter premises
managed by an authority in which children are being looked after, or where they are
being detained or their education, health or welfare needs are being attended to.[2]
Secondly, in order to conduct formal investigations the Commissioner is required to
produce terms of reference (or to outline the substance of the allegations) and to give
notice of the proposed investigation to the body subject of the investigation, as well as
according it the right to comment on the matters being investigated.[3]

1   See paras 1.99, 1.100, 1.101.
2   Commissioner for Children and Young People (Northern Ireland) Order 2003, arts 20 and 21.
3   Commissioner for Children and Young People (Northern Ireland) Order 2003, art 16(3).

1.103   The actual conduct of the formal investigation is within the discretion of the
Commissioner, and there is no obligation on him (or her) to hold an oral hearing or to
allow particular persons to be legally represented.[1] However, where a person or
authority may be adversely affected by the report of the investigation then that
person or authority must be given the opportunity to present oral, or other evidence,
and to test the evidence against them in cross-examination.

1   Commissioner for Children and Young People (Northern Ireland) Order 2003, art 16(8).

1.104   The report of the formal investigation must not mention individuals by name
nor must it mention them in such a way that those persons can be identified. If the
report contains a recommendation that the authority take certain action, the Commissioner can give it three months to demonstrate that the recommendation has been
complied with, or the authority can make a statement explaining why it does not
intend to comply.[1] If the authority opts for the latter course, or if the Commissioner
thinks that its response has been inadequate, the Commissioner can reply to the
authority, giving it a further month to comply with the recommendation.[2] Further
failure to comply does not attract a specific sanction, but the Commissioner is
empowered to maintain a register of such responses, so it will ultimately be possible
for the public to become aware of the manner in which the authority responded or
that it did not respond, as the case may be.

[1]　Commissioner for Children and Young People (Northern Ireland) Order 2003, art 19(1).
[2]　Commissioner for Children and Young People (Northern Ireland) Order 2003, art 19(3).

INITIATING LEGAL ACTION

1.105　The Act also empowers the Commissioner to institute legal proceedings, to intervene in existing legal proceedings, or to act as *amicus curiae* (literally 'friend of the court') in cases touching on the rights or welfare of children and young people.[1] In order to do so, however, the Commissioner must be satisfied that the case raises a question of principle or that 'special circumstances make it appropriate for him to do so'.[2] This power would allow the Commissioner to institute judicial review proceedings for example, in respect of a law or practice that affected children's rights, presumably without the necessity of obtaining an individual litigant. This power to intervene legally is, however, limited by the fact that where the Commissioner has previously conducted a formal investigation of the matter then such legal intervention is not possible. The reverse situation also applies, namely that where the Commissioner has previously exercised his power to institute legal proceedings, a formal investigation may not be conducted.[3]

[1]　Commissioner for Children and Young People (Northern Ireland) Order 2003, art 14.
[2]　Commissioner for Children and Young People (Northern Ireland) Order 2003, art 14(3).
[3]　Commissioner for Children and Young People (Northern Ireland) Order 2003, art 17.

Northern Ireland Human Rights Commission

1.106　The Northern Ireland Human Rights Commission (NIHRC), established under the Northern Ireland Act 1998, has the statutory task of ensuring that 'law and practice in Northern Ireland is compatible with human rights law'.[1] As pointed out above,[2] international human rights law includes not just the ECHR, but a whole range of international treaties and instruments. In accordance with this statutory task the Commission has produced reports on the compatibility with human rights law, of law and practice relating to the elderly, for example.[3] A similar report that may also have a significant impact on social work practice is the Commission's report on the juvenile justice system, 'In our care: Promoting the rights of children in custody'.[4] It has also made submissions in response to consultation documents on matters such as the legislation dealing with the Commissioner for Children and the Protection of Children and Vulnerable Adults. The Commission has adopted a policy of commenting on periodic reports submitted by the UK under its international human rights law obligations and has, for example, commented on the UK's second submission to the UNCRC.

[1]　Northern Ireland Act 1998, s 69(1).
[2]　See para 1.73.
[3]　'Enhancing the Rights of Older People in Northern Ireland', NIHRC, November 2001.
[4]　NIHRC, March 2002.

Role in legislative process

1.107 The Commission has a particular role in the legislative process, ensuring that legislation enacted by the Assembly is compatible with human rights law. The Assembly may refer a Bill to the Commission to have it determine whether the Bill is compatible with human rights,[1] which, as we have seen above, includes a broader range of legal instruments than the HRA. The Commission may also intervene of its own accord, if it considers that it is appropriate to do so.[2] To date the Commission has responded, not only to published Bills, but also to consultation documents, which often form an earlier, less formal stage in the legislative process.[3] The Commission is not in a position, however, to declare an Act or a Bill invalid, because the legislative proposal does not, in its view, respect international human rights law. It remains to be seen what will happen where the Commission and the Assembly disagree about the effect of a particular enactment on the human rights of persons living in Northern Ireland.

[1]   Northern Ireland Act 1998, s 69(4)(a).
[2]   Northern Ireland Act 1998, s 69(4)(b).
[3]   A vast range of responses to legal and policy developments impacting on Northern Ireland is available on the Commission's website: www.nihrc.org.

Initiating legal action and conducting investigations

1.108 The Commission may take cases in its own name[1] or it may support cases taken by particular individuals where it considers that an important element of human rights law is involved. The House of Lords has also confirmed that the Commission may intervene as *amicus curiae* in appropriate cases.[2] The investigatory powers accorded to the Commission are considerably less effective than those given to the Commissioner for Children. Section 69(8) of the Northern Ireland Act 1998 provides it with the powers to carry out an investigation, but not the powers necessary to compel enforcement with that investigation such as the power to compel disclosure of documents or to require witnesses to testify, matters which became clear in its investigation into the juvenile justice system.[3]

[1]   Northern Ireland Act 1998, s 69(5)(b).
[2]   *Re Northern Ireland Human Rights Commission* [2002] UKHL 25, [2002] All ER (D) 140 (Jun).
[3]   NIHRC, Annual Report 2000–2001, 'Investigation into the Care of Young People in Custody.'

Bill of Rights for Northern Ireland

1.109 The Commission has proposed a Bill of Rights for Northern Ireland, as it was required to do under the Northern Ireland Act 1998,[1] which would include a wide range of protected rights and would apply only to those living in Northern Ireland. In drawing up its draft Bill of Rights[2] the Commission drew from the extensive range of international human rights treaties and proposed the protection of rights in a wide variety of circumstances, not just those already protected by the ECHR. The proposed rights include language rights, social economics and cultural rights, education rights, rights concerning identity and communities, and rights to equality, as well as the rights of women and children. Whether this proposed Bill of Rights is adopted will be a decision likely to be made by the UK government. If it is adopted it will probably be in the form of a Westminster Act of Parliament.

[1]   Section 69(7).
[2]   'Making a Bill of Rights for Northern Ireland – a consultation by the NIHRC', NIHRC, September 2001.

Legal structure of health and personal social services system

1.110   The final matter that must be addressed in this chapter is the legal organisation of health and social service delivery in Northern Ireland. Unlike the position in England and Wales, where responsibility for health matters and for the delivery of social services are split between separate agencies, ie agencies with responsibility for one area or the other, in Northern Ireland responsibility lies with integrated agencies delivering both health and social services.

Department of Health and Personal Social Services and Public Safety

1.111   The Department of Health and Personal Social Services and Public Safety, established by the Departments (Northern Ireland) Order 1999, is one of the ten Northern Ireland Executive departments, and oversees the operation of the health and social care system in Northern Ireland. In particular, its responsibilities are to devise, implement and recommend policy and legislative developments in the fields of health and personal social services. In this manner the Department 'shapes' the activities of the boards and trusts.[1]

[1]   Any reference to 'Department' in this book is a reference to the DHSSPS.

1.112   A particularly important agency within the Department is the Social Services Inspectorate (SSI) whose main function is to review the quality of social work and social care services. Detailed consideration of the role of the SSI is given in chapter 2.[1]

[1]   See paras 2.71–2.79.

Health and social services boards

1.113   At present there are four area health and social services boards – Eastern, Southern, Northern and Western – covering all of Northern Ireland and having their legislative basis in the Health and Social Services (Northern Ireland) Order 1972.[1] These boards are serviced by the Central Services Agency, established under article 26 of the 1972 Order, which 'administers, on behalf of Boards, payments in respect of family health services. Payments are made to general, medical and dental practitioners.'[2]

---

[1] Health and Personal Social Services (Northern Ireland) Order 1972, art 16 and the Health and Personal Social Services (Establishment and Determination of Areas of Health and Social Services Boards) Order (Northern Ireland) 1972.

[2] DHSSPS Equality Scheme 2002, p 56.

Health and social services trusts

1.114 Within each of these boards is a range of community and hospital trusts totalling 19 in number, owing their separate legal existence to the Health and Personal Social Services (Northern Ireland) Order 1991, art 10.[1] (The legislative basis of each individual trust is based on secondary legislation made under the 1991 Order). Broadly stated, the split between the boards and trusts is intended to create a purchaser-provider split, with the boards funding the trusts to provide services within their geographical areas, on foot of an 'HSS contract' between them[2] or under an authorisation made by the board, with the approval of the department.[3] The functions that may be the subject of such authorisations have been outlined by the department in regulations.[4] The process of securing the department's authorisation to allow a trust to carry out some of the boards' functions begins with the trust submitting a scheme to the board explaining how it intends to exercise its functions. The board must then approve the scheme, and pass it to the department for its approval.[5] In this way, powers and duties of the boards can be performed under such contracts and schemes of authorisation, by trusts, so that although the statutory duty may lie with a board, it is a trust that will implement that duty.

---

[1] This organisational structure is likely to come under scrutiny in the Assembly's review of public administration in Northern Ireland and has already been the subject of consideration in the report of the Acute Hospitals Review Group (DHSS, 2001, chapter 8).

[2] Health and Personal Social Services (Northern Ireland) Order 1991, art 8.

[3] Health and Personal Social Services (Northern Ireland) Order 1994, art 3.

[4] Health and Social Services Trusts (Exercise of Functions) Regulations (Northern Ireland) 1994, as amended by Health and Social Services Trusts (Exercise of Functions) (Amendment) Regulations (Northern Ireland) 1996, 1997 and 2003.

[5] Health and Personal Social Services (Northern Ireland) Order 1994, art 4.

Special agencies

1.115 One further element of the health and social services institutional infrastructure are Departmental agencies, of which there are ten. These agencies, of which the Northern Ireland Guardian Ad Litem Agency (NIGALA) is an example, focus on discrete issues or tasks and are not territorially or geographically based. The general legal basis of such agencies is found in the Health and Personal Social Services (Special Agencies) (Northern Ireland) Order 1990, with secondary legislation providing the specific legal powers and duties of the special agencies. So, for example,

NIGALA was established under secondary legislation made under the 1990 Order, namely the Northern Ireland Guardian ad Litem (Establishment and Constitution) Order (Northern Ireland) 1995.

Chapter 2

Accountability

Introduction

2.1 This chapter focuses on the mechanisms by which social workers are made accountable for their actions, other than by their employing organisations. One might argue that not dealing with social workers' obligations to their employers distorts the picture of the network of accountability presented in this chapter. There is no doubt that the employer-employee relationship dominates social workers' professional lives, and accountability there is achieved in a variety of ways; by the setting of performance targets, and the conducting of appraisals or reviews of performance, or even through financial scrutiny of social workers' activities. However, the relationship is not unique to the social work profession and like all such relationships the exact terms may differ so significantly from job to job that providing generic advice or guidance is almost impossible. Furthermore, and more significantly for the purposes of setting the terms of reference for this chapter, the relationship may not be an effective and objective form of accountability because it is affected by matters internal to the employing organisation, like budgetary concerns or personal relationships for example, that have little to do with the propriety or otherwise of the social worker's actions. Because the focus of this chapter is on accountability achieved by agencies external to the employing organisation, the mechanisms examined here should be free from any such influence and should be capable of being more objective. (There is discussion, however, of two matters that touch on the theme of accountability in the context of the employer-employee relationship, namely 'whistle-blowing', ie employees disclosing grave misconduct by their employers or others[1] and making employment-related complaints to the Ombudsman.)[2]

---

[1] See para 2.134.
[2] See para 2.54.

2.2 Neither does this chapter focus on internal complaints' mechanisms, (ie procedures allowing members of the public to complain to the social worker's employing organisation) even where these have a statutory basis. Admittedly, social workers may be more likely to encounter such schemes in the course of their careers than any of the professional, administrative or legal systems of regulation discussed here. However, the large number of such schemes and the variation in their content means that this chapter can do no more than acknowledge their role in the overall scheme of accountability. However, later in this chapter the Independent Review process, whereby complainants who continue to be dissatisfied with the relevant internal complaints mechanism can appeal to an independent external body, is explained.[2]

[1]   See para 2.66.

Professional regulation and legal accountability

2.3   The two main methods of accountability that form the focus of this chapter are, first, professional or administrative regulation and secondly, legal accountability. Matters examined under the first heading include the newly created Northern Ireland Social Care Council, the Office of the Ombudsman, the Social Services Inspectorate, the Health and Personal Social Services Regulation and Improvement Authority and the Health and Social Services Councils. Legal accountability of social workers is achieved in a number of different ways. First, through the tort of negligence, and the tort of misfeasance in public office, which are applied to activity performed by them in the course of their professional activities. Secondly, the courts can be asked to carry out a judicial review of actions or decisions of Health and Social Services authorities carrying out statutory, or other public functions and, thirdly, by the establishment of statutory inquiries. The issue of 'whistle-blowing' in the public interest, is also discussed under this heading.

Assessing social workers' accountability

2.4   How effective is this array of accountability mechanisms? The measures examined here clearly differ from one to the other in terms of their effect on individual social workers because some of them only focus on systems failures, rather than seeking to ascribe blame to particular individuals, and the direct punitive consequences for individual social workers may be non-existent. In short, their different powers and terms of reference mean that not all of them will have immediate consequences for individual social workers.

2.5   Nevertheless, taken together this accountability architecture has quite a significant impact on social workers and the social work profession. Although particular elements are not intended to focus on the actions of a particular social worker, the very nature of the exercise may result in the individual coming under close scrutiny. Adverse reports, comments and references, can have significant negative consequences for a social worker's career. Undoubtedly some of these mechanisms only have an impact at more general levels. However, even those mechanisms may make it possible to draw lessons for the future and require health and social services authorities to address the systematic faults identified therein. This sort of approach might be argued to have a longer lasting impact than simply pillorying one social worker and making that person a scapegoat.

2.6 Not all commentators agree that these accountability measures are efficacious. Brayne and Preston-Shoot, in 'Accountability, administrative law and social work practice: redressing or reinforcing the power imbalance?',[1] are disparaging about mechanisms such as those outlined here. These review or redress mechanisms operate ex post facto, they argue, and therefore play only a peripheral role in shaping the general approach taken by service providers and their social work employees. In particular, they assert, they fail to help service users because they are 'limited in [their] ability to empower service users as the stakeholders with perhaps the greatest need of assistance to develop a voice in the debate. It confers only procedural rights to fairness, information, informed use of discretion and reasons for decisions, rather than substantive rights to needs satisfaction or social justice.'[2]

[1] (1999) 21 JSWFL, pp 235–255.
[2] (1999) 21 JSWFL 235 at 249.

2.7 This view, I suggest, underplays the benefit to service users of identifying and conferring such rights upon them. More crucially, this view suggests that these accountability mechanisms have a substantive role to play in the determination of substantial rights and entitlements that they cannot deliver. If they were in a position to do so, they would be appeal mechanisms, reviewing the substantive merits of decisions, and not engaged in supervising the manner in which those decisions are taken by the relevant authority. If these mechanisms were engaged in reviewing the substantive merits of decisions it could be argued that they would in effect be usurping the functions of the relevant authorities. For example, Brayne and Preston-Shoot assert that judicial review is limited in its scope and effect because it does not seek or attempt to secure the redressing of the imbalance between the client and the service provider. However, this is to misunderstand the role of judicial review in public and constitutional law and that of the courts in this context. The purpose of judicial review is to ensure conformity in the legal order by supervising the exercise by public bodies of their legal powers. It cannot act as an assessor of the correctness or otherwise of the public body's decision because of the specialised nature of the subject matter in question.

Accountability and social justice

2.8 The limitations of the accountability mechanisms examined here arise, I suggest, from the manner in which the system of health and personal social services delivery has been constructed and is not the fault of the accountability infrastructure itself. A more radical realignment, or re-structuring, of the legal basis for the delivery of health and social services is required for this sort of impact to arise. The goals of needs satisfaction and social justice can only be achieved by altering the basis on which the relevant authorities deliver these services by requiring them to consider these matters when making service delivery plans. Some would argue that achieving such goals is the function of the political system and accountability in a sense lies at the political level. Thus, whether social justice is attained is not a matter for the individual health and personal social services authority in delivering its statutory and non-statutory programmes but a matter for government generally and thus a matter for the electorate. Some matters are in the realm of political accountability, the argument goes, and it is unrealistic to expect accountability mechanisms to be able to cope with more significant questions about social justice and needs satisfaction. Others would argue that these goals are best reflected in social and economic rights. Health and personal social services authorities should, this argument runs, be required to act in accordance with these rights – in the same manner that they are required to act in accordance with the rights in the HRA – and that if this were the case, these goals could be achieved.

Northern Ireland Social Care Council

2.9 The most significant change in recent years in the regulation of the social work profession has been the establishment of the Northern Ireland Social Care Council (NISCC), whose overall function is to regulate 'social care workers', and which replaces the Central Council for the Training and Education of Social Workers (CCETSW) and the Training Organisation for Personal Social Services (TOPSS). The Council is established under the Part I of the Health and Personal Services Act (Northern Ireland) 2001, and is the equivalent of the Scottish Social Services Council (SSSC), the Care Council for Wales (CCW) and the English General Social Care Council (GSCC). It represents the range of sectors in the social care professions, maintaining a balance between service-users, carers, social care workers, employers, unions, professional associations and educational institutions. The nature of the powers and duties given to the Council means that it is a significant departure in the regulation of the social care professions, and it will wield considerable influence on the development of social care training and education.

Social care workers

2.10 The Council's main role is to maintain standards amongst the social care workforce with the aim of increasing the protection of service-users, their carers and the public. One should note that its role is not confined to professionally qualified social workers but to all working in the social care professions. 'Social care workers' are statutorily defined as:[1]

- those engaged in 'relevant' social work (which includes social work in connection with any health, education, probation or personal social services provided by any person);
- those employed at, or who manage, a children's home, a residential care home, a nursing home,[2] a day care setting, a residential family centre;
- or who are supplied by a domiciliary care agency to provide 'personal care'[3] to

persons in their own homes. (Note that it does not extend to persons who are paid directly by a person to provide such personal care, and those individuals will not be required to register).

Regulations may provide for a broadening of this classification to include persons who would not otherwise by caught by this definition. This includes those who are employed for the purposes of aiding a Board or Trust to fulfil its personal social service functions but who are not directly engaged in providing those services, as well as those providing 'personal care' privately for any person, or who work in or manage an organisation that supplies 'personal carers'. The definition can also be extended to those employed by private sector organisations engaged in the provision of services similar to those provided, under statute, by Boards or Trusts. Those have been enrolled on qualifying social work education programmes have been included within the definition of 'social care worker'.[4] Regulations have extended the definition of social care worker to include those who work in, or manage, a children's home, and those who manage a residential care home or a day care setting and are not registered with another professional regulatory body.[5]

[1] Health and Personal Services Act (Northern Ireland) 2001, s 2.
[2] Children's homes are defined in the Children (Northern Ireland) Order 1995, art 119(3), and the other facilities are defined in the Registered Homes (Northern Ireland) Order 1992, art 3.
[3] See the Registered Homes (Northern Ireland) Order 1992, art 3(4).
[4] Northern Ireland Social Care Council (Description of Social Care Workers) Order (Northern Ireland) 2004 and Northern Ireland Social Care Council (Description of Persons to be treated as Social Workers) Regulations (Northern Ireland) 2004.
[5] The Northern Ireland Social Care Council (Description of Social Care Workers) Order (Northern Ireland) 2003.

2.11   Social workers should note that the construction of the statutory definition means that they are considered part of the wider classification of 'social care worker' and hence material relating to social care workers will usually apply to them as well. However, on occasion the Council will direct itself to social workers only, without including the other social care professions. Accordingly, as the registration categories are developed this will mean that the Council will be in a position to deal either generically with all social care workers, or with particular registration categories of social care worker.

Council's powers

2.12   In order to fulfil its role, the Council has been accorded a number of legislative powers relating to: (1) the registration of the social care workforce; (2) the regulation of professional social work education and training; (3) the promotion and development of education and training on social care; and (4) the issuing of Codes of Practice.

Registration of social care workers

2.13   Perhaps the most significant development in the Health and Personal Services Act (Northern Ireland) 2001 is the requirement for the Council to maintain a register of social care workers[1] with registration remaining valid for three years, after which time the social care worker must re-register.[2] The registration of all social care workers will clearly take quite some time, and as a result the Council has decided to register social care workers on a phased basis, with social workers, managers and staff of residential child care facilities being registered as the first priority group in April 2003. Social work students will be registered from 2004.

[1]   Health and Personal Social Services Act (Northern Ireland) 2001, s 3.
[2]   In order to re-register, the social care worker must furnish evidence of having complied with the post-registration training and learning requirements set out in the NISCC (Registration) Rules 2003, Sch 3: see para 2.18.

2.14   The different types of occupation and activity engaged in by social care workers will be reflected in the fact that there will be different levels of registration requirement, which will be dependant on the type of work the social care worker performs and the qualifications required to occupy that post. The general conditions that govern registration are that an individual is: (1) of good character; (2) physically and mentally fit to perform some or all of the work in question; and (3) that he or she has the necessary training or educational qualifications.[1] Registration is governed by the NISCC (Registration) Rules 2003.

[1]   Health and Personal Social Services Act (Northern Ireland) 2001, s 5(1). The Registration Rules 2003, r 4(3) appear to have added a fourth criterion, namely 'good conduct'.

Good character

2.15   It remains to be seen whether this first requirement has any practical utility and adds anything to the existing control mechanisms for persons applying from within the UK. Applicants with a criminal record, or with a record that indicates that they have been a risk to children and/or vulnerable adults in the past, should, in the past, have featured in Pre-Employment Consultancy Scheme (PECS) vetting checks, or, in the future, in checks under the Protection of Children and Vulnerable Adults (Northern Ireland) Order 2003[1] and are unlikely to have secured employment in the social care professions in any case. The Registration Rules 2003 require an applicant to furnish evidence of good character, which can include references from employers or other persons acceptable to the Council. The Council has indicated that this provision will allow it to seek other information about applicants from outside the UK, to whom PECS and the Criminal Records Bureau would not apply.[2] (The costs of making these checks will have to be borne by the applicant). It is not clear whether a record of criminal activity which does not suggest that the applicant is a danger to children and/or vulnerable adults will result in the Council concluding that a registration applicant's character does not meet the requisite standard. Registered social workers are required to furnish the Council with details of changes to information provided at the time of registration. This requires them to provide details of criminal convictions, for example, acquired after the date of registration.[3]

[1]   See chapter 6, para 6.152.

2   Explanatory Notes for Draft Registration Rules for Social Care Workers, Consultation Document, June 2002.
3   NISCC (Registration) Rules 2003.

Physical and mental fitness

2.16 The second requirement requires applicants to complete a statement of physical and mental health confirming that they are fit to perform all, or some, of the work relating to the registration category. The Registration Rules 2003 allow the Council to require the applicant to provide a medical certificate, although the Council anticipates that it will not have to avail of this power in standard applications.[1] This requirement must, however, be interpreted in light of the Disability Discrimination Act 1995[2] and the obligation on employers to make reasonable adjustments in the workplace to accommodate qualified personnel with physical or mental impairments. It will not be open to the Council to refuse to register an otherwise suitably qualified applicant simply in the basis that he or she had, or has, some physical or mental impairment.

1   Explanatory Notes for Draft Registration Rules for Social Care workers, June 2002, para 10.
2   See chapter four, para 4.19.

Educational qualifications

2.17 In respect of social workers, the third requirement means that they must have completed an educational qualification approved by the Council[1] or an equivalent qualification obtained outside the jurisdiction.[2] The list of approved qualifications for social workers is set out in the NISCC (Registration) Rules 2003.[3] Training and education courses for other social care workers need not have been approved directly by the Council, but it does have the power to stipulate which educational qualifications are required before an applicant can be registered as a particular category of social care worker.[4]

1   Health and Personal Social Services Act (Northern Ireland) 2001, s 5(1)(c) and (2). The Council may make rules about the provision of courses, and the content, and completion, of them: s 10 (as amended by the Health and Personal Social Services (Quality, Improvement and Regulation) (Northern Ireland) Order 2003, art 46).
2   Section 11.
3   Schedule 1.
4   Health and Personal Social Services Act (Northern Ireland) 2001, s 5(2)(b).

2.18 This mandatory registration regime comes into existence at the same time as changes in social work educational qualification requirements are about to be implemented. From 2004 all new social workers will be required to study to social work to degree level over a three-year period, followed by an assessed year in employment, before being entitled to be registered. Applications for registration must be made within three years of qualification for those undertaking the new social work degrees. Any applicant for registration must also satisfy any other rules of conduct or competence that the Council may impose. All new registrants must confirm that they have read and understood the Council's Code of Practice for Social Workers and confirm that they agree to abide by it. The Council is further authorised to require registrants to undertake further training[1] and re-registration will be dependent upon successful completion of compulsory professional developments requirements set by the Council. At present the Council requires registered social care workers to complete 15 days, or 90 hours, of study, training, courses, reading, teaching or other activities 'which could reasonably be expected to advance the social care worker's professional development, or contribute to the development of the profession as a whole.'[2]

[1]   Health and Personal Social Services Act (Northern Ireland) 2001, s 12.
[2]   NISCC (Registration) Rules 2003, Sch 3.

Refusal to register

2.19   Where the Council refuses to register an applicant, or to renew a registration, or intends to register an applicant subject to certain conditions the matter must be referred to the Registration Committee.[1] The Committee may not deal with a refusal to register or to renew registration where there are proceedings current or pending before the Conduct Committee.[2]

[1]   NISCC (Registration) Rules 2003, r 11.
[2]   NISCC (Registration) Rules 2003, r 7(2). On Conduct Committee, see para 2.33.

2.20   This five-person committee, chaired by a lay person who is not a member of the Council, will then determine the issue of registration, at a private hearing, conducted with regard to the rules of natural justice and the right to a fair hearing,[1] but with no oral testimony from witnesses, other than the applicant.[2] Evidence that might not be admissible in a court of law may be admitted in this hearing.[3] The Registration Committee may grant or refuse the applicant to register or renew registration, with or without conditions attached. It may also refer an application for renewal to the Council's Preliminary Proceedings Committee,[4] where a complaint of misconduct has been made against an applicant.[5]

[1]   NISCC (Registration) Rules 2003, r 16(1). On the rules of natural justice and the right to a fair hearing, see paras 2.122–2.126.
[2]   NISCC (Registration) Rules 2003, r 15(1).
[3]   NISCC (Registration) Rules 2003, r 15(3).
[4]   See para 2.26.
[5]   NISCC (Registration) Rules 2003, r 16(16).

Codes of Conduct and Practice

2.21   The Council is required to maintain Codes of Conduct and of Practice, establishing standards for social care workers and for their employers in their treatment of service users, carers and staff.[1] A Code of Practice for Social Care

Workers, and a Code of Practice for Employers of Social Care Workers were finalised in September 2002. The main duties of social care workers according to the former Code are to:[2]

- protect the rights and promote the interests of service users and carers;
- strive to establish and maintain the Trust and confidence of service users and carers;
- respect the independence of service users while protecting them as far as possible from danger or harm;
- respect the rights of service users while seeking to ensure that their behaviour does not harm themselves or other people;
- uphold public Trust and confidence in social care services; and
- be accountable for the quality of their work and take responsibility for maintaining and improving their knowledge and skills.

Each of these duties is elaborated upon further in the Code. The likely impact of this Code can be gleaned from the fact that not only is the Council mandated to consider it when making a decision under the Act, for example, about registration or de-registration and allegations of misconduct,[3] but so too is any public body making a decision about a social care worker employed by it.[4] The Code may also become a benchmark against which the behaviour of social care workers employed by private bodies will be measured in the future.

[1]   Health and Personal Social Services Act (Northern Ireland) 2001, s 9(1).
[2]   NISCC Code of Practice for Social Care Workers, September 2002, p 3.
[3]   Health and Personal Social Services Act (Northern Ireland) 2001, s 9(4) and NISCC Code of Practice for Social Care Workers, September 2002, p 3.
[4]   Health and Personal Social Services Act (Northern Ireland) 2001, s 9(5). A public body must also take the Council's Code of Conduct into account in these circumstances.

2.22   The Code of Practice for Employers of Social Care Workers is 'intended to complement rather than replace or duplicate existing employers' policies and it forms part of the wider package of legislation, requirements and guidance that relate to the employment of staff.'[1] It places a broad range of responsibilities on employers, requiring them to, for example, undertake vetting checks of potential employees, as well as promoting and implementing systems for the promotion of staff welfare and equal opportunities.

[1]   NISCC Code of Practice for Employers of Social Care Workers, September 2002, p 9.

2.23   The Council has also enacted a Code of Conduct, entitled the Northern Ireland Social Care Council (Conduct) Rules 2003, which are discussed below.[1]

[1]   See para 2.25.

Protection of title 'social worker'

2.24   The significance of registration is that the State, by this process, will attempt to ensure that only those who meet these conditions may be employed as social care workers. Thus the legislation allows the Department (the DHSSPS) to make regulations prohibiting persons from working in certain positions unless they are registered.[1] In particular, the use of the title 'social worker' is protected by the Health and Personal Social Services Act (Northern Ireland) 2001, which makes it a criminal offence to use that title, or to suggest or indicate that one is so registered, if it is done with the intent to deceive others.[2] The intention, therefore, is that only those who fulfil the necessary conditions and are registered with the Council may call themselves social workers. (There would, however, be nothing wrong with a social worker who is not registered with the Council using the title of 'social worker' so long as he or she indicated that he or she was unregistered). This presents the possibility that employers may stipulate in the future that some positions may only be open to those validly registered with the Council, or a similar UK agency, or at least capable of being so registered if they have qualified in another EU state, for example.

---

[1]   Health and Personal Social Services Act (Northern Ireland) 2001, s 8(3).
[2]   Health and Personal Social Services Act (Northern Ireland) 2001, s 8(1).

The Register: suspension, removal and restoration

2.25   As one might expect, registration systems usually give rise to issues of suspension or de-registration in particular circumstances. The Council has developed rules allowing for the suspension, or removal, of individuals from the register, and which are entitled the NISCC (Conduct) Rules 2003.[1] The Act does not outline the grounds on which any of these actions may take place, although s 6 mandates the Council to promulgate rules that, amongst other matters, determine the circumstances in which a person may be removed or suspended from the register. However, the Conduct Rules do not specify what those circumstances are, beyond defining 'misconduct' as 'conduct which calls into question the suitability of a Registrant to remain on the Register.'[2] Failure to adhere to the Council's Code of Practice for Social Care Workers will play a part in determining whether a social worker has been guilty of misconduct.[3]

The Conduct Rules establish three Committees to oversee their implementation, namely the Preliminary Proceedings Committee, the Conduct Committee and the Restoration Committee, with each committee consisting of five members[4] and chaired by a lay person.[5]

---

[1]   Under the Health and Personal Social Services Act (Northern Ireland) 2001, ss 6 and 18. Refusal to register for non-conduct related matters is dealt with by the Registration Committee. See para 2.19.
[2]   NISCC (Conduct) Rules 2003, r 2(1). See also NISCC (Registration)Rules 2003, r 13(1) which states that a social worker may be removed from the register for misconduct, or if unfit to plead before the Conduct Committee when charged with misconduct, or if convicted of an offence in or outside of the UK.
[3]   Health and Personal Social Services Act (Northern Ireland) 2001, s 9(4).
[4]   The Committees are quorate when three members are present: NISCC (Conduct) Rules 2003, r 7(3),
[5]   Each Committee is assisted by a legal adviser and a clerk: NISCC (Conduct) Rules 2003, rr 9 and 11 respectively.

Preliminary Proceedings Committee

2.26 As its title suggests, the Preliminary Proceedings Committee's role is generally limited to making preliminary inquiries about the allegations of misconduct and about whether to refer a matter to the Conduct Committee. The Preliminary Proceedings Committee's deliberations will be activated by a referral to it, by an officer of the Council, of any allegations of misconduct or criminal activity made to it in relation to a registered social care worker. The Preliminary Proceedings Committee will also have referred to it not only those cases where the Council receives notification that a registered social worker has been convicted or cautioned for an offence in Northern Ireland but also where a complaint related to the commission of an offence committed outside of the UK, which would also constitute an offence if committed in the UK. Lastly, it will also have referred to it allegations that a registered social worker is seriously impaired, by reasons of physical or mental health, from performing his or her duties.[1]

[1] NISCC (Conduct) Rules 2003, r 7(7).

2.27 Referrals from the Council to the Preliminary Proceedings Committee will only be made where an officer of the Council is satisfied that the complaint relates to specific allegations against an identified individual,[1] requiring the officer to carry out preliminary inquiries if necessary to determine these matters. Anonymous complaints will not be referred to the Preliminary Proceedings Committee unless the Council, after investigation wishes to stand into the shoes of the complainant.[2] Where there are ongoing criminal or professional disciplinary proceedings against the registered social care worker, the Council may, but is not required to, defer investigation or referral of the complaint to the Preliminary Proceedings Committee.[3]

[1] NISCC (Conduct) Rules 2003, r 12(2).
[2] NISCC (Conduct) Rules 2003, r 12(8).
[3] NISCC (Conduct) Rules 2003, r 12(7).

PROCEDURE

2.28 The Preliminary Proceedings Committee's role is to act as a filter mechanism, deciding whether to refer more serious cases to the Conduct Committee.[1] It may also conclude that an Interim Suspension Order is necessary in the short-term to protect the public, on application to it by the Council.[2]

[1] NISCC (Conduct) Rules 2003, r 5(1)(a).
[2] NISCC (Conduct) Rules 2003, r 5(4).

2.29 Proceedings before this Committee are in private, although hearings to consider an Interim Suspension Order may be held in public, at the election of the registered social care worker who is the subject of the complaint.[1] There are two stages to the proceedings before this Committee; the initial consideration and the second consideration. The former is to determine 'whether any complaint referred to it calls into question the suitability of the [social care worker] to remain on the register.'[2] The parties are not present at the initial consideration. Where the

Committee concludes that this is the case it issues a Notice of Referral to the social care worker who is the subject of the complaint and proceeds to the second consideration stage, no earlier than four weeks after the initial consideration stage.[3]

[1]   NISCC (Conduct) Rules 2003, Sch 1, para 2(2).
[2]   NISCC (Conduct) Rules 2003, Sch 1, para 3(2).
[3]   NISCC (Conduct) Rules 2003, Sch 1, paras 3(4) and 4(1).

2.30   At the second consideration stage, the Committee considers written submissions from the registered social care worker, and the Council's recommendations for the disposal of the complaint, but no oral testimony is received unless the it is considering issuing an Interim Suspension Order.[1]

[1]   NISCC (Conduct) Rules 2003, Sch 1, para 5(4).

2.31   The Committee ultimately has four options open to it: (1) decide that no further action need be taken; (2) impose an Interim Suspension Order;[1] (3) direct that further investigations be carried out and adjourn the matter; or (4) refer the matter to the Conduct Committee, via the Conduct Procedure or the Health Procedure.[2] (However, referral to the Conduct Committee can only take place unless the Committee is 'satisfied that there is a real prospect of a finding of misconduct in relation to the complaint').[3]

[1]   The registered social care worker will have a right to be heard where the Committee considers making an Interim Suspension Order. See para 2.42.
[2]   NISCC (Conduct) Rules 2003, Sch 1, para 6.
[3]   NISCC (Conduct) Rules 2003, Sch 1, para 6(2).

2.32   Where the Committee decides to refer the matter to the Conduct Committee, it must send a Notice of Transfer to the registered social care worker, the Council and to the social care worker's employer, giving reasons for the referral and stating whether the Conduct Committee will hear the matter under the Conduct or Health Procedures.[1]

[1]   NISCC (Conduct) Rules 2003, Sch 1, para 7. Where the referral is under the Health Procedure the registered social care worker has 14 days from the date of the Notice of Transfer to be medically examined by a medical adviser nominated by the Council.

Conduct Committee

2.33   As should be clear from the above, it is the Conduct Committee that hears more serious allegations of misconduct or of physical or mental ill-health. The former type of allegation is considered under the Conduct Procedure, while the latter is considered under the Health Procedure. The procedures are extremely similar, though there are some differences between them. All the features of the Conduct Procedure apply equally to the Health Procedure, unless the contrary is made clear.

CONDUCT PROCEDURE

2.34   The procedure before the Conduct Committee begins with a pre-hearing review, within four weeks of the referral of the matter to the Committee. At this hearing, presided over by a legal adviser, the parties – the Council and the registered social care worker – consider a range of practical matters related to the substantive hearing, like the draft charge against the social care worker, the numbers of witnesses to be called, including any expert witnesses, whether there are undisputed facts that may be admitted and whether the social care worker admits to misconduct.[1]

[1] NISCC (Conduct) Rules 2003, Sch 2, para 2(6). Any facts not in dispute between the parties can be the subject of an agreed Statement of Facts: para 2(10).

2.35 The next step involves sending the parties a Notice of Hearing, which outlines the allegations, the time, date and location of the hearing and the rights of the registered social care worker in respect of the hearing.[1] The social worker's current employer is also sent this Notice.[2] Conduct procedure proceedings are generally held in public, although the Committee has the option of hearing the matter in public if the circumstances warrant it,[3] while Health Procedure hearings are usually heard in private.

[1] NISCC (Conduct) Rules 2003, Sch 2, para 4.
[2] NISCC (Conduct) Rules 2003, Sch 2, para 6.
[3] NISCC (Conduct) Rules 2003, Sch 2, para 9(2).

2.36 At the hearing the registered social worker may be represented by a lawyer, trade union official or representative of a professional body. The Committee has an extensive power to admit evidence whether or not it would be admissible in a court of law, subject to the requirements of a fair hearing and of relevance.[1] The burden of proving the allegations of misconduct lies on the Council, and the standard of proof is that of the balance of probabilities, though it is slightly modified such that the 'more serious the allegation, the more cogent the evidence required to prove it.'[2]

[1] NISCC (Conduct) Rules 2003, Sch 2, para 11(1).
[2] NISCC (Conduct) Rules 2003, Sch 2, para 12. This standard of proof is similar to that applied by the courts in Care Order applications. See chapter 6, para 6.137.

2.37 There are three stages to hearings under this procedure, namely: (1) preliminaries and findings of fact; (2) findings of misconduct; and (3) mitigation and sanction. In the first stage, the Committee addresses the registered social worker's fitness to plead his or her case,[1] any admissions of misconduct or agreed Statement of Facts are tabled, witnesses are examined and the Committee, deliberating in private, considers whether the facts have been proven. In the second stage, the question for the Committee is whether the facts proven disclose misconduct by the registered social care worker. In coming to this conclusion the Committee deliberates in private and has regard to the Code of Practice for Social Workers.[2] The third stage involves the registered social care worker making a plea in mitigation prior to the imposition of any sanction. This can involve him or her presenting character references, for example, or providing details of his or her previous disciplinary record.

[1] In the event that the Committee considers that he or she is not fit to plead, the hearing is to proceed under the Health Procedure. NISCC (Conduct) Rules 2003, Sch 2, para 15.
[2] See para 2.21.

2.38   The sanctions open to the Conduct Committee on a finding that the social care worker has committed an act of misconduct are to: (1) direct a record of admonishment be placed in the social care worker's registration for five years; (2) issue a Suspension Order (suspending the social worker's registration for a maximum period of two years); (3) issue a Removal Order (removing the social care worker's name from the register); (4) revoke any Interim Suspension Order imposed by the Preliminary Proceedings Committee.[1] A right of appeal from this decision lies to the Social Care Tribunal.[2]

[1]   NISCC (Conduct) Rules 2003, Sch 2, para 25(1).
[2]   See para 2.44.

HEALTH PROCEDURE

2.39   The procedure before the Conduct Committee where the matter has been referred to it under the Health Procedure is slightly different. In all respects the procedure is the same, except that the Committee usually sits in private,[1] and in determining whether the social care worker as been guilty of misconduct, and in deciding the issue of sanction, the Committee must consider medical reports and medical evidence 'on whether the alleged misconduct may have been caused, or substantially contributed to by the [social care worker's] physical or mental health.'[2] A medical adviser is appointed to the Committee to help it in its deliberations, although he or she will not be a voting member of the panel.[3]

[1]   NISCC (Conduct) Rules 2003, Sch 2, para 28(2).
[2]   NISCC (Conduct) Rules 2003, Sch 2, para 28(3). The social care worker must have consented to the medical examination and to allowing the Committee to examine the report: para 28(4). Where the social care worker had not so consented, the Committee can take that matter into account.
[3]   NISCC (Conduct) Rules 2003, r 10(2) and (6).

2.40   In a Health Procedure hearing, the Conduct Committee may not receive medical reports or other medical evidence unless the social worker has consented to be examined and to allow such reports and evidence to be presented to the Committee.[1]

The range of options open to the Committee at the conclusion of a Health Procedure hearing are the same as those where, in Conduct Procedure hearings, misconduct is proven to have occurred.[2]

[1]   NISCC (Conduct) Rules 2003, r 28(4).
[2]   See para 2.38.

Interim Suspension

2.42   Interim suspension is possible, though only in prescribed circumstances. The two scenarios where this is possible are where the Preliminary Proceedings Committee is considering a case referred to it by the Council,[1] or where the Council makes an application to it that an interim suspension is necessary in the public interest.[2] If either of these situations arises then the Notice of Referral[3] must indicate that the

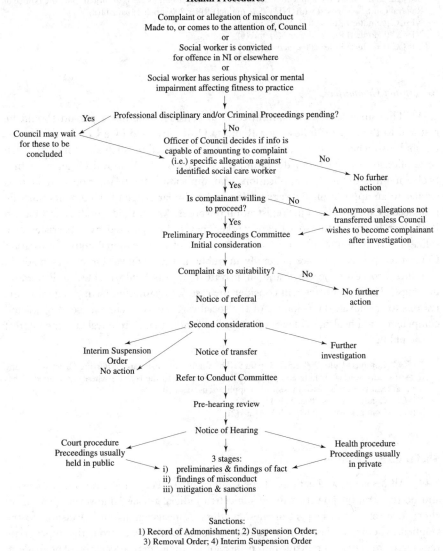

Health Procedures

Complaint or allegation of misconduct
Made to, or comes to the attention of, Council
or
Social worker is convicted
for offence in NI or elsewhere
or
Social worker has serious physical or mental
impairment affecting fitness to practice

Professional disciplinary and/or Criminal Proceedings pending?

Yes → Council may wait for these to be concluded

No → Officer of Council decides if info is capable of amounting to complaint (i.e.) specific allegation against identified social care worker

No → No further action

Yes → Is complainant willing to proceed?

No → Anonymous allegations not transferred unless Council wishes to become complainant after investigation

Yes → Preliminary Proceedings Committee Initial consideration

Complaint as to suitability?

No → No further action

Notice of referral

Second consideration

Interim Suspension Order No action

Notice of transfer

Further investigation

Refer to Conduct Committee

Pre-hearing review

Notice of Hearing

Court procedure Preceedings usually held in public

Health procedure Proceedings usually in private

3 stages:
i) preliminaries & findings of fact
ii) findings of misconduct
iii) mitigation & sanctions

Sanctions:
1) Record of Admonishment; 2) Suspension Order;
3) Removal Order; 4) Interim Suspension Order

registered social care worker can attend, be legally represented, examine and cross-examine witnesses and must provide him or her with a brief statement of the reasons why interim suspension is being considered.[4] An Interim Suspension Order made by the Preliminary Proceedings Committee cannot be for any longer than six months initially, but may be extended for up to two years.[5] Interim suspensions can be reviewed at three monthly intervals, at the election of the Council or the registered social care worker, at a hearing designed for that purpose.[6]

[1]   NISCC (Conduct) Rules 2003, r 5(1)(b).
[2]   NISCC (Conduct) Rules 2003, r 5(4).

3   See para 2.40. Where the application for an Interim Suspension Order is an urgent one, the Notice of
    Referral can be dispensed with. NISCC (Conduct) Rules 2003, Sch 1, para 11(2).
4   NISCC (Conduct) Rules 2003, Sch 1, para 11.
5   NISCC (Conduct) Rules 2003, r 5(5) and (6).
6   NISCC (Conduct) Rules 2003, Sch 1, para 12.

Restoration Committee

2.43   The purpose of this committee is to consider whether a person should be
restored to the register following a Removal Order imposed by a Conduct Committee, and if so whether any conditions need to be imposed on such a restoration. Such
an application cannot be made within three years of the Removal Order or within
twelve months of the last application.[1] An application for restoration is treated as
similar to an application for registration and a similar range of documents must be
produced as are produced for registration purposes. As with the Conduct and Health
Procedure hearings, the social care worker may be represented by a barrister or a
solicitor, a trade union official or a representative of a professional body. Restoration
Committee proceedings are generally in public if the Removal Order was made in
Conduct Procedure hearings and in private if it was made in Health Procedure
hearings.[2] The Committee will consider the case for restoration having regard to the
reasons for removal, the evidence of the social care worker's current good character,
competence and health, evidence of his or her conduct since removal and the interest
of the public.[3]

1   NISCC (Conduct) Rules 2003, Sch 3, para 9. The Committee may make a Barring Order preventing
    the social care worker making an application for restoration to the register where the individual has
    made at least two unsuccessful restoration applications: para 10.
2   NISCC (Conduct) Rules 2003, Sch 3, para 6.
3   NISCC (Conduct) Rules 2003, Sch 3, para 7(2).

Social Care Tribunal

2.44   All decisions and actions of the Council in respect of registration, suspension
and de-registration powers will be subject to judicial review.[1] However, there is an
alternative remedy in respect of these matters. Appeals against any decisions of the
Council, whether to suspend, or remove, a social care worker from the appropriate
register, or to refuse to register him or her for example, may alternatively be made to
the Social Care Tribunal. This tribunal has also been created by renaming, and
re-organising the Registered Homes Tribunal in the 2001 Act.[2] The Tribunal,
established by Part V of the Registered Homes (Northern Ireland) Order 1992, is a
three-member body, the chairperson of which is legally qualified, with the other two
members having relevant experience in social work or in the other social care
professions. It can confirm or vary the Council's decision, either completely or in
part, or substitute any condition which it thinks fit with one of its own choosing. As
the Council will also have responsibility for assessing the equivalence of social work
qualifications obtained in other countries within the European Union and the
European Economic Agreement Area, and hence the ability of social workers

qualified elsewhere to exercise their freedom of movement to come and work in Northern Ireland, some Social Care Tribunal appeals may relate to this aspect of the Council's remit. An appeal, on a point of law, can be made by either by the Council or the individual involved, from the decision of the Tribunal to the High Court. Alternatively, the Tribunal itself can make a case stated to the High Court asking it to determine a particular legal question.[3] The procedure to be adopted by the Tribunal when hearing applications from social care workers about their registration status is set out in the Social Care Tribunals Rules (Northern Ireland) 2003. Under these Rules the hearing should usually be in public,[4] and the appellant may be legally represented,[5] and he or she has the right to give evidence, call, examine and cross-examine witnesses.[6]

[1] On judicial review, see para 2.105.
[2] Section 15.
[3] Registered Homes (Northern Ireland) Order 1992, art 34.
[4] Rule 6.
[5] Rule 5.
[6] Rule 8.

The Ombudsman

2.45 The Ombudsman is a term commonly used to describe what in Northern Ireland are in fact two distinct offices, thought the same person usually occupies both.[1] These offices are those of the Commissioner for Complaints for Northern Ireland and of the Northern Ireland Assembly Ombudsman. The respective statutory bases for these offices are found in the Commissioner for Complaints (Northern Ireland) Order 1996[2] and the Ombudsman (Northern Ireland) Order 1996. The Ombudsman's task is to investigate complaints from the public about the administrative activities of various public bodies.

[1] The Ombudsman issues one annual report covering both offices.
[2] And the Commissioner for Complaints (Amendment) (Northern Ireland) Order 1997.

Commissioner for Complaints and Assembly Ombudsman

2.46 The Commissioner for Complaints might be termed a local government ombudsman and the activities of Health Boards and Trusts come within its remit.[1] The Assembly Ombudsman focuses on the administrative actions of the Northern Ireland Executive Departments (of which the DHSSPS is one, obviously), and on complaints about various tribunals for which those departments are responsible, like the Mental Health Review Tribunal, for example.[2]

[1] Aside from hearing complaints about Trusts and Boards, it also considers those made against local district councils and a range of Northern Ireland-based statutory and non-statutory public sector bodies, but the focus here will be on the relevance of the Commissioner for Complaints for social work practice.
[2] See the Ombudsman (Northern Ireland) Order 1996, Sch 3.

2.47   Bodies subject to investigation by the Commissioner for Complaints, therefore include not only Boards and Trusts, but also health and social services councils,[1] special agencies of the Department, the Central Services Agency,[2] and the Mental Health Commission.[3] Indeed independent health and social services providers, providing services under arrangements made with the statutory sector bodies are also subject to the Ombudsman's jurisdiction.[4]

[1]   See para 2.63.
[2]   See chapter 1, para 1.113.
[3]   See chapter 11, para 11.84.
[4]   Commissioner for Complaints (Northern Ireland) Order 1996, art 8A as inserted by art 3, 1997 Order of the same name.

Maladministration

2.48   Ombudsmen investigate complaints to determine whether there has been maladministration amounting to injustice to the complainant and have traditionally taken a less legalistic approach to the examination of them than that taken by the courts. Maladministration has never been defined in the statutes establishing any of the UK Ombudsmen, and the most oft-quoted explanation of the term is that provided by the Minister, Richard Crossman, sponsoring the original Bill providing for a Parliamentary Ombudsman for Great Britain. He described maladministration in the following terms: 'bias, neglect, inattention, delay, incompetence, ineptitude, perversity, turpitude, arbitrariness and so on.'[1] Consequentially this explanation of the term is often referred to as the 'Crossman Catalogue.' Successive Ombudsmen have taken their cue from this definition and have taken a flexible approach to the interpretation of the term. In particular they have used this freedom to develop a less technical approach to the consideration of the public's complaints, focusing on whether the approach of the administrators amounted to good practice and whether the complainant was treated in an appropriate manner, for example. Examples of maladministration have included avoidable delay, faulty procedures or failing to follow correct procedures, giving misleading or inadequate advice, mistakes in handling claims or discourtesy and failure to apologise properly for errors.

[1]   734 HC Deb (5th Series, col 51).

2.49   A significant limitation in the oversight role played by Ombudsmen is that they are mandated to investigate complaints about administrative matters only, and cannot deal with complaints concerning the merits of a decision taken without maladministration[1] and thus cannot investigate an underlying policy, for example. Thus, the Ombudsman would not be able to field a complaint about the decision of a Trust to close a residential facility and relocate the residents, for example, but could investigate complaints that the residents had not been properly informed of the decision or complaints that the implementation of that policy decision had not been properly handled. This distinction between matters of merits and administrative quality is not always an easy one to draw, although ultimately the Ombudsman makes that decision. The Ombudsman may be judicially reviewed in respect of it, but the courts are reluctant to 'second-guess' the Ombudsman's decision.[2]

[1] Ombudsman (Northern Ireland) Order 1996, art 10(5), and Commissioner for Complaints (Northern Ireland) Order 1996, art 7 (as amended by the 1997 Order of the same name.).
[2] See *R v Parliamentary Comr for Administration (PCA), ex p Dyer* [1994] 1 All ER 375 and *R v PCA, ex p Balchin* [1997] COD 146, and *R v PCA, ex p Balchin (No 2)* (1999) 2 LGLR 87.

2.50 The Ombudsman's jurisdiction is further curtailed by the obligation to decline to investigate where the complainant has an alternative remedy.[1] However, in practice this limitation is not as significant as it might be, because Ombudsmen usually take the view that requiring all complainants to resort to the legal system to resolve their grievances – no matter how tenuous the legal action – would impose an unrealistic burden on complainants.

[1] Ombudsman (Northern Ireland) Order 1996, art 10(3)(b) and the Commissioner for Complaints (Northern Ireland) Order 1996, art 9(3) (as amended by the 1997 Order of the same name).

2.51 All complaints must be usually be made within 12 months for the Ombudsman to have jurisdiction.[1] In Northern Ireland, Ombudsmen have attempted to engage in speedy, informal resolution of many of the complaints made to them, because of the minor nature of many of them and the fact that the complainant is often better served by a quick, although less bureaucratic, resolution of the complaint.

[1] Ombudsman (Northern Ireland) Order 1996, art 11(5), and the Commissioner for Complaints (Northern Ireland) Order 1996, art 10(6).

Sample complaints

2.52 The Ombudsman can investigate a wide variety of complaints against health and social services authorities, including those relating to the exercise of clinical judgment and employment related complaints.[1] These areas of the Ombudsman's competence are discussed below. Other types of complaint can also be entertained by the Ombudsman. For example, the 1999/2000 report contains a digest of a case in which a Trust failed to consider a complaint made under its internal procedures in the proper manner by not giving the complainants an oral hearing, as its procedures required. The Ombudsman recommended that the Trust send a written apology to the complainants and make a payment to them of £200.[2]

[1] See paras 2.53 and 2.54 respectively.
[2] Northern Ireland Ombudsman Annual Report 1999/2000, p 78.

Complaints about clinical judgment

2.53 Although the office of the Commissioner for Complaints has been in existence since 1970, its jurisdiction to deal with complaints about administrative decisions of health and social services bodies and clinical judgments made by health professionals, employed by those bodies, is of more recent vintage.[1] 'Clinical judgment' in this context means decisions by health care professionals about diagnosis, treatment or care of a patient. However, the Ombudsman may not deal with complaints relating to medical negligence or other situations in which the complainant has a remedy before the courts,[2] unless the Ombudsman is satisfied that it is not reasonable in the circumstances for the complainant to exercise that remedy.[3] Furthermore, an investigation will only be carried out where the complainant has exhausted the Trust's or Board's internal complaints mechanisms[4] or where it is not reasonable to expect the complainant to utilise the remedy.[5] These are quite significant restrictions on the Ombudsman's jurisdiction as quite a number of complaints in respect of clinical judgments are likely to include allegations of negligence along with more minor complaints, and unless the latter can be detached from the former, the Ombudsman might not have jurisdiction. Complainants in this situation are also probably more likely to consider seeking legal advice to address their concerns rather than invoking the Ombudsman's jurisdiction. Notwithstanding this combination of factors, this aspect of the Ombudsman's jurisdiction has produced a growing volume of complaints since 1997 when the jurisdiction was conferred on the office. In 2001/02, 107 such complaints were received, up from 12 in 1997.[6] However, almost 40 of them were referred to the body's internal complaints procedure. One of the investigations digested in the 2001/02 Annual Report deals with the decision of a consultant to remove a patient from his list. The Ombudsman criticised the Trust for failing to have a protocol to govern this type of situation.[7]

[1]   Commissioner for Complaints (Northern Ireland) Order 1996, arts 7(10), 8(7), and 9(6), as inserted by Commissioner for Complaints (Amendment) (Northern Ireland) Order 1997.
[2]   Commissioner for Complaints (Northern Ireland) Order 1996, art 9(3)(b), as inserted by Commissioner for Complaints (Amendment) (Northern Ireland) Order 1997.
[3]   Commissioner for Complaints (Northern Ireland) Order 1996, art 9(4)(a), as inserted by Commissioner for Complaints (Amendment) (Northern Ireland) Order 1997.
[4]   Commissioner for Complaints (Northern Ireland) Order 1996, art 9(3)(a), as inserted by Commissioner for Complaints (Amendment) (Northern Ireland) Order 1997.
[5]   Commissioner for Complaints (Northern Ireland) Order 1996, art 9(7), as inserted by Commissioner for Complaints (Amendment) (Northern Ireland) Order 1997.
[6]   Northern Ireland Ombudsman Annual Report 2001/02, p 100. For a breakdown, by category, of these complaints, see p 102.
[7]   Northern Ireland Ombudsman Annual Report 2001/02, p 107.

Employment-related complaints

2.54   The breadth of the Ombudsman's jurisdiction in Northern Ireland is such that, uniquely in the UK, the Ombudsman can also entertain complaints from employees, or job applicants, about matters relating to recruitment, selection and promotion. Thus the Ombudsman regularly entertains complaints about maladministration relating to employment matters. For example, the 2001/02 report has an example of a complaint, against the Causeway Health and Social Services Trust, upheld by the Ombudsman and concerning the Trust's failure's to shortlist the complainant, resulting in a recommendation that the Trust pay the complainant £1000 in compensation and that the Chief Executive issue a letter of apology.[1] The Ombudsman can, therefore, on occasion, provide a remedy in employment disputes where none might otherwise be available.

[1] Northern Ireland Ombudsman Annual Report 2001/02, p 108.

Enforcing Ombudsman's reports

2.55 An Ombudsman's report is not binding on the public body in question. However, in Northern Ireland a unique mechanism exists for the legal enforcement of reports of the Commissioner for Complaints. A complainant may make an application to the county court to have it award damages, or some other suitable remedy, where the Commissioner for Complaints' report discloses maladministration causing injustice by the public body.[1] This enforcement mechanism does not exist elsewhere in the UK, and has been useful in the past in compelling recalcitrant local authorities in particular, to adhere to the Commissioner for Complaints' reports.[2] The county court is confined to deciding the appropriate remedy and there is no question of the hearing resulting in the Ombudsman's report being re-opened.

[1] Commissioner for Complaints (Northern Ireland) Order 1996, art 16.
[2] Ciaran White, 'Enforcing local government ombudsman's reports: the Northern Ireland local government ombudsman's experiences' (1994) 45 NILQ, pp 395–402.

2.56 However, no such mechanism exists for enforcing reports of the Assembly Ombudsman, and ensuring compliance with those reports relies on the pressure generated by adverse publicity. Where a body subject to the jurisdiction of the Assembly Ombudsman refuses to comply with a report of that office, the Ombudsman may make a special reports to the Assembly on that case.[1] However, bodies subject to the jurisdiction of the Assembly Ombudsman do not tend to be resistant to reports that are adverse to them. The threat to report the matter to the Assembly is usually enough to compel career civil servants to comply.

[1] Ombudsman (Northern Ireland) Order 1996, art 17.

2.57 In conducting investigations both the Commissioner for Complaints and the Assembly Ombudsman have the same powers to request documents and require the attendance and examination of witnesses as the High Court.[1] Obstructing the Ombudsman without lawful excuse is tantamount to being in contempt of the High Court.[2]

[1] Commissioner for Complaints (Northern Ireland) Order 1996, art 13 and the Ombudsman (Northern Ireland) Order 1996, art 14.
[2] Commissioner for Complaints (Northern Ireland) Order 1996, art 14 and the Ombudsman (Northern Ireland) Order 1996, art 15.

Redress from Ombudsman

2.58 Recommendations in an Ombudsman's reports can vary quite considerably depending on the extent of the maladministration and particularly the nature of the injustice sustained by the complainant. Therefore, while most recommendations include an amount to compensate the complainant, such a recommendation does not automatically follow from an adverse finding. Other forms of redress might be suggested including a written apology, as well as a commitment on the part of the body in question to implement suitable changes. From the individual social worker's point of view it is worth noting that the complaint is made against the public body, rather than against the individual, although the social worker will of course by interviewed by the Ombudsman's staff if necessary. However, any report issued usually tends to anonymise the identity of both the complainant and the staff members of the body subject to investigation. Even where the Ombudsman concludes that there has not been any maladministration, he or she will occasionally indicate that the administrative policy ought to be reconsidered or re-evaluated.

2.59   The experience of the Ombudsman procedure has been, that because of the latitude given to the incumbent as to how 'maladministration' is to be applied, the effectiveness of the office is affected by the personality of the Ombudsman and the approach taken to the role by the office-holder. An Ombudsman who considers that the role has the potential to indirectly improve the quality of administration will usually apply a more rigorous analysis to the actions of administrators than an Ombudsman who has a less independent view. An effective Ombudsman will challenge the premise on which the administrator proceeds and subject it to rigorous scrutiny, if appropriate, rather than accepting it as a 'given'.

Health and Personal Social Services Regulation and Improvement Authority

2.60   The Northern Ireland Health and Personal Social Services Regulation and Improvement Authority was established by the Health and Personal Social Services (Quality, Improvement and Regulation) (Northern Ireland) Order 2003, with the general duties of keeping the Department informed about the provision of services, their availability and quality, and encouraging improvement in the quality of services.[1] In order to allow it to perform these statutory duties the 2003 Order also requires Boards and Trusts to establish arrangements for the purpose of monitoring and improving the quality of the health and personal social services which they provide, and the environment in which they provide them.[2] One of the Regulation and Improvement Authority's tasks then, is to review these arrangements, or the services actually provided, or to investigate the actual service provision, and to report to the Department where the services are of 'unacceptably poor quality', or where there are 'significant failings' in the way the body is being run.[3]

---

[1]   Health and Personal Social Services (Quality, Improvement and Regulation) (Northern Ireland) Order 2003, art 4.
[2]   Health and Personal Social Services (Quality, Improvement and Regulation) (Northern Ireland) Order 2003, art 34.
[3]   Health and Personal Social Services (Quality, Improvement and Regulation) (Northern Ireland) Order 2003, art 35(3) and (4).

2.61   The 2003 Order also empowers the Department to set minimum standards for the delivery of health and social services,[1] and where there is a failure to comply with these standards the Regulation and Improvement Authority may issue an improvement notice setting out the nature of the failure and the improvements required.[2]

1   Article 38.
2   Article 39.

2.62   In carrying out its functions the Authority has the power to request information of Boards and Trusts, and to enter premises operated or controlled by them to fulfil its functions, and may examine documents retained on those premises.[1]

1   Health and Personal Social Services (Quality, Improvement and Regulation) (Northern Ireland) Order 2003, art 41. The Regulation and Improvement Authority also has similar powers in respect of children's homes, nursing homes and residential homes. Obstruction of an Authority Official exercising his or her powers is a criminal offence.

Health and Social Services Councils

2.63   A further, non-legal, form of accountability is achieved through the Health and Social Services Councils, of which there are four, one for each Health and Social Services Board.[1] (The report of the Acute Hospitals Review Group has suggested the establishment of a single Northern Ireland-wide body to represent consumer interests.[2] If changes are made to the organisational structure for the delivery of health and personal social services in Northern Ireland, then this *de facto* amalgamation of the four Councils may also take place).

1   See chapter 1, para 1.110, for an explanation of the organisation of the health and social services sector in Northern Ireland.
2   DHSS 2001, para 8.45.

2.64   Established by the Health and Personal Social Services (Northern Ireland) Order 1991, article 4, these Councils' duties are to 'represent the interests of the public' in respect of health and personal social services in the relevant Area Board.[1] In particular, the Councils' function is to 'keep under review the operation of the Health and Personal Social Services in its area and to make recommendations for the improvement of those services or otherwise advise the relevant Board upon such matters ... as it thinks fit'[2] giving them a general watchdog role. Their task is not to call individual social workers to account but their brief in surveying the health and social care sector means that they are in a position to comment on matters affecting social workers' duties. This may result in the Council commissioning reports on specific themes or on particular services or facilities, for example, and issuing appropriate advice to the relevant Board. The Council also has a role in dealing with complaints, in that it can advise complainants as to the complaint-resolution options open to them and may even help the complainant articulate his or her concerns.

1   Health and Personal Social Services (Northern Ireland) Order 1991, Sch 1, para 1(a).
2   Health and Personal Social Services Councils (Regulations) 1991, reg 15.

2.65   Each Council is required, in conjunction with its relevant Board, to draw up an annual work programme for the Council and to report on an annual basis to the Department.[1] The Board is required to respond to the report, and to include a list of any steps or actions it has taken in consequence of it.[2] Councils and Boards also meet on an annual basis to discuss matters that may be raised by the Council or the Board.[3] The Councils must also be consulted in respect of any proposals for 'substantial development' or 'variation' of the health and personal social services delivered in their areas.[4] The Boards are obliged to make available 'such information about the planning and operation of health and social services' in its area as the 'Council may reasonably require in order to carry out its duties'.[5] In the event of any dispute between a Council and a Board as to whether material should be disclosed the Department is to decide the matter.[6] Councils also have the power to enter and inspect Board or Trust controlled premises, subject to conditions as are agreed between the Council and the Board, or in the alternative as between the Department and the Council.[7]

[1]   Health and Personal Social Services Councils (Regulations) 1991, reg 16(1).
[2]   Health and Personal Social Services Councils (Regulations) 1991, reg 16(2).
[3]   Health and Personal Social Services Councils (Regulations) 1991, reg 20.
[4]   Health and Personal Social Services Councils (Regulations) 1991, reg 17.
[5]   Health and Personal Social Services Councils (Regulations) 1991, reg 18.
[6]   Health and Personal Social Services Councils (Regulations) 1991, reg 18(3).
[7]   Health and Personal Social Services Councils (Regulations) 1991, reg 19.

Role in Independent Review

2.66   Health and Social Services Councils can also offer help to individuals who remain dissatisfied even after their complaint has been examined, under internal arrangements, by a Board, Trust, family health service practitioner or the independent care sector. Such a person has a right to request an independent review. Councils can aid the individual in drawing up a statement for the Board-appointed convenor whose task it is to decide whether an independent review of the complaint is justified.

2.67   Where a request for an independent review is made to the Trust it should be passed to the convenor, who is a person appointed by the Health and Social Services Board to deal with complaints. The independent review panel is then set up by the convenor and consists of people who are independent of the Trust in question: the convenor, a lay chairperson and another independent member appointed by the Board. Independent professional assessors are also appointed to advise the panel.

2.68   The convenor makes this decision in conjunction with an independent lay chairperson, also appointed by the Board, but no independent review will be established where the matter is the subject matter of legal proceedings or a disciplinary investigation. A refusal to establish an independent review may itself be the subject of a complaint to the Ombudsman/Commissioner for Complaints.[1]

[1]   See para 2.45.

2.69   Where the matter concerns the exercise of clinical or medical judgment the panel will be advised by two independent Clinical Assessors appointed by the Board. The panel determines its own procedure, including whether the complainant and the body should appear before it, but none of the parties appearing may be legally represented. This is where the Councils' role can be valuable because the complainant may have someone from the relevant Council speak on his or her behalf.

2.70   The panel issues a report at the conclusion of the proceedings and the body in question is obliged to inform the complainant of the measures it intends to take to respond to the panel's recommendations. If the complainant is still dissatisfied he or she may complain to the Ombudsman/Commissioner for Complaints. The entire process should take no longer than six months from the receipt of the complainant's request for an independent review to the body's response to the panel's recommendations, or three months if the complaint relates to family health services practitioners.

Social Services Inspectorate

2.71   Accountability is also maintained by the activities of the Social Services Inspectorate (SSI). A professional group based within the Department,[1] the Inspectorate has the task of ensuring the maintenance of standards in the delivery of health and personal social services in Northern Ireland. This involves it inspecting the social care and criminal justice facilities, as well as evaluating those non-statutory organisations that are in receipt of Departmental funding. The Inspectorate is managed by the Chief Social Services Inspector, who makes an annual report to the Minister about matters within the SSI's remit. The Inspectorate is aided in its work by the Social Service Analysis Branch, which provides statistical material to underpin the work of its Inspectors.

[1]   The SSI has no statutory basis but its inspectors avail of various statutory inspection powers that are actually conferred on the Department because they are Departmental employees, see paras 2.74–2.79.

Types of inspection

2.72   The SSI carries out six different types of inspection:

1   Thematic Inspections, examining a particular aspect of social work or contribution by personal social services and criminal justice agencies. An example of this type of report is 'Adopting Best Care: Inspection of Statutory Adoption Services in Northern Ireland', published in 2002;

2   Total Inspections, assessing all of a Board's or Trust's social work services, or the services provided by Juvenile Justice Centres or the Probation Board for Northern Ireland. An example is the 2000 report, 'Report into PBNI funded Hostel Places';

3   Facility Inspections, focusing on the standard of service provided within particular facilities. An example is 'Secure Care: An Inspection of Secure Accommodation at Shamrock House and Linden House', (SSI, 2002);

4   Evaluation of Voluntary Organisations, examining the services provided by voluntary organisations grant aided by the Department. A number of such

evaluations were carried out in 1998, for example, Northlands Centre Evaluation Report; Mencap in Northern Ireland Evaluation Report and Childline in Northern Ireland Evaluation Report;

5   Investigations commissioned by the Secretary of State for Northern Ireland, Ministers, the Departmental Permanent Secretary (ie Chief Civil Servant of the Department), Chief Executive of a Trust or the Chief Inspector. A report into the attempts by a convicted sex offender to gain access to children through volunteer organisations, entitled 'Abuse of Trust: report of the SSI investigation into the case of Martin Huston',[1] was commissioned by the then Minister for Health and Social Services, Michael Mates;

6   Inspections of Registration and Inspection Units, which have responsibility under the Registered Homes (Northern Ireland) Order 1992 for inspecting children's homes, residential services and day centres.[2] These inspections are carried our on a joint basis with the Nursing, Midwifery and Advisory Group and Estate Services Division. Examples of reports of this nature include 'Registration and Inspection Units in Northern Ireland 1999/2000' and a subsequent report entitled, 'Follow-up inspection on the operation of the four registration and inspection units in NI' (both 2001).

[1]   December 1993.
[2]   There are four such units, one for each Area Board. On the structure of health and social services agencies, see chapter 1, para 1.110.

Annual inspection programme

2.73   The Inspectorate's social services inspection programme is agreed on an annual basis by the Central Personal Social Services Advisory Committee.[1] This Committee is comprised of representatives from professional, voluntary and educational bodies and its role is to make proposals for inspection and endorse the inspection programme. (These arrangements do not apply to the inspection of Criminal Justice Services, which as a reserved matter, is within the remit of the Northern Ireland Office).

[1]   Established under the Health and Personal Social Services (Northern Ireland) Order 1972, art 24.

Inspection powers

2.74   The Inspectorate has no separate statutory basis, but a range of legislative provisions confer powers on inspectors appointed, or authorised, by the Secretary of State for Northern Ireland. It is these provisions that authorise SSI inspectors to carry out their tasks, particularly to enter premises for the purposes of inspecting them. In some circumstances inspectors are also given powers to obtain documents and direct questions to staff. These powers are found in diverse statutes and are set out below.

2.75   The Health and Personal Social Services (NI) Order 1972, article 54, is a general inspection power conferred on the Minister allowing him or her to appoint inspectors in respect of any matter covered by the 1972 Order. It is discussed in greater detail under 'Statutory Inquiries'[1] because the generality of the power means that it is often used to establish such inquiries.

[1]   See para 2.130.

2.76   The Adoption (Northern Ireland) Order 1987, article 69 confers a general power on the Department to conduct inquiries or investigations into matters of adoption. Powers of inspection are conferred by article 71, which allows the Department to appoint an inspector to examine any premises where any child coming into contact with the adoption process is being cared for. The inspector may enter the premises at any time and can make reasonable requests to examine relevant records and material.[1]

[1]   Adoption (Northern Ireland) Order 1987, art 71(2).

2.77   Powers of inspection in respect of the Probation Board for Northern Ireland are found in the Criminal Justice (Northern Ireland) Order 1991, article 7, amending the Probation Board (Northern Ireland) Order 1982. This authorises the Secretary of State to appoint an inspector to examine the exercise by the Board, of its statutory functions. Inspection powers extend not only to the Board but also to other organisations and authorities that have entered into agreements with the Board to provide services. The inspector is also given powers of entry,[1] which can be exercised at any reasonable time, making such investigation of the establishment as the inspector deems fit. Powers to request and/or inspect documentation are also granted to Departmental inspectors.[2] Obstructing the inspector is a criminal offence.[3]

[1]   Criminal Justice (Northern Ireland) 1991 Order, art 14(5).
[2]   Criminal Justice (Northern Ireland) 1991 Order, art 14(2) and (3).
[3]   Criminal Justice (Northern Ireland) 1991 Order, art 14(6).

2.78   Inspection duties under the Children (Northern Ireland) Order 1995, are placed on the Department by article 149, which then delegates those to an authorised person,[1] who will usually be an officer of the SSI. Powers to inspect documentation are also provided in the legislation.[2] Further powers for the purposes of these investigations are conferred by article 150, which authorises the officer to enter onto the premises, inspect computer-generated records with the reasonable assistance of the staff, examine the children and the premises. A general power to order inquiries in respect of facilities for children, irrespective of whether the body in question is a statutory or voluntary organisation, is given to the Department in article 152. Lastly, the Department has a general duty, under article 153, to monitor the adequacy of childcare training for the statutory and non-statutory sector and the SSI also fulfils this function.

[1]   Children (Northern Ireland) Order 1995, art 149(2).
[2]   Children (Northern Ireland) Order 1995, art 149(4).

2.79   Although a number of these inspection provisions contain sanctions for failing to allow inspectors entry to premises or access to documents, the reality is that such threats and sanctions rarely have to be invoked. The authority of the SSI, coupled with the importance of the Department's supervisory role in the supervision of health and social services delivery in Northern Ireland, means that it is unlikely that the SSI would need to threaten to avail of these sanctions to facilitate the use of these powers.

In respect of the enforcement of its reports, the SSI expects agencies to make an initial response within eight weeks, which should show whether or not the findings of the report are accepted and how they will be acted upon. Six months after the publication of the report a further response will be sought from it on the action taken to address the findings.

The SSI does not operate on the basis of complaints from the public or social services staff, and as can be seen from the above, its reports relate to facilities or services rather than to individuals, so that individual social workers are not made directly accountable by the SSI. However, the status of the Inspectorate means that considerable attention is paid to its reports and recommendations and, in that indirect way, it has considerable bearing on social work practice.

Tortious liability of social workers

2.80　The focus here is on the social worker's liability to individual persons for their activity in the workplace in the law of torts, principally in the tort of negligence, and, to a lesser extent, in the tort of misfeasance in public office.[1] Both of these torts allow injured persons to claim compensation or damages for injury caused to them, whether physical or mental, by the negligent actions of others or, in the case of misfeasance, by the deliberate and wilful acts of a public servant.

---

[1]　These are not the only torts that may apply in litigation involving health and social service authorities, but they are two of the most significant. Claimants in negligence actions often plead breach of statutory duty as well. This is referred to in the discussion of the *Bedfordshire* case. See para 2.88.

Misfeasance

2.81　Misfeasance in public office is a less commonly pleaded tort that applies to public officials only. It involves imposing liability on a public official for an abuse of the official's powers. The ingredients of the tort have been summarised by the House of Lords in *Three Rivers District Council v Bank of England (No 3) (Summary Judgment)*[1] in the following terms:[2]

'First, there must be an unlawful act or omission done or made in the exercise of power by the public officer. Second, as the essence of the tort is an abuse of power, the act or omission must have been done or made with the required mental element. Third, for the same reason, the act or omission must have been done or made in bad faith. Fourth, as to standing, the claimants must demonstrate that they have a sufficient interest to sue the defendant. Fifth, as causation is an essential element of the cause of action, the act or omission must have caused the claimants' loss.'

1   [2001] UKHL 16, [2001] 2 All ER 513.
2   At para [42] in which the House was drawing from its own decision in *Three Rivers District Council v Bank of England (No 3)* [2003] 2 AC 1, [2000] 3 All ER 1, HL.

2.82   This means that in order to succeed the official must have acted unlawfully, with bad faith and must have known that he or she did not have the power to perform the acts they did. The relative rarity of such situations, and the difficulty in proving the public official's bad faith, help to explain why the tort is not commonly invoked. Furthermore, even where the plaintiff can show bad faith on the part of the official, the employing authority might not be vicariously liable[1] if the official strayed well beyond the scope of his or her employment and 'the unauthorised acts of the [public officials] were so unconnected with their authorised duties as to be quite independent of and outside those duties'.[2] As a result the public official alone might be solely liable to pay damages and may be unlikely to be able to do so. An example of misfeasance arose in *Kuddus v Chief Constable of Leicestershire Constabulary*.[3] In this case the plaintiff reported to a police officer that there had been a theft from his flat. The police officer subsequently forged the plaintiff's signature on a form purporting to withdraw the complaint.

1   See para 2.84.
2   *Racz v Home Office* [1994] 2 AC 45, [1994] 1 All ER 97, HL.
3   [2001] UKHL 29, [2002] 2 AC 122, [2001] 3 All ER 193.

Negligence

2.83   The complex issue that is the tort of negligence has undergone a number of twists and turns in recent years, as one might expect with a common law-created cause of action, with the result that the law is in a state of flux. It is useful at the outset to provide an explanation of the tort generally before proceeding to explain its particular application to social workers. One important point worth noting is that where social workers are the subject of a negligence action arising from their employment, the plaintiff is usually attempting to secure damages, not from the social worker personally, but from his or her employer by virtue of the doctrine of vicarious liability.

Vicarious liability

2.84   Vicarious liability means that employers are liable for the tortious actions of their employees committed in the course of their employment. It is open to an employer to argue that it is not vicariously liable because the employee strayed beyond the scope of his or her authority, in which case the employee will be personally liable. For example, in *Phelps v Hillingdon London Borough Council*,[1] the local authority was capable of being vicariously liable for the actions, or failings, of its educational psychologists, in circumstances were it was alleged that the misdiagnosis of the complainant's condition by those psychologists contributed to their loss.

[1]   [2001] 2 AC 619, [2000] 4 All ER 504, HL. Discussed at para 2.99.

Elements of negligence

2.85   There are a number of elements to the tort of negligence that must be satisfied before liability will be imposed. The leading case of *Caparo Industries plc v Dickman*[1] established that there are three elements to establishing that a defendant is liable:
  (i)   foreseeability;
  (ii)   proximity; and
  (iii) whether it is fair, just and reasonable that the law should impose a duty of care.

'Foreseeability' is the idea that the defendant could have reasonably foreseen that the plaintiff would have suffered damage or loss as a result of his or her actions. 'Proximity' is the notion that the plaintiff must not have been too 'remote' from the defendant such that the defendant would not be under a duty of care towards persons like the plaintiff. The third element of the *Caparo* test is really a fall-back position for the judiciary, allowing it to determine on public policy grounds whether a duty of care should be imposed on the defendant. Essentially then, in order to establish liability in negligence the plaintiff must demonstrate first, that the defendant owed him a legal duty of care, secondly, that the defendant by his or her actions or inactivity breached that duty of care, and thirdly, this breach then resulted in the plaintiff sustaining injury or damage. Failure to establish all three elements will mean that the plaintiff will be unsuccessful.

[1]   [1990] 2 AC 605, [1990] 1 All ER 568, HL.

Social workers and the duty of care

2.86   The central question that has arisen in respect of social workers' liability in negligence has been whether a duty of care ought to be imposed on them at all given the crucial public service role they play. If social workers do not owe a duty of care to others arising from the statutory or non-statutory practice, then clearly they would not be liable in negligence. A common consideration in these cases is whether the imposition of liability on a category of persons will open the floodgates and lead to a rash of claims against public sector professionals.

2.87   This question was considered by the House of Lords in a landmark decision in which a number of cases were heard together. The judgment is commonly referred to as *X (Minors) v Bedfordshire Borough Council*.[1] Two of these cases involved social workers' powers and duties under the Children Act 1989 to intervene to protect children suffering significant harm arising from abuse or neglect. In one of them the allegation was that the social workers' failure to take the children into care resulted in them continuing to suffer shocking levels of abuse and neglect, thereby causing them injury. In the other negligence arose, it was alleged, from the opposite set of circumstances, namely that the decision to take the children into care was an incorrect one and resulted in damage to them.[2]

[1] [1995] 2 AC 633, [1995] 3 All ER 353.
[2] Three other plaintiffs alleged negligence and breach of statutory duty by local authorities in respect of their duties under various education statutes.

2.88 The plaintiffs in the *Bedfordshire* litigation also claimed damages for breach of statutory duty by the local authorities, in conjunction with its claim for damages in negligence. This is a separate tort that public authorities may have to face, though it is often pleaded along with negligence. However, the House of Lords judgment in *Bedfordshire* has defined its scope of application in such a way that it is unlikely to prove as troublesome as negligence for health and social services authorities. In order to succeed with a claim for breach of statutory duty the plaintiffs had to demonstrate that it was Parliament's intention when enacting the legislation that aggrieved private individuals would be compensated in damages in addition to any redress they might have in judicial review:

'The basic proposition is that in the ordinary case a breach of statutory duty does not, by itself, give rise to any private law cause of action. However a private law cause of action will arise if it can be shown, as a matter of construction of the statute, that the statutory duty was imposed for the protection of a limited class of the public and that Parliament intended to confer on members of that class a private right of action for breach of the duty.'[1]

[1] Lord Browne-Wilkinson's speech at 364D.

2.89 Their Lordships considered that the Children Act 1989 was a statutory scheme that allowed social work intervention in certain circumstances and was not designed to give individuals remedies in the law of tort for the actions of social workers.

In respect of the negligence claim, the issue that concerns us here, the House considered that such a claim would only succeed where the manner in which the local authorities had exercised, or failed to exercise, their statutory powers was outside their statutory discretion entirely. In other words, that which the local authorities had, or had not, done, was an unreasonable use of its discretion. It also considered that it would not be 'just and reasonable'[1] to impose a duty of care on social workers in these circumstances because, in short, the fear of being sued might hamper social workers' performance of their statutory child protection duties.

[1] A reference to the third limb of the *Caparo* test, see para 2.85.

Negligence and the European Convention of Human Rights

2.90 There the matter might have rested but for a decision of the European Court of Human Rights some years later in *Osman v United Kingdom*[1] which had to do with an unsuccessful negligence action against the police. Osman's father had keen killed and he himself injured by a former teacher of his who stalked him and had threatened violence in the past, all of which was known to the police. The negligence action alleged that the failure of the police to intervene sooner to arrest Osman's stalker was a contributing factor to the injuries he sustained. Osman's attempt to sue the police had been unsuccessful because the domestic courts had, on the grounds of public policy, declined to impose a duty of care on the police and had applied the precedent established in *Hill v Chief Constable of West Yorkshire*.[2]

[1]   (1998) 29 EHRR 245, [1999] 1 FLR 193.
[2]   [1989] AC 53, [1988] 2 All ER 238, HL.

2.91   In the *Hill* case a relative of a victim of the Yorkshire Ripper attempted to sue the police alleging that their negligence in failing to detect and detain the 'Ripper' at an earlier stage in its investigation was a key factor in the victim's death. The House of Lords struck out the legal action on the basis that public policy dictated that the police should not have to face such negligence actions as it would adversely affect their ability to function. The *Hill* precedent also played a part in the House of Lords decision in *Bedfordshire*, as it did in Osman's case in the UK courts. However, Osman applied to the European Court of Human Rights alleging a breach of his right to a fair trial, and it took a different view to the UK courts.

2.92   The European Court concluded that the striking out of Osman's claims in the domestic courts, on the basis of precedent, without hearing the substance of the claim was a breach of article 6, which guarantees a right to a fair trial.[1] It seemed, therefore, that the reliance on public policy to determine the outcomes of cases like those under scrutiny here, involving the police, social workers and the like, was improper and that the courts in the UK would have to reconsider their approach to the problem of the tort of negligence as it applied to certain types of public servant. In the meantime, the *Bedfordshire* cases were taken to the European Court of Human Rights and surfaced there as *Z v United Kingdom*.[2] In a decision that seemed to fly in the face of its ruling in *Osman*, the European Court concluded that the decision of the House of Lords in *Bedfordshire* was not a breach of the children's right to a fair trial under article 6. (There was, however, a breach of the children's right not to be subject to inhuman and degrading treatment, a right protected by Convention right, article 3,[3] for which the State was responsible, arising from the failure to intervene to protect children from neglect and abuse by taking them into care).[4]

[1]   For the text and a general discussion of Convention right, art 6, see chapter 1, para 1.83 and chapter 6, para 6.23.
[2]   [2001] EHRLR 709.
[3]   For some discussion of Convention right, art 3, see chapter 1, para 1.79, and chapter 6, para 6.21.
[4]   For more on *Z v United Kingdom*, see chapter 6, para 6.21.

2.93   This seemed to restore the status quo established by the House of Lords in the *Bedfordshire* case. Put simply, it would seem to indicate that social workers are not liable in negligence for their actions when operating under legislation like the Children Act 1989. However, in the period between the two European cases – *Osman* *v United Kingdom* and *Z v United Kingdom* – the English courts had occasion to consider the application of the tort of negligence to a number of other public service professions, including social workers.

Reconsideration in UK courts

2.94 In *W v Essex County Council*[1] the courts were faced with a negligence claim by foster parents, and their children against the council, where a foster child placed with them by the council had sexually abused their children. Before agreeing to foster the child the parents stipulated that they were not willing to foster a child who was a known, or suspected sex abuser. Despite this, the local authority proceeded to place a child with the family knowing that he had been cautioned for indecent assault of his own sister and was being investigated for rape. While he was placed with them, he abused his foster parents' children. The parents and their children sought to sue the council and the Court of Appeal and the House of Lords concluded that a duty of care did exist on the facts between the parents and the children on the one hand and the social worker and the local authority on the other, sufficient to allow the matter to go to trial.

[1]   [2001] 2 AC 592, [2000] 2 All ER 237, [2000] 1 FCR 568, HL.

2.95 In two further cases raising similar issues, *S v Gloucestershire County Council* and *L v Tower Hamlets London Borough Council*,[1] the Court of Appeal had another occasion to consider the principles that apply in such cases. Both plaintiffs claimed they had been sexually abused while in foster care and brought negligence actions against the authorities that had placed them. The issue in the appeal was whether the cases should be struck out as disclosing no cause of action and therefore the Court of Appeal had to consider the issue of if, and when, a duty of care could be imposed on public authorities.

[1]   [2001] Fam 313, [2000] 3 All ER 346, [2000] 2 FCR 345, CA.

2.96 No action would lie, it concluded if the subject matter of the claim was 'non-justiciable', that is a matter that the courts did not consider suitable for adjudication by the courts. This would include policy decisions and decisions about the allocation of funds, for example. Decisions or actions based upon the authority's exercise of its discretion would, therefore, normally be immune from negligence actions unless the decision was 'plainly wrong' and was an unlawful use of its discretionary powers. However, decisions of social workers could, by analogy with other professions, be held to be negligent. On an examination of the facts the court allowed S's action to proceed, but struck out L's action on the basis that it disclosed no reasonable prospects of success.

Barrett v Enfield London Borough Council

2.97 The House of Lords also had occasion in the aftermath of *Osman* to consider this topic. In *Barrett v Enfield London Borough Council*,[1] the House was faced with the issue of whether a duty of care could be applied to local authority-employed educational psychologists and social workers for their failure to diagnose learning difficulties in the plaintiff, Barrett, and for their failure to find a suitable adoption placement for him.

¹   [2001] 2 AC 550, [1999] 3 All ER 193.

2.98   The plaintiff in this case had been taken into care when no more than a few months old, and remained there, having been placed in a number of unsuccessful foster arrangements, until he reached 18 years. He alleged that various professionals were guilty of negligence, and once again the salient legal issue was whether a duty of care existed between those professionals and the plaintiff. Their Lordships considered that such a duty could be imposed and that there was a difference between the plaintiff in this case and those in the *Bedfordshire* case. In this case, the fact that Barrett had been in care meant that a duty of care arose, the House of Lords concluded. The fact that he was complaining about matters relating to that time, rather than about whether he should, or should not, have been taken into care distinguished his case from that in *Bedfordshire*.

2.99   The House of Lords also imposed a duty of care on educational psychologists employed by local authorities in *Phelps v Hillingdon London Borough Council*,[1] The plaintiff was a schoolgirl claiming damages for breach of statutory duty under the Education Acts 1944 and 1981[2] and in negligence. Her case was essentially that the local authority's employees had been negligent in detecting and treating her learning difficulties and dyslexia. Lord Slynn of Hadley stated in his speech:[3]

> 'This House decided in *Barrett v Enfield London Borough Council* that the fact that acts which are claimed to be negligent are carried out within the ambit of a statutory discretion is not in itself a reason why it should be held that no claim for negligence can be brought in respect of them. It is only where what is done has involved the weighing of competing public interests, or has been dictated by considerations on which Parliament could not have intended that the courts would substitute their views for the views of ministers or officials, that the courts will hold that the issue is non-justiciable on the ground that the decision was made in the exercise of a statutory discretion. In Pamela's case there is no such ground for holding that her claim is non-justiciable and therefore the question to be determined is whether the damage relied on is foreseeable and proximate and whether it is just and reasonable to recognise a duty of care (*Caparo Industries plc v Dickman*[4]). If a duty of care would exist where advice was given other than pursuant to the exercise of statutory powers, such duty of care is not excluded because the advice is given pursuant to the exercise of statutory powers.'

And later he added:[5]

> '... it is long and well-established, now elementary, that persons exercising a particular skill or profession may owe a duty of care in the performance to people who it can be foreseen will be injured if due skill and care are not

exercised, and if injury or damage can be shown to have been caused by the lack of care. Such duty does not depend on the existence of any contractual relationship between the person causing and the person suffering the damage. A doctor, an accountant and an engineer are plainly such a person. So in my view is an educational psychologist or psychiatrist a teacher including a teacher in a specialised area, such as a teacher concerned with children having special educational needs. So maybe an education officer performing the functions of a local education authority in regard to children with special educational needs.'

What the House of Lords was signalling in *Phelps*, I would suggest, was that it reserves the right not to impose a duty of care on the grounds of public policy, but it is now more reluctant to use that power.

1   [2001] 2 AC 619, [2002] 4 All ER 504, [2000] 3 FCR 102. As with many of these negligence and breach of statutory duty cases, a number of similar cases were judged together. For the purposes of the discussion here, only *Phelps'* factual circumstances are averted to.
2   And the Education (Special Educational Needs) Regulations 1983.
3   [2000] 4 All ER 504 at 517C–F.
4   [1990] 2 AC 605 at 617–8, HL.
5   [2000] 4 All ER 504 at 517J–518A.

Brooks v Metropolitan Police Comr

2.100   The European Court of Human Rights judgment in *Z v United Kingdom* has since been considered by the Court of Appeal in England and Wales in *Brooks v Metropolitan Police Comr*,[1] a negligence action taken against the police by friends of Stephen Lawrence and arising from the racist manner in which the police treated them, following the attack in which Lawrence was killed. As with the other cases examined above, the issue for the Court of Appeal was whether the actions should be struck out and what principles governed that issue. Having surveyed a wide range of cases, many of which are referred to above, the court had this to say:

'That lengthy survey of the authorities leads us to the conclusion that the question whether it is fair, just and reasonable to hold that a duty of care exists in a particular case depends upon the circumstances of that particular case. All or almost all cases involve a balance between competing considerations. The public interest has many strands, which may often point in different directions. ... The considerations of public policy identified by Lord Keith in *Hill [v Chief Constable of West Yorkshire]* remain substantially valid, although they must be weighed against other relevant public policy considerations. One of those considerations is the importance in a particular case of the principle that the public policy consideration which has first claim on the law is that wrongs should be remedied and that very potent considerations are required to override that policy (per Lord Browne-Wilkinson, agreeing with Sir Thomas Bingham MR in *X (Minors) v Bedfordshire CC* [in] the former report,[2] in the passage referred to in para 98 of *Z v United Kingdom*). In the light of the development of the principles in this area of the law by the House of Lords since *Hill*, we do not think that it is appropriate to describe the police as having in every case an "immunity from suit" in respect of allegations of negligent investigation of crime.'

In the event they allowed the plaintiff to proceed with some of his negligence actions.

[1]   [2002] EWCA Civ 407.
[2]   [1995] 2 AC 633 at 745, HL.

Social workers and negligence: the future

2.101   What is the net effect of these cases for social workers' accountability in the tort of negligence? The answer is not a straightforward one. However, it should be clear that social workers can no longer simply rely on the nature of the roles they perform in order to defeat a negligence claim. It will be difficult to argue that the exigencies of public policy require that no duty of care, whatsoever, be imposed on social workers, as might have been considered to be the case in the immediate aftermath of the House of Lords decision in the *Bedfordshire* case.

2.102   The affirmation of the House of Lords decision in that case by the European Court of Human Rights, means that there will be instances, like the exercise of the statutory child protection mandate, where public policy considerations will be sufficient to defeat a negligence action and convince a court to strike it out, but the cases of *Barrett*, *Phelps*, *W v Essex County Council*, and *Brooks* demonstrate that the courts will impose duties of care in certain circumstances, or at the very least, allow the issue to proceed to a full trial to determine whether on the facts a duty of care exists. In that respect, the protracted litigation involving the European Court of Human Rights has let the genie out of the bottle, so to speak, and the situation cannot be restored to the relative simplicity of the law as expressed in the House of Lords' judgment in *Bedfordshire*. The courts, I suggest, will impose a duty of care where a child is already in care (see *Barrett*), or where the social worker has acted in such a manner as to establish a particular relationship, or connection, with the plaintiff (*W x Essex County Council*). Furthermore, *Phelps* demonstrates that the courts will no longer be 'blinded' by the fact that statutory powers or duties underpin the defendant's role, and that the courts will be prepared to draw comparisons with other professionals who are subject to duties of care in respect of some of their activities.

Standard of care

2.103   How then, the average social worker might remark, am I to protect myself, and my employer, from such actions? The cases referred to above related to the issue of whether or not a duty of care existed between the plaintiff and the professional in question. Recall that this is usually only the first matter to be overcome in negligence actions. A further matter to be determined is whether the defendant breached that duty. In deciding this issue the actions, or inactivity as the case may be, of the defendant will be measured or examined against the standard of the reasonable professional having, and exercising, that skill. Another extract from Lord Slynn's speech in *Phelps*, where he in turn quotes a passage from a well known negligence case against doctors, will help to clarify this point:

> 'The recognition of the duty of care does not of itself impose unreasonably high standards. The courts have long recognised that there is no negligence if a doctor "exercises the ordinary skill of an ordinary competent man exercising that particular art".

> 'A doctor is not guilty of negligence if he has acted in accordance with a practice accepted as proper by a responsible body of medical men skilled in that particular art. ... Putting it the other way round, a doctor is not negligent, if he is acting in accordance with such a practice, merely because there is a body of opinion that takes a contrary view.' (*Bolam v Friern Hospital Management Committee*[1])

This means that a social worker will not have acted in a negligent manner if he or she acts in accordance with accepted professional practice. Whether a social worker has broken a duty of care will be measured by assessing the established practice in the area, and the established practice is likely to be determined by reference to standards imposed by the Northern Ireland Social Care Council, or other such councils, by the British Association of Social Workers, or by reference to the expert witness testimony of other social workers.

[1]   [1957] 2 All ER 118, [1957] 1 WLR 582.

2.104   Lastly, liability can also be avoided if it can be shown that even though a social worker was in breach of a duty of care to the plaintiff, the plaintiff would have suffered injury in any event. In short, the defence in those circumstances is that the injury was not caused by, or was not the result of, the social worker's actions or inactivity, as the case may be.

Judicial review

2.105   As explained in chapter 1, much of social work practice is underpinned by legislation that imposes duties on, or grants powers to, public bodies. Public bodies can, of course, only act through their employees, and when it comes to implementing health and social services legislation those actions are often performed by social workers. Social workers may also find themselves implementing non-statutory policies of their employing public authority. All of these actions and decisions are subject to judicial review.

Nature of judicial review

2.106   Judicial review is a particular form of legal action which involves the High Court assessing the legality of the decisions or actions taken by public law bodies in respect of public law matters.[1] The assessment engaged in by the High Court is not concerned with the merits of the decision or action in question, but merely whether it was done in accordance with law. It differs, therefore, from an appeal, where the focus is on whether an earlier court or tribunal made the correct decision. Judicial review plays a crucial role in ensuring public bodies do not stray outside their legislative or common law powers by acting in an *ultra vires* manner.[2] It therefore acts as a check on those bodies exercising such power. A key consideration in many judicial review actions therefore is what powers Parliament conferred on the respondent public body, or what common law powers could it be said to possess.

[1]   For more on judicial review in Northern Ireland, see Paul Maguire, 'Judicial Review in Northern Ireland' in B Hadfield (ed), *Judicial Review: A Thematic Approach* (1995) Gill and Macmillan, Dublin.
[2]   For an explanation of *ultra vires*, see para 2.128.

2.107   However, judicial review can often be the means by which more politically complex and contentious issues are aired in the courts and it is for this reason that judicial review plays such an important role in regulating the activity of public authorities. In chapter 10, for example, two judicial review cases, *Ex p Barry* and *Ex p Tandy*,[1] are discussed. These cases clearly had wider importance for health authorities, because they related to whether the authorities could consider their financial resources when acting under statute. Other examples are encountered throughout this text, especially in the chapter relating to community care law.

[1]   See chapter 10, para 10.28.

Time limits and standing

2.108   Judicial review cases are initiated in the High Court, and must be commenced 'promptly' but in any event within three months of the act, decision or event that is the subject of the proceedings.[1] The applicant must have 'sufficient interest' or standing to commence the action.[2] The meaning of the phrase 'sufficient interest' can cause some difficulty. A clear example of a person with 'sufficient interest' would be the individual most affected by the public body's decision. However, it is more difficult to determine who does not have such an interest, and much will depend on the facts of the case. Public interest type litigation, in which an interested NGO for example, makes a judicial review application to test the lawfulness of some public body's actions, has increased, in Northern Ireland as well as in England and Wales.[3] The courts are, nevertheless, careful to ensure that public bodies are not subject to unnecessary judicial review actions by those with little or no interest in the subject matter of the application.

[1]   Rules of the Supreme Court (Northern Ireland) 1980, Order 53, r 4(1).
[2]   Judicature (Northern Ireland) Act 1978, s 18(4).
[3]   See, for example, *Re Family Planning Association of Northern Ireland* [2003] NIQB 48, 7 July 2003, in which that association challenged the compatibility of Northern Ireland's abortion laws with the HRA.

Obtaining leave to apply

2.109   Judicial review is a two-stage proceeding, with the first stage focusing on whether the court should grant leave to the applicant to bring the matter to a full hearing. The leave hearing is usually quite short. This is because the main issue as this stage is whether the applicant has an arguable case worthy of proceeding to a full hearing, in other words that the case being made has some merit. The issues of whether the applicant has standing, or whether the time limits have been complied with are also canvassed at this stage. Leave to apply for judicial review will not usually be granted unless the applicant has exhausted the available domestic remedies. So, for example, in *R (on the application of Cowl) v Plymouth City Council*[1] the fact that the applicant failed to avail of the local authority's internal procedures for challenging the closure of a residential facility was fatal to the judicial review action.

[1]   [2001] EWCA Civ 1935, [2002] 1 WLR 803.

2.110   The second stage is the substantive hearing of the matter, in which full oral and written arguments are made, and a decision is made as to whether to grant the applicant the remedies sought. The remedies that are available in a judicial review action are:

- an injunction;
- a declaration (which sets out the parties legal rights and entitlements);
- an order of *certiorari* (which has the effect of quashing the decision or action in question);
- an order of *mandamus* (which requires the respondent to perform a certain act, usually to adhere to perform a statutory duty);
- an order of prohibition (which acts much like an injunction in that it prohibits the respondent from acting in a particular fashion and is issued to prevent the respondent taking an unlawful action).

Damages are only issued in a judicial review action if the court would have awarded them in any private law proceedings issued by the applicant against the respondent.[1]

[1]   Rules of the Supreme Court (Northern Ireland) 1980, r 7(1) and the Judicature (Northern Ireland) Act 1978, s 20.

Grounds for judicial review

2.111   The court's assessment of the legality of the respondent public body's actions focuses on the terms of any applicable statute, but also on a number of judicially created or common law principles. This means that it will not be sufficient for the respondent to simply rely on the express terms of the statute to authorise its actions. Merely because a statute authorises a Minister to make such regulations as it 'he or she thinks fit', for example, does not give the Minister carte blanche to act in whatever manner she or she wishes but rather in accordance with these common law principles. These principles, therefore, usually form the grounds for judicial review actions, and have been famously summarised, by Lord Diplock in the *Council of Civil Service Unions v Minister for the Civil Service* (commonly known as the 'GCHQ case'),[1] as 'illegality', 'irrationality' and 'procedural impropriety'.

[1]   [1985] AC 374, HL.

Illegality

2.112 'Illegality' comprises a number of principles, chief among these being the idea that the respondent must not act in an *ultra vires* manner ie outside the powers accorded to it, which of course will usually be found in legislation, and less frequently in common law. But it also comprises a broader notion of *ultra vires*, namely not just whether the legal power exists, but whether the manner in which it has been used is lawful and consistent with Parliament's intention when it conferred the power on the respondent. When exercising a legal power there are a number of ways in which a public body can fail to use the power lawfully.

RELEVANT CONSIDERATIONS

2.113 In exercising a power or fulfilling a duty, a public body should only make its decision on the basis of relevant considerations. These relevant considerations will vary from case to case but are largely derived from the statutory context in which the assessment and decision are being made. For example, in *R(J) v Enfield London Borough Council*[1] the respondent council's failure to give sufficient consideration to the claimant's mental condition in the context of her application to be housed by it, was a successful basis for reviewing the decision. Medical evidence was obviously germane to the issue of how she and her child were to be accommodated, if at all. The corollary of requiring a public body to take relevant considerations into account when making a decision is that the body should not allow its decision to be tainted by irrelevant considerations. The applicant in *Re Donnelly*[2] unsuccessfully argued this ground in his case. He was challenging the Northern Ireland Housing Executive's decision not to evict his neighbours who had been intimidating him and his family. The Housing Executive based its refusal to act largely on the need to ensure the safety of its staff. The applicant argued that this was an irrelevant consideration but the High Court did not agree. The Court of Appeal reversed the High Court's decision on the basis that the Housing Executive did not produce evidence of the threat its staff faced.[3]

[1] [2002] EWHC 432 (Admin), [2002] 2 FLR 1.
[2] (29 January 2003, unreported), HC, transcript available on Lexis.
[3] [2003] NICA 55.

PROPER PURPOSES

2.114 Ensuring that the respondent body acts in lawful manner when exercising its statutory functions also requires the court to examine whether the statutory power is being used for the correct and proper purpose. Using a statutory power to advance a political viewpoint can be considered to be unlawful. The case of *Re De Brun and McGuinness*[1] concerned the refusal of the First Minister to appoint the applicants to a North South Ministerial Conference (NSMC) as he was empowered to do under the Northern Ireland Act 1998, s 52. The First Minister's purpose in doing this was to exert pressure on Sinn Fein to persuade the IRA to decommission, which purpose was collateral to the proper purpose of the section, ie to facilitate the meeting of the NSMC, and therefore unlawful.

[1]   [2001] NI 442, (5 October 2001, unreported), NI CA, transcript available on Lexis.

IMPROPER DELEGATION

2.115 'Illegality' also includes the idea that if statute confers a duty on a particular authority to make a decision that authority may not improperly delegate that duty to another. For example, in *Re Bell*,[1] the Director of Pharmaceutical Services in the Northern Health and Social Services Board had improperly taken the decision to refuse the applicant permission to move her pharmacy practice because that function had been conferred, by statute, on the Board, and only the Board was capable of making that decision.

[1]   [2000] NI 245.

LEGITIMATE EXPECTATION

2.116 An applicant may also claim that he or she has a legitimate expectation arising from a prior practice of, or the promises made by, the respondent body and that the respondent has failed to deliver on those legitimate expectations. Such expectations are generally considered to be of two types: procedural expectations and substantive expectations.

2.117 A procedural legitimate expectation means that the applicant is entitled to expect that the respondent will follow a particular procedure and its operation is illustrated by the case of *Re Buick*.[1] The applicant in this case successfully argued that consultations with certain interested groups had to take place before final decisions in respect of maternity services at Belfast City Hospital could be taken, and this expectation had arisen from the manner in which consultation had been sought previously in regard to the issue.

[1]   (3 June 1999, unreported), HC, transcript available on Lexis.

2.118 Where a substantive legitimate expectation arises it means that the respondent must accord the applicant the benefit that he or she has come to expect. It is usually more difficult to establish a substantive expectation because the applicant is making a claim, not about the process involved in making a decision, but that he or she is entitled to an actual benefit. For example, *Re Morrow and Campbell*[1] involved a successful assertion by two Democratic Unionist Party Northern Ireland Executive ministers that, even though they were not taking their seats at the Executive table, they were entitled to be provided with the papers of Executive meetings. This expectation arose from commitments made to them by the First and Deputy First Ministers in correspondence with the applicants.

[1]   [2002] NI 261, (16 January 2002, unreported), HC, transcript available on Lexis.

OVER-RIGID POLICY

2.119   Another principle often grouped under the 'Illegality' heading provides that an administrator may not apply an over-rigid policy in making its decisions. A public body is free to adopt a policy but must not in applying that policy close its mind to the possibility that the individual case it is considering might justify a departure from that policy. If it fails to keep its mind open to that possibility, and is simply slavishly following a pre-determined policy, then it is failing to exercise its discretion. An example of the application of this principle arose in the case of *Re Lavery*,[1] which concerned the refusal by the Secretary of State to provide protection for a Sinn Fein councillor, Robert Lavery, under the non-statutory Key Persons Protection Scheme because he has adopted a policy of not providing such protection for Sinn Fein in light if its support for political violence. The application of this policy without considering the particular circumstance of the applicant was considered to be the unlawful application of an over-rigid policy.

[1]   [1994] NI 209.

Irrationality

2.120   'Irrationality', the second of Lord Diplock's categories, is a shorthand expression for an established principle that the respondent should not make a perverse or unreasonable decision. This ground is often referred to as 'Wednesbury unreasonableness', the term deriving from the case of *Associated Provincial Picture Houses Ltd v Wednesbury Corpn*[1] which is commonly held to be the case in which this notion of irrationality was first crystallised. A 'Wednesbury unreasonable' decision has been explained in different terms by different judges at various times. Lord Denning, for example, in *Secretary of State for Education and Science v Tameside Metropolitan Borough Council*[2] described such a decision as one 'so wrong that no reasonable person could sensibly take that view'.[3] Lord Diplock himself in the GCHQ case offered the following explanation:[4]

'It applies to a decision which is so outrageous in it defiance of logic or of accepted moral standards that no sensible person who had applied his mind to the question to be decided could have arrived at it.'

In *Nottinghamshire County Council v Secretary of State for the Environment*,[5] Lord Scarman, offered a definition which is similar in many respects to that of Lord Diplock's when he described it as a decision 'so absurd that he [Secretary of State in this case] must have taken leave of his senses'.[6]

[1]   [1948] 1 KB 223, CA.
[2]   [1977] AC 1014, [1976] 3 All ER 665, HL.
[3]   [1976] 3 All ER 665 at 671F.
[4]   [1985] AC 374 at 410G.
[5]   [1986] AC 240, [1986] 1 All ER 199, HL.
[6]   [1986] 1 All ER 199 at 202F.

2.121 A court in assessing the reasonableness of a decision or action will accord the respondent some degree of latitude because the respondent is usually considered to be in better position than the court to assess the appropriate course of action. This is because the respondent body will often have access to information that is not available to the court, or will be in a better position to assess this information than the court. Thus there may be a number of possible conflicting, or contradictory, options open to the respondent, each of which might be considered to be reasonable. The fact that the applicant believes the respondent should have come to another decision is not enough to ground a successful judicial review action on this point. The court, in short, will not substitute its decision for that of the decision-maker, in keeping with the supervisory nature of judicial review.

From the applicant's point-of-view the threshold to overcome in order when pleading 'Wednesbury unreasonableness' is quite high, as can be seen from the explanations of the term offered by members of the judiciary in the examples cited above, so that it is difficult for applicants to succeed with such a claim. However, there are examples of courts quashing decisions on policies on this ground. For example, in *R(L) v Manchester City Council*[1] the local authority's policy of paying foster parents, who were related to the children they fostered, less than was paid to those who were not so related was considered to be irrational. *Re Harkin*[2] concerned the failure of a senior departmental official to consider relevant evidence when reviewing a decision to refuse the applicant benefit payments. This failure rendered the official's decision 'Wednesbury' unreasonable.

[1]   [2001] EWHC Admin 707, [2002] 1 FLR 43. The judge also concluded that this policy infringed Convention right, art 14, which prohibits any discrimination in the exercise of the other Convention rights, and the other Convention right engaged here was art 8. On art 14, see chapter 9, para 9.11.
[2]   (16 February 2001, unreported), transcript available on Lexis.

Impropriety

2.122 'Impropriety' is the third, general, ground for judicial review and refers to the procedures adopted by the respondent in the course of arriving at its decision or in fulfilling certain actions. The manner in which the respondent arrives at its decision on a particular matter must be in accordance with procedures contained in statute, official guidance or circulars, or those deriving from the judicially developed 'rules of natural justice' or from the procedural guarantees contained in article 6 of the Convention rights,[1] where it applies.

[1]   On the HRA generally, see chapter 1, para 1.74.

2.123 A failure by a respondent to adhere to its own procedures will probably result in the court quashing the decision that it has arrived at, thereby requiring it to retake that decision again, with the proviso that it implements its procedures correctly on the second occasion. It is, or should be at any rate, relatively easy for a respondent to comply with its own procedures, but considerably more difficulty is presented when a respondent has to comply with the 'rules of natural justice'. These 'rules' are comprised of two maxims, namely that everyone should be entitled to a hearing (often referred to by its Latin maxim, *audi alterem partem*) and that no one should be a judge in his or her own case (in Latin, *nemo iudex in causa sua*) or as the latter is more commonly known, the rule against bias. The purposes of the natural justice rules is to give individuals certain procedural guarantees where public entities are making decisions with particular importance for those individuals. The two maxims are examined in turn.

RIGHT TO A FAIR HEARING

2.124 Whether an individual is entitled to fair hearing will depend on the significance of the matter to be decided upon, and the more grave that issue the more likely it is the courts will determine that individual should have an opportunity to be heard.[1] Decisions which may affect a person's livelihood or employment circumstances are therefore almost quite likely to give rise to the right to be heard, for example. Furthermore, the fact that someone is entitled to a hearing from a public body does not mean that a body must accord an individual an oral hearing, much less afford them an opportunity to question witnesses and rebut testimony in a quasi-judicial manner.[2] The nature and extent of the hearing to which the individual is entitled will vary from case to case. The rules of natural justice, as can be seen, are extremely flexible, and might be criticised as being too vague to allow social workers and their employing authorities to assess when, and to what extent they apply. Nevertheless, they remain significant procedural requirements to which they must adhere in suitable cases. Careful thought should be given to the applicability of the rules. The best advice is to err on the side of caution and accord individuals the right to be 'heard' in any case of doubt, giving them ample opportunity to present arguments on their behalf.

[1] *Ridge v Baldwin* [1964] AC 40, HL.
[2] *Lloyd v McMahon* [1987] AC 625, [1987] 1 All ER 1118, HL.

RULE AGAINST BIAS

2.125 The second rule, the rule against bias, seeks to ensure that the decision-maker is independent of the parties to the dispute which is to be decided. It has a particular application to proceedings presided over by members of the judiciary. It was of this legal principle that Lord Hoffman fell foul in the litigation dealing with whether General Augusto Pinochet, the former Chilean dictator, could be extradited to Spain. The House of Lords had concluded, by a majority of three to two, that he could be extradited, Lord Hoffman being one of the majority.[1] However, counsel for General Pinochet successfully argued that Lord Hoffman's position as a director of a charitable wing of Amnesty International, who had submitted an *amicus curiae* brief in the case arguing that it was lawful to extradite General Pinochet, infringed the rule against bias and that the House of Lords decision should be quashed.[2] As a result, a differently constituted House of Lords had to reconsider its decision, though it ultimately came to the same conclusion as it had on the first occasion and indicated that General Pinochet could be extradited from the UK.[3]

[1] *R v Bow Street Metropolitan Stipendiary Magistrate, ex p Pinochet Ugarte (Amnesty International intervening)* [2000] 1 AC 61, [1998] 4 All ER 897.
[2] *R v Bow Street Metropolitan Stipendiary Magistrate, ex p Pinochet Ugarte (No 2)* [2000] 1 AC 119, [1999] 1 All ER 577, HL.
[3] *R v Bow Street Metropolitan Stipendiary Magistrate, ex p Pinochet Ugarte (Amnesty International intervening) (No 3)* [2000] 1 AC 147, [1999] 2 All ER 97.

2.126 The rule against bias does not apply with the same force to administrative decision-making but where disciplinary proceedings are held, for example, it may have some application. Decision-makers should therefore be careful to include any person on the decision making panel who might not have an open mind on the issue in question before hearing evidence and making a decision.[1]

[1] *R (McNally) v Secretary of State for Education and Employment* [2001] EWCA Civ 332, [2002] ICR 15, [2002] LGR 584.

REASONS FOR ADMINISTRATIVE DECISIONS

2.127 A respondent body might also find itself in breach of the rules of natural justice for its failure to give the parties the reasons for its decision or actions. Although there is no absolute duty on administrators to give reasons the courts have imposed such a duty from time to time. *Re Jordan,*[1] for example, concerned a failure of the Legal Aid Board to give its reasons to the applicant for refusing his application for legal aid thereby hampering him in his challenge against the Board's decision. A public body will be required to give a reason for its decision where that decision is a quasi-judicial one and the individual must be given the opportunity to know why the decision was taken to allow him or her to decide whether to challenge it.

[1] [2003] NICA 30, 12 September 2003, Court of Appeal.

Ultra vires action

2.128 It is also possible to argue that secondary legislation on which a public body has based its decision is ultra vires or beyond the authority conferred by the primary legislation and therefore the body cannot exercise powers based upon the unlawful secondary legislation. *In re Shields*[1] is an illustration of the operation of this ground for judicial review. The applicant was a police officer whose application for promotion was rejected on the basis that her sickness record exceeded the period allowed by a Force Order issued by the Chief Constable under the Police (Northern Ireland) Act 1998. However, that Act expressly left regulation of the matter of promotion to the Secretary of State and therefore the Force Order issued by the Chief Constable dealing with the relevance of sickness for promotion purposes was, according to the Court of Appeal, *ultra vires* and void. The decision of the Court of Appeal has since been overturned on appeal by the House of Lords.[2]

[1] (24 April 2002, unreported), NI CA, transcript available on Lexis.

²   [2003] UKHL 3, [2003] All ER (D) 81 (Feb).

Human Rights Act 1998

2.129 Furthermore, the Convention rights contained in the HRA, and discussed in chapter 1,[1] can also be pleaded in judicial review actions. Thus for example, *Re Martin Meehan*[2] concerned an allegation that the police had failed to promptly warn the applicant, a prominent Sinn Fein representative, of death threats made against him by loyalist paramilitaries. The applicant argued that the positive obligation on the State to protect his life, under Convention Right article 2, 'the right to life', had been breached by the tardiness of the police actions in communicating this information to him. On the facts the application was unsuccessful. The positive obligation, on Boards and Trusts, arising from Convention right, article 8 features with increasing frequency in judicial reviews arising out of community care decisions.[3]

¹   See para 1.74.
²   [2003] NICA 34, 26 September 2003, transcript available on Lexis.
³   See chapter 10, para 10.11.

Statutory inquiries

2.130 In exceptional circumstances, statutory inquiries may be established to investigate particular matters. This does not occur very often, and a recent example in England and Wales was the Laming inquiry,[1] established to investigate the death of Victoria Climbié, by the Secretary of State for Health[2] and by the Home Secretary[3] jointly. Its powers were quite extensive and allowed it to require the disclosure of documents and to subpoena witnesses relating to death of the child at the hands of her aunt and her aunt's partner and the manner in which the various statutory agencies discharged their statutory responsibilities.

¹   Victoria Climbié Inquiry: Report of an Inquiry by Lord Laming, January 2003.
²   Under the Children Act 1989, s 81, and the National Health Service Act 1977, s 84.
³   Under the Police Act 1996, s 49.

Ministerial inquiries

2.131 Statutory inquiries about any matter dealt with in the Health and Personal Social Services (Northern Ireland) Order 1972 or in the Mental Health (Northern Ireland) Order 1986, may be established in Northern Ireland, by the minister, under the 1972 Order, article 54. Such an inquiry has extensive powers, under Sch 8 to the 1972 Order, including powers to compel the attendance of witnesses and furnish documentation. The Human Organs Inquiry, which reported in June 2002,[1] and which dealt with hospital post-mortem practices and the retention of human organs and tissues, was commissioned under this provision.

¹   Human Organs Inquiry, DHSSPS, Belfast, 2002.

2.132   It is difficult to predict when general statutory inquiry powers will be used, as they are framed in general terms to allow the appropriate minister to invoke them whenever he or she believes it is appropriate, and it is difficult to escape the conclusion that ministers come to that decision only when the political and public pressure is so great that they feel they ought to be seen to react. These occasions tend to be when there appears to have been a significant failure of particular systems and/or where the circumstances of the event are so harrowing and graphic that the public's attention is drawn to the issue. Quite often when such matters arise in Northern Ireland it appears that the relevant minister requires the Social Services Inspectorate (SSI) to investigate the incident in question. Thus, for example, the SSI was directed to produce reports on Martin Huston, a convicted sex offender who managed to infiltrate a number of volunteer organisations working with children,[1] and on the circumstances leading to the suicide of a pensioner, Frederick McLernon, by lying on a railway track.[2]

[1]   An Abuse of Trust: The Report of the SSI Investigation into the case of Martin Huston, DHSS, 1993.
[2]   Community CARE: from Policy to Practice: The case of Frederick Joseph McLernon, DHSS, 1998.

Failure to comply with inquiry and appeals

2.133   Failure to comply with such an inquiry renders a person liable to summary conviction, although no person is required to answer any questions or produce any documents that he or she would not be required to produce in any legal proceedings.[1] There is no provision for an appeal from the decisions or recommendations of any such inquiry, but it is possible to initiate judicial review proceedings in respect of them.

[1]   Schedule 8, para 3(3). On confidentiality, privilege and disclosure in litigation, see chapter 3, para 3.31.

'Whistle-blowing'

2.134   'Whistle-blowing' is the term commonly given to disclosures made by employees, in the public interest, concerning actions of their employers about which the employee believes the public should know. Our interest here is in the legal position of the social worker who finds himself or herself in this position. This scenario does not fit the terms of reference for the chapter explored earlier, in that in this instance the social worker is calling the employer to account. However, it is recognises that social workers, like all employees, are accountable to their employers but that the employer may abuse that form of accountability to prevent or impede the employee acting in a manner which is ultimately for the public good.

Protected disclosures

2.135   Legislation has provided employees who feel compelled to engage in 'whistle-blowing' with some protection from employers who attempt to prevent them from doing so, whether by invoking confidentiality clauses in their contracts threatening to dismiss or discipline them in some way. Where an employee makes a disclosure about a 'protected' matter, then he or she is entitled to the protection of the Public Interest Disclosure (Northern Ireland) Order 1998.[1] A 'protected disclosure' is one that reveals one of the following:[2]

1   that a criminal offence has been committed, is being committed or is likely to be committed;
2   that a person has failed, is failing or is likely to fail to comply with any legal obligation to which he is subject;
3   that a miscarriage of justice has occurred, is occurring or is likely to occur;
4   that the health or safety of any individual has been, is being or is likely to be endangered;
5   that the environment has been, is being or is likely to be damaged; or
6   that information tending to show any matter falling within any one of the preceding sub-paragraphs has been, is being or is likely to be deliberately concealed.

[1]   This amends the Employment Rights (Northern Ireland) Order 1996 by inserting Part VA after Part V.
[2]   Employment Rights (Northern Ireland) Order 1996, art 67A, as inserted by art 3 of the Public Interest Disclosure (Northern Ireland) Order 1998.

2.136 However, in order for the employee to benefit from its protection the disclosure must be made to particular persons. Disclosure to the media therefore will not allow the employee to avail of the protection afforded by the 1998 Order. In the case of a person employed by a Board which is appointed under statute, such as a health Board or Trust, for example, the relevant authority to whom the disclosure must be made is the Department or the Secretary of State for Northern Ireland.[1] Regulations also make it clear that the prescribed body to which disclosure should be made in respect of 'the proper conduct of public business value for money, fraud and corruption in health service bodies' is the Department and auditors appointed by it.[2] A disclosure will also be a protected one if it is made to a legal adviser for the purposes of obtaining advice.[3]

[1]   Employment Rights (Northern Ireland) Order 1996, art 67E, as inserted by art 3 of the Public Interest Disclosure (Northern Ireland) Order 1998.
[2]   Public Interest Disclosure (Prescribed Persons) Order (Northern Ireland) 1999.
[3]   Employment Rights (Northern Ireland) Order 1996, art 67D, as inserted by art 3 of the Public Interest Disclosure (Northern Ireland) Order 1998.

Availing of protection

2.137 A number of other conditions apply before the employee can utilise the benefits of the Order. First, the disclosure by the employee must be made in good faith; secondly, the employee must 'reasonably believe' that the information disclosed is 'substantially true'; thirdly, that he is not making the disclosure for purposes of personal gain; and fourthly, that in all the circumstances of the case, it is reasonable for the employee to make the disclosure.[1] Finally, the employee must also have passed such information to the employer previously, without any resulting action being taken. Alternatively, he or she must reasonably believe that if the information is not disclosed to others then attempts will be made to prevent its disclosure or that if he or she does inform the employer, that they will suffer a detriment as a result.[2]

[1] Employment Rights (Northern Ireland) Order 1996, art 67G, as inserted by art 3 of the Public Interest Disclosure (Northern Ireland) Order 1998.

[2] Employment Rights (Northern Ireland) Order 1996, art 67(G)(2), as inserted by art 3 of the Public Interest Disclosure (Northern Ireland) Order 1998.

2.138   The employee is protected to the extent that any dismissal for making a 'protected disclosure' will amount to unfair dismissal, and any detriment imposed on an employee for making such a disclosure will give rise to the right to make a complaint to an Industrial Tribunal.[1] Compensation may be awarded by the tribunal.

[1] Public Interest Disclosure (Northern Ireland) Order 1998, arts 5, 6, 7, 8 and 9.

Chapter 3

Litigation and the Trial Process

Introduction

3.1 This chapter seeks to provide guidance to social workers about the trial of legal actions, with a particular focus on the role of the social worker both as a witness and in preparing court reports as an official of the court. Matters such as the operation of the rule against hearsay evidence, the discovery and disclosure of documents gathered for the purposes of the court hearing, to other parties, the summoning and examination of witnesses, as well as the confidentiality of the social worker-client relationship in the context of court proceedings are also examined.

3.2 Anecdotal evidence indicates that few social workers are given training regarding court procedures and the operation of the courts. It appears that social workers learn about court procedures, and their role within the court process by experience, because these matters are usually only broached when a case arises. Occasionally, on court observational visits, the role of all participants is explained to newly-qualified social workers but this appears to be the exception rather than the rule. A social worker's exposure to the legal process then, is often, literally as well as metaphorically, on the steps of the courthouse. Greater thought needs to be given to training social work students and practitioners with regard to courtroom procedures.

3.3 When in court, social workers should never feel inadequate or uneasy merely because they are in lawyers' territory, so to speak. Social workers may be guest actors on the legal stage, but their presence there is important because of their specialist knowledge generally and their particular knowledge of the case in question. However, social workers should be aware of the reasons for their involvement and not stray beyond it by, for example, trying to fulfil the lawyers' role. With sufficient preparation and understanding of what is expected, a day in court can become a valuable experience, rather than an occasion for anxiety and dread.

3.4 Social workers' involvement with a court will usually take two forms: (1) report writing or making written documentation available for court; and (2) giving oral evidence. Both of these activities will involve social workers closely in the trial process. This chapter is therefore centred on these activities and the focus is on those aspects of the trial process that will concern social workers when engaging in them. It is necessary at the outset to explain some general features of court procedure and some terms that may arise in the course of a trial.

Court procedure

3.5   Trial procedure is generally adversarial and accusatorial rather than inquisitorial. This means that the trial process is a competitive argument between two sides, involving each side presenting the best case for it, rather than an objective non-competitive inquiry into the facts of a particular set of circumstances. It is not designed to objectively discover the absolute truth of the matter being tried, if such is possible in the first place. The parties are engaged in a struggle with each other, not in a mutual search for the truth. The competitive nature of the process is, in part, an explanation for its reputation as an awesome place for the inexperienced witness under cross-examination.

3.6   However, social workers should note, as discussed below, that the English and Northern Irish courts have taken the view that 'family proceedings' (particularly public law family proceedings)[1] are not completely adversarial and that social workers involved in them should behave accordingly by ensuring that their reports or testimony are not biased towards one side.[2]

---

[1]   For an explanation of 'family proceedings' and 'public law family proceedings', see chapter 6, para 6.28.

[2]   See *Re E (a minor) (Wardship: Court Duty)* [1984] 7 LR 457; *S County Council v B* [2000] 2 FLR 161 and *Re L (Minors) (Police Investigation: Privilege)* [1997] AC 16, HL. In Northern Ireland in *McG v McC* (23 April 2002, unreported), FD, Gillen J in determining the nature of a hearing in the High Court, of an appeal from the county court, referred to the fact that 'there is a strong inquisatorial element in family law cases which reflects the balancing exercise that has to be carried out by the judge.'

Describing the parties

3.7   Social workers should understand the nomenclature used to describe the parties to various types of court action and the order of the hearing of the action. In civil cases[1] the parties are known either as the applicant and the respondent (if the case is a 'family proceeding' under the Children Order, for example) or the plaintiff and the defendant (if the action is a tortious one, for example, negligence or misfeasance).[2] In a divorce case, the party bringing the action will be known as the petitioner and the other party as the respondent. In a criminal case the party pursuing the case will be the prosecution and the party answering the case will be the defence.

---

[1]   For an explanation of the terms 'criminal' and 'civil', see chapter 1, para 1.13.

[2]   See chapter 2, para 2.80.

3.8   Juries are not used in the county court and jury trial is only available in High Court actions for libel, slander, malicious prosecution and false imprisonment. A social worker is therefore only likely to encounter a jury in criminal matters. The function of a jury is to determine issues of fact, leaving matters of law for the judge. Where a judge is sitting alone, he or she has the responsibility of determining both disputes of fact and law.

Order of trial

3.9   The order in which a civil trial in the High Court proceeds will depend generally on whether the defendant/respondent decides to call any evidence.[1] A civil case is always opened by the plaintiff or applicant who may call witnesses if he or she wishes to. Where the defendant/respondent does not call evidence, the plaintiff will sum up his or her case after adducing all the evidence it intends to. Then the defence has an opportunity to sum up its case. However, where the defendant does call evidence it is the plaintiff that will have the last word. In that case, once the plaintiff has adduced his or her evidence, the defendant will then call its witnesses and sum up when that stage is complete. The plaintiff will then sum up its case after the conclusion of the defence's summation. The order of a trial in the county court will usually follow this pattern but is often more flexible in practice and the County Court (Northern Ireland) Order 1980 leaves the matter to the discretion of the judge.[2]

[1]   The order of trial in the High Court is governed by Rules of the Supreme Court (Northern Ireland) 1980 Order 35, r 4 (these rules hereafter described as 'RSC').

[2]   Article 9, per B Valentine, 'Civil Proceedings in the County Court', SLS, Belfast, 1999, para 14.37. The relevant court rules are found at County Court Rules Order 43, r 1(2) (these rules hereafter described as 'CCR').

3.10   The hearing of 'family proceedings' may be more involved because of the involvement of the guardian ad litem, the 'welfare officer'[1] and the child, or children, the subject of the application. Thus, for example, in applications for article 8 orders (determining issues about child rearing),[2] or for Care or Supervision Orders (determining whether the child should be in care),[3] the 'running' order will generally be as follows:

1   the applicant;
2   any party with parental responsibility for the child;
3   other respondents;
4   the guardian ad litem;
5   the child, if he or she is a party to the proceedings and there is no guardian ad litem.[4]

The length of the proceedings may be further added to if the welfare officer is directed by the court to attend to have his or her report considered.[5]

[1]   This is the term used in the Family Proceedings Rules (Northern Ireland) 1996 (these rules hereafter described as 'FPR 1996') to describe the person appointed to compile a report under the Children (Northern Ireland) Order 1995, art 4. See chapter 6, para 6.30.

[2]   See chapter 9, paras 9.99 ff.

[3]   See chapter 6, paras 3.119 ff.

[4]   FPR 1996, r 4.21; Magistrates' Courts (Children (Northern Ireland) Order 1995) Rules (Northern Ireland) 1996, r 21 (Hereafter 'MCR 1996').

⁵ FPR 1996, r 4.14(3); MCR 1996 1986, r 14(3).

Addressing the court

3.11 One minor point worth noting concerns the correct form of address for the judge. In the magistrates' court, the correct form of address is 'Your Worship', in the county court, 'Your Honour' and in the High Court, 'Your Lordship' or 'My Lord'. It may seem like a point of minute detail to mention the correct form of address for the judge, but it will add considerably to a social worker's confidence if he or she is prepared in that respect, and it will eliminate the uncomfortable feeling of being publicly corrected by a judge or members of counsel.

Standard of proof

3.12 The standard of proof is the threshold of proof that a party is required to overcome in order to make out its case, or an aspect of that case. It is for the party making the application, or asserting a matter, to prove that the standard of proof has been overcome. A distinction has to be made between criminal and civil cases since a different standard of proof exists for each. In a criminal case, the standard of proof that the prosecution will have to meet is that the accused is guilty 'beyond a reasonable doubt'. In a civil case, however, all that need be proved to the court is that the events were more likely to have happened in the manner asserted by the applicant/plaintiff than not to have happened in that way. This standard of proof is commonly referred to as the 'balance of probabilities' test. It is impossible to quantify those phrases in percentage terms for example, but clearly the criminal standard of proof is considerably higher than the civil standard. It is these differing standards of proof that explain why a child may be taken into care in a civil law case (because on the balance of probabilities this was necessary in her/her interests), and yet the person who abused the child is walking free (because the criminal case against the abuser could not be maintained 'beyond a reasonable doubt').

3.13 However, the courts sometimes blur the distinction between the tests in certain types of cases. For example, the balance of probabilities test governs applications for a Care Order under the Children (Northern Ireland) Order 1995,[1] but the House of Lords held that where the allegations of abuse are particularly gross and unusual, the evidence required to comply with the standard of proof rises accordingly.[2] Lord Nicholls of Birkinhead explained this idea, and its application to the threshold conditions for taking children into care, in his speech in *Re H*:

> 'The balance of probability standard means that a court is satisfied an event occurred if the court considers that, on the evidence, the occurrence of the event was more likely than not. When assessing the probabilities the court will have in mind as a factor, to whatever extent is appropriate in the particular case, that the more serious the allegation the less likely it is that the event occurred and, hence, the stronger should be the evidence before the court concludes that

the allegation is established on the balance of probability. Fraud is usually less likely than negligence. Deliberate physical injury is usually less likely than accidental physical injury. A stepfather is usually less likely to have repeatedly raped and had non-consensual oral sex with his under age stepdaughter than on some occasion to have lost his temper and slapped her. Built into the preponderance of probability standard is a generous degree of flexibility in respect of the seriousness of the allegation.

Although the result is much the same, this does not mean that where a serious allegation is in issue the standard of proof required is higher. It means only that the inherent probability or improbability of an event is itself a matter to be taken into account when weighing the probabilities and deciding whether, on balance, the event occurred. The more improbable the event, the stronger must be the evidence that it did occur before, on the balance of probability, its occurrence will be established.'

This means that the more horrific the allegations of abuse the more evidence will be required to meet the standard of proof, which, notwithstanding Lord Nicholl's opinion, appears to set the standard higher than the balance of probabilities.[3]

[1]   See chapter 6, para 6.137.
[2]   *Re H (Minors) (Sexual Abuse: Standard of Proof)* [1996] 1 All ER 1, HL, and see *Re J (Freeing without Consent)* (13 March 2002, unreported), HC, Gillen J, in which he applied the House of Lords view. For more on the standard of proof in Children Order public law cases see chapter 6, para 6.137.
[3]   This standard of proof is similar to that which is applied in misconduct proceedings against registered social care workers before the Conduct Committee of the NISCC. See chapter 2, para 2.36.

Discovery and disclosure

3.14   'Discovery' refers to the process whereby one party requires another party to the action, or indeed in exceptional cases a non-party to the dispute, to make available a list of documentation, in its possession or control, which is of relevance to the legal dispute.[1] This documentation can include internal reports, memoranda, minutes of meetings, notes of telephone conversations, in fact any type or form of written material.[2] 'Disclosure' is the term used to describe the process whereby this documentation is made available to the other party for inspection and copying, though colloquially 'discovery' is used to cover both stages of the process.[3] Discovery has a particular significance, therefore, for social workers because it can mean that material only ever intended for internal use may be made available to be used at the trial of an action. Note that court reports, affidavits and witness statements are not disclosed using this process, as discovery is confined to documents that would not ordinarily feature in the trial.

[1]   RSC Ord 25. This Order also governs the availability of discovery in family proceedings, see the FPR 1996, r 2.24 .
[2]   For example, in *Re J (Threshold Conditions: Parental Concessions)* (28 June 2002, unreported), HC, Gillen J referred to entries in the daily contact sheets to corroborate and support evidence that the child, J, was required to take on responsibility for looking after his siblings.
[3]   B Valentine, 'Civil Proceedings in the County Court' SLS, Belfast, 1999, para 11.91. Disclosure is also

used in another context which is outside the scope of this book, namely the exchange of medical reports in personal injury actions, except in medical negligence cases (RSC Ord 25 and CCR Ord 24).

3.15 Discovery takes place after the pleadings have closed (ie all documents outlining the parties' cases have been prepared and lodged with the court) and involve the parties exchanging lists of documents in, or formerly in, their possession 'relating to any matter in question between them in the action'.[1] One month after the exchange of those lists one party serves a notice on the other requiring it to serve an affidavit, within 14 days, testifying to the documents on the list. Swearing the affidavit is a significant step because it is not permissible to mislead or lie to the court, or the other party, in an affidavit. An affidavit that deliberately omitted certain documents, or denied that certain documents were in the possession, or control, of the party swearing the affidavit would amount to contempt of court. At this point the party serving the affidavit also serves a notice on the other side indicating when and where the documents can be inspected. Where the pre-trial discovery process is not adhered to, a court order can be obtained to require the recalcitrant party to comply.

[1]   CCR Ord 15, r 1(1), (2). RSC Ord 24, r 2(1).

3.16 In this affidavit a party can indicate that there are some documents in its possession, which although pertinent to the legal dispute, may be privileged documents and therefore the party objects to their disclosure. Documents are usually privileged[1] because they are communications between lawyer and client, or because public interest immunity[2] may apply to them.

[1]   See para 3.31.
[2]   See para 3.32.

Non-party discovery

3.17 It is even possible, although uncommon, for a non-party (or a third party as they are sometimes referred to) to be required by the courts to make discovery of material that is relevant to the determination of a dispute between two other parties, although this in only possible in High Court[1] or county court proceedings,[2] for personal injury or death. Furthermore, there is no obligation on a non-party to comply voluntarily with a request for discovery.

[1]   Administration of Justice Act (Northern Ireland) 1970, s 32(1).
[2]   County Court (Northern Ireland) Order 1980, art 42B(2).

3.18 The usual manner of obtaining discovery against a third party in civil proceedings is to issue what is commonly called a 'Khanna' subpoena. This subpoena requires a third party to attend in court, in advance of the actual commencement of the litigation, to produce documents which the party serving the subpoena wishes to inspect. It is a slightly artificial exercise, and presents some practical problems. Consequently, the Law Reform Advisory Committee for Northern Ireland has launched a consultation process with a view to amending the law in this area.[1] If those reforms are implemented, social workers' employers may well find themselves required to disclose documentation, in a greater number of cases than heretofore, in respect of litigation to which they are not a party.

[1]   LRAC, Third party Discovery in Civil Proceedings, May 2003.

3.19   In respect of family proceedings, the courts have exercised the power to order disclosure from third parties in certain circumstances, even where the litigation has yet to commence. For example, in *Re S (Disclosure of police records)*[2] the police had information about the death of one child, and the injury of another, gathered from the children's adoptive parents as part of a criminal investigation. The Trust sought disclosure of this information from the police to facilitate its investigation into the welfare of the surviving child. The court ordered this information be made available to the relevant Trust, under strict conditions,[2] for the purposes of considering whether to make a Care Order application.[3] The court noted that the Trust can subsequently be required, by the court, to disclose such information to the individual respondent but only where the judge carries out a balancing exercise:

> 'between the interests of those seeking disclosure and the public interest in maintaining the confidentiality of such records. But at this stage conventionally disclosure will only be ordered if the documents are found to be of real importance to the party's case.'

Disclosure of information, coming to light in family proceedings, to the public is discussed in chapter 6.[4]

[1]   *Re S (Disclosure of Documents held by the Police)* (30 August 2001, unreported), FD, Gillen J.
[2]   The documents were released to the Chief Executive who took responsibility for passing them to the guardian ad litem and the social workers involved in the case.
[3]   Note that the court indicated that the correct procedure for making such an application is by way of Form C2 of the FPR 1996 seeking a *subpoena duces tecum* directed at a police officer requiring him or her to attend in court with the particular documents.
[4]   See para 6.175.

Exchanging reports

3.20   Disclosure is also used to describe the process by which reports are exchanged with, or provided to, other parties. There is no requirement to disclose expert witnesses' reports in non-family proceedings, except in actions for damages where personal injury or death has resulted,[1] although it is often prudent to do so.

[1]   RSC Ord 25, r 1, CCR Ord 24, r 36. However, this requirement does not apply to cases of medical or surgical negligence.

3.21   The exchange of expert witness reports in 'family proceedings' is governed by the Court Rules.[1] Expert witnesses' reports, as well as any other documents on which a party intends to rely, must be disclosed to other parties before the trial, ensuring that the prospect of surprising another party in 'family proceedings' should not arise.

[1]   FPR 1996, r 4.18(1)(b); MCR 1996, r 18(1)(b). On the appointment of experts to carry out medical or psychiatric examinations of children for family proceedings, see para 3.97.

3.22   The sanction for failing to comply with these disclosure rules is that where a party seeks to rely on a document or adduce evidence where it has not made the necessary documentation available to the other parties, or otherwise complied with the rules, then such documents or material cannot be adduced in evidence, without the leave of the court.[1]

1   FPR 1996, r 4.18(3); MCR 1996, r 18(3).

3.23   Other reports will also become available before the trial of the action. A welfare report,[1] or a guardian ad litem's report,[2] becomes available via an officer of the court, or a chief clerk, to whom the report-compiler submits it. The officer of the court (or chief clerk) distributes the report to the other parties, including the guardian ad litem, as soon as possible.[3]

1   See para 3.43.
2   See para 3.43.
3   FPR 1996, rr 4.12(8) and 4.14(1); MCR 1996, rr 12(8) and 14(1).

Impact of discovery

3.24   Material made available as part of the pre-trial discovery process may cast a new and different perspective on the legal issue being tried. Exposure of this sort can be embarrassing for individual social workers, or their employing organisations and may even affect the conduct of the trial and result in some costs being awarded against the social worker's employer. In *Re R (Care: Disclosure: nature of Proceedings)*,[1] for example, the inadvertent failure of the local authority to disclose contemporaneous notes made by witnesses led it to withdraw one of the grounds on which a Care Order was being sought while the case was at hearing. The lengthy judgment offers very specific advice to health and social services authorities in managing Care Order applications. However, for the purposes of understanding the impact of failing to properly disclose documentation it is worth highlighting the fact that the judge required the authority to pay part of the four respondents' costs, judging that the authority's failure to locate and disclose the witnesses' notes had added unnecessarily to the length of the proceedings.

1   [2002] 1 FLR 755.

3.25   In *Re JC (Care Proceedings: Procedure)*[1] the court had reason to address the manner in which the local authority involved in care proceedings offered its evidence, and once again the discovery of documents played a part in the hearing of the application.

The facts of the case are instructive. The father perceived the social workers as being biased and as a consequence the father's advisers sought discovery of all the social workers' notes during the trial. The trial judge had this to say about social worker's duties to the court:[2]

'In my judgment, however, the very difficulties inherent in the performance of the social work role make it all the more important that the evidence of the social worker should be demonstrably fair, balanced and objective. *In particular this means, where value judgements are concerned, that the social worker must include in his or her evidence all the material upon which the judgement is based, both negative and positive, and be able to demonstrate that the judgement which has been reached is a fair one objectively based on all the disclosed material.'* [author's emphasis]

1   [1996] 1 FCR 434, [1995] 2 FLR 77, [1995] Fam Law 543.
2   [1995] 2 FLR 77 at 80H.

3.26   The trial judge explained the background to his comments:[1]

'What happened was this. The assessment of the father took the form of a large number of supervised contacts between himself and JC in which his handling of and interaction with the child was observed by social workers and by JC's foster-mother. All three social workers involved gave evidence, as did the foster-mother. All were clear in their oral evidence that the father loved the child and that there were positive aspects to his care of and interaction with the child. Each, however, had independently formed the opinion that he lacked the basic capacity to care properly for JC and had shown both an inability to learn elementary skills and an incapacity to remember what he had been taught.

Under cross-examination I thought all three witnesses were fair to the father, and each expressed sympathy for him. However, very little of the positive aspects of his parenting emerges from their written statements. Thus in each of the contact periods which was identified, the negative aspects were highlighted.

Furthermore, not all the contact periods were cited in the written evidence. The technique adopted was to select individual contact periods in which points of criticism were highlighted. The impression thus given was both negative and critical.

During the course of the trial, an application was made for discovery of the notes made by the social workers of the contact periods each had observed. Not surprisingly, these give a different and more balanced impression. The points of criticism are, of course, still there, but positive observations are also to be found, not just in periods of contact not mentioned at all in the written evidence of the social workers, but also in the contact periods which had been referred to, and from which negative elements were selected.

I recognise, of course, that a process of selection is inevitable in dealing with a mass of material such as the numerous contact periods observed by the social workers in this case. The point is, of course, that the observations should be seen to be balanced so that the conclusion drawn from them can be seen to have taken into account both their positive and negative aspects.'

In such cases the obligation on the authority to be objective, fair and balanced could not be overemphasised. In particular, when compiling court reports a social worker should include all the material upon which a judgment was based, both negative and positive, and be able to demonstrate that the judgment was objectively based on all the disclosed material. Social workers should remember that internal material might be disclosed in the discovery process that indicates that their evidence is partial in some way.

¹ [1995] 2 FLR 77 at 81E–82B.

3.27 Another matter that may arise from the discovery of internal documents and which the courts have highlighted, is the necessity of maintaining accurate, contemporaneous documentation. In *Rochdale Borough Council v B W*¹ the court made reference to the difficulties that can be caused by inaccurate or mistaken documentation. The local authority made available to the court, without dispute, a number of case conference minutes which had been helpful. However, it emerged in cross-examination that they contained, in some instances, startling inaccuracies. They were all circulated to those present, but the social worker said that although she realised that they ought to be corrected if mistakes were noticed, it was generally a waste of time to try and correct errors. The trial judge noted:

> 'The result is that these documents, which were a vital social work tool, could be dangerously misleading. If minutes were worth taking then they were worth taking accurately, and if the opportunity was given for correction it should be accepted.'

¹ [1991] FCR 705, [1991] 2 FLR 192.

3.28 Internal documentation may also come to light indirectly if affidavits are tendered based on documentary evidence contained within the social worker's employing organisation. (Note that affidavits are sworn documents made in a particular format, and which are normally drafted by counsel, on the basis of evidence tendered by the deponent (ie the person swearing the affidavit). They are not to be confused with court reports¹ or witness statements in family proceedings.² The advantage of an affidavit is that it allows for the introduction of evidence without the necesity of examining the witness. Deponents of affidavits may be cross-examined but it is not common to do so. In *Re A (Minors) (Child Abuse: Guidelines)*,³ Hollings J considered that the affidavits filed by some local authority staff did not represent the full picture of the matter at hand. He felt it necessary to refer to the need for social workers to present all of the evidence relevant to an issue and not to simply highlight those matters beneficial to the case being made by the employing authority making the application:

> '... I have been very concerned in this case to have found that affidavits and affirmations filed on behalf of the local authority appear to have been drafted with a view to presenting the case which they are advancing, that is permanent removal of the children, in the best light, without paying proper regard to the information and material upon which the affidavits are based. The result has been that an exaggerated or one-sided case has been presented in the first place to the court, certainly at the interim stages.'⁴

¹   See para 3.43.
²   See para 3.73.
³   [1992] 1 FLR 439.
⁴   [1992] 1 FLR 439 at 445B–C.

3.29   And in *Rochdale Borough Council v B W*,[1] examined previously on another point, Douglas Brown J made the same point:

> 'Affidavits, particularly affidavits for use in an ex parte hearing,[2] should be drawn with care and should be accurate, balanced and fair, and by analogy with Mareva or Anton Piller applications,[3] ex parte affidavits[4] should contain material, if known, which militates against the relief sought. Local authority solicitors should be particularly aware that they owe a duty to the court in this respect.'[5]

¹   [1991] FCR 705, [1991] 2 FLR 192.
²   One in which only one party is involved owing to the urgency of the situation, for example.
³   Application for certain types of injunctions in commercial proceedings.
⁴   Affidavits tendered in cases, where for reasons of urgency usually, only one party is present in court.
⁵   [1991] 2 FLR at 231H.

3.30   In summary then, social workers should be alert to the fact that other forms of written material, other than court reports, may be sought from them if the information is relevant to the matter that is the subject of the court application. Judicial expectations of social workers presenting evidence that is based on such internal written material is that the evidence should be demonstrably fair, and balanced. It should include all the material upon which a judgment was based, both negative and positive, and be able to demonstrate that the judgment was objectively based on all the disclosed material. Where internal documents are relied upon they should not be misleading and inaccuracies should be corrected as soon as possible after the documents are created.

Confidentiality, privilege and disclosure

3.31   Social workers might wish to argue that disclosure of certain documents ought to be resisted because of the need to protect the confidentiality of their relationships with clients. However, the only confidential, or 'privileged', relationship which the law recognises is that of lawyer and client. Legal professional privilege only applies to written or oral communications between them, made with a view to giving, and receiving, legal advice on any subject, whether or not a court case was pending. Submission for legal advice must be the dominant purpose for which the document was created. If it is considered that certain documents are privileged they will be listed in a particular part of the discovery affidavit that indicates that although the documents exist, it is intended to resist their disclosure by claiming privilege over them. Privilege can be waived by the client, but not by his or her solicitor.[1] Where a privileged document is used to refresh a witness's memory prior to that witness taking the stand, privilege is deemed to be waived over it, allowing the document to be disclosed to the other party.[2]

1 *Hogg v McAteer* (31 January 2002, unreported), HC, Coghlin J.
2 *Great Atlantic Insurance Co v Home Insurance Co* [1981] 2 All ER 485, CA.

Public interest immunity

3.32 In situations where legal professional privilege does not operate to prevent the disclosure of written material, it may be possible for a social worker, or more likely his or her employing organisation to argue that, in certain circumstances, some degree of immunity from disclosure is required. In other words, it may be possible to claim public interest immunity in respect of certain material. Public interest immunity is available where some particular document warrants immunity from general disclosure, in the public interest. This will be an issue for the court to decide.

3.33 Pre-trial applications seeking the immunity of particular documents or information will be made by counsel, probably based on affidavits sworn by senior management explaining why particular information should be exempt from disclosure. In the case of *D v National Society for the Prevention of Cruelty to Children (NSPCC)*[1] the House of Lords refused to require the Society to disclose the identity of an informant who (wrongly) alleged that the plaintiff had ill-treated her child. The plaintiff wished to sue the informant for defamation of character but was required to identify him or her before doing so. The House allowed the NSPCC to benefit from public interest immunity holding that:[2]

> 'where a confidential relationship exists (other than that of lawyer and client) and disclosure would be in breach of some ethical or social value involving the public interest, the court has a discretion to uphold a refusal to disclose relevant evidence provided it considers that, on balance, the public interest would be better served by excluding such evidence … if on balance the matter is left in doubt, disclosure should be ordered.'

1 [1978] AC 171, [1977] 1 All ER 589.
2 Lord Edmund-Davies [1977] 1 All ER 589 at 618d and 619d.

3.34 Social workers should be wary, however, of concluding that public interest immunity can be availed of on a regular basis to thwart full disclosure. Only in very particular circumstances will the doctrine be successfully employed, and the judiciary have warned against excessive and unnecessary reference to public interest immunity.[1] It will usually only be possible to make a successful claim for a public interest immunity where disclosing the information for the purposes of, or in the course of the trial, may jeopardise the activity of the agency in question, eroding public confidence in the organisation. Where the trial judge concludes that the public interest would be best served by preventing disclosure he or she will issue a Public Interest Immunity Certificate (PIIC). However, if the request for a PIIC is refused, then disclosure must take place as the court orders and witnesses will be unable to rely on public interest immunity to justify refusing to answer questions when on the witness stand.[2]

1 *Re R (Care: Disclosure: Nature of Proceedings)* [2002] 1 FLR 755 at 777H. When considering public

interest immunity, any authority or statement which did not consider *R v Chief Constable of West Midlands Police, ex p Wiley*; *R v Chief Constable of Nottinghamshire Constabulary, ex p Sunderland* [1995] 1 AC 274, [1994] 3 All ER 420, HL, should be regarded with caution, and anyone advancing a claim to public interest immunity in respect of material held by a local authority should consider whether the material passed the threshold test, take advice, and set out with particularity the harm that it was alleged would be caused to the public interest by disclosure.

2   Interestingly the NISCC (Conduct) Rules 2003, r 14 (see generally chapter 2, para 2.25). indicate that if the NISCC considers that it should resist disclosure of information about misconduct by social workers it will apply to the court to avoid such disclosure on grounds of public interest immunity.

Data Protection Act 1998 and disclosure

3.35 Material protected under the Data Protection Act 1998, which includes manual files as well as electronic information, can be required to be disclosed by court order, in legal proceedings or otherwise by any rule of law. Furthermore, such protected data can also be disclosed, if necessary, for the purposes of actual or contemplated litigation, or obtaining legal advice or establishing or defending legal rights.[1]

1   Data Protection Act 1998, s 35. See *Guyer v Walton* [2001] STC (SCD) 75 where the applicant, a solicitor, was forced to disclose information relating to clients' accounts.

3.36 Information to which the Data Protection Act 1998 applies is defined as 'personal data' and this includes any information that is capable of identifying a person, including any opinion about, or reference to, that person.[1] The 1998 Act seeks to ensure that such data, including 'sensitive personal data', is not improperly disclosed. Persons on whom personal data is stored (in the language of the Act, 'data subjects') have rights of access to such data,[2] but exemptions exist for the health, education and social work professions,[3] such that specified bodies or persons working in those fields can normally resist any disclosure of personal data to the 'data subject'.

1   Data Protection Act 1998, s 1.
2   Data Protection Act 1998, s 7.
3   Data Protection Act 1998, s 30. This section allows the Home Secretary to enact secondary legislation exempting certain bodies from the application of the Act. This has been done in respect of social work in the Data Protection (Subject Access Modification) (Social Work) Order 2000.

3.37 From the social worker's point of view this exemption extends to various different types of information, namely:

- 'personal data processed by a court and consisting of information supplied in a report, or other evidence given to the court by a local authority, Health and Social Services Board, Health and Social Services Trust, probation officer or other person in the course of any proceedings' under the Magistrates' Courts (Criminal Justice (Children)) Rules (Northern Ireland) 1999;[1]
- personal data processed by Boards, Trusts, by probation committees of the Probation Board for Northern Ireland, education and library Boards, the NSPCC and by guardians ad litem.[2]

The exemption from releasing information in respect of the second category listed here is to the extent that releasing such information 'would be likely to prejudice the carrying out of social work by reason of the fact that serious harm to the physical or mental health or condition of the data subject or any other person would be likely to be caused'.[3] It does not, therefore, allow for a blanket refusal to disclose information but is limited to the circumstances set out here. In regard to the first category referred to here, the exemption from disclosure to the 'data subject' is absolute.[4]

[1] Data Protection (Subject Access Modification) (Social Work) Order 2000, Sch, para 2.
[2] Data Protection (Subject Access Modification) (Social Work) Order 2000, Sch, para 1.
[3] Data Protection (Subject Access Modification) (Social Work) Order 2000, art 5.
[4] Data Protection (Subject Access Modification) (Social Work) Order 2000, art 4.

Family proceedings and disclosure

3.38   There is another context in which confidentiality between social worker and client can arise, however, and that is in relation to all documents compiled, or furnished in, or touching upon 'family proceedings'. Such documents cannot be disclosed, without the leave of the court, except to the parties and their legal representatives, the welfare officer, the guardian ad litem and the legal aid department.[1] This means that where a Trust considers that circumstances warrant it disclosing information or evidence which has emerged in the course of family proceedings then the authority must secure the leave of the court to do so. For example, in *Re C (sexual abuse: disclosure to landlords)*[2] a local authority sought, and secured, permission to disclose a finding made in Care Order proceedings, that a particular person was a dangerous and manipulative paedophile, to the housing association of which the man was a tenant.[3] However, disclosure of such information without the leave of the court will amount to contempt of court.

[1] FPR 1996, r 4.24; MCR 1996, r 24.
[2] [2002] EWHC 234 (Fam), [2002] 2 FCR 385.
[3] See also chapter 6, para 6.175.

3.39   Judicial permission is also required for the disclosure of such material to other public bodies or authorities. Thus, at the end of protracted public law family proceedings it was permissible for a court to order the release of selected case papers to the appropriate health authority, but only on the condition that they could not disclose those to any others without the court's permission.[1] The Northern Ireland High Court came to a similar conclusion in *Re L (Disclosure to a Third Party)*[2] when it considered the issue of whether two medical reports (and the threshold criteria agreed and found to have been proved in the case) should be released to a particular social services unit in England. The father of children in care was now resident in England and the Trust was anxious to be in a position to pass relevant information to their counterparts in England. Gillen J allowed the information to be disclosed:[3]

'In deciding whether or not to grant permission for disclosure, the court has to exercise a discretion, in the process of which it has to carry out a balancing exercise of competing rights and interests. There had to be real and cogent evidence of a pressing need for the requested disclosure. In this case, the fact that other young children are living with M, in circumstances where he has admitted that a child of similar age was sexually abused whilst in his care, amounts to real and cogent evidence of a pressing need for this disclosure. There is no doubt that there is a public interest in preserving faith and encouraging frankness for those who have given evidence to the family court in the belief that it will remain confidential and who have undergone medical examination in such a belief.'[4]

[1]   *A Health Authority v X* [2001] EWCA Civ 2014, [2002] 2 All ER 780, [2002] 1 FLR 1045.
[2]   (5 December 2002, unreported), transcript available on Lexis.
[3]   *Re L (Disclosure of third party)* (5 December 2002, unreported) at para 6.
[4]   See also *Re S (Disclosure of documents held by Police)* (30 August 2001, unreported) High Court, Gillen J. On the issue of disclosure to the public of information obtained in family proceedings, see chapter 6, para 6.175.

3.40   Another issue of considerable importance is the extent to which admissions made in the course of 'family proceedings' may be furnished to other authorities, like the police for example, to facilitate their investigations into the incidents in question. The admissions may not be used in any criminal proceedings but the police, or other authorities may seek a copy of the transcript of the trial proceedings to allow them to carry on their investigation.

3.41   This matter has been considered by the English courts on a number of occasions.[1] In *Re EC (Disclosure of Material)*[2] the English High Court considered the basis on which it would allow disclosure to the police of an admission made by a father in care proceedings that he had killed another of his children. Disclosure of this information involved a balancing exercise between 'the public interest in encouraging frankness on the part of witnesses in children proceedings[3] and, on the other, the public interest in ensuring the prosecution of those who committed serious offences against children.' In that case the court concluded that it would not release the transcript of the trial or the father's admission but would disclose the medical information relating to the death of the baby.

[1]   Most notably by the House of Lords in *Re L (Police Investigation: Privilege)* [1996] 1 FLR 731, HL. There, the House confirmed that a report prepared about the respondent mother at her solicitor's request could be ordered to be disclosed to the police.
[2]   [1996] 3 FCR 52, 1[1996] 2 FLR 123, [1996] Fam Law 603.
[3]   A public interest buttressed by the Children Act 1989, s 98(2) itself.

Writing court reports

3.42   The main concern in this section is with reports that social workers may be ordered by the courts to compile. However, although other reports that employers may order social work staff to prepare are not directly relevant here, the comments made here may be useful when compiling these other types of report, because such material may be required to be disclosed for the purposes of court proceedings, as outlined above.[1]

[1]   See para 3.14.

Types of court reports

3.43 There are a number of different types of report that social workers in Northern Ireland may be required, under statute, to compile, although in some cases only social workers with particular qualifications may be ordered to compile them. These are:

- *Court Welfare Reports* in private law family proceedings, compiled under the Children (Northern Ireland) Order 1995, article 4.[1] Article 4 reports are described in the FPR 1996, r 4 as 'welfare reports' and those designated to compile them as 'welfare officers' with the welfare officer becoming a party to the proceedings. These reports can also be required of persons who are not qualified social workers, although this would be unusual, because the legislation allows the judge to direct any 'suitably qualified person' to complete them;

- *Reports by Guardians ad Litem* for public law and private law family proceedings including Contact and Residence Order applications and adoption proceedings;[2]

- Reports of Board-employed, or agency-employed, social workers in adoption proceedings, commonly called *Reports of the Reporting Officer;*[3]

- *Pre-sentence Reports* by probation officers in criminal proceedings;[4]

- *Guardianship Reports* by Approved Social Workers (ASWs) under the Mental Health (Northern Ireland) Order 1986, stating that the reception of the client into guardianship is 'necessary in the interests of the welfare of the patient'.[5]

In all these circumstances, when compiling a report a social worker is acting as an officer of the court. This means that their primary duty is to the court, rather than to any one of the parties, for example. The report is intended to provide an objective assessment, for the court's benefit, of the matter in question and therefore it is vital that the report does not intentionally or unintentionally mislead the court.

[1] See chapter 6, para 6.71. FPR 1996, r 4 governs welfare reports. These reports are sometimes referred to as 'article 8' reports because they often are compiled in the context of applications for an article 8 order. On article 8 orders, see chapter 9, para 9.101.
[2] For information on GAL reports in Children Order proceedings, see chapter 6, para 6.65. For information on GAL reports in adoption proceedings, see chapter 8, para 8.40.
[3] See chapter 8, para 8.42.
[4] See chapter 5, para 5.78.
[5] Mental Health (Northern Ireland) Order 1986, art 18(2), see chapter 11, paras 11.54–11.55.

Nature of role

3.44 Higgins J in a judicial review action, *Re Downey,*[1] explained, in some detail, the nature of the welfare officer's role in preparing court welfare reports. His comments are equally applicable, however, to the other forms of court report set out above:[2]

'A social worker who prepares a report at the request of a court is a court welfare officer. As such he is an officer of the court appointed for the purpose of reporting to the court. He is not a witness nor is he an expert witness. He is not employed by a party to the proceedings. He is not an expert witness who is relied on by that party nor a witness who may be called on behalf of a party. He is appointed by the court to investigate circumstances relating to a child or a family and to report on those circumstances to the court. It is for the court to decide in its discretion whether he should be called as a witness and examined or cross-examined by any party. He does provide an expertise outwith the experience of the court but nevertheless is in a different category from persons with expertise engaged by a party to advise and if necessary give evidence on behalf of that party. He should not be a person who had previously engaged in conciliation between the parties. He requires to be independent from the parties and to provide on the basis of his investigations a balanced view upon which the court can decide the issue. He is not a person to whom the guidelines relating to expert witnesses should apply.'

---

[1] (11 May 2000, unreported), HC, an unsuccessful challenge to the court welfare report by the father of a child whose Contact Order application had been denied.

[2] A guardian ad litem, for example, is also, as one might expect, considered to be an officer of the court with a duty to safeguard the child's best interests: *Manchester City Council v T* [1994] Fam 181, CA; *Re T (a minor) (Guardian ad litem: Case Record)* [1994] 1 FLR 632, CA.

3.45 This view confirms a similar view taken in the English courts. In *Re M (a child) (children and family reporter: disclosure)*,[1] the English Court of Appeal had occasion to consider the status of the Child and Family Reporter (CFR)[2] in that jurisdiction in the context of deciding whether the CFR needed court permission to disclose information gathered in the context of a contact and residence application, to social services. Thorpe J stated:

'[24] The special status of the court welfare officer was defined by Ormrod LJ in the case of *Cadman v Cadman* (1982) 3 FLR 275 at 277 when he said of the court welfare officers:

"They are not witnesses in the case at all; they are officers of the court, appointed to make reports to the court. They may or may not give evidence and submit themselves to cross-examination. It is a matter entirely for the discretion of the judge as to whether he thinks that would be an appropriate course or not. It does not, by any means, follow that in every case the court welfare officers are to be treated as witnesses. Whatever they are, they are not witnesses. They are independent officers of the court appointed to assist the court."

[25] In other judgments it has rightly been said that they are the eyes and ears of the court able to go where the judge cannot go and to record for him and report to him conversations, observations and impressions which may have a decisive effect on outcome.

[26] All that I accept but in my judgment it does not follow that the CFR acts always under the direction of the judge. If that were ever so, and the history of the evolution of this invaluable service is recorded in the judgment of Butler-Sloss LJ in the case of *H v H; K v K (child cases: evidence)* [1989] FCR 356 at

379, [1990] Fam 86 at 110, it is certainly not so now. The CFR is a member of a newly created service the success of which depends in part on the support of other disciplines including the judiciary. Manifestly the CFR acts independently and exercises an independent discretion as to the nature and extent of his investigations and inquiries and no less in the manner in which he approaches them. He is bounded by only the obvious requirements to cover all the relevant ground and to be even handed. Absent any statutory prohibition on the discretionary communication from CFR to social worker I would not be prepared to find one in the common law or in the inherent nature of the function of the CFR or in the inherent relationship between the CFR and the court.'

1   [2002] EWCA Civ 1199, [2002] 4 All ER 401.
2   This person is an employee of the Children and Family Court Advisory and Support Service (CAFCASS), and performs a similar function to the Court Welfare Officer.

3.46   In the event, the court concluded that its permission was not required before the details could be transmitted from the CFR to the social services and his role as officer of the court did not require him to seek the court's permission to act in a certain way. It is not clear to what extent this precedent would be followed in Northern Ireland, but *In Re N and L (Care Order: Investigations by GAL outside Northern Ireland)*[1] may provide some indicators.

1   [2003] NIFam 1 (22 January 2003) See chapter 6, para 6.69.

Negligently prepared reports

3.47   Social workers should recognise that a court report is not just a source of information for all the parties to the case, but is also a documented reflection of their professionalism. An inadequate, or incomplete report will not merely have the potential to adversely affect the manner in which the case is dealt with, but will create a strong negative impression of the professional competency of the report-compiler. Preparing a report for court should be easier if social workers understand the use to which that report will be put within the legal process, and if they acquaint themselves with the legal process in which they are involved.

3.48   It is not clear whether social workers are liable in negligence for reports which are shoddily prepared and which cause 'damage' or injury to someone. Expert witnesses are not liable in respect of reports that they compile.[1] Whether social workers are liable in such circumstances will depend on the courts finding that a duty of care is owed by social workers to parties or persons who are the subject of a report, and that this duty has been broken, thereby causing the party some injury.[2]

1   See para 3.94.
2   On negligence generally, see chapter 2, para 2.80.

3.49   Social workers performing functions under mental health law, or acting as probation officers, may benefit from the statutory indemnity for those specialised types of social worker. Article 133 of the Mental Health (Northern Ireland) Order 1986 and article 10 of the Probation Board Northern Ireland (Northern Ireland) 1982 allow social workers who are sued successfully for actions performed in good faith under these enactments to be indemnified for any loss.[1]

[1]   For more on indemnity provision for Approved Social Workers under the Mental Health (Northern Ireland) Order 1986, see chapter 11, para 11.27 and for the indemnity provision for probation officers, see chapter 5, para 5.17.

Compiling the report

3.50   It appears that few agencies give training in report writing and consequently many social workers end up relying on sample reports, written on previous occasions by colleagues, to guide them. This practice may not be as helpful as it seems because the quality of past reports may vary and the models chosen may not be as useful for the court as social workers believe. The Children Order Advisory Committee, in its second report, stated that it was 'aware of variations both in the layout and timescales for the filing of Court Welfare Reports by Trusts in private law cases', and proposed that a research study be conducted to improve the current arrangements.[1] This suggests that different practices exist across the Boards and Trusts in respect of the form of reports and the speed with which they are compiled. In this section some general guidance on the compilation of reports is offered.

[1]   Children Order Advisory Committee, Second Report. p 25, paras 2 and 4.

3.51   A social worker's report will supplement the evidence that the court has heard and may be a crucial factor in the court's decision on that particular matter in the case. Written reports play an important role in legal proceedings if only for the fact that they are easier to assimilate than a mass of oral testimony.

3.52   Aside from the guidance that may be derived from judicial statements in the cases outlined in the section dealing with discovery and disclosure,[1] more generic advice might also be useful in compiling reports. At the outset it is worth stating that there is no definitively correct way to compile reports. Content, not form, is the most important feature of any such report. Therefore, the approach taken here is to offer a number of principles that should apply to the preparation of such a report. Adhering to them should ensure that any report can be more easily digested, and prove more helpful to the court in coming to a decision. Admittedly, these principles are inter-related and there is a considerable degree of overlap between them. They are intended to be used as a checklist when writing reports.

[1]   See para 3.14.

(a)   Awareness – 'What is the purpose of this report, and is it clear from it that I understand that purpose?'

3.53   If it is clear from a social worker's report that he or she has an awareness of the relevant facts of the case and of the legal context in which the report arises, the report will be more valuable to the court. The clearer one is about the use to which the report is put the better. The specific purpose of a report will depend on the type of report in question. The legislative basis for the report is a good starting point in terms of determining the court's expectations of that report. For example, a welfare report under the Children (Northern Ireland) Order 1995, article 4, should address matters relating to the child's welfare and requires the report-compiler to be familiar with the paramountcy principle and the welfare checklist.[1]

[1]   See chapter 6, para 6.31.

(b)   Relevance – 'Does everything in the report need to be there?'

3.54   The statutory provision will inform social workers as to the purpose the report will be put and should also help social workers determine what is relevant and what is not. Where it is a marginal decision as to whether material is relevant or not it is probably better for the report-compiler to err on the side of caution and include it to ensure that the court is not deprived of information that may have an impact on the issue at hand. This principle is designed to require the report-compiler to focus on thecentrality of the task. In the compilation of 'welfare reports' the court is entitled to issue directions about the preparation of the report and some guidance may be offered by that process as to what matters are relevant or the relative importance of them.[1]

[1]   See chapter 6, para 6.31. FPR 1996, r 4.15(2)(g); MCR 1996, r 15(2)(g).

(c)   Accuracy – 'Can I defend every word of it?'

3.55   The report should, as accurately as words will allow, reflect the factual situation and the social worker's views, if required. This means that care should be taken that what is written is not ambiguous and that the descriptive words chosen should not be too dramatic, for example. The reason for this is simple. If the report is not accurate, then opposing counsel will expose those inaccuracies and attempt to discredit it. Doubts about accuracy should be expressed and social workers should attempt to check the accuracy of as many facts as possible. It will greatly impress the court if social workers have cross-checked the evidence of a witness. Social workers should also take care to identify matters of fact from matters of opinion. Remember too that material prepared originally for internal use may be made available via the discovery process and the accuracy of a report may be judged against other documentary evidence.

(d)   Complete – 'Have I dealt with all the issues?'

3.56   In any problem situation, there will be a number of central core issues but also a number of less important ones. The latter should not be ignored. For the sake of completeness, these less important issues should be treated, though obviously not to the same depth to which the core issues are treated. Ensuring that the report is complete is commensurate with a social worker's role in providing the court with sufficient information for it to act justly. An example might be the importance of considering unlikely, though feasible, arrangements for the care of children in a court welfare report made in private law proceedings about residence and contact.

(e)   Style and length – 'Is it easily understood and no longer than it needs to be?'

3.57   A report that is short and direct, rather than long and 'waffly', will be more highly valued by the court. Excessive use of jargon should be avoided, though recourse to some jargon is permissible provided that the term is explained on the first occasion it is used and used consistently thereafter. Concentrating on keeping the report to a necessary length should be beneficial because the report should then be more digestible. This is not an excuse to cut the report short, but rather a warning to prevent it being too long. A simple, concise, though precise, writing style will often be far more beneficial than a jargon-laden, 'flowery' style which seeks to impress the reader with the author's knowledge of social work principles and of the factual circumstances of the issue.

3.58   Just as the document itself will have an overall structure so too should the sentences and paragraphs within the report. Avoid sentences that are longer than they need to be, remembering that two shorter sentences will be far more comprehensible that one long one, sub-divided into various clauses. Clarity of expression and of thought should be high in a social worker's mind when compiling the report. Confused or awkward writing will often be something social workers will find difficult to spot themselves and therefore it is a good idea to ask a colleague to read a report before submitting it. Indeed, the 'swapping' of reports between colleagues should form part of everyday practice.

3.59   A social worker should make allowances for all the various stages in the completion of a report and indeed when first instructed to compile such a report, it is advisable to establish a timescale for each stage, leaving time of course for typing, proofreading and any changes that might need to be made.

(f)   Diligence – 'Is this report the best it can be?'

3.60   What is meant here is that in compiling the report social workers should leave no stone unturned. Social workers may emit an anguished sigh at this point and argue that such an exhortation is unrealistic, given the time constraints within which they work. Those constraints are fully appreciated and it is not being suggested that social workers spend an unlimited period of time on a report. Rather, the advice is that what time social workers do have to spend on its compilation should be spent making it the best it can be. Exercising due diligence in writing the report means that sloppiness should be eliminated. (One could indeed express this principle as the 'sloppiness principle', ie do not be sloppy in compiling the report, but these principles are framed in the positive, rather than in the negative).

3.61 As regards the form of the report the following advice is offered. On the front cover include sufficient details to allow the report to be identified. Thus the court, including the county court division, and judge hearing the matter, the case name (including the parties and their designations as applicant, respondent, defendant or appellant) and the case number if appropriate, the date of the court hearing and the identity of the report writer should appear on the cover, with a clear indication that the contents of the report are confidential. It is probably good practice to repeat the essence of the Family Proceedings Rules, r 4.24, that the contents of the report should not be disclosed to other persons, other than those authorised to receive it under that rule, namely the parties, their legal representatives, the guardian ad litem, the legal aid department and welfare officer, without the leave of the court.

3.62 If the report is long, a contents page should be included. On the first, substantive, page of the report it is a good idea for the report-compiler to inform the reader of his or her acquaintance with the subject matter of the report and to set out the sources of information used in compiling the report. Consider beginning the report by stating the obvious because what is obvious to social workers may not be obvious to others. This will probably include a reference to the context in which the report-compiler was instructed to produce the report. Numbering paragraphs and numbered pages will make reference to the report easier for all concerned including the report-compiler if he or she must appear as a witness. Further, if the report involves reference to a considerable number of people a reader may find it useful to have a list of such persons, their titles or occupations and relationships stated at the beginning of the report. Should the reader become confused as to who an individual is, or what that individual's role is in the proceedings, he or she can refer back to this list. Such a list is particularly important where the persons mentioned in the report are family members bearing similar names.

3.63 When people are being interviewed for the purposes of a report they should be aware from the outset of the report-compiler's role and why they are being interviewed. Social workers should also be conscious of the danger of 'leading' such interviewees by suggesting answers to the questions posed or by asking questions which contain the answer within them. A barrister in court is not allowed to ask leading questions of his or her witness and social workers should try to exercise a similar restraint upon themselves in this context. In addition, a report-compiler needs to ensure that the content of interviews, and the context in which statements are made, is clearly set out in the report. The report-compiler's account of those interviews is hearsay evidence, which for reasons which are set out below, is admissible.[1] However, it may be damaging to the acceptability of the report and to the social worker's reputation if inaccuracies are highlighted in cross-examination.

[1] See para 3.101.

3.64 Finally, social workers should ensure that the conclusions of the report flow on from the information provided in the text. Conclusions suddenly appearing at the end of a document without any apparent foundation are not worth the paper on which they are written and will make an easy target for opposing counsel when he or she seeks to destroy the credibility of a report. When stating conclusions social workers should choose words that describe adequately their degree of conviction about the conclusion. Once put down in writing, a person's judgment often acquires greater authority than it might warrant. Thus words like 'probable', 'possible', 'sufficient' and 'considerable', for example, which are used as predictors, or to evaluate matters, have different but important meanings and the report-compiler should think carefully about the consequences of putting them in their conclusions.

Requiring attendance of witnesses

3.65 If counsel representing either party regards certain persons as material witnesses he or she can ensure their attendance at the trial by having a witness summons issued, if the matter is to be tried by the county court,[1] or writ of subpeona served on that person, if the matter is to be heard in the High Court.[2] A witness summons is issued by the chief clerk, or similar officer in a county court and can only be served in Northern Ireland. It requires a person to attend in court to give oral evidence to produce a document in his or her possession. A writ of subpoena, on the other hand, can only be issued by the High Court[3] and can be served anywhere in the UK, requiring attendance at any court. There are two types of such subpoena, a *subpoena ad testificandum*, which requires the person to attend to give oral testimony, and a *subpoena duces tecum* which obliges a person to attend along with certain documents.[4] Refusal to obey either types of subpoena or a witness summons can result in the imposition of a fine or imprisonment, or both, for contempt of court. Where a *subpeona duces tecum* has been served, or a witness summons requiring the recipient to attend along with certain documents, and the witness intends to claim that such documents attract either legal professional privilege or public interest immunity, he or she must attend with the documents and make such a claim before the court.

[1]   CCR Ord 24, r 9(1).
[2]   Judicature (Northern Ireland) Act 1978, s 67, and RSC Ord 38.
[3]   Or the appropriate High Court Office, although such a subpoena can only be served in Northern Ireland. Where the subpoena is required to compel attendance at proceedings to be held in chambers, as will be the case with much of the litigation in which social workers will be involved, the leave of the court must be obtained before the subpoena can be issued (RSC, Ord 32, r 9).
[4]   *Re S (Disclosure of Documents held by the Police)* (30 August 2001, unreported), FD, Gillen J, is an example of the use of a *subpoena duces tecum*. There the application for such a subpoena was made by a Trust to compel a police inspector to attend in court with material relating to S (and his sibling D) which had been gathered by the police in the course of their investigations into the death of one of the children and the infliction of injury on the other. See chapter 6, para 6.184.

Competence and compellability of witnesses

3.66 Not everybody is competent to be a witness. A witness is considered competent if he or she can lawfully give evidence; that is to say he or she conforms with the rules regarding mental capacity, age and understanding and what they have to say can be admitted into evidence. A witness will be compellable if, having refused to give evidence willingly, he or she can be lawfully required to give evidence.

3.67 It is important to be aware that certain persons, for example persons with learning difficulties, may not be competent to act as witnesses. The difficulty arises, not with their ability to relate facts to the court, but with their ability to understand the nature of the oath.

Mental illness and competence

3.68 Persons with a mental illness or impairment are not considered to have sufficient maturity and understanding to give sworn evidence, though this is a rebuttable presumption. This means that evidence can be adduced to show that the person with the mental illness or learning disability is capable of appreciating the significance of giving sworn oral testimony. If this can be shown, then he or she is competent to give oral testimony.

Competence and hearsay

3.69 A person's competency to appear as a witness has consequences for the admissibility of any hearsay evidence attributed to them. A person who is not competent to appear as a witness cannot have his or her evidence admitted as hearsay evidence under the Civil Evidence (Northern Ireland) Order 1997 (discussed below).[1] Social workers should bear this in mind in situations where they are planning to offer hearsay testimony in those circumstances. Concealing the fact that the person who furnished them with the hearsay evidence was not competent to appear as a witness in their own right – because of a mental illness, for example – would have very significant consequences. If this fact is discovered during the trial the evidence will be excluded, and if it is discovered afterwards it would be sufficient grounds for an appeal.

[1]   See para 3.105.

Children and competence

3.70 Formerly, children were considered to be incompetent to be called as witnesses in many cases. However, the Children's Evidence (Northern Ireland) Order 1995 abolished much of the uncertainty over children's competency. The current statutory provisions are found in the Criminal Justice (Children) (Northern Ireland) Order 1998. A child under the age of 14 years may give unsworn testimony in criminal proceedings, so long as the court considers that he or she is capable of giving 'intelligible testimony'.[1] 'Intelligible testimony', the English courts have offered, is simply 'evidence that is capable of being understood.'[2]

[1]   Criminal Justice (Children) (Northern Ireland) Order 1998, art 20(3). This is a matter that can be
      determined by the trial judge without the need for expert evidence: *G v DPP* [1998] QB 919.
[2]   *G v DPP* [1998] QB 919.

Compellability

3.71   Generally speaking, all competent witnesses are compellable, although a
spouse may only be compellable to give evidence against his or her spouse in criminal
trials in respect of certain types of offences, namely those which are sexual offences
against children under 17, and those which involve violence within the home.[1]

Social workers are competent and compellable witnesses in the vast majority of
circumstances. Thus, if social workers are asked to attend court proceedings for some
matter, and they indicate that they do not intend to do so, for whatever reason, they
may then be summoned or subpoenaed[2] before the court to give such evidence, and
failure to comply will result in the imposition of either a fine or a prison sentence.

[1]   Police and Criminal Evidence (Northern Ireland) Order 1989, art 79(3).
[2]   See para 3.65.

Witness statements and affidavits

3.72   With some minor exceptions that allow witnesses to give evidence by way of
affidavit[1] or by deposition,[2] all witnesses must give their evidence by way of oral
testimony.[3] In England and Wales witness statements are prepared before the trial
and exchanged with other parties pre-trial. However, the witness must still attend and
give oral evidence and the witness statement does not supplant the witness's oral
testimony. In Northern Ireland, the only civil proceedings in which witness statements feature are 'family proceedings'. A witness statement is not to be confused
with a court report,[4] as witness statements are simply statements of the evidence that
a particular person will adduce at the hearing of the action.[5] Clearly, the witness is
still required to attend and give his or her evidence in person to the court.

[1]   See para 3.75.
[2]   Tendering evidence by deposition is possible only if the witness cannot attend court, in which case the
      evidence is recorded by an examiner: RSC Ord 39, r 1; CCR Ord 24, r 20(1).
[3]   RSC Ord 38, r 1; CCR Ord 24, r 2; FPR 1996, r 2.40 all reiterate this, in one form or other, and provide
      that generally all evidence shall be taken on oath.
[4]   On Court Reports generally, see para 3.42.
[5]   Or indeed at a directions appointment FPR 1996, r 4.18(1)(a); MCR 1996, r 18(1)(n).

Witness statements and family proceedings

3.73   The FPR 1996 require that witness statements be tendered to other parties
before the hearing of any application under the Children (Northern Ireland)
Order 1995.[1] This statement must be dated and signed by the witness and contain a
declaration as to its veracity.[2] The witness statement is drawn up on the basis of

information tendered by the witness, but the witness should be content, given the declaration as to its truth, that it represents the evidence that he or she intends to give and will be furnished to all other party's involved in the action before the hearing of the matter. A witness will be examined and cross-examined on the basis of this statement although it is the witness's oral testimony that takes precedence. When appearing as a witness, a person should be familiar with his or her statement and with the facts of the case. Barristers and solicitors cannot coach their witnesses but witnesses are not prevented from consulting their statements prior to taking the stand.

1 FPR 1996, r 4.18; MCR 1996, r 18.
2 FPR 1996, r 4.18(1)(a); MCR 1996, r 18(1)(n).

3.74 In the English case of *Re R (Care: Disclosure: Nature of Proceedings)*,[1] the trial judge offered the following advice about the preparation of witness statements following his experience in that case:[2]

> 'The preparation of statements had to be done by someone: (a) with a proper understanding of the relevant legal principles, the issues of the case and the procedures of the court; (b) who had made a proper examination of all the background material and all the relevant files; (c) who had had a proper discussion with relevant witnesses to ensure so far as possible that their statements contained a full and proper account of the relevant matters, including the central matter seen or heard, the sources of hearsay being recorded, and the relevant background to and circumstances in which the matters set out took place; and (d) who had properly considered what further information or material should be obtained. If this work were done properly by the legal advisers, experts would be instructed on a properly informed basis, statements would exhibit appropriate background material and there would be additional appropriate discovery.'

1 [2002] 1 FLR 755.
2 [2002] 1 FLR 755 at 773H–774D.

Affidavits

3.75 Affidavits are documents setting out pertinent factual information about a legal dispute, which are sworn and signed, and the signature witnessed by a Commissioner for Oaths or a solicitor. As with witness statements, affidavits are drafted by counsel using information provided by the deponent. An affidavit may be sworn, in divorce proceedings, by order of the court.[1] In such a case, the purpose of the affidavit is to prove some fact or other without the need to call the deponent of the affidavit as a witness.[2] Evidence is also given by way of affidavit in judicial review actions, and though it is possible for the deponents of those affidavits to be cross-examined it is rarely done. Affidavits will also feature in other family proceedings, like applications for spousal maintenance and for domestic violence orders,[3] for example.

[1]   FPR 1996, r 2.41(1).
[2]   Ordinarily, however, evidence in divorce cases will be given orally.
[3]   See chapter 9, paras 9.75 and 9.17 respectively.

Oral testimony: the barrister's perspective

3.76   It will be of benefit to social workers to understand the barrister's role in court and to assess the examination of witnesses from his or her perspective. A diligent advocate will have planned the questions, or at least the line of questioning, that he or she is going to pursue. The series of questions put to social workers will not have occurred to the barrister as he or she rose to speak. In order to identify such questions, or line of questioning, the barrister will first have decided what his or her objectives are with respect to each witness. Will counsel want to portray a witness as muddled and confused or thoroughly professional? Will the objective be to undermine the value of a witness's testimony or report findings, for example, by impugning the objectivity of that witness ? Whatever the objective, the questions that are asked will be tailored to that end. The examination of witnesses usually focuses on very specific issues and explains why counsel often return to the same points a number of times. The questions posed will also usually be short, and very specific, allowing the barrister maximum control over the progress of the witness's testimony. This will be true of counsel that calls the witness as well as of opposing counsel who will cross-examine the witness. The reason for this is alluded to by Keith Evans, in his guidebook for new practitioners at the Bar, 'Advocacy at the Bar – a beginner's guide'. Evans takes the slightly tongue-in-cheek view that a good barrister will:

> 'treat all [his or her] own witnesses as being potentially foolish, as being dumbly willing to let [the barrister] down if given the chance and as being in need at all times of [an] obtrusive guiding hand.'[1]

[1]   (1983) Blackstone Press, p 120.

Taking the witness stand

3.77   A witness can swear an oath on the Bible to tell the truth, or can affirm, if he or she wishes,[1] although a child witness is only required to promise, rather than to swear.[2] Where a party calls a witness that party will question him or her first. This stage is the examination-in-chief. The function of the examination-in-chief is to have the witness tell his or her story, and testify as to the facts the barrister has called him or her to prove. Leading questions cannot be asked in examination-in-chief, nor indeed at the re-examination stage. It is not easy to define these but essentially leading questions are those questions which contain their own answer. For example, it would be a leading question to ask of a witness:

> 'Were you in Mr Smith's house on the night that he is alleged to have attacked his wife?'

It is acceptable to ask, however:

'Where were you on the night and at the time this attack is alleged to have taken place?'

Witnesses may therefore find it somewhat exasperating to answer some of the apparently pointless questions that counsel asks and may think that a more direct approach would speed the process considerably. However, the prohibition on asking leading questions in examination-in-chief is the reason for this.

[1] Oaths Act 1978, s 5.
[2] Children (Northern Ireland) Order 1995, art 169(1) in relation to Children Order proceedings; Criminal Justice (Children) (Northern Ireland) Order 1998, art 19 in relation to criminal proceedings.

3.78 Once the examination-in-chief is completed opposing counsel has an opportunity to ask questions of the witness. This is known as the cross-examination, and can be the most trying part of witness's experience in court. Occasionally witnesses will not be cross-examined because opposing counsel will feel that there is little or nothing to be gained by doing so. That opposing counsel decides not to cross-examine a witness is not a reflection on the manner in which he or she has performed as a witness.

3.79 Perhaps the two main functions of the cross-examination are: (1) to discredit the evidence of a witness; and (2) to have a witness confirm, at least partially, the opposing side's version of events. Social workers should remember that the barrister is seeking to discredit a witness's evidence, not the witness personally, although this can often only be done by robust and searching questioning of social workers or perhaps by focusing on some aspect of the witness's past, character, or credibility. Obviously a barrister will focus on what he or she considers weak points in the witness's evidence. In cross-examination, where a party has a number of witnesses, a barrister will often attempt to discredit those witnesses' testimony by highlighting differences between their recollections of events and/or between their opinions. This can be done by focusing on minor, or background details of the case and endeavouring to get them to admit to different recollections of the same events.

3.80 If the opposing case involves a mutually incompatible version of facts or events, then opposing counsel is required to put his side's case to witnesses, even though he or she is almost certain that the witness will reject that version. If opposing counsel does not 'put his or her case' to the other party's witness under cross-examination then the judge can exclude the evidence that the opposing counsel intends to adduce.[1] This mandatory requirement, that the barrister 'put his case', explains why counsel may question social workers in the following way:

'I put it to you, Mr Jones, that you were not in Mr Smith's house on the date in question.'

Thus the conclusion of the cross-examination can often appear superfluous and a little odd as the witness denies a number of questions putting forward the opposing view of events. Lastly, leading questions can be asked in cross-examination.

3.81   Once the cross-examination is complete the party calling the witness has an opportunity to re-examine the witness and hence this part of the witness's testimony is known as the re-examination. This is counsel's chance to try and repair the 'damage' done to the witness's evidence in cross-examination. However, the opportunity to cross-examine will not always be taken and much will depend on counsel's assessment of the impact of answers given in cross-examination.

3.82   The cardinal rule regarding appearance in court as a witness is the rather obvious, 'confine yourself to the questions asked of you'. A witness should not attempt to pass comment or interject during the course of the proceedings nor should he or she try to make speeches in answer to questions put to them. Social worker witnesses should not be tempted into giving long-winded answers even if the barrister is nice enough to allow them do so, because eventually he or she will berate the witness for failing to answer the question. And the judge and jury (if there is one) will view the witness as incoherent, confused and less than completely credible witness. Although it is counsel that pose the questions to witnesses, witnesses should address their answers to the magistrate or judge. In essence the advice is that as a witness, a social worker should not be unduly expansive and confine themselves to what needs to be said.

3.83   When giving evidence it is beneficial to give evidence in as reasonable a fashion as possible without being dogmatic or overly combative, whether under examination or under cross-examination. Such an approach is likely to discredit one's testimony. Social workers need to demonstrate that they have arrived at their conclusions having used their professional knowledge and skills and having considered all aspects of the issue at hand.

3.84   Social workers in 'family proceedings' should be well-versed with the contents of their sworn witness statements,[1] since that is what will be used to formulate the questions which will be put by counsel. A witness should be very careful to stay within the confines of his or her statement, and not introduce something new during the trial, since this may create difficulties for both them and the case that is being made. But be aware, as mentioned earlier, a witness's oral testimony takes precedence over a sworn statement and a witness can be asked about items not contained in the witness statement, or can introduce evidence not originally included there.

3.85   Aside from this, witnesses should remember that they are 'under oath' and therefore everything they say should, as far as possible, be the truth. A witness should try to think before answering questions, and speak slowly and clearly so they will be easily understood. This will give a strong impression of confidence in what is being said. The more nervous a witness appears to be, the more likely it is that opposing counsel will spend a considerable length of time in cross-examination in an attempt to 'rattle' him or her and sow seeds of doubt in the witness's mind about the testimony being given.

Referring to notes whilst testifying

3.86   Before testifying witnesses may consult any contemporaneous notes made by them, but this can only be done if the notes or records to which they refer have been made in close proximity to the actual occurrence of the events at issue, otherwise they may actually constitute hearsay evidence.[1] Be aware that if a social worker witness refers to such notes whilst on the witness stand, then opposing counsel is also at liberty to refer to those notes in cross-examination, and may find something in them which he or she can use to undermine the witness's testimony. Furthermore, if social workers' notes constitute a part of a file on the case, the whole file will then be open to scrutiny by opposing counsel.[2] Social workers need to be aware of this latter point when preparing the notes and/or the file for the court hearing. Hearsay evidence is examined below, but it is pertinent to mention here that if someone else has been responsible for compiling part of that file then that part of the file will be considered hearsay evidence, however, that hearsay evidence may be admissible under one of a number of statutory enactments.[3]

[1]   See para 3.101.
[2]   Civil Evidence (Northern Ireland) Order 1997, art 7(5).
[3]   See paras 3.103, 3.105 and 3.114.

Children as witnesses

3.87   The issue of children's competence to act as a witness has been discussed earlier.[1] The focus of attention in this section is on children giving evidence as part of the trial of an action. Where a child is being tried in the Youth Court, or where the offence charged is a sexual offence or one involving violence or cruelty[2] a child witness may give his or her evidence in chief by way of a pre-recorded video, with the leave of the court.[3] Such a child witness must, however, be present in court to facilitate their cross-examination, if necessary. A 'child' for the purposes of these provisions is a person aged under 14 years, if the offence in question is under the Police and Criminal Evidence (Northern Ireland) Order 1989, article 81(3)(a) or (b),[4] or under 17 years if the offence being tried is one under article 81(3)(c) of the 1989 Order.[5] The cross-examination of the accuser may not be carried out by the accused, however.[6] The NSPCC has produced a child witness pack to help children called to appear as witnesses.[7]

[1]   See para 3.70.
[2]   As defined by the Police and Criminal Evidence (Northern Ireland) Order 1989, art 81(3). For children in family proceedings, see para 3.103.
[3]   Children's Evidence (Northern Ireland) Order 1995, art 5, inserting a new art 81A into the Police and Criminal Evidence (Northern Ireland) Order 1989.
[4]   The child can be under 15 years if the video testimony was recorded when the child was under 14 years. The offences in question involve injury or violence to a person.
[5]   The child can be under 18 years if the video testimony was recorded when the child was under 17 years. The offences referred to here are sexual offences.
[6]   Children's Evidence (Northern Ireland) Order 1995, art 5, inserting a new art 81B into the Police and Criminal Evidence (Northern Ireland) Order 1989.
[7]   The Young Witness Pack, 1998.

3.88   The videotape of the child's evidence in chief must be compiled in accordance with the 'Memorandum of Good Practice on Video Recorded Interviews with Child Witnesses for Criminal Proceedings'.[1] A failure to do so can have fatal consequences for the prosecution of an alleged abuser of a child, because the trial judge might refuse to admit the child's video evidence. In *G v DPP*[2] the video evidence was admitted even though the memorandum had not been fully complied with. The English High Court considered that an important factor in deciding whether or not to admit such a video was whether the evidence was reliable.

---

[1]   Home Office 1992. This Memorandum has it origins in the recommendations of the Report of the Inquiry into Child Abuse in Cleveland (1988) (Cm 412) ('the Cleveland Report'), conducted by Dame Elizabeth Butler-Sloss.
[2]   [1998] QB 919.

Acting as an expert witness

3.89   One of the concerns of the law of evidence is that witnesses confine themselves to making statements of fact and not statements of opinion. Generally, opinions are not admissible as evidence when the witness is not describing what he or she saw, or heard, or otherwise experienced, but is expressing a view as to how a particular event might have occurred or what was about to occur. Undoubtedly there will be some occasions where the only way in which a witness can give evidence is to use expressions that describe certain events, such as another person's feelings, for example, that appear to amount to statements of opinion, rather than of fact. Generally, however, only expert witnesses will be allowed to offer opinions in their oral testimony. Thus an expert witness is allowed to offer opinion evidence as well as evidence based on material such as books, journals and the materials of other professionals, articles, reports or statistics which are compiled for purposes other than the case at hand.

Social workers as expert witnesses

3.90   Only those whom the law accepts as being experts are allowed to have their opinions introduced as evidence. Usually an expert witness is identified by professional qualifications and as one would expect expert witnesses usually are doctors, psychiatrists, psychologists etc. However, anyone with considerable knowledge or expertise in the matters at hand may also be regarded by the court as an expert. The decision as to whether or not social workers can be an expert witness is one for the judge and in making that decision he or she must be satisfied of two things; first that the matter before him or her is one of expertise, and second, that the witness in question qualifies as an expert. The classical legal case dealing with qualification as an expert witness is *R v Silverlock*,[1] where the court accepted that a solicitor, who had studied handwriting for ten years, mainly in a non-professional capacity constituted an expert; thereby admitting his opinion as evidence. In stating the test as whether or not the witness is 'peritus' ie skilled in his work, the court rejected the requirement of formal qualifications.

[1]   [1894] 2 QB 766, CCR.

3.91   This suggests that a social worker who has read extensively, attended training courses or specialised in one particular area of practice for a number of years might be regarded as an expert by the court. However, the courts have tended to stress that they may only be allowed to act as expert witnesses if they have a particular qualification or expertise. In *Re N (a minor) (sexual abuse: video evidence)*,[1] a case in which admissibility of the evidence of the local authority social worker and the guardian ad litem as experts in a case of child sexual abuse was in question, the English Court of Appeal considered that:

> 'For the court to rely on opinion evidence – even to admit it – the qualifications of the witness must extend beyond experience gained as a social worker and require clinical experience as or akin to a child psychologist or child psychiatrist.'[2]

The social worker in that case was considered to have the necessary expertise to be considered an expert but that was an exceptional finding based on the social worker's experience of working with Dr Bentovim, a well known child psychiatrist.

[1]   [1996] 4 All ER 225, [1996] 2 FLR 214.
[2]   Guardians ad litem are not considered to have the necessary specialist knowledge to be considered an expert in that case either and should commission expert witness testimony if necessary.

Role of expert witness[1]

3.92   However, even though an expert will be making conclusions based on the evidence that he or she has surveyed, ultimately the task of deciding what actually happened is one for the judge alone. The expert cannot therefore usurp the functions of the trial judge by deciding issues of fact.[2] To illustrate with an example used by one trial judge:[3]

> 'There are particular problems in the reception of expert evidence in separating out that which is admissible from that which is inadmissible. To make the point, take a simple but sadly regular occurrence – an incident of domestic violence. The wife goes to the general practitioner, he takes her history, and he makes his examination. This is not a case where any real diagnosis is required. The proper and relevant evidence from the doctor is that he saw bruises and that the bruising was consistent with an assault. If he gives evidence of the history, that is hearsay and, assuming that it is admissible as such, its weight is a matter for the court's judgment and if the wife does not herself give evidence of those facts then considerable caution must be exercised by the court before relying on the hearsay. What the doctor is not permitted to say is that he believed the wife when she gave him the history, he is not permitted to say that

because of the nature of the injuries he saw, he believed or was fortified in his belief of her having been assaulted, and he is certainly not entitled to say he believed that the husband was the one who had committed such an assault.'

[1]   On the roles and duties of expert witnesses, see A Swann ' The Role and Duties of the Expert Witness', 2002 Vo. 8 No 4 Child Care in Practice 305.
[2]   *Re N (a minor) (sexual abuse: video evidence)* [1996] 4 All ER 225, [1996] 2 FLR 214, applying dicta of Glidewell LJ and Stocker LJJ in *Re S and B (minors) (child abuse: evidence)* [1990] 2 FLR 489 at 498–499 and Morritt LJ in *Re F S (minors)* [1996] 1 FLR 666 at 676–677.
[3]   *Re N (a minor) (sexual abuse: video evidence)* [1996] 4 All ER 225 at 232B–D, [1996] 2 FLR 214.

3.93   Another example was offered in a different case. In *Re S and B (Minors) (child abuse: evidence)*,[1] Glidewell LJ offered this analysis:

'In that role [as an expert witness] her opinions about A's psychiatric state and her propensity to fantasise or invent were properly admissible. To the extent that she was supporting these opinions by an expression of view that A's account of her previous history was apparently credible, this was also admissible. What, however, was not admissible was any direct expression of opinion that A was telling the truth, and not telling malicious lies. The boundary between the two expressions of view is fine, but it does seem to me that Miss Tranter's evidence crossed that line, so that her expression of "little doubt that the accounts given to me by A are accurate" was a matter for the judge and not for her.'

This means that the judge can reject the evidence of experts, even if they are all united in their views, because in the final analysis, the power and the duty to decide the case rests with the judge. However, where the judge does depart from the opinions of experts it is crucial that he or she explain the reasons why the expert's evidence is not being accepted.[2]

[1]   [1990] 2 FLR 489 at 498, CA, Glidewell LJ.
[2]   *Re N-B (children) (residence: expert evidence)* [2002] EWCA Civ 1052, [2002] 3 FCR 259. The judge certainly should not reject the expert's evidence on the basis of the performance on the witness stand of any witness alone.

Duty of expert witness

3.94   An expert witness's duty is to give unbiased evidence.[1] An expert is immune from suit for evidence given in court or tendered by way of a report[2] but is liable for any pre-trial advice given in respect of the merits of a case or the appropriate defence to advance, for example.

[1]   *Robinson v Law* [2000] NIJB 184, Shiel J.
[2]   *Stanton v Callaghan* [2000] 1 QB 75, CA.

3.95   Cazalet J in *Re R (A minor) (Expert's Evidence)*[1] offered detailed criteria on the manner in which experts in child cases should carry out their functions and they are worth reproducing in full here:

'Expert witnesses are in a privileged position; indeed, only experts are permitted to give an opinion in evidence. Outside the legal field the court itself has no expertise and for that reason frequently has to rely on the evidence of experts. Such experts must express only opinions which they genuinely hold and which are not biased in favour of one particular party. Opinions can, of course, differ and indeed quite frequently experts who have expressed their objective and honest opinions will differ, but such differences are usually within a legitimate area of disagreement. On occasions, and because they are acting on opposing sides, each may give his opinion from different basic facts. This of itself is likely to produce a divergence.

The expert should not mislead by omissions. He should consider all the material facts in reaching his conclusions and must not omit to consider the material facts which could detract from his concluded opinion.

If experts look for and report on factors which tend to support a particular proposition or case, their reports should still:

(a) provide a straightforward, not a misleading opinion;
(b) be objective and not omit factors which do not support their opinion; and
(c) be properly researched.

If the expert's opinion is not properly researched because he considers that insufficient data is available, then he must say so and indicate that his opinion is no more than a provisional one.

In certain circumstances an expert may find that he has to give an opinion adverse to his client. Alternatively, if, contrary to the appropriate practice, an expert does provide a report which is other than wholly objective – that is one which seeks to 'promote' a particular case – the report must make this clear. However, such an approach should be avoided because, in my view, it would: (a) be an abuse of the position of the expert's proper function and privilege; and (b) render the report an argument, and not an opinion.

It should be borne in mind that a misleading opinion from an expert may well inhibit a proper assessment of a particular case by the non-medical professional advisers and may also lead parties, and in particular parents, to false views and hopes.'

[1] [1991] 1 FLR 291n.

3.96 In order to comply with the right to a fair trial,[1] a jointly instructed expert must ensure that he or she does not conduct a conference with one of the parties to an action alone and that both parties have the opportunity of commenting on the documents and issues that are being examined by the expert.[2] Furthermore, the witnesses that are interviewed by the expert and whose evidence forms the basis for the expert's report must also be available for cross-examination.

[1] Convention right, art 6, contained in the HRA, Sch 1. See chapter 1, para 1.83 and chapter 6, para 6.23.

2   *Re C (Care proceedings: disclosure of local authority's decision-making process)* [2002] EWHC 1379 (Fam), [2002] 2 FCR 673.

Appointment of experts in family proceedings

3.97   Leave of the court is required, in 'family proceedings', for the appointment of an expert to carry out any medical or psychiatric examination of a child. Where the court's permission is not obtained then the evidence arising out of that assessment or examination cannot be adduced at the trial without the leave of the court.[1] Instructing an expert witness to prepare a report without the court's permission may result in the court imposing any costs falling on other parties as a result of commissioning the unauthorised report.[2]

1   FPR 1996, r 4.19, and MCR 1996, r 19.
2   *Re A (Family Proceedings: Expert Witnesses)* [2001] 1 FLR 723.

3.98   The general, although detailed, advice regarding the instructing of expert witnesses offered in *Re R (Care: Disclosure: nature of Proceedings)* was as follows:[1]

'Letters of instruction to experts should be prepared carefully on an individual basis; precedents should be used only as a basis and a check, and should not simply be reproduced. The expert should consider carefully the terms of the instructions, and whether he or she could fulfil them by applying his or her general approach or an adaptation thereof; it would be sensible to invite the expert to confirm this expressly before embarking on the assessment. Once a report from an expert had been received, it should be considered by all parties and their legal advisers in order to check: (a) that the expert had reported in accordance with his or her instructions; (b) whether the party wished to put any further points to the expert, including points on reasoning, and on relevance of facts or matters; and (c) the role that the expert should play at the hearing and thus whether and if so when, and as to what, the expert should give oral evidence. The local authority should consider and raise with the parties and the court the relevance of the reports of each of the experts. If an expert videoed interviews he should say so in the report and should make those videos available unless he or she wished to raise a particularised point as to why they should not be seen. However, it should only be in exceptional cases that a court be invited to watch videos of interviews conducted by experts, and before it was invited to do so, the relevant parts of the video and the points sought to be derived from them should be clearly identified so that viewing time was kept to a minimum.'

Responsibility for ensuring compliance with this extensive range of duties will lie primarily with solicitors, although clearly other interested persons, including social workers, will have some involvement.

1   [2002] 1 FLR 755.

Hearsay evidence and expert witnesses

3.99 Hearsay evidence, explained below,[1] is only admissible in certain circumstances and its relevance to the evidence of experts is that such evidence invariably includes references to matters, such as research data and statistics for example, which will constitute hearsay if the person relying on them is not the author of them and cannot verify their veracity before the court. Some degree of hearsay evidence must be admitted in the testimony of an expert witness. However, as outlined above when referring to *Re N (a minor) (sexual abuse: video evidence)* and the role of the expert witness, the court has a difficult role in determining what is admissible hearsay in the case of expert witnesses.[2]

Some statutory provisions expressly allow for the admission of hearsay expert evidence.[3]

1 See para 3.101.
2 See para 3.92.
2 The hearsay evidence of expert witnesses in undefended divorce cases in the High Court and the county court is governed by FPR 1996, r 2.45 modifying the application of RSC Ord 38, rr 5 and 19(1) and CCR Ord 38, r 19(1).

Admitting reports of expert witnesses

3.100 Experts' written reports are admissible via the Civil Evidence (Northern Ireland) Order 1997. This is done by simply calling the expert to testify that he or she is the author of the report.

Hearsay evidence

3.101 One of the most complex rules governing what evidence can, and cannot be presented to the court is the rule against hearsay. Hearsay evidence is an out-of-court statement which is adduced in evidence to assert the veracity of the content of that statement. The most obvious example is where a witness attempts to give evidence about something another person told them, in circumstances where the witness is testifying not simply to the fact that the statement was made but that its contents are true. Thus it is hearsay for a witness to adduce in evidence, at a criminal trial, that a bystander had told him that a person matching the description of the accused had been seen running from the scene of the crime. As the rule against hearsay is a common law creation there is no definitive definition of it. A leading textbook explains the concept in the following terms:

'Evidence of a statement made to a witness by a person who is not himself called as a witness may or may not be hearsay. *It is hearsay, and inadmissible, when the object of the evidence is to establish the truth of what is contained in the statement.* It is not hearsay, and admissible, when it is proposed to establish by the evidence, not the truth of the statement, but the fact that it was made'. [author's emphasis][1]

¹   *Subramanian v Public Prosecutor* [1956] 1 WLR 965 at 969.

3.102   The importance of identifying hearsay evidence is that it is inadmissible in criminal proceedings and may only be admitted in civil proceedings if certain conditions are met.¹ Ultimately the admissibility of evidence is an issue for the trial judge, so where a social worker has any doubts about whether or not to introduce any evidence into court the best advice is to attempt to introduce it and let the lawyers argue about its admissibility. Social workers should not take it upon themselves to act as the arbiter of admissibility as they may wrongly exclude evidence that could have been admitted with grave consequences for the conduct of the case.

¹   See paras 3.103, 3.105 and 3.114.

Hearsay and children's cases

3.103   The significance of the rule against hearsay in all civil proceedings has been greatly diminished by statute. The Children (Admissibility of Hearsay Evidence) (Northern Ireland) Order 1996¹ allows hearsay evidence to be admitted in civil proceedings in the High Court or county court, and in any proceedings under the Children (Northern Ireland) Order 1995 or under the Child Support (Northern Ireland) Order 1991 'in connection with the upbringing, maintenance or welfare of a child'.² In admitting such evidence a judge will often weigh the hearsay evidence carefully before arriving at any conclusion.³ The fact that hearsay evidence can be admitted in such proceedings means, for example, that it is not necessary to call the child who is the subject of the application as a witness to testify as to the content of statements he or she may have made to social workers, or other witnesses. It will be sufficient for the court to hear the evidence of the social workers, or others who heard the child make such statements.

¹   Made under the Children Order, art 169(5). The equivalent English legislation is the Children (Admissibility of Hearsay Evidence) Order 1993, SI 1993/621.
²   Regulation 2.
³   See, for example, Gillen J in *Re J (Threshold Conditions Parental Concessions)* (28 June 2002, unreported), FD, a useful example of the use of the 1996 Order. See also *Re an Appeal (2000/11) (Children: Video evidence)* [2001] NI 358 in which the Northern Ireland Court of Appeal considered the purpose of the Admissibility of Hearsay evidence legislation. A video of the children's evidence was considered to have been correctly admitted.

3.104   However, the crucial test is whether the proceedings are in connection with the 'upbringing, maintenance or welfare of a child'. In *Re C (Minors) (hearsay evidence: contempt proceedings)*¹ a woman in whose favour a Non-molestation Order had been made sought to introduce, in proceedings in which it was alleged her husband had acted in breach of the order, the evidence of her children contained in a court welfare officer's report and an affidavit sworn by the minister of her church. Where the proceedings primarily affected the parents, as in this case, but not the children's upbringing, maintenance or welfare, it was probable that children's hearsay evidence would be excluded. The woman could not therefore rely on this provision to introduce the hearsay evidence. In contrast in *F v Child Support Agency*,² a mother of a child, which was either that of her husband or her lover was faced, in child support proceedings, with a refusal of her lover to undergo DNA testing. She was allowed to adduce hearsay evidence of earlier DNA tests that indicated that her lover was the father of the child.[3]

---

[1]   [1993] 4 All ER 690, [1993] 1 FLR 220, [1993] 1 FCR 820, CA.
[2]   [1999] 2 FCR 385, [1999] 2 FLR 244, [1999] Fam Law 540.
[3]   *R v Oxfordshire County Council (secure accommodation order)* [1992] Fam 150, [1992] 3 All ER 660, [1992] 1 FLR 648 is another example in which evidence was admitted under the equivalent English legislation, this time in an application for a Secure Accommodation Order, which although not within the definition of 'family proceedings' was considered to be proceedings about the upbringing, maintenance and welfare of children.

Hearsay and civil proceedings generally

3.105   The Civil Evidence (Northern Ireland) Order 1997[1] provides that evidence is not to be excluded in *any* civil proceedings on the grounds of being hearsay.[2] 'Hearsay' is statutorily defined in this context as 'a statement made otherwise than by a person giving oral evidence in the instant proceedings, which is tendered as evidence of the matters stated'.[3] However, the 1997 Order sets out factors to be considered by the judiciary when estimating the weight to be given to hearsay evidence.[4] In other words the fact that the evidence is admitted even as hearsay is only the first step. The court must then go on to consider the content, and consider what value to place on it. The range of factors set out in the 1997 Order include:

1   any circumstances from which any inference can reasonably be drawn as to the reliability or otherwise of the evidence;

2   whether the party adducing the hearsay evidence gave notice to the other party that it intended to do so and the sufficiency of that notice;

3   whether it would have been reasonable and practicable for the party by whom the evidence is adduced to have produced the maker of the original statement as a witness;

4   whether the statement was made contemporaneously;

5   whether the evidence involves multiple hearsay (ie is third or fourth hand evidence, and not just second-hand evidence);

6   whether any person involved has any motive to conceal or misrepresent matters;

7   whether the original statement was an edited account made in collaboration for another purpose;

8   whether the circumstances in which the hearsay evidence is adduced suggest that a proper evaluation of its weight is being thwarted.

---

[1]   This Order mirrors the content of the Civil Evidence Act 1995 in England and Wales and the Civil Evidence (Scotland) Act 1998.
[2]   Civil Evidence (Northern Ireland) Order 1997, art 3.
[3]   Civil Evidence (Northern Ireland) Order 1997, art 3(3).
[4]   Civil Evidence (Northern Ireland) Order 1997, art 5.

3.106   The impact of this provision can be seen by considering an example. Imagine that in a domestic violence situation a Non-molestation Order,[1] directing a husband to refrain from interfering with his wife, has been breached. At the hearing to consider this breach it is possible for the court to admit evidence given by the wife of matters told to her by her child,[2] provided that the court carries out the assessment referred to above,[3] and is satisfied that other safeguards explored below do not apply.

[1]   See chapter 9, para 9.33.
[2]   See, for example, *C v C* [2001] EWCA Civ 1625.
[3]   Also set out in the Civil Evidence (Northern Ireland) Order 1997, art 5.

Safeguards against abuse

3.107   Three safeguards against the abuse of the modifications made to the hearsay rule by the 1997 Order are included within it to ensure fairness in the trial. The first is that hearsay evidence can only be introduced, under the 1997 Order, if the person who made the original statement that is being sought to be adduced in evidence is competent to be a witness at the trial.[1] For example, where the original statement is made by a person with a history of severe learning difficulties, who would not be competent to be called as a witness, and a person to whom she made that statement seeks to testify about its truthfulness, such hearsay evidence will not be admitted under the Civil Evidence Order because the original maker of the statement could not have been called as a witness.[2] In order for the hearsay evidence of a child to be admitted under the 1997 Order he or she must satisfy the condition for the reception of unsworn evidence of a child.[3] If the child cannot satisfy such conditions, then the hearsay evidence is inadmissible in such proceedings. To illustrate, let us return to the example used previously of the mother giving evidence of matters a child told her, at the hearing into the breach of a Non-molestation Order. In order to admit such hearsay evidence the child must be considered to be competent to testify in his or her own right.[4]

[1]   Civil Evidence (Northern Ireland) Order 1997, art 6. On competence generally, see para 3.66.
[2]   Such evidence may be admissible if it is not considered to be hearsay, ie if it is not being adduced to prove the truthfulness of its content, but merely to show that, for example, the statement had been made. For example, if the statement is adduced to prove the fact that the statement-maker made allegations previously – in order to rebut suggestions that the allegations were of recent vintage – then it will not be hearsay and is capable of being admitted into evidence. Further, such evidence may be admitted under the Children (Admissibility of Hearsay Evidence) Order 1995 if it touches on the upbringing, welfare or maintenance of the children.
[3]   Children (Northern Ireland) Order 1995, art 169(4)(a) and (b) and see para 3.70.
[4]   It is for the party asserting that the person would not be a competent witness to make that case and not for the party seeking to adduce the evidence to prove that the person was competent: *C v C* [2001] EWCA Civ 1625.

3.108   The second safeguard is that if hearsay evidence is admitted under the 1997 Order, such that the maker of the original statement is not called as a witness, the other party is free to call the statement-maker and cross-examine him or her.[1] This means that careful thought should be given as to whether the statement-maker can, and should, be called as a witness. The 1997 Order is not simply an opportunity to avoid having certain witnesses called and allowing other witnesses to give the evidence that the maker of the original statement would have given.

3.109 The third safeguard against possible abuse of this modification of the hearsay rule allows evidence to be called about the original statement-maker for the purposes of attacking his or her credibility, or which would otherwise be put in cross-examination, or which shows that he or she made inconsistent statements in the past.[1] To illustrate this safeguard, recall the example involving the breach of the Non-molestation Order. In that case it would be possible to call other adults who heard the child say something different to that which its mother testified had been said by the child.

[1] Civil Evidence (Northern Ireland) Order 1997, art 6(3).

3.110 Clearly then, the Civil Evidence (Northern Ireland) Order 1997 has not eliminated the significance of designating evidence as hearsay completely. Once the judge in civil proceedings (ie those not concerned about the 'upbringing, maintenance or welfare' of children) identifies evidence as hearsay, the safeguards outlined above must be applied.

3.111 Where hearsay evidence is admitted the judge may well seek corroborating evidence to support it. Corroboration occurs where another independent witness gives testimony that supports the hearsay evidence, or there is some other physical evidence that provides this support. Corroborating evidence is not necessary but will obviously add to the credibility of the hearsay evidence. This means that social workers and their legal advisers must be alert to the need, in the pre-trial preparation stage, to identify hearsay evidence which is intended to be adduced, assessing whether the original statement-maker is competent to testify, why they are not to be called, whether such a person is credible, and the various other matters addressed in the safeguards outlined above and contained in articles 4–6 of the 1997 Order,[1] as well as considering whether there is any evidence to corroborate the hearsay evidence. Indeed, it is good practice to give other parties to the case, advance notice of any hearsay evidence which it is intended to adduce.[2] Note, however, that these safeguards do not expressly apply in proceedings about the 'upbringing, maintenance or welfare' of children, although in practice the trial judge is likely to evaluate the weight of the hearsay evidence by reference to the type of factors outlined in article 5.[3]

[1] See para 3.107.
[2] See B Valentine, 'Civil Proceedings in the County Court' (1999) SLS, Belfast, para 13.13.
[3] For those factors, see para 3.105.

3.112 To summarise, what social workers need to bear in mind is that the court wants the best possible evidence of the facts. If the only evidence of the facts is hearsay, the court will usually want some corroboration of that evidence, to ensure fairness for all the parties to the case. This can mean that virtually all types of written material produced in respect of a file or a case can acquire importance and underscores the importance of paperwork.

3.113 One of the virtues of the adversarial system is said to be the opportunity it provides to test, in cross-examination, the truthfulness of a witness's testimony.

Admitting hearsay evidence undermines that possibility and therefore the courts will be alert to the need to weigh such evidence carefully before arriving at conclusions on the basis of it. Generally, however, it is clear that evidence, which in the past would have been excluded, will now be admitted. It seems that, with respect to in 'children's cases' in particular, the balance has shifted away from excessive observance of legal rules in favour of obtaining as much information as possible, to allow the court be as fully informed as possible before making a decision which will affect a vulnerable child. This emphasises the need for social workers to be vigilant when gathering and compiling evidence in the course of their everyday duties, as well as in the context of forthcoming trials.

Hearsay and case records and documents

3.114   Information contained in documents or recorded in documentary form will amount to hearsay if it is intended to introduce that evidence to prove the truthfulness of the statement contained within it. Yet, clearly, such forms of evidence can be very valuable and in many cases quite reliable. As a result there are statutory provisions that allow the introduction of such evidence.

Computer records

3.115   Computer records were admissible under the Civil Evidence Act (Northern Ireland) 1971[1] provided that the computer was in regular use and in proper order and that the information was of a type usually loaded onto that computer. The Civil Evidence (Northern Ireland) Order 1997 does not have a similar provision. However, if the computer record is to be adduced in evidence to prove the veracity of its contents it will be hearsay evidence if the truth of its content cannot be proven by oral testimony and thus what has been said about hearsay evidence and civil proceedings applies: see para 3.105.

[1]   Section 2.

Documents compiled under duty

3.116   Information compiled in documentary form by a person acting under a duty to record that information, and supplied by a person who may reasonably be supposed to have direct knowledge of it, is admissible if direct oral testimony of the same facts would also be admissible.[1] The advantage of this provision is that it allows information to be admitted, like for example, material recorded by successive social workers in a child's case file, where it was not possible to trace the original social workers who had made the relevant entry. A solicitor taking a statement from a client is not compiling a record so as to allow the client's written statement to be accepted into evidence if the client has since died.[2] In order for this form of evidence to qualify from this statutory provision, a certificate must be signed by a responsible officer of the authority in question stating that the information was compiled under a duty.

1   The Civil Evidence (Northern Ireland) Order 1997, art 9.
2   *Johnson v Gilpins (Protective Wear) Ltd* [1989] NI 294 interpreting the Civil Evidence Act (Northern Ireland) 1971, s 1, the statutory predecessor to the Civil Evidence (Northern Ireland) Order 1997, art 9.

Hearsay and Court Welfare Reports

3.117   The contents of a Court Welfare Report can be adduced into evidence notwithstanding any rule of law 'which would otherwise prevent the court from doing so.' The court may take account of: (a) any statement contained in the report; and (b) any evidence given in respect of the matters referred to in the report, in so far as the statement or evidence is, in the opinion of the court, relevant to the question which it is considering.[1] This provides a further mechanism by which the court can admit otherwise inadmissible evidence in cases where a Court Welfare Report is prepared. This particular formulation has the advantage of allowing the admission of evidence that is in breach of other rules of evidence, and not just the rule against hearsay. Thus, it may allow the admission of material, referred to in the report, which had been secretly recorded, for example, without the authorisation of a court or other authority. However, some rights contained in the HRA may be of significance in the admissibility of such material, such as the right to a fair trial[2] and the right to privacy,[3] and these would have to be considered before the evidence was admitted.

1   Children (Northern Ireland) Order 1995, art 4(4).
2   On the HRA, see chapter 1, para 1.74 and chapter 6, para 6.23.
3   For more on right to privacy, see chapter 6, para 6.11.

Chapter 4

Equality Law

Introduction

4.1 Principles of non-discrimination and tolerance for diversity underpin social work practice. Knowledge of equality law is therefore required in order to reinforce those practice values and to provide social workers with an understanding of how the law protects people from discrimination and seeks to ensure equality of opportunity for all. The law in this area has undergone considerable change in recent years with the advent of anti-race discrimination legislation, the extension of fair employment legislation, and the gradual implementation of the Disability Discrimination Act 1995. The enactment of the statutory duty on public authorities, in the Northern Ireland Act 1998, s 75, requiring them to promote equality of opportunity, also has significance for social workers. Trusts and Boards, amongst other public bodies, are particularly affected by this latter development and some social workers may even find themselves involved in the process of implementing the duty within their employing organisation. It should also be borne in mind that some of the developments in Northern Ireland equality law have been prompted by developments in the law of the European Union, and this influence is likely to be even more evident in future years. Two particular Directives that have had, and will have, an impact on equality law are the Race and Ethnic Origin Directive 2000[1] (REOD) and the Framework Employment Equality Directive 2000[2] (FEED), which, for example, extend statutory protection to include the grounds of sexual orientation and age.

[1] 2000/43/EC.
[2] 2000/78/EC.

Equality legislation

4.2 At present the body of equality law in Northern Ireland is composed of a number of different statutes regulating discrimination in respect of a range of activities.[1] The Sex Discrimination (Northern Ireland) Order 1976,[2] as its title suggests, deals with gender discrimination as well as discrimination against married people. Gender discrimination is unlawful in the fields of employment, education, the availability of goods, facilities and services and in the selling and letting of premises. The Race Relations (Northern Ireland) Order 1997[3] outlaws discrimination on the basis of race, nationality, ethnic or national origin and prohibits discrimination in the same spheres of activity as the Sex Discrimination Order. The Disability Discrimination Act 1995 is a UK-wide statute prohibiting discrimination against disabled persons in employment[4] and in the provision of goods, facilities and services. However, it applies in a limited manner to education[5] and to the provision of transport facilities,[6] and is therefore more limited in its impact than the other anti-discrimination statutes. The Equality (Disability, etc) (Northern Ireland) Order 2000 confers particular powers and duties on the Equality Commission for Northern Ireland[7] to tackle discrimination against disabled persons. Changes to the Disability Discrimination Act 1995 will be made by the Disability Discrimination Act 1995 (Amendment) (Regulations) 2003 when they come into force in October 2004. Political or religious discrimination is governed by the Fair Employment and Treatment (Northern Ireland) Order 1998. In the past, fair employment legislation only dealt with sectarian or political discrimination in the workplace.[8] However, the 1998 Order extended the coverage of that legislation to matters such as the selling or letting of premises and the provision of goods, facilities and services. However, its application to education is limited to higher education only.[9] The Employment Equality (Sexual Orientation) Regulations (Northern Ireland) 2003 deal with discrimination on the basis of sexual preferences but in the workplace only.

[1] Equal pay legislation is also part of equality law, but is not considered here as it relates to the employer/employee relationship, rather than the discriminatory or unequal use of power, which arguably sits at the heart of discriminatory practices. It is the unequal power relationships that engage social work values.
[2] A further Order, the Sex Discrimination (Northern Ireland) Order 1988, makes some amendments to the 1976 Order, but the main legislative enactment is the 1976 Order.
[3] As amended by the Race Relations Order (Amendment) Regulations (Northern Ireland) 2003, which implemented the terms of the Race and Ethnic Origin Directive 2000 into Northern Ireland law.
[4] However, the Act can only be applied to employers with more than 15 employees.
[5] It applies to higher education only. The Special Educational Needs and Disability Act 2001 does deal with discrimination in the primary and secondary education sectors but that Act only applies in England and Wales.
[6] Rather than outlawing discrimination in the provision of transport facilities, it allows the Government to set minimum standards for the accessibility of transportation services.
[7] See paras 4.58 ff.
[8] See the Fair Employment (Northern Ireland) Acts 1976–1989.
[9] Fair Employment and Treatment (Northern Ireland) Order 1998, art 27.

4.3 Formerly, these various enactments were overseen by different agencies, but since 1999 a single body, the Equality Commission for Northern Ireland (ECNI), has statutory responsibility for overseeing compliance with this body of anti-discrimination law.[1] It is proposed to replace these various statutes with one Single Equality Act to be enacted by the Northern Ireland Assembly. However, the complexity of the task, and the suspension of the Assembly in late 2002, has resulted in some slippage in the timetable for the Single Equality Act.

[1] See para 4.57 for its antecedents.

4.4   One other element of Northern Ireland's equality law regime is found in the Northern Ireland Act 1998, s 75 and is commonly referred to as the 'statutory duty'. It requires specified public bodies to have due regard, in the performance of their functions, to the need to ensure equality of opportunity in respect of nine character- istics (religious belief, political opinion, racial group, age, marital status or sexual orientation, gender, disability and whether a person has dependants). It also requires public bodies to have regard to the need to promote good community relations between Catholics and Protestants.

4.5   The net effect of this duty is to require those bodies to assess the impact of their policies and administrative activity on facilitating equal opportunity, ameliorating or eradicating any adverse impacts where they occur. This duty is enforced by the Equality Commission for Northern Ireland and should have the impact of tackling discrimination and disadvantage in a systematic fashion at the level of public sector institutions.[1]

---

[1]   See para 4.75.

4.6   There are a number of other legal provisions that will have, or may in the future have, an impact on combating discrimination and promoting equality. The HRA, as we have seen in chapter 1, imports the ECHR into domestic law. One of the Convention rights is article 14, the right not to be subject to discrimination in the exercise of other Convention rights. This does not outlaw discrimination generally but only where another Convention right is engaged or affected.[1] An example may illustrate its operation. In *Van Raalte v Netherlands*,[2] a provision of Dutch social security law was under scrutiny. It obliged all workers to make contributions to a general childcare fund, irrespective of whether they had children. However, women over the age of 45 years, who were childless, were exempt from making this contribution, but men over that age had to make the payment. Creating such a distinction between men and women over the age of 45 years amounted to a difference of treatment in the manner in which tax was levied on them and the tax interfered with a persons' right to property, which is protected by article 1 of Protocol 1. There was no justification, the court found, for this differential treatment and as a result it found that there was impermissible discrimination, resulting in a violation of article 14, in the exercise of the applicant's article 1, Protocol 1 rights.[3]

---

[1]   Protocol 14 to the ECHR will outlaw discrimination generally when it comes into force. However, in order for that Protocol to be effective it must be incorporated into domestic law, and therefore some amendment of the HRA will be required.

[2]   (1997) 24 EHRR 503, E Ct HR.

[3]   For more on art 14, see chapter 9, para 9.11

4.7   Reference was also made in chapter 1, when discussing the Northern Ireland Human Rights Commission,[1] to its Draft Bill of Rights for Northern Ireland. It is not clear whether that Draft will become law, and if so, whether all of its terms will be included in a future Bill of Rights, but if it does then further equality guarantees will probably be provided therein.[2]

---

[1]   See para 1.109.

2   The Draft Bill of Rights includes Equality provisions in Part 4. See 'Making a Bill of Rights for Northern Ireland – A Consultation by the Northern Ireland Human Rights Commission', NIHRC, September 2001.

Discrimination

4.8   There are important concepts contained in all anti-discrimination enactments and these require explanation in order to appreciate the manner in which the legislation operates. Four types of discrimination are recognised in statute: direct discrimination, indirect discrimination, harassment and victimisation. It is on these concepts that the courts and tribunals will focus when hearing complaints of discrimination. In order to succeed in a particular case, a complainant must demonstrate that one of these forms of discrimination is present in his or her circumstances.

Direct discrimination

4.9   What is commonly referred to as direct discrimination is defined in the various anti-discrimination enactments referred to above as involving less favourable treatment of the complainant on the basis of the characteristic or attribute in question, ie ethnicity, religious belief, political opinion, disability or gender.[1] This assessment of less favourable treatment involves a comparison between persons in the same material circumstances but with different characteristics, ie ethnicity, religious belief, political opinion, disability or gender.[2] (The wording of the direct discrimination provision in the Disability Discrimination Act 1995 differs slightly, but importantly, from that in other statutes, in that it applies to discrimination *for a reason which relates to the disabled person's disability*.[3] The courts have concluded that there is no requirement to engage in a comparison with a non-disabled person. Instead the court or Tribunal merely asks itself whether there has been less favourable treatment of the person with a disability and whether it was motivated by a reason to do with the person's disability, which reason did not apply to others.)[4] The definition of direct discrimination in the Disability Discrimination Act 1995 will be amended when the Disability Discrimination Act (Amendment) Regulations 2003 come into force, to include another form of discrimination. Those Regulations prohibit less favourable treatment *on the grounds of* the person's disability.[5]

1   The definition of direct discrimination is found in the following statutory provisions: religion and politics – Fair Employment and Treatment (Northern Ireland) Order 1998, art 3(2)(a); disability – Disability Discrimination Act 1995, s 5(1)(a); gender – Sex Discrimination (Northern Ireland) Order 1976, art 3(1)(a); sexual orientation – Employment Equality (Sexual Orientation) Regulations (Northern Ireland) 2003, reg 3(1)(a); race – Race Relations (Northern Ireland) Order 1997, art 3(1)(a).
2   The issue of choosing the appropriate comparator received extensive treatment in *Shamoon v Chief Constable of the Royal Ulster Constabulary* [2003] UKHL 11, [2003] 2 All ER 26, [2003] ICR 337, [2003] IRLR 285.
3   Disability Discrimination Act 1995, s 5(1)(a).
4   *Clark v TDG Ltd (t/a Novacold)* [1999] 2 All ER 977, [1999] ICR 951, [1999] IRLR 318, CA, in which the employee was dismissed because he could no longer physically perform the work. The Court

concluded that the comparison was not with others who could not perform the work, but with others who could perform the main tasks of the job. see also *Cosgrove v Caesar and Howie (a firm)* [2001] IRLR 653, [2001] All ER (D) 118 (Jun), EAT.

5   Disability Discrimination Act 1995, s 3A(5), as inserted by the Disability Discrimination Act 1995 (Amendment) Regulations 2003, reg 4.

4.10   The courts have formulated a very simple test to act as a guide in establishing whether direct discrimination has taken place: 'Would the complainant have received the same treatment from the defendant but for his or her [ethnicity, religious belief, etc]?'[1] Motives or intentions of the alleged discriminator are irrelevant. For example, if an employer refuses to employ a person because he or she fears that that person will be harmed by other racist employees, that still amounts to unlawful direct discrimination. In *R v Commission for Racial Equality, ex p Westminster City Council*[2] the High Court found that discrimination occurred when the Council, under pressure from an all-white workforce, refused to employ a black man in its refuse collection section. [3]

1   *James v Eastleigh Borough Council* [1990] 2 AC 751, [1990] 2 All ER 607, HL.
2   [1984] ICR 770; affd [1985] ICR 827, CA.
3   For a Northern Ireland example of religious discrimination, see *Smyth v Croft Inns Ltd* [1995] NI 292.

4.11   Direct discrimination can never be justified, except under the Disability Discrimination Act 1995,[1] and then only if the less favourable treatment is material to the circumstances of the case and is substantial.[2] The issue of whether the discriminatory act can be justified on this test can be subject to analysis by a tribunal, but only as to whether the employer or service provider's view is reasonable.

1   Disability Discrimination Act 1995, s 5(1)(b).
2   Disability Discrimination Act 1995, s 5(4). *Jones v Post Office* [2001] EWCA Civ 558, [2001] IRLR 384, [2001] ICR 805.

4.12   Under race discrimination law, because discrimination occurs where, on racial grounds, a person treats another less favourably than he or she treats, or would treat, other persons,[1] the victim need not suffer less favourable treatment because of his or her own racial origins. A person who is dismissed because he or she refuses to comply with management's instructions to expel black youths from the workplace, for example, will be a victim of racial discrimination despite the fact that he is white.[2] This protection does not apply in respect of sex discrimination law, but may do so in sexual orientation discrimination and fair employment law because of the way direct discrimination is defined in the legislation that deals with those forms of discrimination.[3]

1   Race Relations (Northern Ireland) Order 1997, art 3(1)(a).
2   *Showboat Entertainment Centre Ltd v Owens* [1984] 1 All ER 836, [1984] 1 WLR 384, EAT.
3   Employment Equality (Sexual Orientation) Regulations (Northern Ireland) 2003, reg 3(1)(a); Fair Employment and Treatment (Northern Ireland) Order 1998, art 3(2)(a).

Indirect discrimination

4.13   Indirect discrimination has a more complex statutory definition and is designed to eliminate the adverse impact, on particular groups or persons, caused by the imposition of rules and requirements which, on the face of them, are neutral and do not appear to be discriminatory. The definition of indirect discrimination has been broadened, and made more complex, by the legislation implementing the recent European Union directives referred to earlier. Indirect discrimination is outlawed by all the anti-discrimination legislation referred to above,[1] with the exception of the Disability Discrimination Act 1995 which tackles the issue of adverse impact in a different manner.[2]

---

[1]   These definitions are not identical: Fair Employment and Treatment (Northern Ireland) Order 1998, art 3(2)(b); Sex Discrimination (Indirect Discrimination and Burden of Proof) Regulations (Northern Ireland) 2001, reg 2, amending Sex Discrimination (Northern Ireland) Order 1976, art 3; Race Relations (Northern Ireland) Order 1997, art 3(1)(b) and Race Relations Order (Amendment) Regulations (Northern Ireland) 2003, reg 4(1); Employment Equality (Sexual Orientation) Regulations (Northern Ireland) 2003, reg 3(1)(a).
[2]   See para 4.19 on 'reasonable adjustment'.

4.14   Indirect discrimination occurs where the claimant has been subject to a requirement or condition, provision, criterion or practice which is applied equally to all and thus appears to be neutral in its impact. However, its impact is discriminatory because it adversely impacts upon one group more than another. For example, a requirement that all employees be members of Glasgow Celtic supporters club would clearly have an adverse impact upon the ability of Protestants as fewer of them could meet this condition.

4.15   It might be said that there are two definitions of the term: that which was originally developed in UK domestic law, and that which now derives from European Union law.[1] Some statutes use the UK definition in combination with the EU law definition,[2] whereas others use the EU definition only.[3] The original UK definition assesses whether the proportion of persons of the same race, religion or political opinion as the complainant that can comply with the requirement or condition is considerably smaller than the proportion of persons who are not of that race, religion or political opinion. If the proportion is considerably smaller, then indirect discrimination has occurred, unless the alleged discriminator can show that the requirement or condition was justifiable.[4] In order to succeed with a claim the complainant must have suffered a detriment of some sort. The alleged discriminator may seek to mount a defence on the basis that the requirement or condition was justifiable.[5]

---

[1]   There is in fact a third type of indirect discrimination definition which is used in complaints of sex discrimination in the workplace, and is based on a European Council Directive 97/80/EC. It is similar to the UK domestic definition in that it is indirectly discriminatory to apply a provision, criterion or practice with which a considerably smaller proportion of women can comply, which is not justifiable and works to the detriment of the complainant. For convenience sake this chapter focuses on the two definitions discussed in the text.
[2]   Race Relations Order (Amendment) Regulations (Northern Ireland) 2003. The Fair Employment and Treatment (Northern Ireland) Order 1998 continues to use the UK definition of indirect discrimination until that statute is amended to conform to the Framework Employment Equality Directive.
[3]   Employment Equality (Sexual Orientation) Regulations (Northern Ireland) 2003.
[4]   The complainant must also, of course, have suffered a detriment in order to succeed with his or her claim.
[5]   For example, in *Panesar v Nestlé Co Ltd* [1980] ICR 144n, CA the requirement that employees of the respondent could not have beards if involved in manufacturing confectionery, adversely impacted on Sikhs but was considered to be a justifiable requirement for health and safety reasons.

4.16 It is clear that this is a complex concept that may be difficult to apply. One particular element of the definition worth highlighting relates to the requirement that one pool of people is 'considerably smaller' than the other. There is no statutory definition as to what constitutes a 'considerably smaller' proportion. The courts have taken the view that a 20% disparity between the proportions of the two pools that can comply may meet the requirements of being a considerable smaller proportion. Thus if 55% of the pool of women in question can comply with a particular requirement and 80% of the pool of men are able to comply with it, then the courts usually conclude that the pool of women who can comply is 'considerable smaller'. However, this is a rule of thumb rather than an absolute rule and nothing prevents the courts concluding that a smaller disparity between the two pools of comparators amounts to indirect discrimination, or that a wider disparity does not amount to discrimination.[1]

---

[1]   See *McCausland v Dungannon District Council* [1993] IRLR 583; *Greater Manchester Police Authority v Lea* [1990] IRLR 372 and *Staffordshire County Council v Black* [1995] IRLR 234.

4.17 In the EU law definition, the discrimination arises because the provision, criterion or practice puts persons of the same race or sexual orientation as the complainant, as well as the complainant, at a particular disadvantage when compared to other persons. The alleged discriminator can defend the case if he or she can show that in imposing this provision, criterion or practice, he or she is pursuing a legitimate aim in a proportionate manner. This will require the alleged discriminator to show that there is a genuine, supportable purpose for having the provision, criterion or practice and that the manner in which that purpose is being pursued is reasonable.

4.18 Indirect discrimination is unlawful under all the anti-discrimination statutes with the exception of the Disability Discrimination Act 1995. However, it employs a different mechanism to deal with requirements, practices or arrangements which have an adverse impact on disabled persons, thereby limiting their ability to access employment or avail of services. This alternative mechanism is discussed in the next paragraph.

Reasonable adjustments

4.19 The Disability Discrimination Act 1995 does not outlaw indirect discrimination against disabled persons, but employs a different concept to address matters which have an adverse impact on the ability of disabled persons to access employment, goods and services or further and higher educational facilities. Where an arrangement made by an employer or service provider, or any physical feature of the premises occupied by the employer or service provider, places the disabled person at a substantial disadvantage in comparison to persons who do not have impairments, then the employer or service provider must take reasonable steps to prevent the arrangement having that effect.[1] This is commonly referred to as the concept of 'reasonable adjustment' or the 'duty to make reasonable adjustments'. What is reasonable is determined by reference to a number of factors including the practicability of taking the step and the financial costs of making the adjustment.[2] Clearly what is reasonable will depend on the circumstances and regulations provide guidance as to how this duty might be met in particular situations.[3] Making the reasonable adjustment could involve a wide range of changes, provided that they are directed to facilitating access to the workplace or to the goods, facilities and services. It can include adjustments as simple as making documentation available in different formats for people with visual impairments, providing ramped access to buildings for people with mobility impairments or providing sign language interpreters for sign language users. The essence of the duty is to consider the nature of the physical or mental impairment and then to conceive of ways of altering the terms of the job, or the manner in which the goods, facilities or services are made available, to allow disabled persons to participate meaningfully.

[1] Disability Discrimination Act 1995, ss 6 and 21.
[2] Disability Discrimination Act 1995, s 6(4); see also s 21(5). Guidelines offer advice on the applicability of this provision: 'Code of Practice on Employment and Occupations – DDA 1995', Equality Commission for Northern Ireland, 1996.
[3] 'Code of Practice on Employment and Occupations – DDA 1995', Equality Commission for Northern Ireland, 1996, Section 5.

4.20 Lack of knowledge of the fact that a person is, or is likely to be disabled, will mean that the employer, or service provider, is not under a duty to make reasonable adjustments.[1] However, this does not mean that the he or she can simply ignore the possibility that a person has a disability, and they should make all reasonable inquiries to ascertain relevant knowledge. If the employer has knowledge of the person's disability, then whether or not the duty to make reasonable adjustments has been complied with, is an objective issue, regardless of the employer's, or service-provider's, knowledge, actual or imputed, as to the extent of that disability and the precise extent of its effects. If the employer, or service provider, is found to have breached his or her duty to make reasonable adjustments he or she is prima facie acting unlawfully subject to the defence that the discrimination is justified.[2]

[1] Disability Discrimination Act 1995, s 6(6) and *Wright v Governing Body of Bilton High School* [2002] ICR 1463, EAT.
[2] Disability Discrimination Act 1995, s 5(2)(b).

Justification

4.21 In determining the question of justification, it may be relevant for the employer, or service provider, to show that he or she made all reasonable inquiries of the disabled person and sought all necessary medical advice and carried out a reasonable assessment of that person's condition, but was nevertheless ignorant of the true extent of the disability and its effects, possibly due to lack of co-operation on the part of the employee, such that his or her failure to make a reasonable adjustment was justified.[1]

[1] *Wright v Governing Body of Bilton High School* [2002] ICR 1463, EAT.

Victimisation

4.22   Victimisation arises where a person is the subject of some less favourable treatment as a direct result of initiating his or her legal rights under anti-discrimination law. It occurs where the victim is treated less favourably merely because the discriminator believes, or suspects, that the victim has done, or intends to do, any of following:[1]

- bring proceedings under the appropriate legislation;
- given evidence or information in connection with a case brought by someone else, or made allegations that another person has acted in breach of the relevant statute;
- in any way exercised his or her rights under the appropriate statute.[2]

[1]   Fair Employment and Treatment (Northern Ireland) Order 1998, art 3(4); Race Relations (Northern Ireland) Order 1997, art 4; Disability Discrimination Act 1995, s 55.
[2]   However, the protection does not apply to bad faith allegations: Fair Employment and Treatment (Northern Ireland) Order 1998, art 3(6); Disability Discrimination Act 1995, s 55(4); Race Relations (Northern Ireland) Order 1997, art 4(3); Sex Discrimination (Northern Ireland) Order 1976, art 6(2); Employment Equality (Sexual Orientation) Regulations (Northern Ireland) 2003, reg 4(2).

4.23   However, the judiciary has narrowly construed the application of the victimisation provisions. As a result they will only avail a person if the action taken against him or her follows because it is known, or believed, that he or she has made use of the legislative protection from discrimination and not because of some other reason.[1]

[1]   *Kirby v Manpower Services Commission* [1980] 3 All ER 334, EAT and *Aziz v Trinity Street Taxis Ltd* [1988] 2 All ER 860, CA. In these cases the victimisation allegations failed because in the former the employee was considered to have suffered less favourable treatment because he disclosed confidential information, and in the latter the applicant was dismissed, his employers argued, not because he had commenced an action but because he had secretly taped conversations with other employees for the purpose of proving the racial discrimination against him. For a Northern Ireland example of victimisation see *Northern Health and Social Services Board v Fair Employment Commission*, Court of Appeal, 24 September 1994.

4.24   Victimisation, the courts have held, need not be a conscious act on the part of the alleged discriminator. The complainant will succeed once it can be shown that he or she was being victimised, whether consciously or unconsciously, by the respondent.[1]

[1]   *Nagarajan v London Regional Transport* [2000] 1 AC 501, [1999] 4 All ER 65, HL..

Harassment

4.25   None of the anti-discrimination statutes originally outlawed harassment but the courts and tribunals had, in various cases, determined that harassment came within the definition of direct discrimination.[1] The European Directives referred to earlier[2] – the REOD and FEED – require a statutory prohibition on harassment and as a result appropriate legislative amendments have been made. Harassment is now defined in the various legislative instruments as occurring when 'unwanted conduct' takes places which 'has the purpose or effect of violating the person's dignity or creating an intimidating, hostile, degrading, humiliating or offensive environment for the person.'[3] Conduct shall only be regarded as amounting to harassment if it might reasonably be regarded as having that effect, although in making this assessment the court or tribunal must have particular regard to the perception of the harassed person. This means that the test of whether a person has been harassed is largely an objective one but due regard is given to the sensitivities of the victim.

[1] See, for example, *Strathclyde Regional Council v Porcelli* [1986] IRLR 134, Ct of Sess.
[2] See para 4.1.
[3] Disability Discrimination Act 1995 (Amendment) Regulations 2003, reg 4; the Employment Equality (Sexual Orientation) Regulations (Northern Ireland) 2003, reg 5; the Race Relations Order (Amendment) Regulations (Northern Ireland) 2003, reg 5. The appropriate amendments to fair employment and sex discrimination law have yet to be made.

Aiding others in discriminating

4.26 It is also discrimination for someone to 'knowingly aid' another in the commission of an unlawful act under the legislation.[1] In a number of recent cases the House of Lords has had to consider the application of this concept. In *Anyanwu v South Bank Student Union*[2] the issue of the proper interpretation of the equivalent section in the Race Relations Act 1976[3] arose. The complainants in this case were officers of the student union who were expelled from South Bank University. This had the effect of requiring their contracts of employment with the student union to be terminated. The complainants alleged that the student union had subjected them to racial discrimination and that the University had 'knowingly aided' them in this. The House of Lords considered that the University's actions were capable of infringing the section in so much as there was an arguable case that the University had 'knowingly aided' the alleged discrimination, and remitted that matter back to the tribunal for a re-hearing. In their Lordships' view there was no technical meaning to the phrase 'knowingly aids', and it rejected the Court of Appeal's view that the party aiding the discriminator needed to be a 'prime mover' in order to attract liability. The tribunal should, in its view, give an ordinary view to the meaning.

[1] Fair Employment and Treatment (Northern Ireland) Order 1998, art 35(1)(a); Disability Discrimination Act 1995, s 57; Sex Discrimination (Northern Ireland) Order 1976, art 43(1); Employment Equality (Sexual Orientation) Regulations (Northern Ireland) 2003, reg 25(1); Race Relations (Northern Ireland) Order 1997, art 33.
[2] [2001] UKHL 14, [2001] 2 All ER 353, [2001] 1 WLR 638.
[3] Section 33(1).

Employers' liability and defence

4.27 An employer is liable for the acts of his or her employees, whether or not carried out with the employer's knowledge of approval.[1] In any discrimination proceedings it will be a defence for an employer if he or she can demonstrate that all steps as were 'reasonably practicable' to prevent the discriminatory acts in question taking place were in fact taken.[2] An employer will therefore have staff trained in discrimination matters, and develop anti-discrimination policies and procedures to deal with any allegations of discriminatory conduct, partly to demonstrate that he or she has done all that is reasonably practicable in the circumstances to prevent the commission of discriminatory acts.

1   Race Relations (Northern Ireland) Order 1997, art 32(1); Sex Discrimination (Northern Ireland) Order 1976, art 42(1); Fair Employment and Treatment (Northern Ireland) Order 1998, art 36(1); Employment Equality (Sexual Orientation) Regulations (Northern Ireland) 2003, reg 24(1).

2   Religion and politics – Fair Employment and Treatment (Northern Ireland) Order 1998, art 36(4); disability – Disability Discrimination Act 1995, s 58(5); gender – Sex Discrimination (Northern Ireland) Order 1976, art 42(3); sexual orientation – Employment Equality (Sexual Orientation) Regulations (Northern Ireland) 2003, reg 24(3); race – Race Relations (Northern Ireland) Order 1997, art 32(5).

Protected persons

4.28   The persons protected from discrimination are defined in the relevant enactments but in some cases the courts have had to interpret these legislative definitions to determine whether certain persons fall within the scope of definition. In respect of gender discrimination or religious discrimination this issue does not tend to present a difficulty but the application of race discrimination, political discrimination and disability discrimination legislation has given rise to problems.

Disabled persons with disabilities

4.29   A disabled person[1] for the purposes of the Disability Discrimination Act 1995 is defined as a person with a physical or mental impairment,[2] which has a substantial and long-term effect on his or her ability to carry out normal day-to-day activities.[3] The protection of the legislation extends to those who had such a disability in the past, but no longer do.[4] Guidance issued under the Act[5] provides further detail on how one establishes whether a particular impairment meets this definition, but at a minimum the impairment must have lasted, or be likely to last, for at least 12 months.[6] An impairment affects the normal day-to-day activities if it affects matters such as mobility, memory or concentration, perception of risk of physical danger and physical co-ordination, amongst others.[7]

1   The Disability Discrimination Act 1995 deals with discrimination against disabled persons only. A non-disabled person cannot avail of the 1995 Act to claim that, for example, a disabled person was preferred to them in filling a job vacancy.

2   The onus is on the complainant to adduce medical evidence to show that he or she has a physical or medical impairment: *McNicol v Balfour Beatty Rail Maintenance Ltd* [2002] EWCA Civ 1074, [2002] ICR 1498, [2002] IRLR 711.

3   Disability Discrimination Act 1995, s 1. As regards an impairment having a substantial impact see *Kirton v Tetrosyl Ltd* [2002] IRLR 840, EAT.

4   Disability Discrimination Act 1995, s 2.

5   Disability Discrimination Act 1995, s 3(1).

6   Schedule 1, para 2(1). Recurring impairments also meet this definition, even if at the time of the alleged discrimination the impairment is not actually affecting the person's performance of normal day-to-day activities: para 2(2). Progressive conditions, eg multiple sclerosis, are also covered in the same circumstances if they will significantly impair someone in the future.

[7] Disability Discrimination Act 1995, Sch 1, para 4. Severe disfigurement is automatically covered, Sch 1, para 3(1).

Gender discrimination

4.30 The Sex Discrimination (Northern Ireland) Order 1976 provides protection for men and women and for married persons, but unmarried persons may not avail of the legislative protection where they suspect that married persons have been preferred to single persons.[1] Case law has determined that pregnant women are protected by gender discrimination law and that there is no necessity to compare a pregnant woman with a man who has endured a considerable illness to test whether the decision made in respect of the woman was discriminatory.[2]

[1] The protection of married persons only applies in the field of employment.
[2] *Webb v EMO Air Cargo Ltd* [1992] 4 All ER 929. For a Northern Ireland example of the application of *Webb*, see *Stephenson v FA Wellworth & Co Ltd* [1997] NI 93, NI CA, Carswell LCJ.

4.31 The prohibition of discrimination on gender grounds does not, however, prohibit discrimination on the basis of sexual orientation. In *Pearce v Governing Body of Mayfield Secondary School*[1] the courts confirmed this proposition when it decided that the use of homophobic epithets directed at a lesbian school teacher did not constitute sexual harassment because they were motivated by discrimination on the basis of her sexual orientation and not of her gender. However, the enactment of anti-sexual orientation discrimination legislation has filled this gap in the law to some extent.[2] Further, by virtue of judicial interpretation, sex discrimination legislation does provide protection for transsexuals.[3]

[1] [2003] UKHL 34, [2004] 1 All ER 339, [2003] ICR 937.
[2] See para 4.35.
[3] In *A v Chief Constable of West Yorkshire Police* [2002] EWCA Civ 1584, [2003] 1 All ER 255 a male to female transsexual applied to joint the police force but was rejected on the basis that she would be unable to carry out lawful body searches of female suspects. The Court of Appeal considered that she was entitled to be treated as a female, except if there were factors of public interest to weigh against the interests of the individual in obtaining legal recognition of her gender re-assignment.

Race discrimination

4.32 The 1997 Order outlaws discrimination on the grounds of colour, race, nationality ethnic or national origins[1] and specifically includes Irish Travellers within the definition of protected racial groups.[2] The prohibition of discrimination on the grounds of national origin also means that less favourable treatment of English, Welsh and Scottish persons can amount to racial discrimination.[3] Whether a group qualifies as being an ethnic group capable of benefiting from the protection afforded by the legislation depends on whether they meet the criteria for an ethnic group set out by the House of Lords in *Mandla v Dowell Lee*.[4] These were:

1   a long-shared history, of which the group is conscious as distinguishing it from other groups, and the memory of which it keeps alive;

2   a cultural tradition of its own, including family and social customs and
     manners, often but not necessarily associated with religious observance.

[1]   Race Relations (Northern Ireland) Order 1997, art 5(1). The scope of application of the Race Relations
     Order (Amendment) Regulations (Northern Ireland) 2003 is slightly narrower, however, as it only deals
     with race, ethnic or national origins, reg 4(1).
[2]   Race Relations (Northern Ireland) Order 1997, art 5(3).
[3]   *Griffiths v Reading University Students' Unions* (1997) EOC Discrimination Law Digest, Spring, p 3;
     BBC Scotland v Souster [2001] IRLR 150. Jews are considered an ethnic group: *Seide v Gillette
     Industries* [1980] IRLR 42, EAT.
[4]   [1983] 2 AC 548, [1983] 1 All ER 1062, HL.

4.33   There is also a range of non-essential criteria. Compliance with these is not
crucial, but it does serve to reinforce the view that the group is an ethnic one. They
are:

1   a common geographical origin or descent from a small number of common
     ancestors;
2   a common language not necessarily peculiar to that group;
3   a common literature peculiar to that group;
4   a common religion, different from that of neighbouring groups or from the
     general community surrounding it;
5   being a minority, or being an oppressed, or dominant group, within a larger
     community.

In *Mandla v Dowell Lee*, Sikhs were considered to be an ethnic group and the
requirement that a school cap be worn as part of the school uniform was therefore
held to be indirectly discriminatory, as being a requirement with which a considerably
smaller proportion of Sikhs could comply.[1]

[1]   Jews have also been considered an ethnic group, *Seide v Gillette Industries Ltd* (1980), as have English
     Romanies, *Commission for Racial Equality v Dutton* [1989] QB 783, CA, and Welsh people, *Griffiths v
     Reading University Students' Union* (1997). In *BBC Scotland v Souster* [2001] IRLR 150 it was held that
     English and Scottish people could benefit from protection of the Race Relations Act 1976.

Sectarian and political discrimination

4.34   The prohibition on discrimination of the basis of one's political opinion is not
confined to matters relating to the politics of Northern Ireland. Less favourable
treatment on the basis of one's political opinions about other matters will attract the
protection of the Fair Employment and Treatment (Northern Ireland) Order 1998.[1]
Similarly, the Order can afford protection against sectarian discrimination no matter
what the religious persuasion of the complainant.[2] However, the Order specifically
excludes teachers from the protection of the legislation.[3]

[1]   *McKay v NIPSA* [1994] NI 103, NI CA. However, it does not cover alleged discrimination on the basis
     of different approaches that individuals might have to combating racism: *Gill v NICEM* [2001] NIJB
     299.
[2]   Fair Employment and Treatment (Northern Ireland) Order 1998 does not apply however to employ-
     ment in a private household or to clergyman: art 70(1).
[3]   Fair Employment and Treatment (Northern Ireland) 1998, art 71.

Sexual orientation

4.35   The extension of anti-discrimination law, by the Employment Equality
(Sexual Orientation) Regulations (Northern Ireland) 2003, to include protection
from discrimination on the grounds of sexual orientation is a very recent development with which the Government was required to proceed in order to implement the
terms of the Framework Employment Equality Directive. The legislation applies to
heterosexual, homosexual and bisexual people, but deals only with discrimination in
the workplace, and in that respect it is narrower in its scope than all other
anti-discrimination statutes.

Age discrimination

4.36   While, at present, there is no legislation dealing with discrimination on the
grounds of a person's age, the UK is required to enact such legislation before the end
of 2006, in order to implement the terms of the Framework Employment Equality
Directive. The Equality Unit of the Office of the First Minister and Deputy First
Minister has indicated that it will carry out a consultation process on this issue in
2004.

Particular aspects of anti-discrimination law

4.37   There are a number of features of the anti-discrimination regime that are
worthy of particular attention either because they are unique to Northern Ireland or
because they have a significant effect on the operation of the legislative enactments.

'Genuine occupational qualification'

4.38   Anti-discrimination law does not apply to situations of employment where it is
an essential element of a job that it be done by a person having particular characteristics, whether that means the person must be of a particular religious persuasion,[1] or
of a particular ethnic background[2] or of a particular gender[3] or sexual orientation.[4]
This exemption from the application of equality legislation is commonly referred to
as the genuine occupational qualification (GOQ) requirement, although it is worded
differently in each statute. For example, under the Race Relations Order the
exemption is only available where a person of a particular ethnic persuasion is needed
to perform in a drama, work in an ethnically-themed restaurant, pose as a photo-
graphic or artistic model or provide personal care services to a member of an ethnic
community.[5] Under the Sex Discrimination Order, it is only available in prescribed
circumstances, such as the delivery of care services of an intimate nature or for
authenticity in dramatic performances, for example.[6] The GOQ exemption in sexual
orientation discrimination law is, in contrast, more broadly framed. It allows for an
exemption where the employment is with a religious group. However, it also offers a

more generally worded exemption that 'having regard to the nature of the employment or the context in which it is carried out being of a particular sexual orientation is a genuine and determining occupational requirement.'[7]

1   Fair Employment and Treatment (Northern Ireland) Order 1998, art 70(3), See also art 70(1).
2   Race Relations (Northern Ireland) Order 1997, art 8.
3   Sex Discrimination (Northern Ireland) Order 1976, art 10.
4   Employment Equality (Sexual Orientation) Regulations (Northern Ireland) 2003, reg 8.
5   These specified exemptions appear to be predicated on some stereotypical assumptions about person of minority ethnic origin and may well disappear in the new Single Equality Act.
6   Sex Discrimination (Northern Ireland) Order 1975, art 10(2).
7   Employment Equality (Sexual Orientation) Regulations (Northern Ireland) 2003, reg 8(2).

4.39   The burden of proof lies on the employer to show that the GOQ exemption applies in a particular case. This concept is not found in the Disability Discrimination Act 1995, nor is it possible to stipulate that a person must be of a particular political persuasion to perform a certain task.

Affirmative action

4.40   'Affirmative action' is the phrase used to describe measures validly and lawfully taken under the Fair Employment and Treatment (Northern Ireland) Order 1998 to attempt to increase the numbers of under-represented Catholics or Protestants in a particular setting. The 1998 Order defines affirmative action as 'action designed to secure fair participation in employment of Roman Catholics and Protestants' and includes the adoption of practices encouraging such participation and the modification of barriers.[1] These measures are specifically provided for in the 1998 Order. They do not mean that members of the under-represented group are automatically entitled to be preferred for any vacancy. The measures in question are as follows: (1) encouraging applications from the under-represented community;[2] (2) selecting persons for jobs from amongst those who are unemployed; [3] and (3) providing training for a specific religious denomination if there is an under-representation of that religious community in the workplace generally or in a category of employment.[4]

1   Fair Employment and Treatment (Northern Ireland) Order 1998, art 4.
2   Fair Employment and Treatment (Northern Ireland) Order 1998, art 74.
3   Fair Employment and Treatment (Northern Ireland) Order 1998, art 75.
4   Fair Employment and Treatment (Northern Ireland) Order 1998, art 76.

4.41   Note that 'affirmative action' applies only to religious or political discrimination and not to other forms of discrimination, and that its scope is very narrow. 'Affirmative action' is often referred to as 'positive action'[1] and is sometimes erroneously referred to as ' positive ' or 'reverse' discrimination. 'Positive discrimination' means, in the context of employment, that persons of the under-represented group are positively preferred over other equally qualified applicants in order to boost the numbers of the under-represented group in that workplace. It is generally unlawful to engage in positive discrimination.

[1]   See, for example, Employment Equality (Sexual Orientation) Regulations (Northern Ireland) 2003, reg 29.

4.42   While 'affirmative action' strictly speaking only applies to fair employment law, there are measures in the other statutes that allow for special measures to be taken to increase the chances of achieving more representative workplaces.[1]

[1]   Race Relations (Northern Ireland) Order 1997, arts 35, 36 and 37; Sex Discrimination (Northern Ireland) 1976, art 48; Employment Equality (Sexual Orientation) Regulations (Northern Ireland) 2003, reg 29. The last mentioned is the most broadly worded of these provisions.

Equality of opportunity

4.43   One might imagine that because the concept of 'equality of opportunity' is so central to equality law that it features in all the legislative enactments and has been well-defined. However, this is not the case. It features in the Fair Employment and Treatment Order 1998 only and is there defined as meaning that a person of one religion has the same opportunity as persons of another religion in respect of employment matters, such as recruitment, retention and promotion.[1] It also features in the section 75 statutory duty, although it is not defined there.[2]

[1]   Fair Employment and Treatment (Northern Ireland) Order 1998, art 5.
[2]   See para 4.75.

Enforcement I

4.44   Enforcement of anti-discrimination law is effected in the relevant tribunals and courts, and by the Equality Commission for Northern Ireland. These two types of enforcement are distinguished by the fact that enforcement in tribunals and courts is instigated by individuals and focuses on particular complaints made by those individuals. Enforcement by the Equality Commission, on the other hand, focuses more generally on the policies and procedures adopted in particular industries, sectors of society, or companies, in order to combat discrimination more generally.

Tribunals and courts

4.45   Individuals must apply to the Industrial Tribunal where they have complaints of racial, gender or disability discrimination in respect of employment matters, while the Fair Employment Tribunal hears complaints of religious or political discrimination in the workplace.[1] The time limits within which one must initiate a complaint are quite short. Complaints to the Industrial Tribunal about employment related discrimination must generally be made within three months of the date of the act complained of.[2]

[1]   The resolution of complaints by conciliation is provided for in a number of the statutes. Such conciliation is carried out by the Labour Relations Agency but its jurisdiction is dependent on the consent of both parties or there being a reasonable chance of success: Fair Employment and Treatment

(Northern Ireland) Order 1998, art 88. Under the Equality (Disability, etc) (Northern Ireland) Order 2000, art 12, the Commission can make arrangements for providing conciliation in disability discrimination cases but the legislation forbids Commission staff members from being involved in this conciliation, thus preventing 'in-house' conciliation within the Commission. Note that CAFCASS does not operate in Northern Ireland.

2   Sex Discrimination (Northern Ireland) Order 1976, art 76(1); Fair Employment and Treatment (Northern Ireland) Order 1998, art 46(1); Race Relations (Northern Ireland) Order 1997, art 65; Employment Equality (Sexual Orientation) Regulations (Northern Ireland) 2003, reg 41; Disability Discrimination Act 1995, Sch 3, Pt 1, para 3.

4.46   Complaints about discrimination in the provision of goods, facilities and services or in the selling and letting or premises or in respect of education are dealt with by the county courts. However, where the complaint is about education and the legislation outlaws discrimination in the sector, then the complaint must first be made to the Department of Education, and it has two months to deal with the complaint before court proceedings can commence.[1] The time limit for initiating litigation in the county court in regard to other forms of discrimination is six months.[2] These time limits may be extended if the tribunal (or the court, as appropriate) thinks it just and equitable to do so.[3]

1   Fair Employment and Treatment (Northern Ireland) Order 1998, art 40(5).
2   Fair Employment and Treatment (Northern Ireland) Order 1998, art 46(2); Race Relations (Northern Ireland) Order 1997, art 65(2); Disability Discrimination Act 1995, Sch 3, Pt 1, para 6; Sex Discrimination (Northern Ireland) Order 1976, art 76(2).
3   Fair Employment and Treatment (Northern Ireland) Order 1998, art 46(5); Race Relations (Northern Ireland) Order 1997, art 65(7); Employment Equality (Sexual Orientation) Regulations (Northern Ireland) 2003, reg 41(3); Disability Discrimination Act 1995, Sch 3, Pt 1, paras 3(2) and 6(3). See for example *Fennell v University of Ulster* (21 May 1999, unreported), NI CA, McCollum LJ, transcript on Lexis.

4.47   It has been argued that a specialist anti-discrimination tribunal should be established to hear all complaints of discrimination, irrespective of the nature of the complaint and the sphere of activity to which it relates.[1] This issue may be ventilated further in the debates about the content of the Single Equality Bill.

1   Submission to initial consultation by Office of First Minister and Deputy First Minister on a Single Equality Bill for Northern Ireland, Committee on the Administration of Justice, Belfast, 2001.

4.48   An appeal can be made by way of case stated to the Court of Appeal, from decisions of the Industrial Tribunal[1] and Fair Employment Tribunal,[2] and from decisions of the county court.[3]

1   Industrial Tribunals (Northern Ireland) Order 1996, art 22 and Rules of the Supreme Court (Northern Ireland) 1980, Order 61.
2   Fair Employment and Treatment (Northern Ireland) Order 1998, art 90.
3   County Courts (Northern Ireland) Order 1980, art 61.

Remedies

4.49   The remedies available from a tribunal, where the respondent has discriminated against the complainant, are as follows:[1]

(1)   a declaration as to the parties' legal rights and entitlements;

(2)   an award of compensation, including damages for injury to feelings;[2] or

(3)   a recommendation that the respondent take particular action to reduce the effect of the discrimination either against the complainant or against others more generally.

An employer's liability in respect of his or her employees and the possibility of defending such an action are discussed elsewhere.[3]

[1]   Fair Employment and Treatment (Northern Ireland) Order 1998, art 39; Race Relations (Northern Ireland) Order 1997, art 53(1); Disability Discrimination Act 1995. s 8(2), (to be renumbered s 17A by the 2003 Regulations); Sex Discrimination (Northern Ireland) Order 1976, art 65(1); Employment Equality (Sexual Orientation) Regulations (Northern Ireland) 2003, reg 36(1).

[2]   However, no compensation award may be made for indirect discrimination if there was no intention to discriminate: Fair Employment and Treatment (Northern Ireland) Order 1998, art 40(5); Race Relations (Northern Ireland) Order 1997, art 54(3); Sex Discrimination (Northern Ireland) Order 1976, art 66(3); Sex Discrimination (Northern Ireland) Order 1976, art 65(1B) and the Employment Equality (Sexual Orientation) Regulations (Northern Ireland) 2003, reg 36(2) does allow compensation in these circumstances, in employment cases, but only where the tribunal intended availing of the other two remedial possibilities as well. There is no limit on the compensation that can be awarded by an Industrial or Fair Employment Tribunal.

[3]   See para 4.27.

4.50   However, where the action is taken in respect of non-employment matters the only remedy usually available is that of damages, although the normal jurisdiction of he county court is replaced by the unlimited jurisdiction of the High Court[1] (see Disability Discrimination Act 1995 for example).

[1]   Fair Employment and Treatment (Northern Ireland) Order 1998, art 40; Race Relations (Northern Ireland) Order 1997, art 54(2); Sex Discrimination (Northern Ireland) Order 1976, art 66(2).

Conduct of the hearing and the burden of proof

4.51   Prior to the hearing of the matter, the complainant may address written questions to the respondent in order to obtain information about the matter to be tried, although the respondent is not obligated to provide answers. Any equivocation in the answers, or any deliberate refusal to answer, entitles the court or the tribunal to draw adverse inferences.[1]

[1]   Fair Employment and Treatment (Northern Ireland) Order 1998, art 44(2); Race Relations (Northern Ireland) 1997, art 63(2); Disability Discrimination Act 1995, s 56(3); Employment Equality (Sexual Orientation) Regulations (Northern Ireland) 2003; Sex Discrimination (Northern Ireland) Order 1976, art 74(2).

4.52   As discussed in chapter 3, the standard of proof in civil law matters is proof on the balance of probabilities and the onus of discharging that burden lies on the applicant.[1] However, in anti-discrimination matters, in certain circumstances, the burden of proof will shift to the respondent. This situation has also been brought about by European Union law.

[1]   See para 3.12.

4.53   Where the complainant proves facts which could allow the tribunal to conclude that he or she had been the victim of discrimination, in the absence of an adequate explanation from the respondent, the tribunal must uphold the complaint unless the respondent proves that he or she did not commit or is to be treated as having committed the discriminatory act.[1] This means that where the complainant mounts a credible case of discrimination the onus effectively shifts to the respondent to defend the case and offer an explanation for his or her actions. If the respondent does not do this, then the complainant will succeed.

[1]   Disability Discrimination Act 1995 (Amendment) Regulations 2003, reg 9; Sex Discrimination (Indirect Discrimination and Burden of Proof) Regulations (Northern Ireland) 2001, regs 4 and 5; Race Relations Order (Amendment) Regulations (Northern Ireland) 2003, regs 42 and 43.

Cost of pursuing a case

4.54   The usual rule as regards legal costs is that 'costs follow the event', that is to say that the losing party pays both its own costs, plus the costs of the other party. This rule applies in county court proceedings under the various enactments but not, however, to proceedings in the Industrial or Fair Employment Tribunals. Furthermore, legal aid is not available for actions either in the tribunals or in the county court. The Equality Commission may support a complainant's case financially but this will depend on his or her case meeting criteria devised by the Commission. The Commission is permitted to assist complainants[1] on the grounds that the case raises a question of principle, or that it is unreasonable, because of the complexity of the case or for other reasons to expect the applicant to proceed unaided. However, because of budgetary constraints the Commission is likely to only support a case where it meets its detailed criteria for support which elaborate on these general statutory criteria.[2]

[1]   Equality (Disability etc) (Northern Ireland) Order 2000, art 9(2); Fair Employment and Treatment (Northern Ireland) Order 1998, art 45; Race Relations (Northern Ireland) Order 1997, art 64; Sex Discrimination (Northern Ireland) Order 1976, art 75.
[2]   'Enforcement Policy for the Provision of Advice and Assistance', Equality Commission for Northern Ireland, December 2002.

Enforcement II

4.55   This section discusses the enforcement powers of the Equality Commission and the various ways in which it is empowered to implement equality legislation. These enforcement powers seek to deal with systemic inequalities, by altering work practices and occupational cultures for example, rather than provide a remedy for individuals.

Equality Commission for Northern Ireland

4.56   The Equality Commission for Northern Ireland, as was outlined above, also has a role to play in implementing Northern Ireland equality law. The Northern Ireland Act 1998 sets out its general statutory duties,[1] but at present the details of its powers are found in the various statutes that govern this area of Northern Ireland law. The gradual development of anti-discrimination law has resulted in the Commission acquiring different powers to deal with different types of discrimination, with those powers being scattered throughout the various enactments. Presumably the enactment of the Single Equality Act will be an opportunity to harmonise the Commission's powers to the highest standard possible to provide it with common powers to combat the various types of discrimination. The Equality Commission has pointed out that there is a non-regression clause in the European Directives mentioned earlier:

> 'whereby implementation of the Directives cannot be used to lower pre-existing national standards. In order to achieve universality across the grounds protected, the 'best standard' within existing regimes would have to be applied across all grounds.'[2]

[1] Northern Ireland Act 1998, s 74.
[2] ECNI, ' Response to the Odysseus Trust/Lord Lester of Herne Hill Draft Equality Bill', January 2003, p 3.

4.57 The Equality Commission was established by the Northern Ireland Act 1998, and it replaces a number of bodies that previously exercised statutory functions in this area. These included the Fair Employment Commission, the Commission for Racial Equality for Northern Ireland, the Equal Opportunities Commission (which dealt with gender discrimination), and the Northern Ireland Disability Council (which had a limited role in the implementation of the Disability Discrimination Act 1995). The Equality Commission is the only unitary equality body in the UK. In Great Britain the task of tackling discrimination is variously undertaken by the Commission for Racial Equality, the Equal Opportunities Commission and the Disability Rights Commission, although there are suggestions that a combined Human Rights and Equality Commission will be developed some time in the future.[1]

[1] See Joint Committee on Human Rights, 6th Report (2002–03) HL Paper 67-I, HC 489-I, paras 189 ff.

Powers

4.58 The Commission's powers, broadly stated, allow it to investigate alleged unlawful discrimination in a particular workplace or industry and to engage in enforcement action where it finds unlawful discrimination to have taken place. These enforcement actions can include issuing enforcement notices, non-discrimination notices, securing undertakings not to discriminate or otherwise punishing persistent discrimination.[1]

[1] See paras 4.62, 4.68 and 4.70. The Commission also has powers in respect of discriminatory adverts, which for reasons of space cannot be dealt with here: Fair Employment and Treatment (Northern Ireland) Order 1998, art 34; Disability Discrimination Act 1995, s 11; Race Relations (Northern Ireland) Order 1997, art 29, and the Sex Discrimination (Northern Ireland) Order 1976, art 39.

Investigations

4.59 As might be expected, the Commission has formidable investigation powers. However, its precise investigatory powers depend on the category of discrimination that is the subject of the investigation.

Under the Fair Employment and Treatment (Northern Ireland) Order 1998, the Commission's main investigatory power is the power to investigate practices to determine what action is necessary to promote equality of opportunity.[1] The conduct of these article 11 investigations is governed by Sch 2 to the 1998 Order. In conducting those forms of investigation the Commission must give notice in writing of the investigation to the person or persons involved and also provide written details of the scope and purpose of the investigation.[2] All persons who are subject to investigation are entitled to comment on matters under investigation and to furnish evidence.[3] The investigation is conducted in private[4] and the Commission has powers to compel compliance with the investigation.[5]

[1]   Fair Employment and Treatment (Northern Ireland) Order 1998, art 11.
[2]   Fair Employment and Treatment (Northern Ireland) Order 1998, Sch 2, para 2.
[3]   Fair Employment and Treatment (Northern Ireland) Order 1998, Sch 2, para 3.
[4]   Fair Employment and Treatment (Northern Ireland) Order 1998, Sch 2, para 4.
[5]   Fair Employment and Treatment (Northern Ireland) Order 1998, Sch 2, para 7.

4.60   The Commission's equivalent investigatory powers in respect of disability, race and sex discrimination are referred to as 'formal investigations'.[1] These investigations can be for any purpose related to the fulfilling of the Commissioner's general statutory duties to combat discrimination. Before commencing a formal investigation the Commission must establish the terms of reference of any such investigation, and issue and serve a notice to the person being investigated informing them of the investigation and to allow them the opportunity of making oral or written submissions.[2]

[1]   Equality (Disability etc) (Northern Ireland) Order 2000, art 5. The detail of how they must be conducted is included in Sch1, Pt 1; Sex Discrimination (Northern Ireland) Order 1976, art 57; Race Relations (Northern Ireland) 1997, art 46.
[2]   Sex Discrimination (Northern Ireland) Order 1976, art 58; Race Relations (Northern Ireland) 1997, art 47; Equality (Disability etc) (Northern Ireland) Order 2000, Sch 1, Pt 1, para 3(4).

4.61   Under disability discrimination law, the necessary conditions before such investigations can be allowed are that the Commission considers that an unlawful act has taken place, or that there has been a failure to comply with a non-discrimination notice or a failure to comply with an undertaking made in an agreement.[1] No such conditions appear on the face of the sex or race discrimination legislation, but as a result of case law a number of conditions also apply before a formal investigation can be conducted under those statutes.[2] This case law requires the Commission to conduct what is known as a 'preliminary inquiry' before launching the formal investigation. It allows the entity which is to be the subject of the investigation to be given reasons why the investigation should proceed and to allow it to present arguments that there is no necessity for the investigation if it wishes.[3]

[1]   Equality (Disability etc) (Northern Ireland) Order 2000, Sch 1, Pt 1, para 2(1),
[2]   *Hillingdon London Borough Council v Commission for Racial Equality* [1982] AC 779, HL and in *Re Prestige Group plc* [1984] IRLR 166, HL.
[3]   For a Northern Ireland example of the application of the principles in the *Hillingdon* and *Prestige* cases (see previous footnote) see *Re Belfast Telegraph's Application* (29 November 2001, unreported), Coghlin J, transcript on Lexis, in which the newspaper unsuccessfully challenged the commencement of a formal investigation under sex discrimination law.

Undertakings and agreements in lieu of action

4.62 Undertakings and agreements are essentially methods of settling cases with the Commission where it uncovers discriminatory practices in the course of one of its investigations, or in some other way. Undertakings are commitments made to the Commission whereby the party making the undertaking agrees to act in a certain manner in the future, normally to promote equality of opportunity.

4.63 Under the Fair Employment and Treatment (Northern Ireland) Order 1998 there are two types of such undertaking in respect of employment matters; one that may be made following an Article 11 investigation[1] into practices adopted or used by an employer[2] or a second type, a 'voluntary undertaking', which can be made at any other time.[3] If a party refuses to make an undertaking when directed to do so by the Commission, the Commission can issue a Notice.[4] Such a Notice can also be served if the party does not comply with the undertaking, irrespective of whether the undertaking was made voluntarily or not. Alternatively the undertaking can be enforced by an application by the Commission to the Fair Employment Tribunal.[5] A failure to comply with the Tribunal's ruling may result in the President of the Tribunal certifying the failure to comply to the High Court or imposing a fine of £40,000.

[1] See para 4.59.
[2] Fair Employment and Treatment (Northern Ireland) Order 1998, art 12.
[3] This can include situations where evidence emerges in the course of proceedings before a court or tribunal: art 13(1)(b).
[4] Fair Employment and Treatment (Northern Ireland) Order 1998, art 14(1). A right of appeal against this notice may be made to the Fair Employment Tribunal: art 15.
[5] Fair Employment and Treatment (Northern Ireland) Order 1998, art 16.

4.64 Undertakings may also be sought by the Commission in respect of sectarian or political discrimination in the further and higher education sector, the selling or letting or premises and the availability of services.[1]

[1] Fair Employment and Treatment (Northern Ireland) Order 1998, art 43.

4.65 Undertakings also feature in the Commission's powers to issue a 'notice about goals and timetables'.[1] This type of notice is used to set targets for achieving 'progress that, in the opinion of the Commission, can reasonably be expected to be made towards fair participation'[2] in the entity concerned. Where undertakings are in existence the Commission can issue such a notice, which outlines the period within which the person to whom it is addressed should make progress in establishing equality of opportunity between Catholics and Protestants in the work place.

[1] Fair Employment and Treatment (Northern Ireland) Order 1998, art 60.
[2] Fair Employment and Treatment (Northern Ireland) Order 1998, art 60(2).

4.66 Undertakings also feature in the Race Relations Order,[1] but not in the Sex Discrimination Order. Those undertakings are available where the Commission is satisfied that a person has committed a discriminatory act and they can commit the person subject to them to change certain practices, or not to carry out certain acts.

These undertakings can deal with discrimination in the provision of goods facilities and services, selling and letting premises, and the education sector.

[1]   Race Relations (Northern Ireland) Order 1997, art 62.

4.67 'Agreements in lieu of action' are found in disability discrimination law and are similar to undertakings but the main difference is the Commission is also a party to such agreements. In essence the Commission undertakes not to initiate enforcement action if the person or entity agrees to perform certain agreed actions.[1] They are enforced by way of an application to the county court.[2]

[1]   Equality (Disability etc) (Northern Ireland) Order 2000, art 7.
[2]   Equality (Disability etc) (Northern Ireland) Order 2000, art 7(8).

Non-discrimination notices

4.68 These notices can be issued by the Commission to signify that it considers that the recipient has been involved in discrimination in the past and they direct that person or entity not to perform such discriminatory acts again.[1] Such notices can only be served if, in the course of a formal investigation into racial, disability or gender discrimination, the Commission considers that an unlawful act has been performed. (Non-discrimination notices are not available under the Fair Employment and Treatment (Northern Ireland) Order 1998 or the Employment Equality (Sexual Orientation) Regulations (Northern Ireland) 2003). Before issuing such a notice the Commission must give notice to the party to be affected by it that it intends to issue the notice, giving that person an opportunity to reply.

[1]   Race Relations (Northern Ireland) Order 1997, art 55; Equality (Disability etc) (Northern Ireland) Order 2000, art 6; Sex Discrimination (Northern Ireland) Order 1976, art 67.

4.69 A non-discrimination notice under disability discrimination legislation can require the recipient to set up an 'action plan',[1] while those under race and gender discrimination law can require him or her to provide the Commission with specific information. Non-discrimination notices last for five years. They can be enforced within that period under disability discrimination law, by the Commission making an application to the county court if there is a failure to comply, or if the Commission reasonably believes that the recipient does not intend to comply.[2] Under racial or gender discrimination law, non-discrimination notices are enforced by having the Commission commence a formal investigation into failure to comply with a non-discrimination notice.[3]

[1]   Disability Discrimination Act 1995, Sch 1, Pt III, para 14.
[2]   Equality (Disability etc) (Northern Ireland) Order 2000, Sch 1, Pt II, para 12.
[3]   Race Relations (Northern Ireland) Order 1997, art 57; Sex Discrimination (Northern Ireland) Order 1976, art 69.

Persistent discrimination

4.70 Where the Commission is of the view that a person or entity, which a tribunal or court has determined has discriminated or harassed persons in the past, is likely to commit further similar acts, it can apply to the county court for a form of statutory injunction prohibiting it from committing such acts.[1] Such orders can last for five years.

[1] Fair Employment and Treatment (Northern Ireland) Order 1998, art 41; Race Relations (Northern Ireland) Order 1997, art 59; Sex Discrimination (Northern Ireland) Order 1976, art 71; Equality (Disability etc) (Northern Ireland) Order 2000, art 8. There is no persistent discrimination provision in the Employment Equality (Sexual Orientation) Regulations 2003.

Codes of Practice

4.71 The Commission has quite extensive powers to issue Codes of Practices for employers, service-providers, and those involved in the housing and education sectors, which they can then use as guidance to help them comply with their statutory duties.[1] Codes of Practice, therefore, use practical examples and accessible language to illustrate methods of acting in a lawful manner to achieve equality of opportunity. These Codes are not themselves legal documents, and failure to act in accordance with them does not render an act an unlawful one nor does it render a person liable to any proceedings. However, the tribunals and the courts often make reference to them in assessing whether a person or a company has behaved lawfully.[2] It will obviously be easier to defend oneself from allegations of discrimination if one has acted in accordance with the Codes.

[1] The power to make Codes of Practice are found at the following points in the legislation but not all statutes allow for the making of a full range of Codes: Fair Employment and Treatment (Northern Ireland) Order 1998, art 9(1) and 9(3); Equality (Disability etc) (Northern Ireland) Order 2000, art 11; Disability Discrimination Act 1995, s 53(1); Race Relations (Northern Ireland) Order 1997, art 45; Sex Discrimination (Northern Ireland) Order 1976, art 56A; Employment Equality (Sexual Orientation) Regulations (Northern Ireland) 2003, reg 32.
[2] For example, the Commission can use the Codes of Practice issued under the Fair Employment and Treatment (Northern Ireland) Order 1998 to determine whether 'equality of opportunity' is being afforded. Under art 11(8) of the Equality Order 'any provision of a code which appears to a court or tribunal to be relevant ... shall be taken into account in determining that question'. See also the Race Relations (Northern Ireland) Order 1997, art 45(10), and Disability Discrimination Act 1995, s 53(4), which allows a court or tribunal to take in account any failure to adhere to a Code of Practice.

Monitoring staff composition

4.72 Alone of all the equality enactments, the Fair Employment and Treatment (Northern Ireland) Order requires employers with more than ten employees to register with the Commission[1] and monitor the religious composition of their staff members, and of those applying for positions, and then file this information on an annual basis to the Commission.[2]

[1] Fair Employment and Treatment (Northern Ireland) Order 1998, art 48.
[2] Fair Employment and Treatment (Northern Ireland) Order 1998, arts 52 and 54. Article 55 requires employers to conduct periodic reviews every three years, based on this information, to assess whether Catholic and Protestant communities are enjoying 'fair participation' in that workplace, and hence these are referred to as 'Article 55 reviews'.

4.73   The Commission can seek undertakings from employers in regard to their monitoring duties. If an employer refuses to make such an undertaking, or if the undertaking is made, but not complied with, the Commission can issue a notice, which is similar to that issued in respect of other types of undertaking under the Race Relations (Northern Ireland) Order 1997. It is also open to the Commission to make an application to the Fair Employment Tribunal, where the employer fails to comply with an undertaking.

4.74   A further sanction exists for non-compliance with aspects of these monitoring requirements. Where an employer is guilty of certain offences to do with its monitoring duties, public sector authorities are prohibited from entering into contracts with that firm.[1] This aspect of the Fair Employment legislation is commonly referred to as 'contract compliance', as it attempts to secure compliance with the legislation using commercial disincentives.

[1]   Fair Employment and Treatment (Northern Ireland) Order 1998, art 64.

Section 75: statutory equality duty

4.75   Section 75 of the Northern Ireland Act 1998 imposes a duty on a wide range of public bodies and authorities to combat inequality, and is commonly referred to as the 'statutory duty'. The specific terms of the main duty[1] are that in carrying out its duties a public authority is to:

'have due regard to the need to promote equality of opportunity—

(a)   between persons of different religious belief, political opinion, racial group, age, marital status or sexual orientation;

(b)   between men and women generally;

(c)   between persons with a disability and persons without; and

(d)   between persons with dependants and persons without.'

[1]   Subsection 1. Subsection 2 includes an ancillary duty: 'Without prejudice to its obligations under sub-s (1), a public authority shall in carrying out its functions relating to Northern Ireland have regard to the desirability of promoting good relations between persons of different religious belief, political opinion or racial group.' The relationship between the two subsections is not entirely clear. However, sub-s (1) is stated in stronger terms than sub-s (2).

4.76   The public bodies subject to this duty are all those coming within the jurisdiction of the Northern Ireland Ombudsman,[1] those government departments subject to scrutiny by the UK Parliamentary Ombudsman and which have been specially designated by the Secretary of State for Northern Ireland to comply with s 75,[2] as well as those public bodies on whom the Secretary of State imposed the duty.[3]

[1]   See chapter 2, para 2.45.
[2]   This includes government departments such as the Department of Trade and Industry and the Department of Culture, Media and Sport.
[3]   Those designated to comply with the duty include the British Council, and HM Customs & Excise.

4.77 The section 75 statutory duty seeks to ensure equality of opportunity by requiring public sector organisations to assess, on a systematic basis, the manner in which they carry out their functions to see whether any inequalities arise from the body's activities. The belief is that by placing the duty on public sector bodies to ensure equality of opportunity in the manner in which they function, a more co-ordinated approach to achieving equality of opportunity can be maintained. The approach taken in section 75 represents a significant shift in the enforcement of equality law, which has traditionally focused on enforcement by an individual, through the appropriate courts and tribunals, or by an agency exercising its powers to investigate particular industries or industrial sectors. Section 75 involves the public agency taking responsibility for ensuring equality of opportunity in the sphere of activity under its control. The approach take in section 75 is often referred to as 'mainstreaming equality', encapsulating the idea that the assessment of the impact of a public body's activities on equality of opportunity should occupy a central and continuing role in the management of the public body.

Equality Schemes and Equality Impact Assessments

4.78 In order to comply with the statutory duty in section 75 a public body is first required to produce, on a quinnenial basis, a document known as an 'Equality Scheme'.[1] The purpose of the scheme is to demonstrate the manner in which the public body intends to fulfil the duties imposed on it by section 75. In compiling the Equality Scheme the public body will first have to determine which of its functions should be included in it. This process is commonly referred to as 'screening'. A public body screens its functions by considering which of them may have an impact on equality of opportunity.

[1]   Northern Ireland Act 1998, Sch 9, para 2.

4.79 There are a number of particular matters that must be dealt with in the Equality Scheme.[1] Thus, it must include reference to the mechanisms by which the public body intends to consult with the public on proposed policies, and on amendments to existing policies, that may have an impact upon the promotion of equality. It must also monitor any adverse impact these changes in their activities might have on compliance with that duty.[2] The process of monitoring any possible adverse impact is conducted by carrying out an 'Equality Impact Assessment' (EQIA), discussed below.[3] The results of EQIAs must be published and the Equality Scheme must indicate how this is to be done. Furthermore, the Equality Scheme is to indicate how staff will be trained about equality matters and how the public is to have access to information about the public body's services. To aid public bodies in compiling these Equality Schemes the Equality Commission has issued guidelines as to the form and content of the schemes.[4]

[1]   Northern Ireland Act 1998, Sch 9.
[2]   Northern Ireland Act 1998, Sch 9, para 4(2)(b)and (c).
[3]   See para 4.80.
[4]   Northern Ireland Act 1998, Sch 9, para 4(3); 'Guide to the Statutory Duties: A Guide to the

Implementation of the Statutory Duties on Public Authorities arising from Section 75 of the Northern Ireland Act 1998', Equality Commission for Northern Ireland.

4.80   Certain details must be contained in any Equality Impact Assessment produced by the public body. The EQIA must contain the aims of the policy to which the assessment relates and give details of any consideration given by the authority to:

(a)   measures which might mitigate any adverse impact of that policy on the promotion of equality of opportunity; and

(b)   alternative policies which might better achieve the promotion of equality of opportunity.[1]

More significantly a public body must take the result of an EQIA into account when making any decision about a policy adopted, or proposed to be adopted, by it.[2] The Commission has produced a document offering practical guidance for the compilation of EQIAs.[3]

[1]   Northern Ireland Act 1998, Sch 9, para 9(1).
[2]   Northern Ireland Act 1998, Sch 9, para 9(2).
[3]   Section 75, Northern Ireland Act 1998: Practical Guidance on Equality Impact Assessment.

4.81   One important way of identifying any adverse impact in the performance of a public body's functions is to analyse any statistical data relating to the performance of them. For example, significant imbalances in the gender composition of persons availing themselves of a particular service should alert the public body to the possibility that it is delivering the service in a manner which makes it less likely that one gender, rather than the other, can avail themselves of it. The body may therefore have to consider alternative ways of delivering the same service or consider that the unequal take-up of that service can be explained in other grounds. As a consequence, data collection and evaluation are crucial to the effective operation of the section 75 process. Considerable amounts of data have been collected by public bodies in the past in respect of the religious affiliations of employees, service users and others, but there is a clear dearth of information dealing with minority ethnic communities, persons with disabilities, and persons of different sexual orientation, for example. The section 75 duty has therefore prompted many public bodies to fill this information gap by monitoring the performance of their functions on the basis of these other characteristics.

Monitoring implementation

4.82   A crucial element in the effectiveness of the section 75 duty is the manner in which its implementation by public bodies can be overseen and supervised. Furthermore, members of the public must be in a position to make complaints about the manner in which the duty has been complied with.

Approving the Equality Scheme

4.83   The Statutory Duty Unit of the Commission has the responsibility of reviewing and approving Equality Schemes. There are a number of stages to the assessment of an Equality Scheme. First, a desk audit is carried out to establish the compatibility of the scheme with the Commission's guidelines. This is followed by a 'consultation audit' that allows the Commission to establish whether, and to what extent, the public body has consulted with interested groups and considered their views. The Commission's conclusions arising from these audits are then communicated to the public body for its consideration.

4.84 Where the Commission does not approve the scheme its only statutory option is to refer the matter to the Secretary of State, informing the Assembly at the same time that it is doing so.[1] The Secretary of State has the option of approving the scheme or returning it to the public body with a recommendation that it be revised.[2] The Secretary of State's decision will be communicated to the Assembly. Interestingly, the public body is not required to re-submit a revised Equality Scheme under this element of the enforcement mechanism and need only do so if it wishes.[3]

[1]   The Commission has devised a protocol for this purpose, Annual Report 2000–2001, p 17.
[2]   Northern Ireland Act 1998, Sch 9, para 7. The Secretary of State has a third option namely to devise an Equality Scheme for the public body but it is difficult to imagine that this option will ever be invoked.
[3]   Northern Ireland Act 1998, Sch 9, para 8(1).

Complaint by the public

4.85   There is provision for ensuring compliance with the section 75 duty founded on a complaint made by the general public but it does not accord that a complainant with a right of action and the pursuit of the complaint is, in effect, relinquished to the Equality Commission. Any such complaint must be made within a year of the complainant coming to know of the matters alleged[1] and the complainant is required to give the public authority the opportunity to address the complaint before proceeding to the Equality Commission. This in effect means that the complainant would be best advised to notify the public body of the complaint before the expiry of the 12 month deadline for making the complaint to the Equality Commission to avoid the danger that the tardiness of the public body in dealing with the complaint means that the limitation period for making a complaint to the Commission has expired.

[1]   Northern Ireland Act 1998, Sch 9, para 10(3).

4.86   The Equality Commission then investigates the complaint and on completing that investigation sends a report to the complainant, the public body and the Secretary of State.[1] However, no specific sanction exists for compelling the public body to comply with its statutory duty. If the Commission's investigation recommends that certain action be taken by the public body, but such action is not taken within a reasonable time, then the Commission has the power to refer the matter to the Secretary of State who may then 'give directions' to the public body.[2] At the same time that it refers the matter to the Secretary of State, the Commission must also notify the Assembly that it has referred the matter to him or her.[3]

1   Northern Ireland Act 1998, Sch 9, para 11(2). It must also notify the Assembly of the fact that it is sending a report to the Secretary of State and furnish it with a copy.
2   Northern Ireland Act 1998, Sch 9, para 11(3)(b). If the Secretary of State gives any such directions then he or she must notify the Assembly that they have done so.
3   Northern Ireland Act 1998, Sch 9, para 11(4).

4.87   Where the public body complained against is a government department which falls under the jurisdiction of the UK Parliamentary Ombudsman, the above enforcement mechanism is amended, because such a body is not answerable to the Secretary of State for Northern Ireland, but to other Secretaries of State. If on reviewing such a body's Equality Scheme the Commission concludes that it should be revised, then it can request the government department to do so. The department then has six months within which to decide whether to make the revisions. If it does not make the revised scheme, it has the option of writing to the Equality Commission at the conclusion of the six month period outlining its reasons for not complying with the Commission's request.[1] The only option open to the Commission then is for it to lay a report before both the Westminster Parliament and the Assembly.[2]

1   Northern Ireland Act 1998, Sch 9, para 12(4).
2   Northern Ireland Act 1998, Sch 9, para 12(5).

Role of judicial review

4.88   It should be clear from the above that the mechanisms for enforcing the statutory duty are weak and the Commission lacks an effective sanction to ensure implementation of the section 75 duty. It appears to rely on a process of 'naming and shaming' in the Assembly, (or in the case of a UK government department, in the Westminster Parliament) to coerce a recalcitrant public body to comply with its recommendations. One unresolved issue is whether a member of the general public also has the right to apply to the High Court for a judicial review[1] of the alleged failure of a public body to comply with its statutory duty.

1   On judicial review generally, see chapter 2, para 2.105.

4.89   Orthodox judicial review principles require an applicant to have exhausted alternative remedies first and this would seem to mean that the complainant would be required to complain to the Commission to have it review the Equality Scheme before he or she can proceed to judicial review. However, the Commission can only entertain section 75 complaints that relate to the manner in which the public body has adhered to its Equality Scheme and in which it has carried out its EQIAs. It cannot, for example, deal with complaints that a public body has 'screened' out of the section 75 process an element of its functions that ought to have been included in its Equality Scheme. Therefore in cases where the Commission cannot entertain the complaint the complainant should be able to proceed immediately to judicial review.

4.90   However, one potential difficulty with any section 75 judicial review action is likely to arise from the fact that the complainant's assertion that the public body is failing to comply with its statutory duty involves an implicit suggestion that the

Equality Commission has failed to supervise the public body properly in respect of its section 75 obligations. This is likely to make any judicial review action even more complex.[1]

[1] Section 75 has featured in some judicial review applications. For example, see *Re Murphy's Application* (4 October 2001, unreported), Kerr J, transcript on Lexis, in which it was unsuccessfully argued that the Secretary of State was subject to section 75, and *Re D's Application* (19 September 2002, unreported), Coghlin J, transcript on Lexis, where the High Court concluded that section 75 was a factor for the Department to consider before using it powers under the Roads (Northern Ireland) Order 1993 to deal with an Orange Order arch which blocked the pavement. The decision was overturned on appeal but the Court of Appeal made no reference to the section 75 arguments.

Chapter 5

Criminal Justice System

Introduction

5.1 This chapter gives an overview of the criminal justice process from arrest to sentencing. It therefore explains, for example, the roles performed by various state agencies in the criminal justice system, the rights and entitlements of arrested people and the sentencing options open to the courts. However, it focuses in greater detail on matters of particular interest to social workers, including acting as an appropriate adult during the detention process,[1] and the role of probation officers in the criminal justice system. Finally, the role of probation officers in supervising sex offenders after their release from prison is also explored as these are elements of the criminal justice system in which social workers have a particular interest. Actual and proposed changes to the system, made by the Criminal Justice Review Commission, (set up on foot of the Belfast/Good Friday Agreement), are also examined. There has been considerable legislative development in the field of criminal justice in recent years and the main enactments that feature in this chapter are the Criminal Justice (Northern Ireland) Order 1996, the Criminal Justice (Children) (Northern Ireland) Order 1998, and the Justice (Northern Ireland) Act 2002.

[1] See para 5.46.

Role of social workers and social services

5.2 Obviously, social workers have limited direct involvement with the criminal justice system, but there are a number of ways in which their work relates directly to it. First, there is the activity of probation officers, working under the auspices of the Probation Board for Northern Ireland. Secondly, social workers may become involved, as appropriate adults, in the interviewing of juveniles and mentally disordered people suspected of criminal offences. A third relationship exists between social services and the criminal justice authorities arising from the powers and duties in the Children (Northern Ireland) Order 1995 in respect of children services generally, but in particular in respect of 'children in need', and from the obligation on social services to produce Children's Services Plans. The first two matters are dealt with in this chapter, and the third matter is referred to here and also in chapter 7.

5.3   The Children Order imposes a duty on every Board to take reasonable steps designed to reduce the need to bring criminal proceedings against children in its area and to encourage children within the Board's area not to commit criminal offences.[1] It is through the production of Children's Services Plans that Boards present evidence of the manner in which they are complying with this duty.

The Children (1995 Order) (Amendment) (Children's Services Planning) Order (Northern Ireland) 1998 requires every Health and Social Services Board to prepare and publish plans for the provision of children's services within its area and to keep those plans under review.[2] The most recent Children's Services Plans for the four Area Boards cover the period 2002–2005.[3]

[1]   Children (Northern Ireland) Order 1995, Sch 2, para 8(a)(ii), (b).
[2]   It does this by inserting a new paragraph in the Children (Northern Ireland) Order 1995, Sch 2.
[3]   For more on children's services plans, see chapter 7, para 7.10.

Agencies and institutions

5.4   As might be expected, there is a range of statutory agencies with responsibility for criminal justice matters, with very recent additions being made to this list of agencies, in line with recommendations of the Criminal Justice Review Commission. As a result, the operation of the criminal justice system in Northern Ireland is in a state of transition.

Criminal justice system in Northern Ireland

5.5   Various criminal justice agencies have banded together to form 'Criminal Justice System Northern Ireland'. These agencies are the Police Service of Northern Ireland, the Northern Ireland Prison Service, the Probation Board for Northern Ireland,[1] the Northern Ireland Court Service, the Department of the Director of Public Prosecutions and the Northern Ireland Office. However, each agency retains its distinct legal and administrative status and 'Criminal Justice System Northern Ireland' has not acquired any extra powers or duties that gives it a unique or special role in the criminal justice process.

[1]   See para 5.9.

Prisons and juvenile justice centres

5.6   There are three penal establishments in Northern Ireland: (i) HMP Magilligan, Co Derry, a medium security prison housing male prisoners only, many of them on short term sentences; (ii) HMP Maghaberry, Co Antrim, a high security prison housing male prisoners and all female prisoners in Northern Ireland;[1] and (iii) HM

Young Offenders' Centre, Hydebank, Co Antrim, accommodating young offenders and male prisoners on remand. A probation unit is found at each of Northern Ireland's prison establishments.

Northern Ireland has only one juvenile justice centre, located at Rathgael, Bangor, County Down, that is a secure facility for the detention of children found guilty of offences and whom the court considers require detention in a custodial setting. A new purpose-built juvenile justice centre is to be built on the existing site and to be ready for 2006.[2]

[1]   Including all female remands and young offenders.
[2]   NIO press release, 'New Youth Justice Agency launched', 31 March 2003.

Prosecuting offences

5.7   At present, the prosecution of criminal activity is divided between the police and the Office of the Director of Public Prosecutions (DPP).[1] The former are responsible for the prosecution of many of the offences tried in the magistrates' court, while the latter undertake the prosecution of offences in the Crown Court. (The DPP will occasionally try more serious offences in the magistrates' court[2] but the vast majority of prosecutions in those courts are conducted by the police).[3] This situation is about to change with the implementation of the Justice (Northern Ireland) Act 2002.

[1]   The statutory basis for the office of the DPP is found in the Prosecution of Offences (Northern Ireland) Order 1972.
[2]   These would be offences like the following: assault occasioning actual bodily harm, criminal damage, minor sexual assaults.
[3]   For an account of the prosecution of offences in Northern Ireland, see 'Review of Criminal Justice System in Northern Ireland', Stationery Office, 2000, paras 4.15–4.41, pp 54–60.

5.8   The 2002 Act will establish a Public Prosecution Service for Northern Ireland,[1] which will have the duty to 'take over the conduct of all criminal proceedings which are instituted in Northern Ireland on behalf of any police force',[2] and which will be headed by the DPP. These changes arise from recommendations of the Criminal Justice Review Commission. The Commission considered that the practice of having the police prosecute offences was out of line with international standards.[3]

[1]   Section 29.
[2]   Section 31.
[3]   'Review of the Criminal Justice System in Northern Ireland', Criminal Justice Review Commission, March 2000, Recommendation 17, para 4.127.

Probation Board for Northern Ireland[1]

5.9   Although the possibility of making Probation Orders with respect to offenders has been available since the Probation of Offenders Act 1907 and an organised

Probation Service was in existence for some time, the Probation Board for Northern Ireland (PBNI) was only put on a statutory footing in 1982, in the Probation Board (Northern Ireland) Order of that year.

[1] See Colette Blair, 'Prisons and Probation', a research report produced for the Criminal Justice Review Commission, 2000 for an assessment of the feasibility of making greater alignment between the prison and probation services.

5.10 The PBNI's powers and duties are outlined in articles 4 and 5 of the Order, as amended. As well as being required to 'serve the maintenance of an adequate and efficient probation service', it must also ensure that 'arrangements are made for persons to perform work under Community Service Orders'[1] and 'provide such probation officers and other staff as the Secretary of State considers necessary to perform social welfare duties in prisons and young offenders centres'. (It is the Board's duty to select, and to appoint, probation officers for each magistrate's court district).[2] It is open to the Secretary of State for Northern Ireland to prescribe other duties for the PBNI to undertake. The Board undertakes no 'civil work', that is to say that it does not provide reports for children or family proceedings, leaving such matters to social workers employed by health and social services authorities.[3]

[1] For more on Community Service Orders, see para 5.102.
[2] Probation Board (Northern Ireland) Order 1982, art 5(1).
[3] On reports in family proceedings, see chapter 6, para 6.31.

5.11 The PBNI, a non-Departmental public body,[1] comprises a maximum of 18 members, appointed by the Secretary of State for Northern Ireland for three year terms, and serviced by a full-time secretary. There are a number of differences between the organisation and delivery of probation services in Northern Ireland and the remainder of the UK. Structurally the probation service differs from others in the UK in that it has no link with local authorities, whilst operationally the key differences are that: (i) the service in Northern Ireland is community-based and does not, therefore, include members of the judiciary or magistracy (although lay panel-lists are included);[2] and (ii) it has never undertaken any civil work.[3] Other important differences are that probation is available in Northern Ireland for all those aged 10 years and over, whereas in England it is available for those over the age of 16 years only, and that no system of parole exists in Northern Ireland, although remission is available and there are 'home leave' and pre-release schemes. Those serving fixed-term sentences qualify for 50% remission.[4]

[1] The perceived benefit of this status is that is grants the PBNI greater independence from government than if it were a 'next steps agency', as is the prison service, for example. See Colette Blair, 'Prisons and Probation', 2000 for a discussion of these issues and the feasibility of integrating prison and probation services.
[2] See para 5.28 discussing the Youth Court.
[3] The probation service in Great Britain had responsibilities for producing reports in matrimonial and family proceedings.
[4] Prisons and Young Offenders Centres Rules (Northern Ireland) 1995, r 30. Paramilitary prisoners serving sentences for offences committed before the signing of the Belfast/Good Friday Agreement on 10 April 1998 were released under the Northern Ireland (Sentences) Act 1998.

5.12 The work of the service is headed by a Chief Probation Officer (CPO) who is aided in his task by the Director of Operations, to whom a number of Assistant Chief

Officers report. The service operates through field teams, prison-based teams and two specialist teams based in Belfast. The PBNI supervises approximately 2700 statutory clients at any one time, though as a result of financial constraints it has had to curtail the services it provides to non-statutory clients. Particular aspects of probation officers' work, including the compilation of court reports and the supervision of community disposals, are examined when considering the sentencing options open to a court.[1]

---

[1]   See paras 5.77 ff.

PROBATION OFFICERS

5.13   Probation officers become involved at the latter stages of the criminal process, ie after conviction but before sentencing, and can remain involved with offenders long after the trial has been concluded where they have responsibility for supervising an offender's compliance with a court order.

5.14   Probation officers might be perceived as playing a dual role; on one hand they operate as officers of the court, yet on the other, because of their involvement in the provision of welfare services to prisoners, prisoners' families and people recently released from prison, they could be described as specialised social workers endeavouring to assist their clients. Indeed this latter perspective of probation officers is re-enforced by the view that possession of either a Certificate of Qualification in Social Work or a DipSW is a necessary qualification for appointment as a probation officer.[1] The nature of the role played by the probation service over the years has also changed, as the previous CPO recognised some years ago.[2] She acknowledged, when considering the changes in the external environment in which the PBNI worked, that:

> 'the probation service was required to undertake and assume a role on public protection so that the focus shifted from advising, assisting and befriending the low risk repeat property offender to supervising the higher risk potentially violent repeat offender'.

In short, a 'risk assessment and management culture' appears to have superseded the 'rehabilitation culture' that previously characterised the probation services throughout the UK.

---

[1]   Chief Executive's Introduction, PBNI Annual Report 2001–02 expressing approval of the government's decision to retain the social work qualification as the core requirement for probation officers.
[2]   PBNI Corporate Plan 1999–2002, p 15.

5.15   There are four main areas of work in which a probation officer is likely to be engaged: (1) courts; (2) community supervision; (3) prisons; and (4) offenders' families. There are statutory provisions relating directly to the first two only, whilst the latter two are non-statutory areas of work, or perhaps more accurately, areas with respect to which statutory provisions are enabling, rather than directive. For that reason the focus in this chapter is on the first two categories.

GENERAL DUTY

5.16   There is a general statutory duty on probation officers which governs all the work engaged in by them. It is outlined by the Probation Board (Northern Ireland) Order 1982, article 14A,[1] and requires probation officers:

'(a)   to supervise persons placed under their supervision and to advise, assist and befriend those persons,

(b)   to enquire in accordance with any direction of the court into circumstances or home surroundings of any persons with a view to assisting the court in determining the most suitable method of dealing with him and

(c)   to perform such other duties as may be prescribed or imposed by or under any statutory provision or as the Probation Board may direct'.

[1]   As inserted by the Criminal Justice (Northern Ireland) Order 1996, Sch 5,

LEGAL LIABILITY FOR INJURY OR DAMAGE

5.17   The rules and principles relating to the legal liability of social workers for injury or damage caused by them in the course of their employment, and dealt with in chapter 2,[1] are modified in their application to probation officers.[2] PBNI staff are exempted from personal liability for acts done on the basis of a statutory provision if: (a) the officer acted reasonably; and (b) in the honest belief that his or her statutory duty required or allowed him or her to do it.

[1]   See para 2.80.
[2]   Probation Board (Northern Ireland) Order 1982, art 10.

5.18   However, the PBNI remains liable for acts of its staff members. The practical effect of this is that individual officers will not have to pay out of their own pockets if injury or damage is caused as a result of their actions, provided, of course, the PBNI thinks that officer's actions are reasonable and that the officer honestly believed that statute allowed him or her to do what was done. The PBNI itself will remain liable to pay compensation to the injured party by virtue of the doctrine of vicarious liability.[1] Disciplinary proceedings may be brought against an officer who strays beyond what is permissible but those proceedings will not result in compensation for injured parties and therefore will provide little satisfaction for them.

[1]   See chapter 2, para 2.84.

Youth Justice Agency

5.19   The Youth Justice Agency (YJA) has been established to co-ordinate the youth justice system,[1] and replaces the Juvenile Justice Board.[2] The YJA is a 'next-steps agency' under the aegis of the Northern Ireland Office. The establishment of just such an agency was, like so many other recent developments in the Northern Ireland criminal justice system, recommended by the Criminal Justice Review Commission.[3] The Commission was strongly of the view that the YJA would have no responsibility

for the development of juvenile justice policy, merely its implementation, and that
another unit or entity would have a policy review and development function.[4]

[1] On the youth justice system, see para 5.26.
[2] The Juvenile Justice Board had originally been established to fulfil this task, under the Criminal Justice
(Childrens') (Northern Ireland) Order 1998, art 56(1), but it has since been abolished by the Juvenile
Justice Board (Transfer of Functions) Order (Northern Ireland) 2003, effective from 1 April 2003.
[3] Review of the Criminal Justice System in Northern Ireland, para 10.101.
[4] Review of the Criminal Justice System in Northern Ireland, para 10.102.

Chief Inspector of Criminal Justice

5.20 The Justice (Northern Ireland) Act 2002 also provides for the establishment of
a Chief Inspector of Criminal Justice[1] whose duty it will be to carry out inspections of
the PBNI, the YJA, organisations with responsibility for providing juvenile justice
centres or attendance centres, as well as arrangements for secure accommodation
under Custody Care Orders[2] administered by Boards and Trusts, amongst others.[3]
Some of these organisations will also be subject to scrutiny by other agencies[4] and the
Chief Inspector is not to carry out an inspection if he or she concludes that the
agency or organisation is subject to adequate inspection by some other body.[5]
However, the Chief Inspector is forbidden by statute from carrying out an investigation of individual cases.[6] The Chief Inspector's programme of inspections is to be
produced in advance and the Inspector can be ordered to carry out certain inspections
by the Secretary of State.[7] He or she has extensive powers of investigation and any
obstruction of an inspection is a criminal offence.[8]

[1] The origins of this post also lie in the Criminal Justice Review Commission's report: Review of the
Criminal Justice System in Northern Ireland, March 2000, para 15.72.
[2] See para 5.129.
[3] Justice (Northern Ireland) Act 2002, s 46. This list also includes the police and the Public Prosecution
Service.
[4] See chapter 2. These bodies could include the Social Services Inspectorate, and the Health and
Personal Social Services Regulation and Improvement Authority, for example.
[5] Justice (Northern Ireland) Act 2002, s 46(2).
[6] Justice (Northern Ireland) Act 2002, s 47(6)(a).
[7] Justice (Northern Ireland) Act 2002, s 47.
[8] Justice (Northern Ireland) Act 2002, s 48.

Life Sentence Review Commissioners

5.21 A 'life sentence' is a custodial sentence imposed by a court where the crime
committed is particularly grave or serious. For some offences, like murder for
example, the imposition of a life sentence is mandatory. The effect of a life sentence is
that a person is detained in prison for the minimum period of time prescribed by the
sentencing judge, a period referred to as the 'tariff'.[1] Upon release from prison he or
she is liable to be recalled to prison at any time, by the Secretary of State, where they
engage in any other illegal activity or breach the conditions of their licence, without
the necessity of facing a further trial. Adult life sentence prisoners are commonly
referred to as 'lifers', whilst offenders aged less than 18 years are colloquially referred

to as 'SOSPs', an acronym for 'Secretary of State's Pleasure', because those offenders are 'detained during the pleasure of the Secretary of State'.[2]

[1] Life Sentences (Northern Ireland) Order 2001, art 5(1).
[2] Criminal Justice (Children) (Northern Ireland) Order 1998, art 45(1).

5.22 'Lifers' and 'SOSPs' are released by the Secretary of State but he or she acts on advice from the Life Sentence Review Commissioners. Of these Commissioners, at least one must be a lawyer, one a medical practitioner, one a person with knowledge of the supervision or aftercare of discharged prisoners, and one must have knowledge of the treatment of offenders or the issue of delinquency. A prisoner must be released where he or she has served their tariff and the Commissioners have recommended it.[1] However, the Commissioners can only make such a recommendation if they conclude that 'it is no longer necessary for the protection of the public from serious harm that the prisoner should be confined.'[2] The prisoner is entitled to refer his or her case to the Commissioners once the tariff has expired, or, alternatively when two years have passed since the last, unsuccessful, referral.[3] All proceedings before the Commissioners are conducted according to the Life Sentence Review Commissioners' Rules 2001. Probation officers are required to submit a report on the prisoner for these proceedings.[4] This report details the prisoner's family circumstances, opportunities for employment, the local community's attitude towards the prisoner and the victim, the prisoner's response to supervision and the risk of re-offending, amongst other matters.[5]

[1] Life Sentences (Northern Ireland) Order 2001, art 6(3).
[2] Life Sentences (Northern Ireland) Order 2001, art 6(4).
[3] Life Sentences (Northern Ireland) Order 2001, art 6(5).
[4] Life Sentence Review Commissioners' Rules 2001, Sch 1, Pt B, para 4.
[5] Reports on the prisoner's performance and behaviour in prison can also be sought by the Commissioners and this may involve prison-based probation staff providing some information as well: Life Sentences Review Commissioners' Rule 2001, Sch 1, Pt B, para 3.

5.23 When 'Lifers' and 'SOSPS' are released from prison they are said to be 'on licence,' which literally means that the prisoner is released on the permission of the Secretary of State. The licence may include conditions, for example, requiring the prisoner to submit to supervision by a probation officer. The Secretary of State may revoke the prisoner's licence, thus recalling him or her to prison, on the recommendation of the Commissioners, or may do so of his or her own accord if it appears 'that it is expedient in the public interest to recall that person before such a recommendation is practicable.'[1] Any prisoner recalled to prison in this manner can challenge the decision to recall him or her in writing to the Secretary of State,[2] but only after he or she has returned to prison. The Secretary of State is required to refer the case of any 'Lifer' or 'SOSP' recalled from licence to the Life Sentence Review Commissioners.[3]

[1] Life Sentences (Northern Ireland) Order 2001, art 9(1) and (2).
[2] Life Sentences (Northern Ireland) Order 2001, art 9(3)(b). It would also be possible to challenge it by way of judicial review. See chapter 2, para 2.105.
[3] Life Sentences (Northern Ireland) Order 2001, art 9(4).

5.24 The supervision of 'Lifers' and 'SOSPs' on licence also forms part of the duties of probation officers. As noted above, it is possible that one of the conditions that the Secretary of State attaches to the licence is that the licensee is subject to the supervision of a probation officer. Licensees are required to meet with their supervising officer on a regular basis and a change of employment or residence requires the permission of the supervising officer. Other restrictions may be included in the licence according to the circumstances of the crime. After a substantial period, normally several years, if the licensee has shown that he or she has settled in the community and his or her behaviour has not given rise to any cause for concern, the supervising conditions are usually cancelled. Otherwise they are retained for as long as is thought necessary. They can, of course, be retained for the duration of the licensee's life. The liability of the licensee to be recalled at anytime does continue, however, despite the revocation of the supervising conditions.

Aspects and features

5.25   This element of the introductory section focuses on particular aspects or features of the criminal justice system, as opposed to office-holders and agencies, that may be of interest to social workers, providing them with further introductory details on the operation of the criminal justice system.

Youth justice system

5.26   The Justice (Northern Ireland) Act 2002 attempts to bring coherence to the juvenile justice system by establishing a 'youth justice system' and enacting principles that underpin its activities. The principal aim of the youth justice system 'is to protect the public by preventing offending by children'[1] and all organisations involved in that system must have regard to that aim 'with a view (in particular) to encouraging children to recognise the effects of crime and to take responsibility for their actions'.[2] A range of new disposals have been introduced,[3] many of them modelled on developments in England and Wales,[4] although there are some innovations unique to Northern Ireland. The recommendations of the Criminal Justice Review Commission on juvenile justice matters were influential in the making of these significant changes.[5] One very significant alteration is the modification of the youth justice system to include 17-year-old offenders within its remit.[6] This change has met one of the criticisms and reservations expressed by the UN Committee on the Rights of the Child in its previous reports dealing with the UK.[7]

---

[1]   Justice (Northern Ireland) Act 2002, s 53.
[2]   Justice (Northern Ireland) Act 2002, s 53(2) with a view (in particular) to encouraging children to recognise the effects of crime and to take responsibility for their actions. This principle might be said to justify the restorative justice initiatives discussed at paras 5.62 and 5.124.
[3]   See para 5.129 on Custody-Care Orders.
[4]   See S Mullan and D O' Mahony, 'A Review of Recent Youth Justice Reforms in England and Wales', NIO Research and Statistical Series Report NO 8, October 2002.
[5]   See 'Review of Criminal Justice System in Northern Ireland', NIO, 2000, chapter 10.
[6]   Justice (Northern Ireland) Act 2002, s 63 and Sch 11.

[7] For the UNCRC's reaction to this development and its other views on juvenile justice in the UK, see its concluding observations on the UK's second report in CRC/C/15/Add.188, 9 October 2002, para 59.

5.27 One feature of the youth justice system worth noting is that organisations subject to supervision by the Chief Inspector of Criminal Justice[1] are to have regard to the welfare of children dealt with by the system and to the principle that any delay is likely to be prejudicial to the children's development.[2] This latter element is similar to the 'no-delay' principle[3] found in the Children (Northern Ireland) Order 1995, although the former cannot be said to import the 'paramountcy principle'[4] into the youth justice system. 'Having regard to' the child's welfare is not the same as requiring the child's welfare to be the paramount consideration in any decision that has to be made. Nonetheless, it can be seen that there is some relationship between the Children (Northern Ireland) Order 1995 and the principles underlining the youth justice system.

[1] See para 5.20.
[2] Justice (Northern Ireland) Act 2002, s 53(3).
[3] See chapter 6, para 6.39.
[4] See chapter 6, para 6.34.

YOUTH COURT

5.28 Children aged 17 years and under, charged with summary offences,[1] are tried in the Youth Court. The Youth Court is, in effect, the magistrates' court hearing charges against children.[2] However, unlike the magistrates' court, there is lay participation in the Youth Court, similar to that in the Family Proceedings Court.[3] Two lay panellists sit with the resident magistrate, one female and one male. The layout and operation of the Youth Court must conform to certain guidelines,[4] partly to fulfil the UK's obligations under Convention right article 6, to provide individuals with a fair trial.[5] In *VT v United Kingdom*,[6] the European Court of Human Rights concluded that the children convicted of the murder of Jamie Bulger had not been given a fair trial because they had not been able to participate fully in the trial. This inability to participate fully in the trial arose as a consequence of the operation and layout of the trial court. The Guidelines, therefore, about the conduct of trials in the Youth Court require, amongst other matters, that all participants to be seated at the same level, that the trial be carried out in language the child can understand, that the barristers and the judge are not robed and that the child and his or her lawyers can communicate with each other during the trial.

[1] See para 5.73.
[2] The Youth Court was formerly known as the juvenile court. The Criminal Justice (Children) (Northern Ireland) Order 1998, art 27(1) provides that juvenile courts are to be known as Youth Courts.
[3] On the Family Proceedings Court, see chapter 1, para 1.58, and chapter 6, para 6.45.
[4] 'The Youth Court in Northern Ireland: Guidelines for Operation and Layout', Northern Ireland Court Service, 2003.
[5] See chapter 1 and chapter 6, para 6.73.
[6] (1999) 30 EHRR 121.

OTHER ASPECTS OF THE YOUTH JUSTICE SYSTEM

5.29   There are other features of the youth justice system that are worth noting because they modify the usual principles that apply in the adult criminal justice system. One of the most important of these modifications relates to bail. There is what might be described as a legislative presumption that children should be granted bail. An accused child is to be released on bail unless the offence with which they have been charged is one involving violence or a sexual assault or is one which, if it were committed by an adult, would render him or her liable to a prison term of 14 years, and the court 'considers that to protect the public it is necessary to remand him in custody'.[1]

[1]   Criminal Justice (Children) (Northern Ireland) Order 1998, art 12.

5.30   Other modifications of the youth justice system are less significant but are important nonetheless because they are designed to protect the child or to otherwise recognise the vulnerability of the accused child. For example, children who are detained in a police station, or who are charged with an offence must not be allowed to associate with adult suspects,[1] and a person with responsibility for their welfare must be informed when they are arrested.[2] The oath that is administered in the youth court is also altered to require the child to 'promise', rather than 'swear', by Almighty God, thus helping to ensure that the child understands the duty on him or her.[3] Unsworn testimony can be adduced from a child under the age of 14, provided he or she can provide 'intelligible testimony',[4] and reporting restrictions, preventing the publishing of the child's name, for example, are imposed in respect of Youth Court proceedings and may be imposed in respect of other criminal proceedings.[5] And one other final example of these modifications can be found in the prohibition on the use of the words 'conviction' and 'sentence' in respect of children tried summarily, ie in the Youth Court, an attempt to avoid the pejorative labelling of child offenders for minor offences.[6]

[1]   Criminal Justice (Children) (Northern Ireland) Order 1998, arts 9 and 16.
[2]   Criminal Justice (Children) (Northern Ireland) Order 1998, art 10.
[3]   Criminal Justice (Children) (Northern Ireland) Order 1998, art 19.
[4]   Criminal Justice (Children) (Northern Ireland) Order 1998, art 20.
[5]   Criminal Justice (Children) (Northern Ireland) Order 1998, art 22.
[6]   Criminal Justice (Children) (Northern Ireland) Order 1998, art 5.

Age of criminal responsibility

5.31   The age of criminal responsibility is the age at which children are deemed to be responsible, in the criminal law, for their actions. The law in this regard is the same as it is in England and Wales. The age of responsibility is ten years.[1] Children under ten years are thus not criminally responsible for their actions, while those above that age are responsible and may be subject to the criminal law in the same way that adults are. This is one of the lowest ages of criminal responsibility in Europe,[2] and it has attracted adverse comment from the UNCRC in its recent commentary on the UK's second periodic report.[3] Children are defined are those aged 17 years or under,[4] while those aged between 18 and 21 years are referred to as 'young offenders'.

[1] Criminal Justice (Children)(Northern Ireland) Order 1998, art 3.
[2] The age of criminal responsibility is lower in Scotland, and the Republic of Ireland, where it is eight years and seven years respectively.
[3] CRC/C/15/Add.188, 9 October 2002, para 59.
[4] Criminal Justice (Children) (Northern Ireland) Order 1998, art 2, as amended by the Justice (Northern Ireland) Act 2002, s 64 and Sch 11.

5.32 The Criminal Justice Review Commission did not recommend any alteration in the age of criminal responsibility but did suggest that alternative forms of disposal should be developed for those children aged under 14 years.[1] This recommendation has manifested itself as the Custody Care Order and is unique to Northern Ireland,[2] though it is similar to the Detention and Training Order found in England and Wales.

[1] 'Review of the Criminal Justice System in Northern Ireland', Criminal Justice Review Commission, March 2000.
[2] See para 5.129.

Restorative justice

5.33 'Restorative justice' is a topic of current debate and discussion amongst criminal justice policy-makers, criminal justice agencies and academics. It is not capable of one single definition but refers to a process whereby the offender is made to understand the impact of his or her crime on the victim, sometimes by encountering the victim face-to-face. It is an alternative to the prosecution of the offender in the normal manner and is usually used with less serious offences. Restorative justice schemes usually require the offender to admit the offence and to consent to involvement in the restorative justice programme. It has not been part of the Northern Ireland criminal justice system in the past, but was considered by the Criminal Justice Review Commission as part of its report.[1] The Commission considered a number of aspects of restorative justice and recommended that restorative justice approaches be developed for juvenile offenders.[2] This recommendation has been implemented in the form of the new youth conferencing provisions, discussed below.[3] It did not recommend the immediate adoption of similar initiatives for adults, but suggested that pilot schemes be developed and carefully evaluated before any such programmes would be applied across all of Northern Ireland.[4]

[1] 'Review of the Criminal Justice System in Northern Ireland', Criminal Justice Review Commission, March 2000.
[2] 'Review of the Criminal Justice System in Northern Ireland', Criminal Justice Review Commission, March 2000, para 9.53.
[3] See paras 5.124 and 5.62.
[4] 'Review of the Criminal Justice System in Northern Ireland', Criminal Justice Review Commission, March 2000, para 9.54.

Prisoner Release Victim Information Scheme

5.34 Under a new scheme, which came into effect on 1 July 2003, the victims of criminal offences will be able to receive information about the temporary or permanent release of an offender who committed crimes against them. Where the actual victim is a vulnerable person (ie aged under eighteen years, or otherwise physically or mentally vulnerable), a close family member[1] or legal guardian[2] can be provided with the information instead. A number of agencies and public bodies are jointly considering how to implement this scheme.[3]

[1]   This phrase includes the victim's spouse, parent, adult child, sibling, grandparent or someone with whom they are living, or have lived: Prisoner Release Victim Information (Northern Ireland) Scheme 2003, art 2(4).
[2]   The option of allowing the legal guardian to receive the information only applies to 'vulnerable' victims of crime.
[3]   PBNI Business Plan 2002/03, Strategic Partnerships with the Statutory Sector, 'Objectives'.

5.35   The information that will be released in respect of offenders eligible for temporary release includes the date at which the offender will be eligible for such release, any decisions taken in respect of applications for temporary release, and any conditions imposed on such release. Where an offender is about to be discharged, the information that may be transmitted to the victim includes the date on which it is anticipated that the offender will be discharged, and any licence, or probation conditions to which the offender will be subject.

5.36   In the case of 'Lifers', or 'SOSPs',[1] information can include the minimum period of imprisonment before the offender becomes eligible for release, any consideration being given to the his or her discharge and any licence, or probation, conditions attached to the offender's release. There are exceptional circumstances in which the transmission of the information will be refused, for example, because it would constitute an unwarranted interference with the rights of the imprisoned offender, or because the term of imprisonment imposed was less than six months.[2]

[1]   See para 5.21.
[2]   A full list of such circumstances is proved in the Scheme regulations. Prisoner Release Victim Information (Northern Ireland) Scheme 2003, art 5.

Confidentiality and withholding information

5.37   The issue of confidentiality and privilege was discussed in chapter 3 in the context of the litigation process, and it was explained there that the only privileged relationship recognised by the law was that of lawyer and client.[1] Duties of confidentiality owed by social workers to their clients do not justify them refusing to disclose information when requested to do so as part of legal proceedings, whether as witnesses or where required to produce written documents on discovery. The issue of confidentiality that is examined here is whether social workers must disclose to the police any information they acquire about criminal offences in the course of their professional duties.

[1]   See para 3.31.

5.38   Unlike the position in England and Wales, there is an offence of withholding information about arrestable offences that applies to the public generally, and this offence appears, therefore, to require social workers to disclose information in their possession about criminal offences to the police. The Criminal Law Act (Northern Ireland) 1967, s 5, makes it a criminal offence to fail, within a reasonable time, to report to a constable, any knowledge, or belief, that an arrestable offence[1] has been committed.[2] It provides that:

> 'where a person has committed an arrestable offence, it shall be the duty of every other person, who knows or believes (a) that the offence or some other arrestable offence has been committed; and (b) that he has information which is likely to secure, or to be of material assistance in securing, the apprehension, prosecution or conviction of any person for that offence; to give that information, within a reasonable time, to a constable and if, without reasonable excuse he fails to do so, he shall be guilty of an offence.'

[1] 'Arrestable offence' is defined in the Police and Criminal Evidence (Northern Ireland) Order 1989, art 26. See para 5.42.
[2] The equivalent offence in England and Wales is the Criminal Law Act 1967, s 5, which only criminalises the withholding of information for financial or similar gain.

5.39 However, the offence is rarely the subject of a prosecution and when it has been used it has usually been in respect of the withholding of information about paramilitary crime.[1] The courts have acknowledged that there may be some defences in certain instances. Duress may be a defence.[2] If a person withholds information from the police because of a direct threat of violence from a criminal he or she may be able to claim that they committed the offence of withholding information under duress. It will also be a defence if a person asserts that the reason that they did not inform the police was because to have done so would have amounted to self-incrimination.[3] There is also some speculation that certain people – like doctors, priests, and lawyers – can claim that their communications with their 'clients' are not subject to the requirement to disclose.[4] Note, however, that there is no indication that social workers can make a similar claim to that which might be made by doctors, priests and lawyers.

[1] *R v MacLean* (22 May 1992, unreported), Court of Appeal (Criminal Division), reported on Lexis; *R v Donnelly* [1986] NI 54. See also *Sykes v DPP* [1962] AC 528, [1961] 3 All ER 33, HL, for a discussion of the (now abolished) equivalent offence in common law.
[2] *R v McLean* (22 May 1992, unreported), Court of Appeal (Criminal Division), reported on Lexis.
[3] *Rv Donnelly* [1986] NI 54.
[4] *Sykes v DPP* [1962] AC 528, [1961] 3 All ER 33, HL.

Arrest, detention, treatment and questioning

5.40 The criminal process commences with the arrest of a suspect. Criminal suspects with whom social workers are likely to become involved will usually be arrested under the Police and Criminal Evidence (Northern Ireland) Order 1989 (hereafter referred to as 'PACE'). The main arrest provisions will be considered in due course but first a few general points about arrest because social workers can be, and are, called to act as appropriate adults for certain types of detainee[1] and must, therefore, have some understanding of the arrest, detention and questioning process.

¹   See para 5.46.

5.41   If a police officer asks someone to 'accompany them to the police station to help them with their inquiries' that person is not necessarily under arrest and may be free to leave whenever he or she desires.¹ There is no 'halfway house' between being arrested and not being arrested, within which the police may detain and question you. One is either arrested or one is not. The purpose of arrest is to question someone in order to ascertain whether there is enough evidence to charge or prosecute that person for the offence in question. It is not, or at least it should not be, a 'fishing expedition' whereby the police trawl for general information about people or places, rather than specific information about the crime that the detained person is suspected of committing. The police are entitled to use such force as is reasonably necessary in order to effect the arrest.

¹   PACE, art 31, confirms that a person voluntarily attending at a police station shall be entitled to leave at will, unless placed under arrest.

PACE detention

5.42   The PACE powers of arrest allow detention for a maximum of 96 hours¹ and relate to two types of offence. The first is the 'arrestable' offence.² This an offence carrying a penalty set in law and any other offence for which the term of imprisonment is at least five years or which is specifically outlined in PACE, art 26(2). This will include, of course, a broad range of serious offences, for example, murder, arson, rape and theft. The second type might be described as the 'non-arrestable' offence and is outlined by PACE, art 27. A police officer may arrest, without warrant, a person on reasonable suspicion of committing a non-arrestable offence if it appears impracticable or inappropriate to serve a summons, essentially because the identity of the suspect is in doubt, or because the police officer believes it necessary for the protection of persons and property or because the police officer believes it necessary to protect a child or other vulnerable person from the suspect. However, most arrested persons are arrested on suspicion of having committed an arrestable offence.

¹   The initial arrest validates detention for a period of 24 hours. The period of detention can be extended for a further 12 hours by a police officer not below the rank of superintendent. Two further periods of extension are also possible but they must be granted by a magistrates' court. The total period of detention cannot exceed 96 hours.
²   PACE, art 26.

5.43   Someone must be told that he or she is under arrest as soon as is practicable after arrest, if not otherwise informed.¹ The detainee must be told of the reason for his or her arrest, and a caution must be administered as well. The caution will be as follows:

'You are not obliged to say anything in answer to the charge[s] unless you desire to do so, but whatever you say will be taken down in writing and may be given in evidence upon your trial. Do you wish to say anything in answer to the charge[s]?'

[1]   PACE, art 30.

5.44   The arrested person must be brought to a 'designated' police station – the larger police stations are designated – if arrested outside of such a station and if the detention appears likely to last longer than six hours.[1] An arrested person can be searched 'on the spot', ie at the time of arrest, for items he or she might use to escape or which might be evidence relating to an offence, as can the premises where he or she was when arrested, provided there are reasonable grounds for believing that such a search is necessary. Such searches cannot involve the removal of outer clothing.[2]

[1]   PACE, art 32.
[2]   PACE, art 34.

PACE Codes of Practice

5.45   Codes of Practice have been made, outlining the treatment persons arrested and detained under PACE can expect. The Codes of Practice are not legally binding and failure to adhere to them is not a criminal offence, nor does it render a detention invalid. However, breach of them may give rise to disciplinary proceedings against the police officer in question and, often more crucially, may in certain circumstances justify the court in refusing to accept as evidence statements made in circumstances where the Codes were not observed.

Five codes have been made,[1] of which two are of most relevance to social workers because they relate to the role of an appropriate adult and will therefore be examined here.[2] These are Code C, 'The Detention, Treatment and Questioning by police officers', and Code D, 'The identification of persons by police officers'.[3] These Codes contain all the elements of an appropriate adult's duties and should a social worker ever be required to act in this position he or she should make use of them.[4]

[1]   Police and Criminal Evidence (Northern Ireland) Order 1989, arts 60 and 65.
[2]   See para 5.46. for an explanation of the role of the appropriate adult and the circumstances in which he or she will be involved.
[3]   The remaining Codes are: Code A, Code of Practice for the Exercise by Police Officers of Statutory Powers of Stop and Search; Code B, Code of Practice for the Searching of Premises by Police Officers and the Seizure of Property found by Police Officers on Persons or Premises; Code E, Code of Practice for the Tape Recording of Interviews of Persons Suspected of the Commission of Criminal Offences which are held by Police Officers at Police Stations. In England and Wales a Code F, dealing with video recording of police interviews, has been issued.
[4]   There is a useful alphabetical index at the end of each code, which can used to access those provisions that deal with the role of the appropriate adult.

Role of appropriate adult

5.46   The appropriate adult is the person whose function it is to protect the interests of children[1] and the 'mentally disordered' (as the Codes of Practice refer to them) whilst in police detention under PACE. (An appropriate adult may also be involved in situations where a visually impaired person, or someone who is unable to read, is detained. This involvement would entail the appropriate adult checking documentation, and perhaps even giving help in signing documentation).[2] The role can be a daunting one, and consideration ought to be given to reconsidering the manner in which individuals are trained and chosen to complete the tasks involved, particularly now that its scope has been expanded.[3] The importance of the role of the appropriate adult can be gauged by the fact that no interviews should take place with a child or mentally disordered suspect unless the appropriate adult is present.[4]

[1]   The Codes refer to 'juvenile' rather than children, having been issued prior to the changes brought about by the Criminal Justice (Children) (Northern Ireland) Order 1998 and the Justice (Northern Ireland) Act 2002.
[2]   Code C, section 3.8.
[3]   See C White, 'Re-assessing the social worker's role as an appropriate adult', Journal of Social Welfare and Family Law 2002 vol 24, p 55.
[4]   *R v Ham* (1995) 36 BMLR 169, CA. Appeal against conviction allowed as a result of the failure to have an appropriate adult present when mentally disordered suspect was interviewed. Conviction quashed.

5.47   The appropriate adult must be informed of the fact of, and reason for, the detention of the child or mentally disordered person (as the case may be), and be asked to the police station as soon as practicable. Where the police are unsure that the detainee is a child, mentally disordered or impaired or suffering from a serious visual or hearing impairment, the Codes provide that the police should err on the side of caution and appoint an appropriate adult anyway.[1] Code C sets out the role of the appropriate adult:

'Where the appropriate adult is present at an interview, he should be informed that he is not expected to act simply as an observer, and also that the purposes of his presence are, first, to advise the person being questioned and to observe whether or not the interview is being conducted properly and fairly, and secondly, to facilitate communication with the person being interviewed.'[2]

The role of the appropriate adult has now been extended to include participation in Youth Conferences, the new element of the youth justice system introduced by the Justice (Northern Ireland) Act 2002.[3]

[1]   Code C, section 1.5 and 1.7.
[2]   Code C, section 11.12.
[3]   See paras 5.62 and 5.124.

Who can act as an appropriate adult?

5.48   In the case of a mentally disordered or impaired person, those that can fulfil the role are: (i) a relative, guardian or other person responsible for his or her care or custody; or (ii) someone with experience of dealing with mentally disordered or impaired persons; or (iii) failing either of the above, some other responsible adult aged 18 or over, although police officers or employees of the Police Authority for Northern Ireland cannot perform this function.[1] The Codes suggest that it is more satisfactory if the appropriate adult is someone who has experience of the person's mental impairment, rather than a relative lacking such a qualification, although the wishes of the detainee should be respected, if practicable.[2]

¹ Code C, section 1.8(b).
² Code C, Note 1D.

5.49   In the case of a child, a social worker can act as an appropriate adult but so also can the child's parent or guardian or, if he or she is in care, a staff member of the Department or a Board or Trust.[1] The parent or guardian of a juvenile should be the appropriate adult unless he or she is suspected of involvement in the offence or of being its victim.[2] However, Code C specifically cautions against foisting an estranged parent or guardian on a child to act as his or her appropriate adult, if the child expressly and specifically objects to his or her presence.[3] If a child admits an offence to a social worker, another social worker should be the appropriate adult in the interest of fairness.[4] It is also probably not advisable for a social worker to act as the appropriate adult where he or she is the person who alerted the police to the crime, and identified the suspect as the possible perpetrator.[5] Only as a last resort should a solicitor act in such a role.[6]

¹ Code C, section 1.8(a).
² Code C, Note 1B.
³ Code C, Note 1D. See also *DPP v Blake* [1989] 1 WLR 432. The competence of the persons chose to act as an appropriate adult can also be very significant. *R v Morse* [1991] Crim LR 195 – father of juvenile of such low intelligence that he could not have acted as adviser to the juvenile.
⁴ Code C, Note 1C.
⁵ *DPP v Morris* (8 October 1990, unreported), QB (Crown Office List).
⁶ However, this rule is not so strictly set out in respect of Youth Conferences. There the child's legal representative may act as an appropriate adult. Criminal Justice (Children) (Northern Ireland) Order 1998, art 3A(4)(a), as inserted by the Justice (Northern Ireland) Act 2002, s 57.

Fulfilling the duties of the appropriate adult

5.50   Even though the roles of the appropriate adult and that of the solicitor are to be considered separate and distinct, the nature of the appropriate adult's role requires him or her to have some relevant legal knowledge. The following extract from the English Court of Appeal's judgment in *R v Lewis*[1] demonstrates that the role of the solicitor and that of the appropriate adult clearly overlap:

'... It is true that there is a difference between an appropriate adult for this purpose and a solicitor, although their functions may be very similar. An appropriate adult may have a greater insight into the disabilities of a mentally handicapped person who is suffering from a low IQ. *Nevertheless, the functions of such an appropriate adult and a solicitor are largely the same, namely to see that the accused fully understands his rights, fully understands that he does not have to say anything unless he wishes to do so, to see that the interview is conducted correctly and that the police do not abuse their position, and that the accused is able to make himself clearly understood and clearly understands what is being put to him. In those respects the functions of an appropriate adult and a solicitor are similar.*' [Author's emphasis]

This passage sets out in a concise fashion the core responsibility of the appropriate adult. Evidence which has been unfairly or improperly obtained or which has been obtained using oppressive means can be declared inadmissible by the court trying the accused.[2] The court has a broad discretion in respect of the admissibility of evidence in criminal proceedings and it is difficult to provide precise advice as to when it will conclude that the police have 'overstepped' the mark. However, the value of the appropriate adult is that he or she will be able to testify about what transpired in the police interviews and in the custody suite, while the suspect was in police detention. This testimony will help the court in deciding whether the evidence that has been obtained should be admitted or not. The further value of the appropriate adult lies in the fact that he or she will be present during the police interviews and has the opportunity of intervening if, in their opinion, the circumstances warrant it. The fact that audio recordings are usually made of police interviews has eased the burden of the appropriate adult in monitoring the conduct of the interview quite considerably.[3] The following paragraphs offer some advice for those who are called to perform the duties of an appropriate adult.

[1]   [1996] Crim LR 260, CA.
[2]   PACE, arts 74(2) and (3) and 75(1).
[3]   Code E deals with the audio-recording of police interviews.

ON ARRIVAL AT THE POLICE STATION

5.51   It is useful for the appropriate adult to have a copy of the Codes of Practice, and in the event that he or she does not have a personal copy, a copy should be available at the police station. If the appropriate adult is unfamiliar with the Codes an index to the Codes can be used to find those sections relevant to the appropriate adult. The suspect should be informed of his or her rights[1] (orally and in writing) in the presence of the appropriate adult.[2]

[1]   These rights are: (1) right to contact a solicitor; (2) right to contact another person; (3) right to consult codes; and (4) right to obtain a copy of the custody record.
[2]   Code C, section 3.10. However, if the written notice of these rights, required by section 3.2, have already been given to the suspect then further copies need not be given in the presence of the appropriate adult: section 3.11.

5.52   The suspect should not have been interviewed before the arrival of the appropriate adult, unless there are exceptional circumstances in which the urgency of the situation requires the suspect to be interviewed in order to prevent continuing crime or protect a person from imminent danger.[1] The appropriate adult should consider calling a solicitor for the suspect, even where the suspect is reluctant to adopt that course of action.[2]

[1]   Code C, section 11.16.
[2]   Code C, section 3.11 and section 6.

5.53   The appropriate adult should consult with the suspect in private but should be aware that the conversation is not privileged and the appropriate adult can be required to testify as to its content.[1] For this reason the appropriate adult should not be party to the consultations between the suspect and his or her solicitor. The conversation between the appropriate adult and the suspect should be confined to matters relating to conditions of detention and treatment – such as whether the suspect has any complaints about his or her detention, for example[2] – and the physical and mental state of the suspect. The appropriate adult should also take the opportunity to explain his or her role to the suspect.

[1] See chapter 3, para 3.31, on legal professional privilege.
[2] Conditions of detention and treatment are dealt with in Code C, sections 8 and 9 respectively.

IN THE INTERVIEW

5.54 The main task of the appropriate adult during the interview is to ensure that it is not being conducted in an unfair and improper manner. No further guidance is offered in the Codes as to what is 'unfair' or 'improper', and so the appropriate adult will have to use his or her individual skill and judgement in making such an assessment. The appropriate adult should ensure that the suspect understands the questions being put, and on occasion it may be necessary to point out to the police any ambiguities in the suspect's answers arising from his or her age or mental illness about which the police might not be aware. One of the concerns of appropriate adults is whether they will be perceived as interfering if they make interventions of this nature and whether they will, as a result, be removed from the interview room. The police may order the appropriate adult to leave but only if he or she is obstructing the interview and this is something that rarely happens. In any event, expelling the appropriate adult will cause the police some administrative hassle as they cannot proceed with the interview without another appropriate adult being present.

5.55 A number of 'routine' physical matters should also be checked during this element of the detention such as whether the interview room is adequately heated, lit and ventilated,[1] whether the interviewing officers have identified themselves by name and rank[2] and whether breaks are being taken 'at recognised meal times' and whether short breaks are being allowed every two hours or so.[3]

[1] Code C, section 12.4.
[2] Code C, section 12.6.
[3] Although these matters may seem trivial they may have greater significance for vulnerable suspects than for other adult suspects and affect the propriety of the interview.

REVIEWS OF DETENTION

5.56 The police are required to review the necessity of continuing the suspect's detention periodically and the first review should take place after six hours of detention. The appropriate adult is entitled to make representations to the police officer carrying out the review.[1]

[1] Code C, section 15.2.

ON COMPLETION OF THE INTERVIEW

5.57 At the end of the interview the appropriate adult, or the suspect's legal adviser, should be given the opportunity to sign the interview record or the audio recording of the interview.[1] Generally speaking, any actions taken by the police after the completion of the interview should be taken in the presence of the appropriate adult, including the taking of fingerprints, photographs and intimate and non-intimate body samples.[2] Where the suspect has given consent to being involved in identity parades or procedures, or to the taking of fingerprints, body samples or photographs, his or her consent will only be valid if given in the presence of the appropriate adult.[3] Note, however, that fingerprints and non-intimate body samples can be taken without consent and the failure to consent to the taking of intimate body samples is a matter that may be commented upon in court. Children who are charged and not released must be sent to a 'place of safety', and where the appropriate adult is a social worker the expectation is that he or she will organise this place of safety. However, in practice many child suspects are detained in secure facilities.[4]

[1]   Code C, section 11.13.
[2]   For example, all information sought or given in respect of identity parades or procedures must be given or sought in the presence of the appropriate adult (Code D, section 1.15).
[3]   Code D, section 1.13. Such consent must be in writing.
[4]   See para 5.66.

Prosecution process

5.58 This section outlines salient elements of the criminal justice process, from the ending of the detention period through to the sentencing of the convicted defendant. It explains how prosecutions are commenced and provides an explanation of some key stages in the process.

Cautioning and diversion

5.59 Not all cases will reach the courts and there is considerable interest in mechanisms that divert less serious offenders, particularly juveniles, away from the criminal justice system proper while ensuring that the alternative does operate to deter re-offending.

Having completed their questioning of the suspect, the police can elect to caution a person rather than prosecute him or her. Cautioning schemes exist for both adults and juveniles and are administered according to Home Office guidelines and thus are conducted in the same manner as in the remainder of the UK.

Cautions are used quite regularly as a way of dealing with children under the Juvenile Liaison Scheme. Children who come to the attention of the police are referred to the scheme, and officers consider whether to prosecute, take no action, or issue a caution or warning. They are two types of caution used with children, an informal 'warning and advice' and a formal 'restorative caution'.[1] In 2000/01, 12,862 such referrals were

The prosecution process in Northern Ireland
Source: Digest on Information on the Northern Ireland Criminal Justice system, NIO, 1992

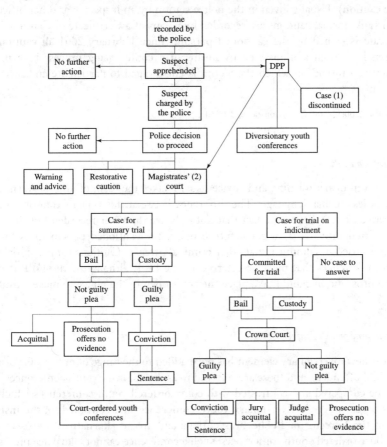

(1) A case will be under continual review, and may be discontinued at any stage before the hearing, withdrawn at court, or the prosecution may offer no evidence. In addition, the charge may be altered up to the final decision of the court.

(2) Although the majority of prosecutions are handled by the Police, certain offences are prosecuted by the DPP, while some are prosecuted by private organisations (including government agencies such as the Inland Revenue).

made to the scheme. 1,314 resulted in cautions,[2] 6,494 resulted in a warning and advice, 2,503 saw the police take no further action, while 443 were prosecuted in the courts.[3]

[1] For an explanation, see para 5.60.
[2] Of these 43 were restorative.
[3] Annual Report of Chief Constable 2000/01, p 65. The remainder were still pending.

Formal caution

5.60 A formal caution is one given by the police in circumstances where they consider that sufficient evidence exists to prosecute the accused successfully and where the offender admits to having committed the crime and consents to the issuing of a caution. (In the case of a child, his or her parents must also consent to the issuing of the caution). Usually given in the police station by an inspector or other officer of higher rank, formal cautions are recorded by means of a Certificate of Caution. This certificate is signed by the cautioned person. Since February 2001 all cautions of children have been administered by means of a conferencing process known as a 'restorative caution', in which the victim is encouraged to participate and meet the offender.[1]

[1]   Annual Report of the Chief Constable, 2000/01, p 65.

Warning and advice

5.61   An informal warning and advice usually takes the form of an oral warning or letter, in less formal language. The difference between this type of caution and the restorative caution lies in the fact that not only are the latter recorded but they may also be cited in court if, at some future point, the cautioned person finds him or herself accused of committing another criminal offence. Cautions cannot initially be issued for offences that must be referred to the DPP, although if the DPP decides that no prosecution should take place then it is open to the police to make a caution.

Diversionary youth conferences

5.62   A new diversionary element has been added to the range of options for dealing with child offenders, and these are referred to as diversionary youth conferences[1] and are to be compared and contrasted with court-ordered youth conferences which are discussed elsewhere.[2] Diversionary youth conferences are convened on the instructions of the Director of Public Prosecutions and are an alternative to prosecution. Like court-ordered youth conferences, such a conference cannot take place unless the child consents to it taking place and also admits the offence.[3] A diversionary youth conference has three options open to it: first, to conclude that no action be taken against the child; secondly to direct that the child be prosecuted for the offence or thirdly, to subject the child to a youth conference plan. If the DPP accepts the recommendation that the child adhere to a youth conference plan, this will prevent the initiation or continuance of any prosecution.[4]

[1]   Criminal Justice (Children) (Northern Ireland) Order 1998, art 10A, as inserted by the Justice (Northern Ireland) Act 2002, s 58.
[2]   See para 5.124.
[3]   Criminal Justice (Children) (Northern Ireland) Order 1998, art 10A(3)(a) and (b), as inserted by the Justice (Northern Ireland) Act 2002, s 58. If the child at any time withdraws this agreement to participate the conference must be terminated: art 10B(1).
[4]   Criminal Justice (Children) (Northern Ireland) Order 1998, art 10A(7), as inserted by the Justice (Northern Ireland) Act 2002, s 58.

5.63   Youth conferences involve meetings to determine how the child will be dealt with for the offence, and is attended by a youth conference co-ordinator (as chairman),[1] the child, a police officer and an appropriate adult.[2] The victim of the crime may also be present, as may the child's legal adviser. (If additionally the child is already the subject of another disposal for previous offences which require his or her supervision, the supervising officer may also be in attendance).[3] Nothing said or done in the youth conference meeting is admissible in any criminal proceedings.[4] The conduct of a youth conference is governed by statutory rules.[5]

[1]   This person will be a civil servant specially designated for this purpose: Criminal Justice (Children) (Northern Ireland) Order 1998, art 3A(3), as inserted by the Justice (Northern Ireland) Act 2002, s 57.
[2]   Criminal Justice (Children) (Northern Ireland) Order 1998, art 3A, as inserted by the Justice (Northern Ireland) Act 2002, s 57.
[3]   Criminal Justice (Children) (Northern Ireland) Order 1998, art 3A(4)(c), as inserted by the Justice (Northern Ireland) Act 2002, s 5.
[4]   Criminal Justice (Children) (Northern Ireland) Order 1998, art 3A(9), as inserted by the Justice (Northern Ireland) Act 2002, s 57.
[5]   Youth Conference Rules (Northern Ireland) 2003.

Charging the detainee

5.64   If the suspect is not cautioned for the offence at the end of the permitted detention period, he or she must either be charged or released without charge. Charging someone with an offence is one way of commencing the prosecution process and takes place when there is sufficient evidence to justify it. Another method of commencing the prosecution process is for a summons to be issued by a magistrate or a justice of the peace following a complaint made to him or her by a police officer. This method is explained later.[1]

[1]   See para 5.72.

5.65   The custody officer determines whether there is sufficient evidence to charge. If the suspect is charged then he or she will again be cautioned in the same way as they were when first arrested. The caution will be administered orally, but the suspect is also to be given written notice of the caution and written notice of the particulars of the offence, the name of the police office in the case, his or her police station and reference number.[1] The charging of a child or mentally ill or impaired person should take place in the presence of the appropriate adult.[2] Both the appropriate adult and the vulnerable person are given the written notice showing the particulars of the offence charged, the name of the officer and his or her station address.[3]

[1]   Note that this form of caution differs to the caution described in para 5.59, which is a way of disposing of or concluding the prosecution process.
[2]   Code C, section 16.1B.
[3]   Code C, section 16.4.

Detaining children in a place of safety

5.66   Having charged the suspect, the custody officer must order his or her release, either with or without bail, unless he or she believes that the suspect will not attend in court, or has given a false name or address, or will commit further offences, or, in the case of a juvenile, that continued detention is in the juvenile's interests.[1] Children may then be detained in a 'place of safety', which includes a juvenile justice centre.[2] This power is commonly used[3] where, at the end of the detention process, the custody officer seeks to release the child into the care of the appropriate adult but he or she refuses to take responsibility for the child, or, in the case of social workers who act in that role, that there is not suitable accommodation in the social service sector for the child. A recent research report noted that 'custody sergeants often have no alternative but to send such persons to Lisnevin[4] or Rathgael[5] to appear in court the next day, when Social Services refuse to receive them.'[6]

[1]   Police and Criminal Evidence (Northern Ireland) 1989, art 39(1).
[2]   Police and Criminal Evidence (Northern Ireland) 1989, art 39(8).
[3]   In 2002, 219 juveniles were detained in this manner under PACE. K Quinn and J Jackson, 'Detention and questioning of young persons in Northern Ireland,' NISRA, September 2003, p 38.
[4]   This was another secure Juvenile Justice Centre in Northern Ireland that has since been closed.
[5]   Northern Ireland's only secure juvenile justice centre. See para 5.115.
[6]   K Quinn and J Jackson, 'Detention and questioning of young persons in Northern Ireland,' Northern Ireland Statistics and Research Agency, September 2003, p 38.

Remand on bail or in custody

5.67   A person released on bail is said to be remanded on bail, while someone who is refused bail is remanded in custody. Bail can be granted initially by the custody officer, and this form of bail is commonly referred to as 'police bail'.[1] Those who are charged and not released on police bail must be brought before a magistrates' court as soon as practicable but usually not later than the day after which they are charged.[2] The decision to refuse bail can be challenged in the magistrates' court and in the High Court. The decision whether or not to grant bail involves an assessment of a number of factors, including whether there is a likelihood of the accused absconding, the severity of the penalty, the nature of the offence and the strength of the evidence.

[1]   Police and Criminal Evidence (Northern Ireland) 1989, art 48. Police bail can be subject to certain conditions, like the requirement to attend, on a regular basis, at a police station.
[2]   Police and Criminal Evidence (Northern Ireland) 1989, art 47(2) and (3).

5.68   A person remanded on bail may be required to comply with certain conditions, such as attending periodically at a police station or observing a curfew. He or she may also be required to reside in a bail hostel. Bail hostels are residential facilities, provided or funded by the PBNI,[1] to which persons awaiting trial are sent, if the courts believe they require a substantial measure of supervision, as well as support, during the remand period. Only persons over the age of 17 are sent to them. Residents usually reside at the hostel until the next court appearance. These are usually used where the alleged offence involved is one against property, rather than one involving violence.

[1]   Under the Probation Board (Northern Ireland) Order 1982, art 5(a).

Remanding children and mentally disordered suspects

5.69 There is a legislative presumption that children be released on bail where the offence is not a serious one and the court has no concerns about the need to protect the public.[1] However, if the circumstances warrant denying bail, then the child is to remanded to a juvenile justice centre or, if aged over 15 years and the court considers that he is likely to injure himself or other persons, to a Young Offenders' Centre.[2] Where a child is denied bail, the court must explain in open court its reasons for refusing to grant it.

[1]   Criminal Justice (Children) (Northern Ireland) Order 1998, art 12. See para 5.29.
[2]   Criminal Justice (Children) (Northern Ireland) Order 1998, art 13.

5.70 An accused person, whom it is suspected has a mental disorder, may be remanded to hospital for assessment of his or her mental health if a Part II doctor[1] gives evidence that there is reason to suspect the accused is suffering from mental illness and the court is of the opinion that 'it would be impracticable for a report on his mental condition to be made if he were remanded on bail'. The magistrates' court may only exercise this power, however, if the accused has been convicted or consents to the court making such an order or where the court is satisfied that the accused did the act with which he or she was charged.[2] The person cannot be remanded for more than 28 days at a time under this procedure, or for more than 12 weeks in total.

[1]   See chapter 11. A 'Part II doctor' is one who is exercising powers under Part II of the Mental Health (Northern Ireland) Order 1986.
[2]   Mental Health (Northern Ireland) Order 1986, art 42.

5.71 A further power is available to the Crown Court to remand the accused person in hospital for treatment instead of remanding him or her into custody.[1] It may only make such an order on the evidence of a Part II doctor that the accused is suffering from a mental disorder to the extent that his or her detention for treatment in hospital is warranted. The maximum single remand period is also 28 days, with an overall limit of 12 weeks.

[1]   Mental Health (Northern Ireland) Order 1986, art 43(1).

Prosecution by way of summons

5.72 The fact that a detainee is released without charge does not mean that a prosecution cannot, or will not, take place. A prosecution can be, and most prosecutions are in fact, initiated by the issuing of a summons – a document issued by a justice of the peace or clerk of petty sessions requiring the accused to answer in court the charges made out in the summons – rather than following the charging of the detainee. A summons is issued after the police investigation has been completed and the DPP's office has examined the police file on the matter.

Indictable and summary offences

5.73   There are two types of criminal offence: summary and indictable. Summary offences are tried in the magistrates' court, whilst indictable offences are tried in the Crown Court, although there is a preliminary stage, called the 'committal stage' in the trial of indictable offences, which takes place in the magistrates' court.[1]

Summary offences are usually less serious than indictable offences. The key difference between the two types of offence is that trial in the magistrates' court will not be before a jury, whilst those in the Crown Court will, with the exception of 'scheduled' offences,[2] be before a jury.[3] Statutes usually prescribe which offences are triable on indictment or which are triable summarily, although there are some offences which are triable either summarily or on indictment, sometimes at the election of the accused, sometimes at the election of the prosecution.

[1]   For more on court structure, see chapter 1, para 1.49.
[2]   'Scheduled offences' are those contained in the Terrorism Act 2000, Sch 9, and essentially amount to offences of a paramilitary nature.
[3]   Previously one other difference was that the accused in a trial in the magistrates' court had no prior knowledge of the strength of the case against him or her but that has been altered by the Criminal Procedure and Investigation Act 1996.

Committal stage

5.74   Committal proceedings take place in the magistrates' court and are the preliminary stage in the trial of an offence on indictment. The purpose of such proceedings is to discover whether there is sufficient evidence to 'commit' the accused to the Crown Court for trial. If, in the opinion of the magistrate, there is not enough evidence to do so then the accused must be 'discharged' (ie released), though because he or she was not formally acquitted, re-trial at a later date is a possibility. However, in most cases the magistrate will conclude that there is sufficient evidence and commit the accused for trial in the Crown Court.

There are two types of committal proceedings, a preliminary inquiry and a preliminary investigation. In the former, the evidence of the witnesses is given as written witness statements, whereas, in the latter, the witnesses are called to give evidence and may be cross-examined. The former type of committal proceeding is more common that the latter.

Arraignment

5.75   This is the part in the proceedings when the charges are formally put to the accused and he or she is required to indicate whether they plead 'guilty' or 'not guilty'. This part of the prosecution takes place in the Crown Court and marks the first occasion on which the accused appears in that court. If the accused pleads 'not guilty' a date will be set for his or her trial, and a decision will be made to remand the accused on bail or in custody. Where the accused does not attend at the arraignment a bench warrant will be issued for his or her arrest.

Trial process

5.76 As the social worker's involvement in the trial will be limited, any relevant or pertinent information regarding litigation is set out in chapter 3.

Sentencing

5.77 One of the elements of the criminal justice process of greatest concern to social workers will be the sentencing process, because probation officers will be involved in preparing pre-sentence reports before the court passes sentence and in supervising any community-type disposal order made by the courts. Sentencing of a convicted person may, or may not, follow immediately after the determination of guilt, but the courts have the power to defer sentence,[1] and in some cases must do so,[2] to allow the preparation of the pre-sentence report.

[1] Criminal Justice (Northern Ireland) Order 1996, art 3; Magistrates' Court (Northern Ireland) Order 1981, art 50. See para 5.82.
[2] In respect of child offenders a Pre-sentence Report must always be obtained unless the offence is very serious: Criminal Justice (Northern Ireland) Order 1996, art 9(5).

Pre-sentence Reports

5.78 The production of Pre-sentence Reports (PSRs) (formerly known as 'Social Enquiry Reports' until the implementation of the 1996 Order) on offenders, to aid the courts in deciding what sentence to impose on them, is one of the main functions of the probation service. Broadly speaking these are compiled as a result of enquiries made by the probation officer into the offender's home and family circumstances. A 'pre-sentence report' is defined, in the Criminal Justice Order 1996 as a report in writing which is made, or submitted, by a probation officer, or a social worker of a Board or Trust with a view to assisting the court in determining the most suitable method of dealing with an offender; and which contains information as to such matters, presented in such a manner as may be prescribed by rules made by the Secretary of State.[1]

[1] Criminal Justice (Northern Ireland) Order 1996, art 2(2). No rules detailing the content of PSRs have been made by the Secretary of State although standards have been agreed between the PBNI and sentencers.

5.79 It should be noted that although PSRs may be prepared by persons other than probation officers, in reality almost all PSRs will be compiled by probation officers. In the past a PSR might have been prepared by a social worker in respect of a child who was in care at the time that he or she was alleged to have committed the offence, but this should not be the case now.[1]

[1]   Juvenile Justice Centre Order Probation Standards, Directory of Probation Resources, PBNI, March 2002.

5.80   In discussion with sentencers, the PBNI has agreed revised standards to allow the production of abbreviated PSRs, known as Specific Sentence Pre-sentence Reports (SSRs).[1] An SSR is 'intended to provide the sentencing court with useful but limited information about a defendant and offences to assist the court to determine whether the defendant is suitable for a specific sentence envisaged by the court. Its purpose is to speed up the provision of information to assist the court to pass sentence without delay',[2] and is most often used where the court is considering imposing a Community Service Order or a Probation Order, without any additional requirements. SSRs are intended for use for less serious crimes, involving adults only. SSRs are prepared by the Court Duty Officer and are usually prepared on the day on which they are requested.[3]

[1]   PBNI, Annual Report 2001/2, 'Activity Report', 'Courts'.
[2]   Directory of Probation Resources, PBNI, March 2002.
[3]   Particular forms, SSR1 Form and SSR 2 Form have been devised for the purpose of completing these abbreviated forms of PSR.

5.81   Probation officers, as might be expected, are acting as officers of the court in this instance[1] and therefore their role is to present information to the court regarding the offender, assess the utility of the various disposal options available to the court and then make a recommendation. It is not the role of a probation officer when preparing PSRs to act as an advocate for the offender. PBNI standards[2] for the preparation of PSRs require the report-compiler to set out his or her report under the following headings:

● Introduction
● The offender in his or her life setting
● Offence analysis
● Risk of harm to the public and the likelihood of re-offending
● Conclusion

In order to inform the fourth element of the report the probation officer is expected to carry out an assessment of the likelihood of the offender committing further offences.[3] The probation officer is mandated to 'obtain all available information which is relevant to the offender, the offences and the purposes of the report', and is required to 'include an account of the steps taken to obtain all relevant information'.[4] A PSR is to be completed usually within 20 working days of the request from the court (or within 15 days if the offender is remanded in custody), unless the court specifies another date.[5]

[1]   For a general commentary on the social worker as an officer of the court see chapter three, para 3.44.
[2]   Directory of Probation Resources, PBNI, March 2002.
[3]   Directory of Probation Resources, PBNI, March 2002, Pre-Sentence Report Standards, Standards 2 and 3.
[4]   Directory of Probation Resources, PBNI, March 2002, Pre-Sentence Report Standards, Standards 6 and 7.

5   Directory of Probation Resources, PBNI, March 2002, Pre-Sentence Report Standards, Standard 11.
    The offender, and if appropriate his or her parent or guardian is to be shown a copy of the draft PSR
    (Standard 10).

5.82   Before making a Probation Order, Community Service Order, Combination Order or Supervision Order,[1] a court must have a Pre-sentence Report before it, unless exceptionally it considers that it is in the circumstances of the case unnecessary for it to do so.[2] However, in the case of youth offenders the court must always have a Pre-sentence Report, unless the offence for which the youth has been convicted is an indictable one.[3] Notwithstanding this general requirement to have a pre-sentence report made available before the sentencing stage, the failure of the court to obtain a PSR prior to making one these Community Orders does not invalidate that order.[4] The probation officer compiling a report on a child charged with an offence will have the benefit of material gathered by social workers, as the Youth Court is obliged to make social services aware of the fact that the child has been charged, as well as notifying the probation service.[5]

1   All of these disposals are explained at paras 5.95, 5.102 and 5.107.
2   Criminal Justice (Northern Ireland) Order 1996, art 9. Where it comes to this conclusion it must state
    so in open court.
3   Criminal Justice (Northern Ireland) Order 1996, art 9(5).
4   Criminal Justice (Northern Ireland) Order 1996, art 9(6).
5   Criminal Justice (Children) (Northern Ireland) Order 1998, art 11.

5.83   A copy of the report is to be given, by the court, to the offender or his or her legal advisers (or if the offender is a youth and is not represented by a legal adviser then to his or her parent/guardian, if present in court).[1]

The courts received 6,979 requests for PSRs in 2001/02.[2] Just over two thirds of these were requested for use in the magistrates' courts, 17% for use in Youth Court cases, 12% in Crown Court cases, with the remaining 2% being requested in appeal cases.[3] In the past, the rate of acceptance of recommendations made in probation reports varied considerably from court to court. However, no contemporary figures are available and it is therefore difficult to say whether this remains the case.[4]

1   Criminal Justice (Northern Ireland) Order 2003, art 32, replacing the Criminal Justice (Northern
    Ireland) Order 1996, art 34, and adding a new art 21A.
2   PBNI Annual Report 2001/02, Appendix G. This represented a small decline from the 7,605
    requested in 2000/2001.
3   This percentage of PSRs that deal with appeals will always be quite small because it is only where the
    reports were not prepared for the original trial that they are prepared afresh for the appeal.
4   In the juvenile court the rate of acceptance of recommendations in 1991 was 60%, whilst for the
    magistrates' courts and the Crown Court it was 69% and 33% respectively (Corporate Plan, p 13). The
    considerable divergence in these statistics between the magistrates' court and the Crown Court may be
    partly explained by the serious nature of offences heard in the latter courts and the restricted scope for
    making a non-custodial disposal within them.

Sentencing options

5.84   The following diagram sets out the main options open to a court when an accused is convicted. A description and explanation of each option is provided and

Disposals available to the courts

Source: Digest of Information on the Northern Ireland Criminal Justice system, NIO, 1992

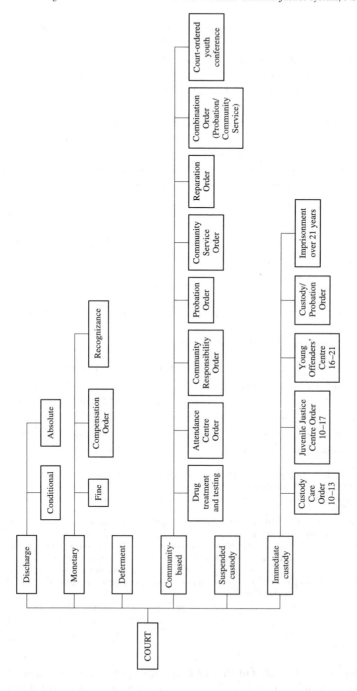

the role of probation officers in respect of those options is discussed. The specialised options that are available for juveniles and mentally disordered offenders only are discussed separately.[1]

[1]   See paras 5.113 and 5.132.

5.85   The range of options may be broadly divided into those which are custodial in nature, and those which are community-based disposals (ie do not involve incarceration in prison). The 1996 Criminal Justice Order uses the terms 'Community Order' to refer to Probation Orders, Community Service Orders, Combination Orders and Attendance Centre Orders, while 'custodial sentences' is the term used to refer to sentences of detention in a prison, a Young Offender's Centre and detention at the Secretary of State's Pleasure.[1]

[1]   Criminal Justice (Northern Ireland) Order 1996, art 2(2).

Discharge

5.86   The option of discharging an offender arises where even though he or she is convicted, the court, having had regard to the circumstances of the offence, including the nature of the offence and the character of the offender, decides that it is 'inexpedient to inflict punishment' and concludes that it is better to discharge the offender. There are two possible types of discharge, absolute and conditional.[1]

[1]   Criminal Justice (Northern Ireland) Order 1996, art 4.

ABSOLUTE DISCHARGE

5.87   The effect of an absolute discharge is that, although convicted, the offender is not subject to any punishment. The option of an absolute discharge is used where the offence committed is a trivial one or where the court believes that there is little likelihood of the offender re-offending. The offender is not left with a criminal record, although if he or she should be prosecuted for a criminal offence in the future then the discharged conviction can be revealed at the trial.

CONDITIONAL DISCHARGE

5.88   One might class this sentencing option as a Probation Order without the requirement for supervision. The court can impose a condition that the offender commit no further offence for a specified period (up to a maximum of three years) and if the offender does commit any further offence he or she may be sentenced for the original offence as well as the 'new' (ie subsequent) one.[1] Conditional discharges are more common than absolute ones. The court is obliged to explain to the offender in simple language the effect of choosing such a disposal. A conditional discharge differs from a suspended sentence[2] in that, in regard to the former, no specific sentence has been set which will be activated by the commission of the subsequent offence.

¹   On making the conditional discharge the court may require the offender to act as surety for his or her
own good behaviour or if the offender is under 14 years the offender's parent or guardian. Where the
offender is aged between 14 and 17 years the court has a choice as to whether the offender or the
parent/guardian should be the surety (Criminal Justice (Northern Ireland) Order 1996, art 7).
²   See para 5.108.

Monetary

5.89   These sentencing options involve the offender (or his or her parent/guardian, in the case of a juvenile) paying out a sum of money as a punishment, as compensation to the victim or as surety for the offender's future good behaviour.

Fine

5.90   This is the most familiar and the most usual form of punishment, with 78% of all offenders in magistrates' courts in 1991 being fined. Imprisonment can of course follow should the offender default on the payment of the fine. A fine imposed on a child must be paid by its parents and the courts must require the parents of a young person to pay if it he or she is aged less than 16 years and the court may order the parents to pay it if he or she is older than 16.[1]

¹   Criminal Justice (Children) (Northern Ireland) Order 1998, art 35(1).

Compensation Order

5.91   Available for adults and juveniles, these orders, as their title suggests, enable courts to order the offender to make direct monetary reparation to the victim. A court can require the offender to pay compensation for any personal injury, loss or damage resulting from an offence.[1] Such an order can be combined with other disposals and can be made by both the Crown Court and magistrates' courts, although the latter cannot make an award over £2,000. One of the advantages with them is that they avoid the expense and need for civil litigation between the victim and the offender in order to allow the former to be compensated.

¹   Criminal Justice (Northern Ireland) Order 1980, art 3(1).

5.92   As with fines, compensation ordered to be paid in the case of a child under 16 years must be paid by a parent and in the case of a child older than that age, the court has a discretion to order the parent to pay the compensation.[1]

¹   Criminal Justice (Children) (Northern Ireland) Order 1998, art 35(1).

Recognizance

5.93   A recognizance is an undertaking to behave in a certain way or to perform some particular obligation, which in the context of the criminal justice system usually means that the offender will 'be of good behaviour', and involves a sum of money being offered as a guarantee that the undertaking will be observed. The practical effect of breaking a recognizance is that the sum will be forfeited. Those who make recognizances are usually referred to as being 'bound over'. The courts may 'bind over' offenders to keep the peace or be of good behaviour.[1] Where a child is charged with an offence then a court can, in addition to or in lieu of any other order, order his or her parents or guardian to enter into a recognizance as security for his or her good behaviour. Such an order cannot be made without giving the parent an opportunity to be heard but, if they have been requested to attend and fail to do so, then they can be bound over in their absence.

[1] Criminal Law Act (Northern Ireland) 1967, s 7(5) and the Magistrates' Courts (Northern Ireland) Order 1981, art 127(1) and for children, the Criminal Justice (Children) (Northern Ireland) Order 1998, art 36(1).

Community disposals

5.94 Although community disposals – that is, sentencing options that are non-custodial and deal with the offender in the community – appear to be 'soft' options, they are in many respects more effective than imprisoning someone, as prison tends to have less effect on preventing re-offending. They are certainly cheaper options. Figures produced in the past demonstrated that it cost more to imprison an offender than to subject him or her to a Probation Order.[1]

[1] It the 1990s, it cost £6,000 per month to imprison someone, whilst the administration of a Probation Order costs approximately £1,300 and an average length Community Service Order about £600 ('Crime in the Community', HMSO, 1993, p 51).

PROBATION ORDER

5.95 A Probation Order means that an offender is put under the supervision of a probation officer for a period of between six months and three years with a view to 'securing the rehabilitation of the offence, protecting the public from harm or preventing the commission of further offences'.[1] The consent of the offender to the making of the Probation Order is necessary for all offenders over the age of 14 years.[2] Probation Orders are available for all offenders, including children.

[1] Criminal Justice (Northern Ireland) Order 1996, art 10(1).
[2] Criminal Justice (Northern Ireland) Order 1996, art 11(3). In March 2002, 32% of all probationers were 'young people', ie aged between 10 and 17. PBNI Annual Report 2001/02. 33% of them were young adults, ie aged 18 to 25 and 35% were adults aged 26 years and older.

5.96 An offender subject to a Probation Order is required to reside in the magistrates' court district specified in the order and to be subject to supervision by a probation officer.[1] In particular the offender is required to remain in touch with the probation officer, informing the officer of any change in his or her address.[2] Additional requirements can be added by the courts, such as a requirement to attend at, and participate in, alcohol or drug treatment programmes.[3] However, the court is given a wide discretion as to the nature of any such additional requirements. Schedule 1 to the 1996 Order sets out the particulars of any such additional requirements.

1   Criminal Justice (Northern Ireland) Order 1996, art 10(2).
2   Criminal Justice (Northern Ireland) Order 1996, art 10(6).
3   Criminal Justice (Northern Ireland) Order 1996, art 11.

Additional requirements

5.97   There are five additional requirements that a court may attach to a Probation Order and they relate to: (1) residence; (2) participation in prescribed activities; (3) attendance at a day centre; (4) medical treatment; and (5) substance abuse treatment.

5.98   The court can require the offender to reside in a certain location, perhaps a probation hostel,[1] for a certain period of time, although before doing so the court must consider the offender's home circumstances.[2] Alternatively it may include a condition that the offender attend at a certain location to engage in certain prescribed activities. However, this sort of additional requirement can only be made where the court has consulted with the probation officer, and it is satisfied as a result that it is a feasible for the offender to comply with the requirement.[3] This requirement is subject to a 60-day limit, ie the court can only order the offender to attend at, or participate in, activities for that length of time. It is also possible for the court to impose a requirement for the offender to attend at a day centre, although once again prior consultation with a probation officer is necessary and the requirement cannot require the offender's attendance at that centre for any more than 60 days. A court requirement directing the offender to undergo medical treatment for a mental condition can only take place on the basis of evidence presented by a doctor accredited for the purposed of Part II of the Mental Health (Northern Ireland) Order 1986.[4] The fifth specific type of additional requirement provided for in the legislation is a requirement that the offender undergo treatment for alcohol or drug dependency. The prerequisite for the imposition of the requirement is that offender's dependency caused, or contributed to, the offence.[5] Clearly, where an offender is subject to this sort of requirement the nature and extent of the supervision by the probation officer is altered significantly, and the probation officer is only required to be involved to ensure the requirement is being complied with.[6]

1   Probation (Northern Ireland) Order 1982, art 5(a) allows the Board to 'provide and maintain probation and bail hostels.' Probation hostels are 'premises for the reception and care of persons who may be required to reside there by a Probation Order': art 2.
2   Criminal Justice (Northern Ireland) Order 1996, Sch 1, para 1.
3   Criminal Justice (Northern Ireland) Order 1996, Sch 1, para 2. Obviously, any third parties involved in the facility or activity with which the offender will be involved must also consent to the making of this additional requirement: para 2(3).
4   Criminal Justice (Northern Ireland) Order 1996, Sch 1, para 4. For more on the role of Part II doctors, see chapter 11.
5   Criminal Justice (Northern Ireland) Order 1996, Sch 1, para 5.
6   Criminal Justice (Northern Ireland) Order 1996, Sch 1, para 5(5).

5.99 The court must also explain to the offender, in ordinary language, why it is making the order, the consequences of that order and the consequences if the offender fails to comply with its terms.[2] It is also required to give the probation officer assigned to the court copies of the order and he or she must then furnish the offender and the supervising probation officer with copies.[2]

[1] Criminal Justice (Northern Ireland) Order 1996, art 10(3).
[2] Criminal Justice (Northern Ireland) Order 1996, art 10(4).

5.100 A range of alternative consequences may flow from the breach of a Probation Order:[1]

(i)   a fine can be imposed without prejudice to the continuance of the order;[2] or

(ii) if the offender is a child, and the original order was a Probation Order, then an Attendance Centre Order can be made;[3]

(iii) the court can make a Community Service Order;[4] or

(iv) if the order was originally made by a magistrates' court then the court can deal with the offender in any manner in which that court could have dealt with him or her.[5]

This last option terminates the Probation Order. If the original order was made by a Crown Court then a magistrates' court can commit him or her to custody or on bail to that court.[6] The Crown Court has the same options for punishing the offender as are open to the magistrates' court.[7]

[1] Criminal Justice (Northern Ireland) Order 1996, Sch 2.
[2] Maximum fine is £1,000: Criminal Justice (Northern Ireland) Order 1996, Sch 2, para 3(1)(a).
[3] Criminal Justice (Children) (Northern Ireland) Order 1998, art 37.
[4] Criminal Justice (Northern Ireland) Order 1996, Sch 2, para 3(1)(b).
[5] Criminal Justice (Northern Ireland) Order 1996, Sch 2, para 2.
[6] Criminal Justice (Northern Ireland) Order 1996, Sch 2, para 3(3).
[7] Criminal Justice (Northern Ireland) Order 1996, Sch 2, para 4.

5.101 The courts made 1,081 Probation Orders in 2002/03, a decrease of 2% from the previous year's figure.[1] The supervision of people on a Probation Order forms the single biggest client group for the PBNI, with 1,283 of its 2,716 clients in March 2003 being subject to a Probation Order. PBNI standards provide that a detailed work plan be devised with the offender within fifteen days of the making of the order, which workplan is then reviewed every four months. Home visits take place on a weekly basis during the first four months and on a bi-weekly basis for the next four months and then on a monthly basis. Detailed standards exist in respect of enforcement, with the supervising probation officer mandated to commence breach proceedings where formal warnings have not been adhered to or if there is a danger to the public or to the offender.

[1] PBNI Annual Report 2002/03, Appendix K, p70.

COMMUNITY SERVICE ORDER

5.102 Community Service Orders (CSOs) are available for offenders aged 16 years and over, except where the penalty for the offence committed is fixed by law.[1] The idea is that the offender performs a number of unpaid hours of work in the community. The court can sentence the offender to carry out a number of hours of community service, totalling not less than 40 hours and not more than 240.[2] Consent of the offender is needed before an order can be made, and the court must be satisfied, having consulted with a probation officer if necessary, that the offender is a suitable person to carry out the work envisaged, and that arrangements can be made for the offender to carry out the work.[3] The court must explain to the offender in ordinary language why it is choosing to make a CSO, the purpose and effect of the order and the consequences of failing to comply with the order.[4] The probation officer must pass a copy of the order to the offender. The offender is required to complete the work set by the court within a year of the making of the order,[5] and is also required to report to his or her probation officer and to notify him or her of any change in address.[6]

[1]   Criminal Justice (Northern Ireland) Order 1996, art 13.
[2]   Criminal Justice (Northern Ireland) Order 1996, art 13(2).
[3]   Criminal Justice (Northern Ireland) Order 1996, art 13(4).
[4]   Criminal Justice (Northern Ireland) Order 1996, art 13(7).
[5]   Criminal Justice (Northern Ireland) Order 1996, art 14(2). This period can be extended by the court either on the application of the offender or of the probation officer: Criminal Justice (Northern Ireland) Order 1996, Sch 2, para 15.
[6]   Criminal Justice (Northern Ireland) Order 1996, art 14.

5.103   A breach of a Community Service Order is enforced in the same manner as a breach of a Probation Order,[1] with the exception that if a court punishes an offender who is in breach of a Community Service Order by requiring him or her to do further community service, the aggregate total of both Community Service Orders must not exceed 240 hours,[2] and the number of community service hours imposed as a punishment cannot exceed 60.[3]

In 2002/03, the courts made 728 CSOs, an increase of 7% from the previous year. In that year the PBNI supervised 654 persons on a CSO, of whom 13% were 'young people' aged between 10 and 17 years, 52% were young adults (ie aged 18–25) while the remaining 36% were adults.[4]

[1]   See para 5.100.
[2]   Criminal Justice (Northern Ireland) Order 1996, Sch 2, para 6(3)(b).
[3]   Criminal Justice (Northern Ireland) Order 1996, Sch 2, para 6(3)(a).
[4]   PBNI Annual Report 2002/03, Appendix K, p 71. 617 of PBNI clients in March 2003 were fulfilling the terms of a CPO.

5.104   Probation officers are responsible for making risk assessments of all potential work placements and of each offender. The offender should commence work on the allotted task no later than ten days after the sentence.[1] As with Probation Orders, enforcement of Community Service Orders by the supervising probation officer is governed by detailed standards, and written warnings are given before the probation officer becomes responsible for initiating enforcement proceedings. However, enforcement proceedings can be issued without the need for warnings, if the failure to adhere to the order would result in danger to the public or the offender.

[1] Directory of Probation Resources, PBNI March 2002, Community Service Standards, Standards 1.2 and 4.1.

CUSTODY-PROBATION ORDER

5.105 A Custody-Probation Order (CPO) requires the offender concerned to serve a custodial sentence and on release from custody, to be subject to supervision by probation officers,[1] and can only be made where a court has determined that a custodial sentence of at least 12 months is justified.[2] The period of supervision is longer than one year but no longer than three years,[3] and before a CPO can be made the offender must consent to it.[4] An offender will normally readily give his or her consent however, because the net effect of the CPO is to reduce the period of time that the offender spends in prison.[5] In making the CPO, the court is required to indicate, in open court, what custodial sentence it would have passed had the offender not consented.[6] The total number of CPOs made by the courts in 2002/03 was 317.[7] As of March 2003, probation officers were supervising 617 persons subject to CPOs.

[1] Criminal Justice (Northern Ireland) Order 1996, art 24.
[2] Criminal Justice (Northern Ireland) Order 1996, art 24(1).
[3] Criminal Justice (Northern Ireland) Order 1996, art 24(1)(b).
[4] Criminal Justice (Northern Ireland) Order 1996, art 24(3).
[5] There is no set or pre-determined period of reduction of the custodial period. That is simply left to the court's discretion (Criminal Justice (Northern Ireland) Order 1996, art 24(2)).
[6] Criminal Justice (Northern Ireland) Order 1996, art 24(5).
[7] PBNI Annual Report 2002/03, Appendix K, p 70 representing an increase of 33% from the number made the previous year.

5.106 In terms of the involvement of PBNI staff, the dual aspects of this order require fairly extensive input by probation staff. At the beginning of the custodial element of the order the offender is interviewed (within two days of the commencement of the sentence) with a view to drafting a 'career plan' to be produced no later than the twentieth day of the sentence.[1] This plan is reviewed at six monthly intervals and on the last occasion two weeks prior to the release of the offender, when a Probation Work Plan is developed. The offender then reports to his or her supervising probation officer no later than two days after release. Probation Order standards then apply to the probation element of the sentence.

[1] Directory of Probation Resources, PBNI, March 2002 Custody Probation Order Standards, Standards 1.1 an 1.2.

COMBINATION ORDER

5.107 A Combination Order (CO) is a disposal involving a probation element and a community service element. The probation element must be for a period of between one and three years while the community service element must be between 40 and 100 hours.[1] The other limitation on the application of Combination Orders is that they are only available to offenders aged 16 years or over. As with other orders, before making the order the court is required to indicate in open court why this option is being chosen and also to explain its effect to the offender in ordinary language.

The Combination Order is the least popular of the community-based disposals available to the courts for adults, with only 119 being made in 2002/03. This is also reflected in the PBNI 's workload as only 129 persons subject to a CO were clients of the Board in March 2003.[2]

[1]   Criminal Justice (Northern Ireland) Order 1996, art 15(1).
[2]   PBNI Annual Report 2002/03, Appendix K, pp 70–71.

SUSPENDED SENTENCE

5.108   A court may impose a term of imprisonment on an offender but it may feel that, for exceptional circumstances, it should not be served and thus it may be suspended. However, should the offender commit an imprisonable offence – as opposed to an offence for which he or she may not be imprisoned, for example some road traffic offences – within the period of suspension, then the suspended sentence may be reactivated.

5.109   Sentences of up to seven years can be suspended for between one and five years, whilst sentences of up to two years in prison or in a YOC can be suspended for between one and three years.[1] On making the suspended sentence the court has to explain to the offender, in ordinary language, his or her liability should he or she commit an imprisonable offence. A suspended sentence is treated as a sentence of imprisonment for all legislative purposes, except legislation that provides for disqualification from, or loss of office of persons sentenced to imprisonment.

[1]   Treatment of Offenders Act (Northern Ireland) 1968, s 18, as amended by the Treatment of Offenders (Northern Ireland) Order 1989, art 9.

DRUG TREATMENT AND TESTING ORDER

5.110   This order can be imposed where the court is satisfied that the offender has a drug abuse problem and can last for between six months and three years.[1] During the period of the order the offender is required to submit himself or herself to treatment designed to reduce his or her dependency on drugs. The offender will also be under the supervision of a probation officer during the period of treatment.[2] The order cannot be made without the offender's consent. It is only available for offenders aged 17 years or over.

[1]   Criminal Justice (Northern Ireland) Order 1998, art 8.
[2]   Criminal Justice (Northern Ireland) Order 1998, art 9(7).

5.111   Drug Treatment and Testing Orders are reviewed by the court that made them on a monthly basis to ensure that the offender is adhering to the regime.[1] The supervising probation officer is required to make a report at these review hearings. At these review hearings the court can deal with any breaches of the order. Where the offender is not complying with the terms of the order the court can vary the terms of the order, or it can revoke it and deal with the offender in the same manner as if it were the court before which he or she had been convicted of the offence.[2]

1   Criminal Justice (Northern Ireland) Order 1998, art 10(1).
2   Criminal Justice (Northern Ireland) Order 1998, art 10(4)(5) and (8).

Immediate custody

5.112   A court may feel that a community disposal is not appropriate and decide to send an offender to a penal establishment immediately on conviction. Young offenders serve custodial sentences in the Young Offenders' Centre (YOC), whilst only offenders aged over 21 years are sent to prison.[1] Offenders aged 17 or under may only be detained in a Juvenile Justice Centre.[2] However, a court may not pass a custodial sentence, including a sentence of detention in a YOC or a Juvenile Justice Centre, where the offender is not legally represented, unless the offender has been refused legal aid, or having been informed of the opportunity to apply for it, declined that invitation.[3]

The release of prisoners serving determinate sentences is governed by remission rules as no system of parole operates in Northern Ireland.[4] Prisoners serving life sentences are recommended for release by the Life Sentence Review Commissioners.[5]

1   Prisoners' rights are outlined in the Prisons and Young Offenders Centres Rules (Northern Ireland) 1995. These govern such matters as visiting rights, and correspondence rights and PBNI produces a pamphlet summarising these. The various prison establishments in Northern Ireland are set out in para 5.6.
2   The rights of children detained under a Juvenile Justice Centre Order are set out in the Juvenile Justice Centre Rules (Northern Ireland) 1999.
3   Criminal Justice (Northern Ireland) Order 1996, art 18.
4   See para 5.11.
5   See para 5.21.

Child offenders

5.113   The applicability of the options outlined above to children is outlined where appropriate. However, there are some options that are available for children only. It is these that are be dealt with in this section.

There are two custodial options for children, namely detention in a juvenile justice centre under an eponymous order[1] or detention in secure accommodation under a Custody Care Order in the case of child offenders younger than 14 years.[2] However, where a child commits certain serious offences – offences which in the case of an adult would carry a term of imprisonment of 14 years or more, not being an offence carrying a penalty fixed by law, and the court is of the opinion that no other method of dealing with the case is suitable – it may sentence the offender to be detained, in such place as the Secretary of State decides, for a specified period.[3] The child can thus be detained at a YOC, a juvenile justice centre or a prison. Children detained in this way can be released on the licence of the Secretary of State, although licences may be revoked and the offender recalled on the same basis as an 'SOSP'.[4]

1   See para 5.114.
2   See para 5.129.

³   Criminal Justice (Children) (Northern Ireland) Order 1998, art 45(2).
⁴   See para 5.21.

Juvenile Justice Centre Order

5.114   This is the main custodial option available for children, although it is not intended to be purely a custodial option, but rather an opportunity to help the juvenile, through training and guidance, to steer clear of criminal activity on release. In order to facilitate that aim, Juvenile Justice Centre Orders (JJCO) also provide for post-release supervision.

5.115   A JJCO is normally for a period of six months, unless the court specifies a longer term.[1] In any event it cannot be longer than two years. One half of the prescribed period is spent in the Juvenile Justice Centre, while the remaining half is spent under the supervision of a probation officer. A juvenile justice centre is a secure facility to which children found guilty of offences may be sent if the Youth Court considers that a custodial sentence would be justified. There is only one juvenile justice facility in Northern Ireland, located at Rathgael, Bangor, County Down. JJCOs have recently become available for 17 year old offenders, although there are some limitations on imposing them on that age category.[2]

¹   Criminal Justice (Children) (Northern Ireland) Order 1998, art 39(2).
²   Criminal Justice (Children) (Northern Ireland) Order 1998, art 39(3A), inserted by the Justice (Northern Ireland) Act 2002, s 64. The offender must not reach adulthood during the Order, and must not have had a custodial sentence imposed on him or her in the previous two years. A PSR is also required.

5.116   After the JJCO is made by the court the Probation Board's Court Duty Officer interviews the child and his or her parents, if possible, with this information being forwarded to the juvenile justice centre. PBNI staff will engage with the child on the basis of a workplan. Before the child's release from the juvenile justice centre, a supervision plan is agreed, and this will be signed by the child and his or her parents. The supervising probation officer will maintain a high level of contact in the first three months, meeting with the child at least twice a week. Thereafter the level of supervision will depend on the risk posed by the child.

5.117   Breach of the supervisory element of a JJCO renders the juvenile liable to a fine of £200 if he or she is less than 14 years, or a fine of £1,000 if older than that age. A court may also order the juvenile to be detained in a juvenile justice centre for a period of 30 days.[1]

¹   Criminal Justice (Children) (Northern Ireland) Order 1998, art 40(2), or to a YOC if aged 17.

5.118   In 2002/03, 46 JJCOs were made by the courts and 33 juveniles were subject to supervision by probation officers as of March 2003.[1] The rights and entitlements of children serving JJCOs are set out in the Juvenile Justice Centre Rules (Northern Ireland) 1999, and contain a number of general principles that should influence the operation of any such Centre.[2] These principles include the following matters:[3]

'(f)   children in custody shall be treated with fairness, dignity and respect at all times and in a manner which takes account of personal circumstances and they shall be entitled to contribute when decisions which affect them are made;

(g)   children in custody will be treated equally and will have access to services and facilities without discrimination on the basis of religion, race, ethnic origin, gender, language, sexual orientation, disability, political opinion, nationality, birth, economic or other status;

(h)   the custodial environment shall, so far as is possible, be stable and control will be maintained as befits the needs and interests of the children, the community and the good order of the centre;

(i)   a child will be encouraged to maintain links with his family and/or those having responsibility for his welfare and will be assisted in other respects to prepare for release from custody;

(j)   a child will retain all rights and privileges except those removed as a necessary consequence of his detention in a juvenile justice centre.'

[1]   PBNI Annual Report 2002/03, pp 70–71.
[2]   These Rules also deal with the management of the Centre.
[3]   Juvenile Justice Centre Rules (Northern Ireland) 1999, r 3.

Attendance Centre Order

5.119   These are orders, available for offenders aged from 10 to 16 years, requiring the offender to attend at a centre for instruction or training given by teachers.[1] Because the legislation requires the court to consider the accessibility of the attendance centre from the offender's home, Attendance Centre Orders are not very common. The order specifies the total number of hours an offender must attend for. In any event it should be 12 hours, unless the offender is a child aged less than 14 years and the court is of the opinion that 12 hours would be excessive or, in the case of an offender aged over 14 years, that 12 hours is not enough. In the latter case the court may order the offender to attend for up to 24 hours. The court will also set the date for the first attendance with subsequent attendance dates and times being set by the centre manager. Attendance at an attendance centre should be organised so as not to interfere with any educational or work commitments that the offender has. Offenders can only be required to attend once in any one day and then only for a maximum of three hours.[2] An Attendance Centre Order can also be made where an offender is in breach of a Probation Order.[3]

[1]   Criminal Justice (Children) (Northern Ireland) Order 1998, art 37.
[2]   Criminal Justice (Children) (Northern Ireland) Order 1998, art 37(6).
[3]   See para 5.100.

Reparation Order

5.120   A Reparation Order is a very recent addition to the range of sentencing options for child offenders. It involves the child offender making some non-financial reparation to the victim or to the community at large,[1] but is an option not available to the court where the sentence for the offence is imprisonment for life. The order cannot involve the offender making reparation for more than 24 hours and the consent of the victim to the making of the order is necessary as well.[2] (Children under the age of 14 years are not required to make reparations for more than one hour per day, while those aged 14 and older cannot be required to make reparations for more than four hours per day).[3] All elements of the order must be performed within six months of the making of the order. Detailed responsibilities of the child and of the supervising probation officer are set out in the Reparation Order Rules (Northern Ireland) 2003.[4]

[1]   Criminal Justice (Children) (Northern Ireland) Order 1998, art 36A, as inserted by the Justice (Northern Ireland) Act 2002, s 54.
[2]   Criminal Justice (Children) (Northern Ireland) Order 1998, art 36C, as inserted by the Justice (Northern Ireland) Act 2002, s 54.
[3]   Reparation Order Rules (Northern Ireland) 2003, r 4.
[4]   Rules 2 and 3.

5.121   Before making the order the court must consider a written report from a probation officer or a social worker,[1] which will indicate the type of reparation requirement that it would be appropriate to impose on the offender and his or her attitude to that proposal. This form of report clearly contains more information than would usually be contained in a PSR. The Reparation Order cannot be made unless the offender consents to it.[2] The court must state in open court why it is of the view that a community sentence is not possible before imposing the Reparation Order. As with many other forms of non-custodial disposal the court is required to explain in open court, in ordinary language the reasons for making the order, its effect and the consequences of not complying with it.

In the event of a breach of a Reparation Order a court may impose an Attendance Order on the offender or alternatively revoke the Reparation Order and deal with the offender for the original offence for which it was imposed on the same basis as it could if it were the trial court.[3]

[1]   Criminal Justice (Children) (Northern Ireland) Order 1998, art 36A(4), or indeed any other person designated by the Secretary of State.
[2]   Criminal Justice (Children) (Northern Ireland) Order 1998, art 36B, as inserted by the Justice (Northern Ireland) Act 2002, s 54.
[3]   Criminal Justice (Children) (Northern Ireland) Order 1998, Sch 1A, paras 3(1)(a) and 4, as inserted by the Justice (Northern Ireland) Act 2002, Sch 10.

Community Responsibility Order

5.122   A Community Responsibility Order (CRO) is another sentencing option established by the 2002 Justice (Northern Ireland) Act. It requires the offender to undergo 'relevant instruction in citizenship' and to carry out a number of hours of practical activities – no less than 20 and no more than 40 – as the supervising probation officer or social worker considers appropriate in light of that instruction.[1] The phrase 'relevant instruction in citizenship' is also defined by statute as instruction dealing with:

'(a)   citizenship (including, in particular, the responsibilities a person owes to a community);

(b)   the impact of crime on victims;

(c)   and factors relating to the offender which may cause him(sic) to commit offences.'[2]

The offender's duties are to attend at the designated place of instruction or activity and to carry out the instructions of the probation officer or social worker, and to keep in touch with that officer or social worker, notifying him or her or any change of address.[3] As with a Reparation Order, the consent of the offender is required before the court is in a position to make it, and all elements of the order must be completed within six months of the making of the order. The details of the supervising probation officer's duties are set out in the Community Responsibility Order Rules (Northern Ireland) 2003.[4]

[1]   Article 36E, as inserted by the Justice (Northern Ireland) Act 2002, s 54. Children under 14 are, however, limited to no more than two hours activity per day with those aged 14 or over limited to four hours per day. Community Responsibility Order Rules (Northern Ireland) 2003, r 3.
[2]   Criminal Justice (Children) (Northern Ireland) Order 1998, art 36E(3), as inserted by the Justice (Northern Ireland) Act 2002, s 55.
[3]   Criminal Justice (Children) (Northern Ireland) Order 1998, art 36G(1) and (2), as inserted by the Justice (Northern Ireland) Act 2002, s 55.
[4]   Rule 2.

5.123   Where the child fails to comply with a CRO a court may impose an Attendance Centre Order or a Community Service Order on him or her, or it may revoke the original order and sentence the child for the original offence as if it were the trial court.[1]

[1]   Criminal Justice (Children) (Northern Ireland) Order 1998, Sch 1A, paras 3(1)(b) and 4, as inserted by the Justice (Northern Ireland) Act 2002, Sch 10.

Court-ordered youth conferences

5.124   'Youth conferencing' is a restorative justice initiative that will be implemented in Northern Ireland in 2004[1] and is perhaps the most ambitious and radical of the new sentencing options introduced by the Justice (Northern Ireland) Act 2002. Its aim 'is to agree a plan of action for dealing with an offence and an offender in accordance with restorative justice principles'.[2] Youth conferences will be possible at two points in the criminal justice system. First, as a diversionary measure 'steering' children away from the usual criminal process. These are referred to as diversionary youth conferences.[3] Secondly, the courts may order a youth conference to be convened after the child has been convicted.[4]

[1]   An NIO press release indicates that 'youth conferencing will be piloted in the Greater Belfast area with further rollout next year [2004]. It will initially apply to 10 to 16 year olds and it is expected that 17

year olds will be included by next autumn [2004].' NIO Press Release, 18 December 2003, 'Youth Conference Service For Victims And Offenders by John Spellar.
2   Research and Statistics, Strategy and Programme 2002/3–2-4/5 Northern Ireland Statistics and Research Agency, p 9.
3   See para 5.62.
4   Criminal Justice (Children) (Northern Ireland) Order 1998, art 33A, as inserted by the Justice (Northern Ireland) Act 2002, s 59.

5.125   In regard to the second type, which is the focus in this section, a court that has found the child guilty of an offence must direct that a youth conference be held, unless the child has been found guilty of a serious indictable offence, or a scheduled offence,[1] which if committed by an adult, would attract a fixed sentence.[2]

1   An offence under the Terrorism Act 2000, Sch 9, ie a paramilitary offence.
2   Criminal Justice (Children) (Northern Ireland) Order 1998, art 33A(2), as inserted by the Justice (Northern Ireland) Act 2002, s 59.

5.126   As with diversionary youth conferences, the child's consent to participate is necessary to commence a court-ordered youth conference and if at any time the child withdraws that consent the conference must conclude.[1] These youth conferences are conducted on the same basis as diversionary youth conferences.

1   Criminal Justice (Children) (Northern Ireland) Order 1998, art 33A(6) and (7) as inserted by the Justice (Northern Ireland) Act 2002, s 59.

5.127   Court-ordered youth conferences have three options open to them; (1) to recommend that the court deal with the child; (2) that a youth conference plan be devised; and (3) that the child be subject to a custodial sentence as well as to a youth conference plan.[1] At the conclusion of the youth conference a plan of action will be devised, which, not surprisingly is called the 'youth conference plan'. The range of options that may be covered in this plan are set out in the legislation:[2]

'(a)   apologise to the victim of the offence or any person otherwise affected by it;

(b)   make reparation for the offence to the victim or any such person or to the community at large;

(c)   make a payment to the victim of the offence not exceeding the cost of replacing or repairing any property taken, destroyed or damaged by the child in committing the offence;

(d)   submit himself to the supervision of an adult;

(e)   perform unpaid work or service in or for the community;[3]

(f)   participate in activities (such as activities designed to address offending behaviour, offering education or training or assisting with the rehabilitation of persons dependent on, or having a propensity to misuse, alcohol or drugs);

(g)   submit himself to restrictions on his conduct or whereabouts (including remaining at a particular place for particular periods); and

(h)   submit himself to treatment for a mental condition or for a dependency on alcohol or drugs.'

The fact that the child has been the subject of a youth conference plan may be cited in future criminal proceedings.[4]

1   Criminal Justice (Children) (Northern Ireland) Order 1998, art 33A(5), as inserted by the Justice (Northern Ireland) Act 2002, s 59.
2   Criminal Justice (Children) (Northern Ireland) Order 1998, art 3C(1), as inserted by the Justice (Northern Ireland) Act 2002, s 57. The aspects of the plan must be completed within one year.
3   This option is only open to children aged 16 years or over.
4   Criminal Justice (Children) (Northern Ireland) Order 1998, art 3C(7), as inserted by the Justice (Northern Ireland) Act 2002, s 57. The aspects of the plan must be completed within one year.

YOUTH CONFERENCE ORDER

5.128   This is a court order requiring the child who has been made subject to a youth conference plan by a court-ordered youth conference to comply with the terms of that plan.[1] A Youth Conference Order is only to be made with the consent of the child, in circumstances where the court considers that the seriousness of the offences warrant making the order. Breach of any order is to be dealt with in the same manner as a breach of a Community Responsibility Order or a Reparation Order.[2]

1   Criminal Justice (Children) (Northern Ireland) Order 1998, art 36J, as inserted by the Justice (Northern Ireland) Act 2002, s 60. Note that a Youth Conference Order cannot be made in respect of a diversionary youth conference.
2   Criminal Justice (Children) (Northern Ireland) Order 1998, Sch 1A, as inserted by the Justice (Northern Ireland) Act 2002, Sch 10. See paras 5.123 and 5.121.

Custody Care Order

5.129   A Custody Care Order (CCO) is a form of disposal unique to Northern Ireland (although it is similar to the Detention and Training Order available in England and Wales) and, as stated earlier, is the result of the Criminal Justice Review Commission's recommendations relating to the age of criminal responsibility.[1] The Commission decided against recommending a change to the age of responsibility and decided instead to recommend a order which would make 10–13 year olds responsible for their criminal conduct but which would involve social services, rather than the youth justice authorities providing for their accommodation needs.

A CCO only applies to child offenders aged less than 14 years and is an order placing the child in secure accommodation, followed by a period under supervision, with the overall period determined by the court. A CCO is usually for six months but is not to exceed two years in length.[2] The child is to be kept in secure accommodation for one half of the period of the order and under supervision for the other half.[3]

1   'Review of the Criminal Justice System in Northern Ireland', 2000, para 10.69.
2   Criminal Justice (Children) (Northern Ireland) Order 1998, art 44A, as inserted by the Justice (Northern Ireland) Act 2002, s 56. If the order is for longer than six months the court must state it reasons for departing from the usual length of order in open court: art 44A(5).
3   Criminal Justice (Children) (Northern Ireland) Order 1998, art 44A(6).

5.130   Where the child would reach the age of 14 years during the period of time in custody the court has the option of directing that the child be held in a juvenile justice centre and not in secure accommodation.[1] The order can only be made if the court concludes that a custodial sentence is not appropriate.

During the period that a child is in secure accommodation under a CCO, the child qualifies as a 'child in need'[2] under the Children (Northern Ireland) Order 1995 and certain, though not all, of the provisions in the 1995 Order that relate to 'children in need' apply to it.[3]

[1]   Criminal Justice (Children) (Northern Ireland) Order 1998, art 44A(8).
[2]   For more on 'children in need' see chapter 7, para 7.16. See, in particular, *R (Howard League for Penal Reform) v Secretary of State for the Home Department* [2002] EWHC 2497 (Admin), [2003] 1 FLR 484.
[3]   The provisions that apply are arts 26, 27(1), (2)(b), (e), (f), (8); 28(2); 29(1), (2), (4), (6); 30; 31; 34, 35(1); 36(1), (4); 45; 73. Article 29(4) applies with exception of sub-para (a) and art 34(1)(a) applies but to Secretary of State rather than Department. Articles 5(7); 52(3) to (6), (7)(a) and (9); 53(1) to (9) all apply as if the child were in care.

5.131   If the child escapes from the secure accommodation he or she may be arrested without warrant by a police officer and is liable to a further punishment of a further period of 30 days' detention under a CCO or alternatively the court may revoke the Care Order and treat the offender as if he or she had just been found guilty of the original offence.[1]

Supervision of the non-custodial part of the order is by probation officers and breach of this element of the order can result in a child not older than 14 years being fined £200 or being subject to a period of dentition in secure accommodation of 30 days, or if older than 14, a fine of £1000, or 30 days in a juvenile justice centre.

[1]   Criminal Justice (Children) (Northern Ireland) Order 1998, art 44C(3).

Mentally disordered offenders

5.132   Mentally disordered offenders convicted in either the Crown Court or magistrates' court can be subject to particular types of disposals, namely Hospital Orders and Guardianship Orders (except for offences with penalties fixed by law).[1] Patients admitted to hospital under a Hospital or Guardianship Order are treated under Part II of the Mental Health (Northern Ireland) Order 1986.[2]

[1]   Mental Health (Northern Ireland) Order 1986, art 44.
[2]   See chapter 11.

Hospital Order

5.133   A Hospital Order can be made on the oral evidence of a 'Part II doctor'[1] and the written or oral evidence of one other medical practitioner that the offender is suffering from mental illness or severe mental impairment of a nature or degree which warrants his or her detention in hospital for medical treatment. The court must also be of the opinion that having regard to all the circumstances, including the nature of the offence and the character and the antecedents of the offender, that this is the most suitable means of dealing with the case.

[1]   See chapter 11. A 'Part II doctor' is one exercising powers under the Mental Health (Northern Ireland) Order 1986.

Guardianship Order[1]

5.134   Before a court may make one of these orders evidence from three people is required: (i) a 'Part II' doctor; (ii) another medical practitioner; and (iii) an Approved Social Worker.[2] The medical personnel give evidence that the offender is suffering from mental illness or severe mental handicap of a nature or degree which warrants reception into guardianship, whilst the Approved Social Worker gives written or oral evidence that it is necessary in the interests of the welfare of the patient that he or she should be received into guardianship. If the court is then of the opinion that, having regard to all circumstances, a Guardianship Order is the most suitable way of dealing with him or her, it can issue such an order. A Guardianship Order is available for use with offenders aged 16 years and over.[3]

[1]   On guardianship generally under the Mental Health (Northern Ireland) Order 1986, see chapter 11, para 11.51.
[2]   For an explanation of an ASW see chapter 11, para 11.16.
[3]   Mental Health (Northern Ireland) Order 1986, art 44(3)(a).

Restriction Order

5.135   Where a Hospital Order has been made and it appears to the court that, having regard to the nature of the offence, the antecedents of the person and the risk of his or her committing further offences if set at large, that it is necessary for the protection of the public from serious harm to do so, it may make a Restriction Order.[1] This attaches special restrictions to the Hospital Order, the effect of which is that the release of the offender is at the discretion of the Secretary of State and that the offender's right to make an application to the Mental Health Review Tribunal[2] to review the necessity of his or her detention is suspended. The Secretary of State can bring a Restriction Order to an end if satisfied that it is no longer required for the protection of the public.[3] A Responsible Medical Officer[4] has the responsibility of making reports on an offender subject to a Restriction Order. These reports are made at the direction of the Secretary of State and the legislation provides that there must be at least one a year.

[1]   Mental Health (Northern Ireland) Order 1986, art 47.
[2]   See chapter 11, para 11.88.
[3]   Mental Health (Northern Ireland) Order 1986, art 48(1).
[4]   See chapter 11.

Interim Hospital Order

5.136   An Interim Hospital Order is also available, allowing the court to place the offender in the care of the Department for admission and detention in a hospital, if the accused has been convicted but not yet sentenced.[1] It can be made on the oral evidence of a Part II doctor and the written or oral evidence of another medical practitioner that the offender is suffering from mental illness or severe mental impairment and that there is reason to suppose that the mental disorder from which he or she is suffering is such that it may warrant a Hospital Order.[2] Such an order can be made into a Hospital Order at a later hearing, or indeed renewed, without the need for the accused to be present, provided the accused has the opportunity of being represented at that hearing. Interim Hospital Orders can be made for a maximum of 12 weeks but are renewable for periods of 28 days on the written or oral evidence of a Residential Medical Officer (RMO) that continuation of the order is warranted. However, an extended Interim Hospital Order cannot last for longer than six months.[3] The Department must be given an opportunity by the court, to make representations before a Hospital or Interim Hospital Order can be made.[4]

[1]   Mental Health (Northern Ireland) Order 1986, art 45.
[2]   Mental Health (Northern Ireland) Order 1986, art 45(1).
[3]   Mental Health (Northern Ireland) Order 1986, art 45(4).
[4]   Mental Health (Northern Ireland) Order 1986, arts 44(5) and 45(3).

Probation officers and post-release supervision of sex offenders

5.137   Probation officers may be involved in the supervision of certain types of offender upon their release from prison. One type, 'Lifers' released on licence, has already been examined.[1] Another group of supervisees include sex offenders released from prison under the remission scheme,[2] or released as part of a Custody-Probation Order,[3] or released on licence under the 1996 Criminal Justice (Northern Ireland) Order.[4] The focus here is on the role of probation in respect of the supervision of sex offenders.[5]

[1]   See para 5.23.
[2]   See para 5.11.
[3]   For Custody-Probation Order, see para 5.105.
[4]   See para 5.141.
[5]   For supervision of sex offenders in the community generally, by social workers, for child protection purposes, see chapter 6, para 6.151.

5.138   Probation officers are involved in the administrative structures that deal with sex offenders post-release. Area Sex Offenders Risk Management Committees, of which there are six, have the responsibility of considering the approach to be taken to particular sex offenders under the Multi-Agency Sex Offender Risk Assessment Management Manual.[1] PBNI staff chair these committees, which report to a Northern Ireland-wide Sex Offenders Strategic Management Committee.[2] It is the function of the police to assess the risk posed by the offender, using standardised assessment methods, and where that risk is high the Area Committee will consider a particular offender's case. If it is felt necessary, an inter-agency plan is formulated by the Area Committee, with the Strategic Committee having the duty to review it in the case of very high risk offenders.

1   For more on the MASRAM Manual, see chapter 6, para 6.174.
2   PBNI Annual Report, 2002/03, p 58.

5.139   Probation Board standards for the supervision of sex offenders[1] require workplans to be established within 15 days of the court orders, which are then reviewed every four months. The supervising officer maintains once weekly contact with the offender from the outset making one visit per month to the offender's place of residence and one unannounced home visit per month until the first review. Contact with the offender can be reduced thereafter.[2]

1   The PBNI Sex Offender standards do not offer a definition of 'sex offenders' so it is difficult to say how it is determined that a particular offender should be subject to these standards.
2   'Sex Offender Supervision Standards', PBNI Directory of Probation Resources.

Release of 'Schedule 1' offenders

5.140   It is PBNI practice to inform social services if a 'Schedule 1' offender[1] (a range of offences of a sexual or violent nature against children) is released, either on licence or on the expiry of his or her sentence. These reports are made shortly before the release date and contain information relating to the prisoner, including medical reports, if appropriate, and a report of the prison-based probation officer. Informing social services in this manner allows them to determine whether any form of intervention into the life of the offender is necessary if, for example, a male 'Schedule 1' offender, convicted of an offence that suggests he may be of danger to young children, moves in with a woman and her children.[2]

1   A prisoner convicted of an offence under the Criminal Justice (Children) (Northern Ireland) Order 1998, Sch 1.
2   For more on the powers and duties of social workers in this type of situation see chapter 6, para 6.151.

Sex offenders released on licence

5.141   Obviously, where a court had made a community-based disposal in respect of a sexual offence, probation officers will be involved in the usual manner. However, they will also be involved where a sex offender is released from prison on licence under the Criminal Justice (Northern Ireland) Order 1996, article 26(1), rather than under the remission rules, before the completion of the custodial sentence imposed.[1] For non-sex offenders, release from prison under the remission rules marks the end of their punishment. However, in respect of sex offenders released on licence, probation officers continue to supervise the offender until the expiration of the period of time in custody imposed by the trial judge.[2] Thus, a sex offender released on licence under this provision, having served two years of a four year sentence, remains liable to supervision for the remaining two years, whereas a non-sex offender will not be liable to supervision.

1   Criminal Justice (Northern Ireland) Order 1996, art 26. The trial judge must indicate at the sentencing stage that this article is to apply: art 26(1)(b)(ii).

2   Criminal Justice (Northern Ireland) Order 1996, art 26(2).

5.142   The release of a sex offender on licence under article 26 is only possible if the sentencing court has sanctioned the possibility. It must consider two criteria when deciding whether a person can be released on licence, first the protection of the public from serious harm and secondly, the prevention of re-offending and the rehabilitation of the offender.

5.143   The terms and conditions of the sex offender's licence should be confirmed no later than four weeks before the offender's release. The terms that usually apply include the offender's responsibility to maintain contact with the supervising officer, to adhere to his or her instructions, to live in an approved location, to remain in the jurisdiction only travelling outside it with the permission of the supervising officer, and not to jeopardise the objectives of the supervision. Breach of the licence conditions renders the offender liable to a fine of £1,000 or a suspension of the licence for six months and a recall to prison. The commission of further offences can also result in a recall to prison as well as the imposition of a further sentence for the more recent offence.

Registered sex offenders

5.144   Probation officers may also be involved in the supervision of sex offenders who are required to register their names and addresses under the Sex Offenders Act 1997[1] and who have been sentenced to Community Orders or who have been released on licence. Probation officers will carry out similar supervisory duties to those they would perform if the offender were a non-sex offender. However, where a probation officer considers it necessary, because there are concerns about the risk posed by the offender, he or she must refer that offender's case to the appropriate Multi-Agency Sex Offender Risk Assessment and Management Committee, in line with the Multi-Agency Sex Offenders Risk Assessment Management Manual.[2]

Chapter 6

Child Protection

Introduction

6.1   This chapter deals with the legal and administrative procedures that are relevant to the protection of children, the area of work in which most social workers will be employed.[1] Interspersing explanation of the legislation and case law with child protection statistics, departmental and other guidance, it provides an up-to-date snapshot of contemporary child protection practice and trends.[2]

[1]   'Crossing Borders', Social Work Mobility Study, NSWQB and CCETSW(NI), 2001, p 14. In 1997 56% of social work graduates employed in social work posts were engaged in family and child care services.
[2]   For an historical overview of the development of child protection service in Northern Ireland, see 'A Better Future – 50 Years of Child Care in Northern Ireland 1950–2000' DHSSPS 2003, Paul Martin.

Types of harm

6.2   The child protection system aims to protect children from abuse and neglect, which can take many different forms. The Departmental Guidance, 'Co-operating to Safeguard Children', provides a description and explanation of four forms of abuse.[1] Physical injury and sexual abuse are, of course, included within the Department's typology, but so too are emotional abuse and neglect. Physical abuse is described as ' the deliberate physical injury to a child, or the wilful or neglectful failure to prevent physical injury or suffering.' Sexual abuse is defined as 'forcing or enticing a child to take part in sexual activities' and these sexual activities may include non-contact activities as well as contact-based sexual acts. Neglect is the 'persistent failure to meet a child's physical, emotional and/or psychological needs, likely to result in significant harm' and emotional abuse is defined as the 'persistent emotional ill-treatment of a child, such as to cause severe and persistent adverse effects on the child's emotional development.'

[1]   DHSSPS, Belfast, 2003, p 13.

6.3 Perhaps surprisingly, approximately 40% of children are included on the Child Protection Register for reasons of neglect. The following table shows the number of children on the CP Register in 2002 and the reasons for their inclusion on the register.

PERCENTAGE OF CHILDREN ON THE NORTHERN IRELAND PROTECTION REGISTER BY CATEGORY OF ABUSE[1]

Category	1998	1999	2000	2001
Sexual abuse	17.1	17.3	15.9	13.4
Physical abuse	20.6	20.9	19.8	24.0
Neglect	40.1	38.1	37.0	37.2
Emotional abuse	13.6	13.6	15.8	13.9

[1] 'A Better Future – 50 Years of Child Care in Northern Ireland 1950–2000' DHSSPS 2003, Paul Martin, Table 10, p 164.

6.4 The numbers of children on the CP Register throughout the 1990s has remained relatively stable, as the table below indicates.

NUMBERS ON NORTHERN IRELAND PROTECTION REGISTER 1991–2001[1]

Year	Number	Rate per 100
1991	1,502	3.3
1992	1,446	3.1
1993	1,345	2.9
1994	1,476	3.1
1995	1,523	3.2
1996	1,551	3.3
1997	1,400	3.0
1998	1,386	3.0
1999	1,463	3.2
2000	1,483	3.2
2001	1,414	3.1

Obviously, those children included on the register are not the total number of children about whom there are child protection concerns, as only the most serious cases where the child is continuing to suffer, or is likely to suffer significant harm will be included on the register. In fact, the UK government has committed itself in its reports to the UNCRC to reducing the number of children included on the register.[2] However, the figures do give a clear indication of the types of harm that children endure.[3]

[1] 'A Better Future – 50 Years of Child Care in Northern Ireland 1950–2000' DHSSPS 2003, Paul Martin, p 163.
[2] UK's second periodic report to UNCRC, CRC/C/83/Add.3, 25 February 2002, para 8.7.1(d). The commitment was that the numbers of children on the 'at risk' registers would have halved by 2002 from the 1997 figures.
[3] Interestingly, most children placed on the register are there for reasons of neglect or potential neglect.

Children's services and child protection

6.5 In order to gain an holistic impression of the role social services authorities play in supporting troubled families it is necessary to understand that the delivery of child and family services and compulsory intervention under the Children (Northern Ireland) 1995 Order must be seen as seeking to achieve the same aim, namely that children are not hampered in achieving their potential by being at risk of harm. There is a relationship between the child protection system and the delivery of children's services which affects the manner in which the former operates. Where social services staff encounter a family in crisis in which children may be suffering harm, they will usually first assess whether the situation can be ameliorated by providing services to that family generally, or the children. In other words, Trusts will not necessarily have immediate recourse to the courts for legal orders. They may instead consider how best to tackle the situation using the full range of services and skills available to them. The range of matters dealt with in the next chapter, 'Children's Services', may therefore arise for consideration before the Trust seeks the court-sanctioned, compulsory intervention measures which are the subject of this chapter.

6.6 'Co-operating to Safeguard Children' refers to findings of Department of Health-sponsored research into the operation of the Children Act 1989 in England and Wales to underline the importance of understanding the relationship between children's services and child protection. The research demonstrated that 'child protection enquiries were inappropriately used by some professionals as a means of obtaining services for children in need' and that 'too often enquiries were too narrowly conducted as investigation into whether abuse or neglect had occurred without considering the wider needs and circumstances of the family.'[1] In short, the delivery of children's services must be considered as part of wider child protection strategies.

[1] 'Co-operating to Safeguard Children' DHS Belfast 2003, p 18, para 3.13.

Public law and private law Orders

6.7　The salient legislative enactment in the field of child protection is the Children (Northern Ireland) Order 1995, Northern Ireland's near equivalent to the Children Act 1989.[1] Like the 1989 Act, it provides for compulsory intervention by social services authorities when the threshold condition of 'significant harm' is reached, allowing the courts to issue a Care Order, or a Supervision Order, as appropriate. Such orders are commonly referred to as 'public law' orders because they involve intervention by the State, and to distinguish them from the 'private law' orders available where the parents of a child, or those with parental responsibility, are involved in a dispute about how the child is to be reared.[2] Public law orders are Care Orders, Supervision Orders, Education Supervision Orders, Emergency Protection Orders, Child Assessment Orders, and Secure Accommodation Orders, while the following are private law orders: Parental Responsibility Orders, Family Assistance Orders and Article 8 orders, ie namely Residence, Contact, Specific Issues and Prohibited Steps Orders.

[1]　For further insight into the operation of child protection services in England and Wales, see the Department of Health's 1995 series of publications, entitled 'Child Protection: Messages from Research' and another series published by the Stationery Office entitled, 'Studies in Evaluating the Children Act 1989.'

[2]　Such orders are provided for in the Children (Northern Ireland) Order 1995, art 8 and discussed in chapter 9, para 9.101.

6.8　Considerably more private law business than public law business comes before the courts, with the ratio of private law proceedings to public law proceedings being approximately 5:1. In the financial year 2001/02, applications were made for public law orders in 913 cases, with 844 of these being disposed of. In contrast applications were made for 5,027 private law orders with 4,596 of these being disposed of.[1]

[1]　COAC, Third Report, Table 21B, p 69.

6.9　There is a degree of crossover between public law and private law because of the fact that a court may make a private law order of its own volition in any application before it.[1] This means that even where the application is one for a Care Order or Supervision Order, for example, the court may make a Residence Order stipulating with whom the child is to live, if it believes that to be the correct course of action, even though no application for such an order had been made to it. Naturally, a court will carefully evaluate the impact of such a step before taking it, and that the person in whose favour the Residence Order is made is willing and capable of caring for the child.[2] The second way in which there may be a crossover between the public law orders and private law orders is where the court is faced with a number of different applications in respect of the same children. For example, while a Trust may make an application for a Care Order in respect of a child, one of the child's grandparents might seek a Residence Order, arguing that they are in a position to care for him or her and that it is in the child's best interests that he or she be reared by them.

[1]　Children (Northern Ireland) Order 1995, art 10(1)(b).

[2]　See, for example, *Re B (children) (residence: interim care order)* [2002] EWCA Civ 1225, [2002] 3 FCR 562 in which the judge at first instance refused the social service authority's application for an interim

care order, instead classifying the problem as a private law dispute about residence and making a shared residence order. The circumstances were that although the mother and father were engaged in a contact dispute, the mother had displayed aggressive behaviour toward the children and had threatened the children's father that she would kill herself and them. The Court of Appeal overturned the judge's decision.

Human Rights Act 1998

6.10   The applicability of the HRA to social services activity generally is examined in Chapter 1.[1] Those Convention rights that are likely to have more applicability to child protection functions are examined here, though it is not suggested that only those rights examined here may be engaged by the child protection process. The Convention rights examined here are articles 3, 6 and 8.

[1]   See para 1.74.

Article 8: Respect for private life and family life

6.11   Because in carrying out their child protection functions social workers are intervening directly in families' lives, article 8, the right to family and private life, is engaged and this right is examined in some depth here.[1] However, this right is not absolute and it may be infringed if a number of conditions are met. If these conditions are held to have existed in a particular situation then the public authority will be held to have acted lawfully.

[1]   Social workers should obviously be aware that this does not mean that art 8 will not feature in other activity in which they are engaged, merely that the obvious applicability of art 8 to the subject matter of the chapter warrants its treatment here, rather than in any other chapter.

6.12   The full text of article 8 is as follows:

'Everyone has the right to respect for his private and family life, his home and his correspondence.

There shall be no interference by a public authority with the exercise of this right except such as is in accordance with the law and is necessary in a democratic society in the interests of national security, public safety or the economic well-being of the country, for the prevention of disorder or crime, for the protection of health or morals, or for the protection of the rights and freedoms of others.'

6.13   The permissible grounds for interfering with the right are contained in paragraph two and much of the discussion about the compatibility of a public authority's actions with the right will centre on this paragraph. There are a number of elements of paragraph two that a public authority needs to satisfy before the courts conclude that it has acted lawfully.

6.14   First, the interference must be 'in accordance with law'. These means that the public authority must have a statutory or common law,[1] basis for its actions. In respect of child protection matters, this legal basis will usually be found in the Children (Northern Ireland) Order 1995. In respect of disclosing information about suspected sex abusers to the public, for example, the legal basis is found in common law.[2]

[1]   For an explanation of 'common law', see chapter 1, para 1.48.
[2]   See para 6.175.

6.15   Secondly, there must be a 'legitimate aim' for any such interference with the right. This does not normally present a problem in respect of child protection matters as the aim in such work is always to protect the child, which in terms of article 8(2) is an attempt to protect the rights of others.

6.16   Thirdly, the actions of the public authority must be 'necessary in a democratic society'. This means that there must be a 'pressing social need'[1] for the interference, thereby requiring the public authority to provide sufficient evidence to justify the interference, and preventing it from simply asserting that it believed the interference was necessary. Clearly, the 'pressing social need' test is satisfied if a child is suffering from significant harm. However, the European Court of Human Rights has stipulated that a legitimate aim must be pursued in a manner that is 'proportionate' to the aim being pursued, and it is in respect of this requirement that many child protection interventions will be measured. The proportionality of the public authority's intervention means that the authority must show that the manner in which it is achieving the aim of protecting the child is appropriate having regard to the authority's state of knowledge and the danger, both immediate and long-term, posed to the child. Therefore, on an application for a Care Order, for example, the courts must assess whether there are less draconian measures open to the Trust that might provide adequate and appropriate protection of the child. If it concludes that such other options are suitable then the granting of a Care Order would be a disproportionate way of achieving the aim of protecting the child. The granting of the Care Order would therefore, in those circumstances amount to a violation of the parents' right to family life and thus the court must decline to make it.

[1]   See, for example, *Dudgeon v United Kingdom* (1981) 4 EHRR 149 in which the European Court of Human Rights considered that there was no pressing social need to criminalise all homosexual activity.

6.17   One further concept deriving from the European Convention of Human Rights is relevant to the application of Convention right, article 8. The European Court of Human Rights developed a concept to reflect the fact that it had a supervisory role in assessing the compatibility of legislation and State action with the Convention rights. State authorities, 'by reason of their direct and continuous contact with vital forces of their countries, are in a better position that the international judge to give an opinion on the "necessity" of a "restriction" or penalty',[1] leaving the states with a 'margin of appreciation'. This 'margin of appreciation' is intended to respect the fact that the authorities with responsibility for a particular issue are usually better placed to make fine distinctions between choosing one course of action and another. However, it does not mean that the authorities may do as they please. In cases under the HRA this margin has been referred to as the 'discretionary area of judgment'.

[1]   *Handyside v United Kingdom* (1976) 1 EHRR 737.

6.18 Some examples will illustrate the application of article 8.[1] In *KA v Finland*[2] the parents of a child who had been in care for some years sought to have him returned to them but the social services authorities refused. The European Court of Human Rights considered that there is a positive obligation on State authorities to ensure that children are taken into care for the shortest period of time necessary. To this end they need to re-consider, on a continuing basis if necessary, the re-unification of the children with their parents, if this is possible. In that regard the social service authorities had, on the facts of the case, violated Article 8 because they had failed to take sufficient steps towards a possible reunification of the parents and their child. The court, therefore, emphasised the importance of concepts discussed earlier, namely the need for proportionality when intervening in a family, and the positive obligation[3] to ensure that individuals can exercise their article 8 rights.

[1]   See also *P, C and S v United Kingdom* discussed in chapter 1, para 1.84, an example of the breach of art 8 (and art 6) involving the UK.
[2]   [2003] 1 FLR 696, [2003] 1 FCR 201.
[3]   On positive obligations see chapter 1, para 1.80 and chapter 6, para 6.21.

6.19   *Kutzner v Germany*[1] provides another example of a failure by State authorities to adhere to its positive obligation under article 8 to consider the possible re-unification of children in care with their parents. In that case the parents were people with learning difficulties. The courts considered that it was questionable whether the authorities had given sufficient consideration to other measures of support for the children's parents as an alternative to taking the children into care.

[1]   [2003] 1 FCR 249.

6.20   *Elsholz v Germany*[1] involved a child-rearing dispute between the unmarried parents of a child. At or about the age of five years the child was reported as stating that he no longer wished to see his father. The father's subsequent application for access was rejected as the court was not prepared to enforce contact because to do so would involve the child in a conflict of loyalty between his mother and father, and it was clear such contact would take place against his mother's will. The courts also refused permission for the father to produce expert psychological evidence and his appeal was dismissed without a hearing. The European Court of Human Rights considered that these last two factors in particular involved the court in overstepping its margin of appreciation.[2]

[1]   [2000] 2 FLR 486.
[2]   Note that the European Court concluded that States have a narrower margin of appreciation when deciding child-rearing disputes between parents, than they do when deciding whether to take children into care: para 49. The court also found a breach of Convention right, art 6.

Article 3: Torture, inhuman and degrading treatment

6.21   Article 3, the right guaranteeing freedom from inhuman and degrading treatment and punishment and torture[1] is also relevant to the child protection process. As outlined in chapter 1,[2] the European Court of Human Rights concluded, in *Z v United Kingdom*,[3] that a failure by a local authority in England and Wales to institute child protection procedures in the applicant's case, with the result that the child continued to be neglected by its parents, amounted to a breach of article 3.[4] As explained in chapter one, the Convention rights also impose positive obligations on States and thus where a person's rights are being violated by another person, the State is obligated to do what it can to bring that violation to an end. The Court explained its decision:[5]

> 'The obligation on high contracting parties under ... the Convention to secure to everyone within their jurisdiction the rights and freedoms defined in the Convention, taken together with Article 3, requires states to take measures designed to ensure that individuals within their jurisdiction are not subjected to torture or inhuman or degrading treatment, including such ill-treatment administered by private individuals. These measures should provide effective protection, in particular, of children and other vulnerable persons and include reasonable steps to prevent ill-treatment of which the authorities had or ought to have had knowledge.
>
> There is no dispute in the present case that the neglect and abuse suffered by the four child applicants reached the threshold of inhuman and degrading treatment. This treatment was brought to the local authority's attention, at the earliest in October 1987. It was under a statutory duty to protect the children and had a range of powers available to them, including removal from their home. The children were however only taken into emergency care, at the insistence of the mother, on 30 April 1992. Over the intervening period of four and a half years, they had been subject in their home to what the child consultant psychiatrist who examined them referred to as horrific experiences. The Criminal Injuries Compensation Board had also found that the children had been subject to appalling neglect over an extended period and suffered physical and psychological injury directly attributable to a crime of violence. The Court acknowledges the difficult and sensitive decisions facing social services and the important countervailing principle of respecting and preserving family life. The present case however leaves no doubt as to the failure of the system to protect these child applicants from serious, long-term neglect and abuse.'

[1]   The text of the article simply reads, 'No one shall be subjected to torture or to inhuman or degrading treatment or punishment.' The applicability of art 3 to corporal and physical punishment of children is discussed in chapter 1, para 1.79.

[2]   See para 1.80.

[3]   [2001] 2 FCR 246, [2001] 2 FLR 612, [2001] Fam Law 583

[4]   See also *E v United Kingdom* [2003] 1 FLR 348 in which the European Court of Human Rights also determined that there had been a breach of art 3 (and art 13 – the right to an effective remedy) arising from the failure of social services to protect children known to be at risk. See also *DP v United Kingdom* [2003] 1 FLR 50, [2002] 3 FCR 385, where there was no violation of art 3 because the authorities were not aware of the harm being suffered by the child.

[5]   At paras 73 and 74.

6.22   Article 3 has been interpreted by the European Court of Human Rights as outlawing three different types of punishment or treatment: torture, inhuman treatment or punishment, and degrading treatment or punishment, with torture being the most severe form of ill-treatment, and degrading treatment being the least severe. Not all forms of ill-treatment will infringe article 3. In order to engage the Article, treatment must meet the test for degrading treatment, namely 'treatment that arouses in the victim a feeling of fear and anguish and inferiority capable of humiliating and debasing the victim and possibly breaking his or her physical or moral resistance.'[1]

[1] *Ireland v United Kingdom* (1978) 2 EHRR 25, para 167.

Article 6: Right to fair trial

6.23 The main element of the right to a fair trial is contained in the guarantee, in article 6(1),[1] that:

'In the determination of his civil rights and obligations or of any criminal charge against him, everyone is entitled to a fair and public hearing within a reasonable time by an independent and impartial tribunal established by law.'[2]

This guarantee contains a number of elements, as can be seen. First, that there will be a fair and public hearing, secondly, that such a hearing will take place within a reasonable time and thirdly, that the matter will be heard by someone who is independent of the parties and whose role has been established by common law or statute.

[1] Article 6(2) and (3) provide guarantees that apply to the trial of criminal offences only.
[2] The remainder of the paragraph provides that 'Judgment shall be pronounced publicly but the press and public may be excluded from all or part of the trial in the interest of morals, public order or national security in a democratic society, where the interests of juveniles or the protection of the private life of the parties so require, or to the extent strictly necessary in the opinion of the court in special circumstances where publicity would prejudice the interests of justice.'

6.24 The first of these protections is the most general and can be the most difficult to apply. In *P, C and S v United Kingdom*,[1] for example, as explained in chapter 1,[2] the judge's decision to continue to hear the Care Order and Freeing Order applications in circumstances where the applicant had to represent herself, was a breach of article 6. The complexity of the case required her to have legal representation.[3] The court stated that it was not convinced that the importance of proceeding with expedition, which attaches generally to child care cases, necessitated the draconian action of proceeding to a full and complex hearing (of the Care Order application), followed within one week by the freeing for adoption application, both without legal assistance being provided to the applicants.[4] Although it was doubtless desirable for S's future to be settled as soon as possible, the court considered that the imposition of one year from birth as the deadline appeared a somewhat inflexible and blanket approach, applied without particular consideration of the facts of this individual case. S was, according to the care plan, to be placed for adoption and it was not envisaged that there would be any difficulty in finding a suitable adoptive family (eight couples were already identified by 2 February 1999). Yet although S was freed for adoption by the court on 15 March 1999, she was not in fact placed with a family until 2 September

1999, a gap of over five months for which no explanation has been given, while the adoption order which finalised matters on a legal basis was not issued until 27 March 2000 more than a year later. Her placement was therefore not achieved by her first birthday in May in any event. It is not possible to speculate at this time as to how long the adjournment would have lasted had it been granted in order to allow the applicant P to have representation at the care proceedings, or for both parent applicants to be represented at the freeing for adoption proceedings. It would have been entirely possible for the judge to place strict time limits on any lawyers instructed, and for instructions to be given for re-listing the matter with due regard to priorities. As the applicants pointed out, S was herself in a successful foster placement and unaffected by the ongoing proceedings. The court did not find that the possibility of some months' delay in reaching a final conclusion in those proceedings was so prejudicial to her interests as to justify what the trial judge himself regarded as a procedure which gave an appearance of 'rail-roading' her parents.

1   [2002] 2 FLR 631, [2002] 3 FCR 1, [2002] Fam Law 811.
2   Paragraph 1.84.
3   The European Court concluded that there had been a violation of the right to fair trial notwithstanding the fact that the applicant's lawyers had withdrawn owing to her unreasonable instructions.
4   Paragraph 98.

6.25   Another example of the applicability of article 6 is *W v United Kingdom*,[1] which pre-dates the Children Act 1989 and the Children (Northern Ireland) Order 1995. In that case the lack of an effective judicial mechanism to allow the parents of a child in care to challenge a decision of the social services authority to restrict access to their child was a breach of article 6.[2] Although the parents could have judicially reviewed the authority's decision, that process would not have allowed them to examine the merits of the decision, merely its legality.[3] The right to a fair trial, therefore, means that not only must one have an opportunity to 'have one's day in court' as it were, but the opportunity to avail of the courts must be as complete as it can possibly be, allowing both parties a reasonable opportunity to present their cases under similar conditions.[4]

1   (1988) 10 EHRR 29, E Ct HR.
2   Contact in care is now dealt with by the Children (Northern Ireland) Order 1995, art 53 and where a Trust wishes to restrict contact between parents and child it needs court sanction if that period is to extend beyond 72 hours. See chapter 7, para 7.39.
3   On judicial review generally, see chapter 2, para 2.105.
4   This is referred to as the 'equality of arms'. See *Neumeister v Austria* (1979–80) 1 EHRR 91.

6.26   However, article 6 does not apply to all decision-making but only to matters involving the determination of a person's 'civil rights and obligations' and criminal charges against him or her. The issue in social work law is likely to be whether the decision that social services have taken can be considered to amount to a determination of a person's civil rights and obligations thus attracting the protections outlined in article 6(1). The European Court of Human Rights has grappled with the question of how to define the phrase 'civil rights and obligations' on a number of occasions, and the case law can be confusing. However, it is clear that it does not apply to administrative decisions or conclusions arising from investigations which are not determinative of the applicant's civil rights in that they do not involve a final adjudication of the matter.[1] This is the case even where those investigations come to conclusions that are significant for the purposes of any ultimate trial. As a consequence the English Court of Appeal has determined that article 6 does not apply to child protection case conferences,[2] although it does, of course, apply to the court proceedings that might arise from decisions made by such conferences.

[1]   *Fayed v United Kingdom* (1994) 18 EHRR 393.
[2]   *R (Haley) v Harrow London Borough* [2001] EWCA Civ 87, Laws LJ at [61].

6.27   *Nuutinen v Finland*[1] provides an example of a failure to provide a trial within a reasonable time, one of the other guarantees in article 6(1). The case concerned the applicant's paternity, custody and access rights to his daughter. Paternity was confirmed a little over a year after the first application, and a series of court cases followed over the next few years about custody and access. The court concluded that the length of the overall substantive and enforcement proceedings (five years and five months) had exceeded a 'reasonable time', and that part of the problem had been that the social services authority had been given excessive periods of time within which to respond.[2]

[1]   Application no 32842/96, Decision of 27 June 2000.
[2]   Note, however, that there was no breach of Convention right, art 8 because the court accepted that the interference with the applicant's family life rights, between himself and his daughter was compatible with the Convention.

Family proceedings

6.28   'Family proceedings' is the term used to describe proceedings under the Children (Northern Ireland) Order 1995 and other legislative enactments related to child and family disputes.[1] It includes, therefore, most of the public law and private law proceedings outlined in this chapter[2] and in chapter 9, including applications for domestic violence orders under the 1998 Family Homes and Domestic Violence (Northern Ireland) Order, matters relating to divorce and maintenance,[3] as well as the inherent jurisdiction of the High Court to deal with children.[4] It also includes adoption proceedings under the Adoption (Northern Ireland) Order 1987.[5] 'Family proceedings' cases in the High Court and county court are governed by the Family Proceedings Rules (Northern Ireland) 1996 (hereafter referred to as FPR 1996),[6] while those at magistrates' court level, in the family proceedings courts, are governed by the Magistrates' Courts (Children (Northern Ireland) Order 1995) Rules (Northern Ireland) 1996. A specialised 'family proceedings' court structure has been created to deal with family proceedings and case can be allocated within that structure.[7]

[1]   Children (Northern Ireland) Order 1995, art 8(3).
[2]   With the exception of Emergency Protection Orders, Child Assessment Orders, Secure Accommodation Orders and Recovery Orders.
[3]   Provided for by the Matrimonial Causes (Northern Ireland) Order 1978 and the Domestic Proceedings (Northern Ireland) Order 1980.
[4]   See para 6.149.
[5]   See chapter 8. For completeness sake it is worth mentioning that the phrase 'family proceedings' also

includes proceedings under the Human Fertilisation and Embryology Act 1990, s 30 and the Matrimonial and Family Proceedings (Northern Ireland) Order 1989, Pt IV, which are outside the scope of this book.

⁶ As these court rules are made under the Family Law (Northern Ireland) Order 1993, art 12, they do include rules relating to Emergency Protection Orders, Recovery Orders and Child Assessment Orders.

⁷ See para 6.45.

6.29   The documents produced for some family proceedings, such as applications for Article 8 Orders, Care and Supervision Order applications, amongst others,[1] are not to be disclosed to other people, other than the parties, the legal representatives, the guardian ad litem, the court welfare officer, and the legal aid department without the leave of the court.[2]

¹   For the full list, see FPR 1996, r 4.1(2) and MCR 1996, r 1(2).
²   FPR 1996, r 4.24 and MCR 1996, r 24.

Court Welfare Officers

6.30   In England and Wales, court welfare officers are employed by a single agency, entitled CAFCASS (Child and Family Court Advisory and Support Service), thereby providing a dedicated service to parties involved in family law proceedings.[1] CAFCASS does not operate in Northern Ireland and no dedicated agency offers a court welfare service. However, individual social workers, employed by Trusts, may be required by the courts to complete reports in 'family proceedings.'[2] When occupying such a role, social workers are referred to as 'court welfare officers' and their reports as 'court welfare reports', although occasionally the reports might be referred to as 'Article 4' reports, reflecting the provision of the 1995 Order under which they are made. (Guardians ad litem produce separate reports to court welfare officers, where the former is required to produce a report[3]).

¹   CAFCASS provides court reports for private law cases, in which they are termed 'child and family reporters' and it also provides guardians ad litem for public law cases.
²   Under the Children (Northern Ireland) Order 1995, art 4.
³   Paragraph 6.65.

Court Welfare Reports[1]

6.31   No specific guidance is provided in the relevant court rules in regard to the compilation of these reports, although the judge may, in a directions hearing,[2] issue directions relating to the preparation of the report.[3] Obviously, the content of the report will reflect the type of order sought by the applicant and the welfare officer should have regard to the statutory criteria for securing the order sought. Furthermore, the social worker is acting as an officer of the court, and the guidance on compilation of court reports offered in chapter 3 is pertinent.[4] The welfare officer must furnish his or her report at least 14 days before the relevant hearing.[5] He or she can be required to submit to questions about the report at the hearing at which the report is considered,[6] and indeed 'Best Practice Guidance' recommends that he or she be available for cross-examination by both.[7]

[1]   For issues of hearsay evidence in court welfare reports, see chapter 3, para 3.117.
[2]   These are periodic reviews of family proceedings cases conducted with a view to managing the cases efficiently.
[3]   FPR 1996, r 4.15(2)(g), and MCR 1996, r 15(2)(g).
[4]   See paras 3.42 ff.
[5]   The report will then be distributed to the other parties and the guardian ad litem by the chief clerk or other proper officer: FPR 1996, r 4.14(1); MCR 1996, r 14(1).
[6]   FPR 1996, r 4.14(3); MCR 1996, r 14(3).
[7]   COAC, 'Best Practice Guidance', para 3.1.2.

6.32   Court welfare reports are extremely common in public law cases but less so in private law cases, because there will not usually be a need for them. They might, however, be ordered in private law cases where the animosity between the parents, for example, makes it difficult for the court to determine the issue before it, with allegation and counter-allegation flying back and forth and serious concerns being raised about the nature of the care being given to the children.

Principles of the Children (Northern Ireland) Order 1995

6.33   The 1995 Order enshrines a number of concepts, or principles, that are intended to govern the determination of any application made under the Order. These principles, therefore, apply to all cases brought under the 1995 Order, and to any others that relate to the welfare or upbringing of a child, and are intended to operate for the benefit of the children who are the subject of these proceedings.

Paramountcy principle

6.34   The Order provides that in proceedings in which a child's upbringing is being determined, that the child's welfare shall be the paramount consideration.[1] Note that this principle applies to a wider range of proceedings than merely 'family proceedings' under the Children Order, although it does not apply to applications for secure accommodation orders. The fact that the child's welfare is paramount means that it is the overriding factor in the court's decision with the practical effect of 'trumping' the concerns of others, including those of the parents. The classical definition of paramountcy is attributed to Lord McDermott in a case, *J v C*[2], pre-dating the Children Order by many year. He explained that paramountcy connotes:[3]

> 'A process whereby, when all the relevant facts, relationships, claims and wishes of parents, risks choices and other circumstances are taken into account and weighed the course to be followed will be that which is most in the interests of the child's welfare as that term is now understood … [It is] the paramount consideration because it rules upon or determines the course the followed.'

[1]   Children (Northern Ireland) Order 1995, art 3(1).
[2]   [1970] AC 668, HL.

³   [1970] AC 668 at 710–711, HL.

6.35   It was originally thought when the HRA was implemented, that the paramountcy principle might contravene Convention right article 8 because it appeared to demote the rights and interests of other family members. However, the courts have indicated that there is nothing in the Convention that suggests that the court should not apply the 'best interests' principle.¹ From a practical point of view, the paramountcy principle, although not directed to the Boards, Trusts and the National Society for the Prevention of Cruelty to Children (NSPCC), has the effect of requiring them to make the child's welfare their primary focus.

¹   See *Dawson v Wearmouth* [1999] 2 AC 308, [1999] 2 All ER 353, [1999] 1 FCR 625, [1999] 1 FLR 1167, HL.

Welfare checklist

6.36   In deciding applications for Article 8 Orders,¹ or for Care Orders, Supervision Orders and Education Supervision Orders, the courts are directed, in particular, to have regard to a number of the child's characteristics and circumstances.² These matters are set out in a list form, in no particular order of importance, in article 3(3) of the 1995 Order and are commonly referred to as the 'welfare checklist'. The full list of these matters is as follows:

(a)   the ascertainable wishes and feelings of the child concerned (considered in the light of his age and understanding);

(b)   his physical, emotional and educational needs;

(c)   the likely effect on him of any change in his circumstances;

(d)   his age, sex, background and any characteristics of his which the court considers relevant;

(e)   any harm which he has suffered or is at risk of suffering;

(f)   how capable of meeting his needs is each of his parents and any other person in relation to whom the court considers the question to be relevant;

(g)   the range of powers available to the court under the Children Order in the proceedings in question.

¹   See chapter 9, para 9.101.
²   Note that the 'welfare checklist' does not, therefore, apply to Emergency Protection Orders and Child Assessment Orders.

6.37   The courts are not required to slavishly or programmatically refer to each and every item in the checklist and therefore a judgment is not inadequate merely because a judge fails to refer to each element of the checklist explicitly.¹ The welfare checklist will, of course, be very significant for social workers and guardians ad litem who are required to compile court reports in proceedings where the welfare of a child is being decided.

¹   *Re SM (Interim Care Orders: Exercise of Judge's Discretion)* [2002] NI Fam 11, 2 May 2002, Gillen J.

'No order' principle

6.38 Article 3(5) directs that when faced by an application for a court order under the 1995 Order, the courts are not to make an order, unless to do so would result in a positive benefit to the child. The exact instruction is that a court 'shall not make the order, or any of the orders, unless it considers that doing so would be better for the child than making no order at all.' This principle is designed to require the courts to consider whether any order that it proposes making will in fact make a material improvement in the child's circumstances, because the suspicion was that, in the past, courts made unnecessary orders. If the proposed order would not make such an improvement, then the court is not to make it.[1] The principle is commonly referred to as the 'No Order principle' or, on occasion, as the 'non-intervention principle'. As a consequence, courts hearing 'family proceedings' have taken to pronouncing an 'order of 'No Order'', where they are of the view that this principle applies. So, for example, in the period covered by the Children Order Advisory Committee's[2] Third Report – October 2001 to December 2002 – 8% of all orders made were 'orders of 'No Order'.[3]

---

[1] For guidance on the application of this principle generally, see *Re X and Y (leave to remove from jurisdiction: no order principle)* [2001] 2 FCR 398, [2001] 2 FLR 118, relying on the House of Lords' decision in *Dawson v Wearmouth* [1999] 2 AC 308, [1999] 2 All ER 353, [1999] 1 FCR 625, [1999] 1 FLR 1167. However, one condition imposed in *Re X and Y* was subsequently disapproved of, namely the suggestion that the burden of proof is on the party seeking the application to show that it would be better for the child if an order were made.
[2] See below para 6.70.
[3] COAC, Third Report, p 15.

'No delay' principle

6.39 The Children Order also instructs the courts to have regard to the general principle that any delay in determining the court application is likely to prejudice the welfare of the child.[1] As a result, the courts engage in active case management of 'family proceedings', seeking to have the parties identify and narrow, the precise points of dispute between them. This process of case management involves the courts in holding 'directions hearings' at which the progress of the case is monitored.[2] The duty on the courts, when administering 'direction hearings', is to draw up a timetable ensuring the proceedings are disposed of with the minimum of delay and permitting the giving of direction on a range of issues, including the submission of statements of evidence and the filing of reports, as well as the attendance of witnesses. The conduct of directions hearings are dealt with in the COAC's 'Best Practice Guidance'[3] and a directions hearing checklist is also provided,[4] which is intended to prompt the court and the parties to consider a wide range of matters, from the availability of witnesses and the disclosure of documents, to the identification of the core issues between the parties.

---

[1] Children (Northern Ireland) Order 1995, art 3(2), 'The court shall have regard to the general principle that any delay in determining the question is likely to prejudice the welfare of the child.'
[2] Power to conduct these directions appointments or hearings is found in the FPR 1996, r 4.15 and MCR

1996, r 15. Directions given under these Rules may not be appealed to the High Court: *Re E, E1 and A (Appeal from the Family Care Centre)* [2003] NI Fam 11, High Court, 29 May 2003, Gillen J. Further, contact orders should not be made in directions hearings except in specific circumstances: *Re S (Direction Hearings)* [2002] NI Fam 18, 28 June 2002, Gillen J. A specific power to set the timetable of proceedings where applications are made for Care Orders or Supervision Orders is provided in the Children (Northern Ireland) Order 1995, art 51.

³   COAC, 'Best Practice Guidance', 2003, Chapter 3.1.
⁴   COAC, 'Best Practice Guidance', 2003, Chapter 3, appendix B.

6.40   However, the 'no delay' principle is easily stated but difficult to observe in practice. The Children Order Advisory Committee (COAC), in its third report, highlighted the growing delay in the completion of 'family proceedings'. Since the implementation of the Children Order, in November 1996, the average length of time it takes to dispose of cases has increased quite considerably in each of the court tiers, as the table below indicates:

DURATION OF CASES IN WEEKS[1]

Title	Case Types	High Court	FCC	Other County	FPC	Other Magistrates	Average
1997	Private	14.8	12.0	3.4	9.4	7.9	8.9
	Public	4.6	20.7	–	9.1	5.2	8.3
	Total	**9.2**	**14.2**	**3.4**	**9.4**	**7.8**	**8.8**
1998	Private	20.6	23.5	17.2	15.6	7.6	14.8
	Public	9.3	20.8	–	13.2	5.0	12.4
	Total	**13.3**	**23.0**	**17.2**	**15.2**	**7.5**	**14.4**
1999	Private	29.8	34.4	4.0	18.2	7.6	18.5
	Public	24.6	37.2	–	15.3	8.6	16.7
	Total	**27.6**	**35.0**	**4.0**	**17.8**	**7.7**	**18.2**
2000	Private	19.2	43.4	–	19.4	13.5	19.8
	Public	23.2	40.1	–	16.8	0.1	18.7
	Total	**20.9**	**42.3**	**-**	**19.0**	**11.5**	**19.6**
2001	Private	30.8	54.0	–	20.6	–	22.0
	Public	25.9	44.3	–	17.3	–	20.4
	Total	**29.2**	**50.9**	**-**	**20.2**	**-**	**21.7**

[1] COAC Third Report, Table 8, p 21.

6.41 This development has led the COAC to establish a sub-committee on delay to investigate the reasons behind it, although its preliminary view is that 'while aspects of effective case management/timetabling might be improved upon, the root causes of delay do not lie within the courtroom per se.'[1] However, the Committee did indicate in its Second Report that the high number of interim orders being issued may be at least partly responsible for the rising delay in the disposal of Children Order cases.[2] It has initiated research into the phenomenon of growing delay to determine what the causes of this delay are and whether the periods of delay can be reduced, and the sub-committee has now reported.[3]

[1] COAC Third Report, p 22.
[2] The total number of interim orders, ie in both public law and private law proceedings, has risen from 2,540 in 1997 to 6,068 in 2001. COAC Third Report, p 19.
3 Children Order Advisory Committee, Delay Sub-Committee, Report 2003.

6.42 One limitation with the 'no delay' principle may be that no sanction applies for the breach of it. The principle is simply an instruction to the courts and no consequences flow from the failure to adhere to it. As the COAC itself has hinted, delay of this nature might, in certain circumstances, amount to a breach of a child's right not to be subject to inhuman and degrading treatment under Convention right, article 3.[1]

[1] COAC Third Report, p 33. However, this would require the child to be suffering the minimum amount of harm to require the protection of art 3, namely that the child was suffering at least degrading harm. On art 3, see chapter 1, para 1.79, and this chapter, para 6.21.

Parental responsibility

6.43 One further important concept crucial to the operation of the 1995 Order is that of 'parental responsibility', defined as 'all the rights, duties, powers, responsibilities and authority which by law a parent of a child has in relation to the child and his property.'[1] People with parental responsibility acquire a legal status with regard to the child that allows them to take decisions that affect the child's life. Mothers and married fathers acquire parental responsibility automatically, while unmarried fathers may acquire it in a number of different ways.[2] This concept is also central to the operation of private family law.[3]

[1] Children (Northern Ireland) Order 1995, art 6.
[2] An unmarried father can acquire parental responsibility by agreement with the mother, by securing a parental responsibility order from the courts, by marrying the child's mother, or by having his name included on the child's birth certificate: Family Law Act (Northern Ireland) 2001, s 1, amending the Children (Northern Ireland) Order 1995, art 7.
[3] See chapter 9, para 9.7.

Admissibility of hearsay evidence

6.44 In the past, hearsay evidence was generally inadmissible in all civil proceedings, with the consequence that social workers often had to be very careful how they gathered and presented evidence in child protection investigations. It also meant that the direct testimony of the child who was the subject of the proceedings would often be required, as it was not possible for another witness, like a social worker for example, to testify as to what the child had told him or her. Considerable changes have been made in the law relating to hearsay evidence as it applies to proceedings dealing with the upbringing, maintenance or welfare of a child, and in civil proceedings generally.[1] In short, therefore, hearsay evidence is admissible in a far greater number of cases now than in the past. It is within the trial judge's discretion to determine how much weight to attach to such evidence, however.

[1] See chapter 3, paras 3.103 and 3.105. These changes have been made by the Children (Admissibility of Hearsay Evidence) (Northern Ireland) Order 1996 and the Civil Evidence (Northern Ireland) Order 1997.

'Family proceedings' court structure

6.45 The implementation of the Children Order also saw a restructuring of the courts to deal with 'family proceedings' in order to counter some of the problems that had been identified in the past with the expeditious determination of cases. For the purposes of hearing 'family proceedings', the Youth Courts[1] have been designated as Family Proceedings Courts, and the three county courts that deal with 'family proceedings' are designated as Family 'Care Centres'.[2] The third element of this structure is the Family Division of the High Court. Appeals from the refusal of a Family Proceedings Court to make an order under the 1995 Order are made to a Care Centre.[3]

[1] See chapter 1, para 1.58.
[2] These Care Centres are based in Belfast, Craigavon and Derry.
[3] Children (Allocation of Proceedings) Order (Northern Ireland) 1996, art 15.

6.46 Applications for a wide range of orders under the Children Order must be made, in the first instance, to the Family Proceedings Court if no other cases in respect of the children are in existence in another court.[1] These applications are referred to as 'free-standing' applications. Where, however, a case is already in existence in respect of the same children, then the application must be made to the court that is hearing that other matter.[2] In this way the courts avoid the difficulties created by having a number of different matters about the same family being heard in different courts. Therefore, if an application has been made for a Care Order, for example, and that application has been transferred to a Care Centre, any further applications for article 8 orders, for example, should be made to that court.

[1] Children (Allocation of Proceedings) Order (Northern Ireland) 1996, art 3.
[2] Children (Allocation of Proceedings) Order (Northern Ireland) 1996, art 3(2)–(5).

Allocation of proceedings

6.47 Furthermore, even though an application is made to the Family Proceedings Court, this does not mean that the application will be heard in that court. The

Children (Allocation of Proceedings) Order (Northern Ireland) 1996 allows cases to be transferred between the three tiers of the family proceedings structure if the gravity, importance or complexity of the matters involved in the case warrants the transfer.[1] The courts must consider a number of matters when assessing the gravity, importance and complexity of matters, including the number of parties involved, any novel or difficult point of law or any complicated or conflicting evidence about the child's welfare. Transfers of this nature can take place either upon application of one of the parties or by the court of its own volition.[2] The transfer of cases is also governed by the paramountcy principle. Re-transfer from a higher level of the court system to a lower level is also possible where the circumstances that gave rise to the transfer in the first place no longer apply.[3]

[1] Children (Allocation of Proceedings) Order (Northern Ireland) 1996, arts 5–8. Where a case is transferred to the Family Care Centre from the Family Proceedings Court then the Family Care Centre must transfer the matter to the High Court if it considers appropriate to do so: art 10.

[2] Where a Family Proceedings Court rejects a request to transfer a matter to a Family Care Centre, then an application can be made to the Care Centre to have it determine whether the matter should be transferred: Children (Allocation of Proceedings) Order (Northern Ireland) 1996, art 9. No such procedure exists where the Family Proceedings Court rejects the request to transfer a case to the High Court.

[3] Children (Allocation of Proceedings) Order (Northern Ireland) 1996, arts 11–14.

CASES TRANSFERRED TO FCCS FROM FPCS ETC[1]

	Belfast FCC	Derry/ Londonderry FCC	Craigavon FCC
1997	13	5	0
1998	25	8	2
1999	77	10	0
2000	75	13	0
2001	101	38	9

CASES TRANSFERRED FROM FPCS TO HIGH COURT[2]

Year	Number of Cases
1997	18
1998	19
1999	15
2000	20
2001	33

CASES TRANSFERRED FROM FCCS TO THE HIGH COURT[3]

	Belfast FCC	Derry/ Londonderry FCC	Craigavon FCC
1997	1	1	0
1998	3	2	0
1999	11	2	0
2000	26	5	0
2001	20	11	7

6.48   The transfer of cases between the various tiers of this structure is not a common occurrence in Northern Ireland, however. The previous tables show the pattern of transfer between the three tiers since the implementation of the Children Order.

[1]   COAC Third Report, Table 3, p 16.
[2]   COAC, Third Report, Table 4, p 16.
[3]   COAC, Third Report, Table 5, p 17.

6.49   The main reason for transfer to the Family Care Centre from the Family Proceedings Court is the complexity of the cases, with this being the reason in approximately two-thirds of cases.[1] The principal reason for transfer from the Family Proceedings Court to the High Court is the need to consolidate proceedings in respect of the same children, while transfer from the Family Care Centres to the High Court is usually based on the complexity of the case (approximately 50% of transfers), with 40% being transferred for reasons of consolidation, and 10% being transferred for reasons of complexity.[2]

[1]   COAC Third Report, p 16.
[2]   COAC Third Report, p 17.

6.50   The Children Order Advisory Committee, in its Second Report, has speculated on the reasons for the low number of transfers and has suggested that there may be a number of explanations, including the fact that in Northern Ireland, in contrast to the position in England and Wales, the Family Proceedings Courts are chaired by resident magistrates who are legally qualified.[1] Both the Northern Ireland Resident Magistrates' Association and the Northern Ireland Youth and Family Courts Association[2] are of the view that cases are being heard at the appropriate level and that those which need to be transferred are being transferred.[3]

[1]   COAC, Second Report, pp 19 and 20.
[2]   The members of this Association sit as Law Panellists in Family Proceedings Courts.

[3] COAC Third Report, p 16.

6.51 *Re T, C, P, M and B (Children (Allocation of Proceedings) Order (Northern Ireland) 1996)*[1] saw the High Court offer some guidance on the types of cases that would merit transfer to it. Gillen J suggested that:

> 'whilst the category of cases appropriate for determination in the High Court is never closed examples of appropriate criteria will include cases which possess one or more of the following features:
>
> voluminous and/or complex issues of law;
> unusually complex psychological or emotional issues;
> considerable expenditure of public monies;
> particularly vulnerable parties and/or unusually uncooperative litigants; and
> unusually long defended cases.'

[1] [2003] NI Fam 9, High Court of Northern Ireland, 2 May 2003, Gillen J.

6.52 Appeals from a Family Care Centre to the High Court should only be on the limited basis that the trial judge has made an error of law or has completely misused his or her discretion in relying on certain evidence.[1]

[1] *McG v McC* (23 April 2002, unreported), High Court, Gillen J drawing on the views expressed in *G v G* [1985] 2 All ER 225, [1985] FLR 894, HL. For a fuller explanation of this point, see chapter 9, para 9.13.

Administration of child protection

6.53 A number of different bodies are involved in the administration of the child protection system in Northern Ireland, and there are some differences to the system that applies in England and Wales. The Department, as one would expect, sets the tone for the operation of the child protection system in the Guidance issued by it. Seven volumes of guidance have been issued under the Children Order, of which volumes one and six are the most directly relevant to child protection.[1] Volume one outlines the court orders available under the 1995 Order as well as other legal issues, while volume six, entitled 'Co-operating to Safeguard Children',[2] outlines the manner in which the child protection system is intended to operate.[3] The various administrative elements of the system are examined in this section.

[1] The other five volumes are: Volume 2, Family Support Child Minding and Day Care; Volume 3, Family Placements and Private Fostering; Volume 4, Residential Care; Volume 5, Children with a Disability, Volume 7, Schools Accommodating Children.
[2] DHSSPS, Belfast, 2003.
[3] Volume 6 is, therefore, broadly similar to the Department of Health's 2003 volume of guidance for England and Wales, entitled 'Co-operating to Safeguard Children'.

Area Child Protection Committees

6.54 Each of the four area Health and Social Services Boards[1] has an Area Child Protection Committee (ACPC). The function of an ACPC is to monitor and supervise the overall administration of the child protection system in that Health Board Area by taking a 'strategic approach to child protection'.[2] As part of its duties, ACPCs develop, and review, area-specific inter-agency policies and procedures for the protection of children to the relevant Trusts within its Area. These are based on 'Co-operating to Safeguard Children'.[3]

[1]   See chapter 1, para 1.113.
[2]   'Co-operating to Safeguard Children', DHSSPS, Belfast, 2003, p 35, para 4.2.
[3]   'Co-operating to Safeguard Children', DHSSPS, Belfast, 2003, p 35, para 4.14.

6.55   ACPCs have a number of other duties including the development of inter-agency training, the setting of objectives, performance indicators and establishing thresholds for intervention for child protection work and the implementation of public communication strategies to advance the goal of child protection.[1]

[1]   ACPCs are also required to maintain a link with the Northern Ireland-wide Sex Offender Strategic Management Committee. For more on the this Committee see chapter 5, para 5.138.

6.56   Membership of an ACPC includes representatives of all those engaged in child protection work in the Board's area, including professionals employed by the Board and Trusts, Child Protection Panels, GPs, the police, probation, the Youth Justice Agency, the NSPCC, and the Council for Catholic Maintained Schools.

Case Management Reviews

6.57   One significant duty performed by ACPCs is the undertaking of Case Management Reviews if a child dies in circumstances where abuse or neglect are suspected as having been a factor in his or her death.[1] The purpose of such reviews is to assess the manner in which the child protection system operated and whether any lessons can be learned from the case.[2] An ACPC should also consider conducting such reviews where a child has 'sustained a potentially life-threatening injury' or serious and permanent impairment of health or development' through abuse or neglect, or where a case gives rise to concerns about the way in which child protection services are functioning in a particular area.

[1]   'Co-operating to Safeguard Children', DHSSPS, Belfast, 2003, Chapter 10.
[2]   A case management review is distinct from an inquiry or investigation instigated by the Department under the Children (Northern Ireland) Order 1995, art 152. See chapter 2, para 2.78.

6.58   'Co-operating to Safeguard Children' advises that there are a number of purposes to a case management review, namely to establish the facts of a case, establish whether lessons can be learned from the cases, what those lessons are if any and how inter-agency work can be improved. The Guidance specifically counsels against viewing case management reviews as enquiries into how a child died and who was culpable, as these matters are properly the task of the Coroner's Court and the criminal courts.[1]

[1]   'Co-operating to Safeguard Children', DHSSPS, Belfast, 2003, paras 10.9 and 10.10, p 95.

6.59   The decision as to whether a case management review should be undertaken should be made within one month of the case coming to the attention of the chairperson of the ACPC, with the terms of reference and an action plan for the review developed by the end of the second month. The review should in the normal course be completed within five months of the decision of the chairperson of the ACPC to initiate it.[1]

[1]   'Co-operating to Safeguard Children', DHSSPS, Belfast, 2003, paras 10.18 and 10.19, p 98.

6.60   One minor, though important point to note is that where a guardian ad litem is expected to contribute to the review the prior permission of the court must be required his or her involvement because of the confidential nature of 'family proceedings' and material produced for those proceedings.[1]

[1]   'Co-operating to Safeguard Children', DHSSPS, Belfast, 2003, p 99, para 10.24, and FPR 1996, r 4.24.

Child Protection Panels

6.61   Each Trust within an Area Board has a Child Protection Panel (CPP). These panels are composed of representatives of those involved in the child protection system in the Trust's area. Similar agencies to those represented on ACPCs are represented on the CPPs.[1] CPPs assess the manner in which the child protection system functions in its Trust Area. In particular the CPP has the task of implementing the ACPC's policies and procedures. The CPP is in a good position to assess practical operational issues and it should monitor and evaluate the manner in which local services interact and advise the ACPC and local agencies on resource needs.[2]

[1]   CPPs in community Trusts are chaired by the Trust's director of social work, and those in hospital Trusts are chaired by a senior member of medical or nursing staff. 'Co-operating to Safeguard Children', DHSSPS, Belfast, 2003, p 42, para 4.22.
[2]   'Co-operating to Safeguard Children', DHSSPS, Belfast, 2003, p 40, para 4.18. CPPs are also mandated to co-operate with the relevant agencies in implementing the 'Multi-agency Procedures for the Assessment and Management of Sex Offenders' (MASRAM), see chapter 5, para 5.138.

National Society for the Prevention of Cruelty to Children

6.62   The legislation, both in Northern Ireland and in England and Wales, allows certain 'authorised persons' to apply for court orders and to intervene in the lives of children suffering harm.[1] The National Society for the Prevention of Cruelty to Children (NSPCC), a private charitable organisation, is, and has been in the past, the only such authorised person. However, the number of cases in which it is the initiating party is now quite small and its designation as an authorised person might be said to reflect the historical development of the child protection regime when voluntary, philanthropic effort, rather than statutory agencies took the lead role in child protection matters. The NSPCC predates the present-day social services regime, having been an authorised person for the purposes of the 1908 Children Act, for example. For the purposes of the Children Order, the NSPCC may function through any of its officers.[2]

1   Children (Northern Ireland) Order 1995, art 49(2)(a).
2   Children (Northern Ireland) Order 1995, art 49(2)(a).

Northern Ireland Guardian ad Litem Agency

6.63 Guardians ad litem are appointed in public and certain private law family proceedings,[1] though more usually to the former, and in adoption proceedings, and work under the aegis of the Northern Ireland Guardian ad Litem Agency (NIGALA).[2] There is no agency in Northern Ireland equivalent to the English body, CAFCASS (Child and Family Court Advisory Service), which combines the activities of guardians ad litem, reporting officers in adoption proceedings and court welfare officers in private law proceedings.[3]

1   The cases in which guardians may be appointed are referred to as 'specified proceedings'. These include cases involving the making or discharging of Care or Supervision Orders, or in which article 56 investigations have been ordered, or for applications for a EPO or a CAO, and those where residence and contact with a child in care have initially been refused.
2   NIGALA was established by the Northern Ireland Guardian ad Litem (Establishment and Constitution) Order (Northern Ireland) 1995.
3   For an explanation of the role of 'court welfare officers', see chapter 9, para 9.3.

6.64 Guardians ad litem are qualified social workers with considerable experience of child and family work, who are appointed by the court, with the principal task of providing an independent report to the court on the child's circumstances along with an assessment of the options of dealing with the child which will be in its best interests. Guardians are appointed from panels of persons qualified to carry out the relevant tasks.[1] In 2001, guardians appointed in care proceedings completed 244 cases, while those appointed in emergency protection and secure accommodation proceedings completed 45 and 31 cases respectively.[2] Guardians are also appointed in adoption proceedings.[3]

1   Guardian ad Litem (Panel) Regulations (Northern Ireland) 1996.
2   NIGALA, Annual Report, 2000–01, Table 2B.
3   See chapter 8, para 8.35.

Guardian ad litem reports

6.65 Guardians are appointed, in specified proceedings,[1] by the court[2] to prepare a report for the court to assist it in determining the application before it. GALs also have other responsibilities like appointing, and, if necessary, instructing solicitors.[3]

1   For an explanation of specified proceedings see para 6.63, note 1.
2   Under the Children Order 1995, art 60(1) and FPR 1996, r 4.11.
3   Details of the guardian's role are set out in: COAC 'Best Practice Guidance', 2003, Chapter 8.

6.66 A guardian's report in 'family proceedings' is compiled, and filed not less than seven days before the date of the final hearing.[1] In compiling the report (and performing any other duties), the GAL is specifically directed to have regard to the paramountcy principle.[2] The guardian is also specifically directed to advise the court on the following range of matters and these will therefore have a considerable bearing on the contents of their reports to the court:[3]

(a)   whether the child is of sufficient understanding for any purpose, including for the purpose of refusing to submit to medical or other assessments;

(b)   the child's wishes in respect of the matter at dispute;[4]

(c)   the appropriate forum for, and timing of, the proceedings;

(d)   the options open to the court for the child, the suitability of each option and what order should be made;

The guardian may also be asked by the court to furnish advice on a particular matter and is entitled to offer advice on matters on which he or she considers that the court should be informed.

[1]   FPR 1996, r 4.12(8), MCR 1996, r 12(8). They are then distributed by the chief clerk or other proper officer to the other parties.
[2]   Children (Northern Ireland) Order 1995, art 3(2), see chapter 6, para 6.34.
[3]   FPR 1996, r 4.12(5); MCR 1996, r 12(4).
[4]   Including whether the child wishes to be present at the hearing.

6.67   In order to carry out his or her duties the guardian is empowered to make whatever investigations are necessary including conducting interviews, inspecting documents[1] and obtaining professional assistance, like separate legal representation for example.[2] In respect of legal representation, the guardian is empowered to instruct a solicitor to advise the child. The solicitor must establish the ability of the child to give instructions, taking into account the views of the GAL and any experts. If the child is not considered to be competent to instruct the solicitor, the task of doing so falls to the GAL.

[1]   The power to inspect documents is found in the Children (Northern Ireland) Order 1995, art 61.
[2]   FPR 1996, r 4.12(3)(a); MCR 1996, r 12(2)(a).

6.68   Interestingly the High Court has noted, that in carrying out his or her duties, the duty of the guardian, per the 1995 Order, is to be an appointment 'for the child', as opposed to being an appointment to 'represent the child'. Accordingly, the court suggests, the guardian has a very wide role, namely to place before the court anything which he or she considers to be in the best interests of the child.[1]

[1]   *Re N and L (Care order: Investigations by Guardian ad Litem outside Northern Ireland)* [2003] NI Fam 1, High Court of Northern Ireland, 22 Jan 2003, Gillen J.

6.69   The breadth in the guardian's powers of action means, the High Court has determined, that there is no restriction on a guardian travelling outside the jurisdiction in order to carry out a task, like interviewing relevant persons, in order to complete his or her report. *Re N and L (Care Order: Investigations by Guardian ad Litem outside Northern Ireland)* established that, unlike the position in adoption proceedings,[1] guardians ad litem appointed under the Children Order could use their own discretion as to whether it was necessary to travel outside the jurisdiction, to the Republic of Ireland, as part of the report-compiling process.

[1]   See *Re K (a minor) (Adoption; child born outside the jurisdiction)* [1997] NIJB 212, High Court of Northern Ireland, Higgins J. See chapter 8, para 8.40.

Children Order Advisory Committee

6.70   This Committee was set up to advise Ministers on the progress of Children Order cases through the courts, to harmonise practice in the various courts dealing with family proceedings and to advise on the impact of the Children Order generally. It is not part of the child protection system per se, but in its role of assessing and monitoring the overall implementation of the Children Order, the Committee obviously comments on matters of importance to the child protection system. Its membership is drawn from the judiciary,[1] the legal professions and the social work and social care professions, thereby giving its views and recommendations considerable weight. It has issued three reports on the progress in implementing the Order, the latest covering the period January 2001 to March 2002.[2]

[1]   The Committee's chair since its establishment has been the Judge of the Family Division of the High Court.
[2]   Children Order Advisory Committee Third Report, DHSSPS and NI Court Service, Belfast, January 2003.

6.71   Its sub-committees address specific themes in the administration of the Children Order and a number of those sub-committees are in the process of addressing matters which will have a significant impact on the implementation of the Order. Two sub-committees of note are the Sub-Committee on Best Practice Guidance and the Sub-Committee dealing with the separate representation of children in private law proceedings. The former has issued guidance on best practice[1] in court procedures and this guidance seeks to 'ensure consistency of practice in all Children Order cases and thereby reduce delay.'[2] The latter sub-committee is dealing with a much-discussed topic across the UK. The discussion is fuelled by the sense that children's views, in private law proceedings, are obscured by those of their parents and the sense that, as a matter of right, children ought to have the opportunity of having their interests represented.

[1]   COAC, 'Best Practice Guidance', 2003.
[2]   COAC, Third Report, DHSSPS and NI Court Service, Belfast, January 2003, p 28.

6.72   The Committee is supported in its work by three Family Court Business Committees (FCBCs) located in the three Family Care Centres, and social workers may encounter these if they fill the role of guardian ad litem, as one of the tasks of a FCBC is to ' ensure that the guardian ad litem is aware of the needs of the courts'.[1]

[1]   Children Order Advisory Committee Third Report, DHSSPS and NI Court Service, Belfast, January 2003, p 8.

PSNI CARE Units

6.73   The Police Service of Northern Ireland (PSNI) handles child protection referrals made to it in its Child Abuse and Rape Enquiry (CARE) units. These CARE units, as they are commonly referred to, were established to provide a specialised service in tackling certain types of crime, while at the same time, providing a service that is particularly sensitive to the concerns of victims.

Stages of child protection investigation

6.74 'Co-operating to Safeguard Children' sets out four broad stages to a typical child protection investigation, as the diagram below indicates, and outlines social workers' duties at each stage. Those stages are referral, investigation, the case conference and the review stage. Obviously the exact shape of each investigation will depend on the circumstances encountered by social workers and the typology suggested in the Guidance is not a definitive one, and is merely indicative.

A short précis of these stages is provided here, and reference is made to the type of court order that might be sought, or legal issue that might arise at each stage, although, of course, the need for court intervention can arise at different times, in different ways. Child protection concerns can involve the police as well as social services and so both agencies will need to co-ordinate their activities. Inter-agency co-operation between the police and social services is governed by a Joint Protocol[1] and Joint Protocol Investigations are also explained. The legal aspects of child protection and the various court orders that may be sought are then explored in detail in the following section.

[1]   The full title is the 'Protocol for Joint Investigation by Social Workers and Police Officers of Alleged and Suspected Cases of Child Abuse' and it is now in its third edition.

Joint Protocol investigations

6.75 Social services and the police have, for some time, recognised the need to co-ordinate their investigations into suspected child abuse to ensure that each can fulfil its functions in a manner which best serves the child. Both are concerned about children's welfare, although the former's concerns are dealt with by the civil law, and those of the police, by the criminal law. These co-ordinated investigations are governed by a Joint Protocol agreed between the police, the four Area Boards and the NSPCC. The net result of this protocol has been that only those who have been trained under the Joint Protocol are involved in the investigation of incidents of alleged, or suspected abuse and not surprisingly these investigations are referred to as 'Joint Protocol investigations'.

Stages of Joint Protocol investigation

6.76 In substance the stages of a joint protocol investigation do not differ greatly from that carried out by social services alone, as both processes have the same purpose, namely to establish what harm the child has suffered, if any, and who can be deemed responsible. The stages do differ to those of a social services child protection investigation but the key is that all agencies are aware of their particular responsibilities and the roles played by other agencies.

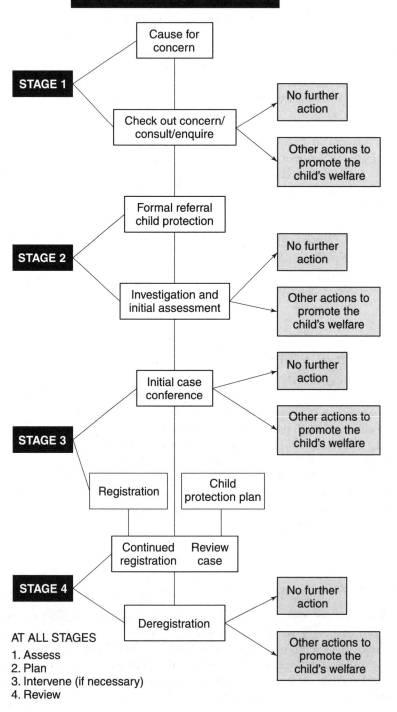

THE CHILD PROTECTION PROCESS

Cause for concern

STAGE 1

Check out concern/ consult/enquire

No further action

Other actions to promote the child's welfare

Formal referral child protection

STAGE 2

Investigation and initial assessment

No further action

Other actions to promote the child's welfare

Initial case conference

No further action

Other actions to promote the child's welfare

STAGE 3

Registration

Child protection plan

Continued registration   Review case

STAGE 4

Deregistration

No further action

Other actions to promote the child's welfare

AT ALL STAGES
1. Assess
2. Plan
3. Intervene (if necessary)
4. Review

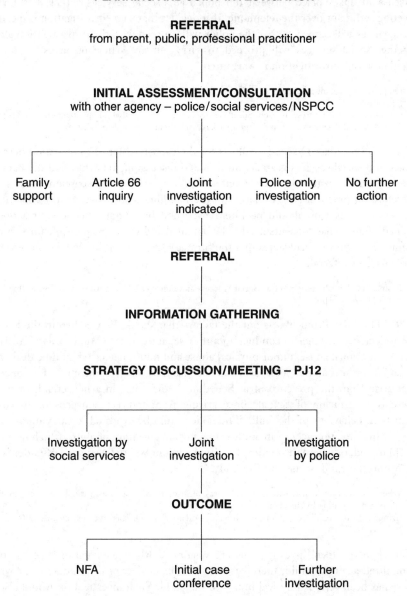

FLOWCHART REGARDING INITIAL ASSESSMENT, CONSULTATION, PLANNING AND JOINT INVESTIGATION

REFERRAL
from parent, public, professional practitioner

INITIAL ASSESSMENT/CONSULTATION
with other agency – police/social services/NSPCC

| Family support | Article 66 inquiry | Joint investigation indicated | Police only investigation | No further action |

REFERRAL

INFORMATION GATHERING

STRATEGY DISCUSSION/MEETING – PJ12

| Investigation by social services | Joint investigation | Investigation by police |

OUTCOME

| NFA | Initial case conference | Further investigation |

Source: Protocol for Joint Investigation by Social Workers and Police of alleged suspected child abuse, p.12.

Deciding on Joint Protocol investigation: strategy discussion

6.77 The key decision at the outset is to determine whether there is to be a joint investigation or not. Consideration will also have to be given at this stage to whether a Joint Protocol investigation with the police is warranted.[1] To this end a 'Strategy Discussion' takes place between the police and social services, either in a formal meeting setting or over the telephone. If it decides that some investigation is merited, the agencies will agree whether the police will proceed with their investigation alone, whether social services will proceed to carry out an Article 66 investigation[2] or whether a joint investigation is warranted.[3]

[1]   On joint protocol investigations see below.
[2]   See para 6.95.
[3]   One other possibility presents itself. Social services could consider that no investigation is necessary or warranted and decide instead to deliver a package of support measures to the family.

6.78   The Strategy Discussion allows for the early transfer of information between police and social services is an action-oriented discussion, very different in character from a Child Protection Case Conference.'[1] A Strategy Discussion must focus therefore on practical issues relating to the handling of the investigation, including matters such as who should be interviewed and by whom, what urgent action is needed, if any, what consents need to be obtained and who is responsible for securing them. The Joint Protocol states that the Strategy Discussion should take place within three days of referral.

[1]   Protocol for Joint Investigation by Social Workers and Police Officers of Alleged and Suspected Cases of Child Abuse, p 18.

6.79   The Joint Protocol sets out the factors that should be weighed in the balance when deciding whether to conduct a joint or separate investigation.[1] Cases involving purely emotional abuse, minor physical abuse and minor neglect should be dealt with by social services alone. Social services will also have sole responsibility for concerns that arise from the presence of a 'Schedule 1' offender[2] in a household, or where there is a suspicion of sexual abuse arising from indirect concerns or the over-sexualised behaviour of the child. The police could be expected to carry out a single agency investigation where an adult is making an allegation of abuse which occurred in childhood, or where the victim is a young adult or where the alleged offender is not known to the child or the child's family.

[1]   Where the decision is taken to proceed by way of a Joint Protocol investigation, this fact should be evidenced in writing by the completion of a PJI1 form.
[2]   Criminal Justice (Children) (Northern Ireland) Order 1998, Sch 1 as amended by Justice (Northern Ireland) Act 2002.

6.80   Joint Protocol investigations are warranted where a sexual offence has been committed against a child, there has been serious neglect or ill-treatment,[1] or where there has been serious physical injury to the child. Such investigation would also be warranted where a 'looked after' child,[2] or a child who is on the Child Protection Register, sustains injuries. Situations involving suspicion of organised or institution-alised abuse will, of course, be investigated under the Joint Protocol. Cases of minor injury may need to be explored to determine whether the circumstances suggest that although the individual injury is minor, other factors render it serious and therefore one that ought to be the subject of a Joint Protocol investigation.

1 Neglect or ill-treatment to such an extent that prosecution under section of the Children and Young Persons Act (Northern Ireland) 1968 would be warranted.
2 See chapter 7, para 7.34.

Referral to social services

6.81 This initial stage involves the engagement of social services staff, where they come to know of children who are or who are likely to be, suffering significant harm. Social workers may become aware of such children themselves or they may have such cases referred to them by other agencies, like teachers or community nursing staff for example. In any event, once they become aware of them a duty to investigate arises.[1] Within 24 hours of the referral the child must be seen and interviewed by a social worker, and an assessment made as to whether there is a possibility of significant harm, how the concern has arisen, what urgent action if any is needed and whether the child and its family have any other needs at that time.[2]

1 On the 'duty to investigate' see para 6.95.
2 'Co-operating to safeguard children', DHSSPS, Belfast, 2003, p 45, para 5.12.

6.82 An initial assessment is to be made of the child within seven days of the referral and this should result in the development of an initial plan, which 'sets out the actions to be taken and support mechanism which can be put in place immediately to manage the risks to the child identified at this point.'[1] It may also be necessary to intervene to protect the child from immediate harm and the initial plan must consider this possibility. Whether the child is in need of immediate protection will depend on the nature and source of the harm that the child faces. If the situation warrants urgent action to provide protection for the child then an Emergency Protection Order[2] or an Interim Care Order[3] may have to be sought or the police may consider that it is appropriate to exercise their powers of police protection.[4] However, one less drastic solution is to seek the parents' assistance and have the alleged abuser leave the child's place of residence voluntarily. If this voluntary co-operation is not forthcoming then the possibility of securing an exclusion order attached to an Emergency Protection Order should be considered. A child that has run away from its parents, or those with parental responsibility for it, might become the subject of a recovery order.[5] The second stage of the assessment process should then be completed within 15 days of the referral.

1 'Co-operating to Safeguard Children', DHSSPS, Belfast, 2003, p 47, para 5.20.
2 See para 6.100.
3 See para 6.114.
4 See para 6.105.
5 See para 6.112.

6.83 Where the assessment indicates that the child has suffered, or is likely to suffer, significant harm 'Co-operating to Safeguard Children' advises that 'in most cases it will be necessary to proceed to an initial case conference at this stage.'[1]

1 'Co-operating to Safeguard Children', DHSSPS, Belfast, 2003, p 48, para 5.24.

Interviewing children

6.84   A few points are worth making about the task of gathering evidence about the child and its circumstances, and making appropriate assessments of the child. An assessment of the child will usually be carried out on the basis of the parents' consent. However, where that consent is not forthcoming, the Trust or the NSPCC will have the option of applying for a Child Assessment Order[1] in order to carry out any necessary examinations and assessments. (It might also be possible to carry out such examinations on the basis of permission granted by the court when an Emergency Protection Order is made).

[1]   See para 6.103.

6.85   Interviews with children for the purpose of investigating child protection concerns should be conducted according to Northern Ireland Office Guidelines entitled 'Memorandum of Good Practice on Video Recorded Interviews with Child Witnesses for Criminal Proceedings'.[1] The advantage of video recording such interviews is that the video may subsequently be used in any criminal or civil proceedings as the child's evidence-in-chief, thereby saving the child the ordeal of having to re-present his or her story in the witness box.[2] However, the child may of course be cross-examined on the content of his or her video evidence.

[1]   It is commonly referred to as the 'Memorandum of Good Practice' and accompanies the Children's Evidence (Northern Ireland) Order 1995.
[2]   On the admissibility of this type of evidence, see chapter 3, paras 3.87 and 3.88.

6.86   One of the matters that must be addressed in the strategy discussion, if the discussion concludes that the child is suffering, or is likely to suffer significant harm, is whether the interview with the child should be conducted jointly by police and social services staff. One of the benefits of a joint interview is that it helps to reduce the number of interviews the child has to endure and the numbers of occasions when the child is called to outline its story.

6.87   The guidance offered in the Joint Protocol emphasises the importance of the joint interviewers agreeing a detailed plan for conducting the interview. When the joint interview has been completed the interviewers must report back to their respective managers and a decision will then be taken as to whether a Child Protection Case Conference needs to be held immediately or whether the initial plan of the investigation needs to be altered.

Child protection case conference[1]

6.88   One of the key administrative stages of a child protection investigation, the initial conference brings together family members and professionals from various statutory agencies to share information and decide on the need for registration of the child on the Child Protection Register under at least one of the following eight categories: suspected or potential neglect, suspected or potential sexual abuse, suspected or potential physical abuse or suspected or potential emotional abuse. Each

Trust is required to maintain a register of children within its area who are subject to child protection plans, with the result that in practice there a number of such registers.[2] The child's parents, and the alleged abuser(s) should also be allowed to submit their views to the case conference, although this does not necessarily mean that they must be allowed to participate at the actual conference.[3]

[1]   Where the child is not yet born, a pre-birth child protection case conference can be convened to decide what action should be taken.

[2]   The Department maintains a list of custodians of registers in Northern Ireland.

[3]   See para 6.116.

6.89   The first conference should take place within a maximum 15 days of the first Strategy Discussion.[1] It will discuss reports prepared by some of the participants arising from their dealings with the child and the family, and particularly a report from social workers summarising the result of the initial assessment and the enquiries to date.

[1]   'Co-operating to Safeguard Children', DHSSPS, Belfast, 2003, p 48, para 5.46.

6.90   If the child is registered on the Child Protection Register a named key worker is appointed and recommendations made for a core group of professionals to carry out inter-agency work as part of the Child Protection Plan. Where the child's name is placed on a register, the child should be informed, if old enough, as should the child's parents.[1] The fact that a child is not considered to be at risk of future or continuing harm, and should not therefore be put on the register, does not mean, however, that social services should end their involvement with the child as the child, or his or her family, may be suitable candidate for children's services.

[1]   The child's school should also be notified.

6.91   An (internal) appeal can be made against the decision of a case conference to register, or de-register, a child. The relevant ACPC's policies and procedures determine the procedure by which this may be done. In the event that the complainant is unhappy with the decision made on appeal, he or she may judicially review the decision of the case conference.

Post-Case Conference

6.92   Upon registration the comprehensive assessment of the child should be completed, thereby allowing the initial child protection plan to be developed. The child protection plan, which sets out each statutory agency's duties and each agency's role in regard to the care of the child, and will also deal with its role in respect of the remainder of the family and the issue of the need for treatment for the abuser, should be based on a comprehensive assessment.[1] The child protection plan also plays a crucial role in the application for a Care Order. These steps should be completed before the first review is held.

[1]   'Co-operating to Safeguard Children'. DHSSPS, Belfast 2003, p 57 and 58, paras 5.71 and 5.72.

Child protection review conference

6.93   The final stage is focused on the implementation of the child protection plan with a commitment to carrying out regular reviews of the extent to which the child is being adequately safeguarded and his or her registration status. The first review case conference should normally take place within three months of the initial case conference, with further reviews taking pace on a six monthly basis.[1] Court orders might well be part of the child protection plan and would then be sought as part of the implementation of the plan. The purpose of a case review is to examine the current level of risk and ensure continued protection, review the protection plan and consider whether registration should be continued or ended. For reasons alluded to in the introduction to the chapter, the decision to de-register the child does not mean that the need to continue delivering services to the child and his or her family has disappeared. The review case conference will also have to assess the implementation of the child protection plan and may perhaps have to finalise particular features of it.

[1]   'Co-operating to Safeguard Children'. DHSSPS, Belfast 2003, p 58, para 5.75. The review date is set at initial case conference but if issues arise before then a review can held.

Legal elements of child protection investigation

6.94   This section explores the various types of court orders that may be sought and legal issues that may arise in a child protection investigation. Note that matters relating to hearsay evidence and expert witness evidence are dealt with in chapter 3.[1]

[1]   Paragraphs 3.101 and 3.89 respectively.

Duty to investigate

6.95   Article 66 of the 1995 Order places a duty on Trusts to investigate the circumstances of any child which it believes is suffering or is likely to suffer, significant harm. Even if the Order did not impose such a duty, it would in effect be imposed by the Human Rights Act, because a failure on the part of social services authorities to intervene in a situation where a child was suffering significant harm would be a breach of that child's Article 3 Convention rights, as determined in *Z v United Kingdom*.[1]

[1]   [2001] 2 FCR 246, [2001] 2 FLR 612. See para 6.21.

6.96   The duty to investigate does not require the Trust to initiate any action or make any applications in respect of the child and this appears to be a gap in the legislative scheme. In an English case, *Nottingham County Council v H*,[1] the court highlighted the fact that although the authority could be ordered to carry out the investigation the court had no power to require it to make a subsequent application. As outlined above, this failure to act may now amount to a breach of the positive obligations on social services authorities to protect the child from article 3-type harm, namely its rights not to be subject to inhuman and degrading treatment or punishment. If the Trust decides not to act then it must report its decision to court, with its reasons for not doing so and the details of any action that it intends to take.

¹   [1994] Fam 18, [1994] 1 FCR 624, HL.

6.97   A court may also order an investigation to be carried out if in the course of family proceedings it appears to it that a Care Order or a Supervision Order may be appropriate. Such a direction is made under article 56 and hence these investigations are usually called 'Article 56 investigations'. Article 56 investigations might be ordered in private law applications where the court is reluctant to make an order in favour of either of the child's parents unless the wider circumstances of the child's welfare are investigated by social services because the court considers that the child is, or may be suffering or at risk of suffering, significant harm. As a result a Trust might become involved because it considers it appropriate to apply for a public law order, even though the case began as a private law matter.

6.98   The report of the Trust's investigation must be furnished within eight weeks of the direction being given,¹ and must outline its reasons for not applying for a Care or Supervision Order if that is the conclusion it arrives at.² While the Trust is carrying out an investigation, the court can make an Interim Care, or Supervision, Order if it believes that the threshold criteria in article 50(2) are made out.³ This is the only occasion in which the court can make a public law order without an application being made.

¹   Children (Northern Ireland) Order 1995, art 56(4).
²   Children (Northern Ireland) Order 1995, art 56(3).
³   On interim orders, see para 6.114.

6.99   The court has a similar power where it discharges an Education Supervision Order (ESO) because it can, at that point, order the Trust to investigate the circumstances of the child.¹ It may also make a similar direction where an education and library Board notifies a Trust that a child is persistently failing to comply with the directions made under an ESO.²

¹   Children (Northern Ireland) Order 1995, Sch 4, para 7(2).
²   Children (Northern Ireland) Order 1995, Sch 4, para 9.

Emergency Protection Order

6.100   As its title indicates, this order is intended for use in urgent cases to protect a child in the short-term. Technically, almost anyone can apply for an EPO including, for example, a neighbour or relative, although in almost all circumstances Trusts seek them. The grounds for securing an order differ according to the identity of the applicant. Where the applicant is a Trust it must show that, in the course of fulfilling its 'duty to investigate',¹ it is being unreasonably frustrated in its attempts to gain access to the child.² The NSPCC must meet a similar test.³ If the applicant is neither a Trust nor the NSPCC, he or she need only show that there is reasonable cause to suspect that the child is likely to suffer significant harm unless removed to, or allowed to remain in, a safe place.⁴

[1]   See para 6.95.
[2]   Children (Northern Ireland) Order 1995, art 63(1)(b).
[3]   Children (Northern Ireland) Order 1995, art 63(1)(c).
[4]   Children (Northern Ireland) Order 1995, art 63(1)(a).

6.101   An EPO can only last for eight days,[1] although it may be extended for a further seven days on one occasion only.[2] One advantage to the Trust of securing an EPO is that because no application may be made to discharge the order within the first 72 hours, it gives the Trust some degree of time to decide what actions are to be taken in respect of the child. The second advantage is that the person to whom the order is addressed acquires parental responsibility[3] for the duration of the order. This means that the Trust is in a position to make similar decisions to those that a parent might make in caring for the child, although it is limited to exercising parental responsibility in manner that is reasonably required to safeguard the welfare of the child.[4]

[1]   Children (Northern Ireland) Order 1995, art 64(1). Where the child is in police protection (see para 6.105) at the time the EPO is made the eight day period is deemed to have commenced when the child was first taken into police protection: art 64(2) .
[2]   Children (Northern Ireland) Order 1995, art 64(4) and (5).
[3]   See paras 6.43.
[4]   Children (Northern Ireland) Order 1995, art 63(5)(b).

6.102   An application for an EPO can be made ex parte[1] allowing the Trust to move at speed if the occasion warrants it. In making such an order, a court may make directions regarding the contact the child's parents are to have with him or her, and it can also make directions allowing the child to be physically or medically examined.[2] An EPO can also be used where the whereabouts of the child are unknown because in making the order the court may order that someone with knowledge of child's whereabouts disclose that information[3] and can authorise entry to premises to search for the child.[4]

[1]   This means it can be made by one party alone, without the parents or those with parental responsibility being notified.
[2]   Children (Northern Ireland) Order 1995, art 63(6), although the child can, if of sufficient understanding, refuse to submit to a medical or any other examination or assessment: art 63(7).
[3]   Children (Northern Ireland) Order 1995, art 67(1).
[4]   Children (Northern Ireland) Order 1995, art 67(3).

Child Assessment Order

6.103   A Child Assessment Order (CAO),[1] as its title suggests, allows a child to be assessed to ascertain whether he or she is suffering harm.[2] It is intended to be sought where there is reasonable cause to suspect that the child is suffering significant harm, but there is no immediate risk and an assessment is appropriate, and the parents, or those with parental responsibility, have refused to co-operate with social services in allowing the child to be assessed or examined.[3] Consequently, when social workers begin dealing with a case they will usually seek the co-operation of the child's parents, hoping that recourse to the courts for an order is not necessary, but knowing that a refusal to co-operate will be central to the application for a Child Assessment Order. A CAO can last for no more than seven days,[4] and the assessment of the child away from his or her home place must be authorised by the court in making the order.[5]

1   Children (Northern Ireland) Order 1995, art 62.
2   A child of sufficient understanding can, however, notwithstanding the making of the order, refuse to submit to medical or other examination: Children (Northern Ireland) Order 1995, art 62(8). This formulation might be said to be a statutory version of the '*Gillick* competency' principle encountered in chapter 1, para 1.52.
3   The exact legislative formulation is that it is unlikely that any, or any satisfactory, assessment will be made unless the order is made: Children (Northern Ireland) Order 1995, art 62(1)(c).
4   Children (Northern Ireland) Order 1995, art 62(5).
5   Children (Northern Ireland) Order 1995, art 62(9).

6.104   A court is not to make a CAO if it considers that there are grounds for making an EPO and it ought to make the latter order.[1] In contrast with an EPO, only Trusts or the NSPPC may apply for a CAO.

1   Children (Northern Ireland) Order 1995, art 62(4).

Police protection

6.105   Where a police officer has reasonable cause to believe that a child would otherwise be likely to suffer significant harm, he or she may remove the child to suitable accommodation and the child is then said to be in 'police protection'.[1] Police protection lasts for a maximum of 72 hours.[2] No court application is necessary. Police protection is used in situations of such urgency that there may not be time to secure an ex parte EPO.[3] Police protection does not give the police powers to search premises for the child, but they may on occasion be able to rely on a provision in the Police and Criminal Evidence (Northern Ireland) Order 1989,[4] which allows them to search premises for the purposes of 'saving life or limb or preventing serious damage to property'.[5]

1   Children (Northern Ireland) Order 1995, art 65.
2   Children (Northern Ireland) Order 1995, art 65(8).
3   See *Re B (A Child) (Care Proceedings: Diplomatic Immunity)* [2002] EWHC 1751 (Fam), [2003] Fam 16, [2003] 1 FLR 241, for example, where a child attended at school with very severe laceration marks on her body consistent with having been beaten. She initially gave conflicting explanations for the marks, and was then taken into police protection when she explained that her father had beaten her.
4   Article 19(1)(e).
5   Note too that if an EPO has been issued, the court may have attached a power to it justifying entry to premises to search for the child, and this may be another way of dealing with the limited powers of search accorded to police officers in the child protection context.

6.106   As soon as practicable after taking the child into police protection, the police officer must ensure that the child's circumstances are inquired into by a designated police officer. The designated officer must release the child if he or she does not consider that, on completing the inquiry, there is still reasonable cause to believe that the child would be likely to suffer significant harm. The designated officer then has a number of different duties with respect to the child, including notifying the Trust that the child is with the police. The police do not acquire parental responsibility for the child during the period of police protection. During the period that the child is in police protection, the police must allow contact between him or her and a range of people, including its parents and those with parental responsibility, if they consider it reasonable and in the child's best interests to do so.

Secure Accommodation Order

6.107   This order, which sanctions the detention of a child in a locked or closed facility is only available where certain conditions are met, namely that the child has a history of absconding from care placements or where he or she is in danger of causing significant harm to themselves.[1] A Trust may keep a child in secure accommodation if it considers that these conditions are met, without the authorisation of a court, for a maximum period of 72 hours in any 28-day period.[2] After that time period has expired, court sanction is needed to detain the child in secure accommodation. Court authorised placement in secure accommodation cannot be longer than three months initially, but renewals of that authorisation for periods of up to six months at a time, are possible.[3] Where a Trust intends making such an application, if must, as far as it is practicable, make this known to the child's parents, those with parental responsibility, the child's independent visitor[4] or others whom it considers should be informed.[5] The Trust's Statement of Evidence should set out the list of relevant incidents and give reasons why the Trust considered that the criteria for granting the order are made out.[6] The evidence should demonstrate that the application is being sought as a matter of last resort.[7] Trusts are obliged to appoint panels of persons to review secure accommodation placements, and such review must take place within one month of the placement and on three monthly intervals thereafter if the child remains in secure accommodation.[8]

[1]   Children (Northern Ireland) Order 1995, art 44.
[2]   Children (Secure Accommodation) Regulations (Northern Ireland) 1996, reg 6(1).
[3]   Children (Secure Accommodation) Regulations (Northern Ireland) 1996, regs 7 and 8.
[4]   See chapter 7, para 7.37.
[5]   Children (Secure Accommodation) Regulations (Northern Ireland) 1996, reg 9. The child must also be informed that the application is to be made and, by virtue of the application of Convention right, art 6 and case law, allowed the opportunity to consult with legal representatives.
[6]   COAC, 'Best Practice Guidance', 2003, para 3.1.27, number 9 of the list of considerations.
[7]   Children Order Guidance and Regulations Volume 4, para 15.5, and COAC, 'Best Practice Guidance', 2003, para 3.1.27, number ten of list of considerations.
[8]   Children (Secure Accommodation) Regulations (Northern Ireland) 1996, reg 10.

6.108   At present there are only 14 secure accommodation places in Northern Ireland and this does not meet the demand for such places. The insufficiency of secure accommodation places has been a matter of concern for the COAC in its last two reports.[1] These secure accommodation places are provided at the Lakewood Regional Centre, Bangor, Co Down.

[1]   COAC Second Report, p 27, Third Report.

6.109   Initially, there was a concern that secure accommodation orders were in breach of Convention right, article 5, the right to liberty, but that concern has been dispelled by the English High Court's decision in *Re K (a child) (Secure Accommodation Order: right to liberty)*.[1] The court concluded that detention under a secure accommodation order was for the purpose of the child's 'educational supervision.'[2]

[1]   [2001] Fam 377, [2001] 1 FLR 526, CA.
[2]   Detention of a minor on this basis is permitted by art 5(1)(d).

6.110   The Court of Appeal in England has determined that although secure accommodation order proceedings are not criminal charges which would attract the benefit of all the procedural guarantees in Convention right, article 6 (the right to a fair trial) nevertheless a child facing such an application should be given the benefit of the guarantees in article 6(3),[1] given the importance of such proceedings.[2]

[1]   Those guarantees include the right to be informed promptly of the evidence to be adduced, adequate time to prepare a defence, the opportunity to examine witnesses, the opportunity to mount a defence and access to an interpreter if necessary.
[2]   *Re M (a child) (secure accommodation)* [2001] EWCA Civ 458, [2001] 1 FCR 692, [2001] 2 FLR 169.

6.111   The Northern Ireland case of *In Re AK (Secure Accommodation Order)*[1] addressed the issue of whether the child had to be in secure accommodation before the court order was sought. The High Court determined that a child should be in such secure accommodation prior to the making of the application for authorisation, although there might be exceptional circumstances that would justify the order being made, even though the child was not yet in such secure accommodation. This issue was revisited in *North and West Belfast Health and Social Services Trust v DH*[2] where an application was made for a secure accommodation order for a child who had been in the care of the Trust but had since absconded. It was argued that if the order was not made he would lose his place in the secure facility and this was an exceptional circumstance that justified departing from the principle in *Re AK*. However, Higgins J considered that proceeding in the absence of the child might infringe his right to fair hearing and the circumstances were not exceptional. Accordingly the application was adjourned generally.

[1]   [2000] 3 FCR 289, [2000] 1 FLR 317.
[2]   (27 June 2001, unreported), High Court of Northern Ireland, Higgins J.

Recovery Order

6.112   If a child is unlawfully taken away from the person responsible for him or her, then a court may make a Recovery Order.[1] The person responsible for the child may have acquired this responsibility by virtue of a Care Order, an Emergency Protection Order or by virtue of the fact that the child is in police protection. The order may also be sought if the child is missing, or has run away, or is staying away from that person. Only a designated police officer[2] or those with parental responsibility by virtue of a Care Order, or an EPO can apply for a Recovery Order.[3]

[1]   Children (Northern Ireland) Order 1995, art 69.

²   See para 6.106.

³   Children (Northern Ireland) Order 1995, art 69(4). See *Re R (Recovery Orders)* [1998] 2 FLR 401, [1998] 3 FCR 321 in which responsibility for a child was shared between his mother and the school principal. An issue subsequently arose about whether a recovery order could be made where the child stayed away from school remaining with his mother.

6.113   The order directs the person who is in a position to produce the child to do so and it authorises the child's removal by any authorised person. It requires people with information about the child's whereabouts to disclose it to police, or the court, and it can authorise the police to enter specified premises, using reasonable force if necessary.[1]

¹   Children (Northern Ireland) Order 1995, art 69(3).

Interim Care and Supervision Orders

6.114   The courts can make interim Care or Supervision Orders[1] where any application for one of those orders is adjourned or where it orders an 'Article 56 investigation'.[2] However, in order to make an interim order the court must have 'reasonable grounds' for believing that the threshold conditions are made out.[3] Interim orders can be for up to eight weeks in the first instance and for a maximum of four weeks on the second, and subsequent occasions that the court deems an interim order appropriate.[4] The court can direct that physical or medical examinations take place during the period of the interim order, although if the court considers that the child is mature enough to make an informed decision then such directions can only be given with the child's consent.[5]

¹   Children (Northern Ireland) Order 1995, art 57.
²   See para 6.95.
³   Children (Northern Ireland) Order 1995, art 57(2).
⁴   Children (Northern Ireland) Order 1995, art 57(4). Technically, an ICO is not renewed at a subsequent hearing but is made afresh, the court being satisfied that there are grounds for making the order. See *Re SM (Interim Care Orders: Exercise of judge's discretion)* [2002] NI FAM 11, 2 May 2002, Gillen J.
⁵   Children (Northern Ireland) Order 1995, art 57(6). There is an 'echo' of the '*Gillick*' principle in this provision. See chapter 1, para 1.52.

Excluding the abuser

6.115   Amendments to the Children Order mean that where a court is making an Interim Care Order[1] or an EPO,[2] it has the option of adding a condition that excludes the alleged abuser from the premises in which the child resides, or a defined area around the premises in which the child resides, or indeed any other defined area. However, it can only do so if there is reasonable cause to believe that the exclusion of that person would mean that the child would cease to suffer, or cease being likely to suffer, significant harm. The genesis of this statutory provision was the concern that the removal of the child from its usual residence in the course of a child protection investigation in order to protect it from the alleged abuser, resulted in further disruption to the child's life. It was considered better to leave the child to live on in its home place and remove the alleged abuser.

1 Children (Northern Ireland) Order 1995, art 57A as amended by the Family Homes and Domestic Violence (Northern Ireland) Order 1998, art 29(2).
2 Children (Northern Ireland) Order 1995, art 63A as amended by the Family Homes and Domestic Violence (Northern Ireland) Order 1998, art 29(4).

Child protection conference and alleged abuser's rights

6.116 The courts have determined, in a number of judicial review actions, that alleged abusers have a right to be aware of the allegations being made against them in the child protection conference and a right to counter these allegations.

6.117 In *R v Norfolk County Council Social Services Department, ex p M*[1] the applicant first knew that he had been named as the abuser of a child who had been placed on the Child Protection Register, when he received a letter from the local authority after the case conference had been concluded. As a result, alleged abusers should be allowed to participate in some part of the child protection conference to provide them with the opportunity to know of, and counter, the allegations against them. However, in *R v Harrow London Borough Council, ex p D*[2] the applicant was unsuccessful in her judicial review of the decision to name her on the Child Protection Register as the alleged abuser because she had been given the opportunity to make written submissions to the case conference and that was considered sufficient opportunity to meet the allegations levelled against her. The requirement, as far as the courts are concerned, is to accord the alleged abuser his or her natural justice rights and this does not necessarily mean that he or she must be allowed to attend in every case.[3]

1 [1989] QB 619, [1989] 2 All ER 359.
2 [1990] Fam 133, [1990] 3 All ER 12, CA.
3 On natural justice rights in judicial review, see chapter 2, para 2.122.

Family Assistance Order

6.118 A Family Assistance Order (FAO) is a type of order that is infrequently made,[1] although it may be issued by court of its own volition in any family proceedings. In an FAO the court will order a suitably qualified person to 'advise, assist and (where appropriate) befriend' any person named in the order.[2] Thus, if in the course of an application for an 'Article 8 order'[3] a court considers that the family could benefit from the involvement of social workers, or other social care workers, it is open to it to make an FAO. However, the drawback with the order is that the consent of every person named in it (with the exception of any children) is necessary before it can be made,[4] and that the circumstances are exceptional.[5] An FAO lasts for six months or such shorter period as the court decides.[6]

1 For an example, only six were made in 2002, Judicial Statistics for Northern Ireland, 2002, Table F7.
2 Children (Northern Ireland) Order 1995, art 16.
3 See chapter 9, para 9.101.
4 Children (Northern Ireland) Order 1995, art 16(3)(b).

⁵   Children (Northern Ireland) Order 1995, art 16(3)(a).
⁶   Children (Northern Ireland) Order 1995, art 16(5).

Care Order, Supervision Order, and Education Supervision Order

6.119   The main public law orders available for the protection of children are Care Orders and Supervision Orders. The threshold conditions for securing these orders are identical and furthermore, a court faced with an application for a Care Order may, of its own volition, make an order for a Supervision Order and vice versa.

6.120   What then is the difference between the two types of order? Practically, the matter is a question of suitability: which of them will afford sufficient protection for the child. From a legal point of view, there is some difference between the two. The crucial legal distinction is that the Trust only acquires parental responsibility for a child subject to a Care Order. One other difference lies in the fact that a Care Order lasts until the child reaches 16 years,[1] whereas a Supervision Order only lasts for one year, with the possibility of subsequent extension for a maximum of three years.[2] Moreover, where a Supervision Order is not being complied with the only sanction is to return to court to have its terms varied or discharged.[3]

[1]   Children (Northern Ireland) Order 1995, arts 50(4) and 52(1).
[2]   Children (Northern Ireland) Order 1995, Sch 3, para 6.
[3]   Children (Northern Ireland) Order 1995, art 54(1)(c).

6.121   Before making either of these orders, the court must be satisfied about the arrangements that the Trust intends to make in respect of the care of the child. These arrangements will be set out in the Trust's Care Plan.[1]

[1]   See para 6.140.

6.122   A third, specialised, type of order may be sought, namely an Education Supervision Order. As its title indicates, its purpose is to deal with poor educational attainment.[1] The threshold criteria do not apply to the granting of this order.

[1]   Children (Northern Ireland) Order 1995, art 55.

6.123   Children who are subject to Care Orders are considered to be 'looked after children'[1] and the Trust must conduct periodic reviews of their cases. Trusts also owe a number of other duties to 'looked after children' and these are outlined in chapter 7.[2]

[1]   Children (Northern Ireland) Order 1995, arts 25(1)(a), and 25(7)(a).
[2]   See chapter 7, para 7.34.

Care Order

6.124   As mentioned above, the threshold conditions for securing a Care Order[1] are the same as those that apply for Supervision Orders. These threshold conditions are explored in detail below,[2] but essentially they require the Trust to demonstrate that the child has suffered, or is likely to suffer, significant harm.

[1]   Children (Northern Ireland) Order 1995, art 50(1)(a).
[2]   See para 6.134.

6.125   The effect of a Care Order is quite considerable, as it accords the Trust parental responsibility and allows the child to be removed from its home and placed in care, usually foster care.[1] This does not extinguish the parental responsibility of the child's parents or others with such responsibility. However, the consequence of the Care Order is that they will not be able to exercise that parental responsibility while the child is in care and indeed, while the Care Order is in force, the Trust may determine the extent to which the people with parental responsibility may fill that role with respect to the child.[2] The child's parents, and others with parental responsibility, will be able to remain in contact with the child and indeed the Trust is mandated to ensure that this sort of contact continues.[3]

Of the public law orders made by the courts, Care Orders are the most common with approximately one half of all public orders made in 2000/01 and 2001/02 being Care Orders.[4]

[1]   On the legal basis underpinning fostering see chapter 8, paras 8.10 ff. The granting of the Care Order does not mean that the child will necessarily be placed outside the home and many children subject to a Care Order continue to be cared for by their parents, at home.
[2]   Children (Northern Ireland) Order 1995, art 52(3)(b), although the Trust may only do this to promote and safeguard the welfare of the child: art 52(4).
[3]   See the Children (Northern Ireland) Order 1995, art 53. See chapter 7, para 7.39.
[4]   COAC Third Report, p 65 and Figure 6, p 82. EPOs featured in 14.3%; ESOs in 7.6%; and 'Article 53 contact' orders in 6% of cases.

6.126   The COAC has highlighted a minor, although important, matter about the administration of Care Orders. It reported that no mechanism exists to enable the transfer of a Care Order from one Trust to another, something which can cause a difficulty where the child's family moves from one Trust's area into another Trust's area. On a similar point, the Committee has noted that no legislation exists which allows Care Orders made in Northern Ireland to be recognised, for the purposes of transfer, in England and Wales.[1]

[1]   COAC Second Report, p 30.

Supervision Order

6.127   These orders require the Trust to advise, assist and befriend the supervised child, [1] and can only be granted if the same threshold conditions that apply to the granting of Care Orders are met.[2] In doing so the Trust is to take such steps as are reasonably necessary to give effect to the order and to seek its variation or discharge if it is not working properly or is no longer necessary.

[1]   Children (Northern Ireland) Order 1995, art 54.
[2]   See para 6.134.

6.128   As outlined above, the Trust does not acquire parental responsibility for the child under a Supervision Order, and if it encounters difficulty in implementing its planned activity under such an order its only remedy is to return to court to seek to have the order varied or discharged. Of course, in certain circumstances, where the Trust encounters such difficulties in performing its duties it may feel justified in applying for a Care Order, although this would involve making a fresh application.

6.129   The Supervision Order allows the supervising social worker to issue directions about a range of aspects relating to the child's upbringing, including the child's place of residence and involvement in specific programmes.[1] However, the supervisor cannot require the child to undergo any medical or psychiatric treatment or examination and the order must specifically provide for this in order for it to be carried out.[2] The order may also be directed to any person having responsibility for the child, although it may only do so with the consent of that person.[3] Schedule 3, of the 1995 Order sets out the full range of matters that may be addressed in a Supervision Order.

[1]   Children (Northern Ireland) Order 1995, Sch 3, para 2(1).
[2]   Children (Northern Ireland) Order 1995, Sch 3, paras 4 and 5.
[3]   Children (Northern Ireland) Order 1995, Sch 3, para 3.

DISCHARGE OF CARE ORDER AND SUPERVISION ORDER

6.130   Care Orders and Supervision Orders can be brought to an end by a court order, which can be applied for by the Trust, the child's parents or others with parental responsibility, or indeed even by the child.[1] A court, faced with an application to discharge a Care Order can, rather than acceding to the application, make a Supervision Order instead.[2] The making of a residence order in favour of any other party will automatically discharge the Care Order.[3]

[1]   Children (Northern Ireland) Order 1995, art 58(1) and (2).
[2]   Children (Northern Ireland) Order 1995, art 58(4).
[3]   Children (Northern Ireland) Order 1995, arts 8(1) and 9(1).

Education Supervision Order

6.131   An ESO may only be made where the court is satisfied that the child is 'not being properly educated'[1] with 'proper education' being defined as 'receiving efficient full-time education suitable to his age, ability and aptitude and to any special educational needs'.[2] The order puts the child under the supervision of a designated education and library Board for a maximum period of one year,[3] although this can be extended for period of three years.[4] The supervisor shall then 'advise, assist and befriend, and give directions to the supervised child and his or her parents, in such a way as will, in the opinion of the supervisor, secure that he is properly educated.'[5] The supervisor is required, before issuing any direction, to ascertain the feelings and wishes of the child and its parents and must give due regard to those wishes and feelings.[6]

1 Children (Northern Ireland) Order 1995, art 55.
2 Children (Northern Ireland) Order 1995, art 55(3).
3 Children (Northern Ireland) Order 1995, Sch 4, para 5(1).
4 Children (Northern Ireland) Order 1995, Sch 4, para 5(4) and (5).
5 Children (Northern Ireland) Order 1995, Sch 4, para 2(1).
6 Children (Northern Ireland) Order 1995, Sch 4, para 2(2) and (3).

6.132 Persistent failure by the parents to adhere to directions of the supervising officer is a criminal offence.[1] Where the child is the one who will not comply with the supervising officer, he or she must inform the appropriate Trust and request them to investigate the child's circumstances.[2] Obviously, where an ESO is not having the desired effect due to the failure of the child or its parents to comply with it, then wider child protection concerns may be raised and these might be more properly dealt with in Care Order proceedings, for example.

1 Children (Northern Ireland) Order 1995, Sch 4, para 8.
2 Children (Northern Ireland) Order 1995, Sch 4, para 9.

6.133 Little use has been made of ESO, although there has been an increase in their use over the years that the Children Order has been in force. The COAC has suggested a number of reasons for the limited use made of them, which reasons include the fact that inter-agency discussion and co-operation between education and library Boards and social services staff has reduced the need for them, the fact that the Education Welfare Service attempts to resolve the child's non-attendance pattern by ensuring resource to other services and the fact that these orders may appear to be ineffective and lack effective enforcement.[1]

1 COAC Second Report, pp 31–32.

Threshold conditions

6.134 Before a court can make either a Care Order or a Supervision Order, it must be satisfied that the threshold conditions are met. These are that the child is suffering, or is likely to suffer, significant harm; and that the harm, or likelihood of harm, is attributable to:

> '(i) the care given to the child, or likely to be given to him if the order were not made, not being what it would be reasonable to expect a parent to give to him; or (ii) the child's being beyond parental control.'[1]

1 Children (Northern Ireland) Order 1995, art 50(2).

6.135 Harm is defined as 'ill-treatment or the impairment of health or development'[1] but no definition of 'significant' is provided in the legislation. The legislation does go on to provide that:[2]

> 'Where the question of whether harm suffered by a child is significant turns on the child's health or development, his health or development shall be compared with that which could reasonably be expected of a similar child.'

The issue of how one identifies a child with whom the health and development of the child the subject of the proceedings can be compared can be difficult, as there may be a number of variables that might affect the validity or usefulness of the comparison made.[3] Departmental guidance suggests that:[4]

> 'the meaning of "similar" in this context ... may need to take account of environmental, social and cultural characteristics of the child. The need to use a standard appropriate for the child in question arises because some children have characteristics or handicaps which mean they cannot be expected to be as healthy or as well-developed as others.'

[1]   Children (Northern Ireland) Order 1995, art 3. 'Harm', 'development' and 'ill-treatment' are further defined in the legislation: Children (Northern Ireland) Order 1995, art 2.
[2]   Children (Northern Ireland) Order 1995, art 50(3).
[3]   *Re O (A Minor) (Care Order: Education: Procedure)* [1992] 4 All ER 905, [1992] 1 WLR 912, [1992] 2 FLR 7, Ewbank J in the context of the facts of that case considered that a 'similar child' was 'a child of equivalent intellectual and social development who has gone to school and not merely a child who may or may not go to school.
[4]   Children (Northern Ireland) Order 1995, Regulations and Guidance, Volume 1, p 59, para 9.24.

6.136   Although the word 'significant' qualifies the type of harm the child must be suffering or is likely to suffer, it is not defined in the 1995 Order, although the courts have offered some guidance on its interpretation. In *Humberside County Council v P*,[1] the English High Court stated that 'significant' meant 'considerable, noteworthy and important'.

[1]   [1993] 1 FLR 257, [1993] 1 FCR 613.

6.137   As is the case with all civil litigation, the standard of proof in Care Order and Supervision Order applications is proof in the balance of probabilities. This means that the onus is on the applicant Trust to satisfy the court that, on the balance of probabilities, the child has suffered or is likely to suffer significant harm. However, the House of Lords has considered the application of the 'balance of probabilities test' to applications for these orders. In *Re H (minors) (sexual abuse: standard of proof)*[1] the House of Lords was faced with a case in which the eldest of the mother's four daughters alleged that her stepfather had sexually abused her. She was fostered, and the local authority sought Care Orders in respect of her three siblings. The issue for the Law Lords was to determine 'the requisite standard of proof' for proving that her sisters were 'likely to suffer significant harm'.[2]

[1]   [1996] AC 563, [1996] 1 All ER 1, [1996] 1 FCR 509, [1996] 1 FLR 80, HL.
[2]   This issue was considered more recently in an unreported English Court of Appeal decision in which the trial judge concluded, drawing on Lord Nicholl's speech in Re H, that if it was determined that one child had suffered harm, then the issue of whether others were likely to suffer significant harm was determined on the basis of whether there was a real possibility that the other children would suffer significant harm '... a possibility that cannot sensibly be ignored having regard to the nature and gravity of the feared harm in the particular case'. *Re K (Children) (care order)* (11 December 2002, unreported) Thorpe, Collins LLJ.

6.138   The Law Lords considered that 'likely to suffer significant harm' did not mean 'more likely than not', and that 'likely is being used in the sense of a real possibility, a possibility that cannot be sensibly ignored having regard to the nature and gravity of the feared harm in the particular case.'[1] However, more controversially, and perhaps more confusingly, a majority of the Law Lords considered that although the balance of probabilities test applied to establishing facts, so that one had to prove, on the balance of probabilities, that the facts on which the prognosis of risk was based had occurred, the more serious the allegation the more evidence was required to meet that standard of proof. Lord Nicholls offered the following explanation:[2]

> 'The balance of probability standard means that a court is satisfied an event occurred if the court considers that, on the evidence, the occurrence of the event was more likely than not. When assessing the probabilities the court will have in mind as a factor, to whatever extent is appropriate in the particular case, that the more serious the allegation the less likely it is that the event occurred and, hence, the stronger should be the evidence before the court concludes that the allegation is established on the balance of probability. Fraud is usually less likely than negligence. Deliberate physical injury is usually less likely than accidental physical injury. A stepfather is usually less likely to have repeatedly raped and had non-consensual oral sex with his under age stepdaughter than on some occasion to have lost his temper and slapped her. Built into the preponderance of probability standard is a generous degree of flexibility in respect of the seriousness of the allegation.'

Although the result is much the same, this does not mean that where a serious allegation is in issue the standard of proof required is higher. It means only that the inherent probability or improbability of an event is itself a matter to be taken into account when weighing the probabilities and deciding whether, on balance, the event occurred. The more improbable the event, the stronger must be the evidence that it did occur before, on the balance of probability, its occurrence will be established. '

The practical effect of this for social workers is that they must gather sufficient evidence to prove that certain events probably did happen, but the more unusual the allegations, the more tenacious and thorough they need to be in obtaining that evidence.

[1]   [1996] 1 All ER 1 at 15F, per Lord Nicholls.
[2]   [1996] 1 All ER 1 at 16F.

STATEMENT OF FACTS TO THRESHOLD CRITERIA

6.139   As indicated in chapter 3, there is an obligation on parties in public and private law family proceedings to file Statements of Evidence, setting out the matters which that party intends to adduce in evidence. Good practice now also requires the Trust to submit a 'Statement of Facts to Threshold Criteria' in Care Order proceedings.[1] This document summaries the factual evidence the Trust has gathered, or concerns that it continues to have, which are germane to the threshold criteria. Where all the matters in this statement are agreed by all the parties, it should be signed by the appropriate social worker and each of the respondents. Where there are disputed facts these should be identified, allowing the court to hear evidence about those matters. However, the task of deciding whether the facts contained in the statement, or adduced in evidence, meet the threshold criteria remains one for the court alone.

[1]   COAC, 'Best practice Guidance', 2003, para 3.1.30. The guardian ad litem should be shown the document and asked whether he or she approves it.

Care plan

6.140   A care plan sets out the long-term arrangements for the child's care when it has been taken into care. A care plan must be created for every child that is 'looked after'[1] and should be made before the child becomes looked after, except where the child is brought into care on an emergency basis, in which case it should be completed as soon as possible after the placement is made.[2] In particular, a care plan is obviously required whenever an application is made for a Care Order as the court cannot make an order until it is satisfied with the plan. It is not to be confused with a placement plan, which deals with the day-to-day arrangements for the care of the child.[3]

[1]   See chater 7, para 7.34.
[2]   Children (Northern Ireland) Order 1995 Guidance and Regs, Volume 3 (Family Placements para 2.2).
[3]   Placement plans are made under the Arrangement for Placement of Children (General) Regulations (Northern Ireland) 1996 and are explained in chapter 7, para 7.34.

6.141   The core of the care plan records the overall plan for the child, this plan having been decided at the child protection case conference. This plan may only be altered thereafter in a statutory review, commonly known as 'Looked After Children' reviews.[1] There are a wide range of options that may be adopted in respect of the 'looked after' child. He or she may remain with his or her family with support services being provided by the Trust, returning to his or her birth family within a specified period. Alternatively supported or independent living in the community might be the plan chosen for the child, or the plan may aim for the eventual adoption of the child. However, the ethos of the Children Order is that the plan should be developed with a view to returning the child to its birth parents at some point in the future, if that is at all possible. It is also necessary for the authorities to adopt this approach in order to act in a manner that is compatible with Convention right, article 8. The plan will outline why this particular option has been chosen and will detail the steps or tasks that need to be completed in order to achieve it. It must record whether there have been discussions with the child's parents and others with parental responsibility and whether they have agreed with the plans for the child.[2] As noted in chapter 8, in which adoption is explored, the concept of 'permanency planning'[3] is gaining credence in social work practice. 'Best Practice Guidance' requires that it also be considered as an option in all Care Order applications.[4] In appropriate cases the Trust is to consider the possibility of 'concurrent' or 'twin track' planning'.[5]

[1]   These are held under the Children (Northern Ireland) Order 1995, art 45. See chapter 7, para 7.38.

2   A detailed list of likely necessary contents is provided in COAC, 'Best Practice Guidance', 2003, para 3.1.5.
3   See chapter 8, para 8.7.
4   COAC, 'Best Practice Guidance', 2003, para 3.1.6.
5   *Re D and K (Care Plan: Twin Track Planning)* [1999] 4 All ER 893, [2000] 1 WLR 642, [1999] 3 FCR 109, [1999] 2 FLR 872.

CONCURRENT PLANNING

6.142 'Concurrent planning' is defined as 'the process of working towards family reunification, while at the same time establishing an alternative permanent plan.'[1] This means that the Trust pursues two options in the care plan at the same time, namely rehabilitation of the child within its natural family within a limited time or adoption outside of the family. The Trust is not confined to examining the possibility of adopting the child only when the possibility of returning the child to its family is exhausted. The purpose of this twin track approach is to lead to a speedier, permanent resolution of the child's position, without pre-judging the final determination.

1   Bracewell J in *Re D and K (Care Plan: Twin Track Planning)* [1999] 4 All ER 893, [2000] 1 WLR 642, [1999] 3 FCR 109, [1999] 2 FLR 872, explaining the US origins of the concept.

6.143 Where the plan is for adoption the care plan should contain a timescale for advancing the adoption, all possible information relating to the identity of the prospective adopters and the proposed date for the presentation of the case to the adoption panel.[1] This information would also be provided, so far as possible, where a 'twin track' approach is pursued.

1   COAC, 'Best Practice Guidance', 2003, para 3.1.6(e).

6.144 A court faced with an application for a Care Order is not to make the order until it is content with the care plan. This particular requirement has presented the courts with some interesting issues. For example, in *Re S and D (Children: Powers of Court)*[1] the judge accepted the threshold criteria for a Care Order had been made out, but he was less happy with the care plan which had as its ultimate goal the rehabilitation of the child with his family, an approach that the judge did not consider to be safe. The judge refused to make the Care Orders, issuing Supervision Orders instead and an injunction preventing the mother from taking the children from their foster homes. This approach was overturned by the Court of Appeal which considered that faced with this dilemma the court had to take 'the lesser of two evils' and make the Care Orders.

1   [1995] 2 FLR 456.

6.145 Once the care plan has been approved and the Care Order made there is no statutory mechanism under the Children Order by which the parents, or others with parental responsibility, can involve the courts, where they allege that the Trust has failed to implement the care plan. The English Court of Appeal considered that, in light of the Article 8 Convention rights of the child and its parents, it would develop a mechanism to allow the courts to review the care plan. It proposed that elements of the care plan be 'starred' and that where a starred milestone was not met within a reasonable time period, the social services authority or the guardian ad Litem would have to apply to court. The House of Lords considered this proposed method of dealing with care plans in two conjoined appeals namely, in *Re S (Minors) (Care Order: Implementation of Care Plan)* and in *Re W (Minors) (Care Order: Adequacy of Care Plan).*[1] The Law Lords considered, however, that the Court of Appeal's proposal was a misapplication of the HRA and rejected its proposed method of dealing with care plans. Where the parents of a child in care were in dispute with the social services authority about the application of the care plan, their remedy was to proceed under the HRA.

[1]   [2002] UKHL 10, [2002] 2 AC 291, [2002] 1 FCR 577.

6.146   In regard to the content of the care plan, Lord Nicholls took the opportunity to offer the following advice:[1]

'... when deciding whether to make a care order the court should normally have before it a care plan which is sufficiently firm and particularised for all concerned to have a reasonably clear picture of the likely way ahead for the child for the foreseeable future. The degree of firmness to be expected, as well as the amount of detail in the plan, will vary from case to case depending on how far the local authority can foresee what will be best for the child at that time.'

[1]   [2002] 2 AC 291 at 325G.

Relationship of criminal proceedings to care proceedings

6.147   It is possible that criminal proceedings and care proceedings can arise in respect of the same incidents and the relationship of both sets of proceedings can be problematic. Article 171(2) of the Children Order does provide some degree of protection for the accused whose actions are also to be the subject of inquiry in care proceedings because he or she is the alleged abuser. It establishes that any statement or admission shall not be admissible in evidence against the person making it, or the maker's spouse, in criminal proceedings. However, this does not prevent the police using the information to conduct a criminal investigation, although they cannot use that information in the actual prosecution.[1] This protection is balanced by a requirement that witnesses in applications for Care or Supervision Orders, or for Emergency Protection Orders or Child Assessment Orders may not refuse to answer a question on the grounds of self-incrimination[2] nor may they refuse to testify.[3]

[1]   *Oxfordshire County Council v P* [1995] Fam 161, [1995] 1 FLR 552.
[2]   Self-incrimination arises where a witness is asked a question, an affirmation answer to which would incriminate him or her in criminal activity.
[3]   Children (Northern Ireland) 1995, art 171(1).

6.148   Occasionally the issue arises whether the application for Care or Supervision Orders should proceed when there are pending criminal charges against one of the parties involved, like for example, the child's parents. The danger is that the accused's ability to obtain a fair trial in the criminal proceedings will be jeopardised if the care proceedings are held first. This issue has recently been considered in the Northern Ireland courts in *Re L1 and L2 (Care Proceedings: Criminal Trial).*[1] Relying on the fact that the evidence for the criminal proceedings had already substantially been collected, the protection afforded by article 171 and that any delay would impact adversely on the children, the trial judge considered that there was no necessity to postpone the care proceedings until the determination of the criminal trial. The COAC's 'Best Practice Guidance' suggests that where there may be concurrent criminal and care proceedings that Trusts in the case of public law applications and the applicant's solicitor in the case of private law applications should be in position to inform the judge as to the current position regarding the disposal of the criminal matter.[2] The main object of this exercise, it provides, is 'to timetable both the criminal and the care proceedings, to decide which should be heard first, and to ensure that each is heard without unavoidable delay.'[3]

[1]   [2002] NI Fam 12, 16 October, High Court of Northern Ireland, Gillen J.
[2]   Chapter 5.
[3]   COAC, 'Best Practice Guidance', 2003, para 5.4.

Wardship and the inherent jurisdiction of the High Court

6.149   Wardship is the process by which a child is made a ward of court for its own protection. The significance of wardship is that no decision can be made in respect of a ward of court without the court's permission. The inherent jurisdiction of the High Court refers to the innate, historical and non-statutory power of that court to make court orders to protect children. The paramountcy principle applies to wardship and inherent jurisdiction applications.

6.150   In the past the wardship jurisdiction was the method by which most children came into the care of the State. The Children (Northern Ireland) Order 1995, however, restricts the availability of wardship, and the inherent jurisdiction of the High Court, so that Trusts may not now seek to use wardship to protect a child when alternative orders, like Care Orders, Supervision Orders, Specific Issues Orders or Prohibited Steps Orders are available.[1] Furthermore, the leave of the court is required before a Trust may bring a wardship or inherent jurisdiction application.[2] As a result, wardship and inherent jurisdiction applications now relate to matters that cannot be dealt with by way of any of the applications mentioned above, such as whether a child should have a hazardous liver transplant operation even though its parents objected to the procedure.[3] Another case in which the inherent jurisdiction of the High Court was used was that of the conjoined twins, Mary and Jodie, who would certainly die without medical intervention, but one of whom would likely die as a result of the medical procedure.[4]

[1]   Children (Northern Ireland) Order 1995, art 173(1). On specific issues and prohibited steps orders see chapter 9, para 9.106.

2   Children (Northern Ireland) Order 1995, art 173(2). Article 173(3) sets out the criteria for granting leave.
3   *Re T (A Minor) (Wardship: Medical Treatment)* [1997] 1 All ER 906, [1997] 1 WLR 242, [1997] 1 FLR 503, [1997] 2 FCR 363, CA. The social services authority was granted permission to proceed with the transplant because it was in the child's best interests.
4   *Re A (Children) (Conjoined Twins: Surgical Separation)* [2001] Fam 147, [2000] 4 All ER 961, [2000] 3 FCR 577, CA.

Monitoring sex offenders and suspected abusers

6.151   Public concern about the possibility of convicted, or suspected, child sex abusers gaining access to children has increased in recent years and has influenced a number of legislative and administrative developments designed to protect children and vulnerable adults. This has resulted in the establishment of a sex offenders register under the Sex Offenders Act 1997, the overhaul of vetting checks for social services staff, and the monitoring of sex offenders in the community on the completion of their sentences. In this section, the operation of the Sex Offenders Act 1997 and the processes for vetting staff with significant access to children are explored, as are the principles that govern the disclosure of information about convicted and suspected child abusers. (The law relating to the supervision of sex offenders in the community after completion of their sentences is set out in chapter 5,[1] as it is largely a matter for probation officers).

1   See paras 5.137.

Protection of children and vulnerable adults

6.152   The system of checking the background of social services staff and others who had access to children was previously known as the Pre-Employment Consultancy Scheme (PECS). For a judicial assessment of the compatibility of the equivalent English system with the HRA, see *R v Secretary of State for Health, ex p C.*[1] PECS had been established in the 1980s, but underwent some revision following the publication of the SSI's report, 'An Abuse of Trust', in December 1993 dealing with the infiltration, by a convicted sex offender, of a number of voluntary and statutory organisations.[2] The Department of Education for Northern Ireland also contributed to this aspect of child protection by maintaining a list of persons who were prohibited from working in educational establishments, which was colloquially known as 'List 99'.[3]

PECS and 'List 99' have now been put on a statutory basis in the Protection of Children and Vulnerable Adults (Northern Ireland) Order 2003,[4] a similar statutory scheme to that found in the equivalent legislation in England and Wales, the Protection of Children Act 1999.[5]

1   [1999] 1 FLR 1073.
2   'An Abuse of Trust: the report of the SSI investigation into the case of Martin Huston', DHSS, 1993
3   The Department of Education in Great Britain also maintained a similar list for Great Britain, and also referred to as List 99.

4   The 2003 Order allows the Department to include persons on the new statutory lists who were on included on PECS when the Order was brought into force: Protection of Children and Vulnerable Adults (Northern Ireland) Order 2003, arts 10 and 41.

5   The coverage of the English Act has been extended to vulnerable adults.

Maintaining the lists

6.153 The 2003 Order requires the Department to maintain two lists, one of persons unsuitable to work with children and the other of persons unsuitable to work with vulnerable adults.[1] A 'vulnerable adult' is defined as:

(a) an adult to whom accommodation and nursing or personal care are provided in a residential care home or nursing home;

(b) an adult to whom any 'prescribed service' is provided in his own home under arrangement made by a domiciliary care agency or a prescribed person; or

(c) an adult to whom 'prescribed services' are provided by a health services body or at a private hospital.[2]

with the Department making regulations to identify the 'prescribed services'.

1   Protection of Children and Vulnerable Adults (Northern Ireland) Order 2003, arts 3 and 35 for children and vulnerable adults respectively.

2   Protection of Children and Vulnerable Adults (Northern Ireland) Order 2003, art 48(6).

6.154 The Department compiles the list on the basis of information supplied to it by child care and other organisations that work with children,[1] or in the case of vulnerable adults, the employers of those care workers who work with them.

1   Protection of Children and Vulnerable Adults (Northern Ireland) Order 2003, arts 4 and 36 are the duties to refer for children and vulnerable adults respectively. Child care organisations must relay this information to the Department, whereas non-child care organisations have a discretion as to whether to do so: Protection of Children and Vulnerable Adults (Northern Ireland) Order 2003, art 4(1). Other organisations, like the Northern Ireland Social Care Council, the H&SS Trusts and the Nursing and Midwifery Council may also refer information to the Department if is considers that no other organisation will do so: art 6. The art 4 duty to disclose is enforced by art 19.

6.155 The Department adds people to the lists where it feels that the evidence provided to it by an organisation leads it to reasonably consider the individual to be guilty of misconduct (whether or not in the course of his employment) which harmed a child (or vulnerable adult) or placed a child (or vulnerable adult) at risk of harm[1] making the person unsuitable to work with the appropriate client group.[2] The information provided by these organisations relates to one of the following range of circumstances, with appropriate changes to the text below in the case of vulnerable adults:

- the organisation has dismissed the individual on the grounds of misconduct (whether or not in the course of his employment) which harmed a child or placed a child at risk of harm;

- the individual has resigned, retired or been made redundant in circumstances such that the organisation would have dismissed him, or would have considered dismissing him, on such grounds if he had not resigned, retired or been made redundant;

- the organisation has transferred the individual to a position within the organisation which is not a child care position because he or she has harmed or placed a child at risk of harm;

- the organisation has suspended the individual or provisionally transferred him to a position which is not a child care position, but it has not yet decided whether to dismiss him or to confirm the transfer;[3]

- the organisation becomes aware of information that suggests the person was or could have placed children at risk of harm after he or she has been dismissed, resigned, made redundant or transferred to another position within the organisation.[4]

1   'Harm' is defined by reference to the Children (Northern Ireland) Order 1995, art 2(2).
2   Protection of Children and Vulnerable Adults (Northern Ireland) Order 2003, arts 4(7) and 36(7).
3   Protection of Children and Vulnerable Adults (Northern Ireland) Order 2003, arts 4(2) and 36(2).
4   Protection of Children and Vulnerable Adults (Northern Ireland) Order 2003, arts 4(4) and 36(3).

6.156   A similar duty to refer information to the Department is imposed on employment agencies and nursing agencies so that where such an agency decides not to include a person on its books in the future because it fears he or she may put a child (or vulnerable adult) at risk of harm, or where it will only offer that person work which is not a care position, it too must relay information to the Department to allow it to consider whether to add the person to the appropriate statutory list.[1]

1   Protection of Children and Vulnerable Adults (Northern Ireland) Order 2003, arts 5 and 37.

6.157   The Department may include the individual on the list on a provisional basis[1] but before definitively including that person on the list it must allow him or her an opportunity to respond to the allegations.[2]

1   Protection of Children and Vulnerable Adults (Northern Ireland) Order 2003, arts 4(4)(b) and 36(4)(b).
2   Protection of Children and Vulnerable Adults (Northern Ireland) Order 2003, arts 4(5)(a) and 36(5)(a).

Appeals against inclusion

6.158   A person included on either of the two statutory lists can appeal his or her inclusion to the Social Care tribunal.[1] In respect of the DHSSPS's List of persons unsuitable to work with children, if the Tribunal is not satisfied that either of the following situations apply, namely:

(a)   that the individual was guilty of misconduct (whether or not in the course of his employment) which harmed a child (or vulnerable adult) or placed a child (or vulnerable adult) at risk of harm; and

(b)   the individual is unsuitable to work with children (or vulnerable adults),

then it must determine the appeal in the person's favour.[2] An individual who is found guilty of misconduct in a criminal trial cannot in his or her appeal before the Social Care Tribunal, challenge any finding of fact on which the conviction was based arising from the criminal trial.[3]

¹   Protection of Children and Vulnerable Adults (Northern Ireland) Order 2003, arts 11 and 42. Established under the Health and Personal Social Services Act (Northern Ireland) 2001 and explained in chapter 2, para 2.44. A person may also appeal the decision not to remove his or her name from the list to the Tribunal see para 6.159. Where there are criminal or civil proceedings arising out of the alleged incident of misconduct the individual cannot appeal to the Tribunal before a period of six months has elapsed since the conclusion of those proceedings: art 11(5).
²   Protection of Children and Vulnerable Adults (Northern Ireland) Order 2003, arts 11(3) and 42(3).
³   Protection of Children and Vulnerable Adults (Northern Ireland) Order 2003, art 11(4).

Appeal against continued inclusion

6.159   An individual also has the right to appeal to the tribunal to have his or her name removed from the list but this right is heavily curtailed.[1] In order to proceed with such a challenge, the individual requires the leave of the tribunal and this may only be granted where the person has been on the list for ten years[2] and has not made any other application, and only then if the tribunal considers that the individual's circumstances have changed in the meantime.[3] Where a person has been removed from the list the Chief Constable or a director of a Trust may apply to the High Court to have that person restored to the list if the High Court has 'reasonable cause to believe that an order is necessary to protect children in general, or any children in particular, from serious harm from him.'[4]

¹   Protection of Children and Vulnerable Adults (Northern Ireland) Order 2003, arts 12 and 43.
²   Protection of Children and Vulnerable Adults (Northern Ireland) Order 2003, arts 13(4) and 44(4). Five years if he or she was a child at the time they were included: arts 13(3) and 44(3).
³   Protection of Children and Vulnerable Adults (Northern Ireland) Order 2003, arts 13(5) and 44(5).
⁴   Protection of Children and Vulnerable Adults (Northern Ireland) Order 2003, arts 14(2)(b) and 45(2)(b).

Statutory basis for 'List 99'

6.160   'List 99' has been put on a statutory footing by the Protection of Children and Vulnerable Adults (Northern Ireland) Order 2003. This has been done by amending two provisions of the Education and Libraries (Northern Ireland) Order 1986, namely article 70(2)(e) (which allows the making of regulations for prohibiting or restricting the employment or further employment of teachers) and article 88A(2)(b) (which allows the making of regulations for prohibiting or restricting the employment, or further employment, of non-teaching staff). As a result the grounds for excluding a person from working in educational establishments have been extended to include misconduct, unsuitability to work with children and inclusion on the Department's list of persons unsuitable to work with children maintained under the 2003 Order.[1] People included on 'List 99' also have a right to invoke the Social Care Tribunal.[2]

¹   Protection of Children and Vulnerable Adults (Northern Ireland) Order 2003, art 15(4) and (5).
²   See chapter 2, para 2.44.

Using the lists

6.161   Where it is proposed to offer a person a child-care position, or a position within an educational establishment, a check will be made against these lists.[1] A check with the Criminal Records Bureau, which deals with criminal records and the equivalent statutory lists for Great Britain, will also disclose whether a person is listed on either of the equivalent lists there. All child care organisations are to be given access to this facility, while the Department can, in regulations, specify which non-child care organisations may request checks of be carried out against the lists.[2]

[1]   Protection of Children and Vulnerable Adults (Northern Ireland) Order 2003, art 17.
[2]   These bodies are termed 'accredited organisations'. This process of accrediting organisations should allow a greater range of bodies to use these lists.

6.162   Inclusion in either of the two Departmental lists, or on the statutory form of 'List 99', has very significant consequences for the employability of the person included on them. Where a person is included on the list of those unsuitable to work with children, a child care organisation may not employ that person, or if it already employs him or her it must transfer that person to a non-child care position.[1] A person included on the statutory 'List 99' may not be employed in an educational establishment. Where a person is included on the list of pepole unsuitable to work with vulnerable adults, that person may not be employed by those organisations that provide care for vulnerable adults.[2]

[1]   Protection of Children and Vulnerable Adults (Northern Ireland) Order 2003, art 16. A person included on these lists also commits an offence when they apply for a 'regulated' position. See para 6.167.
[2]   Protection of Children and Vulnerable Adults (Northern Ireland) Order 2003, art 46.

Disqualification Order

6.163   Where a person is convicted of certain types of criminal offences,[1] the court in passing sentence is required to make a order which indicates that the person is prohibited from working with children.[2] This latest addition to the range of mechanisms designed to protected children is referred to as a disqualification order. It is designed partly to deal with the situation where the offence for which the accused is convicted is not a sexual offence for the purposes of the Sex Offenders Act 1997, or does not ordinarily disclose that the offender might pose a risk of harm to children. However, the manner in which the offence was committed might reasonably give rise to concerns that the offender would be a danger to children. The making of the disqualification order by the sentencing judge can serve as a method of alerting others in the future to the dangers posed by the offender.

6.164   The minimum requirements[3] before a disqualification order must be made are that the sentence imposed involves at least 12 months imprisonment[4] or a hospital or guardianship order under the Mental Health (Northern Ireland) Order 1986.[5]

[1]   Set out in the Schedule to the 2003 Order and includes offences under the Criminal Law Amendment Act 1885, ss 4, 5, 6, and 7 (respectively, defilement of girl under 14, defilement of girl under 17,

permitting defilement of young girls on premises, abduction of girl with intent to have carnal knowledge); Infanticide Act (Northern Ireland) 1939, s 1 (infanticide); offences under the Children and Young Persons Act (Northern Ireland) 1968, ss 20, 21, 22, 23 (respectively cruelty to children, causing or encouraging seduction or prostitution of girl under 17, indecent conduct towards child, allowing child or young person to be in brothel.)

2   Protection of Children and Vulnerable Adults (Northern Ireland) Order 2003, arts 23(4) and 24(4).

3   Protection of Children and Vulnerable Adults (Northern Ireland) Order 2003, art 25.

4   This includes detention in a YOC, or detention at the Secretary of State's pleasure under the Criminal Justice (Children) (Northern Ireland) Order 1998, art 45.

5   See chapter 5, paras 5.133 and 5.134.

6.165   The individual may appeal against the disqualification order, or may apply to the Social Care Tribunal to have it reviewed. However, before the application to the Social Care Tribunal can be heard, the tribunal must first give leave, and as with challenges to inclusion on the new statutory lists, a review cannot be carried out of a disqualification order within ten years of the making of the order and unless the person's circumstances have changed.[1]

1   Protection of Children and Vulnerable Adults (Northern Ireland) Order 2003, art 28.

6.166   In the proceedings before the tribunal, the only issue is whether the person is unsuitable to work with children[1] and, thus, the hearing before the tribunal cannot become an opportunity to challenge the court's factual findings or an open-ended opportunity to 're-hash' the entire incident. As with the statutory lists, the Chief Constable, or a Director of Social Services, may apply to have a disqualification order re-imposed if there is reasonable cause to believe that this step was necessary to protect children from serious harm.[2]

1   Protection of Children and Vulnerable Adults (Northern Ireland) Order 2003, art 27.

2   Protection of Children and Vulnerable Adults (Northern Ireland) Order 2003, art 29.

6.167   It is an offence for a disqualified person, or a person included on either of the two statutory lists, to apply for a job which involves access to children[1] and it is also an offence for a person to employ such a person in such a position. A defence is available to the former that he or she did not know, nor could he or she reasonably be expected to know that the offender was disqualified from working with children.[2]

1   The Order stipulates a broad range of occupations and positions which it refers to as 'regulated positions' from which the person is disqualified, and this list includes positions where the employee has direct access or indirect access to children, or otherwise occupies a position of responsibility in respect of health and social services activities: Protection of Children and Vulnerable Adults (Northern Ireland) Order 2003, art 31.

2   Protection of Children and Vulnerable Adults (Northern Ireland) Order 2003, art 30(3).

Sex Offenders Act 1997

6.168   The main purpose of the Act is to require a person convicted, cautioned, or found guilty (but insane) of certain sex offences[1] to notify the police of his or her date of birth, name and address and to continue to do so for the requisite period, whenever he or she changes their name or address.[2] This allows the police to keep up-to-date information about certain types of sex offenders and to facilitate the compilation of a register of such offenders.[3] The police can also request the offender to submit to having his or her photograph or fingerprints taken in order to verify the offender's identity.[4] In complying with the notification requirement, the sex offender is commonly referred to as 'signing the sex offender register.' Sex offenders must also notify the police when they leave the UK, giving a range of details about their travels.[5]

[1] Sex Offenders Act 1997, s 1(1). The list of sex offences to which the Act applies are set out in Sch 1 to the Act.

[2] Initial registration with the police must take place within three days: Sex Offenders Act 1997, s 2(1), as amended by the Criminal Justice and Courts Service Act 2000, Sch 5, para 2(1).

[3] The Act only applies, however, to those cautioned, convicted or found not guilty but insane after the commencement of the legislation, or to those in prison, released on licence, or awaiting sentence at the time it was implemented: s 1(2) and (3). For information on sex offenders in the criminal justice system, see chapter 5, para 5.137.

[4] Sex Offenders Act 1997, s 2(6A) and (6B), as inserted by the Criminal Justice and Court Services Act 2000, Sch 5, para 3.

[5] Sex Offenders Act 1997, s 2(6D), as inserted by the Criminal Justice and Court Services Act 2000, Sch 5, para 4.

6.169 The period for which the sex offender will be required to keep the police informed of the relevant details will depend on the sentence imposed. For example, those sentenced to prison for a term of 30 months or more will be required to register indefinitely, while those who get six months or less in prison will only be required to register for seven years.[1] The table below provides the relevant information:

TABLE: PERIODS OF NOTIFICATION UNDER TEH SEX OFFENDERS ACT 1997

Length of prison sentence [2]	Notification period
> or = 2.5 years	Indefinite
Hospitalised under Restriction Order[3]	Indefinite
> 6 months but < 2.5 years	10 years
< or = 6 months	7 years
Hospitalised without Restriction Order	7 years
Any Other Disposal[4]	5 years

Those convicted of sex offences outside the UK must comply with the notification requirements once they become UK citizens or residents.[5] Failure by a sex offender to keep the police notified of the relevant information is, without a reasonable excuse, an offence.[6] Home Office research has shown that the compliance rate in the UK is quite high.

[1] Sex Offenders Act 1997, s 1(4).

² The requirement to notify also applies to children and young people who were subject to a Juvenile Justice Centre Order or sent to the YOC for the appropriate period: s 4(1)(c) and (d), but the notification period is halved: s 4(2).

³ See chapter 5, para 5.135.

⁴ For other sentencing options, see chapter 5, para 5.84.

⁵ Sex Offenders Act 1997, s 7(2).

⁶ Sex Offenders Act 1997, s 3.

Sex Offender Order

6.170   This is a relatively new civil order, issued where the court considers that it is necessary to protect the public from harm from sex offenders.[1] The police can apply to the court for such an order where the offender has acted 'in such a way as to give reasonable cause to believe that an order under this section is necessary to protect the public from serious harm from him.'[2] The court has a broad discretion to prohibit the offender from engaging in such activity as it considers 'necessary for the purpose of protecting the public from serious harm' from the offender.[3] The classic example of a situation in which a Sex Offender Order might be sought would be one where a known sex offender was adopting a pattern of behaviour identical to that which he followed when committing his offences, thereby giving rise to the fear that he was about to offend again. The original impetus for Sex Offender Orders came from concerns that because the Sex Offenders Act 1997 was not retrospective, offenders convicted before its implementation would not be subject to any monitoring by statutory agencies. However, few orders have been made and they are often an option of last resort for the police as they suffer from some practical drawbacks, such as the considerable staff resources needed to enforce them.[4]

¹ Criminal Justice (Northern Ireland) Order 1998, art 6. Sex offenders in this context are those who have been convicted, cautioned, found not guilty but insane of an offence to which the Sex Offenders Act 1997 applies or an offence committed outside the UK which would be subject to the 1997 Act if committed in the UK.

² Criminal Justice (Northern Ireland) Order 1998, art 6(1)(b).

³ No definition of serious harm is provided in the 1998 Order but Home Office Guidance on the equivalent English provisions explains that 'protecting the public from serious harm from him means protecting members of the public from death or serious personal injury, whether physical or psychological, occasioned by such further offences committed by him. 'Crime and Disorder Act – Sex Offender Order Guidance', Appendix B, para 2.

⁴ 'The police perspective on sex offender orders: a preliminary review of policy and practice', Police Research Series Paper 155, Home Office, 2002.

6.171   The court specifies the length of the order, but in any event it cannot last for less than five years, and during the life of the order the person subject to it is required to comply with the registration requirements of the Sex Offenders Act 1997.[1] Breach of a sex offender order, without a reasonable excuse, is a criminal offence.[2]

¹ See para 6.168.

² Criminal Justice (Northern Ireland) Order 1998, art 6(8).

Restraining Order

6.172   A restraining order may be imposed by the court that imposes a sentence of imprisonment, a hospital or guardianship order on the offender, or which finds the accused not guilty but insane, 'if it is satisfied that it is necessary to do so in order to protect the public in general, or any particular members of the public, from serious harm.'[1] The order may prohibit the offender from doing anything described in the order. Restraining Orders, as can be seen, are intended to operate like Sex Offender Orders by preventing the offender from engaging in certain activity, which might be unremarkable if performed by others, but which in the case of the sex offender suggests that he or she may cause harm.[2]

[1] Sex Offenders Act 1997, s 5A, as inserted by the Criminal Justice and Court Services Act 2000, Sch 5, para 6(1).
[2] The Home Secretary may enact secondary legislation to allow for the enforcement of Restraining Orders in Northern Ireland: Sex Offenders Act 1997, s 10(3A), as inserted by the Criminal Justice and Court Services Act 2000, Sch 5, para 6(3).

Risk assessment and management[1]

6.173   Where a person is arrested, charged, suspected, or convicted of a 'Schedule 1 offence',[2] or is otherwise a sex offender, he or she will be subject to the Multi-Agency Procedures for the Assessment and Management of Sex Offenders (MASRAM).[3] The MASRAM manual establishes a procedure for assessing and managing, the risk posed by such offenders.

[1] 'Co-operating to Safeguard Children' DHSSPS, Belfast, 2003 also sets out guidance for the Risk Assessment and Management of people in non-sexual abuse cases, ie physical abuse, emotional abuse or neglect: p 84, para 7.7–7.14.
[2] Criminal Justice (Children)(Northern Ireland) Order 1998, Sch 1. Although the MASRAM manual deals with convicted offenders, 'Co-operating to Safeguard Children' provides that this range of persons will also be subject to the procedures (p 85, para 7.15). The MASRAM manual appears to refer to offenders convicted of sex offences defined by Sex Offenders Act 1997.
[3] Northern Ireland Office, 2001.

6.174   There are six Area Sex Offender Risk Assessment and Management Committees and one Northern Ireland-wide Sex Offender Management Committee, which oversees the work of the Area Committees, and which in particular is directly involved in the assessment and management of high risk offenders. Area Committees are chaired by PBNI staff and include representatives of the police, the prison service and social services staff. The Area Committees carry out risk assessment of such people based on the guidance in the MASRAM manual. There are three possible categorisations of those subject to assessment. Category 3 classifies someone as 'likely to lead them to seriously harm other people'; Category 2 is applied to those 'whose behaviour gives cause for clear concern with regard to their capacity to carry out a contact sexual offence'; while Category 1 is 'someone whose current behaviour gives no current cause for concern.'

Disclosure of information to public authorities and the public

6.175   One of the concerns in implementing management strategies for convicted and suspect sex offenders and others who may put children at risk of significant harm is whether, and to what extent, public bodies can, and should, disclose information to the public and to other statutory authorities about suspected and convicted sex offenders.

6.176 Widespread disclosure has been rejected as a mechanism for disseminating such information, for practical reasons as much as for legal ones. The UK authorities have rejected the option of pursuing blanket disclosure, retaining discretion to engage in selective disclosure. Thus the Home Office Guidance dealing with the disclosure of information about offenders who feature on the Sex Offenders' register rejects blanket disclosure and opts instead for controlled disclosure at the option of the statutory authorities.[1] This approach has been validated by the courts in *R v Chief Constable of North Wales Police, ex p AB*.[2] That case dealt with the issue of whether the police could disclose to the owner of a caravan site, shortly before the Easter holidays, the fact that two convicted sex offenders were resident on the site. Disclosure was considered lawful provided that disclosure was the exception rather than the rule, and the decision to disclose had been taken with the purpose of protecting the public.

[1] HOC 39/1997.
[2] [1998] 3 All ER 310, CA.

6.177 However, the issue of disclosure becomes more complicated when the information that is sought to be disclosed relates not to convictions, but to suspicions that a person is a sex offender. A number of cases have addressed this issue with perhaps the most significant of these being in *Re C (Sexual Abuse: Disclosure to Landlords)*.[1]

[1] [2002] EWHC 234 (Fam), [2002] 2 FCR 385. See also *Re V and Re L* [1999] 1 WLR 299, [1999] 1 FCR 308, CA; *R v Local Authority in the Midlands, ex p LM* [2000] 1 FCR 736; *R v Devon County Council, ex p L* [1991] FCR 599.

6.178 *Re C* involved an application by a chief constable and a local authority Social Services Director for leave to disclose to the housing association in whose premises C resided, a finding made by a trial judge, when considering a Care Order application, that C was a dangerous and manipulative sex offender.[1]

[1] The trial judge hearing the Care Order application concluded at para 14 that C was 'a cold, chilling, ruthless, devious and manipulative man and I can well see how he would exert power over those who were unable to discriminate good from bad, right from wrong, because of his background.' He added at para 21: 'It follows from what I have said ... that against both wives he has used great violence regularly, violence from a physical and sexual point of view. He is a person who seeks out the vulnerable ... am very satisfied on all of the evidence that has come before me ... that this man poses a grave danger to S. I am satisfied that Mr C is dangerous [and] manipulative, he poses a considerable risk to any child, any child who is young or vulnerable, he poses a great risk to a vulnerable adult whom he can seek to dominate. In short, and I make no apologies for it, I am quite satisfied that this man is a paedophile who poses very great dangers ...'.

6.179 C had a long history of allegations of serious sexual abuse made against him by young children, but none of these had ever resulted in any criminal conviction and he was not subject to the registration regime under the Sex Offenders Act 1997. However, he did have two old cautions for indecent assaults on two six-year-old girls, and two convictions for violence, for which he had received sentences of one month and three months' imprisonment respectively. Because of these allegations, the local authority instituted care proceedings when C's partner gave birth to a child. C was a witness in the proceedings and the court heard evidence of the various allegations referred to above. The Care Order was made, but it was the judge's finding about C that the local authority wished to transmit to others.

6.180   The court concluded that disclosure to the housing association was possible but depended on the court engaging in a balancing act between the rights of the offender and those of the public. However, in order for disclosure to be permitted the onus was on the applicant to demonstrate that there was 'real and cogent' evidence of a 'pressing need' for such disclosure. The judge further required that this 'pressing need' be determined by reference to at least three criteria, first the extent of the authorities' belief in the truth of the allegations, secondly, the extent of the third party's interest in disclosure, and thirdly, the risk posed by non-disclosure.[1] However, the judge rejected the application to allow more extensive disclosure,[2] instead requiring the authorities to make further court applications if they considered it necessary to make wider disclosure of the information to, for example, other housing associations in the area.

[1]   The trial judge outlined the method by which disclosure would be made, and required the police force family protection officer to explain the significance of the court order to the officers of the Housing Association and the importance of abiding strictly to its terms, and even went so far as to draft the terms of the notice that would be issued to them.
[2]   The applicants had also applied for permission to disclose the information to any other Housing Associations, local authorities private landlords in whose area C might live in the future.

6.181   Similar issues arose in a Northern Ireland case, *Re Martin*.[1] This case concerned a man against whom there had been allegations of physical and sexual abuse some years previously and whose children had been on the child protection register. When he began living with another woman who had young children social workers who had knowledge of his history required him to disclose this history to his new partner with the result that the relationship broke down. The judicial review centred on whether there had been a breach of the applicant's article 8 rights to privacy and family life. Relying on *Re C*, the High Court concluded that any interference with the applicant's article 8 rights, in this context, were justified.

[1]   [2002] NIQB 67, 20 December 2002, Weatherup J.

6.182   In summary, information containing details of findings made in family proceedings or suspicions of social services can be disclosed to other members of the general public provided that there has been a proper application of Convention right article 8 and close scrutiny of the necessity of disclosing the information.

Disclosure between statutory agencies

6.183   As one might expect, the issue of disclosure between public or statutory agencies has also arisen. In *Re L (Disclosure to Third Party)*[1] permission was granted for medical reports prepared as part of care proceedings in Northern Ireland to be disclosed to a child protection unit in England, the alleged abuser having moved there to live with a female who was caring for two young children. And in *Re A (Disclosure to Third Party)*[2] the High Court granted leave to allow medical assessments[3] of the parents of children subject to care proceedings to be distributed to the professionals involved in those proceedings and in case conference reviews. Disclosure, however, was only allowed to a defined group of individuals, due consideration having been given to Convention right, article 8.

[1]   [2002] NI Fam 24, 5 December 2002, Gillen J.
[2]   [2003] NI Fam 5, High Court of Northern Ireland, 9 April 2003, Gillen J.
[3]   The Family Proceedings Court had ordered the medical assessments be prepared, but the High Court doubted whether it had such a power under the Family Proceedings Rules: judgment of Gillen J at para 5.

6.184   In *Re S (Disclosure of Documents held by the Police)*[1] the issue was whether the Trust, when investigating its concerns about the care of a child, was entitled to copies of documentation compiled by the police into the criminal investigation of the earlier death of his brother. Gillen J concluded, having considered the application of Convention rights, articles 6 and 8 to this issue,[2] that the documents could be disclosed, although in the first instance only to the Chief Executive of the Trust and to the NIGALA. The documents could further be disclosed to the parents of the children when the Trust and the guardian ad litem thought it appropriate, although the judge considered that this should be done.

[1]   (30 August 2001, unreported), High Court of Northern Ireland, Gillen J. The children at the centre of the case were two Romanian children adopted in a non-Hague Convention adoption. The involvement of social services with the family was the subject of a Social Service Inspectorate report.
[2]   The judge concluded that in respect of art 6 the non-disclosure of documents to the defence in a Public Interest Immunity hearing is not a breach of the right to fair trial, and that in respect of art 8, the European Court's jurisprudence indicated that States had a margin of appreciation in regulating this sort of issue. On Public Interest Immunity, see chapter 3, para 3.32.

Chapter 7

Children's Services

Introduction

7.1　As was explained in chapter 6, there is a close relationship between the delivery of child and family services and the administration of the child protection system. Because the ethos of the Children Order is that children should as far as practicable be raised by their natural parents, with intervention by the State by way of public law orders very much an option of last resort, and a draconian one at that, social workers will normally consider, in the course of a child protection investigation, whether the harm the child is suffering, or the family's problems generally, can be eliminated or ameliorated by the delivery of services to the children or to the family generally. For example, 'Co-operating to Safeguard Children' provides that:[1]

> 'if the second stage assessment rules out that significant harm has occurred, or is likely to occur, the assessment may show that the child is in need as defined by Article 17 of the Children Order.[2] In these circumstances, the Trust's in need assessment procedure should provide a framework for a fuller assessment of the child's needs and the parent's capacity to respond to them.'

[1]　'Co-operating to Safeguard Children', DHSPPS, 2003, p 48, para 5.23. For an explanation of 'Co-operating to Safeguard Children', see chapter 6.
[2]　See para 7.16.

7.2　The provision of children's services, therefore, either to a wide category of children, or to a subset of them, is a method of safeguarding children's welfare where there is no necessity to take them into care.

7.3　This chapter outlines the legal duties imposed on trusts to provide services for children generally and particularly for 'children in need'. It also explores the role of trusts in respect of looked after children who are about to leave care and fend for themselves. The ramifications of the recent legislative requirement, imposed on boards, to draft Children's Services' Plans to identify the manner in which they intend delivering children's services to those living within their areas, are also outlined. The services that are the focus of this chapter includes the full range of publicly-provided, or funded, activities directed at maintaining children's welfare.

These include health and education facilities, for example, as well as services targeted at particular children including family support programmes, early years services, and services for looked after children, to mention a few.

7.4 One other significant recent development that will be focused on at relevant points in the chapter, and which will have considerable implications for the future law and policy in this area, is the publication, by the Department, of a consultation document on the issue of children's services, entitled 'A Strategy for Children in Need – Developing the Strategy'.[1]

[1]   DHSSPS, August 2003.

Children's services and children's rights

7.5 The purpose of the Children (Northern Ireland) Order 1995, and related legislation on this topic, is simply to provide the framework within which the boards and trusts can deliver the appropriate services. Much is left to the discretion of the social services authorities, making the duties imposed on the authorities difficult to enforce, either in judicial review actions[1] or by way of complaint under a trust's internal complaints mechanisms or to the Ombudsman.[2]

[1]   For an explanation of judicial review see chapter 2, para 2.105. The discussion of the nature of the duties imposed in respect of services for children in need explores some of these difficulties. See para 7.20.
[2]   For an explanation of the role of the Ombudsman, see chapter 2, para 2.45.

7.6 The Children's Commissioner[1] may face a similar difficulty in dealing with any complaints that social services authorities are not complying with their statutory duties. However, the Commissioner will be in a position to measure the actions of the authorities against the template of children's human rights contained in the UN Convention on the Rights of the Child (UNCRC) and other international human rights treaties, as well as the Convention rights under the HRA.[2] Thus the Commissioner will be able to assess not only whether the authorities have complied with their duties under domestic law, but also whether those actions are sufficient, in the Commissioner's view, to meet the UK's obligations under international law. It is to be hoped that the Commissioner will interpret the role in this fashion. Note that the State has positive obligations under the HRA,[3] which oblige it to actively engage in protecting or safeguarding the child's rights. The State's obligations are not confined to refraining from unjustifiably interfering with those rights. In the process of delivering children's services, the State is fulfilling its positive obligations by, for example, seeking to protect a child from, *inter alia*, inhumane or degrading treatment or punishment,[4] or by providing an opportunity for the child to pursue its rights to family life with other members of its family.[5]

[1]   For a description of the Children's Commissioner's powers, see chapter 1, para 1.96.
[2]   See chapter 1, para 1.66.
[3]   On positive obligations, see chapter 1, para 1.80.
[4]   Convention right, art 3.
[5]   Convention right, art 8. See chapter 6, para 6.11.

7.7   In any event, the UK does rely on the fact of these statutory duties, and the actual delivery of the associated services, to indicate to the UNCRC that some of the obligations imposed by the Convention are being complied with.[1] In that sense, those responsible for children's services delivery should bear in mind that there is a close relationship between children's services and children's rights, and that the former should be viewed through the prism of the latter.[2]

[1]   See for example, the UK's second periodic report to the Committee, CRC/C/83/Add.3, 25 February 2002, para 7.1 amongst others. For more in the UNCRC, see chapter 1, para 1.70.
[2]   See 'A Strategy for Children in Need – Developing the Strategy', August 2003, p 3, para 2.2 where the Department commits itself to founding the future strategy on the UNCRC.

Differing levels of services

7.8   Children are a varied category of people with very different needs, a fact that must be reflected in the services delivered to them. Children's services are typically categorised into different types, which in turn depend upon the nature of the children's needs and on the statutory powers and duties imposed on the social services authorities. Those responsible for developing Children's Services Plans have taken to using Hardiker's four-level framework in an attempt to explain their differential engagement with children.[1]

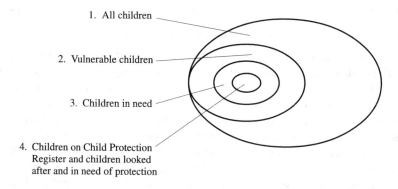

1. All children
2. Vulnerable children
3. Children in need
4. Children on Child Protection Register and children looked after and in need of protection

In this framework, Level 1 represents services provided to the whole population to provide general health care, education services, and leisure facilities, for example. Level 2 represents support for children who are vulnerable, and who could benefit from extra help from a variety of agencies. Services are targeted to individual children, with parental support, and are provided in statutory and voluntary settings. Level 3 represents support to families, or individual children and young people, where there are chronic or serious problems. It is provided through a complex mix of services, which need to work well together in order to provide the best support. Level 4 represents support to families, or individual children and young people, where the family has broken down temporarily or permanently, and the child or young person may be looked after by social services, in youth custody or prison or as an in-patient, for instance, due to disability or mental health problems. The aim of the higher levels of support (Levels 3 and 4) is to affect the family's situation in a positive way, so that the family can be supported through Level 1 services, (and therefore no longer needs specialist services) alongside the mainstream population.[2]

---

[1] Hardiker *The Social Context of Family Life* (1992) used by the Eastern Health and Social Services Board and the Western Health and Social Services Board in their respective Plans for 2002–05 and by the Department in 'A Strategy for Children in Need', p 11, para 5.2.

[2] The description of these levels of service provision is drawn from 'A Strategy for Children in Need'.

7.9 Presented in this way, the range of social services and education facilities operate as an integrated whole, providing appropriate levels of support to appropriate client groups, depending on their vulnerability and need. The reality of children's services' planning and delivery is that it is focused very much on children having particular characteristics, an approach that appears to be dictated in part by resources (and the need to target them) and in part by the fact that some of the duties owed by the trusts and boards are to a statutorily defined category, namely 'children in need',[1] or relate to a particular aspect of children's lives. As a result, Children's Services' Plans have focused on discrete categories of children such as children with a disability, children in conflict with the law, children with mental health problems and children with substance abuse problems, to mention a few.

---

[1] Children (Northern Ireland) Order 1995, art 17. See para 7.16.

Children's Services' Plans

7.10 A statutory amendment of 1998[1] requires every board to prepare and publish plans for the provision of children's services within its area and to keep those plans under review.[2] In preparing or updating its plans, a board is required to consult with trusts, education and library boards, district councils, certain voluntary organisations, the Northern Ireland Housing Executive, the Probation Board for Northern Ireland, the police and other relevant bodies. Guidance on the development of Children's Services' Plans was issued jointly by the Department of Health and Social Services, the Department of Education and the Northern Ireland Office in July 1998. Most of the boards have chosen to establish an Area-wide Children and Young Persons Committee (CYPC), chaired by the relevant Director of Social Services, to produce their Children's Services' Plan. A new dimension to this process has been the introduction, by some CYPCs, of mechanisms to consult with children.[3]

---

[1] The Children (1995 Order) (Amendment) (Children's Services Planning) Order (Northern Ireland) 1998.

[2] The 1998 Order made an amendment to the 1995 Order, Sch 2.

[3] See Eastern Heath and Social Services Board Children's Services' Plan 2002–05, pp 16–17.

7.11 Cross-board co-ordination has also been developed in the relatively short period of time that the requirement to develop Children's Services' Plans has been in existence. The four CYPCs and Children (Northern Ireland)[1] have worked together to attempt to produce a regional approach to the task.[2] The CYPCs have agreed that there are four common themes to their respective reports: promoting social inclusion;

equality and human rights; needs-led planning and resourcing; and coherent and integrated family support. The Department's consultation document, 'A Strategy for Children in Need', envisages a wider role for the CYPCs which would involve it liaising with the Department to draw up regional performance indicators to assess the quality of children's services' delivery, and to consider the ways in which children and young people could become involved in services' planning processes, as well considering a Regional Family Support Strategy.[3] Notwithstanding the important work undertaken by the CYPCs, the clear limitation of the Children's Services' Planning process was that no regional strategy existed for children's social services, but the Department has committed itself to remedying that by developing such a strategy.[4]

[1]   Formerly ChildCare (Northern Ireland).
[2]   Eastern Heath and Social Services Board Children's Services' Plan 2002–05, p 20.
[3]   Eastern Heath and Social Services Board Children's Services' Plan 2002–05, at pp 19, 18 and 33 respectively.
[4]   'A Strategy for children in need', pp 11 ff.

Duties to all children

7.12   One of the main sources of legal obligations placed on trusts in regard to children's services is the Children (Northern Ireland) Order 1995, Sch 2,[1] which contains a wide variety of duties and powers in respect of these services. Some of these are framed with reference to all children, while some are framed in respect of particular categories of children. Those that relate to all children are outlined here. One Law Lord has described the duties and powers as a 'motley collection',[2] and they do cover a disparate range of matters.

[1]   Note that although these were originally imposed on boards, they have since been transferred to trusts. See chapter 1, para 1.110. which outlines the legal structure of social services provision in Northern Ireland.
[2]   See Lord Nicholls in *R (on the application of G) v Barnet London Borough Council* [2003] UKHL 57, [2004] 1 All ER 97.

7.13   One of the general duties imposed on trusts requires them to take 'reasonable steps' to reduce the need to bring legal proceedings against a number of categories of children, including criminal proceedings, proceedings for Care and Supervision Orders or other family proceedings.[1] This duty obviously requires trusts to engage in family and child support activities designed to avoid the necessity of having the courts deal with those children. A similar 'preventative' duty requires trusts to establish support services for children and their families to 'prevent children within its area suffering ill-treatment or neglect.'[2]

[1]   Children (Northern Ireland) Order 1995, Sch 2, para 8.
[2]   Children (Northern Ireland) Order 1995, Sch 2, para 5.

7.14   Trusts are also empowered to establish family centres, at which family members may attend for advice, guidance or counselling or social cultural or recreational activities. They may also provide day care facilities for children who are not in need, either for pre-school children or school-attending children.[1]

[1] Children (Northern Ireland) Order 1995, art 19(3) and (6) respectively.

7.15 The Children (Northern Ireland) Order 1995 also addresses trusts' responsibilities in respect of accommodating children who are not 'in need'.[1] Trusts may provide accommodation for any child within its area (even though a person who has parental responsibility for him or her is able to provide accommodation for the child), if the trust considers that to do so would safeguard or promote the child's welfare.[2] However, the trust's power to provide accommodation must give way to the assertion of a person with parental responsibility that he or she is willing and able to provide accommodation for the child.[3]

[1] The term 'children in need' is explained at para 7.16.
[2] Children (Northern Ireland) Order 1995, art 21(4).
[3] Children (Northern Ireland) Order 1995, art 22.

Children in need

7.16 Much of the discussion about children's services is centred on the term, 'children in need', defined in the 1995 Order. It provides that a child is in need if:[1]

(a) he or she is unlikely to achieve or maintain, or to have the opportunity of achieving or maintaining, a reasonable standard of health or development without the provision of services by an authority under this Part;

(b) his or her health or development is likely to be significantly impaired, or further impaired, without the provision for him of such services; or

(c) he or she is disabled.[2]

[1] Children (Northern Ireland) Order 1995, art 17.
[2] Per the Chronically Sick and Disabled Persons (Northern Ireland) Act 1978, s 1, see chapter 10, para 10.4. Particular duties in respect of disabled children include the requirement to maintain a register of such children within a trust's area: Children (Northern Ireland) Order 1995, Sch 2, para 3 and the provision of services to 'minimise the effect on disabled children of their disabilities': Children (Northern Ireland) Order 1995, Sch 2, para 7.

7.17 Assessment of a child who may be in need is also provided for, so that where it appears to the trust that a child is in need it may carry out an assessment under the Chronically Sick and Disabled Persons (Northern Ireland) Act 1978,[1] the Education and Libraries (Northern Ireland) Order 1986, the Disabled Persons (Northern Ireland) Act 1989[2] or any other relevant statute. The combination of this power, with the requirement on the trust to take 'reasonable steps' to identify children in need in its area converts this into a duty to assess such children.[3]

[1] See chapter 10, para 10.4.
[2] See chapter 10, para 10.5.
[3] See Lord Millet in *R (on the application of G) v Barnet London Borough Council* [2003] UKHL 57, [2004] 1 All ER 97.

7.18 One of the most difficult practical issues for the health and social services authorities when implementing the 1995 Order was how to develop an index, or a typology of need that facilitated the fulfilling of its statutory duty. In 1997, the four boards agreed a list of operational indicators of 'need', which indicated the sorts of factors that suggested that a child was in need. However, the actual method of assessing need was left to individual boards and trusts, giving rise to variations in the quality of assessment from area to area.[1] In contrast, in March 2000, Departmental guidance for assessing children in need was jointly issued by the relevant English departments.[2] As a result it is now proposed that the Department develop similar guidance for Northern Ireland to ensure uniformity of approach and to give social workers the greatest possible amount of guidance.[3]

[1]   'A Strategy for Children in Need', para 7.14, p 19.
[2]   'A Framework for the Assessment of Children in Need and their Families', March 2002, Department of Health, Department of Education and Employment and the Home Office.
[3]   'A Strategy for Children in Need', para 7.21, p 22. Some detail about the Framework guidance is provided in that document.

7.19   The English courts have determined that assessment of a child's needs must normally follow the terms of the Departmental guidance, unless there are good reasons for not doing so, and that the failure to do so may be unlawful. In *R (on the application of AB and SB) v Nottingham City Council*,[1] the council was ordered to carry out such an assessment when its initial assessment did not conform to the essential elements of the 'Framework' guidance. It is to be hoped that the Northern Ireland courts will adopt a similar approach when Northern Ireland-wide guidance is adopted.

[1]   [2001] EWHC Admin 235, [2001] 3 FCR 350.

General duty

7.20   The general duty imposed on trusts in respect of children in need is:[1]
(a)   to safeguard and promote the welfare of children within its area who are in need; and
(b)   so far as is consistent with that duty, to promote the upbringing of such children by their families,

by providing a range and level of personal social services appropriate to those children's needs.[2]

The breadth of discretion accorded to trusts in complying with this duty is readily apparent and one of the enduring difficulties with the children in need duties is how they may be enforced against health and social services authorities given the wide discretion available to them. The equivalent duty in the Children Act 1989, s 17 has been the subject of a number of recent judicial reviews, culminating in a House of Lords decision. Three such judicial reviews were combined as they all touched on the same issue, namely, what is the nature of the duty imposed in art 18/s 17? The facts of each are set out for the purposes of understanding the House of Lords approach.

[1]   Children (Northern Ireland) Order 1995, art 18.

2   In *R (on the application of B) v Merton London Borough Council* [2003] EWHC 1689 (Admin), [2003] 2 FLR 888, the council was of the view that the applicant was not a child, but was aged over 18. The failure of the council to give him an indication of to reasons for coming to this view and allowing him an opportunity to challenge them resulted in the quashing of the council's decision.

R (on the application of G) v Barnet London Borough Council

7.21   In *R (on the application of G) v Barnet London Borough Council,*[1] G was a Dutch national of Somali origin, with a young son. She claimed she left the Netherlands because of social ostracism encountered there in the Somali community on account of her child's illegitimacy, and that she came to the UK to look for the child's father. Applications for income support and for assistance with housing were refused and she then sought assistance from Barnet council as the local social services authority. The local authority considered that the child's needs would be best served by the return of both mother and child to Holland where they were entitled at once to accommodation and other benefits. It did not accept the mother's account of her reasons for coming to London.

[1]   [2003] UKHL 57, [2004] 1 All ER 97.

7.22   In the second case, *R (on the application of W) v Lambeth London Borough Council,*[1] the facts were broadly similar to the case above. W had been assessed as being intentionally homeless and was not entitled to be re-housed under the housing legislation. However, she had two children, aged 16 and 7 years, and sought to be accommodated along with her children on the basis that they were children in need. The social services authority refused to accede to this request but did offer to accommodate the children, if required to do so, under its duty to accommodate children in need.[2]

[1]   [2002] EWCA Civ 613, [2002] 2 All ER 901.
[2]   Children (Northern Ireland) Order 1995, art 18; in England the Children Act 1989, s 17. See para 7.28.

7.23   The third case presented a slightly different legal issue. In *R (on the application of A) v Lambeth Borough Council,*[1] the mother of three children, two of them with autism, was living in a two bedroom flat which was in a very poor condition of repair, with no access to a garden or play area. It was clearly unsuitable accommodation for children with autism. The social services authority assessed the children as being in need and requiring to be accommodated in more suitable premises. The mother argued that once her children were assessed as being 'children in need' the general duty in s 17 'crystallised' into a specific duty and she argued that the social services authority was obliged to provide the suitable accommodation for her and her children.

[1]   [2001] EWCA Civ 1624, [2002] 1 FLR 353.

7.24   Two questions then were being tackled in these cases. First, whether the duty to children in need was capable of giving rise to a enforceable duty in respect of one child, such that the authority had to provide it for that child no matter what the cost? Secondly, did a duty to accommodate a child in need extend to it parents by virtue of

Convention right article 8[1] and provisions of the Children Act 1989?[2] Clearly, if these questions were answered in the affirmative it would have great significance for the way in which social services authorities fulfilled their duties with respect to children in need. However, the Law Lords did not accept the arguments made on behalf of the applicants, answering both questions in the negative.

[1]   See chapter 6, para 6.11.
[2]   Section 23(6) was the relevant provision.

7.25   Lord Hope of Craighead outlined the legislative history of the section to support his view that the duty was not owed to particular children:

'This legislative background serves to reinforce the impression which the structure and language of the legislation itself gives, that the so-called "general duty" in section 17(1) is owed to all the children who are in need within their area and not to each child in need individually. It is an overriding duty, a statement of general principle. It provides the broad aims which the local authority is to bear in mind when it is performing the "other duties" set out in Pt III (see the words in parenthesis in section 17(1)) and the "specific duties" for facilitating the discharge of those general duties which are set out in Pt I of Schedule 2 (see section 17(2)). A child in need within the meaning of section 17(10) is eligible for the provision of those services, but he has no absolute right to them.'

Later he added:

'I think that the correct analysis of section 17(1) is that it sets out duties of a general character which are intended to be for the benefit of children in need in the local social services authority's area in general. The other duties and the specific duties which then follow must be performed in each individual case by reference to the general duties which section 17(1) sets out. What the subsection does is to set out the duties owed to a section of the public in general by which the authority must be guided in the performance of those other duties.'

His Lordship rejected the idea that the 'general duty' crystallised into a specific one whenever the assessment of the child disclosed the nature of his or her need. He also concluded that there was no duty on the local authority to house the child's parents or any other members of its family as they had recourse to the housing legislation. Requiring the social services authority to provide for the child's family members would circumvent the housing legislation and turn the social services authority into a housing authority. One further point worth noting from this decision is that Lord Scott, who was in agreement with Lord Hope, was of the view that in fulfilling its duties under these provisions an authority could take its financial resources into account.[1]

[1]   A further indication of the difficulties that might be faced when persuading the courts to intervene in a children in need dispute, can be gleaned from *R (on the application of T) v A Local Authority* [2003] EWHC 2515 (Admin), [2003] All ER (D) 02 (Nov). The authority took the view that a certain type of placement was more appropriate for the child, but a Barnardo's project recommended a specialist

residential placement. The court quashed the authority's decision but did not direct it to take a certain action, preferring to require it to reconsider its decision.

7.26 Another interesting judicial review involving this duty saw a non-governmental organisation challenge the view, taken by the prison service authorities in Great Britain, that s 17 did not to apply to juveniles in detention. In *R (Howard League for Penal Reform) v Secretary Of State for the Home Department*,[1] the League successfully challenged an assertion to this effect in the Prison Service Orders. However, the court took the view that while juveniles were in detention the social services authority could presume that his or her needs were being met by the Prison Service during the imprisonment and that it would not be unlawful or unreasonable for them to do so. Thus while juveniles in detention qualify for protection under the 'children in need' provisions, the practical limitations arising from their incarceration could thwart the effective implementation of the duty by the social services authority.[2]

[1]   [2002] EWHC 2497 (Admin), [2003] 1 FLR 484.
[2]   This judgment is currently under appeal to the House of Lords. The English courts have also had to consider the difficulties that arise for authorities where the child in question moves from one local authority to another raising the issue of which authority is responsible for assessing the child. *R (M) v London Borough of Barking and Dagenham* [2002] EWHC 2663. A similar problem arose in *R (on the application of Stewart) v Wandsworth, Hammersmith and Fulham, and Lambeth London Borough Councils* [2001] EWHC Admin 709, [2002] 1 FLR 469, and the court concluded that the authority in whose area the children were physically present was responsible for making the assessment.

Day care

7.27 Trusts have a duty to provide 'such day care for children in need within the authority's area who are: (a) aged five or under; and (b) not yet attending schools, as is appropriate.'[1] This duty extends to the provision of after-school day care for school age children in need and during school holidays, although once again the duty is qualified by the fact that the trusts need only provide such day care services as they consider appropriate.[2] It is likely that any applicant would encounter similar difficulties in successfully judicially reviewing the level, and type, of day care services provided to a particular child in need, as have been encountered in the attempts to enforce the s 17/art 18 duty in the judicial review actions discussed above. Trusts are required to review their day care services and the provision of child minding facilities generally within its area on a triennial basis.[3]

[1]   Children (Northern Ireland) Order 1995, art 19(2).
[2]   Children (Northern Ireland) Order 1995, art 19(5).
[3]   Children (Northern Ireland) Order 1995, art 20.

Duty to accommodate

7.28 Trusts are also obliged to place 'children in need', within their area, in accommodation if:[1]

(a)   there is no person who has parental responsibility for him or her;

(b)   he or she is lost or abandoned; or

(c)   the person who has been caring for the child is prevented (whether or not permanently, and for whatever reason) from providing the child with suitable accommodation or care.

The duty to accommodate such children continues after they have reached the age of 16, if the trust considers that the child's welfare is likely to be seriously prejudiced if it does not provide him or her with accommodation.[2]

[1]   Children (Northern Ireland) Order 1995, art 21.
[2]   Children (Northern Ireland) Order 1995, art 21(3).

7.29   Before providing such accommodation the trust must, in so far as is reasonably practicable and consistent with the child's welfare:

(a)   ascertain the child's wishes regarding the provision of accommodation; and

(b)   give due consideration (having regard to his or her age and understanding) to such wishes of the child as the authority has been able to ascertain.[1]

However, a trust's ability to intervene in this manner to provide accommodation must give way to the claims of a person who has parental responsibility for the child and who is willing and able to provide accommodation for him or otherwise arrange accommodation for the child. Where such a person objects to the trust becoming involved in the provision of accommodation, then the trust cannot carry out its plans in respect of accommodation.[2]

[1]   Children (Northern Ireland) Order 1995, art 21(6). The influence of the *Gillick* decision in the formulation of this element of the duty is apparent. On *Gillick*, see chapter 1, para 1.52.
[2]   Children (Northern Ireland) Order 1995, art 22.

7.30   The arrangements for the placement of the child should, 'so far as is reasonably practicable' be agreed, in writing, between the trust, residential home or voluntary organisation, and the parents, or those with parental responsibility, before the placement is made, or if that is not practicable, as soon as is reasonably possible thereafter.[1] The responsible authority must have regard to a range of considerations when making these arrangements, such as health and educational matters.[2] The resultant document is the child's Care Plan.

[1]   Arrangements for Placement of Children (General) Regulations (Northern Ireland) 1996, reg 3(4). This requirement also applies where the child is 'voluntarily accommodated'. See para 7.33.
[2]   Arrangements for Placement of Children (General) Regulations (Northern Ireland) 1996, reg 4(1), Schs 1, 2 and 3.

Removal from accommodation

7.31   Children accommodated under the article 21 provision may, however, be removed at any time by any person with parental responsibility.[1] The trust may not, it appears, refuse to hand the child over on the basis that it is, for example, in the child's best interests that it remains in the accommodation provided by it. Nor may the trust impose a notification period on the person with parental responsibility before the child is handed over. Thus, even if the parents appear late at night seeking the return of their children, and are the worse for drink, for example, the trust does not appear to have the power to refuse to return the children to their parents, even though it may be convinced that this is not the correct course of action.[2] There are a number of ways in which a trust might deal with such a situation, however.

[1]   Children (Northern Ireland) Order 1995, art 22(2).
[2]   See obiter dictum view of Thorpe LJ in *Re G (a child) (secure accommodation order)* [2000] 2 FCR 385, [2000] 2 FLR 259, [2000] Fam Law 716, CA.

7.32   First, where there is a person in whose favour a Residence Order is in force with respect to the child or who has care of the child by virtue of an order made in the exercise of the High Court's inherent jurisdiction with respect to children,[1] and that person agrees to the child being looked after in accommodation provided by, or on behalf of, the trust, the requirement to return the children to anyone with parental responsibility does not apply.[2]

Secondly, if the child has reached the age of 16 years and agrees to be accommodated, its wishes will override those of its parents or any persons with parental responsibility.[3]

Thirdly, if the trust fears that the child will suffer significant harm if it returns to the care of its parents, then public law orders can be sought, such as an Emergency Protection Order[4] or an Interim Care Order,[5] and in the meantime the police might be asked to bring the child into police protection.[6]

[1]   See chapter 6, para 6.149.
[2]   Children (Northern Ireland) Order 1995, art 22(3). Where there is more than one such person, all of them must agree: art 22(4).
[3]   Children (Northern Ireland) Order 1995, art 22(5).
[4]   See chapter 6, para 6.100.
[5]   See chapter 6, para 6.114.
[6]   See chapter 6, para 6.105.

Voluntary accommodation in care

7.33   Children may also come into care, under article 21, because their parents agree to have, or ask to have them accommodated and children that enter the care system in this way are said to be 'voluntarily accommodated' in care. As with the accommodation of children in need, no court order is required as the basis for the trust's involvement is the parents' consent to the accommodation of their children in care, evidenced by a written agreement between the trust and the parents. However, the trust does not have parental responsibility for the child and can only make decisions in respect of the child with parental agreement. In *Re J (Care Proceedings: Disclosure)*,[1] the authority, fearing that a child voluntarily accommodated in care had been abused by its foster parents, had to acquire the birth mother's consent to a medical examination, although it secured this consent in a duplicitous manner, which led the court to write to the chief executive of the authority to highlight the actions of the authority's staff.

[1]   [2003] EWHC 976 (Fam), [2003] 2 FLR 522.

Looked after children: trusts' duties

7.34   All children who are in the care of a trust, or who are being accommodated by a trust,[1] fall within the definition of 'looked after' children, and thus those children in care by virtue of a Care Order, or because they are being accommodated under article 21 of the 1995 Order, are all considered 'looked after' children.[2] The general duty on trusts with regard to looked after children is to safeguard and promote their welfare and make use of such children's services as are available and it considers reasonable.[3] As part of this duty, trusts must establish a Care Plan for each looked after child.[4]

[1]   For a period of 24 hours or more.
[2]   Children (Northern Ireland) Order 1995, art 25. There are approximately 2,500 looked after children in Northern Ireland at any one time. 60% of these are fostered, 30% are normally under the care of a trust by virtue of a Care Order, but living with their parents, and 10% are in residential homes.
[3]   Children (Northern Ireland) Order 1995, art 26.
[4]   Arrangements for the Placement of Children (General) Regulations (Northern Ireland) 1996, reg 3(4). This Care Plan must give consideration to the matters outlined in Schs 1, 2 and 3 to the Regulations.

7.35   Before taking an important decision in respect of a looked after child's life, the trust is to have regard to the child's own wishes and views (due allowance being made for its age and ability to understand the matters in question) and those of the child's parents and anyone else with parental responsibility for the child.[1] The Order does, however, give trusts the flexibility of acting in breach of his duty if it considers that it is necessary to do so to protect the public from injury.[2]

[1]   Children (Northern Ireland) Order 1995, art 26(2) and (3).
[2]   Children (Northern Ireland) Order 1995, art 26(4).

7.36   The trust is obliged to ensure that the child maintains contact with its family and one of the ways of doing this is to keep the child's family members aware of the address at which he or she resides.[1] However, the trust may refuse to disclosure this information if it concludes that informing a person of the child's whereabouts could lead to a prejudicing of the child's welfare.[2]

[1]   Children (Northern Ireland) Order 1995, art 29(2). When drawing up the Care Plan the trust must consider the arrangements for contact. Arrangements for Placement of Children (General) Regulations (Northern Ireland) 1996, reg 4(1) and Sch 1.
[2]   Children (Northern Ireland) Order 1995, art 29(4).

7.37   Trusts do have the power to encourage visitation of the child by his parents, but where such visits have not been taking place within the previous twelve months or taking place infrequently, then the trust is compelled to appoint someone to befriend the child if it considers that it would be in the child's best interests.[1]

[1]   Children (Northern Ireland) Order 1995, art 31.

7.38   Trusts are obliged to carry out reviews of the arrangements for the care of looked after children on a periodic basis, often referred to as 'Article 45 reviews'.[1]

The first review must be carried out within two weeks of the child becoming looked after, with the next review coming no later than three months after the initial review and each subsequent review taking place on a six-monthly basis.[2] Only an 'Article 45 review' may make amendments to the Care Plan. The review records both positive and negative developments in the child's life, including such matters as health and education of the child, developments in its birth family and relationships with the members of his or her family. It also monitors the implementation of the Care Plan and establishes whether the steps that were intended to be taken after the previous review, have in fact been taken.[3] The trust must also conduct 'health reviews' of a looked-after child, once every six months before its fifth birthday and once a year thereafter, unless the child is of sufficient understanding to refuse the examination.[4]

[1] Children (Northern Ireland) Order 1995, art 45.
[2] Review of Children's Cases Regulations (Northern Ireland) 1996, reg 3.
[3] Review of Children's Cases Regulations (Northern Ireland) 1996, regs 4(4), 5 and Schs 1, 2 and 3 set out the content of any such review.
[4] Review of Children's Cases Regulations (Northern Ireland) 1996, reg 6.

Contact with children in care

7.39 A similar duty is imposed on trusts to ensure the maintenance of contact between a looked after child who is in care on foot of a Care Order and its parents. The trust with whom a child made subject to a Care Order is accommodated must allow reasonable contact between the child and his or her parents, guardian and anyone with parental responsibility, unless the court directs otherwise or unless an emergency situation justifies the trust in suspending contact.[1] Indeed, before a Care Order is made, the court is required to consider the trust's arrangements for maintaining contact.[2] A trust must furnish the child, its parents and others with parental responsibility with a written copy of its decision not to allow contact with the child.[3]

If the trust suspends the contact it must be for the purposes of the child's welfare and the period of suspension cannot exceed seven days.[4] If it wishes to block contact for a longer period then the trust must make an application to court.

[1] Children (Northern Ireland) Order 1995, art 53.
[2] Children (Northern Ireland) Order 1995, art 53(11).
[3] Contact with Children's Cases Regulations (Northern Ireland) 1996, reg 2.
[4] Children (Northern Ireland) Order 1995, art 53(6).

7.40 The issue of contact with the child in care can be dealt with by way of an application to the court by any of the interested parties, or the court can deal with the matter of its own volition. The court may also deal with the issue of contact at the same time as it hears the Care Order application and application can be made by the trust, the child, or anyone else with whom the child is to have reasonable contact.[1] The terms of any order for contact can be varied by agreement between the trust and the person with whom the child is to have contact, which gives the trust some degree of flexibility in dealing with the future contact arrangements and allows it to manage the improving or deteriorating relationship between the child and its parents, or those with parental responsibility, without the necessity of requiring a court order on each occasion.[2]

---

[1]   Children (Northern Ireland) Order 1995, art 52(1).
[2]   Contact with Children's Cases Regulations (Northern Ireland) 1996, reg 3. See also *Re W (a child) (parental contact: prohibition)* [2000] Fam 130, [2000] 1 FCR 752, [2000] 1 FLR 502, CA.

Children leaving care

7.41   Children leaving care now have an extended range of entitlements arising from the Children (Leaving Care) Act (Northern Ireland) 2002[1] and there has been a renewed focus on the importance of monitoring the educational attainments and employment rates of children who have left care. Recent statistics show that although the educational qualifications secured by children in care in Northern Ireland compare favourably with those of children in care in England and Wales, nonetheless children in care fare very poorly when compared to children in Northern Ireland generally. For example, over 1 in 10 children leaving care in 2001/02 (14%) had obtained at least 5 GCSEs at grades A*–C. This was more than double the corresponding figure for young people leaving care in England (5%), but only a quarter of the proportion of all Northern Ireland school leavers (58%) achieving these grades.[2] Furthermore, at least 37% of care leavers were unemployed in March 2002, a figure that compares very unfavourably with those for all school leavers in Northern Ireland, of whom only 4% were unemployed. The enactment of the 2002 Act has prompted the establishment of a regional implementation group to ensure the smooth 'roll-out' of the legislation.

---

[1]   The equivalent Act in England and Wales is the Children (Leaving Care) Act 2000.
[2]   Northern Ireland Care Leavers 2001/2, DHSSPS and Department of Education, 2002. This is the first statistical publication of this nature in Northern Ireland.

7.42   The 2002 Act amends relevant parts of the Children Order to outline an enhanced range of duties imposed on trusts in respect of children who were looked after children but have since left care. It operates by reconfiguring the duty, in article 35 of the Children Order, on trusts to provide advice and assistance for a person who is under 21 years and who was formerly a looked after child.[1]

---

[1]   Children (Leaving Care) Act (Northern Ireland) 2002, s 4, replacing the Children (Northern Ireland) Order 1995, art 35.

7.43   Before the looked after child leaves care the trust must advise, assist and befriend the child with a view to promoting his or her welfare when the trust has ceased to look after the child.[1] It must carry out an assessment of his or her needs to determine what advice, assistance and support it would be appropriate for the trust to provide, both while he or she remains looked after, and when the child ceases to be looked after. On the basis of this assessment the trust then prepares a 'pathway plan'. The Department will make regulations setting out the matters pertinent to these assessments, including the persons who are to be consulted, the way in which the assessment is to be carried out and the matters which the trust is to consider when carrying out such assessments.[2]

1   Children (Northern Ireland) Order 1995, art 34A, as inserted by the Children (Leaving Care) Act (Northern Ireland) 2002, s 1.
2   Children (Northern Ireland) Order 1995, art 34A(9), as inserted by the Children (Leaving Care) Act (Northern Ireland) 2002, s 1.

Pathway plans

7.44   A 'pathway plan' is a document setting out the advice, assistance and support that the trust intends to provide for a child.[1] It is to be kept under regular review on the same basis as article 45 reviews under the Children Order.[2] As a result it will make sense for the review of the pathway plan to take place in tandem with the review of arrangements. The pathway plan is to be kept in place, and under review, until the child reaches 21 years.[3] Where, however, an aspect of the plan that relates to education or training is not scheduled to be completed by the time the child reaches 21 years the trust is obligated to continue assisting the child until that aspect of the plan is completed.[4]

1   The Department is to make regulations dealing with the content and review of pathway plans: Children (Northern Ireland) Order 1995, art 34H(2), as inserted by the Children (Leaving Care) Act (Northern Ireland) 2002, s 3.
2   See para 7.38.
3   Children (Northern Ireland) Order 1995, art 34D(3)(b) and (6), as inserted by the Children (Leaving Care) Act (Northern Ireland) 2002, s 2.
4   Children (Northern Ireland) Order 1995, art 34D(7), as inserted by the Children (Leaving Care) Act (Northern Ireland) 2002, s 2.

Personal advisers

7.45   Trusts must also appoint personal advisers to two types of children. First, those who are currently looked after and who may soon be leaving care[1] and secondly, those who have left care and are aged 16 or 17 years.[2] In practice, as the impact of the 2002 Act is unravelled, the same person is likely to be personal adviser to the child while he or she is looked after, and later when the child has left care. Indeed, from the child's point of view this degree of continuity would probably be most welcome. The personal adviser continues to be appointed to the child until he or she reaches 21 years.[3]

1   Children (Northern Ireland) Order 1995, art 34A(10), as inserted by the Children (Leaving Care) Act (Northern Ireland) 2002, s 1.
2   Children (Northern Ireland) Order 1995, art 34C(2), as inserted by the Children (Leaving Care) Act (Northern Ireland) 2002, s 2.
3   Children (Northern Ireland) Order 1995, art 34D(3)(a) and (6), as inserted by the Children (Leaving Care) Act (Northern Ireland) 2002, s 2.

Duty to maintain contact

7.46   A trust has a duty, in respect of children who were looked after but now no longer are, and who are aged 16 or 17 years, to take reasonable steps to keep in touch with that child. Where such a child does not have a pathway plan already provided for him or her one must be established and in order to do so an assessment must be carried out on the child.[1]

[1]   Children (Northern Ireland) Order 1995, art 34C(3) and (4), as inserted by the Children (Leaving Care) Act (Northern Ireland) 2002, s 2.

7.47   Where the trust has lost contact with the child, even though it has taken reasonable steps to maintain contact it must consider how to re-establish contact and take reasonable steps to do so, with the trust being required to continue to take such steps *until it succeeds* [Author's emphasis].[1] A duty to maintain contact continues when the child who has left care reaches 18 years (and continues until he or she reaches 21), although it is less onerous on the trust in that it is simply required to take reasonable steps to maintain contact and to re-establish it if it loses touch with him or her.[2]

[1]   Children (Northern Ireland) Order 1995, art 34C(11), as inserted by the Children (Leaving Care) Act (Northern Ireland) 2002, s 2.
[2]   Children (Northern Ireland) Order 1995, art 34D(2), as inserted by the Children (Leaving Care) Act (Northern Ireland) 2002, s 2.

Duty to support

7.48   An additional duty is imposed on trusts in respect of children who have left care and who are aged 16 or 17 years, in that it must safeguard and promote the child's welfare and must, unless it is satisfied that the child's welfare does not require it, support the child by maintaining him or her, or provide suitable accommodation or other support, including cash.[1] This duty continues in a modified form when the child reaches 18 years in that the trust is obliged to assist such a child to the extent that his or her welfare, education or training needs require it.[2] This duty to support finally concludes when the child reaches 21 years.

[1]   Children (Northern Ireland) Order 1995, art 34C(8), as inserted by the Children (Leaving Care) Act (Northern Ireland) 2002, s 2.
[2]   Children (Northern Ireland) Order 1995, art 34D(4), as inserted by the Children (Leaving Care) Act (Northern Ireland) 2002, s 2.

Provision of advice and assistance

7.49   A more general duty to advise and assist children who were formerly in care, and who are not yet 21 years, has also been added by the 2002 Act.[1] The trust must take appropriate steps to contact such a child to determine whether he or she is in need of advice and assistance generally[2] or, more specifically, in respect of employment, education or training expenses.[3] The advantage to this duty from the point of view of children formerly in care is that it opens the possibility that they may obtain financial support for obtaining educational qualifications that will improve their employment prospects, and this aspect of the duty continues until the person reaches 24 years of age.

[1] Children (Northern Ireland) Order 1995, art 35, as inserted by the Children (Leaving Care) Act (Northern Ireland) 2002, s 4.

[2] Children (Northern Ireland) Order 1995, art 35A, as inserted by the Children (Leaving Care) Act (Northern Ireland) 2002, s 4.

[3] Children (Northern Ireland) Order 1995, art 35B, as inserted by the Children (Leaving Care) Act (Northern Ireland) 2002, s 4.

Transmission of information

7.50 Where a child with whom the trust is to maintain contact, moves to another trust area, the trust on whom the duty lies must inform that other authority. Similar information must be relayed to another trust where a formerly looked-after child that the trust has been advising, assisting or befriending moves into another trust area.[1] In this way, trusts should be aware of the persons who may need assistance living in their area.

[1] Children (Northern Ireland) Order 1995, art 35C(1), as inserted by the Children (Leaving Care) Act (Northern Ireland) 2002, s 4.

7.51 Where a child ceases to be accommodated, and had been accommodated by a voluntary organisation or in a children's home, the accommodation provider must inform the trust in whose area the child intends to live.[1] The intention behind these duties is to avoid the pitfall of formerly looked-after children 'falling between two authorities', as it were, with the result that they fail to receive appropriate support from either of them.

[1] Children (Northern Ireland) Order 1995, art 35C(2), as inserted by the Children (Leaving Care) Act (Northern Ireland) 2002, s 4.

Complaints

7.52 Trusts are obliged to establish systems that allow a person to whom these duties apply to make representations or complaints about the manner in which the trust has, or has not, performed its duties. As outlined in chapter 2, where the person remains dissatisfied by the outcome of these internal complaints procedures it is open to him or her to seek an Independent Review,[1] and if they remain dissatisfied, to complain to the Commissioner for Complaints.[2] In an appropriate case it might also be possible for the individual to seek judicial review of a decision.[3]

[1] See para 2.66. Note that the relevant Health and Social Services Council may assist the complainant in any such independent review.

[2] See para 2.45.

[3] See chapter 2, para 2.105.

Chapter 8

Adoption and Fostering

Introduction

8.1 This chapter outlines the procedural and legal steps of the adoption and fostering processes, including the regulation of intercountry adoption, an increasingly complicated facet of adoption. The role of adoption has changed considerably over time and it is worth considering some of those developments before examining the legal process.

Adoption trends

8.2 The number of children being adopted annually in Northern Ireland has decreased significantly since its peak in the late 1960s and early 1970s accordingly as unmarried motherhood has become less of a stigma than it had been in previous decades.[1] For example, there were 172 adoptions in Northern Ireland in 2001, a significant drop from the 554 adoptions in 1970.[2] Indeed, in 1998 the numbers of adoptions fell to their lowest levels since the 1930s, with 121 children being adopted. Furthermore, decreasing numbers of the children being adopted are infants, ie under one year old at the time of adoption. For example, of the 100 children placed by adoption agencies in 2001/2, only 15 were under 1 year, with 43 aged between 1 year and 5 years and 30 aged between 5 and 10 years. Of the 84 freeing applications made (including consolidated applications), only 6 were made in respect of children aged less than 1 year while 32 were aged between 1 year and 5 years.[3]

---

[1] For an overview of the development of adoption services in Northern Ireland in the post-war period, see Paul Martin, *A Better Future – 50 Years of Child Care in Northern Ireland 1950–2000*, DHSSPS, 2003.

[2] Annual Report of the General Register Office 2002, Table 9.1.

[3] NIGALA Annual Report 2001/2, p 53, Table 8 'Age and Gender of Children in Report Period by Case Type'.

8.3 In recent years there has been an increase in adoption agency placement adoptions and a sudden noticeable fall in step-parent adoptions. (The former arise where the child is made available for adoption via a statutory agency, while the latter can arise where the child's parents have separated but one of them has re-partnered and seeks to have the children of the previous relationship adopted by the new partner). In 2001/02, the Northern Ireland Guardian Ad Litem Agency (NIGALA) became involved in 83 new placement adoptions, an increase from 71 the previous year, while its staff were only appointed in 41 step-parent adoptions, a decrease from the figure of 46 in 2000/01.[1] The drop in the numbers of step-parent adoption applications in the year 2001/02 may be explained by the difficult nature of these adoptions, while there has been a renewed effort to try and adopt more children from amongst those children who are being looked after.[2] However, the split between agency adoptions and step-parent adoptions has altered over recent years, as the table below indicates, and it is too early to say whether this means a downward trend in the number of applications for step-parent adoptions. This table presents information based on the number of children actually adopted, as opposed to placed, and the number of adoptions completed, rather than begun, in one year.

Number of children adopted during the financial years 1997/98–2000/02[3]					
Category	*1997/98*	*1998/99*	*1999/ 2000*	*2000/01*	*2001/02*
Children placed by statutory agencies	*84 (53.5%)*	*54 (41.9%)*	*50 (35.5%)*	*99 (57/ 2%)*	*60 (49.5%)*
Children placed by voluntary agencies	*6 (3.8%)*	*1 (0.1%)*	*7 (5%)*	*4 (2.3%)*	*4 (1%)*
Step-parent Adoptions	*67 (42.7%)*	*74 (57.4%)*	*84 (59.6%)*	*70 (40.5%)*	*60 (49.5%)*
Total	*157*	*129*	*141*	*173*	*124*

All figures expressed as a percentage of the annual total.

[1] NIGALA Annual Report 2001/2, p 53, Table 1' Number of Cases Allocated by Proceedings Type.'
[2] For an explanation of 'looked-after children', see chapter 7, para 7.34.
[3] Based on Table 4, p 62, Paul Martin, *A Better Future – 50 Years of Child Care in Northern Ireland 1950–2000*, DHSSPS, 2003.

8.4   One other feature of the adoption system worth highlighting, is the significant relationship between the child protection system and the adoption system. A number of children who go on to be adopted first come to the notice of social services as child protection cases. By the time the adoption of the child comes to be considered, the child may well be the subject of a Care Order, or, alternatively, the Trust may be applying, in the same proceedings, for both a Care Order and a Freeing Order in respect of the child.[1] In some cases there may be other relations willing to care for the child and who may dispute that adoption is the best plan for the child. In such cases the applications before the court may include applications for 'article 8 orders'[2] – principally for residence or contact – as well as an application relating to the child's adoption.[3] The relationship between the child protection system and the adoption system is likely to grow and to account, in part, for the upward trend in agency placement adoptions, which is counter-balancing the downward trend in step-parent adoptions. This is because the Department has set a target for the adoption of children being looked after of 4% per annum.[4] Given that the annual 'looked after' population is approximately 2,400 children, this target equates to approximately 100 children per annum. The NIGALA noted that in 2001/02 this target had not been achieved in terms of the numbers of children actually adopted who had been placed by adoption agencies, although it had been in the previous year.[5] Research indicates that there is considerable delay in the adoption process with the average time from the child becoming looked after and the granting of an Adoption Order being 4.5 years.[6]

[1]   See, for example, *Re R1 (Care Order: Freeing without Parental Consent)* [2002] NI Fam 25. Where this happens these applications are referred to as 'consolidated proceedings'.
[2]   See chapter 9, para 9.101.
[3]   *Re J (leave to issue application for residence order)* [2002] EWCA Civ 1364, [2003] 1 FLR 114 where the English Court of Appeal stated that such applications should be entertained by the judge and not dismissed on the basis on which they would have been in the past.
[4]   'Priorities for action', DHSSPS, March 2002.
[5]   Annual Report 2001/02, p 20.
[6]   Children Order Advisory Committee, Third Report, p 48, quoting research by Kelly and Ince, 2000.

8.5   Inter-country adoption is an aspect of adoption that has attracted a significant amount of attention in recent years, and there have been important legislative developments in that area to alleviate the difficulties that can arise in such adoptions. However, the annual number of such adoptions is small, with 14 intercountry adoptions being applied for in 2001/02, up from 11 applications the previous year.[1]

[1]   NIGALA Annual Report 2001/02, Table 4, p 17.

Fostering matters

8.6   Fostering is the preferred placement option for children in care, with 66.5% of all such children being fostered in 2000.[1] Fostering is governed by the UK National Standards for Foster Care and by the Code of Practice on the Recruitment, Assessment, Approval, Training, Management and Support of Foster Carers.[2] The Social Services Inspectorate (SSI) carried out a review of fostering in 1997/98, entitled 'Fostering in Northern Ireland: Children and their carers,'[3] which was prompted by the Utting[4] and Kent[5] reports in England and Scotland respectively, dealing with safeguards for children living away from home. The SSI report does not mirror those reports, however, because it was considered that the same concerns as existed in Great Britain did not present themselves in Northern Ireland.[6]

[1] Paul Martin, *A Better Future – 50 Years of Child Care in Northern Ireland 1950–2000*, DHSSPS, 2003, p 25. This figure has increased from 40.6% in 1979, although the equivalent figure for 1954 was 70.2%.
[2] Issued in June 1999 and launched in Northern Ireland in September 1999.
[3] DHSS 1998.
[4] 'People Like Us: The Report of the Review of Safeguarding for Children Living Away from home' Dept of Health and Welsh Office, 1997 Stationery Office.
[5] 'Children's Safeguards Review', 1997 Social Work Services Inspectorate for Scotland, Stationery Office.
[6] Paul Martin, *A Better Future – 50 Years of Child Care in Northern Ireland 1950–2000*, DHSSPS, 2003, p 28.

8.7   There is an increasingly closer relationship between fostering and adoption, with an increasing awareness on the part of the adoption agencies of the benefits of allowing foster carers to adopt the child. Foster carers now form a significant number of non-family adopters. This relationship between fostering and adoption is seen as 'inevitable with the increased emphasis on permanency planning', although this development is at an early stage of development in Northern Ireland.[1] 'Permanency planning' is about 'establishing a foundation for the child's healthy, cognitive, physical and emotional development into adulthood.'[2] Permanency planning should ensure that longer-term strategies for dealing with children who enter the fostering and adoption systems are pursued from the outset. The SSI in its report Adopting Best Care, noted that some Trusts had developed permanency panels or placements panels to address this aspect of adoption. It noted that the aim of these panels 'in general was to prevent drift in planning for looked after children, to promote adherence to the timescale identified in permanency policies to assist social workers in determining the next steps to be taken.'[3]

[1] Paul Martin, *A Better Future – 50 Years of Child Care in Northern Ireland 1950–2000*, DHSSPS, 2003, p 34.
[2] Paul Martin, *A Better Future – 50 Years of Child Care in Northern Ireland 1950–2000*, DHSSPS, 2003, p 60. See 'Permanency planning for children: Adoption – achieving the right balance', DHSS, May 1998.
[3] 'Adopting Best Care', SSI, p 21.

Human Rights Act 1998

8.8   Obviously, Convention right article 8 – the right to private and family life – applies to adoption and fostering.[1] The HRA has the effect of requiring the Trusts, the adoption agencies, adoption panels, and the courts to have regard to its terms when making decisions about adoption.[2]

The key issue in respect of Convention right, article 8 in most adoption cases is likely to be whether the actions of the authorities, which infringe, or restrict, the parents' and the child's rights to family life, are proportionate to the legitimate aim being pursued. The views of Hale LJ, in *Re C and B (Children) (Care Order: Future Harm)*[3] on the application of article 8 where a Care Order was sought, were recited with approval in the adoption case of *Re C (Freeing for Adoption: Contact)*.[4] She had offered the view that any intervention should be against an ongoing intention to reunite the family, if possible, if the actions were to be viewed as proportionate and thus compatible with article 8. The trial judge in *Re C (Freeing for Adoption: Contact)* concluded that the overriding necessity of the interests of the child dictated the making of the Freeing Order.

¹   For a full explanation of art 8, see chapter 6, para 6.11. For an assessment of the relationship of art 8 and the Adoption Act 1976 in England and Wales, see *Re B (a child) (sole adoption by unmarried father)* [2001] UKHL 70, [2002] 1 All ER 641, [2002] 1 WLR 258, [2002] 1 FCR 150, [2002] 1 FLR 196.
²   Section 6. On the HRA, see chapter 1, para 1.74.
³   [2001] 1 FLR 611, CA.
⁴   (12 January 2002, unreported), High Court. Also cited in *Re G and S (Care Order) (Freeing Without Consent) (Contact)* 31 May 2001, unreported High Court, Gillen J.

8.9   There is one other way in which article 8 may arise in adoption proceedings (or indeed in any proceedings dealing with a child's future upbringing) and that is where the child asserts that there is a positive obligation on the State to restore its right to family life, although not necessarily with its birth family. Once again, a quotation from Hale LJ illustrates the point. In *Re W and B; Re W*¹ she stated:²

'In my view there is another way in which a public authority may act incompatibly with the Convention rights in a care case. This is by failing to take adequate steps to secure for a child, who has been deprived of a life with his family of birth, a life with a new family who can become his new 'family for life' to make up for what he has lost ... the notion, ... can be readily inferred from the concept of positive obligations inherent in Article 8.'

She went on to say:³

'Here we are discussing a person who has already been deprived of a large part, if not all of that family life which he is entitled to expect. He is particularly vulnerable, partly because of the reasons which brought him into care and partly because of the risks inherent in the care experience. Where the State has had to deprive someone of their family life, it seems to me that there is a corresponding positive obligation to take reasonable and appropriate steps to fill the gap.'

This view was noted, by Gillen J, in *Re DJ and D*⁴ in support of his decision to granting the Freeing Order in that case.

¹   [2001] EWCA Civ 757, [2001] UKHRR 928.
²   At [55].
³   At [59].
⁴   (25 September 2001, unreported), High Court, transcript available on Lexis.

Fostering

8.10   Fostering occurs when a child is placed by a Trust, or by its parents (or those with parental responsibility), with other persons who will care for, and rear the child. Placement by someone other than a Trust is referred to as 'private fostering' and is subject to the Children (Private Arrangements for Fostering) Regulations (Northern

Ireland) 1996. A child is not privately fostered if he or she is being 'looked after' by a Trust.[1] Foster placement by a Trust is governed by the Foster Placement (Children) Regulations (Northern Ireland) 1996.

[1]   Children (Northern Ireland) Order 1995, art 107(2). On 'looked-after children', see chapter 7, para 7.34.

Foster placement by Trust

8.11   A child is not to be placed with a foster carer until the carer is approved by the authority placing the child.[1] Before approval can be given, the prospective foster carer must supply details about himself or herself and other members of the household and family, including details of his past and present employment, previous experience of caring for children, and any previous criminal convictions recorded against the prospective foster carer or any other adult members of the household.[2] Prospective foster carers must also provide the Trust or voluntary organisation responsible for placing the child with details of two referees, who must then be interviewed.[3]

[1]   Foster Placement (Children) Regulations (Northern Ireland) 1996, reg 3. The placing authority is usually the approving authority.
[2]   Foster Placement (Children) Regulations (Northern Ireland) 1996, reg 3(4)(b) and Sch 1.
[3]   Foster Placement (Children) Regulations (Northern Ireland) 1996, reg 3(4)(a) and Sch 1.

8.12   Armed with this information the authority then considers whether the person is suitable to act as a foster parent and whether the household is a suitable one for the child that may be placed there. This part of the process will involve a social worker visiting the prospective foster carers and checking the information tendered by them with the police and social services.[1]

The authority approving a person as a foster parent is required to maintain a register of all approved foster parents and to maintain case records for them, which information must then be retained for at least ten years.[2]

[1]   In the past, these checks were made under the Pre-Employment Consultancy Scheme and in the future will be made under the lists maintained under the Protection of Children and Vulnerable Adults (Northern Ireland) Order 2003. See chapter 6, para 6.152.
[2]   Foster Placement (Children) Regulations (Northern Ireland) 1996, regs 12, 13 and 14, Where a voluntary organisation maintains these records, a guardian ad litem must be given access to them if he or she requires them: Foster Placement (Children) Regulations (Northern Ireland) 1996, reg 14(4).

Foster care and foster placement agreements

8.13   Even if approval is given, there can be no placement without a written agreement between the foster carer and the authority, referred to as a foster care agreement.[3] The matters to be covered in such an agreement include:[2]
- the amount of support and training to be given to a foster parent;
- the procedure for reviewing the foster parent's approval;
- the prohibition on the administering of corporal punishment;

- the obligation on maintaining confidential any information given to the foster parent in confidence;
- the obligation to care for the child as if he or she were a member of the foster parent's family;
- a requirement to notify the authority of any serious illness or occurrence involving the child.

[1]   Foster Placement (Children) Regulations (Northern Ireland) 1996, reg 3(6)(b).
[2]   Foster Placement (Children) Regulations (Northern Ireland) 1996, Sch 2.

8.14   A second agreement is made between the authority and the foster carer and is referred to as the foster placement agreement.[1] It focuses on the child. It contains all the information that the authority considers necessary to enable the foster carer to care for the child. This information includes:[2]

- the authority's objectives of the placement;
- the child's personal history including cultural, racial and religious background;
- the child's state of health and educational needs;
- the arrangements for the financial support of the child during the placement;
- arrangements for the delegation of responsibility for consent to the medical or dental examination or treatment of the child;
- arrangements for maintaining contact between the child and its family under the Children (Northern Ireland) Order 1995, art 53;[3]
- details of visits and reviews for the purpose of the Review of Children's Cases Regulations (Northern Ireland) 1996;
- circumstances in which prior approval of the authority is needed for the child to stay away from home.

[1]   Foster Placement (Children) Regulations (Northern Ireland) 1996, reg 5(6) and Sch 3.
[2]   Foster Placement (Children) Regulations (Northern Ireland) 1996, Sch 3.
[3]   See chapter 7, para 7.39.

Monitoring foster placements

8.15   The foster parent's approval is reviewed on an annual basis.[1] In placing the child the authority must, where possible, ensure that the foster parent is of the same religious persuasion as the child or that he or she at least gives an undertaking to bring the child up in that persuasion.[2]

Placements are supervised by the authority placing the child, and a supervisory visit is made to the foster parent's home within one week of placement and thereafter on a monthly basis,[3] except where the child is placed in foster care in an emergency, in which case visits take place once per week.[4] Where the child is placed by a voluntary organisation, the Trust carries out a visit within 28 days of the placement and on a six-monthly basis thereafter.[5] Written reports are made of all such visits.[6]

[1]   Foster Placement (Children) Regulations (Northern Ireland) 1996, reg 4(1).
[2]   Foster Placement (Children) Regulations (Northern Ireland) 1996, reg 5(2).
[3]   Foster Placement (Children) Regulations (Northern Ireland) 1996, reg 6(1).

⁴ Foster Placement (Children) Regulations (Northern Ireland) 1996, reg 6(2).
⁵ Foster Placement (Children) Regulations (Northern Ireland) 1996, reg 15, or within seven days of being notified that the child's welfare is not being promoted.
⁶ Foster Placement (Children) Regulations (Northern Ireland) 1996, reg 6(4),

Emergency foster care

8.16 Emergency placement of a child with an approved foster parent is possible, but not for a period of more than 24 hours, where the authority has already approved the emergency foster carer.[1] Such placements are also subject to the requirement to secure a written agreement with the foster parent. This written agreement covers a range of matters similar to those dealt with in a foster care agreement. In particular it allows removal of the child by the authority at any time.

If an immediate placement is necessary, an authority can place the child for a period not longer than six weeks with a person who has not been approved, provided he or she is a relative or friend of the child, has entered into a written agreement (similar to the one just discussed in the above paragraph) and that interviews with the referees, and an inspection of his or her home have been carried out.[2]

[1] Foster Placement (Children) Regulations (Northern Ireland) 1996, reg 11(1).
[2] Foster Placement (Children) Regulations (Northern Ireland) 1996, reg 11(3).

Private fostering

8.17 Where a person proposes to foster a child privately he or she must inform the Trust at least six weeks before doing so, or if the foster carer comes to care for the child in an emergency, then within 48 hours of receiving the child.[1] This notification must be in writing[2] and must contain detailed information about the child, details of the child's parents, or persons with parental responsibility, as well as the proposed foster carer's own details, including details of offences of which he or she has been convicted, or whether he or she is disqualified from acting as a foster carer.[3] The notification must also include details of addresses at which the foster carer has lived in the previous 5 years, and must be updated if the foster carer changes address, or other people come to live in the household.[4] Further notification must be made to the Trust whenever the fostering arrangement comes to an end.[5] Similar notification duties apply to the child's parents (or those with parental responsibility for the child) and to other people involved, whether directly or indirectly, in the proposed fostering arrangement.

[1] Foster Placement (Children) Regulations (Northern Ireland) 1996, reg 4.
[2] Foster Placement (Children) Regulations (Northern Ireland) 1996, reg 7.
[3] Children (Private Arrangements for Fostering) Regulations (Northern Ireland) 1996, reg 4(3) and (4).
[4] Children (Private Arrangements for Fostering) Regulations (Northern Ireland) 1996, reg 4.
[5] Children (Private Arrangements for Fostering) Regulations (Northern Ireland) 1996, reg 5.

Monitoring private fostering

8.18   Where a child is privately fostered the Trust is under a duty to satisfy itself as to the child's welfare.[1] In particular, the Trust must be satisfied of a wide range of matters including:[2]

(1)   the purpose and intended duration of the fostering arrangement;

(2)   the child's physical, intellectual, emotional, social and behavioural development;

(3)   whether the child's needs arising from its religious background, ethnic identity and cultural and linguistic background are being met;

(4)   the final arrangements for the care of the child.

[1]   Children (Northern Ireland) Order 1995, art 108.
[2]   Children (Private Arrangements for Fostering) Regulations (Northern Ireland) 1996, reg 2.

8.19   These visits must take place whenever they are reasonably requested by the child or the foster parents, but in any event every six weeks in the first year of the placement and quarterly thereafter.[1] As might be expected, a written report must be made of all such visits.[2] A Departmental official authorised to make such visits may, at reasonable times, enter any premises where he or she has reasonable cause to believe a child who is being privately fostered is present.[3]

[1]   Children (Private Arrangements for Fostering) Regulations (Northern Ireland) 1996, reg 3.
[2]   Children (Private Arrangements for Fostering) Regulations (Northern Ireland) 1996, reg 3(3).
[3]   Children (Northern Ireland) Order 1995, art 108(3).

Disqualification from private fostering

8.20   As mentioned above, a person who wishes to foster a child privately must disclose any convictions he or she has, as well as the fact that he was at any time prohibited from childminding, or providing day care, or has been prohibited from fostering in the past. These matters are not an automatic bar to the person acting as a private foster carer, as the legislation simply prohibits the person acting in such a capacity unless he has made the relevant disclosures and has obtained the written consent of the Trust to his doing so.[1] The matters that disqualify a person from acting as a foster carer are set out in the Disqualification for Caring for Children Regulations (Northern Ireland) 1996.[2] These include the following:[3]

●   having responsibility for a child who has been the subject of a Care Order;

●   having a conviction for a 'Schedule 1' offence;[4]

●   having had an application to be registered to provide childminding, or day care facilities refused;

●   having a conviction for an offence listed in the Schedule to the 1996 Regulations.[5]

[1]   Children (Northern Ireland) Order 1995, art 109(1).
[2]   These regulations also apply to people seeking to register under the Children (Northern Ireland) Order 1995, art 118, to provide childminding or day care services.
[3]   Disqualification for Caring for Children Regulations (Northern Ireland) 1996, reg 2.
[4]   Criminal Justice (Children) (Northern Ireland) Order 1998, Sch 1.

5   This includes injury or threat of injury to another and offences under the Homosexual Offences (Northern Ireland) Order 1982.

8.21 A Trust can prohibit a person from acting as a private foster carer on the basis that the individual is not a 'suitable person' to foster a child, or that the premises in which the child will be accommodated are not suitable.[1] Alternatively, it is open to the Trust to impose certain requirements on the prospective private foster carer about matters such as the number of children that may be fostered, arrangements for the safeguarding of their health or welfare or other matters about their care.[2]

Where a person is prohibited from acting as a foster carer, or has conditions imposed on them when acting as a foster carer, a right of appeal to the High Court is available, although the appeal must be made within 14 days of the decision complained of.[3]

1   Children (Northern Ireland) Order 1995, art 110(2).
2   Children (Northern Ireland) Order 1995, art 111.
3   Children (Northern Ireland) Order 1995, art 113(1) and (2).

Legal authority of the foster carer

8.22 In the majority of cases the foster carer's authority in respect of the child will be set out in the fostering placement agreement between the foster carer and the Trust. The Trust's legal relationship with the child will in turn be determined by the manner in which the child came to be looked after by it. If the child is in its care on foot of a Care Order, the Trust will have parental responsibility for the child, but if the child is being voluntarily accommodated in care it will not have parental responsibility. In such a case the Trust's legal relationship with the child will be governed by the written agreement that it has with the child's parents.[1] In any event, as outlined above, the foster placement agreement includes arrangements for delegating responsibility for consenting to medical or dental treatment of the child to the foster carer.

1   See chapter 7, paras 7.30 and 7.33.

8.23 However, where the child is privately fostered it may be useful for the foster carer to secure a Residence Order made in his or her favour.[1] This will not only determine the issue of where the child is to live but also gives the person in whose favour it is made parental responsibility for the child. The advantage to the foster carer is that he or she will then be in a position to exercise the powers of a parent.[2] However, leave of the court will be required before the Residence Order application can be made and other restrictions also apply. A person who is, or was at any time within the previous six months, a foster carer of a child may not apply for leave to apply for any article 8 order unless:[3]

(a)   he or she has the consent of the authority;
(b)   he or she is a relative of the child; or
(c)   the child has lived with him or her for at least three years preceding the application.

It may also be possible, even if the foster carer cannot bring an application in his or her own right, for the court to make a Residence Order of its own volition.[4] Without a Residence Order in his or her favour, a private foster parent will not have parental responsibility for the child, unless he or she possessed it before the child was placed with them.

[1]   Children (Northern Ireland) Order 1995, art 10.
[2]   On parental responsibility, see chapter 6, para 6.43.
[3]   Children (Northern Ireland) Order 1995, art 9(3). The period of three years mentioned in para (3)(c) need not be continuous but must have begun not more than five years before the making of the application.
[4]   Children (Northern Ireland) Order 1995, art 10(1)(b) and *Gloucestershire County Council v P* [2000] Fam 1 in which the local authority was opposed to the foster carers obtaining a Residence Order, but the guardian ad litem supported this development. The Court of Appeal considered that the procedural limitations on foster carers did not limit the court's options. However, the High Court in Northern Ireland refused to allow a foster parent to be joined as a party to Care Order proceedings where the foster parent ultimately sought a Residence Order because the facts were not unusual enough to warrant circumvention of the statutory criteria. *Re M (joinder of foster parent)* (27 April 2001, unreported), Gillen J, transcript available on Lexis.

Adoption

8.24   This section identifies the legislative basis for adoption, the appropriate court rules, and the nature of the roles played by the various administrative elements of the adoption system, including the Department, the adoption agencies and adoption panels, and the guardian ad litem.

There are two types of adoption in domestic law, those involving the placement of the child by an adoption agency, and those where the child is placed by its parents, commonly referred to as private adoption. In a private adoption the child cannot be placed with any other person other than a relative of the child.[1] Private placement of a child for adoption outside of this legislatively defined category of relatives is an offence, for both the person making the placement and the person receiving the child.[2] This restriction does not apply to agency adoptions. There is also a difference between the two types of adoption in the period for which a child must be placed with the prospective adopters before an Adoption Order can be made.[3]

It is also an offence to make or give any payment or reward in connection with the adoption of a child,[4] with the exception of adoption allowances paid under the Adoption Allowances Regulations (Northern Ireland) 1996.

[1]   Relatives means a parent, step-parent, grandparent, brother, sister, uncle or aunt: Adoption (Northern Ireland) Order 1987, art 2.
[2]   Adoption (Northern Ireland) Order 1987, art 11. See *In Re R (Inter Country adoption: Consent of Foreign Mother: Arrangements and Payment)* (2 May 2003, unreported), High Court, Gillen J, where this article, and art 59, had to be considered.
[3]   See para 8.48.
[4]   Adoption (Northern Ireland) Order 1987, art 59.

Legislative structure and the role of the Department

8.25   The significant legislative enactments in respect of adoption are the Adoption (Northern Ireland) Order 1987[1] and the Adoption (Intercountry Aspects) Act (Northern Ireland) 2001,[2] which deal with domestic and intercountry adoptions respectively.

The main duty on the courts and the adoption agencies, imposed by article 9 of the 1987 Order, is to have regard for the child's welfare.[3] In doing so they are to have regard to all the circumstances, but in particular they need to be satisfied that adoption will be in the best interests of the child, that the welfare of the child will be safeguarded and promoted throughout its childhood and that the child is going to be provided with a stable and harmonious home. In assessing their satisfaction with these matters they are to have regard to the child's wishes and feelings, so far as is practicable.[4] As might be expected, the Department retains responsibility for overseeing the general delivery of adoption services including the registration and inspection of adoption agencies. These duties are normally carried out by the Social Services Inspectorate (SSI).[5]

---

[1]   This is broadly equivalent to the Adoption and Children Act 2002, which governs adoption in England and Wales, and to the Adoption (Scotland) Act 1978, the relevant legislation in Scotland.

[2]   This is the equivalent of the Adoption (Intercountry Aspects) Act 1999, which incorporates the Hague Convention into the domestic law of Great Britain.

[3]   Adoption (Northern Ireland) Order 1987, art 9.

[4]   Adoption (Northern Ireland) Order 1987, art 9(b).

[5]   For an explanation of the Department's inspection powers in this area, see chapter 2, para 2.76. The SSI carried out an inspection of adoption services in 2000–2001 see 'Adopting Best Care', SSI, 2002.

8.26   The new Regulation and Improvement Authority will also have a role to play in overseeing the quality of service delivery in this area.[1] The Authority will, when regulations are promulgated, be entitled to require Boards and Trusts to provide information about the performance of its adoption and fostering functions, on an annual basis, or otherwise.[2]

The procedural steps of the adoption process are found in the Adoption Agencies Regulations (Northern Ireland) 1989, and, for the High Court, in the Rules of the Supreme Court (Northern Ireland) (Amendment No 6) 1989,[3] and for the county court, in the County Court (Amendment No 3) Rules (Northern Ireland) 1989.[4] (The last two documents are commonly referred to as the 'Adoption Rules', and contain all the necessary forms used in the adoption process). The Adoption Agencies Regulations set out the steps to be taken by the agencies and their adoption panels, while the 'Adoption Rules' detail the procedures before the courts. Adoption matters can be dealt with by both county courts and by the Family Division of the High Court, and are heard in chambers, ie in private.[5]

---

[1]   See chapter 2, para 2.60.

[2]   Health and Personal Social Services (Quality Improvement and Regulation) (Northern Ireland) Order 2003, arts 36 and 37.

[3]   The High Court Adoption Rules appear in the Rules of the Supreme Court (Northern Ireland) as Order 84 (hereafter RSC Order 84).

The County Court Adoption Rules appear in the County Court Rules as Order 50 (hereafter CCR
        Order 50).
    5   Adoption (Northern Ireland) Order 1987, art 65.

Adoption agencies and panels

8.27   Adoption agencies play the central role in the administration of the adoption
system and it is to an adoption agency that prospective adopters[1] must make their
application to be considered as suitable adoptive parents. An adoption agency is a
Trust providing adoption services, or alternatively one of the two registered adoption
societies, namely the Family Care Society[2] and the Church of Ireland Adoption
Society for Northern Ireland.[3] Each of the Western, Southern and Northern Health
Boards has decided to centralise their adoption services in one Trust, while the
Eastern Health Board has two Trusts that provide adoption services. An adoption
panel is composed of no more than ten people,[4] and must include a social worker
employed by the agency, a member of the management committee, a medical adviser,
and at least one person who is not employed by the agency.

[1]   One or two people can make an application, but if the application is made by two people then they
    must be married to one another (Adoption (Northern Ireland) Order 1987, art 14). Adoption by one
    person is provided for in art 15. For convenience, this chapter refers to prospective adopters only.
[2]   Formerly the Catholic Family Care Society.
[3]   In practice, these latter two registered adoption agencies are involved in a very small number of
    adoptions. In 2001/02, the NIGALA was involved in only one adoption matter originating with the
    Church of Ireland Adoption Society and in only three matters generated by the Family Care Society:
    NIGALA Annual Report 2001/02 p 55,'Table 3. The Number of Adoption and Specified Cases by
    Trust and Adoption Agency Area.' Two voluntary agencies are presently unregistered, 'Adopt' and
    'Adoption (UK)'. These agencies exist mainly to provide support for users of adoption services.
[4]   Adoption Agencies Regulations (Northern Ireland) 1989, reg 5(1).

8.28   It is the task of the agency to decide on the suitability of the prospective
adopters, to place a child with prospective adopters and to supervise that placement
and then, with the help of an adoption panel, decide whether to proceed to make an
application for an Adoption Order. An adoption panel has the task of recommending
to the agency whether a child should be adopted or not. Note, however, that the panel
may only recommend the adoption and that the final decision rests with the adoption
agency. Social workers employed by the adoption agencies will have particular
responsibility for supervision placement and preparing court reports.

Adoption agencies' duties

8.29   Agencies must provide counselling services for the child, its parents and the
prospective adopters, as well as explaining to them, both orally and in writing, the
legal implications of the adoption procedures.[1] More pertinently, agencies must
gather a wide range of information about the child, its parents and the prospective
adopters and compile, or have others compile, a variety of reports about the
individuals involved. In particular, written reports must be obtained from a medical
practitioner about health of the child and the prospective adopters.[2] Reports must

also be compiled in respect of the premises in which the child will live, and of the interviews conducted with each prospective adopter's two personal referees.[3] A report must also be sought from the Board in whose area the prospective adopters reside, to ascertain whether or not there is any reason to believe that the proposed adoption would be detrimental to the child.[4] The report assessing the prospective adopters in their own home, and compiled by agency social workers, is commonly called a 'home study report'. Checks are also made with the Pre-Employment Consultancy Service and, in the future, will be made under the lists maintained under the Protection of Children and Vulnerable Adults (Northern Ireland) Order 2003.[5] The detail of the matters to be included in these reports is set out in Parts I to VII of the Schedule to the Adoption Agencies Regulations and report-compilers can use the lists contained there as an aide memoire when completing reports.

[1] Adoption Agencies Regulations (Northern Ireland) 1989, reg 7(1).
[2] Adoption Agencies Regulations (Northern Ireland) 1989, regs 7(2)(c) and 8(2)(c).
[3] Adoption Agencies Regulations (Northern Ireland) 1989, reg 8(2)(d) and (e).
[4] Adoption Agencies Regulations (Northern Ireland) 1989, reg 8(2)(f).
[5] See chapter 6, para 6.152.

8.30 All of this information, along with the agency's observations about it, is then transmitted to the adoption panel for its consideration.[1] The SSI did note, in its inspection of adoption services, that there can be considerable delay, of between one year and six years, between the submission of the prospective adopters' application form and the referral of the matter to the adoption panel.[2] In its view delays of longer than two years were not acceptable. The delay between conducting the home study report and the referral of the applicant to the adoption panel ranged from six months to one year and seven months.[3] The SSI has suggested a model of how to conduct an assessment in 'Adopting Best Care'.[4]

[1] Adoption Agencies Regulations (Northern Ireland) 1989, reg 9.
[2] Executive Summary of 'Adopting Best Care', p 11. The corresponding waiting time for inter-country adoption was between three months and two years, p 12.
[3] 'Adopting Best Care', SSI, 2002, p 79.
[4] 'Adopting Best Care', SSI, 2002, p 81.

8.31 An adoption panel's function is to determine whether to recommend that adoption would be in the child's best interests, whether the prospective adopters are suitable to adoptive parents generally, and in particular whether they are suitable adoptive parents for a particular child.[1] Its determinations in regard to these matters are then made to the agency, which may only make its decision after taking into account the panel's recommendations.[2]

[1] Adoption Agencies Regulations (Northern Ireland) 1989, reg 10(1).
[2] Adoption Agencies Regulations (Northern Ireland) 1989, reg 11(1).

8.32 Where the agency decides that adoption is in the best interests of the child and that the prospective adopters are suitable to adopt the particular child in question, the child may be placed with those prospective adopters. Before the placement occurs, however, the agency sends written proposals of the adoption to the prospective adopters, who must then agree them before the placement can take place.[1]

[1]   Adoption Agencies Regulations (Northern Ireland) 1989, reg 12(1).

8.33   If the placement is to proceed the agency must then send a report on the child's medical history to the prospective adopters' medical practitioner and notify the relevant Health Board and Education and Library Board, and the child's parents of the placement.[1] During the placement the agency has a duty to ensure that the child is visited once a week and that its health is monitored, and that any advice and assistance that it considers appropriate is provided.[2] A review of the placement should take place within three months, and thereafter whenever the agency considers it necessary.[3] A review is required particularly where the child has been freed for adoption for six months or more but has not been placed with a prospective adopter.[4]

[1]   Adoption Agencies Regulations (Northern Ireland) 1989, reg 12(2)(c).
[2]   Adoption Agencies Regulations (Northern Ireland) 1989, reg 12(2)(g), (i) and (j).
[3]   Adoption Agencies Regulations (Northern Ireland) 1989, reg 12(2)(k).
[4]   Adoption Agencies Regulations (Northern Ireland) 1989, reg 13. These reviews continue at six monthly intervals if the child is not adopted and continues to be unplaced.

8.34   Access to an adoption agency's records is governed by the Adoption Agencies Regulations[1] and they prescribe categories of people to whom disclosure can be made, including the Department, the Ombudsman, guardians ad litem, the courts and to others 'as it thinks fit'.[2] A determination as to whether or not to release information to other persons under this provision must now be made in light of any applicant's right to a family life under Convention right, article 8. Any refusal will have to be justified in accordance with the principles in article 8(2).

[1]   Regulation 15.
[2]   Adoption Agencies Regulations (Northern Ireland) 1989, reg 15(2).

Guardians ad litem

8.35   The role of a guardian ad litem (GAL) in adoption proceedings pre-dates the enactment of the Children (Northern Ireland) Order 1995, as it was in the 1987 Order that they were first mentioned in legislation.[1] GALs, operating under the aegis of NIGALA,[2] are appointed by the Master of Care and Protection,[3] to provide the court with an independent assessment of the child and the proposed adoption. Adoption currently forms about one third of NIGALA's annual workload. Details of the contents of the guardian ad litem's report are set out below.

[1]   For role of guardians ad litem in Children Order proceedings see chapter 6, para 6.65.
[2]   For further discussion of the NIGALA, see chapter 6, para 6.63.
[3]   Under the Adoption (Northern Ireland) Order 1987, art 6. On role of High Court Masters, see chapter 1, para 1.63.

8.36   There is a very high correlation between the court order made in adoption proceedings and the recommendation contained in the guardian ad litem's report. In respect of many elements of the Agency's adoption work the final court order may reflect the guardian ad litem's recommendation in 100% of cases, as the Table below, extracted from NIGALA's 2001/02 report indicates:

Table 7   Gal Recommendation in relation to Initial Applications and Court Orders Granted
Case Completed between April 1, 2001 and March 31, 2002

Initial Application Applied for	No. of Applications	GAL Recommendation	Number of GAL Recommendations	Court Order Granted	No. Of Court Orders Granted
Adoption Placement	64	Adoption Order No order	62 2	Adoption Order	64
Adoption Abroad	1	Adoption Order	1	Adoption Order	1
Adoption Step Parent	60 Withdrawn 5	Adoption Order	55	Adoption Order	55
Intercounty Adoption	13	Adoption Order	13	Adoption order	13
Appeal	9 Withdrawn 3	Appeal Rejected	6	Appeal Rejected	6
Care	284 Withdrawn 29	Care Family Assistance No Order Residence Order Substitution of Order Supervision Order	196 3 10 9 1 36	Care Family Assistance No Order Residence Order Substitution of Order Supervision Order	191 3 16 9 0 6
Change of Surname	1	Change of Name	1	Change of Name	1
Contact	50 Withdrawn 8	Contact No Order No Contact	15 23 4	Contact No Order No Contact	18 20 4

Initial Application Applied for	No. of Applications	GAL Recommendation	Number of GAL Recommendations	Court Order Granted	No. Of Court Orders Granted
Discharge of Care Withdrawn 6	46	Adoption Order Order to remain	34 6	Adoption Order Order to remain	34 6
Emergency Protection Withdrawn 5	62	Emergency Protection Extension of EPO	49 8	Emergency Protection Extension of EOP	49 8
Freeing Consolidated	31	Freeing	31	Freeing	31
Freeing [with consent]	5	Freeing	5	Freeing	5
Freeing [without consent] Withdrawn 1	39	Freeing	38	Freeing	38
Investigation Art 56 Withdrawn 5	38	Care No Order Supervision Contact	7 16 7 3	Care No Order Supervision Contact	4 16 10 3
Live Abroad	3	Live Abroad No Order	2 1	Live Abroad No order	2 1

Initial Application Applied for	No. of Applications	GAL Recommendation	Number of GAL Recommendations	Court Order Granted	No. Of Court Orders Granted
Multiple Proceedings Withdrawn 2	14	Care Order	5	Care Order	5
		Discharge of Order	2	Discharge of Order	2
		No Order	2	No Order	2
		Residence Order	2	Residence	2
		Secure Accommodation Order	1	Secure Accommodation Order	1
Residence Withdrawn 13	15	Residence Order	2	Residence Order	2
Secure Accommodation Withdrawn 10	46	Secure Accommodation	27	Secure Accommodation	26
		Care Order	1	Care Order	1
		Order Lapsed	4	Order Lapsed	5
		No Order	4	No Order	4
Supervision Withdrawn 4	10	Care Order	2	Care	2
		No Order	2	No Order	2
		Supervision Order	2	Supervision Order	2
Total	791				

8.37   The Agency does offer, however, that these statistics disguise the fact that 'there is a much wider discrepancy between the initial application made, usually by the HSS Trusts, and the final outcome of the proceedings. This gives some indication regarding the complexity of the negotiations that take place during the court process and the impact that the court proceedings and the role of the guardian ad litem has had on the case.'[1]

[1]   NIGALA 2001/02, Annual Report, p 62.

The legal process

8.38   This section sets out the legal steps in the adoption process, from placement to adoption, and deals with contact between the birth parents and the child during that process.

Application for Freeing Order or Adoption Order

8.39   The legal process of adoption can begin in a number of ways and there are two key court orders in the adoption process, namely a Freeing Order and an Adoption Order. The former, as its title suggests, frees, or makes available, the child for adoption, while the latter completes that process.

The child can be the subject of a Freeing Order application made by an adoption agency either on its own or jointly with the parents.[1] As explained earlier, an application for a Freeing Order can be in consolidated proceedings where the Trust is seeking a Care Order and a Freeing Order in the same proceedings. Alternatively the child might be the subject of an Adoption Order application made by the adoption agency or the prospective adopters provided the requisite period of placement has expired.[2] This period of placement is to allow the adoption agency, or the relevant adoption agency if the placement is a private one, to monitor the child in the home environment of the prospective adopters. Indeed, if the court is not satisfied that the agency has been given sufficient opportunity to engage in this sort of assessment then it is not to make the Adoption Order.[3]

[1]   See para 8.45.
[2]   See para 8.48. The application is made by way of an Originating Summons in the High Court (r 15) and by petition in the county court (r 14), RSC Order 54 and CCR Order 50 respectively.
[3]   Adoption (Northern Ireland) Order 1987, art 13(3).

Guardian ad litem's report

8.40   On the making of either a Freeing or Adoption Order application, the Master of Care and Protection must appoint a guardian ad litem.[1] The guardian is then required to produce a report for the purpose of the court.[2] The guardian ad litem's duties include assessing whether any agreement given to the making of an order has been freely and unconditionally given, that all reasonable steps to identify the father have been taken, and investigating, so far as possible the matters referred to in the application and the Statement of Facts.[3] The guardian ad litem is also required to perform 'such other duties as appear to be necessary' and this element of the guardian ad litem's duties have been the subject of consideration in *Re EJK*,[4] in which the issue before Higgins J was whether the guardian ad litem should travel to Dublin to interview the mother of the child directly, rather than rely on information provided by a social worker in Dublin. The judge reviewed the legislation, in particular the relevant elements of the Adoption Rules dealing with the guardian ad litem's duties, and came to the following conclusion:

> 'It does not seem to me that a guardian ad litem appointed by this court has the right or the power to carry out any investigations outside Northern Ireland [in adoption proceedings]. If such be the practice then it should cease forthwith. If investigations are required outside Northern Ireland, then it is customary to request a corresponding agency in the other jurisdiction, to consider the matter and report in writing. Such requests are invariably complied with in a spirit of comity and mutuality of interest and respect.' [Words in parentheses added]

Higgins J's refusal to allow the guardian to travel outside the jurisdiction contrasts with Gillen J's decision to allow a guardian to do just that in the context of preparing a report in a Care Order application.[6]

---

[1]   Adoption (Northern Ireland) Order 1987, art 66.

[2]   RSC Order 54, r 6 and CCR Order 50, r 5, require the compilation of reports in freeing applications, RSC Order 54, r 18 and CCR Order 50, r 17 govern the compilation of reports in adoption order applications.

[3]   This is an outline of the facts of the circumstances relevant to the child's case, prepared by the agency, and included with the Freeing Order or Adoption Order application.

[4]   (11 June 1997, unreported), High Court, transcript available on Lexis.

[5]   See chapter 6, para 6.68.

8.41   The guardian ad litem's report is confidential.[1] In *Re A (Adoption: Disclosure of Reports of guardian ad litem and Adoption Agency)*[2] the High Court considered a request by the adoptive parents, in an intercountry adoption, that the guardian's report be disclosed to them so that they would be in a position, in future years, to provide the child with as much information about its background as possible. Gillen J considered that there were no pressing reasons for the disclosure of the reports and declined to do so, fearing that a precedent might be set that could damage the confidentiality placed in the guardian ad litem by the birth parents.

---

[1]   RSC Order 54, r 6(6) and CCR Order 50, r 5(6).

[2]   (21 February 2002, unreported), High Court (Family Division), Gillen J.

Adoption agency's report

8.42   The adoption agency is also required to compile a court report for the proceedings,[1] and in Northern Ireland this is commonly referred to as the 'report of the reporting officer'[2] or the 'Appendix G' report.[3] This report deals with the suitability of the prospective adopters and includes an assessment of other 'Article 9' matters. In particular, it provides fulsome detail on the child, its natural parents, the prospective adopters and the actions of the agency, including its reasons for concluding that adoption is in the child's best interests. In the conclusions to the report, the social worker is expected to offer an opinion on whether the order being sought would be in the child's best interests, its likely effect on the natural parents and an opinion on the likelihood of the child's full integration into the prospective adopter's family.

[1]　Adoption (Northern Ireland) Order 1987, art 24. This court report must be compiled to comply with RSC Order 54, rr 3(4)(b) or 22(1) and Part I or Appendix G, and CCR Order 50, rr 2(4)(b) or 21(1) and Form 249B.

[2]　The 'reporting officer' in Northern Ireland has slightly different functions to the 'reporting officer in England and Wales.

[3]　So called because the details of the contents of the report are set out in Appendix G, Part 1 of the Adoption Rules. In the county court, the report should be completed as required by Form 249B of the County Court Adoption Rules.

8.43　Where the order being sought is a freeing application, the 'Appendix G' report is supplied at the time of application,[1] but if an Adoption Order is sought, the 'Appendix G' report is only due within six weeks of the Notice of Hearing (see below).[2]

Where the adoption agency seeks to have a Freeing Order, or an Adoption Order, made without the consent of the child's parents, then it must include in its application to the court a 'Statement of Facts', on which it intends to rely to satisfy the court that the parents' consent can be dispensed with.[3]

[1]　RSC Order 54, r 3(4)b); CCR Order 50, r 2(4)(b).

[2]　RSC Order 54, r 22(2) and CCR Order 50, r 21(1). The only report that will be required at the time of making the Adoption Order application will be a medical report on the child, and only then if the child was not placed by the agency: r 15(5)(b).

[3]　RSC Order 54, r 4(4) re Freeing Order applications and r 16(1) re Adoption Order applications where no Freeing Order was in existence, and CCR Order 50, rr 3(4) and 15(1) respectively.

Notice of Hearing

8.44　Within 14 days of the receipt of the guardian ad litem's report, the applicant must issue a Notice of Hearing to obtain a date for the hearing of the application.[1] As stated previously, the application can be for a Freeing Order or it can be for an Adoption Order. The governing issues in either application will be whether it would be in the child's best interests to have him or her adopted (or freed for adoption, as the case may be)[2] and secondly, whether the consent of the child's parents has been obtained or whether it may validly be dispensed with.

[1]　RSC Order 54, r 8(1) re Freeing Order applications, and r 20 re Adoption Order applications, and CCR Order 50, rr 7(1) and 19 respectively.

[2]　The Adoption and Children Act 2002, which applies in England and Wales, is now harmonised with the Children Act 1989 and the paramountcy principle now applies to adoption under that Act: s 1(2).

Freeing Order

8.45 A Freeing Order, as its name suggests, frees the child up for adoption, thus preparing the way for a later Adoption Order. The original intention when the 1987 Order was enacted was that a Freeing Order would be an expeditious and considerably easier way of dealing with adoption cases. However, Freeing Orders have never proved very popular in Northern Ireland, with only approximately 30 freeing applications being made each year. The NIGALA Annual Report 2000/01 offers some reasons for the low take-up of the Freeing Order option:

'Why has this part of the adoption legislation not lived up to original expectations? Two reasons are cited. One is that, far from being a speedy process, it can be relatively slow. In 2000/01, a freeing application when consolidated with care proceedings (and possible other applications) took an average 13 months to complete compared with an average of 12 months the previous year. Freeing applications heard without consolidation with other applications are of shorter duration, on average between 5–6 months.

The second reason for concern about the freeing legislation is its relevance to the needs of the child, the birth family and the adoptive family in current times. Undoubtedly the new culture of openness created by the Children (Northern Ireland) Order 1995 has permeated adoption practice. Freeing and open adoption involving some degree of on-going contact with the birth family, may be viewed as potentially incompatible and hence militate against the full use of this part of the legislation.'[1]

A Freeing Order can be made either with the consent of the parents[2] or without their consent.[3] Even if the parents consent to the Freeing Order application the court is still under a duty to ensure that it is in the child's best interests that he or she is freed for adoption.[4] If the parents consent, their agreement must be evidenced in the prescribed form.[5]

---

[1] At pp 12–13.
[2] Adoption (Northern Ireland) Order 1987, art 17. However, a mother cannot consent to the Freeing Order application within the first 6 weeks of the child's life (art 16(3)). This particular rule can sometimes arise in non-Hague Convention Intercountry Adoptions. See, for example, *Re R (Inter Country Adoption: Consent of Foreign Mother: Arrangements and payment)* (2 May 2003, unreported), High Court.
[3] Adoption (Northern Ireland) Order 1987, art 18. On unmarried fathers and consent, see para 8.57.
[4] Adoption (Northern Ireland) Order 1987, art 9.
[5] RSC Order 54, Form 3 and CCR Order 50, Form 250.

8.46 On the making of the Freeing Order, either with or without the consent of the parents, all parental rights are vested in the adoption agency, so that the Freeing Order has the effect of extinguishing parental rights and duties as if it were an Adoption Order.[1] Where the parents are withholding their consent to the making of the Freeing Order, the court can dispense with their consent on the same basis as it may in an application for an Adoption Order (see below). It would appear, from the statistics at any rate, that parents do not have a great chance of successfully defending a Freeing Order application. The Children Order Advisory Committee noted that research showed that 94% of all Freeing Order applications in the research study period were granted.[2]

[1]   Adoption (Northern Ireland) Order 1987, arts 17(3) and 18(3). If the parents consent, the application for the order will be made jointly by them and by the adoption agency.
[2]   COAC, Third report, p 49 quoting research by Kelly and Ince, 2000.

8.47   One of the issues that falls to be considered on the making of the Freeing Order is whether the child's parents should be allowed to maintain contact with the child. It is open to the court to make a Contact Order (under the Children (Northern Ireland) Order 1995),[1] although in a number of cases the courts have made use of the 'no order' principle,[2] allowing the Trust the flexibility to deal with the situation as it evolves.[3]

A Freeing Order can be revoked, on application by a parent, if the child has not been placed for adoption within 12 months of the making of the order, on the ground that the former parent wishes to resume parental rights and duties.[4]

Where a Care Order is being sought along with a Freeing Order, the court must deal with the Care Order application first, and, if satisfied that the threshold criteria have been made out, only then should it proceed to consider the Freeing Order application.[5]

[1]   On Contact Orders, see chapter 9, para 9.104.
[2]   See chapter 6, para 6.38.
[3]   See, for example, *Re C (Freeing for Adoption: Contact)*, *Re K (Care Order: Residence Order: Freeing for Adoption)* (17 May 2002, unreported), High Court (Family Division), Gillen J and *Re R1 (Care Order: Freeing without Parental Consent)* [2002] NI Fam 25, High Court (Family Division).
[4]   Adoption (Northern Ireland) Order 1987, art 20.
[5]   *Re D (simultaneous applications for Care Order and Freeing Order)* [1999] 2 FLR 49, cited with approval by Gillen J in *Re G and S (Care Order) (Freeing without Consent) (Contact)* High Court, 31 May 2001, transcript available on Lexis.

Adoption Order

8.48   An Adoption Order[1] can only be made if there is a Freeing Order in existence with regard to the child, or the relevant parental consent has been obtained[2] or can be dispensed with. The making of the Adoption Order extinguishes all parental rights and duties, and they then vest in the adoptive parents.

Furthermore, in order to be eligible to make such an application, the child in question must have been placed with the prospective adopters for a certain period of time. If the prospective adopters are related to the child then this period is 13 consecutive weeks,[3] but if they are not, then the period of continuous placement is for one year.[4]

[1]   The application for an Adoption Order is made under r 15 where the application is to the High Court and under r 14 if to the county court.
[2]   Parental consent must be in the form set out in the Adoption Rules, Form 3.

3   Although the child cannot be adopted before it is 19 weeks old: Adoption (Northern Ireland) Order 1987, art 13(1)(b).
4   Adoption (Northern Ireland) Order 1987, art 13.

8.49   Where it is intended that a child be privately adopted, the prospective adopters must give three months notice, prior to the making of the Adoption Order, to the appropriate Trust to allow it to compile a report on the suitability of the prospective adopters.[1] This is referred to as the Notice of Intention. A child who is the subject of such notice is considered to be a 'protected child' and is to be visited by the Trust from time to time.[2] This report investigates the suitability of the prospective adopters and assesses 'article 9' matters,[3] as well as investigating whether the child was unlawfully placed for adoption, in contravention of article 11. A child adopted from another country, which is not a signatory to the Hague Convention on Intercountry Adoption,[4] will also become a 'protected child' when the child in question arrives in Northern Ireland, because such adoptions are not automatically recognised in Northern Ireland. Therefore, pending the resolution of its legal status such a child would be treated in the same manner as other 'protected children'.

1   Adoption (Northern Ireland) Order 1987, art 22.
2   Adoption (Northern Ireland) Order 1987, art 34. A person with custody of a protected child is required to keep the Trust informed of any change in his or her address. Adoption (Northern Ireland) Order 1987, art 39.
3   See para 8.25.
4   On non-Hague Convention country adoptions, see para 8.78.

8.50   In making the Adoption Order the court is concerned with two matters, namely: (1) whether the adoption would be in the child's best interests and, as referred to above; (2) whether consent has been obtained or may be dispensed with. In concluding whether adoption is in the best interests of the child, a court is sometimes faced with a choice between long-term fostering and adoption. The practical effect for the child may appear the same superficially, in that a person other than its parents will rear him or her. However, the legal effect is different, a difference neatly expressed by Ormrod LJ in *Re H*:[1]

'... adoption gives us total security and makes the child part of our family, and places us in parental control of the child; long term fostering leaves us exposed to changes of view of the local authority, it leaves us exposed to applications and so on, by the natural parent.'

This view was quoted with approval by MacDermott LJ in the case of *Re ML (Adoption: Wardship)*.[2]

1   (1981) 3 FLR 386, CA.
2   (31 October 1997, unreported), High Court.

Dispensing with parental consent

8.51   Parental agreement can be dispensed with, in the case of either a Freeing Order or Adoption Order application, where the parent or guardian:[1]
- cannot be found or is incapable of giving agreement;

- is withholding consent unreasonably;
- has persistently failed without reasonable cause to discharge parental duties;
- has abandoned or neglected the child;
- has persistently ill-treated the child;
- has seriously ill-treated the child, and rehabilitation of the child within the home is not possible.

[1]   Adoption (Northern Ireland) Order 1987, art 16(2).

8.52   The most commonly invoked of these conditions is that the parents are withholding their consent unreasonably. The issue of whether consent could be dispensed with because the parents could not be found was dealt with in *Re R (Inter-Country: Consent of Foreign Mother: Arrangements and payment)*, in which the judge relied on *Re A (adoption of Russian Child)*.[1] In assessing whether the parents cannot be found, the court will examine the actions of the authorities to determine that all reasonable and practical steps have been taken to locate them.

[1]   [2000] 1 FLR 539.

Consent unreasonably withheld

8.53   Consideration of what amounts to the unreasonable withholding of consent will, of course, depend on the circumstances of each case and what is considered to be the child's best interests. However, some general guidance may be offered. In an oft-quoted passage, the late Mr Justice Higgins in *Re Warnock* observed:

> 'There are many cases dealing with the dispensation of parental agreement on the ground that it has been unreasonably withheld. In the leading authority of *Re W (an infant)* [1971] AC 682, it was held that the question is whether at the time of the hearing the parent is withholding his or her agreement unreasonably. The test is reasonableness and not anything else. It is not culpability or indifference or failure to discharge parental duties. It is reasonableness in the context of the totality of the circumstances (see Lord Hailsham's speech in *Re W* at page 699B). It is an objective test: the court must look and see whether it is reasonable or unreasonable according to what a reasonable parent in the parent's place would do in all the circumstances. In the later House of Lords case of *Re D (an infant) (adoption: parents consent)* [1977] AC 602 at 625G, Lord Wilberforce said that this involved considering how a parent in the circumstances of the actual parent but (hypothetically) endowed with a mind and temperament capable of making reasonable decisions would approach a complex question involving a judgment as to the present and the future and the probable impact of these on the child.' [1]

Lord Hailsham's own views in *Re W (an infant)* add further to our understanding of judicial approaches to this issue. He offered the view that:

> '... it does not follow from the fact that the test is reasonableness that any court is entitled to simply to substitute its own view with that of the parent. In my

opinion it should be extremely careful to guard against this error. Two reasonable parents can perfectly reasonably come to opposite conclusions on the same set of facts without forfeiting their title to be regarded as reasonable. The question in any given case is whether a parental veto comes within the band of possible reasonable decisions and not whether it is right or mistaken. Not every reasonable exercise of judgment is right but not every mistaken exercise of judgment is unreasonable. There is a band of decision within which no court should seek to replace the individual's judgment with its own.'[2]

[1] (1 May 1992, unreported).
[2] [1971] AC 682 at 700D.

8.54 Further gloss on the reasonableness test in adoption proceedings was provided in *re K (Care Order; Residence Order; Freeing for Adoption)*,[1] in which Gillen J made reference to two relevant English authorities:

'In *re C (A Minor) (Adoption: Parental Agreement; Contact)*[2] the court suggested that the test may be approached by the judge asking himself whether having regard to the evidence and applying the current values of our society, the advantages of adoption for the welfare of the child appear sufficiently strong to justify overriding the views and interests of the objecting parent. That is an approach that has received further judicial approval in *Re F (Adoption: Freeing Order)*.[3] I consider that Herman McFarlane, Children Law and Practice, Section H at paragraph 124 sets out the appropriate criteria as follows:

(1) The reasonableness of the parents' refusal to consent is to be judged at the date of the hearing.
(2) The judge must take account of all the circumstances of the case.
(3) Whilst the welfare of the child must be taken into account, it is not the sole or necessarily paramount criterion.
(4) The test is an objective one – could a reasonable parent in the position of this parent withhold consent.
(5) The test is reasonableness and nothing else.
(6) The court must be wary not to substitute its own view for that of the reasonable parent.
(7) There is a band of differing reasons, each of which may be reasonable in any given case.'

Gillen J considered further that the mother's incapacity – she had a severe mental impairment and could not instruct solicitors herself and the Official Solicitor had been appointed to represent her interests – was an element in the reasonableness or unreasonableness of her withholding consent, although no more than that.[4] The court must look at the hypothetical 'reasonable parent' with appropriate insight into all the circumstances of the case. In the event he considered that she was unreasonably withholding her consent.

[1] (17 May 2002, unreported), High Court (Family Division), Gillen J.

² [1993] 2 FLR 260, CA.
³ [2000] 2 FLR 505, CA.
⁴ See *Re G and S (Care Order) (Freeing Without Consent) (Contact)* (31 May 2001, unreported), High Court, Gillen J for a similar view.

8.55   *Re Caoimhe Cosgrave*[1] was a case in which the court declined to make the Adoption Order, on the basis that the child's violent father had made progress in controlling his temper and that, with time and effort, there were signs that the parents could establish a relationship with the child and thus the court could not conclude that their consent was being unreasonably withheld.

By contrast, a mother, who had a history of violence and alcohol dependency, making her a vulnerable person, and who refused to consent to the making of a Freeing Order for her child was considered to be unreasonably refusing her consent. Although she had made some progress in tackling her alcoholism and developing parenting skills, experts considered that it would take up to six years before the mother would be in position to care for the child, and consequently, the Freeing Order was made.[2]

¹ (9 December 1999, unreported), High Court, Coghlin J.
² *Re C (Freeing for Adoption: Contact)* (12 January 2002, unreported), Gillen J.

8.56   It is generally irrelevant to the issue of whether consent has been unreasonably withheld that the parents nurse a grievance against the authorities because of the manner in which they have been treated. Only in rare circumstances will a sense of grievance justifiably have an important effect upon a reasonable parent such that they decide not to give consent to the adoption.[1]

Where the decision of the court to dispense with the consent of the parents is appealed the court must be satisfied, before it will overturn the first instance decision, that the decision was 'plainly wrong' and not simply that on balance the trial judge ought to have made a different decision.[2]

¹ *Re ML (Adoption; Wardship)* (31 October 1997, unreported), High Court (Family Division) quoting, with approval, *Re B (a minor)* [1990] 2 FLR 383, CA.
² *Re C and L, Ms M and Mrs O v North and West Belfast HSST* (8 February 2000, unreported), NI CA, Nicholson LJ.

Unmarried fathers and consent

8.57   Where the parties are married the consent of both parents is required. However, where they are unmarried, and the father has not acquired parental responsibility,[1] then it is not necessary to acquire his consent before making the Freeing Order or the Adoption Order. All reasonable steps must be taken to locate the father, however, and his views ascertained.[2] Before the court may make the Adoption Order it must be satisfied that the father has no intention of applying for a Parental Responsibility Order or a Residence Order in respect of the child and that even if he did apply for them, they would be refused.[2]

¹ On parental responsibility, see chapter 6, para 6.43.

² Adoption (Northern Ireland) Order 1987, art 17(6), as inserted by the Children (Northern Ireland) Order 1995.

8.58   Convention right, article 8 also has a relevance for unmarried fathers in the context of adoption, because even though domestic law does not require their consent unless they have parental responsibility, they may nonetheless have a right to family life with the child that the courts must consider before determining the application. The European Court of Human Rights, in *Söderback v Sweden*,[1] has concluded that article 8 can apply to unmarried fathers, but decided in that case that interference with his right to family life was justified as being proportionate to the legitimate aim being pursued and within the State's wide margin of appreciation. Whether the unmarried father has a right to family life with the child that must be assessed will depend on the facts and the nature of the relationship he has enjoyed with the child, and a father with no de facto ties to the child will not be allowed to rely on his article 8 rights.[2]

¹   [1999] 1 FLR 250, [1998] EHRLR 343.

²   *Re H (a child) (adoption: disclosure), Re G (a child) (adoption: disclosure)* [2001] 1 FCR 726 and see *Re J (adoption: contacting father)* [2003] EWHC 199 (Fam), [2003] 1 FLR 933 where the High Court granted a declaration that the local authority was not obliged to contact a father who knew nothing of the child's birth.

8.59   The Northern Ireland courts have had to deal with the unique circumstances created by the death of a mother, who had not consented to the adoption, where the parents of the child had been not married at the time of the child's birth. The father did not have parental responsibility and indeed his application for a Parental Responsibility Order had been previously denied, nor was there any other person with parental responsibility. The court concluded that it could disregard the consent issue and focus solely on whether adoption is in the child's best interests and other related article 9 matters.[1]

¹   *Re NK and TM (Requirement to dispense with parental consent under Article 18 of the Adoption Order (Northern Ireland) 1987)* (16 January 2002, unreported), High Court, Gillen J.

Care plans

8.60   Children who are the subject of adoption proceedings must have care plans developed for them, and these plans must be reviewed periodically. These care plans are similar to those developed for children who are the subject of Care Order or Supervision Order applications.[1] The SSI's inspection of adoption services concluded that most children had a care plan and 'looked-after children' reviews had been convened within, or just outside, the appropriate timescale, but that the standard of them ranged widely, from poor to excellent.[2]

¹   See chapter 6, para 6.140.

²   Executive Summary of 'Adopting Best Care' (2002) SSI, p 8.

Intercountry adoption

8.61   Intercountry adoption is the term that applies to adoption between different countries and there are two types of intercountry adoption: adoption between countries both of which are parties to the 1993 Hague Convention on Intercountry Adoption,[1] and non-Hague Convention adoptions where the other country is not a party to that Convention. The former type of adoption is governed by the Adoption (Intercountry Aspects) Act (Northern Ireland) 2001, while the 1987 Order governs non-Hague Convention adoptions. The latter situation arises because the Adoption Order made by the authorities in the non-Hague Convention country is not recognised in Northern Ireland so the child must be formally adopted, in Northern Ireland, under the 1987 Order, for its new legal status to be recognised.

[1]   Its full title is the Convention on Protection of Children and Co-operation in respect of Intercountry Adoption. The Convention forms a Schedule to the Adoption (Intercountry Aspects) Act (Northern Ireland) 2001.

8.62   One matter that marks out intercountry adoption from adoption within Northern Ireland is that, quite recently, many of the Trusts have begun to exercise a power in the 1987 Order to charge reasonable fees for their services in intercountry adoptions. A fee of £3,000 is charged for services from the 'home study report' to the 'welfare supervision stage' in non-Hague Convention adoptions, and from the 'home study report' to the placement of the child in Hague Convention adoptions.

Adopting from a Hague Convention country

8.63   The Hague Convention on Adoption has a number of objects, namely:[1]

'(a)   to establish safeguards to ensure that intercountry adoptions take place in the best interests of the child and with respect for his or her fundamental rights as recognised in international law;

(b)   to establish a system of co-operation amongst Contracting States to ensure that those safeguards are respected and thereby prevent the abduction, the sale of, or traffic in children;

(c)   to secure the recognition in Contracting States of adoptions made in accordance with the Convention.'

[1]   Hague Convention on Protection of Children and Co-operation in Respect of Intercountry Adoption, art 1. See the Adoption (Intercountry Aspects) Act (Northern Ireland) 2001, Sch.

8.64   The advantage to the prospective adopters of adopting from a Hague Convention country is that the Adoption Order made overseas will be recognised in Northern Ireland.[1] It is also possible for the prospective adopters to adopt a child under the Hague Convention and have the Northern Ireland courts, rather than the overseas courts, make the Convention Adoption Order.

[1]   Adoption (Northern Ireland) Order 1987, art 58ZB, as inserted by the Adoption (Intercountry Aspects) Act (Northern Ireland) 2001, s 13.

8.65 Where prospective adopters wish to adopt a child from another Hague Convention country they must first apply to an adoption agency for a determination of their eligibility to adopt and an assessment of their suitability.[1] The adoption agency is under a duty to provide a counselling service to them, as well as explaining the legal implications of adopting a child under the Convention.[2] Where the agency considers that the prospective adopters are eligible and suitable, it must then gather the information required under the Adoption Agency Regulations (see above) as it would if the adoption were a domestic one, that is it must prepare a 'home study report'.[3] In particular, the agency must obtain written reports from the prospective adopters' doctor, a report about the prospective adopters' home, as well as reports of interviews with referees for the prospective adopters.[4] This report sets out the agency's view that the prospective adopters are eligible to adopt a child under the law of the Convention country from which the child will be adopted, as well as providing an assessment of the prospective adopters' suitability as adoptive parents.[5]

[1] Intercountry Adoption (Hague Convention) Regulations 2003, reg 3(1), The basic requirements are that the prospective adopters must be aged over 21 years and resident in the 'British Islands', defined legislatively as the United Kingdom, Channel Islands and the Isle of Man, for at least one year.

[2] Intercountry Adoption (Hague Convention) Regulations 2003, reg 5.

[3] Part VI, VII of the Schedule to the Regulations.

[4] Intercountry Adoption (Hague Convention) Regulations 2003, reg 6. In the event that the prospective adopters are applying to an agency that is not the Trust for the area in which they live, the agency must also obtain a report from that Trust.

[5] Intercountry Adoption (Hague Convention) Regulations 2003, reg 6(4).

8.66 This report is first sent to the prospective adopters who have 28 days in which they may make any observations they consider pertinent, after which time the report is furnished to the adoption panel.[1] If the agency decides that the applicants are not suitable they have 28 days within which to make further representations.[2] If further representations are made, the matter is referred back to the adoption panel, which makes a fresh recommendation about the applicants' suitability.[3] The agency re-considers this recommendation and either confirms its original view or alters it conclusion. As with domestic adoption, the panel simply makes a recommendation to the agency and the final decision rests with the agency.[4]

[1] Intercountry Adoption (Hague Convention) Regulations 2003, reg 6(5) and (6).

[2] Intercountry Adoption (Hague Convention) Regulations 2003, reg 8(4).

[3] Intercountry Adoption (Hague Convention) Regulations 2003, reg 8(6) and (7).

[4] Intercountry Adoption (Hague Convention) Regulations 2003, reg 8(1).

Central Authority

8.67 In countries where the Hague Convention applies each jurisdiction has a Central Authority through which relevant information is communicated. The Central Authority for Northern Ireland is the Department of Health and Personal Social Services and Public Safety, and where an adoption agency considers prospective adopters suitable to adopt under the Hague Convention process, it sends this information to the Central Authority, along with the original report prepared for its adoption panel.[1] The Central Authority in Northern Ireland then transmits this information to the Central Authority of the State of Origin (ie the country from which the child will be adopted), along with a certificate that the prospective adopters have been assessed as being eligible and suitable to adopt and that the child may reside in the UK.[2]

[1]   Intercountry Adoption (Hague Convention) Regulations 2003, reg 9(1).
[2]   Intercountry Adoption (Hague Convention) Regulations 2003, reg 9(3) and Sch 1.

Article 16 report

8.68   In turn the Northern Ireland Central Authority will receive a report from the State of Origin Central Authority (SOCA), referred to as the 'Article 16 report',[1] which it then transfers to the adoption agency.[2] The 'Article 16 report' includes information about the child's identity, adoptability, background, social environment, family history, medical history and any special needs the child has. It also gives due consideration to the child's upbringing and to his or her ethnic, religious and cultural background, ensures that all necessary consents have been obtained and that the placement is in the child's best interests.

[1]   So called because it is required by art 16 of the Convention.
[2]   Intercountry Adoption (Hague Convention) Regulations 2003, reg 10.

8.69   The agency discusses the content of the 'Article 16 report' with the prospective adopters.[1] It then confirms with the Central Authority that the prospective adopters wish to continue with the adoption and the Central Authority in turn notifies the SOCA that it is prepared to agree with the SOCA that the adoption is to proceed.[2] The next stage in the process is the confirmation by the SOCA, under article 17(c) of the Convention, that the agreement to adopt has been made. However, at this point the child has not been adopted. In order for the adoption to be recognised in Northern Ireland a court in the child's State of Origin must go on to consider whether the requirements for adoption in the country are met and make the Adoption Order.

[1]   Intercountry Adoption (Hague Convention) Regulations 2003, reg 10(2).
[2]   Intercountry Adoption (Hague Convention) Regulations 2003, reg 10(4). Part of the information transmitted at this point includes confirmation that the child will be allowed to reside in, and remain in the UK.

Duties of the adoption agency and prospective adopters

8.70   In the meantime, in preparation for the child's arrival in Northern Ireland, the adoption agency must notify a range of medical and other practitioners, including a paediatrician, the prospective adopters' GP and the relevant Education and Library Board of the child's medical history and related matters.[1]

[1]   Intercountry Adoption (Hague Convention) Regulations 2003, reg 11.

Convention Adoption Order not made in the State of Origin

8.71 Recall that in Hague Convention adoptions, the Adoption Order may be made in the child's country of origin or in Northern Ireland. Where the former applies no further legal steps are required in Northern Ireland. However, in the latter case the prospective adopters must proceed to apply for an Adoption Order in Northern Ireland. In such a case the child is brought to Northern Ireland on foot of an article 17(c) agreement and the prospective adopters have certain duties to fulfil.

8.72 Within 14 days of the child's arrival in the UK, the prospective adopters must notify the Trust with responsibility for their home area of their intention to apply for an Adoption Order.[1] This notification means that the child becomes a 'protected child'[2] and the agency acquires duties to safeguard his or her well-being.[3] Furthermore they must also ensure that the child is not allowed contact with any other person, other than under a Contact Order, and must ensure that the child is not to be known by a new surname and that it is not to be removed from the UK.[4]

[1] Intercountry Adoption (Hague Convention) Regulations 2003, reg 13.
[2] Adoption (Northern Ireland) Order 1987, art 33.
[3] Adoption (Northern Ireland) Order 1987, art 34. See para 8.49.
[4] Intercountry Adoption (Hague Convention) Regulations 2003, reg 14, although it can be removed for periods of less than one month: reg 14(4).

8.73 If the prospective adopters no longer wish to adopt the child, then he or she is to be received into the care of the Trust within seven days of the prospective adopters giving notice of that decision. Indeed, if the Trust is not happy that the continued placement of the child is in his or her best interests, it may demand that the prospective adopters surrender the child to it. In circumstances where the placement breaks down, the Trust may re-place the child with other prospective adopters.[1] If, however, it concludes that it would not be in the child's best interests to be adopted in Northern Ireland, then it must return the child to his State of Origin.[2] Where any of these events occur, the Trust must inform the Central Authority of the developments.

[1] Intercountry Adoption (Hague Convention) Regulations 2003, reg 17(2).
[2] Intercountry Adoption (Hague Convention) Regulations 2003, reg 17(5).

Convention Adoption Order

8.74 A Convention Adoption Order is applied for under the 1987 Order[1] and in order for a child to be adopted in this way, he or she must placed with the prospective adopters for six months.[2] On the making of that Order, the court sends a copy to the Central Authority. The Central Authority then issues a Schedule 2 certificate[3] confirming that a Convention Adoption Order has been made and this is then furnished to the SOCA, the adoptive parents, the adoption agency and, if different from the agency, the relevant Trust.[4] Where the court refuses to make a Convention Adoption Order, then the Trust must prepare a plan for the child's permanent care.[5] The child must be surrendered to the Trust within the period prescribed by the court when it refuses to make the Adoption Order.

[1] Under art 16A, inserted by the Adoption (Intercountry Aspects) Act (Northern Ireland) 2001.
[2] Intercountry (Hague Convention) Act (Northern Ireland) 2001, s 9, amending the Adoption (Northern Ireland) Order 1987, art 13.
[3] Intercountry Adoption (Hague Convention) Regulations 2003, Sch 2.
[4] Intercountry Adoption (Hague Convention) Regulations 2003, reg 20(3).
[5] Intercountry Adoption (Hague Convention) Regulations 2003, reg 21.

Adopting to a Hague Convention country

8.75 It will be less likely that a child permanently resident in the UK will be adopted to another Hague Convention country, but the 2001 Act allows for this possibility. Such a situation arises where a child is the subject of a Freeing Order and a Trust has considered the possibilities of adoption within the UK, Isle of Man and Channel Islands, and considers that adoption outside those countries may be in the child's best interests.[1]

[1] Intercountry Adoption (Hague Convention) Regulations 2003, reg 23.

8.76 The agency must refer the matter to an adoption panel together with the original documents sent to it under regulation 7(2)(e) of the Adoption Agencies Regulations,[1] and a report of a social worker as to why adoption outside the UK, Isle of Man and Channel Islands, may be in the child's best interests.[2] As with domestic adoption, the panel considers the reference having regard to the duty to promote the welfare of the child under Article 9 of the 1987 Order and makes a recommendation to the agency, with the agency having the ultimate responsibility of making the decision.[3] Where the agency concludes that the child should be the subject of a Hague Convention adoption, it must prepare an 'Article 16 report', which will include information about the child's identity, suitability for adoption, background, family history, medical history and the reasons for the agency's decision.[4]

[1] Ie the medical practitioner's report, the information on the child and its parents and the agencies observations on these.
[2] Intercountry Adoption (Hague Convention) Regulations 2003, reg 23(2). This referral to the Panel must be done within 12 months of the Trust's decision that the child's best interests are served by adoption, unless there are exceptional circumstances: reg 23(3).
[3] Intercountry Adoption (Hague Convention) Regulations 2003, reg 24 and 25.
[4] Intercountry Adoption (Hague Convention) Regulations 2003, reg 29.

8.77 The 'Article 16 report' is then communicated to the Central Authority, together with evidence that the child has been freed for adoption, and written observations relating to the child's upbringing and his or her religious, cultural and ethnic background as well as the social work report which accompanied the referral to the adoption panel.[1] The Central Authority then transmits this information to the Central Authority of the Receiving State. The way is open then for the two Central Authorities to make an article 17(c) agreement, although the Northern Ireland Central Authority cannot make such an agreement until the agency confirms that the prospective adopters have visited the child and that both they and the agency are content to proceed with the adoption.[2] No placement of the child can be made by the agency until the Central Authority confirms that the article 17(c) agreement has been made.[3] The Convention Adoption Order can be made in Northern Ireland and if so, copies must be sent to the Receiving State's Central Authority, the adoptive parents and the agency.[4] Where the Adoption Order is made in the Receiving State, the Central Authority is required to furnish the agency with a copy of the Adoption Order, when the Receiving State's Central Authority transmits a copy to it.[5]

[1] Intercountry Adoption (Hague Convention) Regulations 2003, reg 29(2).
[2] Intercountry Adoption (Hague Convention) Regulations 2003, reg 29(5).
[3] Intercountry Adoption (Hague Convention) Regulations 2003, reg 29(6).
[4] Intercountry Adoption (Hague Convention) Regulations 2003, reg 31(2) and (3).
[5] Intercountry Adoption (Hague Convention) Regulations 2003, reg 31(4).

Adopting from a non-Hague Convention country

8.78   As outlined above, where a child is adopted from a non-Hague Convention country the Adoption Order made in that country is not recognised in Northern Ireland, and thus the child must be the subject of an Adoption Order application under the 1987 Order. Such adoptions will be subject to the same legal and procedural requirements of any such application under the 1987 Order.

Restrictions on bringing children to the UK

8.79   Prospective adopters cannot simply operate independently of the adoption service in Northern Ireland and proceed to adopt children from abroad whenever they wish. They must commence the process by applying to an adoption agency for assessment of their suitability to become adopters, and where they bring a child into the UK for the purposes of adoption without meeting certain requirements they will be guilty of an offence,[1] unless they are related to the child, which will be unlikely. The Adoption of Children from Overseas Regulations (Northern Ireland) 2002 set out these requirements. First, the prospective adopters must have applied to the adoption agency. Secondly, the adoption agency must have approved the prospective adopters, and, thirdly, the Secretary of State for Health must have notified the prospective adopters, in writing, that he or she is prepared to issue a certificate that they have been assessed and approved, and that the child will be allowed to enter the UK if the adoption is completed.[2] Furthermore, prospective adopters must notify the relevant Trust, within 14 days of the child's arrival in the UK, of their intention to apply for an Adoption Order.[3] This will be done by filing a Notice of Intention which is similar to that filed in private adoptions in domestic law.

[1] Adoption (Northern Ireland) Order 1987, art 58ZA, as inserted by Adoption (Intercountry Aspects) Act (Northern Ireland) Act 2001.
[2] Adoption of Children from Overseas Regulations (Northern Ireland) 2002, reg 3(2).
[3] Adoption of Children from Overseas Regulations (Northern Ireland) 2002, reg 3(3).

8.80   As with domestic adoption, a 'home study report' is prepared, by the agency in intercountry adoption for the adoption panel's purposes. Assessment of the suitability of the prospective adopters is carried out in the normal way by the adoption panel and the adoption agency,[1] with the agency communicating its final decision to the

Department as to whether it approves the prospective adopters.[2] As with domestic adoption, the panel makes a recommendation to the agency as to whether the applicants are suitable adoptive parents, but the final decision lies with the agency.

[1]   Adoption of Children from Overseas Regulations (Northern Ireland) 2002, reg 4(2).
[2]   Adoption of Children from Overseas Regulations (Northern Ireland) 2002, reg 4(2)(b).

Legal process

8.81   As noted above, the legal process is commenced by the applicants serving a Notice of Intention to adopt[1] within 14 days of the child's arrival in the UK. Of course, the Adoption Order cannot be made until the requisite period of placement has elapsed, namely twelve months,[2] but the application for an Adoption Order can be made before then. While the child is living in Northern Ireland awaiting adoption, it is a 'protected child'[3] and the agency has duties to secure the child's well-being, which are fulfilled in the manner described previously in respect of private adoption.[4] At the hearing of the Adoption Order application the court is concerned with exactly the same matters with which it is concerned in Adoption Order applications for children adopted from within Northern Ireland.[5]

[1]   Under the Adoption (Northern Ireland) Order 1987, art 22(1).
[2]   Adoption (Northern Ireland) Order 1987, art 13(2).
[3]   Adoption (Northern Ireland) Order 1987, art 33.
[4]   See para 8.49.
[5]   See para 8.25.

8.82   A number of legal difficulties can arise with such adoptions, as illustrated in the case of *In Re R (Inter country Adoption: Consent of Foreign Mother: Arrangements and Payment)*.[1] In that case the couple had adopted a child from Russia using an international firm as an intermediary, paying this intermediary almost US\$ 10,000. Before travelling to Russia for the adoption proceedings, the couple contacted their local adoption agency and had a 'home study report' prepared on them. This report was available to the Russian court. The Adoption Order was made and the child brought to Northern Ireland, where the couple then applied for an Adoption Order under the 1987 Order, as they were required to do. In paying sums of money in respect of the adoption, and in facilitating arrangements for placing the child where they were not the child's relatives and thus could not claim that it was a private adoption, the couple were in breach of articles 59 and 11 respectively of the 1987 Order. Breach of these provisions is a criminal offence. However, the judge adopted the approach taken by the English courts in *Re C (adoption: legality)*[2] and considered that the breaches in this case were technical and that the best interests of the child dictated that he make the Adoption Order and disregard these breaches.

[1]   (2 May 2003, unreported), High Court, Gillen J.
[2]   [1999] Fam 128, [1999] 1 FLR 370.

8.83   The English courts have had occasion to consider the phenomenon of 'independent social workers' (ie not employed by an adoption agency) making 'home study reports' for the purposes of intercountry adoptions and have expressed dismay that there appear to have been no prosecutions, under the English equivalent of article 11 of the 1987 Order, for this sort of activity. [1]

[1] *Re M (adoption: international adoption trade)* [2003] EWHC 219 (Fam), [2003] 1 FLR 1111.

Disclosure of records

8.84   An adopted person is entitled, when he or she reaches the age of 18, to obtain disclosure of all records relating to their adoption, sufficient to allow them to obtain a birth certificate.[1] However, people adopted before 10 December 1987 must be referred by the Registrar General, to a counselling service before the information will be released to them. Persons adopted after that date have a choice as to whether to avail themselves of counselling services. Very little information may now be available for persons who were adopted prior to the implementation of the 1987 Order, particularly if they were the subject of private adoptions.

[1] Adoption (Northern Ireland) Order 1987, art 54.

8.85   The Registrar General is required to maintain an Adopted Children's Register,[1] which contains details about the child's birth name, gender, place and date of birth, name, address and occupation of birth parents, and the date of the Adoption Order and the court which made that order. It is this information that adopted children may apply to have released to them after they attain the age of majority. The adopted person can then, if they wish, ask the court to reveal the agency which was involved in the adoption.

[1] Adoption (Northern Ireland) Order 1987, art 50.

8.86   The Registrar General also maintains an Adoption Contact Register which is divided into two parts.[1] The first part contains the details of persons who have been adopted and who wish to contact their relatives, while the second part contains the details of those who were the birth parents or relatives of adopted children and who are amenable to being contacted by the adopted child. The Registrar General is required to transmit to an adopted person whose name is entered in Part I of the register the name and address of any relative in respect of whom there is an entry in Part II of the register.[2] As the Registrar General's Office explains, 'a register provides a safe and confidential way for birth parents and other relatives to assure an adopted person that contact would be welcome and to give a current address.'[3] However, the contact register has only succeeded in uniting two sets of people,[4] although it has only been in operation since 1996.

[1] Adoption (Northern Ireland) Order 1987, art 54A, as inserted by the Children (Northern Ireland) Order 1995.
[2] Adoption (Northern Ireland) Order 1987, art 54A(9), as inserted by the Children (Northern Ireland) Order 1995.
[3] Information leaflet entitled 'Information for adopted people and their relatives', Registrar General's Office, p 2.
[4] Paul Martin, *A Better Future – 50 Years of Child Care in Northern Ireland 1950–2000*, DHSSPS, p 68.

Chapter 9

Law of Relationship Breakdown

Introduction

9.1   It is important, from a practical point of view, that social workers are familiar with those aspects of family law that deal with relationship breakdown, given that a majority of them are employed in the field of family and child care[1] and given the development in recent years of what might be loosely called a family court system, arising from the interconnected nature of most 'family proceedings'.[2] As discussed in chapter 6, 'family proceedings' applications are made either to the Family Proceedings Court or, if another application has been made to the Care Centre or the Family Division of the High Court, to those courts.[3] Transfer of cases between those three courts is also possible.

---

[1]   'Crossing Borders' Social Work Mobility Study, National Social Work Qualifications Board and Central Council for Education and Training of Social Workers (Northern Ireland) 2001.

[2]   Family proceedings are defined in the Children (Northern Ireland) Order 1995, art 8(3) and explained in chapter 6, para 6.28.

[3]   See para 6.45.

9.2   In this chapter, social workers are given an introduction to the main legal provisions relating to the breakdown of marital and non-marital relationships, including the law of divorce, the law relating to the rearing of children, the division of financial assets, and child support, as well as the remedies open to domestic violence survivors. The purpose of the chapter is to give social workers grounding in family law matters of relevance to their clients, thereby deepening their understanding of their clients' legal situations. Furthermore, social workers may occasionally be involved in these legal proceedings as court welfare officers.

As explained in chapter 6,[1] the remedies referred to in this chapter can be referred to as private law remedies, to distinguish them from the public law orders explored in that chapter. To give social workers some perspective of the impact of private law orders and remedies on their clients' lives, it is worth noting that applications for private law remedies form a considerable greater part of the courts' workload than similar public law applications. In 2001–02, 5,108 applications were made for the former and 938 for the latter.[2]

¹ See para 6.7.
² Northern Ireland Court Service Annual Report 2001–02, Table F1, p 130.

Court welfare officers and reports

9.3 As explained in chapter 6,[1] court welfare officers are not employed by a dedicated agency as is the case in England and Wales, but are usually social workers employed by the relevant Trust. Court Welfare Reports are not commonly sought in private law family proceedings, as there usually is no necessity for such a report. A court might order the preparation of a Welfare Report in private law cases where the parents of a child are making serious allegations against each other about the treatment and upbringing of the child, or where an independent assessment of the parties and any children was necessary in the court's view.[2] The timescale within which Court Welfare Reports are produced for private law proceedings is a matter that has concerned the Children Order Advisory Committee.[3]

¹ See para 6.30.
² See, for example, *Re A (abduction: declaration of wrongful removal)* (17 January 2002, unreported), High Court, Gillen J, where the Family Proceedings Court in hearing the Contact Order and Parental Responsibility Order applications ordered the preparation of a Court Welfare Report.
³ See chapter 3, para 3.50.

Guardians ad litem

9.4 While guardians ad litem normally compile reports in public law family proceedings and in adoption proceedings, their expertise might be utilised in other private law cases where the future care and upbringing of the children was in issue, although it is not common. These cases usually involve applications for Residence Orders where the child is in care and guardians are appointed to about a dozen such cases per annum.[1]

¹ For example, guardians ad litem completed nine such applications in 2001/02: NIGALA Annual Report, Table 2A, p 54.

Relationships protected in law

9.5 In the past it could validly be said that family law was concerned primarily, and sometimes exclusively, with married couples. That is no longer the case and some commentators now suggest that parenthood, rather than marriage, is the central defining relationship of contemporary family law.[1] The changing orientation of family law may be said to be a consequence of, and a reaction to, the changing patterns of contemporary family life. Statistics reveal that the number of marriages contracted per annum is falling,[2] the percentage of children born to unmarried parents has increased to approximately one third of all births each year,[3] while the birth rate has declined over the last twenty years,[4] for example. Examples of this focus on parenthood as the key relationship to which family law is to have regard, can be seen in the child support legislation, which imposes maintenance duties on parents irrespective of their marital status,[5] and in the fact that all parents can seek court orders dealing with their children's upbringing, regardless of whether the parents have ever been married to one another.[6]

[1]   See J Dewar and S Parker, 'English Family law since WWII: From Status to Chaos', in Katz, Eekelaar and Maclean (eds), 'Cross Currents, Family law and Policy in the US and England', (2000) OUP.
[2]   In 1968 there were 1,1240 marriages in Northern Ireland, but 33 years later that annual figure had fallen to 7,281: Annual Report of the Registrar General 2002, p 171.
[3]   In 2001, 33% of all births in Northern Ireland were to unmarried parents, 69% of these were jointly registered by the child's parents, suggesting that many of these births were to unmarried parents whose relationship was subsisting: Annual Report of the Registrar General 2002, p 33.
[4]   The birth rate was running at approximately 27,000 births per annum in the 1980s, a rate that had fallen to below 22,000 by 2001: Annual Report of the Registrar General 2002, p 35.
[5]   See para 9.65.
[6]   See para 9.99.

9.6   The changing nature of family law and family life is also reflected in the fact that some statutes now make provision for cohabiting couples, as well as for married couples. For example, as outlined below,[1] the Family Homes and Domestic Violence Order allows individuals in abusive cohabiting relationships to seek court orders. However, same-sex couples receive no statutory recognition at present, but that may have to change with the implementation of the HRA.[2]

[1]   See para 9.17.
[2]   See para 9.11. For more on the law relating to gays, lesbians, bisexuals and transsexuals see Feenan et al, 'Enhancing the rights of Lesbian, Gay and Bisexual People in Northern Ireland', Northern Ireland Human Rights Commission, August 2001.

9.7   The unique, legal consequences of marriage have also dwindled in number over the years, further diminishing the legal differences between the position of the married and the unmarried. However, the remaining, significant legal difference between married and unmarried couples is that the former have access to a range of legal remedies when the relationship breaks down and these remedies are far wider than the remedies that are available to unmarried couples.[1]

This trend towards greater legal recognition of non-marital relationships can be seen in one other aspect of familial legal relations worth noting at this point, namely the extension of circumstances in which parental responsibility can be accorded to unmarried fathers. Parental responsibility, as was explained in chapter 6, is an important concept in the implementation of family and child law. The basis for acquiring parental responsibility in Northern Ireland has been altered by the Family Law Act (Northern Ireland) 2001,[2] so that an unmarried father can acquire that status simply by having his name included on the child's birth certificate. This statutory innovation was introduced in Northern Ireland prior to its introduction in Great Britain.[3]

[1]   See para 9.75.
[2]   Section 1, amending the Children (Northern Ireland) Order 1995, art 7.
[3]   The English amendment was made in the Adoption and Children Act 2002, s 11.

Human Rights Act 1998

9.8   Clearly, various Convention rights apply to family life, particularly articles 8, 12 and 14 and these will be examined here.

Article 8: Respect for private life and family life

9.9   Article 8, the right to privacy, home and family life has been dealt with elsewhere,[1] and little needs to be added at this point other than to emphasise that the right applies to a wide variety of family forms, and not just to traditional nuclear families. Most of the legal matters under discussion in this chapter will not involve the State directly, but will usually involve a dispute between the parents of a child or between a married couple. In such cases, each of the parents and the child can be said to have a right to family life in respect of other members of the family. The courts are under a duty when hearing cases to have regard to the parties' article 8 rights, because of the terms of s 6 of the HRA.[2] As a result a court may be faced with competing article 8 claims from different members of the family, involved in the same dispute. It will have to balance these competing claims and, because invariably whatever decision a court does make will interfere with somebody's article 8 rights, must ensure that its decision is compatible with article 8.[3]

Furthermore, because such disputes involve the family members, and do not involve the State, on occasion the courts may have to make an assessment of the extent to which the State has met its positive obligation[4] under article 8 to facilitate the family members' exercise of their article 8 rights. In other words, the issue will be on what public bodies did, or could have done, to allow the parties to exercise their rights to family and home life and to privacy.

---

[1]   See chapter 1, para 1.83 and chapter 6, para 6.11.
[2]   See chapter 1, para 1.74.
[3]   In applications for orders under the Children Act 1989, s 8 (equivalent of the Children (Northern Ireland) Order 1995, art 8) the courts have concluded that an assessment based on the 'welfare checklist' will suffice for the purposes of fulfilling the balancing exercise in Convention right art 8: *Re H (children) (contact order) (No 2)* [2001] 3 FCR 385, [2002] 1 FLR 22, [2001] Fam Law 795.
[4]   On positive obligations, see chapter 1, para 1.80, and chapter 6, para 6.21.

Article 12: Right to marry

9.10   Article 12 enshrines the right of men and women of marriageable age to marry and found a family, 'according to the national laws governing the exercise of this right'. As a result, a State may establish some limits in its national law on who may, or may not marry and interpretation of this right means it does not apply to same-sex couples.[1] Thus it does not compel a State to allow homosexual or lesbian couples to marry one another, nor to establish a system by which they may record a commitment to one another.[2] The position of transsexuals is discussed later when examining the grounds for annulments.[3]

[1]   See *Rees v United Kingdom* (1986) 9 EHRR 56 at 68 where it states that '"the right to marry" refers to the traditional marriage between persons of opposite biological sex'.

[2]   However, there has been considerable discussion about registration schemes that will allow same-sex couples to record this commitment and to avail themselves of statutory remedies for the distribution of property and assets should the relationship break down, and legislation on this topic may follow. See the consultation document on Civil Registered Partnerships, Department of Trade and Industry, June 2003.

[3]   See para 9.60.

Article 14: Protection form discrimination

9.11   Article 14 prohibits the discriminatory application of the other, substantive, Convention rights. It reads:

> 'The enjoyment of the rights and freedoms set forth in this Convention shall be secured without discrimination on any ground such as sex, race, colour, language, religion, political or other opinion, national or social origin, association with a national minority, property, birth or other status.'

This right does not outlaw discrimination per se, but requires a complainant to argue that his or her ability to exercise another Convention right is hampered and that that restriction is applied to them, but not to others. The following example will help to explain the application of the provision. In *Ghaidan v Godin-Mendoza*,[1] the English Court of Appeal had the opportunity to consider a statute that allowed a person to succeed to a tenancy where the tenant had died and he had lived with the deceased 'as his or her wife or husband'.[2] The purpose of such legislation is obviously to allow the surviving member of a cohabiting couple to remain on in the couple's home even after the tenant has died. The House of Lords had considered previously that this phrase in the statute could not apply to same-sex couples,[3] although ultimately they could obtain some benefit as the statute also allowed the survivor to succeed to the tenancy (albeit a less secure form of that tenancy) as the survivor could be considered to be a member of the deceased's family.[4] However, the Court of Appeal considered, in *Ghaidan v Godin-Mendoza*, that this view of the phrase 'as his or her wife or husband', had to be reinterpreted in light of the HRA.

[1]   [2002] EWCA Civ 1533, [2003] Ch 380, [2002] 4 All ER 1162.

[2]   Rent Act 1977, Sch 2, para 2(2).

[3]   *Fitzpatrick v Sterling Housing Association Ltd* [2001] 1 AC 27, [1999] 4 All ER 705, [2000] 1 FCR 21, HL.

[4]   The legislation also allowed the surviving resident to succeed to the tenancy where he or she had lived with the deceased tenant as a member of the latter's family: Rent Act 1977, Sch 2, para 3(1).

9.12   The statute in question engaged the same-sex couple's article 8 rights, it concluded, because it related to their habitual dwelling place. The court considered that the House of Lords' interpretation of the statutory phrase amounted to a discriminatory application of the statute, in breach of article 14, because its interpretation of it allowed heterosexual cohabiting couples to benefit, but not homosexual cohabiting couples, and there was no justification for that discrimination. Thus the statutory words 'as his or her wife or husband' had to be read to mean 'as if they were his or her wife or husband', thereby broadening its scope of application to homosexual couples.

Appealing family law cases

9.13 As might be expected various statutory rights of appeal exist in respect of family law decisions under various statutes. It is worth remembering, however, that the courts' approach to such an appeal may limit the attractiveness of an appeal to a person who is disgruntled with the lower court's decision. The courts have had to deal with this issue in regard to an appeal from a Family Care Centre to the High Court.[1]

[1] The courts have also had to deal with the issue of appealing directions made by a judge in direction hearings, see chapter 6.

9.14 In *McG v McC*[1] the High Court addressed the issue of what approach it ought to take to the hearing of an appeal against a decision taken by the Family Care Centre. A father wished to appeal the Care Centre's decision to refuse him a Contact Order, and to withhold the father's identity from the child. The issue for the High Court was to determine the nature of the course of the hearing at the appeal. It concluded that appeals from a Family Care Centre to the High Court under article 166 of the 1995 Order should be entertained according to the principles established in an English case, *G v G*.[2] This means that the High Court will not overturn a decision unless it was made under a mistake of law, or in disregard of principle, or under a misapprehension of fact, or involved taking into account irrelevant matters or omitting relevant matters or was plainly wrong, ie outside the generous ambit within which a reasonable disagreement is possible. This means that an unhappy party has a relatively heavy burden when appealing such a decision and must have very cogent reasons why the decision should be overturned. As the judge concluded 'the fact of the matter is that Care Centre judges are vested with a discretion in family law cases where there may be two or more possible decisions, any of which a judge may make without being wrong.' However, it does appear to be the practice that appeals from the magistrates' court to the county court are dealt with by way of full rehearing, that is the matter is reheard afresh with witnesses being called, and full arguments as to facts being presented.[3]

[1] (23 April 2002, unreported), High Court, Gillen J.
[2] [1985] 2 All ER 225, [1985] FLR 894, HL.
[3] See, in *McG v McC* (23 April 2002, unreported), High Court, Gillen J, reference to practice in Northern Ireland in such cases.

Mediation and conciliation services

9.15 Mediation and conciliation have come to occupy a central place in family law reform policy discussions as the significance of having the parties discuss and agree matters relating to their own further relations, in a manner that can help to reduce long term acrimony between them, is increasingly recognised. There is one mediation service operating in Northern Ireland, 'Relate Northern Ireland'. Mediation and conciliation services are, however, accessed on a voluntary basis by couples and parties are not required to avail of them within the formal family justice system.[1] Neither is there any onus on parties' legal advisers to indicate to the court that they have discussed the possibility of mediation and conciliation with the parties, but that they have declined to avail themselves of such service.[2] The proposed Family Law (Divorce etc ...) Bill 2003, which will make changes to Northern Ireland divorce law, will confer powers on the courts to adjourn proceedings to facilitate mediation or reconciliation in divorce proceedings if it considers that there is an advantage to the parties in that approach.[3]

[1]   In England and Wales, Part III of the Family Law Act 1996 contemplated compulsory mediation for some classes of divorcees but feedback from mediation pilot projects has been influential in convincing the authorities not to implement the 1996 Act. See G Davis, 'Monitoring Publicly Funded Family Mediation' Legal Services Commission, December 2000 and G Davis [2001] Fam Law 110, 186, 265, 378.

[2]   Certification by the parties' legal advisers that reconciliation had been considered, and rejected, by the parties was once part of the family law regime in Northern Ireland but no longer is. It is required in the Republic of Ireland, however, under that jurisdiction's divorce and judicial separation regime: Circuit Court Rules (No 1) 1997, Forms 7–10, Schedule.

[3]   Family Law (Divorce etc ...) Bill 2003, cls 5 and 8.

9.16   The Children Order Advisory Committee (COAC)[1] in its Third Report[2] noted that a pilot project for court-mandated family mediation, involving Relate Northern Ireland and the Northern Ireland Court Service, is currently running from October 2002, for a two year period. The project is available in two Family Proceedings Courts and will involve the magistrates adjourning proceedings in appropriate cases to allow mediation settlement to be considered. Where an agreement is reached it can then be made the subject of a court order on the basis of the parties consent, but if no settlement is reached then the matter will return to the courts for adjudication.

[1]   See chapter 6, para 6.70.

[2]   At p 25.

Domestic violence

9.17   Considerable legislative and policy changes have taken place in the field of domestic violence in recent years ensuring an improvement in the mechanisms designed to protect domestic violence survivors. This focus on domestic violence was prompted by research studies that highlighted the flaws with the domestic violence protection services,[1] leading to the establishment of a Northern Ireland-wide Domestic Violence forum in 1995 and the adoption of legislation, the Family Homes and Domestic Violence (Northern Ireland) Order 1998, mirroring much of Part IV of the Family Law Act 1996, the equivalent legislation in England and Wales, although containing some innovations, which are highlighted in the course of the discussion below. The government has recently proposed changes in domestic violence legislation for Northern Ireland, in a document entitled 'Tackling Violence at Home',[2] based on research on the implementation of the Family Homes and Domestic Violence Order conducted by the Office of Law Reform (OLR).[3] These will be referred to where relevant.

[1] McKiernan and McWilliams, 'Bringing it out in the open', HMSO, 1993 and McWilliams and Spence, 'Taking domestic violence seriously', HMSO, 1996.
[2] 'Tackling Violence at Home – The Government's Proposals on Domestic Violence in Northern Ireland', NIO and DHSSPS, October 2003.
[3] 'Review of the Family Homes and Domestic Violence (Northern Ireland) Order 1998', OLR, October 2003.

9.18 The two main types of court orders available under the 1998 Order, and that can made in situations of domestic violence, are Occupation Orders and Non-molestation Orders. Where, however, a victim of domestic violence cannot apply for either of these orders, it may be possible to apply for an order under the Protection from Harassment (Northern Ireland) Order 1997, or he or she may be able to make an application to the county court for an injunction. The availability of these remedies is discussed below in turn.

Occupation Orders

9.19 Occupation Orders are available from the magistrates' court (known for this purpose as the Domestic Proceedings Court) or from the county court, and govern the manner in which the matrimonial, or habitual, home is occupied by those living there or who have lived there.[1] They may be made in other family proceedings, or as 'stand-alone' applications.[2] These orders are available for spouses, former spouses, cohabitants and former cohabitants, although in respect of former spouses and former cohabitants there are some restrictions to the availability of them. These orders may also be sought where the applicant has a legal and/or beneficial interest in the matrimonial or habitual home. This means that where one or more people own the property, then each owner may make an application for an Occupation Order, irrespective of the nature of the relationship between the parties. This means that even though same-sex couples are not ordinarily entitled to apply for an Occupation Order, they may be in a position to do so where both of them jointly own the property, for example. 'Tackling Violence at Home' also considers the possibility of amending the 1998 Order to allow same-sex couples to apply for Occupation Orders.

[1] Family Homes and Domestic Violence (Northern Ireland) Order 1998, arts 11–19.
[2] Family Homes and Domestic Violence (Northern Ireland) Order 1998, art 17(1).

9.20 The popular view of Occupation Orders is that they are the mechanism by which the respondent party can be evicted from the 'family' home. However, a court in making an Occupation Order has a wide range of options open to it, including directing that the:[1]

● applicant remain in occupation;
● respondent permit the applicant to enter the home;
● respondent allow the applicant peaceful enjoyment of the property;

- home be occupied by both parties but that the manner in which they occupy it is be regulated,

in addition to ordering that the respondent's right to live in the property be prohibited, suspended, or restricted, or that the respondent leaves the dwelling place.[2] A court can also require the party in whose favour an Occupation Order is made to make periodical payments to the other party, if the other party has a right to reside in the property by virtue of being a (legal and/or beneficial) owner of the property or by virtue of some contractual provision.[3] In effect these payments amount to a form of rent.

Furthermore, the respondent can be excluded from a defined area around the family home, or other premises that the victim frequents.[4] The Office of Law Reform research reported extensive use of the power to attach exclusion zones to Occupation Orders, with 44.9% of consultees reporting that courts attach such zones to both Occupation Orders and Non-molestation Orders and a further 16.2% reporting that they were attached to Occupation Orders only.[5] Where these exclusion zones are attached to the order they are usually placed around the applicant's home,[6] although they could also be placed around other areas, like the applicant's workplace, the child's school, places of worship, streets, and even town centres. Occupation Orders can also restrain the respondent from selling his or her interest in the home while the order is in force.[7]

---

[1]   Family Homes and Domestic Violence (Northern Ireland) Order 1998, art 11(3).
[2]   Although the respondent can be allowed remove personal effects and specified furniture: art 11(3)(h).
[3]   Family Homes and Domestic Violence (Northern Ireland) Order 1998, art 18(1)(b).
[4]   Family Homes and Domestic Violence (Northern Ireland) Order 1998, art 11(3)(i).
[4]   Review of the Family Homes and Domestic Violence (Northern Ireland) Order 1998, OLR, October 2003, p 15.
[5]   This was the experience of 86% of consultees, Review of the Family Homes and Domestic Violence (Northern Ireland) Order 1998, OLR, October 2003, p 15.
[7]   Family Homes and Domestic Violence (Northern Ireland) Order 1998, art 11(3)(j).

9.21   Occupation Orders have been described as draconian and the courts have advised that, because it overrides any proprietary rights that the respondent may have, an order will only be justified in exceptional circumstances.[1]

Northern Ireland courts made 1,419 Occupation Orders in 2001/02.[2] This figure includes orders made on consent, and Ex Parte Orders. An Ex Parte Order is one which is made in situations of urgency without giving the respondent notice of it. Thus only one side is present when they are issued. In theory, Ex Parte Orders should only be made for a very short period of time, and at the date that the matter returns to court both parties can be present to make their arguments before the court to have it decide whether to make a full order. This aspect of the 1998 Order has been considered by the courts and is discussed below.

---

[1]   *Chalmers v Johns* [1999] 1 FLR 392, [1999] Fam Law 16, [1999] 2 FCR 110, CA.
[2]   Northern Ireland Court Service Annual Report 2001–2, Table E13, pp 118–119.

Criteria

9.22 The criteria for issuing an Occupation Order differ according to the whether the parties are married to one another or not. Where the applicant and the respondent are married to one another the court must have regard to the following:[1]

- the housing needs and resources of each of them and of the children;
- The couple's financial resources;
- The likely effects on health and safety or well being of the couple and the children;
- The conduct of parties in relation to each other and otherwise.

(These criteria also apply where there is no marital, or cohabiting, relationship between the parties, but the applicant is the owner, or one of the owners of the property, that is to say that he or she has a legal and/or beneficial interest in the property).

[1] Family Homes and Domestic Violence (Northern Ireland) Order 1998, art 11(6).

9.23 Where the couple involved are now divorced, and therefore qualify to make applications as former spouses, the court must consider the criteria that apply to spouses as well as some extra criteria:[1]

- the length of time since the parties have lived together;
- the length of time since the dissolution or annulment of the marriage;
- the existence of pending actions under the Matrimonial Causes (Northern Ireland) Order 1978,[2] or under the Children (Northern Ireland) 1995, Sch 1[3] or any actions relating to the (legal or beneficial) ownership of the former matrimonial home.[4]

Any application by a former spouse must be in respect of the former matrimonial home, or the premises that were intended to be the matrimonial home.[5]

[1] Family Homes and Domestic Violence (Northern Ireland) Order 1998, art 13(6).
[2] Actions for divorce, judicial separation, annulment or maintenance. See para 9.50.
[3] Applications for child support maintenance or property for the children. See para 9.72.
[4] For example, actions alleging that one party holds the property on trust for the other. See para 9.96.
[5] Family Homes and Domestic Violence (Northern Ireland) Order 1998, art 13(1)(c).

9.24 If the parties are cohabitants, or were cohabitants,[1] then the court is to have regard to further criteria before determining whether to make an Occupation Order. Cohabitants are defined as 'a man and a woman who, although not married to each other, are living together as husband and wife'.[2] In light of the English Court of Appeal's judgment in *Ghaidan v Godin-Mendoza*,[3] it must be arguable that the exclusion of same-sex couples from this definition of cohabitants is discriminatory and in breach of article 14 taken in conjunction with article 8. This may be a situation that can only be properly tested in an application for a declaration of incompatibility under the HRA.[4]

[1] Family Homes and Domestic Violence (Northern Ireland) Order 1998, art 14.
[2] Family Homes and Domestic Violence (Northern Ireland) Order 1998, art 3(1)(a).
[3] See para 9.11.
[4] See chapter 1, para 1.93.

9.25   Along with the four criteria that apply in respect of spouses, the court, when hearing applications by cohabitants, is also to have regard to the following:[1]
- the nature of parties relationship;
- the length of time they have lived together as 'husband and wife';
- whether there are any children of the relationship or for whom both have parental responsibility;
- the length of time since parties lived together;
- the existence of pending legal actions under the Children (Northern Ireland) Order 1995, Sch 1, or any actions relating to the (legal and beneficial) ownership of the matrimonial home.

Any application must be made in respect of the premises in which they live, or at any time lived, together or in which they intended to live together.[2]

[1]   Family Homes and Domestic Violence (Northern Ireland) Order 1998, art 14(6)(e)–(i).
[2]   Family Homes and Domestic Violence (Northern Ireland) Order 1998, art 14(1)(c).

'Balance of harm' test

9.26   In considering an application for an Occupation Order, the court must consider the application of what is commonly known as the 'balance of harm' test. This dictates that if the court is of the view that the applicant, or any children, will suffer significant harm, then the court must make the order sought, unless the harm likely to be suffered by the respondent or children as a result of the making of the order, is greater than, or as great as, the harm attributable to the respondent's conduct and likely to be suffered by applicant and children, if the order is not made. This test is the same for spouses, former spouses, cohabitants and former cohabitants, a fact that marks a subtle difference between the Northern Ireland legislation and the equivalent legislation in England and Wales.[1]

[1]   See the Family Law Act 1996, Pt IV, ss 33(7), 35(8), 36(8) and 38(5).

9.27   The purpose of the balance of harm test is to require the court to examine the two types of harm, namely that caused by the domestic violence abuser and that which would be caused to the abuser or children if the order is made and their right to reside in the home is curtailed in some way. This is a recognition that where a couple are in dispute, regulating the occupation of the family home by them is likely to cause hardship to one of the parties and it will be necessary to see whether the hardship caused to the party at the receiving end of the order, so to speak, is justified because of the harm that he or she is causing to the party applying for the order.

9.28   The English Court of Appeal has interpreted the balance of harm provision in the following way: if the applicant, or children, are suffering significant harm then the order must be made, unless the balance of harm test dictates otherwise, and the court has no discretion in the matter. However, if no significant harm is being, or likely to be suffered, then the court is not under a duty to make an order, but has a discretion to do so, and must base its decision on the relevant criteria outlined above, which as explained, will differ according to the relationship between the parties.[1]

> [1]   *Chalmers v Johns* [1999] 1 FLR 392, [1999] Fam Law 16, [1999] 2 FCR 110, and *G v G (Occupation Order: Contact)* [2000] 3 FCR 53, [2000] 2 FLR 36.

9.29   This balancing exercise can produce results which appear odd at first glance, as illustrated by *B v B (Occupation Order)*.[1] In that case the husband's violent behaviour towards his wife resulted in her leaving the family home with the son of their marriage and moving into temporary accommodation. The husband was left in occupation, along with a six-year-old child whom he had fathered in a previous marriage. His wife applied for an Occupation Order. The local authority had indicated that if the husband were made homeless by an Occupation Order then it would consider him to have made himself intentionally homeless, with the result that it would not be obliged to house him or his daughter. The Court of Appeal considered that the six-year-old daughter would suffer more harm than the wife and son if she were required to be accommodated on a temporary basis in hostel or B & B type accommodation, as this would have the consequence of requiring her to change schools. Furthermore, there was evidence that the wife and baby would, within a matter of weeks, be re-housed in more suitable accommodation and that had the husband and daughter been required to move to temporary accommodation then they would have to stay there indefinitely. Therefore the Occupation Order was refused.

A court can make an Occupation Order even if the respondent's conduct is unintentional, provided that it is causing, or likely to cause, the applicant or children significant harm.[2]

> [1]   [1999] 1 FLR 715, [1999] 2 FCR 251, [1999] Fam Law 208, CA.
> [2]   *G v G (Occupation Order: Conduct)* [2000] 2 FLR 36, CA. See, however, *Banks v Banks* [1999] 1 FLR 726, [1999] Fam Law 206 where the court refused to make Occupation and Non-molestation Orders against a woman whose conduct derived from a mental illness.

Duration

9.30   Where the parties are spouses, Occupation Orders can be made for any period of time, or until some specified event occurs or until such time as a further order is made.[1] Where however the parties are former spouses, cohabitants, or former cohabitants then the order can only be for a maximum of 12 months, although it may be renewed for 12-month periods without any limit as to the number of renewals.[2] Significant numbers of Occupation Orders are being made for indefinite periods (ie until such further order is made), as the Office of Law Reform research indicates, with 44.1% of consultees stating that this had been their experience. Where the order was made for a specified period of time the most usual duration was one year (31.6% of consultees) or six months (12.5% of consultees).[3]

> [1]   Family Homes and Domestic Violence (Northern Ireland) Order 1998, art 11(10).
> [2]   Family Homes and Domestic Violence (Northern Ireland) Order 1998, arts 13(10) and 14(10).
> [3]   Review of the Family Homes and Domestic Violence (Northern Ireland) Order 1998, OLR, October 2003, p 13.

9.31   This provision in respect of the duration of the orders, involving as it does, the identical treatment of former spouses, cohabitants and former cohabitants, represents a further difference between the Northern Ireland and English legislative regimes. The 1996 Act in England and Wales provides different permissible maximum lengths for the three categories, treating former spouses more generously than cohabitants, and former cohabitants.[1]

[1]   Family Law Act 1996, ss 33(8), 35(10) and 36(10).

9.32   When the 1998 Order was first implemented, it was the practice to issue Ex Parte Orders until some further other order was issued. This approach could be in breach of Convention right, Article 6 – the right to a fair trial[1] – as it may mean that the other party gets no opportunity to contest the making of the order. The High Court, in the case of in *Re Sloan*,[2] held that Ex Parte Non-molestation Orders issued without a return date (ie a date by which the matter could be brought back into court for a full hearing) might be in breach of article 6 as the court had no opportunity to supervise them. The same principle should be applicable to Ex Parte Occupation Orders. The practice of issuing indefinite Ex Parte Occupation Orders should therefore have ended. The research carried out by the OLR established that most Ex Parte Occupation Orders of a finite duration were made for between four and six weeks.[3]

[1]   See chapter 6, para 6.23.
[2]   (27 June 2001, unreported), High Court of Northern Ireland, Higgins J.
[3]   This was the experience of 43.4% of consultees, Review of the Family Homes and Domestic Violence (Northern Ireland) Order 1998, OLR, October 2003, p 13. Only 5.9% reported Ex Parte Orders of shorter duration while 15.3% reported orders of longer duration.

Non-molestation Orders

9.33   Non-molestation Orders (NMOs) are a form of statutory injunction requiring the respondent to desist from interfering, pestering or annoying the applicant. There is no requirement that such behaviour include violence.[1] No statutory definition of 'molestation' is provided, but the term has a long history of judicial use and reference to some case examples helps to explain the term and to appreciate the nature of the protection provided by these orders. One of the classic definitions of the term is attributed to Ormerod LJ in *Horner v Horner*:[2]

> '... I have no doubt that the word "molesting" ... does not imply necessarily either violence or threats of violence. It applies to any conduct which can properly be regarded as such a degree of harassment as to call for the intervention of the court.'

The husband's behaviour in that case amounted to molestation. He accosted his wife at the railway station. He also telephoned the school repeatedly where his wife was employed as a schoolteacher and made disparaging comments about her behaviour to anyone who answered the telephone – usually the school secretary. He also hung scurrilous posters about her on the school railings addressed to the parents of children taught by her.

¹ *Horner v Horner* [1982] 2 All ER 495, 4 FLR 50, CA.
² [1982] 2 All ER 495 at 497G, [1983] 4 FLR 50 at 51G, CA.

9.34 In *Vaughan v Vaughan*¹ the court referred to dictionary definitions of the term 'molestation' to conclude that the husband has molested his wife in breach of a court order where he called at her house early in the morning and late at night, and also called on her at her place of work making a nuisance of himself to her the whole time. Although he used no violence, he had used violence against her in the past.

However, in *C v C (application for non-molestation order)*,² the court did not consider that the respondent's conduct of selling her story to the tabloid press about the parties' relationship, and about her husband's deceitful behaviour towards her, amounted to molestation and refused to continue the Ex Parte Order.

NMOs are more common than Occupation Orders and courts in Northern Ireland issued 3,726 such orders in 2001/02, which figure includes orders made on consent and Ex Parte Orders.³

¹ [1973] 3 All ER 449, [1973] 1 WLR 1159, CA.
² [1998] Fam 70, [1998] 1 FLR 554, [1998] 1 FCR 11.
³ Northern Ireland Court Service Annual Report 2001–2, Table E13, pp 118–119.

Exclusion zones

9.35 These orders are less draconian in their effect because they do not require the respondent to vacate the premises. However, courts can, when making an NMO, establish an exclusion zone around the applicant's home, for example, the inside of which the respondent is not permitted to go. The case of *Re Hilary Glennon*¹ established that even though there is no express reference in the legislation to the creation of an exclusion zone, it is possible for a magistrate, when making a Non-molestation Order, to prescribe such a zone around some particular building or premises within which the respondent is not to go. When considering whether or not to add such a requirement to a Non-molestation Order, the High Court recommended that the judge should follow these steps:

'(a) establish the facts carefully, including the nature and extent of the actual or perceived threat of molestation;

(b) determine whether an exclusion zone provision is necessary to prevent molestation of the applicant and secure his or her health, welfare or wellbeing;

(c) balance the competing interests of the applicant and the respondent being particularly astute to protect the Convention Right of the respondent to freedom of movement;

(d) if satisfied that such a provision is necessary, draft it in such a way as to ensure it is proportionate to the level of threat and balances the competing interests of the respondent. Care should be taken to ensure that an order does not preclude the respondent from attending work, visiting family or friends or engaging in ordinary social or domestic tasks, unless it is necessary to do so to achieve the broader objects of the legislation.'

[1]   (28 June 2002, unreported), High Court of Northern Ireland, McLaughlin J.

'Associated' persons

9.36 NMOs may be sought by any applicant falling within the definition of 'associated persons'.[1] This phrase includes a wide range of persons, the full list of which includes those who:

(a)   are, or have been, married to each other;
(b)   are cohabitees or former cohabitees;
(c)   live, or have lived in the same, household, otherwise than merely by reason of one of them being the other's employee, tenant, lodger or boarder;[2]
(d)   are relatives;[3]
(e)   are engaged to be married, or were engaged to be married;[4]
(f)   in relation to any child, they are both parents of the child; or have had parental responsibility for the child;
(g)   are parties to the same family proceedings.

The breadth of the category of persons eligible to apply for an NMO means that same-sex couples, for example, could be in a position to make an application against one another if they are jointly renting property from a third party. Another example of the impact of the legislation is provided by *Re Sloan*,[5] where a Non-molestation Order was made against a woman arising out of an application by her maternal aunts. However, 'Tackling Violence at Home' suggests the extension of the category of relatives who can avail of the protection afforded by an NMO.[6] Consultees to the OLR research indicated that there were certain persons who could not avail themselves of an NMO, namely cousins, partners of former cohabitants and persons in certain in-law relationships. For example, a person cannot obtain an order against the spouse or cohabitant of his or her sibling, nor can a mother-in-law secure an order against her son-in-law.[7]

[1]   Family Homes and Domestic Violence (Northern Ireland) Order 1998, art 3(3).
[2]   This means that one flatmate can obtain an NMO against another flatmate if these conditions are complied with.
[3]   'Relatives' are defined as the following persons: the father, mother, stepfather, stepmother, son, daughter, stepson, stepdaughter, grandmother, grandfather, grandson or granddaughter of the applicant or of the applicant's spouse or former spouse; or (b) the brother, sister, uncle, aunt, niece or nephew (whether of the full blood or of the half blood or by affinity) of the applicant or of the applicant's spouse or former spouse: Family Homes and Domestic Violence (Northern Ireland) Order 1998, art 2.
[4]   Persons who were formerly engaged must make an application within three years of the termination of the agreement to marry: Family Homes and Domestic Violence (Northern Ireland) Order 1998, art 11(2).

5   (27 June 2001, unreported), High Court of Northern Ireland, Higgins J.

6   'Tackling Violence at Home – The Government's Proposals on Domestic Violence in Northern Ireland', N10 and DHSSPS, October 2003.

7   Review of the Family Homes and Domestic Violence (Northern Ireland) Order 1998, OLR, October 2003, p 9.

9.37   On the facts of a particular case it can be difficult to determine whether a couple were engaged in a cohabiting relationship sufficient to be entitled to apply for a Non-molestation Order. In *G v F (non-molestation order: jurisdiction),*[1] the English High Court was faced with a refusal by the magistrates' court to accept that the applicant and the respondent were a cohabiting couple where the applicant herself admitted that, 'strictly speaking, [the couple] did not did not live together' but that they divided their time between each other's flats, and where, by the respondent's own admission, they had marriage plans, operated a joint bank account, and had cohabited for a short time. The court considered that the equivalent English legislation should be given a purposive construction and that the courts should not construe the legislation narrowly so as to exclude borderline cases, 'unless the facts of the case were plainly incapable of being brought within the statute.'[2]

1   [2000] Fam 186, [2000] 2 FCR 638, [2000] 2 FLR 533.

2   [2000] 2 FLR 533 at 543F.

Duration

9.38   A Non-molestation Order may be made for a specified period or until further order,[1] although as explained above,[2] the High Court has recommended, in the case of *In re Sloan*, that those issued on an ex parte basis be issued[3] for a definite period or with a return date to allow a full inter partes hearing to take place. The English courts have advised that, barring exceptional or unusual circumstances, NMOs should be made for a specified period.[4]

1   Family Homes and Domestic Violence (Northern Ireland) Order 1998, art 20(7).

2   See para 9.36.

3   The court took the view that to refer to an ex parte NMO was slightly misleading as in fact they were full NMOs that happened to be made under art 23, ie without notice to the respondent.

4   *M v W (Non-Molestation Order: Duration)* [2000] 1 FLR 107, [2000] Fam Law 13.

9.39   The Northern Ireland Court of Appeal had further reason to re-assess the issue of the duration of ex parte NMOs in *Wallace v Kennedy.*[1] An Ex Parte NMO had been issued against an individual for a period of one year. He was subsequently charged with breaching that order almost six months after it was made. The magistrate dismissed the summons against him on the basis that a full hearing of the matter should have taken place before then, and that the Ex Parte Order had been issued for too long a period. The Court of Appeal confirmed that a full, inter partes hearing should have taken place sooner and that the magistrate was correct to dismiss the petition. The net effect of this is that Ex Parte Orders should only be used as a short-term protection measure and the full inter partes hearing should take place as soon as it just and convenient.

The OLR research recorded that 52.9% of consultees reported that it was their experience that orders made at contested, inter partes, hearings were for indefinite periods. Where a period of time was specified, 37.5% indicated that the most common duration was one year, with 14.7% indicating that their experience was that six months was the common period.

1   [2003] NICA 25, 25 June 2003.

Enforcement

9.40   The protection provided by domestic violence legislation is only as effective as the mechanisms established to enforce the orders issued by the courts. Breach of either a Non-molestation Order or an Occupation Order amounts to contempt of court. The burden of proof in contempt proceedings is the criminal burden of proof because a finding that one party has acted in breach of a court order may attract criminal penalties.

9.41   The English courts have considered the principles that apply when contempt of court proceedings are pursued for a failure to obey the terms of an order. In *Hale v Tanner*,[1] the Court of Appeal set these principles out as follows:
- (i) that imprisonment was not the automatic consequence of the breach of an order, and there was no principle that it should be imposed on the first occasion;
- (ii) that in an appropriate case, particularly if no actual violence had been proved, there were a range of options to consider: the court could make no order, adjourn the case, impose a fine, requisition assets, or make a Mental Health Order;
- (iii) that if imprisonment was appropriate, the length of the committal should be decided without reference to whether or not it was to be suspended;
- (iv) that since the length of the committal reflected the court's disapproval of the disobedience to its order and was to secure compliance in the future, the seriousness of what had taken place had to be viewed in that light;
- (v) that the length of the committal had to bear some reasonable relationship to the maximum sentence of two years' imprisonment;
- (vi) that the sentence could be suspended in a wider range of circumstances than in criminal cases, and it did not have to be an exceptional case;
- (vii) that the length of the suspension required separate consideration, although it was often appropriate for it to be linked to continued compliance with the order underlying the committal;
- (viii) that the context of the case, which could be aggravating or mitigating had to be borne in mind;
- (ix) that any concurrent proceedings, based on either the same facts or some of the same facts, in another court should be borne in mind and the outcome might have to be taken into account in considering what the practical effect was upon the contempt proceedings; and

(x) that it would usually be desirable to explain very briefly the reasons for the choices made in the particular case.[2]

---

[1]　[2000] 1 WLR 2377, [2000] 3 FCR 62, [2000] 2 FLR 879.
[2]　The court sentenced him to 28 days' imprisonment for his contempt in breaching the order by telephoning his former cohabitant.

9.42　Breach of a Non-molestation Order is also a criminal offence,[1] but the breach of an Occupation Order is not an offence unless there is in existence alongside the order, a Non-molestation Order.[2] Therefore, if the alleged abuser enters the family home, for example, in breach of an Occupation Order this will not automatically amount to a criminal offence unless a Non-molestation Order is also in existence in respect of his wife. The effectiveness of the 1998 Order is also partly enforced by conferring a power of arrest, without a warrant, on the police where a person commits a criminal offence by breaching an order.[3] The Northern Ireland approach differs to that taken in England and Wales where the court must attach a power of arrest to each NMO or Occupation Order in order to confer the power on the police to arrest a person in breach of the terms of the order, although such powers of arrest are made in virtually all cases.

---

[1]　Family Homes and Domestic Violence (Northern Ireland) Order 1998, art 25(a). The same enforcement powers apply to breach of an exclusion requirement attached to an Interim Care Order or Emergency Protection Order. See chapter 6, para 6.115.
[2]　Family Homes and Domestic Violence (Northern Ireland) Order 1998, art 25(b).
[3]　Family Homes and Domestic Violence (Northern Ireland) Order 1998, art 26, making appropriate amendments to the Police and Criminal Evidence (Northern Ireland) Order 1989, art 26(2).

9.43　A novel feature of the 1998 Order which has yet to be implemented, and which has the potential to radically alter the manner in which civil law Domestic Violence Orders are enforced, is found at article 35. It allows a representative of a domestic violence survivor to make applications for Occupation and Non-molestation Orders on behalf of the survivor. In fact, it may also allow the police, or other statutory or voluntary agencies to make the application. However, secondary legislation bringing this provision into force has not yet been enacted. 'Tackling Violence at Home' also raises the possibility of establishing a register of persons against whom Domestic Violence Orders have been made, similar to the sex offenders' register.[1]

---

[1]　'Tackling Violence at Home – The Government's Proposals on Domestic Violence in Northern Ireland', NIO and DHSSPS, October 2003, p 41.

Contact with children

9.44　A particularly difficult issue to consider in the context of domestic violence is whether a domestic violence abuser should be allowed to continue to have contact with any children of the relationship and if so, what safeguards need to be imposed to ensure the safety of the other partner.

Domestic violence against a partner does not automatically disqualify a parent, or someone with parental responsibility, from maintaining contact with a child. The ethos of the Children (Northern Ireland) Order 1995 is that parents should maintain relations with their children and that the courts should facilitate that, wherever possible. However, clear difficulties present themselves where the pursuit of that contact involves the abuser and the survivor encountering one another, with the possibility that the abuse will re-occur. The 1998 Order seeks to deal with this problem.[1] It directs the courts, when deciding whether to make a Residence or Contact Order, to consider whether the child has suffered or is at risk of suffering any harm through seeing, or hearing, ill-treatment of another person by a person who is, or whom the court considers should be subject to a Non-molestation Order.[2]

[1]   Family Homes and Domestic Violence (Northern Ireland) Order 1998, art 28, inserts a new art 12A into the Children (Northern Ireland) Order 1995.
[2]   This approach differs slightly to that in England and Wales where the courts assess the impact of domestic violence on the children on the basis of the principles set out in *Re L (a child) (contact: domestic violence)*; *Re V (a child) (contact: domestic violence)*; *Re M (a child) (contact: domestic violence)*; *Re H (children) (contact: domestic violence)* [2001] Fam 260, [2000] 4 All ER 609, [2000] 2 FCR 404, [2000] 2 FLR 334, CA, rather than on the basis of statutory instruction. The Northern Ireland courts also use these principles when dealing with the issue of domestic violence and contact.

9.45   The practical value of this is that where a father, who has been abusive to the mother of their child, seeks a Residence Order or a Contact Order[1] in respect of that child, the court must have regard to the effect on the child of witnessing, or having witnessed, this abuse. This does not mean that in all circumstances that the father's application will be denied but it will have a practical bearing on the type of order made, if any. For example, an abusive father applying for a Contact Order may have the type of contact he is allowed restricted to telephone calls and to letters.

[1]   See para 9.101.

Protection from harassment and county court injunctions

9.46   Some individuals in abusive situations or relationships may not be able to avail themselves of the protection offered by the 1998 Order, because they do not fall within the categories of people entitled to apply. They may, however, be in a position to apply for court orders under other legislation. The Protection from Harassment (Northern Ireland) Order 1997 was originally enacted to deal with concerns raised by 'stalking' but was drafted in such broad terms that it has been possible for applicants to utilise it in a wide range of situations. For example, in *Re Shay Donnelly*[1] the applicant for judicial review had previously obtained an order under the protection from harassment legislation against his neighbours, arising from their sectarian and paramilitary harassment of him and his family. The judicial review action sought to challenge the Northern Ireland Housing Executive's refusal to evict the applicant's neighbours.[2]

[1]   (29 January 2003, unreported), High Court, Weatherup J. This case is discussed in chapter 2 at para 2.113.
[2]   See also, for example, *Daiichi UK Ltd v Stop Huntingdon Animal Cruelty* [2003] EWHC 2337 (QB), [2003] All ER (D) 194 (Oct), where orders were made under the English protection from harassment legislation, against animal rights' activists who were seeking to prevent companies carrying out laboratory experiments on animals.

9.47 'Harassment' is not defined in the Order but it does state that 'the person whose course of conduct is in question ought to know that it amounts to harassment of another if a reasonable person in possession of the same information would think the course of conduct amounted to harassment'.[1] In order for such harassment to entitle the victim to seek a judicial remedy there must have been at least two incidents of that type of behaviour.[2] Harassment is both a crime[3] and activity that can give rise to a civil law remedy.[4] The person being harassed may apply to the High Court or the county court for an injunction under the 1997 Order. Any breach of such an injunction entitles the harassed person to apply for an arrest warrant in respect of the person harassing him or her.[5]

Furthermore, the 1997 Order also makes it an offence to put another in fear of violence, on at least two occasions, where he or she knows or ought to know that their conduct will give rise to this fear.[6] A person is taken to know that his or her actions will put another in fear of violence 'if a reasonable person in possession of the same information would think the course of conduct would cause the other [person][7] to have the fear that violence will be used against him or her in the future.

[1] Protection from Harassment (Northern Ireland) Order 1997, art 3(2).
[2] Protection from Harassment (Northern Ireland) Order 1997, art 2(3).
[3] Protection from Harassment (Northern Ireland) Order 1997, art 4.
[4] Protection from Harassment (Northern Ireland) Order 1997, art 5(1).
[5] Protection from Harassment (Northern Ireland) Order 1997, art 5(3).
[6] Protection from Harassment (Northern Ireland) Order 1997, art 6(1).
[7] Protection from Harassment (Northern Ireland) Order 1997, art 6(2).

9.48   In sentencing a person for the commission of either of these offences, ie the offence of harassment or the offence of putting a person in fear of violence, the court may also issue a Restraining Order, prohibiting that person from doing anything in that restraining order.[1]

Even where it is not open to an applicant to apply under the 1997 Order, an avenue of redress may still be available by way of an application to the county court for an injunction restraining a person from acting in a certain manner. These applications are made under the County Courts (Northern Ireland) Order 1980.[2]

[1] Protection from Harassment (Northern Ireland) Order 1997, art 7. 'Tackling Violence at Home – The Government's Proposals on Domestic Violence in Northern Ireland', NIO and DHSSPS, October 2003, p 41 considers whether Restraining Orders should become more widely available.
[2] Article 13.

Termination of relationships

9.49   This section outlines the legal mechanisms by which a married couple can terminate their relationship. It also provides an overview of the law with regard to some of the major issues facing the parties when their relationship breaks down, including spousal maintenance, child support, property division and child rearing.

Divorce, judicial separation and annulment

9.50   There are three remedies available to a married couple whose relationship has broken down and who wish to formally terminate that relationship. These remedies are divorce, judicial separation and annulment. Each of these three remedies has different consequences for the couple's marriage.

Divorce terminates the marriage, freeing the parties to marry again, while a decree of judicial separation brings to an end the obligation on the parties to live with one another, but does not terminate the marriage. As a result the parties remain married, although judicially separated, and unable to remarry. An annulment is a decree whose effect is that the marriage is deemed never to have occurred because of some fundamental flaw at the time the parties participated in the wedding ceremony.

9.51   A petition of nullity differs greatly from the other two remedies in that in considering such a petition the courts must consider whether that fundamental flaw was present at the time the parties married and it is of no avail to the parties to say that their marriage is now irretrievably broken down. The advantage to the parties is that if the civil annulment obtained in the courts is accepted by the relevant church body, the parties will be free to marry in church at a later occasion. Even if it is not accepted for this purpose, obtaining the civil decree of nullity will usually make it easier to secure a church annulment, which will facilitate remarriage in church.

Divorce

9.52   Parties may divorce one another if their marriage has irretrievably broken down.[1] The fact of the irretrievable collapse of the marriage must be proved by establishing that one of five factual situations has arisen. These are that:[2]

- the respondent has committed adultery;
- the respondent has deserted the petitioner for a period of at least two years;
- the respondent has behaved in such a manner that it is intolerable for the petitioner to continue to live with the respondent (commonly referred to as 'unreasonable behaviour');
- the parties have lived apart for two years and the respondent consents to the divorce petition;
- the parties have lived apart for a period of five years.

These facts are commonly, although, erroneously, referred to as the 'grounds' for divorce. The first three facts are usually referred to as the 'fault' facts, while the last two facts can be referred to as the 'no fault' facts. There are two stages to the granting of a divorce decree. After the hearing of the petition by the judge in chambers, a decree nisi is granted. At a later stage, not less than six weeks later,[3] a decree absolute is issued, and it is at that point that the marriage is terminated.

[1]   Matrimonial Causes (Northern Ireland) Order 1978, art 3(1).
[2]   Matrimonial Causes (Northern Ireland) Order 1978, art 3(2).
[3]   Matrimonial Causes (Northern Ireland) Order 1978, art 3(6).

9.53 In Northern Ireland the majority of divorce decrees are granted on the basis of the no-fault facts, with almost 75% of all divorces in 2002[2] being granted on the basis of those facts. And of the no-fault facts, two years' separation with consent is the most common.[1]

Of the fault facts, desertion features very infrequently as a basis for the granting of a divorce decree with only five decrees made on the basis of this fact in 2002. The most frequently invoked fault fact is 'unreasonable behaviour' which featured in approximately 24% of divorce decrees nisi in 2002.[3] This pattern of favouring the no-fault facts over the fault facts is in stark contrast to the position in England and Wales where approximately two-thirds of divorces in 2002 were on fault based facts.[4] This contrast may be explained by the fact that the normal practice in Northern Ireland is for the parties to apply for the divorce decree many years after they have separated. Quite often, during the period of separation, the parties have availed themselves of other remedies to resolve matters relating to the division of property and the rearing of the children, or they may have agreed these matters privately with the help of their legal advisers.[5]

[1] Northern Ireland Judicial Statistics 2002, Northern Ireland Court Service, p 23, Table B30.
[2] In 2002, two thirds of the decrees nisi in which no-fault facts were cited involved the two years' separation plus consent fact. Northern Ireland Judicial Statistics 2002, Northern Ireland Court Service, p 23 Table B30.
[3] Northern Ireland Court Service, p 23, Table B30.
[4] 'Population Trends 113', Report: Divorces in England and Wales during 2002, Table of Facts proven at divorce and to whom granted, 2002.
[5] See 'Unravelling the system: Divorce in Northern Ireland', Archbold, White, Murtagh, McKee and McWilliams, Stationery Office 1999.

9.54 Desertion does not feature very frequently in divorce petitions because in order for the petitioner to succeed the respondent must have been in desertion for a period of two years or more. Where these factual circumstances arise the respondent will usually be happy to consent to a two years' separation petition in any event. Divorces based on the adultery fact formed about 8% of the overall total number of decrees nisi in 2001/02,[1] and the declining stigma of adultery means that it is no longer very difficult to prove because in some cases the respondent will admit to it, or indeed may have separated from the petitioner and moved in with his or her new partner.

[1] Northern Ireland Court Service, p 23, Table B30.

9.55 'Unreasonable behaviour' petitions feature a wide range of unsavoury behaviour. Research has shown that of the particular incidents that are cited in 'unreasonable behaviour' petitions, domestic violence and drunkenness are the most prominent.[1] The court assesses the behaviour involved from the point of view of the reasonable person, assessing what would be intolerable for that particular petitioner to have to deal with. As the High Court has offered, 'the words [of the statute] prima facie suggest an objective test but it is clear from the authorities that the court must have regard to the particular petitioner and respondent in assessing what is reasonable' and the conduct must be of a 'grave and weighty character'.[2] In *Lenaghan v Lenaghan* the court did not consider that the respondent's flirtatious behaviour with

other men on some occasions, or the fact they socialised independently, was sufficiently grave and weighty conduct to amount to 'unreasonable behaviour'. A finding
that one party has engaged in unreasonable behaviour can be made even where the
parties continue to live together.[3]

[1]   'Unravelling the system: Divorce in Northern Ireland', Archbold, White, Murtagh, McKee and
McWilliams, Stationery Office 1999, p 78.
[2]   *Lenaghan v Lenaghan* (21 December 1995, unreported), High Court, Girvan J, transcript available on
Lexis, although not as grave and weighty as would have been required under the law prior to the
Matrimonial Causes (Northern Ireland) Order 1978 to ground a divorce petition on the basis of
'cruelty'. Girvan J had reason to revisit his judgment in *Lenaghan* in *W v W* [1998] NI 207 and alter his
view as to what conduct was sufficient to show 'unreasonable behaviour'.
[3]   *W v W* [1998] NI 207, High Court, Girvan J, in which episodes of adultery, and general marital
disharmony and conflict amounted to unreasonable behaviour.

Reform of divorce law

9.56   Northern Ireland divorce law is about to be reformed after an extensive period
of consultation.[1] The five facts upon which a divorce petition may be based will be
amended when the Family Law (Divorce etc ...) Bill 2003 is enacted. It proposes
amalgamating the three fault facts into one fault fact, namely 'behaviour so intolerable that the petitioner cannot be expected to live with it'.[2] It also proposes that the
periods of time for which the parties must live apart in order to avail themselves of
the no-fault facts should be altered from two years to one year, and from five years to
two years respectively. The abridgement of these time periods is a reflection of the
fact that divorce is usually a long and protracted event in Northern Ireland and that
consequently long, formal periods of separation are not necessary to convince the
courts that a divorce decree is warranted.

[1]   'Divorce the new law in Northern Ireland', OLRNI, April 2002.
[2]   Family Law (Divorce etc ...) Bill 2003, cl 2, amending the Matrimonial Causes (Northern Ireland)
Order 1978, art 3.

9.57   The Bill also proposes to amend the requirement for the petitioner to attend in
court for the hearing of the divorce petition, a difference in the divorce procedure
that marks the system in Northern Ireland out from that in England and Wales,
where such a requirement does not apply.[1] Where the petition is to be based on the
no-fault facts and the court does not consider that the interests of the children
require the petitioner's attendance it may dispense with that requirement.[2]

[1]   The 'Special Procedure' relieves petitioners of the obligation to attend for the hearing. This procedure
is commonly referred to as 'Divorce by Post'.
[2]   Family Law (Divorce etc ...) Bill 2003, cl 3, amending the Matrimonial Causes (Northern Ireland)
Order 1978, art 3.

Judicial separation

9.58   A decree of judicial separation may be obtained on the same basis as a decree
of divorce. Such a decree, as with divorce decrees, can be made by the county court or

the High Court. A decree of judicial separation is not to be confused with any order of the magistrates' court dealing with maintenance for a spouse or the children of the marriage. The confusion can arise from the fact that in practice many people refer to a magistrates' court order that deals with these issues, where the parties have experienced marital breakdown, as a 'Separation Order'.

A court when faced with a judicial separation petition may also make all the orders about the division of the property and about residence and contact with the children that may be made by a court in the course of a divorce petition.

9.59   The number of judicial separation decrees per annum in Northern Ireland is quite small with 15 being pronounced in 2002.[1] The fact that the decree of judicial separation does not dissolve the marriage and prevents the parties remarrying means that unless the person has a conscientious, or religious, objection to divorce, or unless they wish to prevent the other party from remarrying, he or she is likely to prefer to seek a divorce decree.

[1]   Northern Ireland Judicial Statistics 2002, Northern Ireland Court Service, p 23, Table B30.

Annulment

9.60   An annulment is available where a marriage can be deemed to be void or voidable because at the time of the marriage a state of affairs existed which affected the very essence of the marriage contract. A marriage will be void if:[1]

- the parties are not respectively male and female;[2]
- one of the parties was already validly married at the time of the marriage ceremony;[3]
- one of the parties was younger than 16 years of age;[4]
- the parties were knowingly, and wilfully, in breach of the formalities of the marriage ceremony;[5]
- the parties are within the prohibited degrees of relationship, ie they fall within the range of relations who are prohibited by statute from marrying one another. Thus a man, to take the male example, may not marry his mother, sister, grandmother, daughter, aunt, and granddaughter and may only marry his mother-in-law and step-daughter in limited circumstances.[6]

[1]   Matrimonial Causes (Northern Ireland) Order 1978, art 13.
[2]   A recent case has alleviated the difficulty caused for transsexuals in meeting these requirements, see *Goodwin v United Kingdom*, where art 12 was violated by the State's refusal to allow a transgendered person to have their gender re-assignment legally recognised, thus facilitating their marriage to a person of the opposite gender to their 'new' gender status.
[3]   The party already married commits the offence of bigamy.
[4]   Where a person is aged between 16 and 18 years of age, he or she requires parental consent before marrying. However, the absence of this consent is not, curiously, fatal to the validity of the marriage.
[5]   These formalities are those set out in the Marriage (Northern Ireland) Order 2003.
[6]   His mother-in-law's husband must be dead before he marries her and he can only marry his stepdaughter if their respective spouses are dead and she was not a child of his family.

9.61   A marriage will be voidable if, at the time of the marriage:[1]

- the respondent to the annulment petition wilfully refused to consummate the marriage;
- either of the parties was incapable of consummating the marriage;
- the petitioner was mentally disordered so as to be unfit for marriage, or consented to the marriage under duress or by virtue of a mistake about the identity of the other party at the time of the ceremony, or as a result of unsoundness of mind;
- the respondent was suffering from a communicable venereal disease at the time of the marriage;[2]
- the woman was pregnant by someone other than the husband, and this fact was not known to him.

The last three grounds may only be availed of within three years of the date of marriage.[3] None of the grounds are available to a petitioner if he or she knew that they had the option of seeking an annulment of the marriage on the basis that it was voidable, but indicated to their spouse that they would not do so.[4]

[1] Matrimonial Causes (Northern Ireland) Order 1978, art 14.
[2] It is not clear whether HIV/AIDS is included within the range of communicable diseases.
[3] Matrimonial Causes (Northern Ireland) Order 1978, art 16(2), although leave to institute proceedings can be granted if the person had a mental disorder and the court considers it just to do so: art 16(4).
[4] Matrimonial Causes (Northern Ireland) Order 1978, art 16(1).

9.62 The difference between a void marriage and a voidable one is that the former lacks any legal standing from the outset and the law refuses to recognise that there was ever a marriage between the parties. Thus, if a man marries a woman, whom he believes to be aged 18, but who is in fact 15 years old, such a marriage has no legal validity despite the fact that the parties have voluntarily undergone a wedding ceremony. A marriage can be declared void on the petition of any person and indeed there need not even by a decree made by the courts, once it is clear that one of the conditions above have been fulfilled. A voidable marriage can only be brought to an end on the basis of a petition brought by one of the parties to the marriage, and is considered only to have been invalid from the point at which the court issues the decree of nullity.[1]

[1] Matrimonial Causes (Northern Ireland) Order 1978, art 18.

9.63 The same remedies in respect of financial, property and child rearing issues are available in respect of annulment as are available on a petition for divorce or judicial separation. Decrees of nullity are quite rare with only a handful being sought each year in Northern Ireland and where petitions are successful they are usually on the basis of wilful refusal, or incapacity, to consummate the marriage.[1]

[1] Two annulment decrees were made in 2002. Northern Ireland Judicial Statistics, Northern Ireland Court Service, p 23, Table B30. The Law Reform Advisory Committee has issued a consultation document on the law of nullity. See 'Nullity of Marriage' Discussion Paper No 10, October 2003.

Unmarried cohabitants

9.64 Obviously none of the three remedies examined above are available to an unmarried cohabiting couple. As a result, a cohabiting relationship can be ended without the need to have recourse to the courts. However, as with married couples, substantive issues like the division of assets, child support maintenance and child rearing will often have to be dealt with. Issues related to the division of property must then be addressed in court actions other than by way of applications ancillary to divorce, judicial separation or annulment.[1] The Child Support Agency can determine child support for children, irrespective of the marital status of their parents[2] and the courts can entertain applications about property and lump sums for children where their parents part.[3]

[1] See para 9.96.
[2] See para 9.65.
[3] See para 9.72.

Maintaining the children

9.65 A key issue for the parties to a relationship that has broken down, is what levels of child support maintenance the non-resident parent must provide. The calculation of child support maintenance was formerly a matter exclusively for the courts but since 5 April 1993, when the Child Support (Northern Ireland) Order 1991 came into force, this matter is now largely one for the Child Support Agency (CSA), although the courts have some residual role to play.

All natural parents have a duty to maintain their children financially[1] and where a child is cared for predominately by one parent and the other parent does not reside with the child,[1] then the parent with care *may* (and in the case of parents with care in receipt of benefits, *must*) apply to the CSA to have it determine the amount of child support maintenance payable by the non-resident parent.[3] However, where a parent with care in receipt of benefits states that he or she, or the child, would be at risk of suffering harm or undue distress as a result of making the application to the CSA, then that parent will be relieved of the obligation.[4]

[1] Child Support (Northern Ireland) Order 1991, art 5.
[2] Child Support (Northern Ireland) Order 1991, art 4(2) and (3).
[3] Child Support (Northern Ireland) Order 1991, arts 7(1) and 9(1) respectively.
[4] Child Support (Northern Ireland) Order 1991, art 9(2).

9.66 However, the CSA's remit only extends to the calculation and collection of maintenance, that is periodic payments of money. Where the parents, or one of them, is particularly wealthy, it may be sensible for the parent with care to seek lump sum payments, or to have property transferred from the non-resident parent to the child.[1]

[1] See para 9.72.

Child support

9.67 Where a parent with care is in receipt of benefits he or she must apply to the CSA to have it determine child support maintenance or risk a reduction in their benefits.[1] If the parent with care is not in receipt of benefits then he or she is not obliged to make the application to the CSA.[2] However, the courts now only have jurisdiction in child support cases in limited circumstances and so such a parent may not have a choice as to how to proceed.

The current levels of child support are determined by the Child Support, Social Security and Pension Act (Northern Ireland) Act 2000. This established that a non-resident parent must pay 15% of his or her assessable income by way of child support, with this figure rising to 25% for two children, and 30% for three or more children.[3] This is referred to as the basic rate. Three other rates apply where the non-resident parent's income falls below certain levels.[4]Where the non-resident parent's weekly income is between £100 and £200, a reduced rate applies. If the non-resident parent's income is less than £100, or is in receipt of certain benefits or his or her partner is in receipt of them, a flat rate applies. A nil rate applies where the non-resident parent's income is less than £5 per week or he or she is under 16, or a full time student, or in prison.

[1] Child Support (Northern Ireland) Order 1991, art 9(1).
[2] Child Support (Northern Ireland) Order 1991, art 7(1).
[3] Child Support, Pensions and Social Security Act (Northern Ireland) 2000, s 1(3), Sch 1, Pt 1, para 2(1).
[4] Child Support, Pensions and Social Security Act (Northern Ireland) 2000, Sch 1, paras 3, 4 and 5.

9.68 Reductions in the child support maintenance payable[1] can be made where the non-resident parent is financially responsible for children, or step-children, arising out of any new relationship.[2] Reductions are also available to the non-resident parent where he or she is involved in caring for the children for at least one night per week.[3] The amount payable may also be reduced to cater for special expenses that the non-parent has incurred as a result of maintaining contact with the child for example, for costs incurred in travelling to work; for costs attributable to a long-term illness (or disability) of the non-resident parent or a dependant; for costs associated with debts incurred before the child's parents separated where these debts were for the benefit of the parents or the child, or other financial commitments incurred prior to the introduction of the CSA's regime in 1993 from which it would be unreasonable to expect the absent parent to withdraw, or costs incurred in supporting the children of any 'new' family that the absent parent has acquired.[4]

Reductions can also be made in respect of property transfers made to the parent with care, before 5 April 1993, in return for the payment of a lower amount of maintenance than would have been paid had the transfer not taken place.[5] Conversely, the absent parent can have the amount of child support maintenance payable raised where the absent parent is seeking to avoid some of his or her responsibility by, for example, claiming unreasonably high housing costs, or travelling costs, or is in possession of valuable assets which do not, however, generate any income.[6]

[1] In the vernacular of the child support legislative regime, these are referred to as 'variations'.
[2] Child Support (Northern Ireland) Order 1991, Sch 1, Pt 1 para 2(2), and the Child Support (Maintenance Calculations and Special Cases) Regulations (Northern Ireland) 2001, reg 3.
[3] Child Support (Northern Ireland) Order 1991, Sch 1, Pt 1, para 7, and the Child Support (Maintenance Calculations and Special Cases) Regulations (Northern Ireland) 2001, reg 7. The

reduction for overnight care of the child is one seventh for between 52 and 103 nights per year; two sevenths for 104–155 nights; three sevenths for between 156 and 174 nights, and one half for 175 nights or more.

⁴ Child Support (Northern Ireland) Order 1991, Sch 4B, Pt I, para 2(2), as amended, and the Child Support (Variations) Regulations (Northern Ireland) 2001, regs 10, 11, 12, 13 and 14.

⁵ Child Support (Northern Ireland) Order 1991, Sch 4B, Pt I, paras 3 and 4, as amended and the Child Support (Variations) Regulations (Northern Ireland) 2001, regs 16, 17, and 18.

⁶ Child Support (Northern Ireland) Order 1991, Sch 4B, Pt I, para 5, as amended and the Child Support (Variations) Regulations (Northern Ireland) 2001, regs 19 and 20.

9.69 Failure to make the child support maintenance payments determined by the CSA renders a parent liable to imprisonment or disqualification from driving before a court.[1] Alternatively, the CSA may impose penalty payments on the defaulting party, although these must not exceed 25% of the amount outstanding.[2]

A parent who is unhappy with the decision made in respect of child support maintenance can appeal that decision to the Child Support Appeal Tribunal.[3] A right of appeal also exists in respect of this tribunal to the Child Support Commissioner,[4] and a decision of the Commissioner can be appealed to the High Court, but only on a point of law.[5] However, an appeal against the CSA's determination that a particular person is the father of a child is to be made to the magistrates' court, and not to the Child Support Appeal Tribunal.[6]

[1] Child Support (Northern Ireland) Order 1991, art 36A, as inserted by the Child Support, Pensions and Social Security Act (Northern Ireland) 2000, s 16.
[2] Child Support (Northern Ireland) Order 1991, art 38A, as inserted by the Child Support, Pensions and Social Security Act (Northern Ireland) 2000, s 17.
[3] Child Support (Northern Ireland) Order 1991, art 22.
[4] Child Support (Northern Ireland) Order 1991, art 25.
[5] Child Support (Northern Ireland) Order 1991, art 26.
[6] Child Support Appeals (Jurisdiction of Courts) Order (Northern Ireland) 2002, arts 3 and 4.

Courts' residual jurisdiction

9.70 The CSA does not have jurisdiction to determine child support maintenance in the following cases and as a result the parties must apply to the courts as they alone have jurisdiction to set the level of maintenance. The situations in which the CSA does not have jurisdiction are where:

1 a previous maintenance agreement, dating from before 5 April 1993, or an agreed Maintenance Order (see below), is in existence;[1]
2 the child is aged 16–18 years and is not in full-time non-advanced education, ie not in second level schooling;[2]
3 the application is for maintenance which would be used solely to pay the child's educational or training fees;[3]
4 top-up payments are appropriate, ie where the children have wealthy parents;[4]
5 the child is disabled;[4]
6 the person being assessed is the child's stepfather and not its natural and biological father;[6]
7 one of the parents is not resident in the UK.[7]

¹   Child Support (Northern Ireland) Order 1991, art 7(10), as amended. The court's power to make a
    Maintenance Order by consent derives from art 10(5).
²   Child Support (Northern Ireland) Order 1991, art 3(1), as defined by the Child Support (Maintenance
    Calculation Procedure) Regulations (Northern Ireland) 2001, Sch 1, paras 1 and 2. This includes
    children enrolled on BTEC and HND courses amongst others.
³   Child Support (Northern Ireland) Order 1991, art 10(7).
⁴   This arises where the non-resident parent's income is above the level of assessable income, which is
    currently fixed at £2,000 per week, Child Support (Northern Ireland) Order 1991, Sch 1, Pt 1,
    para 10(3).
⁵   Child Support (Northern Ireland) Order 1991, art 10(8) and (9).
⁶   See the definition of 'parent' in the Child Support (Northern Ireland) Order 1991, art 2(2).
⁷   Child Support (Northern Ireland) Order 1991, art 41(1).

9.71   The reference to an agreed Maintenance Order above refers to cases where the parties are divorcing and they wish to have all property and financial matters dealt with by the courts. They may avoid the inconvenience of having the CSA deal with child support maintenance while the courts deal with other financial issues between the parties. This can be done if the parties make an agreement as to the amount of maintenance to be paid and then have the court convert that agreement into a court order. However, where such a Maintenance Order has been in force for a year or more, it is open to one parent to apply to the CSA for a maintenance assessment from the agency, notwithstanding the existence of the Maintenance Order.[1]

¹   Child Support, Pensions and Social Security Act (Northern Ireland) 2000, s 2, amending the Child
    Support (Northern Ireland) Order 1991, art 7(10).

Property and lump sums for children

9.72   The CSA only has jurisdiction to determine periodic payments and the courts retain jurisdiction to make Lump Sum Orders and Property Adjustment Orders for all children.[1] The practical effect of this is that where the non-resident parent has considerable wealth or owns property, the parent with care can apply to the courts to have some part or all of the interest in the property transferred to the child or to have them order that lump sums be paid over to the child. (The courts will, of course, also be able to order periodic payments in the circumstances outlined above where the CSA does not have jurisdiction).[2]

¹   Children (Northern Ireland) Order 1995, art 15 and Sch 1 .
²   See para 9.70.

9.73   Lump Sum Orders and Property Adjustment Orders are similar sorts of orders to those which can be made in favour of one of the parties to a divorce, judicial separation or annulment petition.[1] In making such orders, or any Periodical Payments Orders, the court is to have regard to all the circumstances of the parties including the following matters:[2]
(a)   the income, earning capacity, property and other financial resources which each [of the parents] has or is likely to have in the foreseeable future;
(b)   the financial needs, obligations and responsibilities which each [of the parents] has or is likely to have in the foreseeable future;
(c)   the financial needs of the child;

(d)   the income, earning capacity (if any), property and other financial resources of the child;

(e)   any physical or mental disability of the child;

(f)   the manner in which the child was being, or was expected to be, educated or trained.

---

[1]   See para 9.87.

[2]   Children (Northern Ireland) Order 1995, Sch 1, para 5.

9.74   However, the courts will be alert to the necessity of ensuring that the benefit of the court order is for the child and that the parent with care does not in fact obtain a benefit.[1]

It is also possible for a parent to make an application to the courts in respect of a child who is over the age of 18 years but remains in full-time education to have the courts order periodical payments or a lump sum where the court is satisfied that there are special circumstances for doing so, thus allowing the possibility that the child will need to be supported through full-time education.[2]

---

[1]   See, for example, *A v A (minor) (Financial provision)* [1994] 1 FLR 657.

[2]   Children (Northern Ireland) Order 1995, Sch 1, para 3.

Providing for the spouse

9.75   As part of the petition for divorce, judicial separation or annulment, the parties can make applications to the court to have it deal with financial matters between them. This aspect of the legal proceedings is referred to as 'ancillary relief', the idea being that the issues being decided are ancillary to the main business, which is the petition for divorce, judicial separation or annulment as the case may be. In reality of course the parties are often more interested in the ancillary relief proceedings than the petition for divorce, judicial separation or annulment as the latter is usually a foregone conclusion and the former have implications for the parties' futures.

9.76   One of the legal consequences of marriage is that the parties undertake to maintain each another, a duty which does not arise, obviously, where the parties are merely cohabitants. This common law duty is about to be abolished by the Family Law (Divorce etc ...) Bill 2002[1] but the historical importance of the duty to maintain will continue to be reflected in the fact that statute provides mechanisms by which one spouse can secure an order for maintenance against another.

---

[1]   Clause 10.

Maintenance for spouses

9.77   Maintenance may be obtained from the Domestic Proceedings Court[1] or the High Court, when the marriage has broken down but is still subsisting (referred to here as 'maintenance short of divorce'), or from the county court or High Court, where one of the couple has petitioned for divorce, judicial separation or annulment.

[1]   See chapter 1, para 1.59.

Maintenance short of divorce

9.78   Maintenance may be secured without the need to launch divorce, judicial separation or annulment proceedings where the respondent party has failed to properly maintain the applicant or where the respondent has committed adultery, deserted the applicant, or engaged in unreasonable behaviour.

Maintenance Orders can be granted by the High Court where the respondent has reasonably failed to maintain his or her spouse or the children of the family.[1] In determining the amount of maintenance the court has first regard for the children's welfare and assesses all the circumstances but particularly a range of factors similar to those that are relevant when the court is hearing ancillary relief petitions in the context of divorce, judicial separation or annulment.[2]

[1]   Matrimonial Causes (Northern Ireland) Order 1978, art 29.
[2]   See the Matrimonial Causes (Northern Ireland) Order 1978, art 27(2)(a)–(g) as amended.

9.79   Maintenance Orders can also be granted by the Domestic Proceedings Court. In that court an application for maintenance can be made by one spouse not only where the respondent has failed to reasonably maintain the applicant spouse or children, but also where the respondent spouse has committed adultery, deserted the applicant spouse or engaged in unreasonable behaviour.[1] The range of factors to which the court is to have regard before making a Maintenance Order in the Domestic Proceedings Court are the same as those where the application for maintenance is made in the High Court for failure to reasonably maintain. There is a clear overlap between the basis on which maintenance may be secured from the Domestic Proceedings Court and the High Court on the one hand, and the facts that need to be proved in a petition for a decree of divorce or judicial separation on the other. This may explain why the public is occasionally confused about the effect of the Maintenance Order made in the Domestic Proceedings Court, believing that it amounts to a 'Separation Order' or some other order terminating the marriage.[2]

[1]   Domestic Proceedings (Northern Ireland) Order 1980, art 4.
[2]   'Unravelling the system – Divorce in Northern Ireland', Archbold, White, McWilliams, McKee and Murtagh, Stationery Office, 1999, pp 215–6.

9.80   Research into divorcing patterns in Northern Ireland has shown that considerable use is made of the magistrates' courts by couples in troubled relationships, and that much of the early legal resolution of matrimonial disputes, in relation to financial and child rearing matters, takes place in that forum.[1]

[1]   'Unravelling the system – Divorce in Northern Ireland', Archbold, White, McWilliams, McKee and Murtagh, Stationery Office, 1999, pp 161 ff, for example.

Maintenance on divorce, judicial separation or annulment

9.81 Maintenance from the divorce court is only available quite obviously if a divorce petition has been made (or alternatively, as outlined above, a judicial separation or nullity petition). Maintenance pending the final outcome of the petition is available and this is referred to as 'maintenance pending suit'.[1] The other, more long-term form of spousal maintenance, however, arises from court orders made as part of the ancillary relief proceedings. These orders are for periodical payments, either secured or unsecured, by one party to the other.[2] Secured periodical payments are simply a more certain form of payment because, for example, the maintenance is paid from an account containing funds designated for that purpose.

[1] Matrimonial Causes (Northern Ireland) Order 1978, art 24.
[2] Matrimonial Causes (Northern Ireland) Order 1978, art 25(1)(a) and (b).

9.82 In determining the amount of maintenance that a spouse is to receive, the court has regard to a number of factors set out in the Matrimonial Causes (Northern Ireland) 1978.[1] These are:

(a) the income, earning capacity, property and other financial resources which each of the parties to the marriage has or is likely to have in the foreseeable future, including in the case of earning capacity any increase in that capacity which it would in the opinion of the court be reasonable to expect a party to the marriage to take steps to acquire;

(b) the financial needs, obligations and responsibilities which each of the parties to the marriage has or is likely to have in the foreseeable future;

(c) the standard of living enjoyed by the family before the breakdown of the marriage;

(d) the age of each party to the marriage and the duration of the marriage;

(e) any physical or mental disability of either of the parties to the marriage;

(f) the contributions which each of the parties has made or is likely in the foreseeable future to make to the welfare of the family, including any contribution by looking after the home or caring for the family;

(g) the conduct of each of the parties, if that conduct is such that it would in the opinion of the court be inequitable to disregard it;

(h) in the case of proceedings for divorce of nullity of marriage, the value to each of the parties to the marriage of any benefit which, by reason of the dissolution or annulment of the marriage, that party will lose the chance of acquiring.

The court is mandated to take all the circumstances of the case into account, 'first consideration being given to the welfare' of any children.[2] Where the court is intending to make a property, lump sum or Periodical Payments Order in respect of the children, it must consider other factors:[3]

(a) the financial needs of the child;

(b) the income, earning capacity (if any), property and other financial resources of the child;

(c) any physical or mental disability of the child;

(d) the manner in which he was being and in which the parties to the marriage expected him to be educated or trained;

(e)   the matters mentioned in relation to making financial or property orders for the parties to the marriage and referred to in the paragraph above at (a), (b), (c) and (e).

1   Article 27(2).
2   Matrimonial Causes (Northern Ireland) Order 1978, art 27(1).
3   Matrimonial Causes (Northern Ireland) Order 1978, art 27(3) as amended.

9.83   Recall that the courts may only make an order for maintenance in the child's favour where the CSA does not have jurisdiction to determine child support maintenance.[1] Note the parties' conduct is not a factor that the courts are required to assess when making Ancillary Relief Orders, and normally their conduct is irrelevant to such issues, unless the conduct is 'obvious and gross'.[2]

1   See para 9.70.
2   *Wachtel v Wachtel* [1973] Fam 72 at 89–90.

9.84   It is important to realise that the UK does not operate a community property regime and there are no set shares, or percentages, of the family property to which an applicant is entitled. Marriage alone does not entitle a spouse to half of his or her spouse's property. The wide discretion available to the courts, or more properly the High Court Master or district judge who decides these matters[1] when considering ancillary relief applications, means that it is difficult to predict exactly what the court will decide. Allied to this, the wide variation in the circumstances of each couple means that it is difficult to rely on outcomes in previous cases as precedents to be used by future applicants. In general terms, legal advisers attempt to negotiate a total package of ancillary relief measures, rather than dealing with each item individually. In doing so they will often pay particular attention to the necessity of providing housing for the children and the party with whom they will reside.

1   On High Court Masters, see chapter 1, para 1.63.

9.85   Notwithstanding the range and breadth of the statutory factors that must be considered by a court faced with an application for an Ancillary Relief Order the courts have attempted to provide further guidance to married couples and their legal advisers. In *White v White*[1] the House of Lords examined the application of the statutory criteria. In that case the parties were quite wealthy and had amassed marital assets totalling £4.5m. The wife was granted £1.5m of these assets by the Court of Appeal, which allowing for the parties' costs was approximately 40% of the total marital assets. She appealed to the House of Lords seeking an equal share. The House of Lords suggested that judges should have regard to the principle of equality in such cases, but did not go so far as to say that there was a presumption that property be equally divided between divorcing spouses:

'Sometimes, having carried out the statutory exercise, the judge's conclusion involves a more or less equal division of the available assets. More often, this is not so. More often, having looked at all the circumstances, the judge's decision means that one party will receive a bigger share than the other will. Before reaching a firm conclusion and making an order along these lines, a judge would always be well-advised to check his tentative views against the yardstick of equality of division. As a general guide, equality should be departed from only if, and to the extent that, there is good reason for doing so. The need to consider and articulate reasons for departing from equality would help the parties and the court to focus on the need to ensure the absence of discrimination.'

1   [2001] 1 AC 596, [2001] 1 All ER 1, [2000] 2 FCR 555, HL.

9.86   The courts have reconsidered this issue in further cases, like for example, *GW v RW*,[1] where the wife was awarded 40% of the family assets, the court departing from a position of equality to reflect the duration of the marriage and the fact that the husband had amassed significant wealth before the marriage.[2]

1   [2003] EWHC 611 (Fam), [2003] 2 FLR 108, [2003] 2 FCR 289.
2   See also *C v C (variation of post-nuptial settlement: company shares)*[2003] EWHC 1222 (Fam), [2003] 2 FLR 493, where the court awarded the wife 30% of the husband's shares in a Cayman Island company, having regard to his role in setting it up and the fact that the wife was awarded sole interest in the matrimonial home.

Property and assets on divorce, judicial separation or annulment

9.87   The redistribution of property by the courts is also possible on a petition for divorce, judicial separation or annulment. The court carries out this redistributive task on the same basis as it determines spousal maintenance, namely having regard to all the circumstances of the case, but in particular the matters and factors referred to above.[1] There are two types of order that can be made, namely a Property Adjustment Order and a Lump Sum Order.

1   Matrimonial Causes (Northern Ireland) Order 1978, art 27. See para 9.82.

Property Adjustment Order

9.88   A court can, on application to it, make a number of orders in respect of the property of one of the spouses. It can order the transfer of ownership of the property from one person to another.[1] Secondly, it may settle the benefit of any property to which one party is entitled on the other party, or on the children. Thirdly, it can vary any existing settlement of property in favour of any member of the family.[2] The court can also if it wishes, order the sale of any property owned by the parties.[3]

1   See for example, *JMcC v AMcC* [1982] NI 342 in which the husband was ordered to transfer his interest in the matrimonial home to his ill spouse, and that the wife make a lump sum payment to her husband within three months of the transfer.
2   Matrimonial Causes (Northern Ireland) Order 1978, art 26.
3   Matrimonial Causes (Northern Ireland) Order 1978, art 26(4).

Lump Sum Order

9.89   In respect of other financial assets, the court may make a Lump Sum Order.[1] A Lump Sum Order is an order that the respondent pays a large single sum of money to the applicant, rather than spreading the payments over a period of time as is the case with periodical payments. Clearly, such orders will usually only be appropriate where the parties have considerable capital reserves.

[1]   Matrimonial Causes (Northern Ireland) Order 1978, art 25(1)(c) and (f).

Pensions and divorce, judicial separation and annulment

9.90   In an ancillary relief application the courts may also make orders in respect of the parties' pension entitlements. There are three options open to the court in respect of pensions: pension splitting, pension earmarking and pension offsetting.

Pension splitting

9.91   First, it may split any pension to which the respondent contributes, between the parties by making a Pension Sharing Order.[1] This means that the value of the pension will have to be calculated and the court then considers what percentage of that value should be awarded to the applicant having regard to the same statutory factors that the court assesses when making Property Adjustment Orders, Lump Sum Orders or Periodical Payments Orders.[2] The purpose of pension splitting is to provide the applicant with a sum that will allow him or her to establish a pension of their own. The advantage of this approach is that the parties' obligations in respect of pensions are resolved definitively at this point.

[1]   Matrimonial Causes (Northern Ireland) Order 1978, art 23A, as inserted by the Welfare Reform and Provisions (Northern Ireland) Order 1999, art 18 and Sch 3.
[2]   See para 9.82.

Pension earmarking

9.92   Secondly, the court may engage in pension 'earmarking'.[1] This involves the court in determining the size of the share to which the applicant will be entitled when the pension matures, but no apportionment of the existing value of the pension takes place. In effect, a percentage of the future value of the pension is earmarked for the applicant.

Pension off-setting

9.93   The third option open to the court is for it to set-off the share of the pension to which the applicant would be entitled against some other assets, which are then transferred to the applicant. The respondent's pension remains intact, but the applicant receives another benefit in lieu of obtaining a share of the respondent's pension, like, for example, a share in a property.

[1]   Matrimonial Causes (Northern Ireland) Order 1978, art 27C.

'Clean break' settlements

9.94   Where possible, and where appropriate, the courts are directed to consider making Ancillary Relief Orders that ensure that the parties continuing obligations to one another are terminated as soon as possible after the divorce as the court thinks just and reasonable.[1] This phenomenon is referred to as the 'clean break' settlement and involves the court considering whether a limited number of periodical payments would be appropriate or whether a Lump Sum Order might be possible. The court is directed to calculate the number of periodical payments that 'would be sufficient to enable [that spouse] to adjust without undue hardship to the termination of his or her financial dependence on the other [spouse].'[2] The court can also prevent one spouse from making any other applications for Ancillary Relief Orders as methods of achieving this 'clean break'.[3]

[1]   Matrimonial Causes (Northern Ireland) Order 1978, art 27A.
[2]   Matrimonial Causes (Northern Ireland) Order 1978, art 27A(2).
[3]   Matrimonial Causes (Northern Ireland) Order 1978, art 27A(3).

9.95   It is clear that clean break settlements are usually only an option where the parties have the financial wherewithal to sever the ties between them. The legislation directs the courts to have regard to the possibility of making a 'clean break' as between the parties to the marriage and therefore there can never be a 'clean break' of the responsibilities the parents owe to their children.

Property division and former cohabitants

9.96   As stated above, unmarried cohabitants cannot avail themselves of the ancillary relief regime that is open to married couples whenever the latter seek to divorce, judicially separate or annul their marriages. The practical effect of this is that cohabitants do not have access to the redistributive powers available to married couples (and examined above)[1] and must, therefore, rely upon general property law concepts to resolve property and financial disputes between them.[2]

[1]   See para 9.87.
[2]   Note that disputes about child support maintenance will be resolved under the Child Support Legislation, see para 9.67 or exceptionally, under the Children (Northern Ireland) Order 1995, Sch 1, see para 9.72.

9.97   Usually the single, most valuable asset that cohabitants will own is the house in which they have resided together. Difficulties arise where at the time of breakdown of the relationship the habitual home is (legally) owned by one of them alone. The non-owning party may then seek to establish that he or she has an (beneficial) interest in the title of the property by virtue of any direct contributions that he or she has made to the purchase price. Alternatively he or she may claim that they have such an interest by virtue of an agreement, arrangement or understanding between the parties, coupled with actions that suggest that the parties intended that both of them would own the property, such actions indicating that the non-owning party relied on the agreement, arrangement or understanding. This concept is referred to as a constructive trust, and means that the party that is the sole legal owner is deemed to hold the property on trust for both cohabitants. It is a difficult doctrine of which to avail oneself and has given rise to much controversy and judicial and academic discussion over the years.[1] Contributions of a non-financial nature, such as home-making activities, child rearing for example, will not entitle the non-owning party to a share in the property. In the leading case, *Lloyds Bank plc v Rosset*,[2] the wife claimed an interest in the family home arising from her participation in, and supervision of, renovation works on the property. The House of Lords rejected this claim, indicating that it was doubtful whether anything less than a direct contribution to the acquisition of the property would suffice.[3]

---

[1]   See, for example, Wragg, 'Constructive trusts and the unmarried couple', 1996 Fam Law 298–300, Cardner, 'Fin de siecle chez Gissing v Gissing', 1996 LQR 378. Lind and Barlow, 'A matter of trust: the allocation of property rights in the family home', 1999 Legal Studies 468–488', S Wong, 'Constructive trusts within the family home: lessons to be learned from other common law jurisdictions,' 1998 Legal Studies 369.
[2]   [1991] 1 AC 107, [1990] 1 All ER 1111, HL.
[3]   However, once the court has determined that the non-owning party is entitled to some share in the property, the courts take a more liberal view in assessing the size of that share. See *Drake v Whipp* [1996] 2 FCR 296, CA and *Midland Bank plc v Cooke* [1995] 4 All ER 562, CA, for example.

9.98   The Law Reform Advisory Committee has issued a discussion document on the topic of the division of legal interests in the habitual home on the breakdown of cohabitants' relationship.[1] It proposes that the habitual home be considered the joint property of both cohabitants where the property is bought by one of them, for example, unless they agree otherwise in writing. This regime would apply where the cohabitants had lived together for a period of two years within the preceding three, or had a child together. This regime would only apply to property purchased after the couple became a qualifying couple.

---

[1]   Matrimonial Property, Discussion Paper No 5, LRAC, 1999.

Child rearing

9.99   The issue of the care of children post-relationship breakdown is provided for in the Children (Northern Ireland) Order 1995. The 1995 Order significantly altered the regime for considering disputes between parents about the upbringing of the children and in doing so replaced the terms of 'custody' and 'access' with those of 'residence' and 'contact' respectively. A range of orders, referred to in Northern Ireland as 'Article 8 orders',[1] is available to the court in situations of disputes between the child's family members. In determining any Article 8 application, the court will obviously have regard to the paramountcy principle and the 'welfare checklist'.[2] These orders are available to the child's parents or other parties, irrespective of whether the parents were, or are, married. Article 8 Orders can be made by the court of its own volition, without the need for a parent or other person, to make an application, if it thinks the circumstances warrant it, in any 'family proceedings'.

[1] In England and Wales these are referred to as 'Section 8 Orders' this being the relevant section of the Children Act 1989 which makes provision for these orders.
[2] See chapter 6, paras 6.34–6.39.

9.100 Article 8 applications are referred to as private law applications because they do not usually involve agencies of the state as participants and to distinguish them from the public law applications, principally for Care Orders and Supervision Orders, in which the state is seeking to protect the best interests of the child.[1] However, the fact that Article 8 Orders can be made in any 'family proceedings' means that the same legal hearing may have to determine competing applications for public law and private law orders.

[1] See chapter 6, para 6.7.

Article 8 Orders

9.101 There are four types of 'Article 8 Order', namely Residence Order, Contact Order, Specific Issues Order and Prohibited Steps Order, which can be made in respect of children under the age of 16 years or for those over 16 in exceptional circumstances.[1] Applications for any of these orders must be made to the Family Proceedings Court, or where other proceedings are in existence in respect of the child, to the court hearing those other proceedings.[2] These orders are usually sought by the child's parents, or grandparents or some other relative, although people who are not the child's parents may require the leave of the court to bring the application.[3] A Trust may not apply for, or have granted in its favour, a Residence Order or a Contact Order. Even where no application has been made to it, the court is also entitled to make an Article 8 Order of its own volition.[4] The vast majority of Article 8 applications were for Residence and Contact Orders. For example, in 2001/02, 2,466 applications were lodged for Contact Orders, while 1,684 were lodged for Residence Orders. However, in contrast, only 258 applications were lodged for Prohibited Steps Orders and 119 for Specific Issues Orders.[5]

[1] Children (Northern Ireland) Order 1995, art 9(6) and (7).
[2] See chapter 6, para 6.45. However, where the application under the Children (Northern Ireland) Order seeks to vary an order previously made by the Domestic Proceedings Court then the application should be made to that court. See *Re Robb* (20 April 2000, unreported), High Court, Higgins J.
[3] Children (Northern Ireland) Order 1995, art 10(5) and (9). See for example, *Re C (grandparents: application for leave)* High Court, Gillen J, 2003 NIFAM 13, in which leave was granted to the child's grandfather to apply for a Contact Order where he had previously been convicted of child sexual abuse.
[4] Children (Northern Ireland) Order 1995, art 10(1)(b).
[5] Northern Ireland Court Service Annual Report 2001–02, Table F3, Free Standing Proceedings by Type, p 132.

Residence Order

9.102 A Residence Order determines with whom the child is to live and accords parental responsibility to the person in whose favour it is made.[1] Thus, for example, if the child's grandparents secure a Residence Order to have the child reside with them, they will acquire parental responsibility for the child. This does not extinguish the parental responsibility that any other person has for the child. The purpose of the order is simply to formally establish the child's accommodation arrangements.

1   Children (Northern Ireland) Order 1995, art 12(1) and (2).

9.103   It may be made in the form of a Shared, or Joint Residence Order in which the court directs that the child is to live with both parents. *Re R (Shared Residence Application: Contact)*,[1] Gillen J had occasion to assess just such an application and relied on the leading English authority, *Re D (Shared Residence Order)*.[2] This latter case established that it is no longer the case that there must be exceptional circumstances before a Shared Residence Order will be made, signalling a shift of attitude on the part of the courts towards granting more Shared Residence Orders.[4] However, on the facts, Gillen J concluded that such an order would not be in the child's interests in the case before him, as the level of disharmony and mistrust between the child's parents was so great that it would affect the child. However, Shared Residence Orders are not very common and it is more usual that both parents will agree, perhaps for a variety of reasons, that the child is to reside with its mother.[4]

A child who is the subject of a Residence Order is not to become known by a new surname, nor is he or she allowed to leave the UK for period longer than one month, without the written permission of others with parental responsibility or the leave of the court.[5]

1   (24 October 2002, unreported), High Court, transcript available on Lexis.
2   [2001] 1 FLR 495, CA.
3   However, the decision does appear to rely heavily on the fact that the children were spending significant amounts of time in both parents' houses in any event.
4   See 'Unravelling the system: Divorce in Northern Ireland', Archbold, White, Murtagh, McKee and McWilliams, Stationery Office 1999, which demonstrates this pattern, albeit in respect of court orders made prior to the implementation of the Children (Northern Ireland) Order 1995.
5   Children (Northern Ireland) Order 1995, art 13(1) and (2). See *L v L (leave to remove children from jurisdiction: effect on children)* [2002] EWHC 2577 (Fam), [2003] 1 FLR 900, [2003] Fam Law 310 in which the court granted the mother permission to emigrate to the US.

Contact Order

9.104   A Contact Order is directed to the person with whom the child is residing and requires him or her to allow the child to have contact with specified people. This contact can take various forms including indirect contact (by writing or by telephone, for example), supervised or unsupervised contact or 'staying contact' whereby the child is permitted to stay overnight in the other parent's home. For example, in *MF v MF*,[1] faced with an application by a father for a Contact Order in circumstances where the judge accepted that he had sexually abused his children, the trial judge ordered indirect contact, namely the sending of birthday cards, to be permitted.

1   (11 April 2003, unreported), High Court, Weatherup J.

9.105 The principles governing the setting of contact have been set out by the English Court of Appeal in *Re P (Contact: Supervision)*:[1]

'(1) overriding all else, ... the welfare of the child is the paramount consideration, and the court is concerned with the interests of the mother and the father only insofar as they bear on the welfare of the child;

(2) it is almost always in the interests of a child whose parents are separated that he or she should have contact with the parent with whom the child is not living;

(3) the court has power to enforce orders for contact, which it should not hesitate to exercise where it judges that it will overall promote the welfare of the child to do so;

(4) cases do, unhappily and infrequently but occasionally, arise in which a court is compelled to conclude that in existing circumstances an order for immediate direct contact should not be ordered, because so to order would injure the welfare of the child;[2]

(5) in cases in which, for whatever reason, direct contact cannot for the time being be ordered, it is ordinarily highly desirable that there should be indirect contact so that the child grows up knowing of the love and interest of the absent parent with whom, in due course, direct contact should be established.'

As can be seen from this quotation, there is a strong presumption in favour of granting Contact Orders because of the underlying ethos in the Children (Northern Ireland) Order 1995 that children should, as far as possible, maintain relationships with their parents, whatever the status of their parents' relationship. This issue of contact in cases of domestic violence has already been examined.[3] Similar types of difficulties can arise in respect of contact and parental abuse of the children. In *Re NS and JAS and JBS*,[4] the judge considered that the allegations of sexual abuse had not been made out on the balance of probabilities and ordered a detailed regime of contact beginning with supervised contact and proceeding to unsupervised contact.

[1] [1996] 2 FLR 314.
[2] Citing *Re D (A Minor) (Contact: Mother's Hostility)* [1993] 2 FLR 1 at 7G, per Waite LJ. This case concluded that while the hostility of a parent to allowing the other parent contact would not decide the issue there were occasions in which that hostility might justify the refusal of contact.
[3] See para 9.44.
[4] (5 July 2002, unreported), High Court, Weatherup J, transcript on Lexis.

Specific Issues and Prohibited Steps Orders

9.106 The remaining two types of order are used when the parents are in dispute about some particular aspect of their child's welfare or upbringing. A Specific Issues Order decides a particular dispute between the parents, or others with parental responsibility. Such an order would be appropriate to determine an argument about where a child should be educated, for example.[1] A Prohibited Steps Order prevents the party to whom it is addressed from engaging in a particular act, or carrying out some step, without the permission of the court. This order might be employed where the parents were in dispute about whether a child should receive a blood transfusion in the event of an accident.[2]

---

[1]   See, for example, *Re W (children) (education: choice of school)* [2002] EWCA Civ 1411, [2002] 3 FCR 473.

[2]   Although see an unusual use of a Prohibited Steps Order in *Re G (a child)* [2002] EWCA Civ 1547, where the order prohibited the child's father from publishing details of the case on the Internet. See also *Re H (a child: parental responsibility)* [2002] EWCA Civ 542, in which the father was granted a Parental Responsibility Order but the court granted the mother a Specific Issues Order according her full autonomy in regard to the child's health and a Prohibited Steps Order preventing the father from trying to ascertain the location of the child.

Enforcement of Contact Orders

9.107   The enforcement of Contact Orders has proven to be a very controversial contemporary topic. Parents in whose favour court orders have been made are becoming increasingly vocal about the difficulties they experience in ensuring contact with their children, in the face of, what they allege is unwarranted hostility, from the parent with whom the child resides. The normal method of enforcing court orders is by way of contempt of court proceedings, and the penalties for acting in contempt of court are a fine or a term of imprisonment. However, imposing a fine or prison sentence on the parent with whom the child resides clearly present difficulties. Monetary penalties will affect that parent's ability to provide for the child and imprisoning the parent will raise immediate problems about the care of he child. As a result, these penalties are imposed as a last resort, prompting the allegation from parents with Contact Orders, who feel contact is being frustrated, that the State is not doing enough to safeguard their right to family life. This matter has already been the subject of a case before the European Court of Human Rights. In *Glaser v United Kingdom*,[1] the court heard a complaint from a father that his wife was refusing to obey a Contact Order and that the courts were not enforcing that order in an effective manner. The complainant's wife had disappeared with the children soon after the Contact Order was made. The High Court ordered court officials to seek and locate them, ordered Government agencies to disclose any information they had as to the current address or whereabouts of the children, and invited the Official Solicitor to act as guardian ad litem for the children, who also conducted his own investigations into their whereabouts. The European Court of Human Rights rejected his complaint on the basis that the English courts were doing all that was possible to enforce the order. The court concluded that the obligation on national authorities to take measures to facilitate contact by a non-custodial parent after divorce was not absolute, and the key consideration was whether the authorities had taken all necessary steps to facilitate contact as could reasonably be demanded in the special circumstances of each case. It also rejected his complaint that there had been a breach of his right to a fair trial[2] within a reasonable time, because having regard the nature of the dispute, the three year period in enforcing the order was not unreasonable.

¹ [2001] 1 FLR 153, [2000] 3 FCR 193.
² Convention right, art 6. See chapter 6, para 6.23.

9.108 Because imprisonment and fining the non co-operative parent is a measure of last resort, the courts can take novel approaches to the problem of obstructed contact. In *Re M (intractable contact dispute: interim care order)*,¹ the court was faced with a parent who had falsely persuaded her children that they had been physically and sexually abused by their non-residential father and their paternal grandparents, with whom the children had previously enjoyed a normal relationship. The result had been the cessation of contact. The parent's conduct was affecting the children in such a way that the court decided to order the English equivalent of an Article 56 Investigation² to see whether it would be appropriate for a Care or Supervision Order to be made in respect of a child. The children were suffering significant harm in the residential parent's care. As a result of making the Article 56 Investigation Order, an Interim Care Order was subsequently made since it had been impossible to conduct an assessment of the children at home. When the case was finally concluded a Residence Order, was granted to the father. However, this was an unusual method of dealing with the problem of obstructed contact and depended on its facts, and not every situation will give rise to the need for an Article 56 Investigation.

¹ [2003] EWHC 1024 (Fam), [2003] 2 FLR 636.
² See chapter 6 para 6.95. The order was made under the Children Act 1989, s 37

9.109 The recalcitrant parent can indeed be committed to prison if the circumstances warrant it. In *A v N (Committal Refusal of Contact)*¹ the mother repeatedly breached the court order, maintaining, despite DNA evidence that the father was not in fact the father of the child and relying on his violence towards her. She was initially sentenced to six weeks' imprisonment suspended for six months, but when she failed to allow supervised contact on the next occasion, the Suspended Order was activated. In refusing her appeal against this decision, the court noted that the child's welfare was a material factor to be considered but not a paramount one, and that there was a limit to the court's forbearance faced with the woman's intransigence.

¹ [1997] 1 FLR 533, CA.

9.110 This issue has become so pressing that the Lord Chancellor's Department has published a report examining methods by which contact could be made to work.¹ It concluded that it was necessary to retain the traditional penalties for acting in contempt of court by breaching a court order, but that the courts required new statutory powers to supplement these penalties.² In this respect the report endorsed suggestions by CAFCASS that what is required 'is an approach that gives practitioners more time to work with parents and children within a framework of an existing order, such as supervised contact centres, child counselling, perpetrator programmes, information giving meetings, conciliation meetings prior to initial directions and psychological assessments.'³ These non-punitive elements would precede the exercise of punitive options.

¹ Advisory Board in Family Law (Children Act Sub-Committee) 'Making Contact Work' – A report to

the Lord Chancellor on the Facilitation of Arrangements for Contact between children and their non-residential parents and the enforcement of court orders for contact, February 2002.

2   Advisory Board in Family Law (Children Act Sub-Committee) 'Making Contact Work' – A report to the Lord Chancellor on the Facilitation of Arrangements for Contact between children and their non-residential parents and the enforcement of court orders for contact, February 2002, at paras 14.47 ff.

3   Advisory Board in Family Law (Children Act Sub-Committee) 'Making Contact Work' – A report to the Lord Chancellor on the Facilitation of Arrangements for Contact between children and their non-residential parents and the enforcement of court orders for contact, February 2002, at para 14.51.

Chapter 10

Community Care Law

Maura McCallion

Introduction

10.1 Community care is generally considered to be the provision of social care and some health care, other than in a hospital setting. Community care services can include such things as support offered to a person at home, access to respite and day care, family placements, the provision of sheltered housing, placement in group homes and hostels or residential and nursing homes.

Although what is now known as community care has always existed in some form, in 1991 proposals for improving the management and delivery of community care services were set out in the government policy paper, 'People First: Community Care in Northern Ireland in the 1990s'.[1] The fundamental principle, as outlined in this document, is that a person who needs care and support should be encouraged and assisted in order to enable him or her to live, with as much independence as possible, in the community, as opposed to living in an institution. A review of community care was commissioned by the government in 2001 and the first report in 2002 re-committed the government to the 'People First' principles, but also outlined a strategic approach to developing services.[2]

This chapter looks at the legislative framework for the provision of community care services and considers the law around key issues such as assessment, and more recent developments in relation to carers and direct payments.

[1]   DHSS, 1991.
[2]   Review of Community Care, report of first phase, DHSSPS, 2002.

The legal framework

10.2 The law relating to community care in Northern Ireland is not contained in one piece of legislation. There are at least six important community care statutes, and of course, as explained in chapter 1,[1] social workers and social services staff also need to comply with human rights and equality legislation. In addition to the main statutes governing service provision, there is a range of other legislation which may be relevant in different contexts, for example, regulations governing the payment of benefits,[2] or the running of residential and nursing homes.

Trusts are also issued with guidance in various forms, such as Departmental circulars on hospital discharge, or circulars relating to assessment or good practice guidance. Generally, guidance does not impose legally binding obligations although it does carry significant weight in any dispute about the assessment of need and the provision of services and will usually be relevant in any judicial review application.[3]

The 'People First' guidance is an important, general document to be taken into account in considering policy and practice. There are also more specific pieces of guidance on issues such as consenting to service provision, carers' assessments and direct payment, that may be relevant in certain instances. In order to understand the duties placed on Trusts it is important to be aware of the most significant community care statutes and to consider some of the main features of that legislation.

[1]   See paras 1.66 ff.
[2]   For example, the Social Security (Disability Living Allowance) Regulations (Northern Ireland) 1992.
[3]   For an explanation of judicial review, see chapter 2, paras 2.105 ff.

Health and Personal Social Services (NI) Order 1972

10.3   The Health and Personal Social Services (NI) Order 1972 (HPSS 1972) is the key piece of legislation governing the provision of health and social services care in Northern Ireland. It has been amended several times and the updated version can be accessed on the Stationery Office website.[1] The Order imposes a number of duties, the most significant of which include the following:

- a duty on the Department,[2] to provide or secure the provision of, integrated health services in Northern Ireland and to provide or secure the provision of personal social services in Northern Ireland designed to promote the social welfare of the people of Northern Ireland;[3]

- a duty to make arrangements, to such extent as the relevant Trust considers necessary, for the prevention of illness and the care, and after-care of a person suffering from illness;[4]

- a duty to make available advice, guidance and assistance, to such extent as the Trust considers necessary, and to make such arrangements and provide, or secure the provision of, such facilities as it considers suitable and adequate in order for it to discharge its duty under Article 4.[5]

[1]   See www.hmso.gov.uk, and chapter 1, para 1.37 on finding legislation generally.
[2]   Although these duties were originally imposed on the Department, subsequent legislation transferred these duties to Health Boards and then, in the 1990s, to Trusts. See chapter 1, para 1.114.
[3]   HPSS 1972, art 4.
[4]   HPSS 1972, art 7(1).
[5]   HPSS 1972, art 15(1).

Chronically Sick and Disabled Persons (NI) Act 1978

10.4 The Chronically Sick and Disabled Persons (NI) Act 1978 (CSDP 1978) contains specific duties in relation to a person who is chronically sick or has a disability. The language used in the definition is very much of its time. However, it remains the definition with which social services staff must work. Sections 1 and 2 outline the duty to share information and make such arrangements as are necessary for the provision of social welfare services to meet the needs of any person coming within the definition of chronically sick and disabled.

Persons covered by the CSDP 1978 are those who are 'blind, deaf or dumb, and other persons who are substantially handicapped by illness, injury or congenital deformity and whose handicap is of a permanent or lasting nature or are suffering from a mental disorder within the meaning of the Mental Health (NI) Order 1986'.[1]

The range of services that can be provided include: practical assistance in the home; the provision of or assistance in obtaining wireless, television, library or similar recreational features; the provision of lectures, games, outings or other recreational facilities or assistance in taking advantage of educational facilities available; travel arrangements for the purposes of participating in services; assisting in arrangements for the carrying out of any works of adaptation to the home; facilitating the taking of holidays; the provision of meals and the provision of, or assistance in obtaining, a telephone.[2] Section 2 has given rise to considerable litigation, discussed later.[3]

[1] CSDP 1978, s 1(1).
[2] Section 2.
[3] See paras 10.21, 10.28 and 10.30.

Disabled Persons (NI) Act 1989

10.5 The specific duty imposed by the 1989 Act, in relation to the assessment of people who come within the definition of chronically sick or disabled,[1] is that an assessment must be carried out, when requested by either a person meeting the definition or by his or her carer, to establish whether there is a need for the provision of services under the CSDP 1978, s 2. This means that there is a specific right to an assessment and if an assessment is requested, then the Trust must arrange it.

Care should be taken when reading this Act as several sections have not been brought into force.[2]

[1] CSDP 1978, s 4.
[2] Sections 1, 2, 3, 4(b), 8(2) and 8(3) are not yet in force.

Mental Health (NI) Order 1986

10.6 The operation of the Mental Health Order 1986 and its use for persons with a mental disorder is discussed in chapter 11, but it is worth noting here that the Order also places a general duty on Trusts to promote mental health, secure the prevention of mental disorder and promote the treatment, welfare and care of persons suffering from mental disorder.[1]

[1]   Mental Health (Northern Ireland) Order 1986, art 112.

Children (NI) Order 1995

10.7 While all the above provisions apply equally to children and adults, the Children (NI) Order 1995 creates certain rights and duties specific to children, which may be relevant in the context of the provision of community care services. Thus, for example, Trusts are under a general duty, by virtue of article 18 of the Order, to safeguard and promote the interests of 'children in need', which includes disabled children, and are empowered to provide a wide range of services. Children's services are discussed in chapter 7, although the rights of their carers are discussed here.

In relation to child carers and those who care for children with a disability, the Children (NI) Order 1995 has recently been amended by the Carers and Direct Payments Act (NI) 2002, to include a duty to assess the needs of child carers and carers of disabled children, when requested, and to consider what services to provide, where appropriate.[1]

[1]   New arts 17A and 18A have been inserted into the Children (Northern Ireland) Order 1995.

Carers and Direct Payments Act (NI) 2002

10.8 The Carers and Direct Payments (NI) Act 2002 (CDPA 2002) covers two distinct areas. It gives new rights to carers and it also extends the scope of direct payments. The carers' rights elements[1] of the CDPA 2002 came into effect on 1 April 2003, with the remainder due to commence on 19 April 2004.

[1]   The Carers and Direct Payments (2002 Act) (Commencement No 1) Order (Northern Ireland) 2003 brought ss 1, 2, 4, 5, 7 and 10 of the Act into operation on 31 March 2003.

Assessment of carers

10.9 For the first time, carers now have a statutory right under the CDPA 2002 to an assessment of need when requested.

Prior to the introduction of this legislation, departmental guidance recommended that Trusts follow the principles of the carers' legislation in England and Wales which afforded a more limited right to assessment.[1]

[1]   Carers (Recognition and Services) Act 1995.

Direct payments

10.10   Direct payments were first introduced to Northern Ireland in 1997, by the Personal Social Services (Direct Payments) (NI) Order 1996 (DPO 1996), which has since been amended by the Personal Social Services (Direct Payments) (Amendment) Regulations (Northern Ireland) 2000. The CDPA 2002 repeals and replaces the 1996 Order and new regulations will be enacted to replace the 2000 Regulations.

Direct payments mean that the person who needs assistance is given money to purchase his or her own service rather than having a service arranged or provided by a Trust. At present, the majority of those over 18 years old who could manage direct payments with assistance are entitled to request them. The CDPA 2002 extends the groups of people who can get direct payments to those with parental responsibility for disabled children, disabled parents with parental responsibility for children in relation to their own needs, and service users aged 16 or 17.[1] Carers will also be able to access direct payments to meet their own caring role needs.[2]

[1]   CDPA 2002, s 9, inserting a new art 18C into the Children (Northern Ireland) Order 1995.
[2]   CDPA 2002, s 8.

Human Rights Act 1998

10.11   In common with many other areas of social work law, Convention right, article 8 – right to respect for private and family life, home and correspondence – is most likely to be the most relevant right to providers and users of community care services.[1] Examples of scenarios in which article 8 is engaged in the field of community care services include those where there is a serious lack of effective domiciliary care services being delivered to a person, or where a person is placed in a residential care setting who wishes to remain at home. *R (Bernard) v Enfield London Borough Council*[2] is a good example of the breach of the positive obligation imposed by article 8 caused by the failure of the authority to act. In this case the local authority delayed in arranging adapted accommodation, including essential washing and toilet facilities, for a woman with a disability, leading to considerable distress for her and her family. The local authority was ordered to pay £10,000 damages.

However, it has been confirmed by the Court of Appeal in England and Wales that not all acts of maladministration by social services authorities will necessarily reach the threshold required for an article 8 claim.[3] The court emphasised that they would look both at the level of culpability involved in the failure to act and the severity of the consequences. It stated that isolated acts of even significant carelessness will not reach the article 8 threshold.

[1]   For text, and discussion, of article 8, see chapter 6 paras 6.11–6.20. Social workers should of course be aware that other Convention rights may also be applicable.
[2]   (2002) 5 CCL Rep 577.
[3]   *Anufrijeva v Southwark London Borough Council* [2003] EWCA Civ 1406, [2004] 1 All ER 833.

Section 75: statutory equality duty

10.12   As explained in chapter 4,[1] the Northern Ireland Act 1998, s 75 imposes a duty on public bodies to have due regard to the need to promote equality of opportunity between different specified groups of people including people of different ages, people with and without disabilities, and those who are carers and those who are not. This equality duty is relevant to all community care decisions, including individual service decisions and wider strategies.

[1]   See paras 4.75 ff.

Assessment of need for community care services

10.13   The legislation noted above sets the framework for decisions made by Trusts. The connection between the legislation and an individual is apparent when a Trust makes a decision about whether the legislation applies to his or her particular circumstances and thereafter whether services should be provided. This decision-making process is generally known as assessment of need.

Purpose of assessment

10.14   Assessment of need has a central role to play in the provision of community care. Correct assessment is crucial to the provision of appropriate care to meet a person's needs. Some of the statutory duties and powers directed to Trusts (and set out above) requires them to assess need. This is where a person who is a carer or is chronically sick or disabled makes an assessment request.

Departmental guidance widens the scope for assessment to those who, although not within the definition of chronically sick or disabled, may require a service because of, for example, old age. If the person appears to need care then it is not necessary for them to make a specific request for an assessment. 'People First, Care Management: Guidance on Assessment and the Provision of Community Care'[1] requires Trusts to assess the care needs of any person who appears to them to be in need of community care services and to decide, in the light of that assessment, whether they should provide, or arrange for, the provision of any services.

While this is Departmental guidance and does not carry the weight of legislation, a Trust deviating from it would have to show good reason for doing so. Moreover, whilst there is no duty in the 1972 Order to assess, there is a duty to make arrangements and provide, for example, home help, as considered suitable and adequate[2]. In order to meet a person's needs, those needs must be identified and this is generally done by an assessment.

[1]   DHSS, 1991.
[2]   HPSS 1972, art 15.

Accessing assessment

10.15 There are several ways in which a person's need for an assessment may be triggered. Some of these are set out below. A person may:

- apply for a place in residential accommodation or in a nursing home or for some domiciliary services;
- be referred by a general practitioner or a professional officer of the Trust (including hospital staff);
- be referred by a voluntary organisation;
- be referred by an informal carer seeking assistance or by a relative or some other person because of perceived unmet needs. [1]

---

[1] These methods of accessing assessment are set out in People First, Care Management: Guidance on Assessment and the Provision of Community Care, DHSS, 1991, para 5.1.

Type of assessment

10.16 Once it has been determined that a person requires an assessment, the decision must be made as to what level of assessment is required. Some people will require a higher level of assessment than others. In some cases, a person's needs are readily apparent and an assessment can be carried out with relative ease to identify those needs. However, in certain cases it will be necessary for a comprehensive multi-disciplinary assessment to be carried out to ensure that all the needs of the individual have been identified. The comprehensive assessment should always be carried out when a decision is to be taken about moving into residential care or back home from care. [1]

It is up to the Trust, having regard to all the relevant factors, to determine what type of assessment a person requires and to arrange for the assessment. There is no effective legislative description of what the assessment process should involve except that contained in s 3 of the Disabled Persons (NI) Act 1989 and the guidance issued on this section [2] where the details of what a formal assessment should include are set out. However, this particular section has never been brought into force. [3]

Section 3, if brought into force, would require Trusts to enable people to make representations as to their needs, to be provided with a written statement of need and to have a right of review. [4] The guidance states that assessments should record individual views about what is required to facilitate living in the community, the professional view of those requirements, any discrepancies, with explanations, which services it is not possible to provide and why, or that there are no needs requiring services, the carer's ability to continue to provide care, those services which it is intended will be provided with timescales if possible and a clear statement of a right of appeal and procedures [5]. This more detailed approach to what an assessment document should cover reflects the 'People First' principles for community care. However, a failure to follow every aspect of the guide would be difficult to challenge given that the legislation is not in force.

[1]   People First, Care Management: Guidance on Assessment and the Provision of Community Care, DHSS, 1991, para 6.6.

[2]   Disabled Persons (Northern Ireland) Act 1989 – Guide to Good Practice, published by the four HSS Boards, June 1992.

[3]   The equivalent legislation in England and Wales has not been brought into force: Disabled Persons (Service, Consultation and Representation) Act 1986, s 3.

[4]   Disabled Persons (Northern Ireland) Act 1989 – Guide to Good Practice, published by the four HSS Boards, June 1992, p 17.

[5]   Disabled Persons (Northern Ireland) Act 1989 – Guide to Good Practice, published by the four HSS Boards, June 1992, p 17.

10.17   The guidance does state that pending s 3 being brought into force, it is good practice to provide at least a letter confirming the nature of the discussions which took place and the agreements reached as a result, and that a thorough re-assessment should be carried out on a request for review.[1]

The 'People First' assessment guidance noted above does give some guidelines on what an assessment should cover but it is not as detailed as the Guide to Good Practice under the Disabled Persons (Northern Ireland) Act 1989. There is no standard assessment tool for community care services although it is expected that one will be developed as a result of the Community Care Review,[2] which took place in 2002. The 'People First' guidance states that comprehensive assessment should include physical, mental and social functioning and suggests that the areas to be covered include:[3]

- physical health;
- mental health;
- capacity for the activities of daily living and self care;
- abilities and lifestyle;
- the contribution of informal carers;
- social network and support;
- housing;
- finance;
- environmental factors.

All appropriate agencies and professions involved with a person, and his or her problems, should be brought into the assessment procedure. These may include, for example, social workers, family members, physiotherapists, occupational therapists, speech therapists, dieticians, dentists, general medical practitioners, community psychiatric nursing staff, housing officers, social security officials, home care assistants and voluntary workers.

[1]   Disabled Persons (Northern Ireland) Act 1989 – Guide to Good Practice, published by the four Health Boards, June 1992, p 18.

[2]   Review of Community Care, First Report, April 2002, DHSSPS.

[3]   People First, Care Management: Guidance on Assessment and the Provision of Community Care, DHSS, 1991, para 7.2.

Taking users' views into account

10.18   It is important that the user's views are taken into account, even if they have a low level of capacity. This was highlighted in the English case of *R v North*

Yorkshire County Council, ex p Hargreaves[1] in which it was held that the social services authority had failed, in breach of the English guidance, to ascertain the user's preferences in relation to respite care. They had not directly questioned her but they had taken into account the views of her brother (who acted as her carer) who described himself as his 'sister's spokesman'. The authority had great difficulty in communicating with the sister because of her learning disability and also because of her brother's protective attitude. Nevertheless, its decision as to appropriate respite care was unlawful as a result of failure to comply with guidance.

[1] (1994) 1 CCL Rep 104.

Notification of outcome of assessment

10.19 Once the assessment process has been completed, the individual and his or her carer should be informed of the result of the assessment and given the contact name of an individual to contact for any further discussion.[1] Whilst there is nothing in legislation compelling Trusts to provide written copies of assessments, guidance states that a written statement should always be provided on request.[2]

Furthermore, the Data Protection Act 1998 gives a person the right of access to personal data held on him or her. When a person requests a copy of the assessment, it should be provided within 40 days from the date of request.[3]

[1] People First, Care Management: Guidance on Assessment and the Provision of Community Care, DHSS 1991, para 10.4.
[2] People First, Care Management: Guidance on Assessment and the Provision of Community Care, DHSS 1991, para 10.4.
[3] Data Protection Act 1998, s 7.

Assessment and housing need

10.20 The issue of assessing and meeting housing needs for a person who is ill or has disabilities is complex. Both the Northern Ireland Housing Executive (NIHE) and Trusts have duties in relation to housing.

The Housing Executive has no statutory obligation to adapt the homes of its tenants to meet their need. In practice, NIHE is committed to carrying out adaptations to its own homes where they have assessed a need, or where there has been a recommendation from the Trust, despite the lack of statutory obligation.[1] Similarly, registered housing associations adapt their properties as they are able to access Departmental funding on the basis of a social services recommendation.[2]

The Housing Executive has an obligation under the Housing (Northern Ireland) Order 1992,[3] to operate a disabled facilities grant scheme[4] which is open to tenants, landlords and owner occupiers and the purpose of which is to allow applicants to carry out appropriate adaptations to their properties. NIHE carries out assessments of need following recommendations from a Trust and then carries out a financial assessment as to the amount of grant aid to be offered.[5]

1   See further, Joint Fundamental Review of the Housing Adaptations Service, NIHE 2003.
2   Joint Fundamental Review of the Housing Adaptations Service, NIHE 2003, p 19, para 2.3.
3   Article 52.
4   Housing Renovation etc Grants (Reduction of Grant) Regulations (Northern Ireland) 1997 details the means test applied to grant applications.
5   The means test operated for disabled facilities grants is restrictive. It has been the subject of a human rights challenge: *Re Lorraine McHugh*, High Court, Kerr J, (2003) judgment forthcoming. A Departmental review of the means test was announced in 2002.

Role of Trusts

10.21   Housing is one of the main areas which should be assessed as part of multi-disciplinary community care assessment.[1] Under articles 4 and 15 of the HPSS 1972, Trusts must meet an assessed social welfare need, including a need for residential or other accommodation. Thus while the NIHE has no specific statutuory duty to meet in terms of the accommodation of disabled persons, the Trusts do have such a duty.

There is also a duty to meet the needs of children with disabilities for accommodation under the Children (Northern Ireland) Order 1995.[2] This sits alongside the obligation to promote the upbringing of the child within his or her family.[3]

Trusts are under a statutory duty to provide assistance in arranging for the carrying out of adaptations to the home, or to provide additional facilities designed to secure greater safety, comfort or convenience, where either is necessary to make to meet a person's housing needs.[4] This is the basis for many community occupational therapy assessments.

Although the NIHE has agreed to assess the need for, and to carry out, adaptation to its properties that are occupied by people with disabilities, the only statutory obligation in this area remains with the Trust. This means that if there is a failure by the NIHE to assess or meet needs correctly, the Trust may be considered to have failed in its obligation to assist in the arranging for the adaptation of the home.[5] There has been litigation on the extent of the Trust's obligation under the CSDP 1978, s 2(3)[6] and it has been held that Trusts are not under an obligation to guarantee that adaptations are carried out. However, there is still legal debate as to whether this interpretation of the legislation is correct.[7]

1   People First, Care Management: Guidance on Assessment and the Provision of Community Care, DHSS, 1991, para 7.2.
2   Article 17, see chapter 7, para 7.16.
3   Children (Northern Ireland) Order 1995, art 18(b). See chapter 7, para 7.20.
4   Chronically Sick and Disabled Persons (Northern Ireland) Act 1978, s 2(e).
5   *Re Withnell's application for Judicial Review* (2004) unreported.
6   *Re Judge's application for judicial review* (2001) NIJB 85.
7   *Re Lorraine McHugh*, High Court, Kerr J, (2003) judgment forthcoming.

Assessment of carers

10.22   Carers are central to the continued operation of community care. The work involved in regular and substantial caring for a relative or friend can be intensive and draining. Over the years, the role of carers has gradually been given more recognition through government guidance on assessment of need. In 2002, legislation was passed establishing an independent right for a carer to request an assessment of their needs as a carer.[1] In addition, for the first time Trusts were empowered to provide services directly to a carer.[2]

[1]   Carers and Direct Payments (NI) Act 2002, s 1.
[2]   Carers and Direct Payments (NI) Act 2002, s 2.

Statutory duty to assess

10.23   As outlined above, the legislative framework for social services assistance of carers is the Carers and Direct Payments Act (Northern Ireland) 2002. A carer is defined as person aged 16 or over, who provides, or intends to provide, a substantial amount of care on a regular basis for another person.[1] There is special provision for carers who are under 16 years of age.[2]

There is now a statutory duty on Trusts to carry out an assessment of a carer's ability to provide, and to continue to provide care, where such an assessment is requested and where the Trust considers the person cared for to be someone for whom it may provide personal social services.[3] The person cared for does not need to be receiving, or willing to receive, services.

Where the Trust is aware of a carer, it must notify that carer of their right to request an assessment.[4] Trusts must also take such steps as are reasonably practicable to ensure that information is available to carers regarding their right to assessment.[5]

[1]   Carers and Direct Payments (NI) Act 2002, s 10.
[2]   Carers and Direct Payments (NI) Act 2002, s 4. See below para 10.26, 'Young carers'.
[3]   Carers and Direct Payments (NI) Act 2002, s 1.
[4]   Carers and Direct Payments (NI) Act 2002, s 7(2).
[5]   Carers and Direct Payments (NI) Act 2002, s 7(1).

Provision of services to carers

10.24   For the first time, Trusts are empowered to provide services directly to the carer.[1] A Trust is obliged to consider whether the carer has needs in relation to the care provided, whether these are needs which could be satisfied by services which the Trust could provide, and if so whether to provide them.

Trusts may provide a service to a carer by delivering a service to the person for whom they care, if agreed.[2] An example might be a sitting service to allow the carer to go out. The service should not include anything of an intimate nature, except in prescribed circumstances as set out in regulations.[3] The regulations allow an intimate service to be provided, for example, help with toileting, if the person cared for requests assistance.[4] In certain circumstances assistance can be given even if the person has not requested assistance.[5] This can be done where the person cared for is unable to give consent to the provider assisting them and there is a likelihood of serious personal harm to the person cared for if help is not given. Even if the person cared for could have given consent but does not do so, the regulations allow the assistance to be given in the absence of agreement if the provider believes that the likelihood of serious personal harm is imminent.

Trusts are entitled to charge the carer for services provided. If a service, for example, respite care, could be provided, either to the carer directly or to the service user as part of the user's care package, the Trust must decide to whom the service will be provided. In making that decision it must not take into account the means of either person, ie it cannot decide to provide it to a particular person because it can recover a charge from them.

The legislation also empowers the Department to make regulations that will allow Trusts to issue vouchers for short term breaks.[6]

[1]   Carers and Direct Payments (NI) Act 2002, s 2.
[2]   Carers and Direct Payments (NI) Act 2002, s 2(3).
[3]   Carers (Services) and Direct Payments Regulations (NI) 2003.
[4]   Carers (Services) and Direct Payments Regulations (NI) 2003, reg 2(2)(a).
[5]   Carers (Services) and Direct Payments Regulations (NI) 2003, reg 2(2)(b).
[6]   Carers and Direct Payments (NI) Act 2002, s 3.

Guidance on carer's assessments

10.25   The guidance issued under the CDPA 2002[1] states that an essential component of the assessment is to identify the impact of the caring role on the carer in light of various factors, for example, the carer's age, general health and well-being, employment status and other commitments. It also notes that the assessment should recognise that people caring for those with mental health problems have responsibilities that are not necessarily based on physical tasks.

The emphasis is clearly on individual needs-based assessment and not limited to whether the carer would benefit from any services which are already available. The guidance encourages creativity and flexibility in the services which can be provided, or arranged, to meet assessed need, including travel vouchers and driving lessons. In considering services for carers, the guidance suggests two tests, either the service will help the person care or it will help to maintain the carer's own health and well-being.[2]

[1]   Carers and Direct Payments Act (NI) 2002: Guidance, DHSSPS, March 2003.
[2]   Carers and Direct Payments Act (NI) 2002: Guidance, DHSSPS, March 2003, para 2.2.1.

Young carers

10.26   The duties placed on Trusts by the guidance apply to all carers. However, in respect of young carers, the guidance points out that this category of carers are not expected to take on the same level of caring responsibilities as adults and recognition must be given to the impact of caring responsibilities on educational and social opportunities.[1] The practical impact might then be that increased services are provided to the person cared for in order to remove the caring role from the child, rather than delivering services to the child to assist them in continuing to care.

[1] Carers and Direct Payments Act (NI) 2002: Guidance, DHSSPS, March 2003, para 2.3.1.

Future change – carers' strategy and the Community Care Review

10.27 In April 2002, the Department published 'Valuing Carers', the report of a working group which had been set up to look at carers in Northern Ireland and their needs. A number of recommendations on the support of carers have been made and these are due to be implemented by an inter-departmental working group.[1]

The initial report of the Community Care Review Project Board[2] also highlights the needs of carers. It noted that the 'People First' key objective of ensuring that service providers make practical support for carers, a high priority had only been partially met, if at all.[3]

Trusts were then asked as a result of the Community Care Review recommendations to take immediate action to provide carer support and to protect and develop respite services.[4] It stated that there should be as few changes as possible to personal care services to allow carers to plan their lives outside of their caring role. Trusts were also asked to consider the development of a support group in their area.

In the medium to long term, the Boards are to carry forward a project on developing a range of services which would provide practical support for carers, focusing on the potential for an extensive range of community based services such as respite and sitting services.

[1] Valuing Carers – Proposals for a Strategy for Carers in Northern Ireland, DHSSPS, 2002.
[2] Review of Community Care, First Report, DHSSPS, 2002.
[3] Review of Community Care, First Report, DHSSPS, 2002, p 59.
[4] Review of Community Care, First Report, DHSSPS, 2002, pp 59 and 60.

Resources and assessment of need: the courts' approach

10.28 There has been considerable legal discussion about whether or not social services can take their own financial resources into account when assessing a person's needs and two cases have gone as far as the House of Lords.

If a Trust can take into account its limited budget when assessing whether a person has a need for a service then there a possibility that a need will not be recognised as such because of the Trust's financial difficulties. The relevant legislation does not suggest that budget factors should be a part of the assessment process but budget holders have argued that the needs of people must be seen in the context of how much money is available.

The House of Lords dealt with this point in *R v Gloucestershire County Council, ex p Barry*.[1] This case concerned the obligations of social services under the Chronically Sick and Disabled Persons Act 1970, s 2(1), the applicable legislation in England and Wales (which is a near equivalent of CSDP 1978).

Mr Barry was a 79-year-old man with a disability who had been assessed by social services as needing home care assistance including cleaning and laundry services. Those services were initially provided to Mr Barry but were later withdrawn when the local authority encountered a shortage of financial resources. The authority wrote to around 1,500 people who were on the lowest priority level for the home care service telling them that their service would be either reduced or withdrawn. Some of those people who were receiving their service under the 1970 Act applied for a judicial review of the decision and the original court's decision was appealed.

The Court of Appeal held that the duty to assess need could not be connected to the financial position of the local authority. However, the House of Lords, held by a majority decision, of three to two, that a local authority could take into account its own resources when assessing both a disabled person's needs and whether services (for example, practical assistance in the home) were required to be provided to meet that need. This meant that a local authority could, when its budget was reduced, re-assess a person as having less need, by changing its eligibility criteria, because it had fewer resources. Then, even though his or her personal needs had not changed, the person may no longer be eligible for assistance and the service could be withdrawn or reduced.

It was noted, however, that once it is established that there exists a need that it is necessary to meet, then a failure or delay in meeting that need could not be justified on the basis of a lack of financial resources.[2]

In a later case, *R v East Sussex County Council, ex p Tandy*,[3] a differently constituted House of Lords considered the duty of a local authority under the Education Acts of 1993 and 1996 and came to the conclusion that the resource arguments in the *Barry* case were largely restricted to cases concerning the Chronically Sick and Disabled Persons Act 1970, s 2.

The House of Lords had to decide whether or not the local authority's resources were a relevant factor to take into account in deciding to reduce Beth Tandy's home tuition service to three hours per week, from five hours per week.

In a unanimous judgment, the House of Lords held that the duty owed under the Education Act 1993 was a specific duty which was owed to each child individually, and that there was nothing in the legislation setting out the statutory duty to indicate that local authorities could take their resources into account when deciding such matters.

Although there appears to be little difference between this case and the earlier *Barry* case, the judges distinguished the two cases on the basis that the needs in the 1970 Act were not of the same magnitude as those under the Education Acts.

¹   [1997] AC 584, [1997] 2 All ER 1, HL.
²   [1997] AC 584, [1997] 2 All ER 1, HL, Lord Clyde.
³   [1998] AC 714, [1998] 2 All ER 769, HL.

10.29   The present position in Northern Ireland is complex. Following the *Barry* case, when performing their duties under the chronically sick and disabled persons legislation, Trusts can take their available resources into account during the assessment process under this legislation when making a decision as to whether or not a need exists, ie a Trust can decide that the provision of certain services is not necessary. For example, a Trust might decide that in light of its budget, it is not usually going to be necessary for it to provide laundry services to those resident in its area. Assessments carried out on individuals will be done on the basis of this policy. General judicial review principles[1] apply, however, so the Trust cannot, for example, fetter its discretion and must not act irrationally in placing undue weight on the resources factor. An HRA assessment is also necessary if a Convention right is engaged and, as stated earlier, Convention right, article 8 may be engaged in many community care situations.[2] However, once it has been decided that a service is needed in an individual case then it must be provided regardless of the availability or otherwise of resources.

In relation to assessments for services such as residential care, which cannot be provided under the Chronically Sick and Disabled Persons (Northern Ireland) Act 1978, but are provided directly under article 15 of the HPSS 1972, there is more scope for an argument that resources should not be taken into account at the stage of assessing need. However, a recent judgment in Northern Ireland has found that resources can be taken into account thereafter in deciding when need can be met.[3] There is less clarity on whether a Trust could decide not to meet a need at all because of a lack of resources.

¹   On judicial review generally, see chapter 2, paras 2.105–2.129.
²   See chapter 1, paras 1.74 ff, for a discussion of HRA generally and chapter 6, paras 6.11–6.27 for discussion of the content of arts 3 and 8.
³   *Re Hanna's application for judicial review* (2003) unreported at 9.

Meeting assessed needs

10.30   Once it has been established that a person has needs, the next consideration is whether these will be met by the provision of a service. It is necessary to check whether the Trust is under a statutory duty to meet the need, or whether it merely has a power to do so and may exercise its discretion in considering whether to provide the service.

If there is a statutory duty imposing an obligation to meet need, the Trust cannot refuse to meet an assessed need on the grounds of lack of resources. Trusts can only take their available resources into account during the assessment process when making a decision as to whether or not a need exists.

Where there is simply a power to provide a service, the Trust is able to exercise its discretion. However, it must exercise its discretion properly, otherwise its decision may be subject to judicial review. This means, for example, that where a Trust has a policy, it should comply with that policy and the policy must be fair, reasonable and non-discriminatory. It is also essential that the policy is not so rigid that it does not take account of individual circumstances. If it appears that there has been an abuse of discretion, a person who has been refused a service may be able to seek a judicial review of the Trust's decision.

It is often the case that a Trust will not refuse to provide the service but will operate a waiting list due to financial constraints. As noted, a Trust must carry out a statutory duty and where no time limit for doing so is set down in the legislation, the law implies that it should be carried out within a reasonable period of time.[1] This allows someone who has been on a waiting list for a considerable amount of time to take court action to force the Trust to provide the service.[2]

The only Northern Irish judgment on delay in meeting need concerned a woman whose discharge from hospital was delayed for over seven months due to a lack of Trust funding to pay for a bed in a nursing home for her. It was argued that the delay in meeting the assessed need for a nursing home placement was unlawful. However, the court held that article 15 of the HPSS 1972 does not place a Trust under any mandatory duty to fulfil any specific need once that need has been assessed. This allowed a lack of resources to be taken into account and the Trust were held to have acted lawfully.[3] This case is being appealed to the Court of Appeal in Northern Ireland.

[1]   Reasonableness might be considered with regard to factors such as any Departmental guidance and the impact on the individual.

[2]   A number of potential judicial review applications against Trusts on this point have settled prior to proceedings being issued, and so there is not definitive decision on this point.

[3]   *Re Hanna's application for judicial review* (2003) unreported.

10.31   For a person who has been placed on a waiting list for a service and who feels that there has been excessive delay, there is also the option of making a complaint to the Ombudsman on the grounds of maladministration.[1]

Sometimes a Trust will wish to meet an assessed need by providing a particular service, but the person in need may wish a different service to be provided. In those circumstances it is important to check that both services actually meet the person's need. Consideration should be given to whether the suggested service meets a person's particular psychological or cultural needs. If the services are equally suitable in terms of meeting needs, the Trust may take into account its resources at this stage, ie it can have regard to the fact that one option is more cost-effective in deciding which service to offer. This was established in the English case *R v Lancashire County Council, ex p RADAR*[2].

[1]   For an explanation of the jurisdiction and role of the Ombudsman, see chapter 2, para 2.45.

[2]   [1996] 4 All ER 421, CA.

Care management

10.32   A 'care management' approach to community care is emphasised in the 'People First' guidance. Care management involves publicising services, assessment, planning, monitoring and review. It is different from a service management approach in its focus on tailoring services to meet individual needs, rather than fitting clients into existing services.[1]

[1] Care Management: Guidance on the Assessment and the Provision of Community Care, DHSS, 1991, chapter 4.

Care packages

10.33 Once a comprehensive individual assessment has been completed and a decision has been taken that care can, and should be arranged, it is the responsibility of the Trust to design appropriate care arrangements in consultation with the person, his or her informal carers, and all the care professionals involved.

The 'People First' guidance emphasises that care arrangements should begin with the needs and wishes of the person and his or her carers, and that Board or Trust staff should, as far as possible, aim to provide or arrange the provision of services which will meet those particular needs and wishes.[1] This guidance also states that Trust staff should consider at the outset, whether it is possible to provide a package of care to support the person at home as the principle of preserving or restoring independent living is paramount.[2]

[1] Care Management: Guidance on the Assessment and the Provision of Community Care, DHSS, 1991, chapter 3.3.
[2] Care Management: Guidance on the Assessment and the Provision of Community Care, DHSS, 1991, chapter 8.5.

Consent to suggested services

10.34 Consent to services is necessary as no-one can be forced to receive a service. This is outlined in the Departmental guidance on consent, 'Reference Guide to Consent for Examination, Treatment or Care'.[1] It covers personal care services, by their nature intrusive. The guidance commences by stating, 'it is a general legal and ethical principle that valid consent must be obtained before .... providing personal care'. This principle also derives from Convention right, article 8 because everyone, no matter their level of capacity, has a right to respect for their private life, which includes their physical and psychological integrity. This right should not be interfered with unless the person consents to the intervention, for example, a bathing service, and the intervention is proportionate to the aim to be achieved, for example, the protection of health.

[1] DHSSPS, 2003, p 1, para 1.

10.35 If a person is genuinely unable to consent, the Trust should still consider whether the action taken is minimal in its interference, that is if it does not unduly impact on the person's dignity and serves a legitimate and defined purpose such as the protection of health. Because article 8 also protects the right to respect for family life and home, whether or not a person is able to express a view, the Trust must consider whether its proposals, for example, the removal of a person to a residential home, interfere with these rights and whether or not the interference can be justified.

If a care assessment is being carried out then the staff member discussing the care needs with an adult without the capacity to consent should make an assessment of their ability to make such a decision or offer a view. A note should be placed on file in relation to this assessment of capacity.

10.36   The guidance reminds practitioners of the fact that capacity to understand can be temporarily affected by confusion, fatigue or pain, for example, and that there should not be a presumption that this person will always be incapable of consenting or expressing a view.[1]

A significant time for ensuring that consent is obtained, and that those with a low level of capacity are helped to achieve capacity threshold for at least some decisions, is when a comprehensive assessment is being carried out to look at hospital discharge options. When there is pressure of time it is tempting to listen to the views of an articulate relative rather than working with the person being assessed. A person's seemingly irrational refusal of a particular type of service is not a ground to decide that that person is incapable. The key is whether or not the person has an understanding[2] of what is entailed in their decision.

It is emphasised that social workers and all other social care staff should take all steps that are reasonable in the circumstances to facilitate communication with a person with a low level of capacity, using communication aids, simple language and visual aids.[3]

[1]   Reference Guide to Consent for Examination, Treatment or Care, DHSSPS, March 2003, chapter 1, para 2.3.
[2]   Reference Guide to Consent for Examination, Treatment or Care, DHSSPS, March 2003, chapter 1, para 2.4.
[3]   Reference Guide to Consent for Examination, Treatment or Care, DHSSPS, March 2003, chapter 1, paras 2.6 and 2.7.

10.37   The Convention right that outlaws discrimination in the operation of all the other Convention rights – article 14[1] – means that decisions about a person's private life should not be made on the basis that they will be incapable of making their own decision simply because they have a learning disability, or are of a certain age. Otherwise there will be a breach of article 14 in conjunction with article 8.

Before consent can be validly given to a care plan the user needs to understand the nature and purpose of the services proposed. More detailed guidance on adults without capacity is given.[2] A carer or family member cannot consent to care on behalf of the adult without capacity. However, the Trust can make decisions and provide services 'in the best interests' of the person.[3]

In determining the person's best interests the Trust should take account of the individual's values and preferences when competent, their psychological health, well-being, quality of life, relationships with family/carers, spiritual and religious welfare and financial interests.[4] Good practice would involve asking people close to the person about their values and preferences, unless the person has previously indicated that particular people should not be involved.

It should not be necessary to refer a case for a court ruling on what the person's best interests are unless there is a dispute, the implications of the decision are particularly serious or the person is resisting a service. If a court ruling is needed then an application should be made to the High Court for a declaration as to what are the best interests of the person in the particular circumstances. If the person is sufficiently lacking in capacity as to be unable to instruct a solicitor then the Trust should make a referral to the Official Solicitor,[5] who is able to act on his or her behalf at the hearing.[6]

The English case of *Re F (Adult Patient)*[7] involved a dispute between social services and family members, about whether a young adult with a learning disability should stay in a care home or return to the family home from where she had been removed as a child. The family members argued that their article 8 rights were engaged. The local authority was concerned about the risk of abuse on return to the family home. The court exercised its inherent jurisdiction and approved the decision of the authority, commenting that the right to respect for family life was not an issue of 'ownership', but was there to protect what is positive and benign about family life.[8]

A decision about best interests, and the factors taken into account should be recorded on file in the event of any future dispute. If the issue is contentious it would be wise for social workers and other social services staff to record the HRA analysis carried out as well. An English court has recently held that public authorities must show that they have carried out such an analysis at the time.[9]

---

1   For an explanation of art 14, see chapter 9, para 9.11.
2   Reference Guide to Consent for Examination, Treatment or Care, DHSSPS, March 2003, chapter 2.
3   Reference Guide to Consent for Examination, Treatment or Care, DHSSPS, March 2003, chapter 2, para 3.1 and *Re F (Adult Patient)* (2000) 3 CCL Rep 210, CA.
4   Reference Guide to Consent for Examination, Treatment or Care, DHSSPS, March 2003, chapter 2, para 1.4
5   See chapter 1, para 1.65.
6   Reference Guide to Consent for Examination, Treatment or Care, DHSSPS, March 2003, chapter 2.
7   [2001] Fam 38, 3 CCL Rep 210, CA.
8   [2001] Fam 38, 3 CCL Rep 210 at 227, CA, Sedley LJ.
9   *R (Madden) v Bury Metropolitan Borough Council* [2002] EWHC 1882, (2002) 5 CCL Rep 622.

Confidentiality

10.38   In relation to discussing case details and releasing information to a carer or relative, Trusts must be aware of the legal position on protection of confidential information. Difficulties in protecting the adult with incapacity from abuse may arise where information is released to people who do not act in their best interests or where the Trust fails protect their rights by restricting access to assessment documents. The Data Protection Act 1998 aims to protect personal data.[1] The person in question is known as the 'data subject'. Where a data subject lacks capacity to understand the information or request access to it, the legislation permits Trusts to release the information in certain circumstances.

¹   On the Data Protection Act 1998 generally, see chapter 3, para 3.35.

10.39   Any material relating to a person's physical or mental health is 'sensitive personal data' and this can be released in three situations.¹ These are first, where it is necessary to do so to protect the vital interests of the data subject or another person, secondly, where it is needed in connection with legal proceedings or legal advice or for establishing, exercising or defending legal rights, and thirdly, where it is necessary for the administration of justice or other exercise of other statutory functions. Most applications by a carer for release of assessment documents due to dissatisfaction with the level of care provided should be covered. These three tests must be read in light of the HRA, in particular article 8 and a balance has to be struck between the public and private interests in maintaining the confidentiality of the information and the public and private interests in requiring disclosure. The Trust does need to consider the right to respect for private life of the person with incapacity very carefully in a case where a potentially abusive third party requests access to information. While a person other than the data subject can ask for information to be released, it appears that the information can only be given to the data subject and the person requesting the information would need to obtain the information from the person lacking capacity.²

¹   Data Protection Act 1998, Sch 3.
²   Data Protection Act 1998, s 7.

Monitoring the care plan

10.40   It was recognised in 'People First' that a person's care needs may change over time and must be monitored. It is therefore recommended that a single professional worker should be assigned as a personal contact to each individual. This person should take responsibility for designing and assembling a package of services tailored to his or her needs and for ensuring that the services are effectively co-ordinated, delivered and monitored.¹

¹   Care Management: Guidance on Assessment and the Provision of Community Care, DHSS, 1991, chapter 8.2.

Direct payments

10.41   A Trust can ensure that need is met by providing or arranging a service, or by making a cash payment to allow the person in need to secure their own service.¹ This latter method is known as a direct payment. The direct payment cannot be used to buy a service from certain people, including relatives living in the same house as the person receiving the direct payment, unless it is necessary to do so in order to meet the person's need or promote the welfare of the child in need.[2] This aims to minimise the risk of financial abuse.

[1] HPSS 1972, art 15 and the CDPA 2002, s 8.
[2] Personal Social Services (Direct Payments) Regulations (NI) 1997, reg 3, as amended. These regulations are due to be replaced in 2003 by regulations made under the Carers and Direct Payments Act (NI) 2002.

10.42 Any assessed need which is a personal social service is covered by the direct payment provisions. This includes, for example, help with bathing, home help, adaptations and respite care. There is a restriction as regards the purchasing of residential care with a direct payment to four weeks within any twelve month period. However, if the periods of residential care are less than four weeks and more than four weeks apart, then it is possible to start afresh each time in the computation of the four week maximum.

Assessments for direct payments

10.43 Direct payments can only be offered to someone who has been assessed as needing personal social services or services to meet needs as a carer, or a service under article 18 of the Children (NI) Order 1995. The fact that someone has indicated an interest in receiving direct payments should not alter the assessment of need process. The process should be needs-led.

The assessment process must also include an assessment of whether the person is eligible for direct payments, whether they are appropriate and whether the person is able to manage them.[1] The person who is considering direct payment will also require time to think through what this will involve. The assessment period should take account of the time that this will involve.

A judgment on whether or not someone will be able to manage direct payments should be made with regard to their individual circumstances and Trusts should not automatically exclude groups of people. A person may be able to manage the direct payments with appropriate support. The Trust, however, would have to be satisfied that such support is available for a sustainable period.[2]

[1] Personal Social Services (Direct Payments) (NI) Order 1996 – Guidance for Boards and Trusts, DHSSPS, April 2000, para 26. This guidance is due to be replaced by new guidance in 2003.
[2] Personal Social Services (Direct Payments) (NI) Order 1996 – Guidance for Boards and Trusts, DHSSPS, April 2000, paras 26–36.

10.44 If the assistance required is with managing the money then this is acceptable as long as the person for whom the direct payment is made has control over how support is delivered to meet assessed need. The payment can be made to a third party and detailed management of finances can be carried out by an agent. The assistance which someone might need is not restricted to help with managing finances, but could also cover, for example, assistance with managing day to day relationships with staff.

ENSURING DIRECT PAYMENTS ARE USED TO MEET ASSESSED NEED

10.45   It is necessary for the Trust to discuss with the recipient how he or she intends to use the direct payments. The Trust may set conditions on the use of the payments, although such a condition should not undermine the aim of enabling more choice and individual control.

If there is a local register of approved providers then the Trust should bring it to the attention of the person, if the providers consent to their details being passed on. Direct payments cannot be used to purchase Trust services but can be used to purchase from agencies, self-employed individuals or from people who become direct employees of the person receiving direct payments.[1]

Direct payments can also be used to purchase equipment or carry out adaptations which would otherwise have been provided by, or arranged through, the Trust. This does not extend to adaptations which would be paid for by the NIHE through a disabled facilities grant. If the payment is to be used to purchase equipment then the Trust needs to ensure that the person has the appropriate knowledge or specialist support to ensure that what is purchased is safe, appropriate and cost-effective.

[1]   Personal Social Services (Direct Payments) (Northern Ireland) Order 1996 – Guidance for Boards and Trusts, DHSSPS, April 2000, paras 42 and 44.

Best value

10.46   The Department has advised that Trusts should not make direct payments unless they are at least as cost-effective as the services which they would otherwise arrange.[1] However, in considering cost-effectiveness, a factor is long term 'best value', which could mean that higher costs for preventative services may be cost-effective in the long term. Trusts can also consider that the benefit to the individual of the choice and independence afforded by direct payments is at least as cost-effective as arranging the services and the consequent loss of that independence.

[1]   Personal Social Services (Direct Payments) (NI) Order 1996 – Guidance for Boards and Trusts, DHSSPS, April 2000, para 50.

The level of direct payment

10.47   The direct payment must be sufficient to enable the person receiving it to secure the service to a standard that the Trust considers acceptable. The Trust has to consider costs such as national insurance, employer's and public liability insurance, sick pay, maternity pay and VAT.

If the service can be secured to an acceptable quality by a cheaper method, then the guidance states that the Trust will not be obliged to provide for the extra associated costs of the preferred method of the person receiving the payment.[1] This does impact to some extent on the flexibility of the scheme.

Direct payments are not treated as taxable income and will not affect social security benefits or independent living fund payments.

---

[1] Personal Social Services (Direct Payments) (NI) Order 1996 – Guidance for Boards and Trusts, DHSSPS, April 2000, para 52.

Charging

10.48 If a person would usually be charged for a service arranged or provided by the Trust, then they should be charged for the direct payment. The practical impact is that the amount of direct payment is reduced.

Monitoring

10.49 If an emergency arises where the person is unable to arrange for the service to be provided, the Trust has a responsibility to ensure that the care needs are met.[1] The Trust should consider whether it could provide assistance to the individual to allow continued independence rather than automatically arranging for the service to be provided to the person.

---

[1] Personal Social Services (Direct Payments) (Northern Ireland) Order 1996 – Guidance for Boards and Trusts, DHSSPS, April 2000, para 74.

Ending direct payments

10.50 Either the Trust or the individual may decide that direct payments should be stopped. If Trusts are considering withdrawing direct payments they should give a previously agreed amount of minimum notice of their intention. If no notice is to be given, this should only be in exceptional circumstances, which should have been clearly explained to the person receiving the payments when they were first agreed.[1]

At the start of the process, the Trust should also discuss how any ongoing contractual responsibilities to employees, for example, would be handled should the direct payments be discontinued.

---

[1] HPSS 1972, art 15.

Repayment of direct payments

10.51 The Trust can seek repayment of money paid out by direct payment if it is not satisfied that it has been used to secure the required services, if the person has not complied with a condition of the direct payment or contravened the regulations, for example, as regards the person providing the care.

Third party schemes

10.52 The legislation[1] in Northern Ireland allows payments to be made to third parties, either individuals or organisations, to secure services and there is no obligation to provide services directly.

These third party schemes continue to be possible despite the introduction of direct payments. They are more flexible in that the payment could be made to a relative of the person with a disability who lives in the same household in return for their provision of the service.

[1]   HPSS 1972, art 15.

Paying for services

10.53 The funding of community care services comes from a number of sources including Trust and voluntary sector spending and the charging of individual users. The law on charging for care is complex.

Financial assessment

10.54 Once an assessment of need has been carried out and a decision taken as to what services are to be provided or arranged to meet the individual's needs, a financial assessment may be carried out to determine whether or not a person will have to pay for, or make a contribution to, the cost of providing the services.

The rules which apply in relation to charging for domiciliary services are different to those which apply to residential and respite care. The principal difference is that Trusts have a duty to impose charges for residential accommodation, whereas there is only a power to charge in respect of the whole range of non-residential services.[1] Notwithstanding this important distinction, however, there are some fundamental principles which apply to all aspects of charging.

All decisions about the provision of services must be made independently of any consideration of a person's ability to pay. This means that assessment of need is the first stage in the process and must be carried out before any consideration of the financial situation. People who receive disability benefits should be treated in the same way as those who do not.[2]

The second stage is a consideration of a person's ability to pay. Public authorities, such as Trusts, must act reasonably and therefore some regard has to be had to whether or not it is reasonable for the person to pay the charge under consideration.[3]

It is also important to note that where a person has been assessed as needing a service, social services may not refuse to provide the service if he or she is unable, or fails, to pay the charge imposed. A Trust may take legal action to recover any charge as a debt but is legally obliged to continue to provide the service to meet the assessed need.

[1] HPSS 1972, art 15(4).
[2] A Departmental Circular dated 3 June 1999 confirmed that receipt of disability benefits should not be taken into account in decisions about the provision of community care services.
[3] See chapter 2, paras 2.105 ff.

Charging for domiciliary services

10.55 Once a person has been assessed as requiring domiciliary services (also known as non-residential services), the Trust must exercise its discretion in deciding whether or not to charge for those services.

Trusts are allowed to recover such charges (if any), as they consider appropriate in respect of any services provided under article 15 of the 1972 Order.[1]

There is no specific legislation regulating the imposition of charges for domiciliary services. Historically, domiciliary personal social services have attracted a relatively low level of charges or have been provided free of charge.

Departmental circular HSS (SS) 1/80 sets out a means test for one aspect of non-residential services: home help. The definition of home help includes most personal social services including personal care, cleaning, laundry and shopping services. This model home-help scheme outlines the criteria for assessment and charging of individuals aged under 75. Those over 75 are not charged. The circular is regularly amended to take account of increases in social security benefits which are applied when assessing a person's ability to pay for the service. A Trust must have regard to this circular when carrying out a financial assessment.

[1] HPSS 1972, art 15(4).

Charging for residential care

10.56 When a person is assessed as requiring nursing or residential care, the Trust will undertake a financial assessment to see whether or not he or she can pay, or requires assistance paying the residential care fees.

Everyone who is assessed as having a need for nursing care is not required to pay towards the cost of that nursing care, regardless of their means.[1]

A Trust can arrange to pay the cost of the accommodation for everyone who it has assessed as needing the placement and must then recover such a charge from the person as assessed as appropriate up to the full cost of the placement after deduction of the nursing care cost. Some people contract privately with the residential or nursing home.

[1] Health and Personal Social Services Act (Northern Ireland) 2002, s 1. The effect is that those who have nursing care needs after assessment are entitled to at least £100 per week of Trust funding towards the cost of care.

Meeting the cost of care

10.57   The cost of the care placement to the Trust, made up of personal care and accommodation costs, is then either met by the person entirely from their own resources or through a mixture of the person's income and benefits and Trust funding. In order to establish the level of charge to be recovered, the Trust will look firstly at the person's capital, and then, if he or she has less than the capital limit, the Trust will look at income.

The capital and income rules which Trusts must follow in conducting a financial assessment for a person entering residential care are similar to those applied in determining entitlement to income support, although there are some significant differences.

Trusts have a duty to charge for residential services. Article 99 of the HPSS 1972 provides for charging for accommodation in Board and Trust managed homes and article 36 of the HPSS 1972 makes provision for charging for accommodation in voluntary or private homes.

In both situations, a financial assessment must be carried out in accordance with the Health and Personal Social Services (Assessment of Resources) Regulations (Northern Ireland) 1993 (as amended) (HPSS 1993) to ascertain the person's ability to pay. Guidance on charging is contained in the Charging for Residential Accommodation Guide (CRAG)[1] which is issued by the Department and is regularly updated.

[1]   DHSSPS, August 2002.

Capital rules

10.58   In order to receive assistance from social services with care fees, a person must not have capital in excess of specified limits. Those limits are set down in the HPSS 1993 and Trusts are not entitled to substitute their own scale for judging a person's ability to pay.[1]

Capital can take many forms and there is no useful definition of what it includes in the legislation or regulations. Capital includes a person's home and any land or property owned by him or her although there are circumstances where the value of a home can be ignored. These are discussed below.

Capital can be distinguished from income because a capital payment is made without being tied to a period and is not intended to form part of a series of payments.[2] Savings count as capital. This includes money in a bank or building society, cash at home, shares and unit Trusts. Fixed term investments are taken into account unless the money is unobtainable. An investment which can be realised before the end of a term, albeit with a loss of interest, is taken into account.

[1]   This was confirmed in the case of *R v Sefton Metropolitan Borough Council, ex p Help the Aged* (1997) 1 CCL Rep 57, CA, where the local authority's policy of waiting until people had only £1,500 left before providing financial assistance was held to be unlawful.

Treatment of the home

10.59 Often one of the major concerns for a person entering residential care is whether or not his or her home will have to be sold in order to meet the invoices for the care home placement. The term home includes the garage, garden and outbuildings, together with any land or other premises which are not occupied, but which it is unreasonable to sell separately.

Since 22 April 2002, when a person enters residential care permanently the value of his or her home will be disregarded for up to twelve weeks. After that, how the property is treated will depend on who is still in occupation.

The value of the home is ignored if any of the following still lives there:[1]
- a partner (including anyone treated as a former partner for income support purposes because the person applying has gone into residential care);
- a relative who is aged 60 or over or is incapacitated;
- a child under 16 whom the person applying is liable to maintain;
- the Trust also has a general discretion to ignore the value of the premises occupied by any third party where this would be reasonable in the circumstances.

The discretion to ignore the value of the home where a person goes into residential care permanently and the home is occupied by a third party is a far wider power to disregard the value of the property than that contained within the income support regulations. The discretion may be exercised, for example, where a long-standing carer or family member under 60 continues to live in the person's property after his or her admission to care.[2]

If the house is taken into account in the valuation of the person's capital it is not always necessary for the house to be sold. The key question is whether any charge for care can be met from other assets or income, for example, rental income which could be obtained from the letting of the property.

---

1   CRAG, DHSSPS, 2002, chapter 7.
2   CRAG, para 7.007, gives the example of someone who has given up their own home to care for the person now entering care.

Other capital disregards

10.60 In certain circumstances, other capital can be disregarded. These include tax rebates, arrears of a number of social security benefits (ignored for up to one year), the surrender value of life assurance, endowment policies or annuities and personal possessions.

However, where personal possessions are purchased in order to enable a person to claim or increase his or her entitlement to assistance with care fees, the value of those may be taken into account.

The value of capital is based on its current market value or surrender value. From this is deducted 10% for expenses attributable to the sale and also the amount of any charge secured on the asset (for example, an outstanding mortgage).[1]

Where more than one person has an interest in a capital asset, other than land, then each person will be deemed to have an equal share of the asset until such time as the asset is sold and each person possesses his or her actual share.

Where the asset which is jointly owned is land, the value of a person's share is the price his or her interest would realise if sold to a willing buyer, minus 10% and the amount of any charge secured solely on the person's share.[2] The resulting value could easily be minimal, as there may be few willing buyers for a part share in a house.

[1]   HPSS 1993, reg 23.
[2]   HPSS 1993, reg 27(2) and CRAG, para 7.012.

Disposal of capital and notional capital

10.61   A person may be treated as possessing actual capital of which he or she has deprived him or herself for the purpose of decreasing the amount that he or she may be liable to pay for residential care.[1]

It is important to note that Trusts have a discretion as to whether or not to assume notional capital and accordingly they should have regard to all relevant factors. As with all decisions made by Trusts, they cannot take account of irrelevant factors and could be challenged if they act irrationally in making their decision, and will be subject to judicial review if they do.

The key issue for Trusts to consider is the motive of the person in disposing of their property. There may be more than one purpose for disposing of a capital asset, only one of which is to avoid a charge for accommodation. CRAG states that avoiding the charge need not be the resident's main motive but it must be a significant one.[2]

CRAG also notes that it would be unreasonable to decide that a person had disposed of an asset in order to reduce his or her charge for accommodation when the disposal took place at a time when he or she was fit and healthy and could not have foreseen the need for a move to residential accommodation.[3]

Nonetheless, the legal test is one relating to the purpose of transferring property or other assets and not about timing.

Where it is held that a person has deliberately transferred an asset to a third party in the six months prior to going into care, or after going into care, the Trust has the power to seek recovery of accommodation costs from the third party.[4] If an asset is transferred to more than one person, then each person is liable for charges up to the value of his or her share of the transferred asset. If assets are deliberately transferred more than six months before going into care, the Trust still has discretion to treat the resident as possessing that asset and to seek recovery of charges from him or her.

In the case of *Yule v South Lanarkshire Council,*[5] the Scottish Court of Session held that the true purpose of any transfer of property could be determined without a specific finding having to be reached concerning the state of knowledge or intention of the resident.

In the case of *Robertson v Fife Council*[6] the court refused to find it unreasonable of the council to hold that a woman who had transferred her home to her children two and a half years before entering residential care had deprived herself of capital for the purpose of reducing liability for care fees. The Council was accordingly entitled to treat the woman as having notional capital from which she could pay the fees.

[1]   HPSS 1993, reg 25.
[2]   CRAG, DHSSPS, 2002, para 6.062.
[3]   CRAG, DHSSPS, 2002, para 6.064.
[4]   HPSS 1972, art 101A.
[5]   (1998) 2 CCL Rep 394.
[6]   2000 SLT 1226.

Income rules

10.62   Once it has been established that a person is not disqualified from assistance by virtue of the amount of capital that he or she has, the Trust will consider his or her income. In order to do this, the Trust must ascertain what the cost of the accommodation will be and also the level of income which the person will have when in care. The Trust will take into account almost all income except an allowance for personal expenses and an amount of savings credit.

The Trust will expect the person to contribute all income above this disregarded amount and if there is still an outstanding fee then it will make up the difference if the overall charge is reasonable.

Preferred accommodation

10.63   A Trust should arrange to provide care in a person's preferred accommodation, subject to the accommodation being available and suitable to his or her needs, and provided that it does not cost more than the Trust would usually expect to pay for care for someone with such needs.[1] Where a person is unable to make a choice because of ill health, then the wishes of the carer should be taken into account.

The cost test is not whether a cheaper option is available but what a Trust would normally pay to meet a person's needs by the provision of residential care.

[1]   'People First', DHSS, 1991, p 46.

Third party agreements to meet excess fees

10.64   If a person chooses a more expensive option, the placement may be arranged by the Trust, providing a third party (for example, a family member or friend) is prepared to meet the difference. In such cases, the Trust will normally pay the full charge and recover the extra cost from the third party. The third party may alternatively enter into a contract with the home. Third party top-ups should only occur where the third party has agreed to pay the additional amount in order that the person entering care can enter a particular home which is more expensive than the Trust considers reasonable.

If the Trust has placed an unreasonable restriction on the amount which it considered reasonable, or if the person's needs can only be met by being placed in a particular home then a request for a third party top-up payment may be improper and open to legal challenge.

Liable relative payments

10.65   Whilst it is only the income and capital of the person in residential care which is taken into account during the financial assessment, once that assessment has been carried out, if the Trust is unable to recover the full cost of the care from him or her, then it can look to see if there are any liable relatives from whom it could recover the outstanding costs.

Trusts are able to claim payment from liable relatives under article 100 of the HPSS 1972. This power is based on the legal principle that spouses are liable to maintain one another and parents are liable for their children's maintenance. However, other relatives, such as children of elderly parents or cohabitees, have no legal liability to fund care or to provide financial assistance.

Continuing care

10.66   There has been a substantial number of legal challenges about the division between health and social care in England and Wales. The reason for this arises from the different charging implications. There can be no charge for health care provided by a health authority whereas social care provided by a social services authority is subject to similar mandatory charging rules as described above.

As noted in chapter 1, health and personal social services are delivered through integrated agencies in Northern Ireland, and the division of responsibility for the two types of care is not so obvious. There is also a different legislative framework for the provision of care.

The result is that in England and Wales there are residents of care homes who have their entire fees met by their local health authority as it is considered that they are eligible for continuing health care outside hospital. Case law has held that free care should be provided where the person has primarily health care needs.[1] This does not occur in Northern Ireland as the equivalent concept of continuing health care is very restricted and would appear to be applied only to those in hospital who have moved from acute wards. No Departmental guidance has been issued in this area.[2]

[1] *R v North and East Devon Health Authority, ex p Coughlan (Secretary of State for Health and Royal College of Nursing intervening)* [2001] QB 213, [2000] 3 All ER 850, 2 CCL Rep 285, CA.
[2] The Health Service Ombudsman for England issued a special report in 2003 criticising the approach of NHS bodies and central government to continuing care. The NHS bodies were held to have been too restrictive in their approach leading to people paying for their care who should have been entitled to free care. The Ombudsman called on the Department of Health to issue clearer guidance: The Health Service Ombudsman, 2nd report, Session 2002–2003, HC 399 (2002–2003).

The future of community care

10.67 The government is considering the cost of implementing the payment of personal care costs by Trusts.[1] If nursing and personal care costs are covered by the State then only the accommodation costs element of a placement would need to be recovered from residents on the basis of their means. This would significantly reduce the cost of long term care for individuals.

The Community Care Review led to the establishment of seven projects. The first project is aimed at examining the scope for development of more preventative and rehabilitative schemes to enable people to remain living in their own homes as long as possible. There will be a second project focused on the spreading of best practice between Trusts. Developing services for carers is the third project. The fourth project is looking at the possibility of developing a single assessment tool for care management. Partnership and the development of a stable and sustainable independent sector alongside good quality public services will be tackled by the fifth project. The sixth project is concerned with the accountability of the various agencies involved in community care. The final project will look at the funding structure for community care, including whether funding levels are adequate to address need. The reports of these project teams will no doubt shape the direction of community care over the next decade.

[1] There are different positions throughout the UK on this issue. Scotland has a system whereby nursing and personal care costs are provided free of charge. In England the government has ruled out the provision of free personal care. The Northern Ireland decision is awaited.

Procedures for challenging Trust decisions

10.68 There is a health and social services complaints procedure which can be accessed by service users unhappy with the service provided by the Trust. The procedure involves an internal stage (or local resolution as it sometimes called), where the complainant utilises the Trust's own complaints process, and an independent review,[1] if the complainant remains unsatisfied. If the complainant remains unhappy at the end of that process, he or she can lodge a complaint with the Northern Ireland Ombudsman.[2]

The Health and Social Services Complaints Procedures Directions (Northern Ireland) 1996 and the Miscellaneous Complaints Procedures Directions (Northern Ireland) 1996 set out the procedure on which Trusts should base their complaints' policies. Departmental Guidance on the implementation of the procedures, 'Complaints: Listening ... Acting ... Improving', is also available.[3] A complaint should normally be made within six months from the date the matter occurred, or six months from the date the matter came to the complainant's notice, provided that is within twelve months of the matter occurring.

The complaints procedure can be useful for resolving disputes at an early stage and for clarifying factual issues between the Trust and the complainant.[4]

However, where the case concerns a dispute about the interpretation of law or the application of the HRA, for example, then the most appropriate way to progress the matter is through judicial review. The complaints procedure does not appear to have been considered to be an effective remedy which needs to be exhausted before lodging a judicial review application. One of the advantages of judicial review is that there is a possibility of obtaining an interim injunction to prevent, for example, a service reduction until the dispute is resolved.

[1]   For an explanation of the role of the Health and Social Services Council in independent reviews, see chapter 2, paras 2.66–2.70.

[2]   On the Ombudsman see chapter 2, paras 2.45 ff.

[3]   HPSS Executive, March 1996.

[4]   *R (on the application of Cowl) v Plymouth City Council* [2001] EWCA Civ 1935, [2002] 1 WLR 803.

Chapter 11

Mental Health Law

Michael Potter

Introduction

11.1   Social workers in the field of mental health commonly perform their duties in complex and emotionally fraught situations. For example, they regularly encounter people with a mental disorder (including mental illness and mental disability) who may be in a disturbed, agitated and/or distressed state, as well as patients' family and/or friends who may themselves be in a heightened emotional state due to the patient's condition. Mental health social workers are often required to make difficult decisions in such emotionally-charged contexts in the knowledge that their decisions could have profound ramifications.

11.2   While providing an overview of mental health law in Northern Ireland, this chapter focuses on those aspects of the law that most closely concern social workers in the mental health field, such as compulsory admission to hospital and guardianship. The chapter draws on research into the role of the mental health social worker recently undertaken in Northern Ireland.[1] It is intended to provide practical assistance for professionals working in this field.

[1]   The author expresses his appreciation to Jim Campbell of the Department of Social Work, Queens University Belfast and Eileen Regan for their assistance in the preparation of this chapter.

11.3   Northern Ireland's mental health law has two dimensions: (1) domestic law, including practice and procedure; and (2) European Convention on Human Rights law (ECHR or European Convention law), now incorporated into domestic law by the HRA.[1]

[1]   See chapter 1, paras 1.74 ff.

The legal framework

11.4   The Mental Health (Northern Ireland) Order 1986 (MHO 1986) is the primary domestic legal source. Amongst other things, the MHO 1986 provides for compulsory admission and detention in hospital and admission into guardianship (including social workers' statutory duty in defined circumstances to ensure that persons are admitted to hospital or guardianship), non-consensual treatment, and the management of a patient's property and affairs.[1] The MHO 1986 also created a new designation – the Approved Social Worker (ASW) – to ensure that social workers exercising powers under the MHO 1986 have undergone relevant training. It is the only area of social work where post-qualifying training is required before social workers are lawfully empowered to discharge certain statutory duties.

[1]　MHO 1986, art 40.

11.5　Companion mental health legislation includes the Mental Health (Nurses, Guardianship, Consent to Treatment and Prescribed Forms) Regulations (Northern Ireland) 1986 (referred to here as 'the Regulations'), and the Mental Health Review Tribunal (Northern Ireland) Rules 1986 (referred to here as 'the Rules'). The Regulations contain some parts of the mental health legal framework, for example provisions governing guardianship and treatment, as well as template forms for applications, recommendations, reports and certificates. The Rules concern procedure in Mental Health Review Tribunal hearings (rules of procedure), which must be applied in light of the HRA.

11.6　Other relevant statutory provision includes the Health and Personal Social Services (Northern Ireland) Order 1972. It allows for State intervention in the lives of persons who appear to be 'at risk' or who require care and attention.[1] Also of relevance is the Children (Northern Ireland) Order 1995, which permits state intervention in the lives of children who have psychiatric conditions.[2]

[1]　See para 11.45.
[2]　See generally chapter 6 and below at para 11.43.

11.7　Pursuant to article 111 of the MHO 1986, there is a Code of Practice that provides advice and guidance on good professional practice relating to the procedures prescribed in the Order. The Code provides useful guidance about various social work duties. A failure to comply with it is not in itself unlawful, but it could be cited as evidence of bad practice and/or illegality if a dispute should arise. Social workers therefore should take time to acquaint themselves with the Code's provisions:

> 'In Northern Ireland a number of academic and professional social workers recently undertook research about the role of the Approved Social Worker (ASW).[1] The study cast considerable light on this aspect of health and welfare provision in Northern Ireland, particularly the difficulties experienced by ASWs in discharging their statutory duties.'[2]

[1]　Britton, Campbell, Hamilton, Hughes, Manktelow and Wilson, 'A Study of Approved Social Work in Northern Ireland.' ISBN 0 85389 757 3.
[2]　Some of the most pertinent findings from this research will be referred to in the chapter as and where appropriate. See also related publications: Manktelow, Hughes, Britton, Campbell, Hamilton, and Wilson, 'The Experience and Practice of Approved Social Workers in Northern Ireland', British Journal of Social Worker (2002) pp 32, 443–461; Campbell, Wilson, Britton, Hamilton, Hughes and Manktelow, 'The management and supervision of Approved Social Workers: Aspects of law, policy and practice', Journal of Social Welfare and Family Law 23(2) (2001), pp 155–172.

Human Rights Act 1998

11.8   The HRA clearly impacts upon the field of mental health care.[1] As a general rule, domestic law must comform with European Convention law, and there are three key Convention rights that concern people with mental health issues, namely articles 3, 5 and 8.

[1]   On the HRA generally, see chapter 1, para 1.74. See also Current Law Statutes Annotated; 1998, chapter 42; see also Simor and Emerson, *Human Rights Practice* Sweet and Maxwell; Keir Starmer, *European Human Rights Law* (1999) Legal Action Group; Keir Starmer with Iain Byrne, *Blackstone's Human Rights Digest* (2001); David Hewitt 'Uncomfortable Truths' (2003) New Law Journal 153, pp 661–662; 'Connecting mental health and human rights' Northern Ireland Human Rights Commission. ISBN 1 903681 405.

ARTICLE 3: TORTURE, INHUMAN OR DEGRADING TREATMENT

11.9   Article 3 prohibits torture or inhuman or degrading treatment or punishment in the care and treatment of people with a mental disorder, including their medical treatment. In the case of *Herczegfalvy v Austria*, the European Court on Human Rights (the European Court) intimated that treatment conforming to psychiatric principles generally accepted at the time, did not contravene article 3.[1] This is known as the 'principle of therapeutic necessity'. Therein, the European Court stated that:[2]

'The position of inferiority and powerlessness which is typical of patients confined in psychiatric hospitals calls for increased vigilance in reviewing whether the Convention has been complied with. While it was for the medical authorities to decide, on the basis of the recognised rules of medical science, on the therapeutic methods to be used, if necessary by force, to preserve the physical and mental health of patients who are entirely incapable of deciding for themselves, such patients nevertheless remain under the protection of article 3, whose requirements permit of no derogation.'

The Court of Appeal in England recently held that the use of seclusion in psychiatric hospitals could amount to 'inhuman or degrading treatment or punishment'.[3]

[1]   (1992) 15 EHRR 437.
[2]   (1992) 15 EHRR 437, para 86.
[3]   *R (on the application of Munjaz) v Mersey Care NHS Trust, R (on the application of S) v Airedale NHS Trust* [2003] EWCA Civ 1036, [2003] WLR 1505. The court held, however, that the seclusion of a patient from other detained patients did not of itself constitute inhuman or degrading treatment or punishment.

ARTICLE 5: RIGHT TO LIBERTY

11.10   Article 5 protects against arbitrary arrest and detention. Pursuant to article 5(1)(e), it is lawful to deny liberty to 'persons of unsound mind' in certain circumstances. The European Court has not provided a precise definition for the concept 'unsound mind'. In *Winterwerp v Netherlands*, it stated:[1]

'The Convention does not state what is to be understood by the words "persons of unsound mind". This term is not one that can be given a definite interpretation: ... it is a term whose meaning is continually evolving as research in psychiatry progresses, an increasing flexibility in treatment is developing and society's attitude to mental illness changes, in particular so that a greater understanding of the problems of mental patients is becoming more widespread.'

¹   *Winterwerp v Netherlands* (1979) 2 EHRR 387, para 37.

11.11   Case law of the European Court specifies a number of requirements that must be fulfilled if a person of unsound mind is to be detained lawfully:
(1)   it must be medically established that the person concerned is of unsound mind;
(2)   the mental disorder must be of a kind or degree warranting compulsory confinement;
(3)   the validity of continued confinement depends upon the persistence of such a disorder; and,
(3)   the detention must be in accordance with applicable domestic legal procedure.¹

¹   *Winterwerp v Netherlands* (1979) 2 EHRR 387; *Ashingdane v United Kingdom* (1985) 7 EHRR 528; and, *Johnson v United Kingdom* (1997) 27 EHRR 296.

ARTICLE 8: RESPECT FOR PRIVATE LIFE AND FAMILY LIFE

11.12   Article 8(1) concerns the right of a person to his or her private and family life, home and correspondence.¹ This obviously applies to people with mental conditions whether they are living at home, in residential accommodation or in a hospital. This right protects against unlawful interference with a person's physical integrity.² But article 8(2) permits interference with article 8(1) rights if such interference is in accordance with law and 'necessary in a democratic society in the interests of public safety, for the prevention of disorder or crime, for the protection of health or morals, or for the protection of the rights and freedoms of others'.³ The Court of Appeal in England recently held that the use of seclusion in psychiatric hospitals breached article 8, unless it could be justified by article 8(2).⁴

¹   For a detailed exposition of art 8, see chapter 6, paras 6.11 ff.
²   *A v United Kingdom* (1998) 27 EHRR 611; *Costello-Roberts v United Kingdom* (1993) 19 EHRR 112; *Osman v United Kingdom* (1998) 29 EHRR 245.
³   Article 8(2).
⁴   *R (on the application of Munjaz) v Mersey Care NHS Trust, R (on the application of S) v Airedale NHS Trust* [2003] EWCA Civ 1036, [2003] WLR 1505.

Mental disorder, capacity and minors

11.13   Currently in Northern Ireland, mental disorder is defined as 'mental illness, mental handicap and any other disorder or disability of mind.'¹ Excluded from this statutory definition are mental conditions caused 'by reason only of personality disorder, promiscuity or other immoral conduct, sexual deviancy or dependence on alcohol or drugs.'[2] The European Convention definition of 'unsound mind' seems broader than the definition of 'mental disorder' contained in the MHO 1986.[3]

Any competent person can be admitted to hospital or receive medical treatment if he or she consents. The law presumes that a person has mental capacity to consent to medical treatment. Under the law, the question as to whether a person lacks mental capacity requires consideration of his or her ability to: (1) comprehend and retain information relevant to a decision; (2) appreciate the significance of the decision; and (3) make a considered decision on the basis of such information.[4]

[1] MHO 1986, art 3(1).
[2] MHO1986, art 3(2).
[3] See the MHO 1986, art 3.
[4] *Re C (Refusal of Medical Treatment)* [1994] 1 All ER 819, *Re MB (Medical Treatment)* [1997] 2 FCR 541, CA, and *Re B (Consent to Treatment)* [2002] EWHC 429 (Fam), [2002] 1 FLR 1090.

11.14   While as a general rule, mentally competent adults of 18 years (full age) can give or withhold consent in matters concerning their health care, the law is different for minors, that is persons under 18 years.[1] The law separately provides for minors aged under 16 years and those aged 16 and 17 years. Whether a minor aged under 16 years has mental capacity (that is, sufficient understanding and intelligence to make a given health care decision) is a question of medical judgement.[2] If such a minor is not found to have the required capacity, (sometimes known as a '*Gillick*-incompetent' minor),[3] a health care decision is made by the parent(s) or guardian(s) of the minor and a relevant medical practitioner.[4]

[1] Age of Majority Act (Northern Ireland) 1969, s 1.
[2] *Gillick v West Norfolk and Wisbech Area Health Authority* [1986] AC 112, [1985] 3 All ER 402.
[3] On *Gillick* competency, see chapter 1, para 1.52.
[4] A parental refusal for medical treatment can be overridden by the courts under parens patriae ('parent for the nation'), but only if the court considers the proposed treatment to be within the minor's best interests: the minor's welfare being the court's paramount consideration: *Re B (A Minor) (Wardship: Medical Treatment)* (1981) 3 FLR 117.

11.15   If a minor is found to have the required capacity (a *Gillick*-competent minor), but refuses to consent to medical care and treatment, the courts can override the minor's wishes on the ground that the proposed care and treatment is in his or her best interests.[1] Judicial decisions about a minor's mental capacity and ability to consent to treatment are premised upon a range of factors, including the minor's age, his or her current mental health and mental health history and his or her level of personal development, understanding and maturity.

The Age of Majority Act (Northern Ireland) 1969 authorises minors, aged 16 and 17 years, to consent to surgical, medical or dental treatment.[2] Similar principles apply for these minors as apply to *Gillick*-competent and *Gillick*-incompetent minors aged under 16 years, as outlined above.[3]

[1] *Re R (A Minor) (Wardship: Consent to Treatment)* [1992] Fam 11, [1991] 4 All ER 177. See chapter 1, para 1.56.
[2] Section 4.
[3] *Re W (A Minor) (Medical Treatment: Court's Jurisdiction)* [1993] Fam 64, [1992] 4 All ER 627, CA.

Role of the social worker in the field of mental health

11.16   The MHO 1986 contains a number of powers that social workers may exercise in respect of the admission of patients to hospital, the reception of patients into guardianship, the continued applicability of guardianship and the removal of patients to a place of safety. But such powers may be exercised only by social workers who have been 'approved by the [responsible authority] as having appropriate competence in dealing with persons who are suffering from mental disorder'.[1] ASWs are social workers specially trained in dealing with persons who are suffering from mental disorder and appointed by the relevant authority to act as an ASW for the purposes of the [MHO]'.[2] To become approved, a social worker must have two years post-qualification experience and have attended an additional training course.

[1]   MHO 1986, art 115.
[2]   Code of Practice, para 1.18.

11.17   Under the MHO 1986, an ASW is under a specific duty of care relating to a patient's hospital admission and his or her reception into guardianship. Article 40 requires an ASW to make an application for admission to hospital or reception into guardianship where the ASW is 'satisfied that such an application ought to be made' and 'having regard to the wishes expressed by relatives or any other relevant circumstances [is]... of the opinion that it is necessary or proper for the application to be made'.[1]

An ASW should make an application for detention in hospital or guardianship only if, having interviewed the patient in a 'suitable manner', he or she is satisfied that '... in all the circumstances of the case it is the most appropriate way of providing care and medical treatment of which the patient stands in need.'[2]

[1]   MHO 1986, art 40(1).
[2]   MHO 1986, art 40(2).

11.18   The Code sets out some interviewing guidance. It explains that the ASW should begin by identifying him or herself to the patient and any family member and/or friend present, using relevant identification. The Code emphasises the need for the ASW to clearly explain both the nature of his or her role and the purpose of the interview. It states that good communication is essential, particularly if the patient has a disability or is a foreign national who does not have fluency in English.[1]

Despite this guidance, recent research undertaken by Manktelow and others reveals that many ASWs experience some difficulty in interviewing patients in a suitable manner.[2] The research revealed that the most common obstacles to good communication included: patients being too disturbed to engage; ASW concerns about their personal safety; and, patients' use of alcohol and drugs.[3]

[1]   Code of Practice 2.16.
[2]   Britton, Campbell, Hamilton, Hughes, Manktelow and Wilson. 'A Study of Approved Social Work in Northern Ireland'. By ISBN 0 85389 757 3; and, Manktelow, Hughes, Britton, Campbell, Hamilton, and Wilson, 'The Experience and Practice of Approved Social Workers in Northern Ireland'; British Journal of Social Work (2002) 32, pp 443–461.

3   Britton, Campbell, Hamilton, Hughes, Manktelow and Wilson, 'A study of Approved Social Work in Northern Ireland', p 55.

11.19 While both the doctor and social worker should be present at the time of the patient's admission, they should interview him or her separately, if possible, to enable their formulation of independent opinions. The holding of separate interviews is not always practicable by reason of the mental and/or emotional state of the patient. Moreover, depending upon the condition of a patient, to prolong the admission process by insisting on separate interviews could conceivably cause an avoidable deterioration in a patient's condition. Consequently, when appropriate the doctor and social worker should jointly interview the patient. Ultimately the issue of separate interviews is a matter to be decided by the ASW and the medical practitioner.

The Code further advises that the ASW must consult other professionals who have been involved with the patient's care.[1] In certain circumstances it further recommends the ASW to take close friends' views into account, noting such consideration should not conflict with the ASW's duty of confidentiality to the patient, particularly in light of a patient's right to privacy under Convention right, article 8.[2]

1   Code of Practice, para 2.19.
2   Code of Practice, para 2.18.

Role of 'the nearest relative'

11.20 The MHO 1986 contemplates the involvement of both professionals and non-professionals in admission to hospital, discharge from hospital and guardianship. The 'nearest relative' is defined under Part II of the MHO 1986 as an individual with a close personal relationship with the patient (usually a relative) who has a statutorily prescribed role relating to hospital admission, discharge from hospital and guardianship.

11.21 Article 32 prescribes the criteria for ascertaining the nearest relative. The established statutory hierarchy for the nearest relative is: spouse; child; parent; sibling; grandparent; grandchild; uncle or aunt; nephew or niece.[1] This hierarchy is operated with a test of 'relational proximity', that is the nearest relative is the first listed person 'who is caring for the patient or was so caring immediately before the admission of the patient to hospital'. Further components of the statutory scheme are summarised below.[2]

1   MHO 1986, art 32(3).
2   People under the age of 18 are disregarded, unless they are either the spouse or parent of the patient. Where two people appear in the same category, the determining factor is seniority. A person cohabiting with the patient as husband or wife (and not being of the same sex) for at least six months is treated as the spouse. However, such a person is not be treated as the spouse if the patient was married and there has been neither permanent separation nor continuing desertion. In practice the decision is a matter for the ASW.

11.22 The ASW is required to take steps to identify the 'nearest relative', and fulfil his or her statutory responsibilities to the nearest relative.[1] Wherever possible the

ASW should ascertain the views of the nearest relative, inform the nearest relative that an application for admission is being considered, and explain the implications of an application.

[1]   MHO 1986, art 5.

11.23   Where there is a difficulty in filling the position of nearest relative, the ASW or a relative or other person with whom the patient is residing may apply to the county court to have him or herself or another specified person appointed to act as the nearest relative.[1] Such an application may be made if the nearest relative: cannot be ascertained; does not exist; is incapable of acting because of mental disorder or other illness; unreasonably objects to the making of an application for assessment or guardianship; or, exercises his or her powers to discharge the patient (or is likely to do so) without due regard to the welfare of the patient or the interests of the public.[2] The court may agree to the application if it finds the proposed person to be 'a proper person to act as the patient's nearest relative and is willing to do so.'[3]

[1]   MHO 1986, art 36.
[2]   MHO 1986, art 36(3).
[3]   MHO 1986, art 36(1).

11.24   The legitimacy of the statutory scheme relating to the designation of the nearest relative has been called into question following the enactment of the HRA. Where a patient objects to the relative designated by the statutory scheme to act in that capacity, (for example, on the ground that said person is unsuitable), there is no statutory provision for re-designation. The failure of the statutory scheme to accommodate the realities of human relationships means that the MHO 1986 can impose a nearest relative upon a patient in circumstances where said relative is entirely unsuitable to perform that role.

11.25   In *JT v United Kingdom*, the patient's nearest relative was her mother.[1] Not only had she a troubled relationship with her mother, she further alleged that she had been sexually abused by her stepfather with whom her mother continued to live. She wanted to nominate her social worker to act as her nearest relative, but her mother refused to consent to this proposal. Legal proceedings were brought on her behalf contending that the fact that the mental health legislation prevented her from changing her nearest relative contravened her article 8 right to private and family life under the ECHR.[2] The UK government conceded as part of a settlement that the legislation should be amended to enable a patient to make an application to a court to have his or her 'nearest relative' replaced where the patient objected on reasonable grounds to a particular individual acting in that capacity.

[1]   [2000] 1 FLR 909.
[2]   [2000] 1 FLR 909.

11.26   Unfortunately the UK government failed to amend the Mental Health Act 1983. Consequently a similar case came before the courts in 2002: *R (on the application of M) v Secretary of State for Health.*[1] Therein the operation of the statutory scheme meant that the patient's nearest relative was her step-father whom she alleged had sexually abused her. It was argued on M's behalf that the lack of flexibility in the system to enable M, or someone on her behalf, to apply to have her step-father replaced by a more suitable person as nearest relative contravened article 8 of the ECHR. Applying the HRA, the High Court in England declared ss 26 and 29 of the English Mental Health Act 1983 incompatible with article 8.[2] This means that although the legislation has been declared by the courts to be contrary to ECHR law, it remains in force until repealed or amended. Hopefully remedial legislation will soon be enacted.

[1]   [2003] EWHC 1094 (Admin), [2003] 3 All ER 672n.
[2]   [2003] EWHC 1094 (Admin), [2003] 3 All ER 672n. The equivalent provisions in the MHO 1986 are arts 32 and 36.

The professional indemnity

11.27 Social workers are required by law to perform their duties to the standard of 'the reasonably skilled professional.'[1] An indemnity clause contained in article 133 of the MHO 1986 partially absolves social workers from criminal and civil liability when exercising their statutory functions under the MHO 1986. The indemnity does not cover actions or omissions in circumstances where a social worker has conducted him or herself in bad faith or without reasonable care. An ASW can be held personally liable for such acts or omissions: for example, failure to make an application for assessment where the ASW was aware the nearest relative was not making an application and the ASW was of the opinion that such an application ought to be made. Consequently social workers must exercise care when discharging their functions under the MHO 1986, and should be mindful of relevant guidance such as that contained in the Code of Practice.

[1]   On negligence and misfeasance in public office, see chapter 2, paras 2.80 ff.

Compulsory admission to hospital

11.28 In certain circumstances people with mental health difficulties can be compulsorily admitted to hospital under both prevailing legislation and the common law.[1] The main statutory mechanism for the compulsory detention of patients is the MHO 1986.

Compulsory detention under the MHO 1986 (sometimes referred to as 'formal detention') comprises of two stages: (1) admission for assessment; and (2) detention for treatment.

[1]   See chapter 1, para 1.48 for an explanation of the term 'common law'.

Admission for assessment

11.29   A person with a 'mental disorder' can be compulsorily admitted to hospital for assessment. If he or she is living in the community, the involuntary admission to hospital can be initiated by an ASW or by the nearest relative on the recommendation of a medical practitioner.[1] More particularly, a person can be admitted for assessment only if he or she is:

(a)   suffering from mental disorder of a nature or degree that warrants his or her detention in a hospital for assessment (or for assessment followed by medical treatment); and

(b)   failing to so detain him or her would create a substantial likelihood of serious physical harm to him or herself or to other persons. [2]

[1]   See para 11.20 on the concept of the nearest relative.
[2]   MHO 1986, art 4(2).

11.30   A nearest relative, or an ASW, can make an application for a person to be admitted to hospital. Most hospital admissions are founded upon a social worker's application.[1] As already discussed above, the ASW is required by law to make an application for assessment in respect of a patient for whom he or she has responsibility where he or she:[2]

(a)   is satisfied that such an application ought to be made; and

(b)   is of the opinion, having regard to any wishes expressed by relatives of the patient or any other relevant circumstances, that it is necessary or proper for the application to be made by him or her.

[1]   In 2001/02, over one half of admissions were social worker applications. See The Mental Health Commission for Northern Ireland Sixth Annual Report and Accounts 2001/2, p 27.
[2]   MHO 1986, art 40(1).

11.31   In considering this duty, the ASW must be mindful of the admission assessment criteria set out above. Before making any such application, an ASW is required to 'interview the patient in a suitable manner and satisfy himself [or herself] that detention in a hospital ... (as the case may be) is in all the circumstances of the case the most appropriate way of providing the care and medical treatment of which the patient stands in need'.[1]

The nearest relative can require the responsible authority to direct the responsible ASW to exercise the article 40(1) duty.[2] Where such a direction is issued, but the ASW decides against making an assessment application, he or she must inform the nearest relative in writing of the reasons for his or her decision.[3]

[1]   MHO 1986, art 40(2); see Code of Practice, paras 2.14 and 2.15.
[2]   MHO 1986, art 40(4); see Code of Practice, para 2.18.
[3]   MHO 1986, art 40(4); see Code of Practice, para 2.20.

Application for admission to hospital by an ASW

11.32   An application for assessment may be made by an ASW.[1] The person who makes an application is known as the applicant.[2] Such application is made on Form 2, and will only be valid if the applicant 'has personally seen' the patient not more than two days before the date on which the application is made.[3]

1   MHO 1986, art 5(1)(b).
2   MHO 1986, art 5(1).
3   The Regulations, and MHO 1986, art 5(2).

11.33 The ASW must consult with 'the person appearing to be the nearest relative' before making an application 'unless it appears to the ASW that in the circumstances such consultation is not reasonably practicable or would involve unreasonable delay.'[1] If a patient is admitted to hospital pursuant to an application for assessment made by an ASW, without consulting the person appearing to be the nearest relative, 'it shall be the duty of that social worker to inform the nearest relative of the patient [of said admission] as soon as may be practicable.'[2]

If the nearest relative objects to an ASW making an application for admission, the ASW concerned must consult with another ASW in relation to the proposed application before proceeding with the application.[3] If, having consulted with this second ASW, the ASW concerned makes an application for assessment, he or she must record the objection of the nearest relative on the application form.

1   MHO 1986, art 5(3).
2   MHO 1986, art 5(5).
3   MHO 1986, art 4.

ASW's role in the nearest relative's application

11.34 A patient's nearest relative can make an application for assessment using Form 1.[1] Under the MHO 1986, where the nearest relative makes the application for admission, the responsible authority is required to arrange for a social worker to interview the patient and provide a social circumstances report for the benefit of the Responsible Medical Officer.[2] Any social worker can discharge this duty. Guidance on the completion of such a report instructs that:

> 'the report will deal with such matters as the past history of the patient's mental disorder, his present condition and the social, familial and personal factors bearing on it, the wishes of the patient and his relatives, and medical opinion. The social worker making the report will need to consult those professionally involved in the case (for example the doctor or community psychiatric nurse) and will consider other options for giving the patient the care and treatment he needs, such as guardianship, admission as a voluntary patient, day care, out-patient treatment, community psychiatric nursing support, primary health care support and support from friends, relatives and voluntary organisations. The social worker's report must be done as soon as practicable as it should be available to the responsible medical officer as early as possible during the assessment period'.[3]

1   The Regulations.
2   MHO 1986, art 5(6).

[3]   DHSS Guide to the MHO 1986, art 20.

11.35   Research undertaken by Manktelow and others revealed that the vast majority of ASWs who participated in their study found it difficult to complete the report within the required timescale (14 days), for reasons such as administrative delays in the report request referral, difficulties in liaising with nearest relatives and pressure of work.[1]

[1]   Britton, Campbell, Hamilton, Hughes, Manktelow and Wilson 'A Study of Approved Social Work in Northern Ireland' p 64; 'The Experience and Practice of Approved Social Workers in Northern Ireland', (2002) 32 British Journal of Social Work, 443–461 at 454.

Conveyance to hospital

11.36   The ASW is responsible for the conveyance or transportation of the patient to hospital where the ASW makes the assessment application. The ASW is also responsible for conveyance where the nearest relative has made the assessment application and requests assistance with conveyance. Useful guidance on conveyance is contained in the Code of Practice.[1]

Conveyance of mental patients to hospital ordinarily involves the ASW, the ambulance service and the police. The ASW should ensure that the form and manner of the patient's transportation to hospital is 'the most humane and least threatening mode of transport consistent with the needs and the safety of the patient and his escort'.[2]

[1]   Paragraphs 2.40–2.49.
[2]   Code of Practice, para 2.40.

11.37   As a general rule, an ambulance should be requested to convey the patient to hospital. The ASW should consider whether he or she should accompany the patient, or whether it is more appropriate for some other professional to fulfil this role. The Code of Practice strongly advises that 'the patient should not be conveyed to hospital by car unless the ASW is satisfied the patient will not endanger himself or others on the journey'; and where a car is used, '… there should always be an escort for the patient other than the driver …'[1]

[1]   Code of Practice, para 2.43.

11.38   Where it is reasonably foreseeable that a patient may become violent or otherwise act in a dangerous manner, the Code advises the ASW to request police assistance. It further stipulates that a patient 'should never be conveyed by private car'.[1] Manktelow and others in their study found that 'aggression and the threat of violence is a frequent factor in compulsory admission as evidenced by the fact that four-fifths of experienced ASW's had requested police assistance'.[2] In the study, the main reason for such ASW requests was protection against physical violence.[3]

The ASW should alert the hospital of the patient's arrival, including the anticipated time, and ensure that the admission documents arrive at the receiving hospital at the same time as the patient. From a legal perspective this is crucial given the ECHR article 5(1) requirement that any deprivation of a person's liberty is in accordance with the relevant national legal procedures. The ASW should also ensure that the admission documents are delivered to the appropriate person in the hospital.

1   Code of Practice, para 2.44.
2   'The Experience and Practice of Approved Social Workers in Northern Ireland', (2002) 32 British Journal of Social Work, 443–461 at 452.
3   Britton, Campbell, Hamilton, Hughes, Manktelow and Wilson, 'A study of Approved Social Work in Northern Ireland' pp 57–60.

11.39 On admission the ASW should remain at the hospital while the admitted patient is examined by a psychiatrist who determines whether the admission is appropriate. The ASW's presence may assist the psychiatrist and other hospital staff in their care of the patient and the discharge of their statutory duties, for example, the ASW may have relevant information.

The admitted patient becomes 'liable to be detained' once the Responsible Medical Officer completes a report stating that 'in his [or her] opinion the patient should be detained in hospital for assessment'.[1] A patient is initially liable to be detained for a period of seven days which can be extended for a further seven.[2]

1   MHO 1986, art 9(4) and (7).
2   MHO 1986, art 9(8).

The temporary holding power

11.40 Provision is made under the MHO 1986 for the compulsory holding or detention of a voluntary in-patient where, for example, he or she tries to leave hospital.[1] This may occur in the following ways:

(1)   a medical practitioner who is a hospital staff member may furnish a report to the responsible authority stating his or her opinion that an application to admit a patient for assessment is necessary. Where such an application is made successfully, the patient concerned may be detained for up to 48 hours;[2] and,

(2)   a mental health nurse may authorise the detention of a patient for up to six hours in circumstances where the nurse believes an assessment application is necessary, but securing the immediate attendance of a medical practitioner for the purpose of furnishing a report under article 7(2) is not practicable.[3]

1   MHO 1986, art 7.
2   MHO 1986, art 7(2). Under art 7A (as amended) there is provision for a medical practitioner in a hospital managed by an HSS Trust other than an authorised HSS Trust to detain a patient for up to 48 hours pending his or her admission to an authorised HSS Trust hospital.
3   MHO 1986, art 7(3).

Detention for treatment

11.41 Detention for longer than 14 days is lawful only if a patient's condition falls within the criteria contained in article 12(1) of the MHO 1986, namely:[1]

(a)   the patient is suffering from a mental illness or severe mental impairment of a nature or degree that warrants his or her detention in hospital for medical treatment; and

(b)   failure to detain the patient would create a substantial likelihood of serious physical harm to him or herself or to other people.

[1]   MHO 1986, art 12(1)(a) and (b).

11.42   Initial detention of a patient for treatment is lawful for a maximum of six months, but can be extended for a second six month period.[1] Thereafter a patient can be detained for periods of up to one year.[2] Under article 13(4) of the MHO 1986 there is a safeguard relating to authorisation of further detention after one year's detention. It requires such authorisation to be made by two psychiatrists, one of whom must be 'a person who is not on the staff of the hospital in which the patient is detained and who has not given either the medical recommendation on which the application for assessment in relation to the patient was founded or any medical report in relation to the patient under articles 9 or 12(1)'.[3]

[1]   MHO 1986, arts 12(1) and 13(1)(a).
[2]   MHO 1986, art 13(1)(b) and (c).
[3]   MHO 1986, art 13(4)(c).

Admission of children and young people

11.43   Children and young people can be lawfully detained under the MHO 1986. The Code of Practice provides guidance to assist practitioners when detaining them.[1] It highlights three issues that always should be considered where admission of children or young persons is a possibility:

(1)   what parent or guardian is legally responsible for the child, if any?
(2)   is the child capable of making his or her own decision? and
(3)   is the child subject to any court or other legal order?

In admitting children and young persons to hospital, the ASW should try to be aware of the child or young person's sensibilities and needs, and as far as reasonably practicable, accommodate him or her as appropriate.

[1]   Paragraphs 2.31–2.36.

11.44   Provision is also made under the Children (Northern Ireland) Order 1995 for interventions concerning children who require psychiatric care and treatment. A supervision order can be imposed where a child requires care that his or her parents are unable to provide.[1] A court can authorise the psychiatric examination of a child subject to a supervision order, if it is satisfied, on the evidence of a medical practitioner, that the child may be suffering from a mental condition that requires treatment and that is medically treatable.[2] A court can also authorise the medical treatment of a child where appropriate.[3]

[1]   Children (Northern Ireland) Order 1995, art 50.
[2]   Children (Northern Ireland) Order 1995, Sch 3, para 4.

³   Children (Northern Ireland) Order 1995, Sch 3, para 5.

Detention under the Health and Personal Social Services (NI) Order 1972

11.45   The HPSS 1972 makes provision for state intervention concerning persons who:[1]

(a)   suffer from grave chronic disease or, being aged, infirm or physically incapacitated, are living in insanitary conditions; and

(b)   are unable to devote themselves, or to receive from persons with whom they reside, or from persons living nearby, proper care and attention.

Such intervention can include the non-consensual removal of such persons to other accommodation where necessary.[2]

¹   HPSS 1972, art 37.
²   HPSS 1972, Sch 6.

11.46   A social worker (who may or may not be an ASW) may initiate proceedings to remove a person from his or her place of residence if the social worker reasonably believes that removal is necessary in the interests of the person concerned or to prevent serious nuisance or injury to a third party. Before doing so, the social worker must initially consult with both the general medical practitioner of the person concerned and a medical officer designated by the health authority. He or she may make a removal application based on the medical certification of the health authority's designated medical officer that such removal is necessary.

11.47   Thereafter the health authority may apply to the magistrates' court within the jurisdiction where the person resides, for an order to remove him or her to a suitable hospital or other place, and can be detained there for up to three months. The health authority must give the nearest relative of the person concerned three days' notice of its intention to apply to the court for a removal order, and the authority must inform the person managing the accommodation where the person is to be received that a removal hearing is to take place. At the hearing, the health and welfare authority must give evidence to substantiate its application. The court also may hear evidence from the person concerned and/or his or her nearest known relative. The person concerned has the right to be legally represented at such a hearing.

Detention under the common law

11.48   Article 127 of the MHO 1986 contemplates the hospital admission and treatment of patients outside the statutory framework prescribed under the MHO 1986. The legal basis for informal or non-statutory intervention is found in the common law 'principle of necessity', as articulated by the House of Lords decision in the English case, *R v Bournewood Community and Mental Health NHS Trust, ex p L.*[1]

Therein an autistic and profoundly mentally retarded 48-year-old man, who was incompetent, was admitted to hospital 'informally'. The psychiatrist considered it unnecessary to admit him under the Mental Health Act 1983 because the man appeared fully compliant and did not resist admission. The lawfulness of the informal admission was challenged by his carers, but the House of Lords held that the non-statutory admission of patients who are incapable of providing informed consent, but who do not object to hospital admission, was lawful.

[1]   [1999] 1 AC 458, [1998] 3 All ER 289, HL.

11.49   The House of Lords' decision was not unanimous. Two of the five Law Lords who heard the case gave dissenting judgements. Lord Steyn stated that the exercise of informal powers deprived the patient of safeguards that applied to formal patients. He maintained that 'the common law principle of necessity is a useful concept, but it contains none of the safeguards of the 1983 Act. It places effective and unqualified control in the hands of the hospital psychiatrist and other health care professionals.' Lord Steyn also pointed out that informal detention was not provided for in the Mental Health Act Code of Practice. The Code subsequently has been amended in England and Wales, but no such step has yet been taken in Northern Ireland.

11.50   In summary, it appears that informal detention is lawful if the action is taken to prevent imminent harm and is in the best interests of the person concerned. It is considered a crisis intervention measure, but whether it is in accord with humane practice and with health professionals' duty of care remains an open question.

Guardianship

11.51   In mental health law, guardianship is an arrangement for people aged 16 or over who suffer from mental illness or have a severe mental handicap, and who require supervision in the interests of their welfare. The appointment of a guardian and the establishment of a legal framework to work with patients with minimum constraint is intended to help the patients live as independent a life as possible within the community.[1] 'The objective is simply to ensure that guardianship is used properly and in a positive and flexible manner.'[2]

The recent Northern Ireland study on the role of ASWs revealed guardianship, in practice, has been found to provide 'a positive framework with which to protect patient welfare.'[3] The study reveals the use of guardianship in Northern Ireland to protect vulnerable adults from family conflict over their welfare and from emotional, physical (including neglect) and sexual abuse. It also revealed that guardianship can be used to assist with the management of financial issues.[4]

[1]   See Code of Practice, para 3.1.
[2]   Code of Practice, para 3.1.
[3]   'The Experience and Practice of Approved Social Workers in Northern Ireland', (2002) 32 British Journal of Social Work, 443–461 at 453.

[4] 'The Experience and Practice of Approved Social Workers in Northern Ireland', (2002) 32 British Journal of Social Work, 443–461 at 452–453.

11.52 Guardianship should form part of a comprehensive care plan devised by the professionals involved in the patient's care. The plan should identify the patient's service needs, in matters concerning accommodation, care, treatment and personal support. Guardianship should be only considered where such a framework is necessary to secure the patient's welfare.[1]

For guardianship to be effective, a number of components are deemed essential:[2]
(1) a willingness on the part of the guardian to take necessary steps to ensure that the service providers deliver the services needed by the patient;
(2) a commitment on the part of the responsible authority to adequately support the guardian;
(3) an appropriate place of residence for the patient taking account of his or her needs for support, care, treatment and protection;
(4) access to necessary day care, education and training facilities as appropriate; and
(5) effective co-operation and communication between all persons concerned in implementing the care plan.

[1] See Code of Practice, para 3.3.
[2] Code of Practice, para 3.4.

11.53 To be received into guardianship, a person must meet two criteria:[1]
(1) he or she must be suffering from mental illness or severe mental handicap of a nature or degree which warrants his or her reception into guardianship; and,
(2) it must be necessary in the interests of the welfare of the person concerned.

[1] MHO 1986, art 18(2).

11.54 The role of the ASW is central in guardianship. The nearest relative also has a role. In considering how to discharge his or her statutory duties, a nearest relative is prima facie entitled to access relevant documentation, including any medical or welfare recommendations, notwithstanding the patient's right to confidentiality or privacy.[1]

A guardianship application can be made by an ASW or the nearest relative.[2] ASWs are subject to a statutory duty to make a guardianship application if the ASW is satisfied that an application ought to be made and that it is necessary or proper for the application to be made by him or her.[3] Form 14 must be used where the ASW makes the application. The applicant must have seen the person concerned not more than 14 days before the date on which the application is made.[4] He or she is required to consult with the nearest relative before making such an application, unless 'such consultation is not reasonably practicable or would involve unreasonable delay.'[5]

[1] *R (S) v Plymouth City Council* [2002] EWCA Civ 388, [2002] 1 WLR 2583, [2002] 1 FLR 1177.
[2] MHO 1986, art 20.
[3] MHO 1986, art 40. See also Code of Practice, para 3.12.
[4] MHO 1986, art 19(2).
[5] MHO 1986, art 19(3).

11.55 An application for reception of a patient into guardianship must be founded on, and accompanied by, two medical recommendations and a welfare recommendation.[1] An ASW provides the welfare recommendation in the prescribed Form 17.[2] If the ASW has made the application, he or she cannot also provide the welfare recommendation: therefore at least two ASW's are required in such an application process.

The welfare recommendation shall include:[3]

(1) a statement that in the ASW's opinion it is necessary in the interests of the welfare of the patient that he or she should be so received into guardianship;

(2) the reasons for such an opinion; and

(3) a statement as to whether the ASW: (a) is related to the patient; and/or (b) has any pecuniary interest in the reception of the patient into guardianship.

[1] MHO 1986, art 18(3).
[2] The Regulations, Appendix 1.
[3] MHO 1986, art 18(3)(b).

11.56 The person named as guardian in the application can be the responsible authority, that is, the Trust. If a person other than the responsible authority is named in the application as the prospective guardian, the application must be accompanied by a written statement to the effect that he or she is willing to act as the guardian. No such person can be appointed as guardian without the approval of the responsible authority.[1]

Where a nearest relative informs an ASW that he or she objects to the making of a guardianship application, no application may be made, unless the ASW consults with another ASW. This requires the involvement of a third ASW in the application process as the applicant ASW cannot discharge this statutory obligation by consulting with the ASW making the welfare recommendation.[2] If after consultation an application is made, notwithstanding the nearest relative's objection, the ASW is required to record the objection on the guardianship application.[3]

[1] MHO 1986, art 18(6).
[2] MHO 1986, art 19(5)(a).
[3] MHO 1986, art 19(5)(b).

11.57 Once completed the application must be forwarded to the responsible authority within seven days of the date of the last medical examination by the doctor who made the medical recommendation.[1] The responsible authority is vested with the power to determine whether or not the application should be accepted. Where a patient is received into guardianship, the responsible authority should forward a copy of the application and the recommendations upon which it is founded to the Mental Health Commission for Northern Ireland.[2] To ensure as far as reasonably practicable that any guardianship arrangement is discharged appropriately, the Code of Practice advises that each responsible authority should prepare a statement establishing policies, practices and procedures that should be followed by those with responsibility for the arrangement.[3]

The guardian, once appointed, has three essential powers:[4]

(1)   to require the patient to reside at a certain place;
(2)   to require the patient to attend for medical treatment, occupation, education or training at specific times and places; and
(3)   to require access to be given at any place where the patient is residing to a doctor, ASW or other authorised person.

[1]   MHO 1986, art 10(2).
[2]   MHO 1986, art 22(5).
[3]   Code of Practice, para 3.20.
[4]   MHO 1986, art 22.

11.58   Guardianship initially lasts for six months. Authority for guardianship may be renewed for a further six months, and thereafter annually.[1] A number of difficulties have been identified with guardianship. In particular, the statutory framework depends upon co-operation from the patient.[2] This can cause problems given the communication constraints that inevitably arise in the care of people with mental illness and mental disability.

[1]   MHO 1986, arts 22(3) and 23.
[2]   See Britton, Campbell, Hamilton, Hughes, Manktelow and Wilson, 'A Study of Approved Social Work in Northern Ireland', ISBN 0 85389 757 3, pp 61–62.

Discharge from guardianship

11.59   A person may be discharged from guardianship by either the Responsible Medical Officer or an authorised social worker. The nearest relative may also discharge the person concerned from guardianship, but this power is subject to the medical and/or welfare officer's agreement.[1]

An authorised social worker is an ASW who has been authorised by the responsible authority to fulfil the discharge duties contained in article 24 of the MHO 1986.[2] An authorised social worker can discharge a patient from guardianship by a written order.[3] He or she is required to make such discharge order 'where he [or she] is satisfied that it is not necessary in the interests of the welfare of the patient that [the patient] should remain under guardianship.'[4]

[1]   MHO 1986, art 24(4).
[2]   MHO 1986, art 24(9).
[3]   MHO 1986, art 24(1).
[4]   MHO 1986, art 24(3).

11.60   A nearest relative seeking to discharge a patient must first give written notification of such intention to the responsible authority at least 72 hours before the time of intended discharge.[1] The nearest relative can discharge the patient pursuant to article 24(1) only if either the Responsible Medical Officer, or the authorised social worker, fail to furnish a written report to the effect that the applicable article 18(2) criteria continue to apply.[2] The nearest relative can attempt to discharge the patient once every six months.[3]

[1]   MHO 1986, art 24(4).

2   MHO 1986, art 24(4)(a)–(b).
3   MHO 1986, art 24.

11.61   Finally, a person can be discharged by a Mental Health Review Tribunal.[1] A tribunal is required under the MHO 1986 to direct the discharge of a patient if it is satisfied that the patient's condition does not fulfil the criteria mentioned above. As the legislation places the burden of proof upon the patient, it seems that this provision is incompatible with human rights law.[2] The current practice of the Mental Health Review Tribunal, however, seems to conform with the HRA.[3] Consequently, notwithstanding the statutory criteria, it would appear that the Tribunal will discharge a patient from guardianship unless it is satisfied by the responsible authority (that is, the Trust) that his or her condition meets the statutory criteria.

1   MHO 1986, art 77(3).
2   *R (H) v London and North East Region Mental Health Review Tribunal* [2001] EWCA Civ 415, [2002] QB 1.
3   See a decision of the Mental Health Review Tribunal for Northern Ireland (with the President of the Mental Health Review Tribunal for Northern Ireland in the Chair) *Re M's application* (February 2003, unreported).

Police intervention powers

11.62   Under the MHO 1986, the police service of Northern Ireland is charged with a number of intervention functions relating to persons with a mental disorder.

Article 129: intervention by warrant

11.63   Article 129 provides authority for a magistrate or justice of the peace, on complaint by an officer of a Board or Trust (for example, a social worker), or a constable (a police officer), to issue a warrant. The issue of a warrant authorises the police, amongst other things, to enter premises, search for a patient and take custody of a patient. The MHO 1986 contemplates the issue of warrant in three main situations, namely:

(1)   Admission to hospital

11.64   The applicant is authorised to convey the patient to hospital where an application has been completed under the MHO 1986 for admission to hospital for assessment. If the applicant finds that it is not reasonably practicable for him or her, or a person authorised by him or her, to fulfil this duty, he or she may request assistance from the police. If there is reasonable cause to believe that a patient is to be found on any premises, the applicant may apply for a warrant that authorises a police officer, accompanied by a doctor, to 'enter, if need be by force, the premises and to take and convey the patient to the hospital specified in the application.'[1]

1   MHO 1986, art 129.

(2) Re-taking of a person liable to be detained who is at large

11.65 Where an officer of a Trust, or a police officer, has reasonable cause to believe that a patient who has absconded or is at large, may be at any premises, a warrant may be obtained authorising a police officer, accompanied by a doctor, to enter the premises and remove the patient, if need be by force.[1]

[1]   MHO 1986, art 129(2).

(3) People at risk

11.66 Where an officer of a Trust or a police officer, has reasonable cause to believe that a person suffering from mental disorder 'has been or is being ill-treated, neglected or kept otherwise than under proper control or being unable to care for himself is living alone', a warrant may be obtained to authorise a police officer, accompanied by a doctor, to enter premises and remove the patient to a place of safety.[1] The person removed may be detained in the place of safety for up to 48 hours.[2]

[1]   MHO 1986, art 129(1).
[2]   MHO 1986, art 129(5).

Article 130: removal of people found in a public place

11.67   If a police officer finds a person in a public place who appears to him or her to be suffering from mental disorder and in 'immediate need of care or control', the officer may remove that person to a place of safety, 'if he [or she] thinks it necessary to do so in the interests of that person or for the protection of other persons.'[1]

A person so removed may be detained for 48 hours to allow a doctor's examination of him and interview by an ASW and to enable any necessary arrangements to be made for his or her care or treatment.[2] A 'place of safety' means any hospital which is willing to temporarily receive such a person, a police station or any other suitable place where the occupier is willing to temporarily receive such people.[3] The police officer is obliged to inform both a responsible person residing with the person concerned and, if not the same person, the nearest relative of the person concerned, that he or she has been removed to a place of safety.

[1]   MHO 1986, art 130.
[2]   MHO 1986, art 130.
[3]   MHO 1986, art 129(7).

Treatment, capacity and consent

11.68   Every adult person is presumed to have the requisite legal mental capacity for making an informed decision about whether he or she consents to proposed medical treatment. However, this presumption is rebuttable if a person's capacity is so reduced by his or her mental condition that he or she does not sufficiently understand the nature, purpose and effects of the proposed treatment, and consequently fails the legal test for competency.[1]

[1]   *Re C (Refusal of Medical Treatment)* [1994] 1 FLR 31.

11.69   In determining whether a person's capacity is so reduced, Lord Justice Butler Sloss held that a patient is unable to make a decision when he or she:[1]

(a)   is unable to comprehend and retain the information which is material to the decision especially as to the likely consequences of having or not having the treatment in question; and/or

(b)   is unable to use the information and weigh it in the balance as part of the process of arriving at the decision.

[1]   See *Re MB (Medical Treatment)* [1997] 2 FLR 426 at 437, CA; *Re B (Consent to Treatment)* [2002] EWHC 429 (Fam), [2002] 1 FLR 1090.

11.70   The common law permits the medical treatment of an incompetent person if such treatment is necessary to preserve the life, health or well-being of the patient concerned, and is in his or her best interests.[1] Moreover, medical practitioners are under a legal duty to administer such treatment. However, such treatment is in the patient's best interests only if it is carried out either to save the patient's life or to ensure improvement or prevent deterioration in his or her physical or mental health.[2] But such treatment cannot be administered where there exists a legally valid 'advance directive' refusing medical treatment.[3]

Ultimately the lawfulness of any proposed medical intervention is a matter for the courts. An interested party may ask the High Court to adjudicate on the lawfulness of proposed treatment. It is standard practice for health authorities to seek judicial approval before undertaking certain procedures, particularly life support withdrawal, sterilisation and abortion. In such circumstances, the Official Solicitor is appointed to represent the patient.[4]

[1]   *Re F (Mental Patient: Sterilisation)* [1989] 2 FLR 376, CA.
[2]   *Re F (Mental Patient: Sterilisation)* [1989] 2 FLR 376, CA.
[3]   *Re T* [1992] 4 All ER 649, CA.
[4]   *Re F (Mental Patient: Sterilisation)* [1989] 2 FLR 376, CA; *Northern Health and Social Services Board v A* [1994] NIJB 1; *Re B (Adult: refusal of medical treatment)* [2002] 2 All ER 449, CA. On the Official Solicitor, see chapter 1, para 1.65.

Psychiatric treatment and the MHO 1986

11.71   Part IV of the MHO 1986 makes special provision for the psychiatric treatment of mental disorder. As a general rule, people who are liable to be detained under the MHO 1986 may be treated for mental disorder without their consent under the direction of the Responsible Medical Officer, regardless of their mental competency.[1] This supersedes the common law governing treatment and consent. To mitigate such permissive statutory powers, safeguards are provided for specified treatments, and are contained in articles 63, 64 and 66 of the MHO 1986. Articles 64 and 69 apply only to patients 'liable to be detained', but not patients who are: admitted for assessment but not liable to be detained; detained under the temporary holding power outlined above;[2] detained under the police powers outlined above;[3] or, subject to guardianship.[4]

[1]   MHO 1986, art 69.
[2]   See para 11.40.
[3]   See paras 11.62–11.67.
[4]   MHO 1986, art 62(2). Other exceptions relate to patients involved in criminal proceedings or under sentence.

Neurosurgery

11.72   Article 63 applies to all patients, not only patients 'liable to be detained'. It prohibits the performance of operations that destroy brain tissue or its functioning, or the administration of hormone implants to reduce sex drive, unless the patient consents and a second medical opinion certifies that the treatment is appropriate 'having regard to the likelihood of the treatment alleviating or preventing a deterioration of the patient's condition.'[1] The second medical opinion must be provided by a psychiatrist appointed by the Mental Health Commission for Northern Ireland, and is commonly known as the second opinion appointed doctor ('SOAD').

[1]   MHO 1986, art 63(2)(b).

Electro-convulsive therapy

11.73   Article 64 provides for a lower level of protection for electro-convulsive therapy (ECT) and the administration of medicines. Such treatment is lawful in three situations:

(1)   where the patient consents, the treatment is lawful only if an authorised psychiatrist certifies that the patient has the mental capacity to consent and has in fact consented to the proposed treatment;[1]

(2)   where the patient is incapable of consenting, an SOAD must certify that the patient is incapable of consenting to the treatment and that the treatment should be given due to its likelihood of 'alleviating or preventing a deterioration of his or her condition';[2] or

(3)   where a patient is capable of consenting, but has refused to consent, a SOAD must certify that, notwithstanding the patient's refusal to consent, the treatment should be given due to the likelihood of it 'alleviating or preventing a deterioration of his or her condition'.[3]

[1]   MHO 1986, art 64(3)(a).
[2]   MHO 1986, art 64(3)(b).
[3]   MHO 1986, art 64(3)(b).

11.74   Using the relevant statutory criteria stated above, which act as safeguards, the SOAD must reach his or her own independent view of the desirability and propriety

of the treatment. Where ECT is concerned, the criteria apply before it is administered. Whereas for medicines, the criteria only come into effect after a detained
patient has received any such medicine (by any means) for a period of three months.[1]
This is known as the 'three months rule'.[2]

[1]   MHO 1986, art 64(1)(b).
[2]   See *R (Wilkinson) v Broadmoor Special Hospital Authority* [2001] EWCA Civ 1545, [2002] 1 WLR 419.

Withdrawal of consent

11.75   Article 66 enables a patient who has consented to treatment under articles 63
or 64 of the MHO 1986 to withdraw his or her consent either before or during a
course of treatment or at any point within a treatment plan. Where consent has been
withdrawn, the treatment may proceed only where statutory provision for non-
consensual treatment exists.

Urgent treatment

11.76   The safeguards prescribed in articles 63 and 64 may be waived where the
administration of treatment is 'immediately necessary' for one of the following
reasons:
(1)   to save the patient's life;
(2)   to prevent a serious deterioration of the patient's condition, as long as the
      treatment is not irreversible;
(3)   to alleviate serious suffering by the patient, as long as the operation is not
      irreversible or hazardous; or
(4)   to prevent the patient from behaving violently or being a danger to him or
      herself or to others, as long as the operation is not irreversible or hazardous,
      and the treatment represents the minimum interference necessary.

11.77   In any of the above circumstances, the following treatments may be administered without the patient's consent or a second opinion:
(a)   surgery affecting brain tissue may be administered to all mental patients,
      including informal mental patients; and
(b)   ECT and medication for psychiatric purposes may be administered to patients
      liable to be detained.

As outlined above, a patient can at any time withdraw consent to any treatment
governed by articles 63 or 64. However, notwithstanding a patient's withdrawal of
consent, a treatment plan may be continued if the Responsible Medical Officer
considers 'the discontinuance of the treatment or of treatment under the plan would
cause serious suffering to the patient'.[1]

[1]   MHO 1986, art 68(2).

Management of incompetent patients' property and affairs

11.78   Where a person becomes unable to look after his or her property and affairs, the law contains a number of mechanisms for substitute decision-making involving the Office of Care and Protection, health and social service authorities, the Department for Social Development, and an enduring power of attorney.

The Office of Care and Protection

11.79   The legal framework regulating the role of the Office of Care and Protection in matters concerning the property and affairs of a person without mental capacity is premised upon Part VIII of the MHO 1986 and Order 109 of the Rules of the Supreme Court (NI) 1980. Legal responsibility for the management of a person's property and affairs may be removed from him or her only if 'after considering medical evidence the court is satisfied that a person is incapable by reason of mental disorder of managing and administering his property and affairs'.[1] An application must be made to the Office of Care and Protection (an office of the High Court) for the appointment of a controller to deal with the daily management of the patient's financial affairs.[2]

---

[1]   MHO 1986, art 97(1).
[2]   Rules of the Supreme Court (NI) 1980, Order 109, r 4.

11.80   Such an application may specify a suitable person who is willing to act as the patient's controller, such as a relative, friend or professional adviser. The Office can direct an Officer of the Court or the Official Solicitor to make such an application if there is no suitable person to do so. Moreover, the requirement to apply in writing may be waived in urgent cases.

In appointing a controller, the Office considers the name stated on the application. Alternatively, where there is no suitable or willing person, the Office may appoint an 'Officer of the Court' or the Official Solicitor. The breadth of a controller's powers are prescribed by the Office in the order of appointment.[1] A court order can discharge the controller if the patient dies, if the court is satisfied that the patient is no longer incapable or if discharge is regarded as otherwise expedient.

The appointment of a controller may be by-passed by a 'short procedure', which is less costly than the normal procedure.[2] This procedure may be used if it appears to the court that the patient's property does not exceed £5,000, or if it is otherwise appropriate to proceed under r 5, and it is not necessary to appoint a controller for the patient. In such a case, the court can direct an Officer of the Court or some other suitable person to deal with the patient's property and affairs.

---

[1]   MHO 1986, art 101(2).
[2]   Rules of the Supreme Court (NI) 1980, Order 109, r 5.

Health and Social Services Authorities

11.81 Health and social services authorities may receive and hold the money and valuables of patients living in local authority accommodation who are incapable by reason of mental disorder of managing their property or affairs.[1] A Trust is empowered to expend that money or dispose of those valuables for the benefit of the patient.[2] Health and social services authorities may not receive or hold patients' monies or valuables exceeding in aggregate £5,000, unless they have permission from the Mental Health Commission for Northern Ireland.[3]

[1] MHO 1986, art 116.
[2] MHO 1986, art 116(3).
[3] MHO 1986, art 116.

Department for Social Development

11.82 In the absence of the appointment of a controller by the Office of Care and Protection, the Department for Social Development can appoint an individual to receive and administer social security benefits that are payable to a person who is 'unable for the time being to act'.[1]

[1] Social Security (Claims and Payments) Regulations (Northern Ireland) 1987, regs 33–34.

Enduring power of attorney

11.83 Under the Enduring Powers of Attorney (Northern Ireland) Order 1987, an individual can create an enduring power of attorney to empower an authorised person to act on his or her behalf in the event of supervening mental incapacity. Such power is regulated by the High Court under a system of registration. This statutory mechanism can be particularly useful for the elderly.

The Mental Health Commission for Northern Ireland

11.84 The Mental Health Commission for Northern Ireland (the Commission) was established by Part VI of the MHO 1986, to 'keep under review the care and treatment of patients including the exercise of the powers and the discharge of the duties conferred by the [MHO 1986].'[1] It performs the responsible task of monitoring the care and treatment of persons with mental disorder, and it has specific responsibility for ensuring the appropriate and lawful exercise of powers under the MHO 1986.

[1] MHO 1986, art 86(1).

The functions of the Commission

11.85 The Commission's functions and duties are contained in articles 86 and 87 of the MHO 1986. Article 86(1) places a general statutory duty upon the Commission 'to keep under review the care and treatment of patients including ... the exercise of the powers and the discharge of the duties conferred or imposed by this Order'. Article 86(2) further places specific statutory obligations upon the Commission, namely:

(a)   to inquire into any case where it appears to the Commission that there may be ill treatment, deficiency in care and treatment or improper detention in hospital or reception into guardianship of any patient, or where the property of any patient may by reason of his or her mental disorder be exposed to loss or damage;

(b)   to visit detained patients;

(c)   to notify the relevant authority where it appears that action is necessary to: (i) prevent ill treatment, (ii) remedy a deficiency in care or treatment, (iii) end improper detention in hospital, or (iv) prevent or redress loss or damage to property;

(d)   to provide advice to relevant authorities on matters pertaining to the MHO 1986 where a matter has been referred to the Commission; and

(e)   to bring matters concerning the welfare of patients to the attention of relevant authorities or people.

The powers of the Commission

11.86 To assist the Commission in the discharge of its above-stated statutory duties, it has various powers, including:

(a)   the power to refer cases to the Mental Health Review Tribunal;

(b)   the power to visit and examine patients; and

(c)   the power to inspect records relating to the detention and treatment of persons.[1]

[1]   MHO 1986, art 86(3). However, this power is vested only in a member of the Commission who is a medical practitioner or a medical practitioner appointed by the Commission for that purpose (see art 87(2)).

11.87 In the exercise of its functions and duties, the Commission may advise or bring a matter to the attention of a body or person (for example, a Trust or a person carrying on a private hospital, a home for people in need, a voluntary home or a nursing home). Where the Commission highlights an issue with a body or person, for example in relation to patient care, it subsequently may serve a notice requiring said body or person within a reasonable period 'to provide to the Commission such information concerning the steps taken or to be taken by that body or person in relation to that case or matter as the Commission may so specify.'[1] The body or person in question is statutorily obliged to comply with the requirements set out in the notice.

---

[1] MHO 1986, art 86(6).

The Mental Health Review Tribunal

11.88 Any person compulsorily detained under the MHO 1986 can make an application to the Mental Health Review Tribunal (the Tribunal), challenging the lawfulness of his or her detention. The Tribunal is composed of three members, namely a legal member, a medical member and a third 'lay' member. It normally convenes at the hospital in which the patient is being held, often in the Boardroom. The jurisdiction of the Tribunal is prescribed in Part V of the MHO 1986. The Tribunal's rules of procedure are contained in the Rules. The Tribunal is, of course, subject to the HRA.[1]

[1] For a useful guide to relevant human rights law see Keir Starmer, *European Human Rights Law* (1999) Legal Action Group.

11.89 When appearing before the Tribunal, a detained patient has the right to representation, including legal representation. He or she will often want to consider the merits of obtaining independent psychiatric evidence, particularly if the psychiatrist in charge of his or her care is opposed to his or her discharge. Advice concerning Mental Health Review Tribunal representation can be obtained from a solicitor, the Northern Ireland Human Rights Commission and voluntary sector organisations such as the Northern Ireland Association for Mental Health and Law Centre (Northern Ireland). Legal aid may also be available if certain financial conditions are met.

11.90 In mental health cases, the Tribunal has discretion to direct discharge.[1] It must direct the discharge of a patient if it is satisfied that the patient's condition does not fulfil the relevant criteria, which states:[2]

(1)   the patient is not suffering from mental illness or severe mental impairment or from either of those forms of mental disorder of a nature or degree which warrants his or her detention in hospital or for medical treatment; and,

(2)   the discharge of the patient would not create a substantial likelihood of serious physical harm to himself or herself or to other persons.

The Tribunal may also :

(a)   direct the discharge of a patient on a future date;

(b)   recommend a patient's leave of absence or his or her transfer to another hospital or into guardianship; and

(c)   further consider a patient's case if there is non-compliance with such a recommendation.[3]

[1] MHO 1986, art 77(1).
[2] MHO 1986, art 77(1).
[3] MHO 1986, art 77(2).

11.91 The MHO 1986 places the burden of proof upon the patient, contrary to the presumption of liberty and the requirements of the HRA.[1] The corresponding legislative provisions in England and Wales (Mental Health Act 1983, ss 71(1) and 73(1)) were declared incompatible with article 5 of the ECHR, by the Court of Appeal, under the HRA.[2] Remedial legislation was subsequently enacted amending the offending provisions and reversing the burden of proof in England and Wales, in compliance with the ECHR.[3] Although the MHO 1986 remains unamended, it seems that the Northern Ireland Mental Health Review Tribunal's practice is to place the burden of proof upon the detaining authority, that is, the Trust.[4]

[1] *Winterwerp v Netherlands* (1979) 2 EHRR 387.
[2] *R (H) v London and North East Region Mental Health Review Tribunal* [2001] EWCA Civ 415, [2002] QB 1.
[3] The Mental Health Act 1983 (Remedial) Order 2001 came into force on 26 November 2001.
[4] See a decision of the Mental Health Review Tribunal for Northern Ireland (with the President of the Mental Health Review Tribunal for Northern Ireland in the Chair) *Re M's application* (February 2003, unreported).

11.92 The social worker has a statutorily prescribed role in Tribunal hearings. Unless not reasonably practicable, the relevant authority, is required to provide an up-to-date social circumstances report on:

(a)   the patient's home and family circumstances, including the attitude of the patient's nearest relative or the person so acting;

(b)   the opportunities for employment or occupation and the housing facilities that would be available to the patient if discharged;

(c)   the availability of community support and relevant medical facilities; and

(d)   the financial circumstances of the patient. In practice this report is usually prepared by the approved social worker with responsibility for the patient. In the body of the report, the social worker must give his or her views on the patient's suitability for discharge.[1]

[1] The Rules, r 6.

11.93 The social worker attends the hearing and may be questioned on his or her report and other relevant matters. Where a Tribunal is minded to discharge a patient, it may be particularly interested in ascertaining whether the patient, if discharged, could be easily transferred into the community, for example, if a suitable place of residence is available for the patient and/or the nature of available community care.

11.94 If a Mental Health Review Tribunal discharges a patient against the professional advice of the Responsible Medical Officer and/or the ASW, the health care professionals in question must recognise that a judicial decision has been made about the patient's liberty. Even if the professionals strongly disagree with the decision and/or regard the decision as irrational or fundamentally flawed, they should think very carefully before re-admitting the person concerned for assessment under Part II of the MHO 1986. Unless there are changed circumstances, or the decision of the court was perverse, the lawfulness of any prompt re-admission would be highly questionable.[1] This matter was recently considered by the Court of Appeal in England in the case of *R (on the application of Ashworth Special Hospital Authority) v West Midlands and North West Region Mental Health Review Board*.[2] Lord Justice Dyson specifically addressed this issue stating:

'when considering whether to resection a patient who has only very recently been discharged by a tribunal, the question that the professionals must ask themselves is whether the sole or principal ground on which they rely is one which in substance has been rejected by the Tribunal. If it is, then in my view, they should not resection. In deciding whether the grounds on which they rely are ones which have been very recently rejected by the tribunal, they should not be too zealous in seeking to find new circumstances. As in the present case, the tribunal will have made an assessment of the degree of the patient's insight into his mental problems, his willingness to comply with the treatment regime in the community, his willingness to engage with doctors, nurses, social workers and so on. If experience of what happens when he is released shows that the tribunal seriously misjudged the patient, then that might well be sufficient evidence of new circumstances: a straightforward application of the proof of the pudding principle. But if the professionals form the view that the tribunal's assessment was wrong not on the basis of what happens upon release, but simply on the basis of their assessment at interview before the patient has actually left the hospital, then it may well be difficult for them reasonably to justify a resection on the basis of circumstances of which the tribunal was unaware. Nothing that I have said affects the ability of the professionals to resection a patient if he does or threatens to do something which imperils or might imperil his health or safety, or that of members of the public'.[3]

---

[1]   A Trust could judicially review a Mental Health Review Tribunal's decision to discharge a patient.
[2]   [2002] EWCA Civ 923, [2003] 1 WLR 127.
[3]   [2002] EWCA Civ 923 at [59]–[60], [2003] 1 WLR 127 at [59]–[60].

11.95   As the senior judge indicated above, and notwithstanding a decision of the Mental Health Review Tribunal, once a patient is discharged, the ASW is yet again subject to the MHO 1986, article 40 duty to make an application for admission for assessment if he or she is satisfied that such an application ought to be made and is of the opinion that it is necessary or proper for the application to be made by him or her.[1] Ultimately an ASW must rely on his or her professional judgement, knowing that he or she may be held accountable for any given decision.[2]

---

[1]   MHO 1986, art 40(1).
[2]   MHO 1986, art 133 protects a social worker against criminal or civil liability in relation to the exercise of powers under the MHO 1986 (or any regulations or rules thereunder) unless the act or omission in question was done in bad faith or without reasonable care.

Recent and ongoing developments

11.96   In Northern Ireland the area of mental health law has come under sharper focus in recent times. In 1998 the UK Government introduced a Green Paper on Mental Incapacity.[1] This generated considerable debate in relation to mental incapacity and substitute decision-making.[2] In October 2002 the DHSSPS initiated a Review of Mental Health and Learning Disability (Northern Ireland), to review law, policy and provision affecting people with mental health needs or a learning disability in

Northern Ireland.[3] The Review is not expected to issue its final report and recommendations until 2005. Most recently, the Northern Ireland Human Rights Commission has published a report on mental health and human rights in Northern Ireland.[4]

[1] 'Who Decides? Making Decisions on behalf of Mentally Incapacitated Adults' Cm 3803.

[2] See for example, 'Commentary on the Government's Green Paper "Who Decides? Making Decisions on behalf of Mentally Incapacitated Adults" pursuant to international human rights law', (M Potter) contained in the Twenty Third Report of the Standing Advisory Commission on Human Rights, 1997–1998.

[3] The Review website is at www.rmhldni.gov.uk.

[4] G Davidson, M McCallion, and M Potter, 'Connecting Mental Health and Human Rights' Northern Ireland Human Rights Commission, ISBN 1 903681 405.

Index

Appropriate adult
 duties
  arrival at police station, on,
   5.51–5.53
  completion of interview, 5.57
  during interview, 5.54–5.55
  introduction, 5.50
  review of detention, on, 5.56
 generally, 5.46–5.47
 qualifications, 5.48–5.49
Approved social worker (ASW)
 Codes of Practice, 11.7
 compulsory admission of persons
  to hospital, and
  application, 11.32–11.33
  conveyance to hospital,
   11.36–11.39
  generally, 11.29–11.31
  introduction, 11.28
  temporary holding power, 11.40
 detention of persons, and
  common law, under, 11.48–11.50
  HPSSO 1972, under, 11.45–
   11.47
  MHO 1986, under, 11.41–11.44
 introduction, 11.4
 professional indemnity, 11.27
 role, 11.16–11.19
**Arbitrary arrest and detention,
 prohibition against**
 mental health, and, 11.10–11.11
Area Child Protection Committees
 case conference, and, 6.91
 case management reviews,
  6.57–6.60
 duties, 6.54–6.55
 function, 6.54
 generally, 6.54–6.56
 membership, 6.56
Arraignment
 criminal justice system, and, 5.75
**Arrest, detention, treatment and
 questioning**
 appropriate adult's role, 5.46–5.47
 Codes of Practice, 5.45
 introduction, 5.40–5.41
 PACE detention, 5.42–5.44
Article 8 orders
 child protection, and
  introduction, 6.7
  welfare checklist, 6.36–6.37
 contact orders
  enforcement, 9.107–9.110
  generally, 9.104–9.105

Article 8 orders – *contd*
  generally, 9.101–9.106
  introduction, 9.99–9.100
  prohibited steps orders, 9.106
  residence orders, 9.102–9.103
  specific issues orders, 9.106
Article 16 report
 inter-country adoption, and,
  8.68–8.69
Article 45 reviews
 looked after children, and,
  7.34–7.38
Assembly Ombudsman
 enforcement of reports, 2.55–2.59
 generally, 2.46
Assessment of carers
 future changes, 10.27
 guidance, 10.25
 introduction, 10.22
 provision of services, 10.24
 statutory basis, 10.9
 statutory duty, 10.23
 young carers, 10.26
Assessment of need
 housing, and, 10.20–10.21
 introduction, 10.13
 notification of outcome, 10.19
 purpose, 10.14
 resources, and, 10.28–10.29
 triggers, 10.15
 type, 10.16–10.17
 user's views, 10.18
'At risk' persons
 generally, 11.45–11.47
 introduction, 11.6
 police intervention powers, 11.66
Attendance centre order
 probation orders, and, 5.97
 sentencing of children, and, 5.119
Attendance of witnesses
 compellability, 3.71
 competence
  children, and, 3.70
  hearsay, and, 3.69
  introduction, 3.66–3.67
  mental illness, 3.68
 generally, 3.65

Balance of probabilities
 standards of proof, and, 3.12–3.13
Barristers
 legal system, and, 1.60
Best interests principle
 child protection, and, 6.35